Tom M████████

427 Haslett St.

East Lansing,

Michigan

ESAR'S JOKE DICTIONARY

ESAR'S JOKE DICTIONARY

By Evan Esar

HARVEST HOUSE, Publishers

NEW YORK

FOREWORD

ENGLISH JOKEBOOKS made their first appearance about 1525 with the publication in London of *A Hundred Mery Talys*. After two centuries of development, jokebooks—or jest books as they were formerly referred to because jokes were originally called jests—culminated in a best seller which set a pattern for generations, the 1739 edition of John Mottley's *Joe Miller's Jests; or, The Wits Vade-Mecum*. It was not until 1774, however, that America produced what was probably its first jokebook, *Shakespeare's Jests, or the Jubilee Jester*.

Since then America, like England, has hatched no end of books of this type. As the jokebook swelled in size, it gradually altered its form. It substituted a subject arrangement for its original numerical sequence. In content, too, it changed, though much more in kind than in quantity. Divergent types of jokes arose as well as numerous new subjects.

Curiously, the four centuries of jokebooks which are behind us produced no scholar to do for jokelore what Johnson or Webster had done for lexicography. Nor did they produce a Roget to organize a large body of jokes upon some sound framework of use and reference. The result is that, whereas the joke has evolved profoundly since the black-letter jest books of the sixteenth century, the jokebook itself has not.

Contemporary jokebooks are generally little more than planless compilations. They are in reality comic storehouses, for their contents are not confined to jokes alone but include different forms of humor. The prevailing practice among compilers is to group the contents under a meager list of general headings; and even when an index is provided, it is usually deficient. Naturally enough, the introductions to jokebooks give no indication of their scope or limitations or basis of selection, nor any comparison with similar books. It is not surprising, therefore, to find them inadequate as reference books, although a number of them are excellent and of general value.

The present work is the first attempt to edit a joke dictionary, and as such it departs radically from all other jokebooks. It provides the reader with a large assortment of the best available jokes—there are over 3,500 examples—and presents this material in convenient dictionary form. Adhering to the dictionary principle of ready reference, this pioneer work has been especially planned to facilitate access to jokes at the least cost of time and effort.

The most important factor in the form of this dictionary is its comprehensive subject list. All jokes are arranged alphabetically by subject, and the number of subject entries is considerably greater than in any other compilation. Jokes will be found listed under all important subjects; and less likely subjects, which do not carry jokes, refer the reader to analogous words which do. Thus, should the reader look for jokes under a common word and not find any listed there, the place where they are to be found will be pointed out. Without such a keyword arrangement, the reference reader would all too often find unlisted the jokes he seeks.

The most valuable element in the alphabetical arrangement of the subject matter is the simplified cross reference system. This derives from the complex nature of the joke itself. Since most jokes cover two or more interrelated subjects, they properly belong under more than one entry. To enable readers to employ the full resources of this dictionary, a subject-word-and-joke-number system has been devised. Under this plan, jokes are numbered below each subject, and cross references are to both the subject word and the joke number under it. In cases where there is only one joke listed under an entry, or where all the jokes listed under an entry are suitable, the subject word alone is indicated.

In the matter of selection no less than in the matter of organization will this work be found basically different from other joke collections. Its scope was determined by the decision to limit it to dictionary size rather than extend it to encyclopedic length, after it had been found possible to cover most common subjects with several thousand items. Even more significant was the decision to restrict the contents to jokes only, thus making this work the first large collection of its kind to do so. All jokebooks lump together a variety of humorous items; and even the least heterogeneous compilations, which exclude verse, contain gags, wisecracks, anecdotes, patter, etc.

Brevity being the soul of wit, all the jokes in this dictionary are brief. Wherever possible, the aim has been to make a long joke short and thus, by eliminating excess verbiage, to sharpen its cutting edge and heighten its humorous effect. The simple situations of these jokes are generally funnier, both in reading and in telling, than the more detailed situations which characterize the longer type of joke. The reader will also find that these abbreviated stories are easier to remember and easier to repeat.

In a work of this kind, the impersonal approach to selection of contents can hardly be overemphasized. As has already been mentioned, the primary consideration was to build a comprehensive subject list. After excluding items which dealt with outmoded topics, it was necessary to avoid dictionary imbalance by decreasing the representation of jokes under the more popular subjects and increasing the representation under those less popular. Then, to lend variety of joke type to variety of joke subject, care was used to include representative examples of insults, apologies, comparisons, puns, double entendres, explanations, nonsense, misinterpretations, mistaken identities, etc.

I am acutely aware that there must be grievous shortcomings in this work and that they are not all due to its pioneer pattern. I fear that my concern with establishing a style for future joke dictionaries may have been purchased at the expense of other considerations. However, this work contains so great a number and diversity of jokes that it should satisfy the humorous taste of every reader. Even in the best of banquets everyone passes up some dishes which are not to his liking.

Finally, I wish to acknowledge my debt to Emil and Eleanor F. for cross referencing the contents, and whose considerable efforts in other respects have made this work possible.

EVAN ESAR.

ESAR'S JOKE DICTIONARY

ABILITY

1

"Why didn't you deliver that message as I told you?" the man scolded his servant. "But I did the best I could, sir," was the reply. "The best you could! Why, if I had expected to send an ass I would have gone myself."

2

The candidate stumping for Congress was loud in his reasons why his rural audience should vote for him. "As a practical farmer myself, I am one of you," he boasted. "I can plow, harvest, shoe horses, milk cows, and the like—indeed, I should like any of you to mention one thing about a farm I cannot do." The momentary silence was impressive until a voice in the rear inquired, "Can you lay an egg?"

3

The farmer's son had just returned home after graduation from college. "The important thing now, father," explained the boy, "is for me to choose a large field where my talent can be employed to the best advantage." "I've already figured that out, son," replied the hardworking father. "You can have that 10-acre cornfield all to yourself."

See also repair, singer[1], talk[4].

ABNORMAL

The inspector was rushing his visit to a somewhat crowded school as much as possible. "Are there any abnormal children in your class?" he asked one worn-looking teacher. "Yes," she replied with a worried frown, "there are two of them who have good manners."

ABSENCE

1

A rainy day found an elegant lady in a mink coat climbing aboard a bus with the common folk. "I don't suppose I have ridden on a bus in over two years," she confided to the rather dour conductor as she paid her fare. "I generally ride in my own car." "Golly!" sneered the conductor, "you can't imagine how we've missed you."

2

An enthusiastic young Sunday School superintendent was out to set a new attendance record. One Sunday he proudly announced the results to the assembly: "Out of our entire school little Alice Gray is the only pupil absent today. Let us hope it is because she is ill."

3

The chairman in addressing the meeting was remarking on the absence of one of the members. "I'm sure we all regret not having Mr. Brown with us tonight," he said. "It's not so much that we miss his vacant chair, but we certainly do miss his vacant face."

4

The preacher had been away on a

long leave, and was now addressing the reunion meeting held for his return. "My happiness at being back is spoiled by only one regret," he announced. "I miss so many of the old faces I used to shake hands with."

See also attendance[3], ostrich[2].

ABSENT-MINDED

1

"What got you into this place, my good man?" asked the visitor in a prison. "Just plain absent-mindedness," responded the prisoner. "Why, however could that be?" inquired the visitor. "Oh, I just forgot to change the engine number of the automobile before I sold it."

2

The absent-minded professor was busy in his study when his wife entered with a paper. "Look at this, Henry," she exclaimed. "This paper carries a report of your death!" "My goodness," replied the professor without looking up, "that's too bad. We must remember to send a wreath."

3

The professor of biology was carefully unwrapping a package before his afternoon class, explaining that he would show them a fine specimen of dissected frog. The package, however, proved to contain two sandwiches, a banana, two radishes, and a hard-boiled egg. The professor scratched his head in bewilderment as he muttered, "But I *know* I have already eaten my lunch!"

See also memory[2], postage[2], remind[1, 2], streetcar[1], surgery[1].

ACCIDENT

1

A policeman was questioning a man pinned under his overturned car. "Married?" he asked. "No," was the reply. "This is the worst fix I've ever been in."

2

The insurance agent was questioning the cowboy who had applied for a policy. "Ever have an accident?" he inquired. "Nope," was the answer. "Not even one?" asked the agent incredulously. "Nope," the cowboy insisted. "Rattler bit me once, though." "And don't you call that an accident?" exclaimed the amazed agent. "Nope; the danged varmint done it a-purpose."

3

There was a long, shrill whistle followed by a thundering crash as the train struck the auto and flung it to one side. After a bit the man and his wife crawled from the wreckage, bruised and shaken. The woman opened her mouth to speak, but was cut off by her husband. "Not a word!" he barked. "I got my end of the car across the tracks all right. You were driving in the back seat, and that's where we got hit."

4

A man slipped on a banana peel, twisted, caught himself, slipped again, and finally went down in a most complicated fall. As his wits cleared, he noted a circle of people about him. "What do these idlers want?" he snapped angrily to a friend. "Oh, they're not idlers," explained the other. "One's a doctor who wants to look you over; that one's a lawyer who will handle your case for you; and this man's a comic film producer who would like to sign you up."

5

Working carefully, they gently extracted the motorist from the wreckage of his auto which had just been hit at the grade-crossing by the limited. "How did it ever happen?" asked one of the rescue party. "There's a clear view for miles in all directions." "That's what makes me mad," stormed the motorist. "You'd think the engineer could have seen me coming in broad daylight!"

See also aviation[3], blame[1], brief[1], clothes[1], injury[2], lawsuit[1], resemblance[3], skating[2], woman-driver[4].

ACCOUNTING

See bookkeeping.

ACCURATE

1

"Yes, sirree," the rabid Californian boasted, "here in God's country we have 365 days of sunshine each year." But the visitor was a little incredulous. "Are you sure you are being quite accurate in that?" he asked. "Well," admitted the Californian, "it's true for most years. Of course, in leap years it's 366 days."

2

The lawyer went to great lengths to impress upon the witness the necessity of telling the exact truth, then asked him: "Do you drive a wagon?" "No, sir," the witness re-

plied. "What!" exclaimed the lawyer, "didn't you just tell my colleague that you did?" "No, I didn't, sir," was the meek response. "Look," stormed the lawyer, "I'm putting it to you on your oath: do you drive a wagon?" "No, sir," was the firm reply. "I drive a horse."

3

The city editor was a stickler for accuracy, and every available space was filled with signs to impress it upon the staff. One day the youngest reporter turned in an account of a public meeting in which he related that, "There were 3,999 eyes turned toward the speaker." The editor shouted for him. "What do you mean by a silly blunder like this?" he demanded. "But it's no blunder," objected the young fellow. "It's strictly accurate. There was a one-eyed man in the audience."

See also counting[2], realism[6].

ACHIEVE

See do, success.

ACQUAINTANCE

1

"Mr. Black," began the shy young man hesitantly, "may I—er, that is, will you—ah, well—" "Certainly, my boy, you may have her, and good luck," smiled the girl's father. "What?" gasped the boy. "Have whom?" "My daughter, of course," answered Black. "Isn't that what you were asking for?" "Oh, no," said the young fellow. "I wanted to ask you to lend me $25." "Don't be silly," barked the father. "Why, I hardly know you."

2

A man encountering another in a hotel lobby felt he knew him though he couldn't recall his name. He held out his hand, saying, "I feel sure that I have met you somewhere, sir." "Quite possibly," responded the other, ignoring the hand, "I've often been there."

3

He had just amazed the rich man's daughter with a proposal of marriage. "What!" she gasped. "You want to marry me?" "Indeed, I do," answered the boy earnestly. "Why, you silly fellow," objected the girl, "you've only known me for three days." "Oh, no," protested the suitor, "it's much longer than that. You see I've worked for two years in the bank where your father has his account."

4

A young man passed two girls on the street and raised his hat to one of them, but was completely ignored. "Why didn't you recognize that fellow?" asked the other girl. "I don't know that I should," was the answer. "Our acquaintance at the seashore last summer was so very slight." "But I thought you promised to marry him," said the first. "Well, yes, I did; but that was all."

5

The man hiring the private car inquired of the owner how many it would hold. "Well," he answered reflectively, "it'll generally hold four, but you can get six in if they're well acquainted."

6

An old rounder was asked if he knew or had ever met a certain gentleman equally notorious for his thirst. "Know him!" the old toper exclaimed. "Well I should hope I do. Why, one night we were out together and I got him so drunk that it took the desk clerk, elevator boy, and the porter to get me to bed."

7

A young man consulted a doctor about his badly inflamed and swollen lips. The diagnosis proved a bit puzzling, so the doctor finally asked, "Kissed anybody lately?" "Yes," the youth admitted, "last night, and quite a few times." "Aha!" exclaimed the doctor. "Undoubtedly a case of lipstick allergy. Before I can treat you properly, you must ask the girl what brand of lipstick she uses." "But I couldn't do that, doctor," cried the boy in horror. "I don't know her well enough to ask her such a thing."

8

Two men met in a smoking car and got to exchanging confidences. One of them finally announced that he was from Springfield. "You are?" said the other. "I don't suppose you happen to know Sammy Johns out there?" "Know him!" exclaimed the first. "Well I should hope I do. We've slept in adjoining pews in the same church for twenty years."

See also dancing[2], fee[2], husband[8], neighbor[8].

ACT

See actor, actress, behavior, do, play[1, 2].

ACTOR

1

A bachelor and his married friend were at the theater together and were admiring the performance of a noted actor. "By George!" whispered the married man, "isn't it wonderful how convincingly he displays affection for the leading lady?" "Yes, it's pretty good," agreed the bachelor, "but then you must remember he's been married to her for fifteen years." "What!" exclaimed the other. "Really married? Gosh, what an actor!"

2

A chorus man, down on his luck, got a small part in a play in which he had only to walk on, sit down, and say, "Well, here I am." But his rehearsals were very poor, and the exasperated director finally shouted, "For Pete's sake, try it again, and this time come on like a man." "Gracious," simpered the fellow, "for $15 a week he wants me to do character parts!"

3

The stage manager called his leading man to him. "After tonight," he said, "I'm going to have you killed in Act I instead of Act III." "Wherefore the change?" boomed the villain. "Because I don't want to run the risk of having the audience do it," explained the manager.

4

A movie actor was suing for breach of contract. In the course of the suit the company's counsel asked, "And do you consider yourself a capable actor?" "Sir," was the response, "I consider myself the world's greatest actor." "Come, now," objected the lawyer, "don't you think that sounds a bit conceited?" "I admit that it may sound so," conceded the actor, "but you must remember that I am under oath."

5

Two strangers seated beside each other at a dinner struck up a conversation. "Well, well, so you're an actor," said the one. "I'm a banker and I'm kept pretty busy, but I'm ashamed to admit that I haven't been in a theater in over ten years." "Oh, don't let it worry you," consoled the actor, "I haven't been in a bank for a much longer time."

See also age[6], architecture[2], audience[5], counting[1], customary[1], imitation[3], precaution[1], publicity[2], salary[5].

ACTRESS

1

An actress was being interviewed and her views and opinions were being discussed. "According to your remarks," said the interviewer, "I take it that you believe in getting married." "Oh, most certainly," replied the actress. "Personally, I have been, am, and am going to be."

2

The conceited actress's boasts were getting more and more extravagant. "And do you know," she confided, "that last year I was offered $4,000 a week to remain in New York?" "Is that so?" remarked the bored listener. "And did the offer come from Hollywood?"

3

The leading lady was extremely thin, and one day at rehearsal she fell to quarreling with a sister actress. At length the leading lady drew herself up haughtily and admonished the other. "Remember, please, that I am the star here." "Yes, I know you are the star," retorted the other as she eyed the slim, bony figure, "but you'd look better, my dear, if you were a little meteor."

ADDRESS

1

It was the history lesson and the new teacher was going over the career of George Washington. "And can you tell me, Sammy," she questioned, "what was Washington's 'Farewell Address'?" "It was Heaven, ma'am," was the prompt reply.

2

The collector announced to the clerk in the outer office, "I'd like to see Mr. Smith about a bill." "Sorry, sir, but he's away on vacation," was the answer. "Well, didn't he leave an address?" the collector persisted. "Yes, sir," responded the clerk. "For bill collectors it's 'Somewhere in South America'."

ADULT

The rural preacher, though unschooled, was ever eager to ornament his remarks with highfalutin words. One Sunday he solemnly announced from the pulpit: "Upon the next Sabbath, brothers and sisters, there will be baptism in the church at the half-hour past ten in the morning. Baptism will be performed upon three adults and five adulteresses."

ADULTERY

The temperance lecturer had herself worked up to fever pitch. She could not find words extreme enough to express her hatred and scorn of liquor. "Why," she ranted, "before I'd put one drop of that vile poison to my lips I'd rather—er, I'd rather—ah, well, I'd rather commit adultery." An impressive hush followed this announcement, in which a voice in the rear could be heard asking, "And who wouldn't?"

See also adult.

ADVERTISING

1

The village Culture Society, of which the local blacksmith was chairman, sponsored a monthly concert. At one of these events the vocalist was loudly applauded after singing "The Village Blacksmith." As he stepped forward to sing the encore, the chairman whispered in his ear, "When you sing that one again, put in a verse about me repairing automobiles too."

2

The advertising man was proposing to the girl of his choice. He had fully outlined the reasons for and benefits to be derived from the union, and concluded by saying, "Remember, this is positively the last day you can take advantage of this astounding offer."

3

An agent was seeking advertisements for the local paper and stopped in the village store. But the old, grizzled proprietor was adamant. "Don't need 'em," he said. "Been in business nigh on 80 years and never advertised." "Could you tell me what that building is on the hill?" inquired the agent. "That's the village church." "Been there long?" was the next question. "Oh, 'bout 300 years," reckoned the storekeeper. "Well," said the agent, "they still ring the bell every week, don't they?"

4

A man shopping for a house got off the train at a suburban station and after looking around inquired of a nearby boy, "Say, son, how far is it to Jones' new block of Kozy Kountry Kottages?" "About a twenty-minute walk," the boy answered. "Twenty minutes!" exclaimed the man. "That's nonsense! The advertisement says five minutes." "Well," rejoined the boy, "you kin believe me or that there ad, whichever you want, but I ain't a-tryin' to sell no houses."

See also ethics[2], publicity[3], signs[1], Sunday school[4].

ADVICE

1

The trial was going very badly indeed for the defendant, so the court advised his lawyer to withdraw with his client and give him the benefit of the best advice he could think of. After about twenty minutes the lawyer returned to the courtroom alone. "Where is the prisoner?" demanded the judge. "Oh, he's skipped," answered the lawyer. "After thinking over his chances here, that's the best advice I could give him."

2

The neighborhood butcher burst into the lawyer's office and demanded of the man behind the desk: "If a dog steals a piece of meat from my shop, is the owner liable for the theft?" "Of course he is," replied the lawyer. "That's what I wanted to know," exploded the butcher. "Your dog just took a dollar steak." "I'm sorry," was the calm response. "Now if you'll just give me another dollar it will cover the fee for my advice."

3

A man red with anger burst into the lawyer's office and shouted, "I want your advice. That so-and-so tailor across the street not only badly overcharged me but didn't have the suit ready on time, and when I objected he told me to go to hell. What should I do? Here's five dollars." "Is this money a retainer?" asked the lawyer. "That's right." "Let's see," said the lawyer, slipping the money into his pocket. "He told you to go to hell? Well, my advice is, don't do it."

4

One farmer met another on the road and hailed him, "Hey, Jed! Got a mule with distemper. What'd ye give that'n o' yourn when he had it?" "Give 'im turpentine," informed Jed. "Giddap!" A week later they met again and the first farmer shouted, "Say, Jed, I give my mule some turpentine like you said, and it killed 'im." "Killed mine, too," confided Jed. "Giddap!"

5

A bum approached a genteel-appearing, elderly man with his tale of woe and request for assistance. The old gentleman refused him, saying, "I'm sorry, my friend, but I have no money, but I can give you some good advice." The tramp sniffed in contempt and said in a disgusted tone, "If you ain't got no money, I don't reckon your advice is worth listenin' to."

6

The town loafer went into the doctor's office and received some definite instructions as to what to do for his ailments. He shook his head dubiously and started to leave, when the doctor called out, "Here, Jim, you forgot to pay me." "Pay you for what, doc?" asked the fellow. "Why, for my advice, of course," said the doctor. "No, sirree," replied the bum with some vehemence. "I ain't a-gonna take it."

See also doctor[4].

AFFECTIONATE

1

A city girl summering in the country had struck up an acquaintance with a farmer boy. Taking a stroll through the fields one evening they came across a cow and a calf rubbing noses in their usual manner. "Ah," sighed the boy timidly, "seeing that makes me want to do the same thing." "Well, go right ahead," encouraged the girl, "it's your cow."

2

The man had his nose in the newspaper and the wife was feeling unusually neglected. "You never speak to me as affectionately as you used to, William," she complained. "Have you stopped loving me?" "There you go again!" growled William. "Stopped loving you! Listen, woman: I adore you, I worship you, I love you more than life itself. Now shut your big mouth and let me read my paper."

3

The girl was looking over some bicycles in a shop and, pointing to one, asked, "What's the name of that bike?" "That's the Belvedere," explained the moony clerk. The girl gave him a stony stare and in an icy tone inquired, "And can you recommend the Belva?"

4

The wife, who weighed about 250 pounds had been much concerned over her husband's illness. However, she greeted the doctor more cheerfully this morning, saying, "I think he's getting better. He took my hand a while ago and called me his little tootsy-wootsy." "Hm!" frowned the doctor, "this is more serious than I thought. It's a bad sign when the patient becomes delirious."

See also actor[1], gift[5].

AFFLICTION

See misfortune, pain, trouble.

AFRAID

See courage, fear, fright.

AGE

1

A census clerk, checking over some questionnaires that had just been filled in, was amazed to note on one the figures 127 and 123 in the spaces for "Age of Father, if living" and "Age of Mother, if living." "Surely your parents can't be this old, can they?" asked the incredulous clerk of the man. "Well, no," was the answer, "but they would be if living."

2

A young man met an elderly rival at the home of a girl they were both courting and, wishing to embarrass and annoy him, asked how old he was. "I can't say exactly," replied the other, "but I can tell you that an ass is older at twenty than a man is at sixty."

3

The streetcar conductor came forward to collect the fare. "How old is your little boy, madam?" he asked the woman. "Just four," the mother answered. As the conductor made change, the little boy looked from one to the other and seemed to feel that further information was in order. "And mother," he said gravely, "is just thirty-three."

4

The woman had been in court before, but the routine questions had to be put to her just the same. "What is your age?" the judge asked. "Thirty," she replied. "Come, now," protested the judge, "you've been giving that age in this court for the past three years." "I know," agreed the woman. "I'm not one of those that says one thing today and another tomorrow."

5

"I've made up my mind that I won't be married until I'm 25," an-nounced the young girl. "And I," returned her elder sister, "have long ago decided not to be 25 until I'm married."

6

"It is my birthday today," declared the handsome and dashing actor importantly. "Is that a fact?" responded his friend calmly. "Congratulations. How old aren't you?"

See also birthday[1], catty[2], longevity[4], office boy[1], size[2], tact[1], wisdom.

AGREEMENT

1

The Weather Man arrived home in great excitement. "Guess what, dear," he exclaimed. "I've been transferred to the South." "That may be good for you," conceded his severest critic. "I've noticed that the weather here doesn't agree with you."

2

"What is the shape of the earth, Willie?" teacher questioned. "It's round," Willie responded promptly. "And how can you prove that it's round, Willie?" continued teacher. "All right, all right," said Willie amiably, "it's square, then. I don't want any argument."

3

The politician's confidential henchman was reporting to him. "Some of your constituents are beginning to disagree rather seriously with you," he said. "Well, keep a close record on them," instructed the Senator, "and when enough disagree with me to form a dependable majority, I'll turn about and agree with them."

4

The couple next door were known throughout the neighborhood as the ideal couple—never a quarrel or harsh word was heard between them. The man was finally asked how it was accomplished. "Why, we just have a simple arrangement that takes care of it," he explained. "In the morning she does exactly as she wants, and in the afternoon I do exactly as she wants."

5

Two self-important politicians of opposite parties met on the train and in discussing the coming primaries found themselves in agreement. "Goodness!" exclaimed one. "This is the first time we have ever agreed on a matter of public policy." "I was just thinking the same thing," replied the other, "and it makes me more than half suspect that I may be wrong about the primaries after all."

See also Democrats[2], frank[3].

AGRICULTURE

See crops, farming, stock raising.

AID

See charity, help.

AIRPLANE

See aviation, aviator.

ALIBI

1

The deputy placed a heavy hand on the shoulder of the desert rat. "The sheriff wants yuh fer that murder over to Lizard Gulch, pardner," he stated. "Hev yuh got a alibi?" "I shore hev," retorted the accused, indignantly, "and a danged good one—thet's the day I bumped off Slim Johnson over to Placer City, and six guys seen me do it."

2

The lawyer was consulting with the man who had engaged him to defend him. "And you say you have a perfect answer to this charge of murdering your wife? What is it?" "It's simple and can't be broken," asserted the client. "She wasn't my wife."

ALIKE

1

It was her silver wedding anniversary and the minister was congratulating her on the achievement. "It requires much patience, tolerance, and understanding to live with the same man for 25 years," he said. "Thank you, Reverend," replied the lady, compressing her lips a little grimly, "but he's not the same man he was when I first got him."

2

His hostess had stuck him with one of the wallflowers and he was dutifully sitting out a dance with her on the moonlit terrace. Overcome with the romance of it all, she gazed into his eyes and sighed, "And couldn't you be happy with a girl like me?" "Perhaps," he conceded with a yawn, "if she weren't too much like you."

See also coincidence, gift[1], man[2], stubborn[1].

ALIMONY

The much-married man was trying to chisel some free advice out of a lawyer acquaintance. "Isn't there some way in which a man can avoid paying alimony?" he inquired. "To be sure," replied the lawyer. "There are two sure-fire ways: he can stay single or stay married."

ALLIGATOR

An Easterner was making his first boat trip on the lower Mississippi and was intrigued by the many alligators they encountered. As an especially big one disported itself, he inquired of the captain, "Is the alligator an amphibious animal?" "Amphibious, hell!" snorted the captain. "That fellow'd take off an arm or a leg in a minute."

ALLOWANCE

"How do you arrange money matters with the wife, Jim?" asked Bill. "Do you give her a personal allowance?" "I tried that, but it didn't work," replied Jim. "Why, what was wrong with it?" "She wouldn't cooperate," explained Jim. "She always spent it before I could borrow it back."

See also marriage[2].

ALMOST

The deacon took a chain to the blacksmith's to have a broken link welded, and left it. Returning some time later he saw the chain lying on the floor and picked it up, only to find that it was still practically red-hot from the repair. He dropped it with a shout of "Hell!" which he immediately amended somewhat sheepishly with, "I almost said."

ALONE

In the course of a sanity trial the lawyer was cross-examining a witness. "And would you say," he asked, "that it was the defendant's habit to talk to himself when alone?" The witness pondered this for a moment, and then answered with due caution, "That's hard to say. You see, I can't recall ever being with him when he was alone."

See also theater[3].

ALPHABET

1

The proud parents were showing off little Johnnie's accomplishments to the visitor, among which they boasted of his knowing the alphabet. "My, that's fine," marveled the visitor. "And what is the first letter, Johnnie?" "A," was the quick response. "That's good," approved the visitor, "and what comes after A?" "All the rest of them," said Johnnie, going back to his blocks.

2

Little Billie was entering school with a group of other beginners and the teacher was attempting to determine the extent of their knowledge. "And what is your name, little boy?" she inquired. "Billy Smith," was the answer. "And do you know your a-b-c's yet?" "Why, hell no!" the little fellow responded in disgust. "I've only been here 10 minutes."

3

"Tommy," reproved his mother,

"why don't you finish your alphabet soup? There's still some noodles left in your plate." "I know," replied the boy, "but they spell spinach."

4

The mother was trying patiently to teach her little girl the alphabet. "And now, dear, what comes after O?" the mother prompted. "Yeah!" was the immediate response.

AMATEUR

The two tennis enthusiasts were talking things over. "Pretty tough about poor old Bill Simms, isn't it?" commented the one. "Why, what's happened to him?" asked the other. "Haven't you heard?" said the first. "Why, he lost his amateur standing and now he can't make a cent."

See also criticism[1], garden[1], musician[1].

AMBITION

1

The elderly fellow who had traveled a great deal was recounting his struggles and adventures to a group of listeners. "It was thirty years ago as a young fellow," he declared, "that one day I determined to go out in the world and seek my fortune. All I had to help me was a dollar bill and my will to make a million." "And how long were you in finding success?" asked a listener. "Success?" the old man's chest swelled proudly. "My boy, today I still have that will and fifty cents in change."

2

The farmer's son was just back from college and the neighbor was inquiring about him. "Is the boy ambitious, Hiram?" he asked. "He sure is," replied the father. "Why, he's figgerin' on bein' so durned rich and successful that already he's startin' to look down on me as a sort o' poor relation."

3

The father was upbraiding his indolent son. "I'm ashamed of you, boy," he scolded. "Why, when George Washington was your age he had made a surveyor of himself and was hard at work." "Yep," yawned the son, "and when he was your age, father, he was President of the United States."

4

The manager was questioning the applicant for the job. "How old are you?" he asked. "Twenty-four," replied the young man. "And just what do you expect to be five years from now?" "Twenty-nine," responded the ambitious young fellow promptly.

5

The hard-working wife of the shiftless loafer had reached the limit of her endurance. "All you've done since we're married," she shouted angrily, "is sit around with your feet on the table. Don't you ever feel any ambition?" "'Course I do, honey," insisted the fellow in a conciliatory tone. "I feel lots of ambition when I sit around; that's why I sits. But soon's I start to work I gets plumb discouraged."

6

The boss insisted on taking a personal interest in the welfare of his employees and encouraging them to try to get on. He approached a meek little clerk and asked him, "And what is your pursuit in life, my man?" "That, sir," replied the clerk who was a commuter, "depends upon whether I'm coming or going. In the morning it's the 8:20 and in the evening it's the 5:15."

See also boss[4], energetic[2, 3], picture[1], wealth[6].

AMERICA

1

One immigrant was extolling the virtues of the New World to another. "America is a wonderful place to live," he said. "Why, they don't even hang you here for murder." "No?" queried the other. "What do they do?" "They just kill you with elocution," was the reply.

2

The American had just returned from a trip abroad and was telling a friend all about it. "So you saw the king's palace, did you?" asked the friend. "What did you think of it?" "Well, to tell the truth I was a little disappointed," admitted the American. "After being used to our movie theaters, filling-stations, and hot-dog stands, I couldn't find it very impressive."

3

The wealthy American girl was attending a party abroad and one of the women present took the occasion to be a little catty. "You American girls are so pallid," she said. "Your complexions are not nearly as rosy as our girls'. I simply can't understand what our noblemen see in your white faces." "Don't kid yourself, sister," the American girl came back. "It's not our white faces they like; it's our greenbacks."

4

"Judging from the rapidly increasing divorce rate," declared the funny man, "I'd say that America is more and more becoming the land of the free." "That may be," said his married friend, "but the maintenance of the marriage rate indicates that it is still the home of the brave."

5

The foreigner and his valet were on their first visit to America and were going by train from New York to Los Angeles. They had been traveling continuously for three days and nights, and the valet had been looking out of the window for some time without speaking. "What are you thinking, Simpkins?" his master asked. "Well, sir," replied the man, "I was just thinking, sir, that Columbus didn't do so much in discovering this country—after all, sir, how could he have helped it?"

6

The New Yorker was showing the sights to a visitor from the West, not forgetting the Battery. "That," he explained, pointing, "is the Statue of Liberty. Fine attitude, what?" "Yes," said the Westerner, who had been riding the subway, "and typically American: hanging to a strap."

7

The foreigner was on his first trip to America and he was being interviewed on the dock. "Tell me, Duke," said the reporter, "what it is that you are most anxious to see in America." "Well," replied the Duke, "I weesh most of all to meet zat famous and prolific Mrs. Beech who had zo many sons in ze last war."

See also government[5], traveler[1].

AMOUNT

1

The hotel manager discovered that a guest had departed without settling his bill, so he wrote him, saying: "My dear Mr. Black: Will you please send us the amount of your bill, and oblige," etc. By return mail came this amiable letter: "Dear Sir: The amount of my bill is $127.19. Happy to be of service. Sincerely yours."

2

The man stood for a while watching the boy fish, and finally spoke. "How many fish have you caught, son?" he asked. "Well," said the boy without looking around, "if I catch this one I'm after now and then two more, I'll have three."

3

The miller was complaining to the farmer about a recent transaction of theirs. "How does it happen," he asked, "that when I measured those twelve barrels of apples you sold me I found them to total nearly three barrels short?" "That's strange," replied the farmer. "They should be right for I sent them in twelve of your own flour barrels." "What!" exclaimed the miller. "You did? Ah, ahem. Guess I must have made a mistake. Let's have a drink."

4

"Johnnie," asked the teacher during the arithmetic lesson, "how many make a million?" Johnnie, a businessman's son, grinned and replied, "Not many, teacher."

AMUSEMENT

The traveling man found himself stranded for the night in a little jerk-water village. In quest of some sort of distraction, he inquired of the hotel clerk, "Is there a movie in town?" "Nope," was the answer. "Well, is there a poolroom, saloon, library, or anything?" he persisted. Again the answer was no. "What in the world do you folks do for amusement around here?" he asked. "Oh," said the clerk, "we go down to the store of an evenin'. They got a new bacon slicer."

ANCESTORS

1

The dowager was inordinately proud of her lineage and never lost an opportunity to boast of it. "Yes, indeed," she informed a friend haughtily, "our family can trace its ancestors back to—back to—well, I can't remember exactly to whom, but, my goodness, we have been descending for centuries."

2

The prissy young fellow was boasting of his family tree. "Oh, yes," he insisted, "my family traces its ancestry clear back to Charlemagne." His friend was a bit skeptical. "I suppose you'll be telling me next that your ancestors were in the Ark with Noah?" he said. "Indeed, no," replied the other disdainfully. "My people had a boat of their own."

3

"I'm joining the army next week,"

boasted the tiresome young man. "But then my family has always been noted for its patriotism. My father was in the last World War, my grandfather in the Boer War, and my great-grandfather fought in the Zulu War when . . ." "Really?" interrupted a listener through a yawn. "And on which side?"

4

The newly-rich woman was trying to create a background for herself. "My ancestors, you know," she informed her bored neighbor, "spring from a long line of peers." "Well, I once had an uncle who jumped off the dock," was the unimpressed reply.

See also evolution[1], Indian[3].

ANGEL

1

A gentleman who made a point of politeness under all circumstances, one day made the remark that he had never seen an ugly woman. A nearby woman with a very flat nose overheard him and put him to the test. "Look at me, sir, and admit I am ugly," she said. "No, madam," countered the gentleman, "like all of your sex you are an angel fallen from the skies, and it is no fault of yours that you landed on your nose."

2

"Mamma," queried the little boy, "do all angels fly?" "Yes, son," said the mother. "Why do you ask?" " 'Cause I heard daddy call the maid an angel yesterday. Will she fly, too, mamma?" The mother's lips compressed grimly as she responded, "Indeed she will, son; tomorrow."

3

Two friends had not seen each other in some years, and on meeting discovered that each had been married during the interval. "What kind of wife did you get, Bill?" asked the one. "Oh, she's an angel, a perfect angel," declared the other. "Man, you're sure lucky," murmured the first enviously. "Mine's still living."

4

The little girl was visiting some friends in New Jersey with her mother, and when bedtime came the strange surroundings and the dark room combined to frighten her a little. "Don't worry, dear," comforted her mother. "Remember that God's angels are all around you." A short while later there was a plaintive cry and the mother hurried to the girl's room. "Mamma," she wailed, "the angels are buzzin' an' buzzin' around me, an' they're *bitin'* me!"

5

A man, usually extremely critical, one day made a point of addressing his wife as "an angel." She was pleased, but puzzled over it all day, and in the evening inquired as to the unexpected honor. "Well," retorted the caustic husband, "for one thing you are always flitting about; for another, you are forever harping on things; and finally, you keep insisting that you never have a thing to wear."

6

The doctor and the lawyer were having rather a bitter argument as to the merits of their respective professions. "Well," the doctor finally conceded, "I don't maintain that *all* lawyers are crooks, but you must confess that your calling doesn't make angels of men." "You're quite right," agreed the lawyer gleefully. "In that respect you doctors have it all over us."

ANGER

See annoyance, insult, offense, quarrel, revenge, temper.

ANNIVERSARY

1

The foreigner had been invited to the golden wedding of a friend of his host and was a little puzzled by it all. "Tell me, please," he inquired of another guest, "this golden wedding, what does she mean?" The guest tried to explain: "Well, it's this way; the man and woman have lived together for 50 years and . . ." "Ah!" exclaimed the other. "I see. And now he will marry her! Most commendable."

2

The wife was inclined to be a little sentimental. "Just think, William," she cooed, "today is our tenth anniversary. Let's kill a turkey for dinner." But the husband, a bit disillusioned, merely growled, "Why kill a poor turkey for something that happened ten years ago and wasn't even its fault?"

3

The little girl was all excited by the preparations for the anniversary party. "Today is my mummy's wedding-day," she boasted to a friend. "Humph!" sneered the other little girl. "*My* mummy was married just *years* ago."

See also remind[1].

ANNOYANCE

An old maid approached a policeman and, pointing to a man sauntering down the street, complained, "Officer, that man is annoying me." "But madam," the policeman objected, "that man isn't even looking at you." "I know he isn't, the brute," was the acrid response. "That's what's annoying me."

ANSWER

1

The history professor propounded to his drowsy class the question, "Which of the two was the greater, Mr. Smith, Caesar or Hannibal?" Smith, caught somewhat off guard, nevertheless jumped to his feet and declared, "when one considers who were Caesar and Hannibal, and thus considering asks himself which was the greater, he must inevitably answer in the affirmative."

2

The lawyer was getting nowhere in his questioning of the calm little woman in the witness-box and his irritation was getting out of hand. "You claim to have had no education," he said bitingly, "but yet you have answered my questions smartly enough." Still unruffled, the woman replied meekly, "You don't have to be educated to answer a lot of silly questions."

3

"Mr. White," asked the instructor after the examination, "how far were you from the correct answer?" To which came the prompt reply, "Two seats over and one down, sir."

4

Teacher was investigating a little

altercation. "And what did you do, John, when Thomas called you a liar?" she asked. "I remembered what you said, teacher, that 'A soft answer turneth away wrath,'" replied John. "Why, excellent," approved the teacher, "and what soft answer did you make?" "I hit him with a rotten tomato," said John grimly.

See also accurate[2], question[3].

ANTS

1

Two little boys were talking over the wonders of nature. Said one, "Aren't ants funny things? They just work and work all the time and never play." "Oh," said the other, "I don't know. Every time you go on a picnic, there they are."

2

An ant climbed atop a wrapped cracker box on a store shelf and saw a pal scurrying along the opposite edge at a great rate. "Where the heck you hurrying to?" inquired the first. "Don't you see?" panted the other, indicating ahead of him. "It says, 'Tear along dotted line'."

APOLOGY

1

A minister approached one of his flock in high anger. "I am told," he said, "that you are saying that I stole the sermon I gave last Sunday. I demand an apology, sir." The parishioner smiled wryly. "I suppose I do owe you an apology," he admitted. "I said you'd stolen the sermon, but when I got home I found it still in the book from which I'd thought you'd taken it."

2

The newspaper editor was fed up on the state of politics. A feature article carried the startling headline: "Half the Legislature Are Crooks!" This, of course, brought a storm of protest from the shifty gentry, and an apology and retraction was demanded, which the editor meekly promised. It appeared the following day entitled: "Half the Legislature Are Not Crooks!"

3

The country editor was confronted by a fierce-looking man who shouted, "That report of my death in your paper was a lie, sir, and I'll horsewhip you publicly if you don't apologize in your next issue." When the next edition appeared it contained the following item: "We regret very much that the notice of Col. Burly's death that appeared in our last issue was not true."

4

"Why so sad-looking, Bill?" inquired a friend. "Aw," said Bill, "I just heard a guy call another fellow a liar, and that fellow said that if he didn't apologize there'd be a fight." "Well, what's in that to make you so sad?" continued the friend. "Shucks," grunted Bill disgustedly, "the guy apologized."

See also explanation[2].

APPEAL

The preacher from a poverty-stricken little church had bothered his bishop with so many appeals for aid that the bishop finally informed him in no uncertain terms that he wanted no more appeals from him.

Nevertheless, the next week brought another letter which said: "Dear Bishop: This is not intended as an appeal. It is meant to be simply a report. I have no pants."

APPEARANCE

1

The young man was just a trifle vain about his appearance. "I daresay," he boasted to the young lady with him, "that you have been out with worse-looking fellows, haven't you?" He waited for the reply that didn't come. "Well, haven't you?" he insisted. "Just a minute, please," returned the girl impatiently. "I'm trying to remember."

2

The girl had just accepted him and he felt humble at his good fortune. "I can't imagine why you'd have me," he marveled. "I know that I'm really not much to look at." "I thought of that," the girl admitted gravely, "but I figure you'll be at the office most of the time."

3

The governor's wife was detailing her husband's accomplishments to the new maid. "And in addition," she said proudly, "my husband is the head of the State militia." "Indeed, mum, and any one might have guessed it," the maid answered dutifully, "what with that fine malicious look he's got."

4

"I had a time with Aunt Milly at the photographer's yesterday," said the nephew wearily. "Why, what was the trouble?" asked a friend. "Well," responded the nephew, "when we tried to get her to look pleasant she didn't look natural, and when she looked natural she didn't look pleasant."

See also corpse[1], fish[3], importance[8], improvement[1], photography.

APPETITE

1

The farmer had struck oil on his land and with all that money available his family decided he needed a trip abroad for his health. On his return his daughter was boasting of the benefits he derived from his travels. "Land sakes," she said, "he looks better and feels better, and his appetite—honest, it would do your heart good just to hear him eat."

2

A famous man was the dinner guest of an over-solicitous hostess who kept insisting to the point of annoyance that he had no appetite, that he was eating scarcely anything, etc., etc. Wearied at last by this persistent chatter, the man spoke up impressively, "Madam, allow me to assure you that though I sometimes eat more than at other times, I never eat less."

3

The naturalist was imparting some gems of information at a social gathering. "The caterpillar," he explained, "is the most voracious of all creatures. Why, in a month it will eat about 600 times its own weight." A somewhat deaf old lady had been following along as best she could, and at this point interrupted to ask, "Whose boy did you say that was?"

See also boarding house[1], eating[1], example[1].

APPRECIATION

1

The group stood in awe at the edge of the Grand Canyon drinking in their first view of this impressive piece of Nature's handiwork. Finally one spoke up in a hushed and humble voice, "I wonder if any of you could possibly find words adequately to describe the magnificence of this scene?" Whereupon a matter-of-fact man in the group announced unhesitatingly, "I think it's very nice."

2

It was a little before the party and the violinist had just laid his instrument aside temporarily. "Oh, that last little number was delightful," gushed the newly-rich hostess. "I loved its freedom and coloring. Was it your own composition?" "No, madam," replied the guest artist with a grimace. "I was simply putting a new string on my violin."

3

The two finishing-school girls were discussing "lit'riture" most learnedly. "And don't you find Dante's *Inferno* a mighty and noble work?" asked the one. "Indeed I do," vociferated the other. "When did you last read it?" "Well," admitted the first, "I haven't got around to it yet. When did you read it?" "Oh, I've never read it either."

4

The organist had just finished his recital when he was approached by an eager lady who asked, "Would you mind playing Handel's 'Largo' for me?" "But," cried the amazed organist, "I just finished playing it." "Oh, dear," sighed the lady regretfully, "I wish I'd known it. That's my favorite piece, you know."

See also book[1], Boston[5], music[3], sermon[9].

APPROPRIATE

1

The man was rummaging about the gift shop but apparently not finding what he wanted. "May I help you, sir?" inquired a clerk. "I'm looking for something suitable for a wedding present," the customer replied. "Ah, then, may I suggest this beautiful picture?" the clerk beamed. "It's titled, 'The Coming Storm'."

2

"Miss Shapely is very particular about her clothes," said one young man to a friend, "and makes a special point of always dressing appropriately. For instance, when she goes walking, she wears a walking suit; when she goes riding, she wears a riding habit; if she goes out in the evening, she wears evening clothes . . ." "Boy, oh boy!" interrupted the friend gleefully. "I'm going to give a birthday party and invite Miss Shapely."

See also funeral[2], lecture[1].

ARCHITECTURE

1

Two ladies were attending a function in the Municipal Auditorium.

In the course of their conversation while the concert was proceeding, one of them looked around and remarked, "This is a nice building. I wonder what style of architecture it is?" "I'm not quite certain," replied the other dubiously, "but I think it's early Reminiscence."

2

Two friends met after a long separation and were talking over old times and acquaintants. "What in the world ever became of Allan?" asked the one. "He wasn't doing so well as an architect," replied the other, "so he went on the stage." "Is that so? And how's he doing there?" "About the same as always," was the answer. "Still drawing poor houses."

3

A famous architect was in town and had been visiting the prominent buildings when he chanced to meet a woman acquaintance. "How nice," she exclaimed. "And what have you been doing in our city?" "I've just been to see the great nave in your new church," explained the architect. "No need to mention names," the woman curled her lip in scorn. "I know perfectly well the man you refer to."

See also self-made[4].

ARGUMENT

1

The farmer and his hired man were examining the pasture fence and found a break in it. Some hair was found clinging to some of the splinters and they both considered it. "Black heifer," concluded the farmer. "Red heifer," opined the hired hand. That evening the hired man informed the farmer he was quitting. "Too danged much argufying around here," he explained.

2

The solicitous lady was inquiring of the old seadog as to his missing leg. "Well, ma'am," the old salt explained, "I falls over the side of the ship and a shark comes along and he grabs me leg." "Mercy!" gasped the lady. "And what did you do?" "I lets him have the leg, o' course, ma'am," the old fellow stated, "I never argues wit' sharks."

See also agreement[2], weapon.

ARITHMETIC

1

Little Sammy approached papa in the evening with his schoolbooks. "Say, pop," he asked, "will you help me with my 'rithmetic problems?" "What are they about, son?" "Teacher says we gotta find the least common denominator," Sammy replied. "Good Gosh!" cried the father in disgust. "Ain't they found that yet? They wuz a-lookin' fer it when I was a boy."

2

The teacher called the racketeer's little boy before her. "Jim, this problem of how much the peddler got for his apples is wrong." "How much off is it, teacher?" the boy asked. "It's a dollar short in the final answer," teacher replied. "Well," the boy pulled out a roll of bills and peeled one off, "I'll just pay off, see, instead of working it out."

3

Teacher was trying to impress Orville with the majesty of mathematics. "It's a fundamental and true science," she explained. "For instance, it shows us that if one man can build a shed in twelve days, twelve men can build it in one day." But Orville was still not convinced. "Then if one ship can cross the ocean in twelve days," he reasoned, "I suppose twelve ships can cross in one day. I don't believe it and I still don't like mathematics."

See also farming[4], good[1], stock raising.

ARKANSAS

A new family moved into Arkansas from another state and, being used to locking everything, put a strong-looking lock on the tool house, among other places. The neighbors came visiting, looked about, and left apparently in a hostile attitude. Puzzled, the newcomer finally asked some of the men what was wrong. "It's the reflection on our honesty," they told him. "Why that lock on the tool house? Don't you know that no one in Arkansas ever stole anything to work with?"

ARMY

1

The two soldiers were exchanging confidences. "What made you come into the army, Corp?" asked the sergeant. "Well, I didn't have a wife and I love war," replied the corporal. "What made you join up, Sarge?" "Me?" returned the sergeant. "Well, I had a wife and I love peace."

2

The wan-looking private had reported on sick-call. "What's wrong with you?" asked the major. "I have a pain in my abdomen, sir," declared the soldier. "Abdomen, my foot!" snorted the major. "You've got a bellyache, man. Don't you know yet that only second lieutenants have abdomens?"

3

Two soldiers were practicing digging slit-trenches. They had been at it all of a long, hot day and one spoke to the other, "Do you remember those posters on the recruiting office saying, 'Enlist and see the world'?" "Sure," said the other, "but why do you ask?" "Well, they didn't say we'd have to dig clear through it to see it."

4

A sweet old lady was paying her first visit to an army post and her attention was attracted to two sentries on duty who passed and repassed each other in silence at regular intervals. Finally, just as they were passing again, she stepped up and spoke to them in pleading tones. "Come, now, boys; why hold a grudge? Why not make up and be friends?"

5

The rookie was passing the mess-hall and stuck his head into the kitchen. "What's on the menu tonight, Cookie?" he inquired. "Oh, boy!" said the cook gloatingly. "Just you wait. Tonight you're going to have thousands of things to eat." "Gee, great!" cried the rookie. "What are they?" "Beans," was the answer.

6

The sergeant was questioning a group of rookies as to why walnut was used to make rifle butts. "Because it's tougher," guessed one. "Nope," said the sergeant. "Because it's more resilient," ventured another. "Nope," repeated the sergeant. "Well, maybe because it looks best," tried a third. "Youse guys is dumb," grunted the sergeant. "It's just because it's laid down that way in army regulations."

7

The Colonel had a name for both his discipline and his pride in his outfit. One day a wandering evangelist chanced into camp and told the Colonel, "In my humble way I am trying to save souls. I have just come from the camp of the 17th Massachusetts where I was able to lead seven men to salvation by . . ." "Major!" roared the Colonel. "Detail ten men for baptism and salvation. I won't have any damned Massachusetts regiment beatin' mine in anything!"

8

The old Colonel had put in forty long years under army routine, and now he was being retired. He took his old orderly with him as a servant and gave him explicit instructions: "Now, George, each morning at five o'clock sharp you wake me up and say, 'Time for parade, sir.' And then I'll say, 'Damn the parade!' and turn over and go back to sleep."

9

The ex-soldier stood perusing the poster in front of the recruiting office, which read, "A chance to serve in nine different countries. Come in and the sergeant will tell you where to go." The old soldier regarded this with reminiscence-dimmed eyes. "I wonder," he mused dreamily, "what are the eight besides the one he used to mention so often?"

10

The Colonel had been promoted and to celebrate was giving his regiment a lavish banquet. At the start he addressed his soldiers: "Fall upon the food without mercy, men—treat it as you would an enemy." Later, as the banquet was ending, he saw a sergeant trying to hide a couple of bottles of wine under his blouse. "What are you doing, sergeant?" he asked. "Obeying orders, sir," was the answer. "What we don't kill of the enemy we're supposed to take prisoner."

See also appearance[3], bread[2], burial[1], invitation[1], officer[3], recruit, revenge[3], soldier, wound.

ART

1

An old gentleman was desirous of clarifying a few points on art. He approached the attendant behind the information desk at a public library and asked, "Where can I find some data on Correggio and his 'Flight into Egypt'?" The girl stopped chewing her gum long enough to inform him, "Everything on aviation in Room 123."

2

The critic was rather conventional in his tastes, so his assignment to review the surrealist exhibit was something of a chore. In the course of his rounds he encountered the sign, "Art Objects," and with a disgusted grunt of assent he muttered, "And who can blame her?"

3

An established artist once undertook to get a picture of a struggling young artist friend shown in an exhibition. Excitedly going with his friend to view it before the exhibition opened, the young artist gasped in horror, "Great Heavens! They're showing my picture upside down!" "Shush!" cautioned the older man. "That's the only way I could get them to accept it."

4

The Newlyriches had just returned from a trip abroad during which they had visited the famous museums. Mrs. Newlyrich was most enthusiastic over a painting depicting the temptation of Adam and Eve by the serpent and the eating of the forbidden fruit. "We were especially interested in the picture," she gushed, "because, you see, we knew the anecdote behind it."

5

Two mothers were taking their children through the art museum. As they passed the statue of the "Winged Victory," one child cried out, "Look at that! She ain't got no head." "Sh!" reproved the other in horror. "That's art. She don't need a head."

See also compliment[5], craftsmanship[6], experience[1], home[1], price[1], realism[3, 4], statue[1].

ARTIST

1

The struggling young artist was having a tough time of it, but the landlord was insistent about the rent. "Let me tell you something," the young fellow blustered, "a few years from now people will be pointing to this wretched hovel and saying, 'Dauber, the artist, used to live there!'" But the landlord was unimpressed. "If you don't have your rent by tonight," he announced, "they'll be able to say it tomorrow."

2

It was the weekly "Art Hour" in school and the teacher was talking about the ability of famous artists. "This artist," she explained, "was so expert that he could change a smiling face into a frowning one with a single stroke of the brush." "Huh, that's nuthin'," murmured one little boy. "My maw kin do that."

3

"Hurrah!" shouted the hungry artist opening an envelope. "Do you remember that painting I sent to the Detroit exhibit? Well, here's ten dollars for it." "Great!" said his friend. "So they decided to keep it?" "Heck, no," jubilated the artist. "The express company lost it."

4

Father was talking with son over his plans for the future. "If you have no objections, father," said the boy, "I have about made up my mind to become an artist." "No, son, I have no objections," agreed the father, "so long, of course, as you don't draw on me."

See also model[1, 2], painting[2], scenery[2].

ASS

1

The temperance lecturer was loudly condemning human stupidity in putting vile alcohol in the stomach. "Suppose," he raved, "I set a pail of water and a pail of beer before a donkey; which would he drink?" "The water," cried a meek and dutiful voice from the balcony. "Exactly," thundered the Dry. "And why would the creature drink the water?" "Because he's an ass," responded the voice gleefully.

2

A non-believer was heckling a simple, religious old fellow about miracles and about Balaam's ass in particular. "How could it be possible," he demanded, "for an ass to talk like a man?" "Well, I can't see," replied the believer with peculiar emphasis, "why it ain't just as easy for an ass to talk like a man as it is for a man to talk like an ass."

3

The lecturer was enthusiastic on his subject of the capability of man for progress and improvement. "Man alone of all creatures," he declared, "possesses this ability to progress. Take the ass, for example: he always has and always will be the same. You never have and never will see a more perfect ass than you do at present." At this point a voice in the back row interrupted, "Brother, you said it."

4

A motorist who was halted by a policeman on some trifling charge became quite angry and ended by calling him an ass. After he had paid his fine in court, the judge admonished him, "You must never call a policeman an ass." "Mustn't I?" inquired the motorist. "Well, is it all right if I call an ass a policeman?" "Why, sure, if it gives you any satisfaction," replied the judge

with a smile. "Fine," said the motorist turning to leave. "Good-by, policeman."

5

The directors' meeting had degenerated into a heated argument and finally one called another an ass. This at once brought general indignation and the demand that the remark be withdrawn. "Certainly, I'll withdraw what I said, Mr. Chairman," agreed the offender, "but I still insist that my opponent is out-of-order." "But how am I out-of-order?" objected the other. "Perhaps a veterinary could tell you," was the grim reply.

See also ability[1], age[2], feeling[5].

ASSIST

See charity, help.

ASYLUM

1

A gentleman of some importance who was visiting an insane asylum was using the telephone but was having difficulty in getting his connection. "Look here, my girl," he shouted to the operator in exasperation, "do you know who I am?" "No, I don't," was the rather pointed reply, "but I know *where* you are."

2

The lady was visiting the asylum and the superintendent was showing her about. "Gracious!" she exclaimed with a shudder. "What a vicious-looking woman that was we just passed in the corridor. Is she dangerous?" "Well, sometimes," admitted the superintendent uneasily. "But why do you allow her such freedom?" insisted the lady. "She's under your control." "No, she's not under my control," sighed the man. "She's my wife."

3

A young miner had been placed in an asylum for treatment and after a few weeks a fellow-worker visited him. "How you gettin' on, Bill?" he asked. "Oh, just fine," was the answer. "That's great," said the visitor. "Guess you'll be comin' back to the mine soon?" "What!" cried Bill. "I should leave a fine comfortable house like this with a swell big garden to come work in a dirty mine? You must think I'm crazy!"

4

Several patients had escaped from one section of an asylum and an inspector was sent to examine the locks and windows. Passing an inmate in the corridor, he thought to test his sanity by asking, "Can you tell me the name of this hospital?" "Hospital!" replied the man sarcastically. "You've got the wrong place, bud. This is the bolt department of the nut factory."

5

Two women inmates were walking around the asylum grounds discussing the hardships and deprivations of their confinement. "What bothers me most of all," said the one, "is that there are no men around the place." The other looked surprised and a little envious. "Gosh!" she exclaimed. "You won't be here much longer. Now you're talking sense."

6

Visitors were going through an asylum and one of them asked the guide how it was determined if a patient was sufficiently recovered to be released. "We've a simple test," he replied. "We have a big trough full of water with a tap we turn on and leave running, and then we tell the boys to empty the trough with buckets." "But what does that prove?" was asked. "Well," replied the guide, "them as ain't nuts no more turns off the tap."

See also college[1], lunatic[3].

ATHLETICS

The young athlete was looking over a selection of track shoes and finally chose a pair. "But," objected the salesman, "this other pair will give you better service in the long run." "Perhaps," said the young man, "but I'm not in any of the long runs. I'm only entered in the fifty-yard dash."

See also record, temperature[2].

ATTEMPT

1

The little boy was standing suspiciously close to the apple barrel, so the grocer leaned over the counter to shout at him, "Say, boy, are you tryin' to steal them apples?" "N-no, sir," was the meek and faltering response. "I'm tryin' not to!"

2

The prisoner was at least sixty. The judge pronounced the sentence: "Thirty years' penal servitude." The old man protested tearfully, "But, your honor, I won't live long enough to serve such a sentence." The judge relented a little and in more kindly tones comforted him, "Don't let it worry you, old fellow; just try your best and do what you can."

See also truthful[1].

ATTENDANCE

1

The Sunday-school superintendent was putting on an attendance drive. "How many of you boys can bring two other boys next Sunday?" he asked. There were no volunteers until at last a new boy raised his hand diffidently. "Please, sir," he said, "I can't bring two, but there's one little guy I can lick and I'll do my damnedest to bring him."

2

The congregation was rather lackadaisical and the minister's best efforts to increase attendance had met with little success. Finally one Sunday he made the announcement: "Brothers and Sisters, the janitor and I will hold our regular prayer meeting next Wednesday evening as usual."

3

The guest conductor of an orchestra was being driven to distraction at rehearsals because invariably at least one member would be missing. At the last rehearsal he tapped for attention and announced: "I wish publicly to thank the first violinist for being the only man in the orchestra with decency enough to attend all rehearsals." The violinist hung his head modestly. "It seemed the least I could do," he said humbly, "since I won't be at the concert tonight."

See also absence[2], premature[1].

ATTENTION

The boy was not doing so well in school and his mother reprimanded him. "I do wish, Johnnie," she said, "that you'd pay a little attention to your studies." "But I do, mom," Johnnie replied. "I pay as little attention to them as possible."

AUCTION

1

A couple had the habit of talking in their sleep. The man was an ardent golfer and the wife was an indefatigable auction goer. One night the husband cried out, "Fore!" and the wife immediately answered, "Four twenty-five!"

2

The auctioneer held up a pair of fine antique silver candlesticks. "Now, then," he called out. "What am I offered on these to give me a start?" "Two-bits!" came a voice from the rear. "What!" cried the auctioneer in horror. "Twenty-five cents for these rare pieces!" "I thought that would give him a start," said the bidder under his breath.

AUDACITY

"What the blue blazes do you want in here?" roared the peevish boss as the meek little clerk slipped into his private office. "Please, sir, may I use your phone?" the clerk requested. "Oh, I suppose so," conceded the boss. "But what for?" "To call my wife, sir," the clerk explained. "You see, she told me to ask you for a raise, but forgot to tell me how much."

AUDIENCE

1

The man at the theater had been long-suffering, but at last he could no longer contain his annoyance at the continued conversation going on behind him. "I beg your pardon," he expostulated, "but I can't hear a word." "Is that so," snapped the gabby man. "And what business is it of yours what I tell my wife?"

2

The famous stage actor had finally succumbed to Hollywood's offers and was making his first picture. "Don't you find it rather strange playing without an audience?" a friend asked him. "Not at all," responded the actor. "It doesn't trouble me in the slightest. You see, I've just finished a road tour in Shakespeare."

3

The small traveling show had not been doing well with its one-night stands in tank towns, but on this night the advance sale had been unusually poor. The worried manager was backstage before the show and found the comedian peeking out at the audience. "How is the house tonight?" he asked. "Better than Peskola," was the answer, "but we've still got them outnumbered."

4

The famous man went back to his little home town for a visit and he was requested to address an audience of his former friends and neighbors. Wishing to show that success had not turned his head and that he was still one of them, he began: "My dear friends—I won't call you ladies and gentlemen as I know you too well for that."

5

"What would you consider the worst possible audience to play to?" queried a friend. "Well," commented the actor reflectively, "I suppose it would be one made up of armless men." "That might be the worst," agreed the friend, "but it seems to me that it would also be the safest."

See also concert[4].

AUTHOR

1

"Sorry, but your story is too highly colored," said the editor, handing back a massive manuscript. "Why, how do you mean?" asked the rejected author. "In the first five pages," explained the editor, "you have the father turn purple with rage, the rival turn green with jealousy, the hero go white with anger, the maiden turn red with blushes, and the coachman turn blue with cold."

2

"At last," announced the budding author with grim satisfaction, "I have written something that I know any magazine will be eager to accept." "Good!" said his friend. "What is it?" "A check for a year's subscription," was the response.

3

An author who barely managed to make a living by his art was being asked questions by a little girl who finally inquired, "What's 'penury' mean, sir?" "Penury, my child," was the weary reply, "means the wages of the pen."

4

The guest was voicing his surprise to the poet's wife that the great man had never dedicated any of his volumes to his spouse. The wife grew thoughtful for a moment, then through pursed lips declared, "I never thought of that before. The first chance I get I must look through his books, and if that's true I'll never speak to him again."

5

"That novelist claims to have taken his characters from real life," explained the admirer of the writer. "Then he should be encouraged to keep on taking them," growled the critic. "The fewer like them we have in real life, the better."

6

The lady of high artistic ideals was taking the popular author to task. "It may be true," she granted sternly, "that your writings have made you rich, but have you written anything that will live?" "Perhaps not, madam," the author admitted genially, "but when it's a question of which shall live, my writings or me, I never hesitate to sacrifice my writings quite cheerfully."

7

"How did your last novel do?" asked the friend. "Well," replied the struggling but self-confident author, "it has been proved beyond all doubt that it isn't one of those trashy best sellers."

See also clothes[2], fame[1], publisher[1].

AUTHORITY

A man approached the librarian of a public library. "I'd like a copy of Dante's *Inferno,* please," he re-quested. The librarian got the book and handed it to him, whereupon he paged through it dubiously for a moment and then inquired, "Is Dante the best authority on the subject?"

AUTOMOBILE

1

The pretty-but-dumb miss was inspecting an automobile and the salesman was trying to explain things to her. "Are you sure you've shown me all the principal parts of the car?" she questioned. "Yes, madam, I have," the salesman replied. "Well, then," insisted the girl doubtfully, "where's the depreciation? My boy-friend told me that's one of the biggest things about a car."

2

The little girl looked up from her school books. "What's a pedestrian, Daddy?" she asked. The long-suffering and experienced father sighed as he responded, "A pedestrian, my child, is a man with a wife, two sons, three daughters, and one automobile."

3

"No," said the old-fashioned man who was still paying off his home, "I have never owned an automobile, but I am very grateful to them for one thing." "And what is that?" inquired his neighbor. "They have made mortgages respectable," was the answer.

4

Anger was exuding from every pore of the woman as she confronted her butcher. "What is the meaning of this," she demanded, "that I find bits of rubber in the hamburger?" The butcher shrugged his shoulders helplessly. "I'm sorry, madam," he apologized, "but it's just another instance of how the automobile is replacing the horse."

5

The city man visiting in the country was watching the actions of a farmer's team. "It's strange how these horses up here still shy at an automobile," he commented to his host. "Oh, I don't know," replied the farmer, "not when you think how strange they must look to horses. Wouldn't you think it kinda queer if you saw my pants comin' down the road without anything in 'em?"

See also cost[1], curious, desertion[3], fireman[2], kiss[3], museum[1], payment[4], pedestrian[2], pull[1], second-hand car, speeding[1], woman-driver[1], wooing[3].

AUTOMOBILIST

See driver, truck-driver, woman-driver.

AVAILABLE

The farmer and his wife had been to the city for a few days to see the sights, and when he was checking out of the hotel a bill for forty-five dollars was handed him. "I'll only pay half of that," the farmer cried. "Why, we didn't eat a single meal here." "We can't help that," the clerk replied, "they were here for you." "Well, how about the way you kissed my wife all the time?" retorted the farmer. "But I did no such thing," cried the man angrily.

"Well," replied the farmer shrewdly, "it was there for you."

AVIATION

1

The plane was flying over the Bay of Naples when the pilot turned to his passenger and asked, "Have you ever heard the expression, 'See Naples and Die'?" "Yes, I have," admitted the passenger. "Why?" "Well," said the pilot grimly, "take a good look—the propeller's just come off."

2

A man met an aviation enthusiast and in discussing his hobby said, "I hear you've put a little kitchen in your plane. How do you like cooking in the air?" "Just fine," replied the other, "especially making flapjacks." "Why flapjacks in particular?" queried the first. "Because you can just put them on and then loop the loop."

3

Two loafers were killing time in idle conversation. "Sam," asked one, "if you were going to be killed would you prefer a shipwreck or an airplane accident?" "Reckon I'd take the shipwreck," answered Sam reflectively. "Why a shipwreck?" asked the other. "Well, if you're in a shipwreck," explained Sam, "there you are; but if you're in an airplane accident, where are you?"

4

The farmer's speed was the horse and buggy, but a friend finally persuaded him to take a ride in his airplane. He made no move nor uttered any word during the trip, but upon being returned to terra firma he turned to his friend and said, "Thanks for the two rides." "What do you mean, two rides?" asked the friend. "You only had one." "Nope," replied the farmer firmly. "Two: my first and my last."

5

It was to be the lady's first airplane ride and she was a trifle nervous over it. "You'll be sure to bring us back safely, won't you?" she asked the pilot with an anxious little smile. "Don't worry, miss," the pilot reassured her gravely. "Of course I will. I've never left any one up there yet."

6

The lady was obviously perturbed at the prospect of her first airplane ride. "S-s-supposing the p-plane should crash?" she stammered fearfully. "Don't be in the least concerned about that, madam," comforted the pilot. "We always keep an extra plane in the hangar for just such emergencies."

See also confidence[2], half[2], parachute[2].

AVIATOR

1

The airman looked down disconsolately from the tangle of his parachute in the tree. "And I was trying to make a record," he complained. "What are you worrying about?" asked the farmer, "you've made one. You're the first man hereabouts who can claim to have climbed down a tree without first having to climb up it."

2

The cadets were talking about a former fellow air-corps student who had been transferred. "Why do you suppose he ever went into the air service anyway?" asked one. "That's easy," responded one of the ground crew. "He was no earthly good."

See also location[5].

AWAKEN

1

"I'd like a good alarm clock," said the customer, "one that will arouse father without awakening the whole family." The clerk shook his head dubiously. "Sorry, madam, but I have never heard of that kind," he said. "We just have the ordinary variety that will awaken the whole family without bothering father."

2

Some repairs had to be made at the factory and the manager called in Mike. "Mike," he said, "I want you to get down at 5 o'clock in the morning to let the repairmen in. Here's an alarm clock to get you up." However, it was 8:30 when Mike came in and was confronted by the scowling manager who asked, "What's the matter? Didn't the alarm go off?" "Oh, sure, it went off, all right," admitted Mike, "only it done it while I was asleep."

BABY

1

The young mother, wishing to announce her baby's arrival in a novel manner, wired a friend simply the reference, "Isaiah 9:6" as that passage begins: "For unto us a child is born, unto us a son is given." The friend, apparently not of a Biblical turn, remarked to her husband, "It seems Jane's had a boy weighing 9 pounds and 6 ounces, but why in the world would she want to name him Isaiah?"

2

"I hear you have a new baby over at your house, Billie," said teacher. "Aw, I don't think he's so very new," replied Billie with a grimace. "According to the way he cries he must have had lots of experience."

3

"How do you like your new little baby sister, Jimmy?" asked a neighbor. "Heck!" said Jimmy disdainfully. "I'd ruther it was a boy 'cause then I could play ball and marbles an' stuff with it." "Well, maybe you could exchange her for a brother," suggested the neighbor playfully. "Can't do that now," was the disgusted answer. "We've used her four days."

4

Billy stood looking at the newly-arrived baby who lay kicking and squalling without let-up. "Mother," asked Billy with a puzzled frown, "did you say the baby came from heaven?" "That's right, dear," answered mother. "Golly!" declared Billy. "I don't blame them for getting rid of him."

5

The little boy was being shown his new baby brother and he seemed especially intrigued by the infant's hairless condition. "Where'd you say he came from?" he asked. "From heaven," he was told. "Well," the boy marveled, "they sure give close haircuts in heaven, don't they?"

6

The little girl was all excited. "We've got a new baby up at our house," she informed the neighbor breathlessly. "Is that so?" exclaimed the neighbor. "And is he going to stay?" "I think so," replied the girl hurrying along, "'cause he's taken all his things off."

7

The bright little girl was quizzing uncle. "Do you know, Uncle John, that a baby was fed on elephant's milk and gained over twenty-five pounds in a month?" she asked. "Ridiculous!" cried uncle. "Why, that's impossible! Whose baby was it?" "The elephant's baby," replied the little girl, scurrying from the room.

8

"Hello, Jim," said the boss, "I hear you have a new little boy at your house." "For goodness' sakes!" gasped the new father glancing about the office nervously. "You can't hear him 'way up here, can you?"

9

The young minister was new at his work and consequently a bit nervous while calling on parishioners. He tickled the chubby cheek of an infant in his mother's arms. "What a fine baby!" he flattered amiably. "How old is he?" "Just six weeks today," answered the proud mother. "My, my," the preacher floundered on. "And is this your youngest?"

10

The hotel was burning briskly, but no sooner had the fireman deposited the rescued woman safely on the walk than she tried frantically to fling herself back into the building, crying, "My baby! I've left my baby in there to burn!" Firemen restrained her and were trying to learn the location of her room when a 290-pound man in gay pajamas and a jaunty hat appeared on a balcony and called down, "Don't worry, Mae, I'm okay." "My baby!" gasped the woman gratefully.

11

"How is your little baby brother?" inquired the sweet old lady. "Can he talk yet?" "Naw, he can't," said the boy disgustedly, "and why should he learn? All he has to do is yell a while and he can get everything in the house worth having."

12

The small boy was taken to see the newly-arrived baby. For a while he looked the infant over in silence, and finally he said, "He's got no hair, has he, father?" The father could only agree. "And he ain't got any teeth, has he, father?" "That's right, son," the father again admitted. "Tell you what I think, father," the boy remarked confidentially, "you've been swindled—he's an old one."

See also Boston[2], cause[2], childbirth[2], diet[4], disturbance[1], doll[1], experience[3], father[2], name[5], newlyweds[2], payment[6], politics[3], pregnancy[2], talk[3], triplets, twins, unlucky[1].

BACHELOR

1

The single man was bemoaning his solitary state. "A bachelor has no one to share his troubles," he complained. "Humph!" grunted the married man. "A bachelor shouldn't have any troubles."

2

"How is it that you have never married?" a friend asked an old bachelor. "Well," said the bachelor reflectively, "I suppose it's because once when I was in a crowd I stepped on a lady's trailing dress. Like a pantheress she turned and snarled, 'You clumsy lout . . .!' Then, seeing it was I, she stopped short, smiled angelically, and cooed, 'Oh, I'm so sorry! I thought you were my husband. It was really nothing at all.'"

3

Two old bums discussed life as they walked along. "Was you ever in love, Weary?" asked Willie. "Yep," responded Weary. "Once when I was a young sprout." "How come you never got married?" continued Willie. "Well, it was this way," explained Weary. "The gal wouldn't marry me when I wuz drunk, and I sure wouldn't marry her when I wuz sober."

See also cookbook[1], escape, marriage[6], proposal[5].

BACTERIA

See germs.

BAGGAGE

See luggage.

BALD

1

The bald-headed man was in a great hurry as he jumped into the barber's chair. "Do you think you can shave me with my collar on?" he asked. "Oh, sure," replied the barber as he tucked a towel under the man's chin. "And I can give you a haircut with your hat on."

2

The small boy sat on his father's knee as they patiently waited for mother to get her hair put up. "What's mummy doing, pop?" the little fellow asked. "She's putting waves in her hair, son." The boy thought this over for a moment, and then spoke up, "No waves for you, huh, pop? You're all beach."

3

The old lady was near-sighted, and the old gentleman seated next to her at dinner was completely bald. While looking to the other side, she unknowingly dropped her napkin. The bald gentleman gallantly stooped to retrieve it and in so doing touched her arm. She turned, took a glance, and said, "No melon, thank you."

4

Timmie's granddad was telling him about the first World War and the battles he had been in. "It was at the battle of Chateau-Thierry, a long time ago," he related, "that my head was grazed by an enemy bullet." Timmie regarded grandpa's shiny pate thoughtfully for a moment, and then observed, "Not much grazing there now, is there, grandpa?"

See also hair[3], memento[3].

BANKING

1

"Father," said daughter with a worried frown, "I'm afraid that the bank you told me to put my money in is in a bad way." "Nonsense, child," scoffed the father. "Why, that's one of the strongest banks in the country. Whatever gave you such an idea?" Daughter was still unconvinced. "I don't see how it can be much of a bank when it sent back one of my checks for a measly $20 marked 'No Funds'."

2

With a change of politics, the local judge found a new job as cashier of the bank. He demurred over cashing a check. "I've no doubt the check is all right, sir," he explained, "but you haven't given proof enough of your identity." "Proof enough!" snorted the man. "Why, I've known you as a judge to hang a man on less evidence." "That's quite possible," agreed the ex-judge, "but when it comes to paying out hard cash you've got to be really careful."

3

The young man was being questioned as to his father's occupation. "He cleans out the bank on Main Street," was his answer. "Well, what is he, the janitor, a robber, or the president?" was the cynical comment.

4

The woman was grimly intent upon her purpose as she inquired of the bank teller, "I wish to know how much money my husband took out of the bank last week?" "I'm sorry, madam," replied the teller, "but I can't give you that information." "And why not? You're the paying teller, aren't you?" demanded the woman. "Yes," he conceded, "but I'm not a telling payer."

5

A husband and wife entered a bank and announced they wished to open a joint account. The husband, being in a hurry, just signed the signature card and rushed out, leaving the details to the woman. "Now, let's see," said the teller. "This is to be a joint account, isn't it?" "That's right," agreed the wife, smiling happily. "Just make it deposit for him, and checking for me."

6

The small-town banker had attained to sufficient wealth and importance to have his portrait done. He chose a dignified but democratic pose, standing with his hands in his pockets. When finished, he had it hung in his office, and all who saw admired and praised it, except one old farmer who snorted, "Humph! 'Tain't like 'im a-tall, him with his hands in his *own* pockets!"

7

The successful banker, mellowed with a few drinks, was detailing his rise to affluence. "I was out of work," he related, "so in order to have something to do I rented an empty store and put up a sign, 'Bank.' The same day a man chanced by and deposited $300. Next day another fellow saw the sign and put in $250. Well, sir, by the third day I'd got confidence enough in the venture to put in $50 of my own money."

8

A Boston woman entered a bank to make a deposit. The deposit slip had spaces marked for listing bills, specie, and checks. The woman entered her bills and checks in their proper places, but puzzled over the "specie" entry. Finally, however, her brow cleared and she wrote *Female* in a firm hand and turned in her deposit.

9

A merchant went into a bank and wanted the cashier to discount his note. But the cashier refused, saying, "I'm sorry, sir, but I can't discount the note unless you get some responsible man who knows you to indorse it." The merchant thought a minute, and then suggested brightly to the cashier, "Well, you know me, and you're responsible—why don't you indorse it?"

See also actor[5], check[2,4], contract[1], identify[4], trust[1].

BAPTISM

See christening.

BAR

See bartender, saloon.

BARBER

1

It was the young barber's first job and the old barber was showing him the ropes. A customer came in for a shave and the older barber gave a few last-minute instructions: "All right, Jim, you try this one and see how you do; but be careful and don't cut yourself."

2

The lawyer in questioning the witness asked, "I believe you are a barber, aren't you?" But the witness was full of the importance of the occasion. "I am," he declared, "a tonsorial artist." "Come now," interposed the judge, "isn't that splitting hairs?"

3

The barber in the little rural shop was more willing than expert. After the ordeal by shaving had been concluded, the pallid customer asked for a drink of water. "Are you thirsty, sir?" inquired the barber. "No," answered the customer weakly, "it's not that. I just want to see if my face still holds water."

4

He was not a regular customer in the shop, so the barber wanted to make him feel at home. "I believe I've shaved you before, haven't I, sir?" he asked amiably. "No, you're just jumping at conclusions," grunted the customer in disgust. "I got that scar in the last war."

See also bald[1], drink[1], haircut, hurry[1], opinion[2], razor, shaving, tired[1].

BARGAIN

1

A bony, anemic-looking woman met a friend on the street. "Why, Anne!" exclaimed the friend. "How thin and pale you look! I thought you were going to winter in Florida for your health?" "Well, I was," admitted Anne, "but a doctor offered me such a marvelous bargain in operations—just think, a major operation for $189—that I just couldn't resist it."

2

The farmer was a born bargainer and the auto salesman was having plenty of trouble selling him. Finally, he thought a demonstration

of the car's performance might help. Explaining its operation, he said, "And now I'll throw in the clutch." "I'll take 'er then," said the farmer triumphantly. "I knew if I held off long enough ye'd throw in somethin'."

BARTENDER

1

The boy had been having a little trouble with his studies in Social Science and he lifted his head from his books to ask, "Papa, what is it they call a person who brings you into contact with the world and things?" Without lifting his rosy nose from the paper, the father replied promptly, "A bartender, son."

2

Two men walking down the street passed another. "Excuse me," said one, "I want to talk to that man." The conversation was long and one-sided, and finally he returned to his waiting friend. "That was my favorite bartender," he explained. "Indeed?" said the other. "And what did he have to say?" "Very little," was the reply. "Just, 'No!'"

See also familiar[1], self-betrayal[1].

BASEBALL

1

He was taking the girl-friend to the game, but by the time she had dressed it was the fourth inning when they got there. "What's the score, Bill?" he asked a nearby acquaintance. "Nothing to nothing," he was informed. "Oh, goody!" exclaimed the girl. "You see, we haven't missed a thing!"

2

The sandlot game was in progress and the kids were going at it hot and heavy. A passing man inquired of one of the fielders as to the score. "Fifty-one to nuthin', favor the other side," he was informed. "They're giving you quite a licking, aren't they?" commented the man. "Heck, no!" retorted the boy. "Just you wait! We ain't been to bat yet."

3

The Sunday afternoon pasture game was short one player so they finally persuaded an old fellow to fill in despite his protests that he had never played and didn't know the game. Nevertheless, when he went to bat he knocked the first ball high over the fence. All stood watching the ball, including the batter, until the crowd started crying excitedly, "Run! Run!" "Shucks!" said the old boy. "Why run? I'll buy you another ball."

4

An Englishman was seeing his first ball game. As inning followed inning he grew increasingly uneasy until at the start of the sixth inning he asked, "I say, old fellow, when do they serve tea?" "Tea!" gasped an American. "They don't serve tea at a ball game." "They don't?" was the amazed response. "Then what's the point of the bloody game?"

5

The girl was sitting bored but patient through her first ball game. At last a fielder made an almost impossible shoe-string catch and the crowd went wild. "What's the excitement about?" she asked her boyfriend. "Why, didn't you see the fielder catch that ball?" he replied

between shouts. "Of course I did," she said calmly. "I thought that's what he's there for."

See also examination[7], indifferent.

BASHFUL

1

The farmer boy and the village girl were equally bashful, but the fellow had screwed up enough courage to walk her home. "Zeke," she implored as they approached her house, "ye won't be a-tellin' anybody that ye beau'd me home, will ye?" "Cracky, Mirandy," said the boy with emphasis, "don't you be a-worryin' — I'm jest as much ashamed of it as you are."

2

Two young men about town one evening were passing a house in which a fair young lady had neglected to pull down the shade. "Gosh!" gasped the one. "That girl isn't at all shy, is she?" "Well, no," said the other, "not exactly. But she most certainly is retiring."

3

The bashful young suitor had been having some trouble in bringing himself to utter those fateful words to the fair lady. At last one evening he made a supreme effort and began, "Ah—Sally, I want to ask—I, er, well—that is, would you, ah—oh, well," he concluded desperately, "do you—er—think that—ah—your mother might give—ah—serious consideration to—ah—becoming my mother-in-law?"

4

The shy young man was having

difficulty in finding sufficient courage to propose to the girl and he kept trying to create situations that would facilitate it for him. One day he took her walking in the cemetery, brought her before the family tomb, and stood awkward and embarrassed for a bit until finally he blurted out, "Mable, dear, wouldn't you like to sleep here someday?"

BATH

1

The former patient called upon the doctor. "Remember me, doc?" he asked. "You cured my rheumatism about a year ago, and you told me to be careful about getting myself wet." "Yes, I recall you," said the doctor. "What can I do for you now?" "Oh, nothing right now, doc," replied the man. "I just wanted to know if it's safe for me to take a bath yet?"

2

The high-school boy was getting dressed with no waste of time as this was to be the big dance of the season. "Did you take a bath, son?" his mother called in. "Heck, no," answered the boy. "Now, look, son," expostulated the mother, "you wouldn't go to that dance without taking a bath, would you?" "Why not?" came the amazed reply. "It's not formal."

3

"G-g-gee, mom," spluttered Tommy through the soap as his mother scrubbed him vigorously, "g-guess you don't like me and want to get rid of me." "Nonsense!" said mother. "Whatever gave you such an idea?" "N-nothin'," replied

Tommy, "'cept it s-seems you're tryin' to rub me out."

See also growth[3], hillbilly[2].

BATTLE

1

It was a dark night and the sergeant was making his rounds when a shell whistled overhead. Without ado, the sergeant dived into the nearest shell-hole, which already held a private on whose stomach he landed and knocked the wind from. There was a ghastly silence, a long tremulous intake of breath, and a shaky voice asked, "That you, sarge?" "Yep," grunted the sergeant. "Oh, boy!" the voice was heavy with relief. "I was just waiting for you to explode."

2

The history teacher was conducting a little quiz and she asked, "What battle was it in which General Wolfe said, 'I die happy,' when he heard the enemy was on the run? Can you tell me, Willie?" Willie hesitated, then replied doubtfully, "I'm not sure, teacher, but it must have been his last."

See also brains[2], courage[1], officer[1].

BEAUTY

The two men hadn't met for many years and they had much to talk of. "And tell me," said one, "is your wife as beautiful as ever?" "Oh, yes," replied the other, "only it takes her a lot longer now."

See also appreciation[1], bride[3], doll[2], mistake[5], reform[4], sarcasm[2], time[3], weeping[3].

BED

1

The traveling man had not slept too well at the little country hotel. Upon leaving, he asked the proprietor, "Could you tell me with what material your beds are stuffed?" "Yes, sir," said the owner proudly, "with the best straw in this part of the country." "How interesting," said the guest. "Now I know where the straw that broke the camel's back came from."

2

The little rural hotel was unusually crowded when the two men applied for lodging. "I'm sorry," said the proprietor, "but I'm afraid I'll have to ask you two to share a room and bed. However, you'll be comfortable as it's a featherbed." At about 3 A.M. one fellow turned stiffly and nudged his partner. "Change places with me, will you, Bill?" he groaned. "It's my turn to lie on the feather."

3

The big, lazy bum thought he'd try the indirect approach. "Say, bud," he stopped the prosperous-looking man, "I wonder would you know where I could get fifteen cents for a bed?" "Certainly, my good man," responded the big-hearted gent graciously. "You just bring the bed to me and if it's worth fifteen cents I'll buy it."

4

It was a little New England inn with more history than comfort, and as the landlord was making out the bill in the morning he was regaling the wan-looking guest with bits of the house's past. "It might interest you to know," he said, "that George Washington once slept in the bed you had last night." "Did he?" replied the tourist weakly. "Boy! He was some sleeper!"

See also bride[2], habit[2], half[1], sleep[2].

BEER

The very proper little old lady had been sipping the first glass of beer she had ever had. After tasting it for a minute or two, she looked up with a puzzled frown and murmured, "How very strange! It tastes just like the medicine my husband has been taking every night for the past thirty years."

See also order[1], saloon[3], shipwreck[2].

BEGGAR

1

The kindly lady could not resist the pleas of the man on crutches. "Here's something for you, my poor fellow," she said pityingly. "It must be terrible to be lame, but think how much worse it would be if you were blind." "How right you are, mum," said the beggar with feeling. "When I wuz blind people wuz always passin' counterfeit money on me."

2

The Newlyriches could have nothing but the best, and consequently their maid had to be cultured and educated. One day the maid announced to her mistress, "Please, ma'am, there's a mendicant at the door." The lady sniffed and waved her hand haughtily. "Send him away," she said, "we've nothing to mend."

3

Two panhandlers were comparing notes on their trade. "Some guys is just heartless," complained one bitterly. "I just tried tellin' a feller that I wuz so flat broke that I'd have to sleep outdoors tonight." "That usually works," commented the other. "Didn't he come across?" "Naw," replied the first disgustedly. "He just told me he was a-doin' the same thing and had to pay a doc big money fer tellin' him to do it."

4

A beggar approached a man on the street one day and after informing him that he hadn't eaten for three days, meekly asked for a penny. Amazed at this request, the man asked what he could do with a cent. "I want to use it," replied the bum, "to find out how much weight I've lost after my three-day fast."

5

The beggar had taken his stand at a busy street-corner in his search for alms. "Sorry, I'm in a hurry now," replied one gentleman he asked, "but I'll give you something on my way back." "Nope, I can't do that," said the beggar curtly. "You can't imagine how much money I've lost giving credit like that."

6

The stranger stopped one of the small town's prominent citizens on the street. "I hit this town broke twelve years ago," he explained, "and asked you for a dollar, and you gave it to me, saying that you never refused such a request." "Yes?" said the important man, smiling expectantly. "Well, here I am again," continued the stranger, "and what I want to know is, are you still game?"

7

The lady was busily engaged in doing her weekly washing, so she had scant patience with the beggar whose knock interrupted her. "Can you help a poor man, mum?" he said in a piteous voice. "You can see I've lost a leg and—" "Well, I haven't got it!" barked the woman, slamming the door in the beggar's face.

See also advice[5], bed[3], blessing, charity[2, 4], penny[2], sympathy[5], tramp, work[2, 4].

BEGGING

1

The beggar was using his most desperate appeal, one that rarely failed to bring results. "Please, sir," he quavered tearfully, "would you give me a loaf of bread for my wife and family?" The man patted his shoulder kindly and replied in tones of deepest sympathy, "I couldn't bring myself to do such a thing, my good man. Why, I wouldn't deprive you of your wife and family for the world."

2

A beggar applied to a well-dressed man hurrying along the street. "Kin ya spare me a dime fer a cuppa coffee, bud?" he asked appealingly. "A dime?" replied the man surprised. "Since when a dime? Coffee's only a nickel." The bum drew himself up in frigid indignation. "Look here, bud," he said haughtily, "are you tryin' to tell me my business?"

See also brief[2], charity, convince[2], grammar[2], rescue[1], tramp, unlucky[2], wish[1], work.

BEHAVIOR

1

The little girl one day ran to her mother in great concern. "Muvver, muvver!" she cried in anxious tones, "how soon is it my birfday?" "It will soon be here, dear," replied mother. "No, no," objected the child impatiently, "I mean is it time yet for me to begin bein' a good girl?"

2

Little Jane had been a "bad girl" and mother had sent her to her room to consider things. After a while she reappeared with a bright and shining face. "Well, mamma," she announced, "I've thought things over and I prayed." "That's fine," approved mother. "That should help you to be a good girl." "Oh, I didn't pray for help to be good," explained the girl. "I asked God to help you put up with me."

3

Little Willie had been acting up and the Sunday school teacher was trying to reprove him gently. "I'm really very much afraid, Willie," she said sorrowfully, "that I'll not meet you in heaven." "Gee! That's too bad," sympathized the boy. "What've you been doing now, teacher?"

4

"Well, Johnnie," asked Auntie at Sunday luncheon, "did you behave well in church this morning?" "Why sure I did," responded Johnnie. "I even heard the lady behind us say that she'd never seen a child behave so."

5

The Arkansas hillbilly was at his favorite occupation: lying in the sun. The flies buzzed around and settled thickly on his face, but it wasn't worth his effort to shoo them away. Finally, a hornet lit amongst the flies and stung his nose, whereupon he slowly wiped his hand across his face muttering, "As long as *some* o' ye won't behave ye'll jist *all* have to git off."

6

Little Jeanne wanted to go to the store with mother, so, in order to placate her, mother promised to bring her something nice if she stayed home and behaved herself. When mother returned she found Jeanne waiting at the gate. "Well, Jeanne, were you a good girl?" asked mother. "Oh, mamma!" exclaimed the child, "I was gooder than good! Why, I was so good I could hardly stand it."

7

Little Margie was fond of playing about in school instead of minding her lessons, but one day she had been so prim and quiet that teacher thought she should praise her a bit. "You've been a very good girl today, Margie," she complimented. "Yeth, ma'am," admitted Margie. "I dist touldn't help it. I dot a stiff neck."

See also rude[1, 2], self-betrayal[2, 4].

BELCHING

1

A drama critic who was known chiefly for two things, his biting criticism and his indigestion, had foolishly put away a big dinner before going to the opening of a new show. His gastric discomfort was not made any easier by the poor quality of the show, and finally he emitted a very clear and distinct burp. A girl in an adjoining seat turned on him reprovingly to whisper, "Can't you wait until later to give your review?"

2

An American with an excessive regard for the proprieties was having dinner with a rotund foreigner, fond of his creature comforts, and his family. As the meal progressed, the host suddenly gave out with a resounding burp. "Oh, gracious!" said the very proper gentleman aghast. "Are you in the habit of doing this before your children?" The other shrugged his shoulders. "Ve have no rules. Sometimes I go first, sometimes de kids go first."

See also volcano[1].

BELIEF

1

The girl looked maliciously after a charming young belle tripping down the street. "There's a girl who's willing to suffer for her beliefs," she observed caustically to her boy-friend. "Why, what belief is that?" he asked innocently. "Oh, she believes that she can wear a number five shoe on a number eight foot," was the biting reply.

2

The backwoods farmer had never been far from his farm, so he was very interested when the neighbor's sailor son came home for a visit. "Tell me, lad," he questioned, "what was the most unusual thing you saw

on your travels?" "I guess about the strangest thing was the flying fish," answered the boy. "Come, now," said the farmer smilingly, "you don't think I'm fool enough to believe that!" "Well," continued the sailor, "once when we pulled up anchor in the Red Sea we found one of Pharaoh's chariot wheels on it." "That I believe," said the farmer. "We've Scripture for that."

See also compromise[3], devil[3], disbelief.

BELLBOY

1

A bellboy moved about the lobby of an elegant hotel whistling as he went. The horrified manager called him aside. "Young man," he said sternly, "you should know that it's forbidden for an employee to whistle while on duty." "But I'm not whistling, sir," explained the page. "I'm paging a guest's dog."

2

After developing a sore thumb on the push-button, the guest bit his lip for control when the bellboy finally stuck his head leisurely in the door. "Did you ring, sir?" the boy asked with a yawn. "Heck, no!" replied the purple guest. "I was tolling—I thought you were dead."

See also hotel[7].

BENEFIT

See charity, favor, help.

BEST

1

It had been a difficult case in domestic relations and the judge pondered long before he spoke. "The best thing you can do," he declared, "is to become reconciled to your wife." "Oh, my!" exclaimed the man, distress in his voice. "And what's the next best thing?"

2

A man of rather mordant wit was having a quarrel with his wife. Finally, after an especially scathing remark, she burst into tears and wailed, "How *can* you say such things to me after I've given you six of the best years of my life!" "Good gracious!" exclaimed her husband, "were *those* your *best?*"

3

The man just arriving in a small town encountered another man waiting for a train to take him away. "Could you direct me to the best hotel in town?" he inquired of the departing stranger. "I can, but I sure hate to do it," replied the other. "Why, how's that?" asked the first. "Because after you get there you'll call me a liar," was the reply.

BET

1

The grumpy old fellow was perusing the menu and brushing aside the waiter's recommendations. "No, no," he snapped, "I don't want any mushrooms. I was nearly poisoned by some I had here last week." The waiter's face brightened as he leaned across the table. "Is that a fact, sir?" he cried eagerly. "Then I *have* won my bet with cook."

2

A man entered a hat shop. "I've just lost a bet," he informed the clerk, "and I'd like to buy a soft hat." The clerk selected one and handed it to the customer, saying, "This is the softest hat we have, sir." The man regarded it dubiously. "What I want," he explained sadly, "is something a little more tender. You see, I've got to eat it."

See also proposal[3], truth[3].

BETTER

1

The street peddler was selling cigars which, according to him, were the best obtainable. "I don't care where you go or what you pay, gents," he shouted, "you can't get better." "You sure can't, brother," spoke a voice in the crowd. "I smoked one last week and I'm not better yet."

2

The boarder's complaints had been so frequent that at last the landlady had had all she could stand. "I think you had better board somewhere else," she said angrily. "You said it, sister," retorted the boarder. "At lots of places."

3

The schoolboy resisted instruction in the domestic arts, and rebelled in particular against sewing. "Look here," said the teacher, trying to placate him, "as a soldier George Washington had to do his sewing, and do you think you're any better than George Washington?" The boy thought this over gravely before he answered, "Well, I'm not sure yet, but time will tell."

4

The wife was highly indignant at her inebriated husband. "My goodness!" she scolded, "couldn't you think of anything better than coming home in such a filthy drunken state?" "Yesh, m'love, I sure could," was the unsteady reply, "but she wassh outta town."

See also steal.

BIBLE

1

The Sunday-school teacher had just finished a detailed account of Jonah and the whale. "And now, Willie, can you tell us what lesson this story teaches?" she asked. "Yes'm," returned Willie. "It teaches that you can't keep a good man down."

2

The minister was reading a text from Holy Scriptures, when an elderly lady interrupted to inquire, "What kind of Bible are you reading from, parson?" "This is the revised version," he replied. "Humph!" she grunted disapprovingly. "The King James version was good enough for St. Paul and it's good enough for me."

3

The teacher of the Sunday school class was calling on her pupils for volunteers to give quotations from the Bible. One little fellow got up and recited, "And Judas went out and hanged himself." He had scarcely finished when another little boy sprang to his feet and quoted, "Go thou and do likewise."

4

The minister was circulating among the various Sunday school classes and he paused to ask one small girl, "Do you come to Sunday school regularly?" "Oh, yes, sir," was the answer. "Then I suppose you can tell me some of the things that are in your Bible?" he continued. "Golly," said the girl, "I can tell you *everything* that's in it. There's mom's recipe for ketchup, sis's snapshots of the boy-friend, one of my baby curls, and the hockticket for pop's watch."

5

The visiting bishop was being shown through the Sunday school and he stopped to inquire of one little girl, "You seem like a bright little girl; can you give me a verse from the Bible?" "Oh, boy! I'll say I can," was the eager reply. "Fine, my dear; let's hear it," urged the bishop, and the girl recited, "The Lord is my shepherd—I should worry."

6

The minister had called rather unexpectedly and while he waited for the lady of the house to make her appearance he conversed with her small daughter. "What is that you have in your hand, my dear?" he asked idly. "Oh, that's my apron that I'm going to put in the wash," replied the little girl. "Mamma just got it all dirty when she grabbed it up to dust the Bible when she saw you coming."

See also baby[1], bigamy[3], neighbor[3], reading[2], talk[3].

BICYCLE

A salesman was trying to talk a farmer into buying a bicycle, but was meeting with considerable sales resistance. "Shucks, I'd sooner spend my money on a cow," said the farmer. "Ah," replied the salesman, "but think how silly you'd look riding around on a cow." "Humph!" retorted the farmer. "Not near as silly as I'd look tryin' to milk a bicycle."

See also affectionate[3].

BIG

See size.

BIGAMY

1

An old Indian on the reservation had a number of wives and the inspector was talking to him about it. "Don't you know that it's against the law to have more than one wife?" he questioned. "Now when you get home you tell all your wives but one that they can't consider you their husband any longer." The Indian was reflective for a moment. "Ugh!" he grunted at last. "You tell 'um."

2

The unlucky fellow was amiable by nature and just couldn't say no, so he ended up with three wives before the year was out. The law stepped in and he was sent to prison for four years, to his apparent relief. As the expiration of his sentence neared, he wrote his lawyer a piteous note in which he queried: "Will it be safe to come out now?"

3

The man with a sense of humor was arguing with a Mormon about polygamy. The Mormon was loud in his insistence that polygamy was perfectly moral. "I defy you, sir," he said with great dignity, "to cite me any passage of Scripture forbidding the practice." But the wit was ready for him and with a twinkle in his eye responded, "Well, how about that passage in the Bible that says no man can serve two masters?"

4

The police judge called the next case. "What's the charge against this here feller?" he asked the policeman. "The charge is bigotry, yer Honor," replied the cop. "He's got three wives." "Three wives!" shouted the judge. "Why you dumbbell, that ain't bigotry, that's trigonometry!"

See also wife[8].

BILL

1

"Imagine my surprise," said a stockbroker genially to one of his clients, "when during this warm spell I got out one of my summer suits to wear and found a big roll of bills in one of the pockets." But the other man must have had experience with stockbrokers for he merely grunted, "Were any of them receipted?"

2

The man had died rather suddenly and every one was doing what he could for the bewildered widow. The doctor called on her and said, "I know what a blow all this has been to you, so I want you to know that I am cutting my bill in half." Tears filled the woman's eyes and she pressed the doctor's hand gratefully. "Bless you, doctor," she quavered, "and I'll be as good as you and forget the other half of the bill."

3

Two men were discussing their household expenses. "The wife used to do all her shopping in two or three stores and run up terrific bills," said one, "but I gave her a talking to and now her bills are much smaller." "Great!" approved the other. "But how did she manage it?" "Very simply," replied the first. "She just buys from thirty or forty stores now."

4

The father of the family returned home one evening to find his little daughter excitedly waiting for him. "A strange man was here to see you today, daddy," she cried as soon as he stepped in. "Is that so? Did he have a bill?" asked father. "Oh, no, daddy," replied the little girl, "just a plain nose like everybody else."

See also amount[1], hotel[8], payment[3, 6], recovery[1, 5].

BILLIARDS

A train wreck forced a traveling salesman to spend the night at a little crossroads village. Desperate for amusement, he resorted to the antiquated pool table at the general store. The balls being all of a uniform dull gray, he inquired, "How do you manage to tell the different colored balls apart?" "Nuthin' to it," replied the proprietor. "You soon git to know 'em by their shape."

BIRD

1

They were strolling in the park and the birds were swooping and circling overhead. Finally, one eagle-eyed birdie made a bull's-eye on her new hat. "Oh, gracious!" the girl exclaimed disgustedly. "Please give me a piece of paper quickly." "Why worry?" asked the boy. "That bird's probably a quarter-mile away by now."

2

Little Junior went to the corner grocery store and asked for some canary seed, but didn't know which brand. "Is it for your mother?" asked the clerk. "Of course not, silly," replied Junior, "it's for the canary."

See also fruit[2], imitation[2].

BIRTHDAY

1

The young lady was planning a birthday party, but her joy was not unmingled with regrets. "Gee!" she sighed sadly to her friend, "I certainly hate to think of my twenty-ninth birthday." "Why is that?" inquired the friend maliciously. "Did something terrible happen on that day?"

2

"Guess what!" confided the little boy to his teacher. "Day after tomorrow is my birthday." "Why, what a coincidence!" exclaimed teacher. "It's mine too!" The little fellow frowned in puzzlement and shook his head. "How can that be," he queried, "when you're so much bigger'n me?"

See also behavior[1], light[2].

BIRTHPLACE

1

The census-taker was questioning the old maid in order to fill out his report. "And in what state were you born?" he questioned her. "Well, er—ah," she stammered, "in—ah—um—the nude, of course."

2

The benign old lady struck up a conversation with the small child playing on a vacant lot. Among other things, she inquired, "And where were you born, my little man?" "I wasn't born at all," replied the boy, not too pleased at being disturbed; "I've got a step-mother."

3

The new cook was so good that the family went out of its way to make her feel at home. "You're from the West, aren't you, Mary?" asked the mistress in a conversational tone. "Sure am, ma'am," was the reply. "Born there, I guess?" was the next question. "Yes'm," was the proud response. "I was originally born in San Francisco, California."

See also meeting[2].

BLACKMAIL

Two young ladies of the chorus were discussing the love affairs of one of their co-workers. "I hear that Ruth's broken off her engagement with George," said one. "I wonder if she's keeping those swell love-letters he wrote her?" "Well, yes and no," replied the other. "To be a little more exact, they're keeping her."

BLACKSMITH

1

The small boy had been looking for a job during summer vacation, but when he came home with the news that he had found one at the blacksmith's shop, his folks couldn't help laughing. "Why, sonny," they said, "you don't mean to tell us that a little fellow like you can shoe horses?" "Maybe not," the boy insisted stoutly, "but I can shoo flies."

2

"Mother! Oh, mother!" cried the little boy, running in all excited. "I've seen a man making a horse!" "Nonsense, son," replied mother, "that couldn't be." "But it is, mother," insisted the boy. "He was just finishing a horse when I saw him and he was nailing on the feet."

See also advertising[1], instructions[2], stuttering[2].

BLAME

1

The tourist couldn't believe his ears when the local policeman told him he was under arrest after the accident. "But, officer," he explained, "I had the right of way, was proceeding slowly, and this man deliberately ran into me—yet you say *I'm* to blame?" "That's right," was the reply. "But it doesn't make sense," objected the tourist. "Why?" "Because," said the cop firmly, "his father's the Mayor, his brother's the Chief of Police, and I'm going steady with his sister."

2

Mother had tried almost everything to keep Tommy away from the cookies. "Now remember, Tommy," she warned, "there's a horrible ghost in that dark closet where the cookies are." "It's sure funny," commented Tommy, "that he's in there all the time and you never blame him when some cookies are gone; you always blame me."

BLESSING

A beggar approached a gentleman of well-to-do appearance and asked for charity. Without a word, the gentleman put his hand in his pocket, and the bum immediately cried out, "May the blessing of the Lord follow you all the days of your life!" But the man only pulled out his handkerchief and started to pass on, whereupon the beggar added with hardly a break "—and never catch up with you."

BLIND

One day a little box with a slot in the top and bearing a sign "For the Blind" appeared on the storekeeper's counter. His customers, with commendable sympathy for the unfortunate, contributed generously of their change. After about a month the box was missing. "What happened to the collection box for the blind?" asked one. The storekeeper chuckled and pointed to the window. "Oh, I collected enough," he said. "There's the new blind."

BLUNDER

See mistake, wrong.

BLUSH

Grandpa was shaking his head sadly over the younger generation. "No, Helen," he told his granddaughter, "girls of today are different." The girl smiled indulgently at the old story. "How do you mean?" she asked. "Well," ex-

plained the old man, "you never see a girl of today blush. It was different when I was a young fellow." "Why, grandpa!" chided Helen. "What in the world did you say to them?"

BOARDING HOUSE

1

The landlady was instructing the new girl. "And always remember, Janie," she stressed, "whenever there's any bad news—family troubles, fickle sweethearts, bad debts, etc.—for any of the boarders, be sure to tell it to them before dinner." "But why, mum?" queried the girl. "Why!" exclaimed the landlady. "You'd be surprised, Janie, what that does for the food bills in the course of a year."

2

The boarders were very hungry, but the sight of the plateful of wafer-thin slices of bread and butter that the landlady set before them was not especially gladdening. "Did you cut these, Mrs. Smith?" inquired one boarder. "Yes, I cut them," was the sharp reply. "All right," said the boarder agreeably. "Then I'll deal them."

3

The newcomer was evidently a seasoned veteran of boarding houses. He came down to breakfast early on his first morning and was greeted with smiles by the landlady. "Will you have tea, coffee, or cocoa?" she inquired sweetly. But he remained unimpressed, sat down quietly, and replied in an even voice, "Whichever you call it."

4

The mother was trying to find a

good boarding house for her son who was entering university. She located a surprisingly nice room and inquired the rent. "I'm willing to let this room at half rates," explained the landlady, "because there's a woman next door who plays the piano almost constantly." "Oh, that won't bother my son," replied the lady, "he's rather deaf." "In that case," said the landlady, "I must have my full price."

5

It was a snowy, blustery night and the elderly boarder sat comfortably by the fireside with the landlady. The coziness and warmth did their insidious work and suddenly he turned to the landlady and murmured, "Will you marry me?" The landlady thought carefully before she answered, "Let's see, you've been here four years, never grumbled about the food or anything, and always paid promptly without question. I'm sorry, but you're too good a boarder to put on the free list."

See also better[2], resemblance[2], tongue.

BOAST

1

A tourist was passing the time of day with the hotelkeeper of the little village. "I was through here about two years ago, and if I recall correctly this place boasts of a choral society, doesn't it?" The hotel man grimaced a little. "We don't boast about it," he replied sadly. "We just do our best to endure it."

2

Two little girls had a quarrel and one took it upon herself to put the other in her place. "You're not so much," she declared. "We have a great big house, three servants, two automobiles, and Mamma has four fur coats." The other girl hesitated a moment, but then retorted with equal pride, "And we've got a big skunk under our barn."

3

The two politicians were having a debate which was rapidly degenerating into an ordinary argument. "I can truthfully say that I never boast," stated the one proudly. "Never boast? Why that's splendid!" replied the other, and then added gleefully, "I don't wonder that you brag about it."

See also display[2], house[4], soldier[1].

BOAT

1

"Don't worry, sir," the captain reassured the nervous passenger. "I've been running boats on this river all my life and I know where every snag, rock, and sandbar is." Just then the boat shivered throughout its length from striking an underwater snag. "See there!" cried the captain triumphantly, "that's one of them now!"

2

A woman taking a boat trip on the Great Lakes emerged from her cabin to see a sailor pumping water from the hold. Going up to a nearby officer, she said, "I see you have a well on this ship." "Oh, yes, madam," the officer replied, keeping a straight face, "we have one for the convenience of the passengers." "That's fine," approved the lady

"I certainly don't like that dirty lake water."

3

The newlyweds went to a lake resort for their honeymoon. The afternoon being beautiful, they had a boat ride as soon as they arrived. The next day the bride's mother received a postcard saying: "Arrived safely. Grand row before supper." The mother laid the card aside with a sigh of regret. "What a pity!" she murmured. "I didn't think they'd start quarreling this soon."

See also hurry[3], jump[1], precaution[3], river[2].

BODY

1

The magician's assistant was a very shapely young lady in her close-fitting garments. As the magician proceeded to saw her in half, he remarked casually, "After the performance, ladies and gentlemen, the young lady's brain will be given to science and, so there will be no waste, the rest will be thrown to the dogs." At once there issued from the rear a deep voice saying, "Woof, woof!"

2

The physiology teacher was calling for common illustrations of body functions. "Willie," she asked, "can you give an everyday example of how the body adapts itself to changing conditions?" "Yes'm," replied Willie. "My aunt put on over 45 pounds in a year and her skin didn't crack."

3

The young medical student wished to be completely up-to-date. "These books on anatomy are all over eight or ten years old," he complained to the professor. "Aren't there any more recent ones?" "These are still fairly valid," replied the professor. "You know, there have been very few new bones added to the body in the last ten years."

4

The teacher in the elementary physiology class was trying to illustrate the workings of metabolism. "It might seem hard to believe," she told her class, "but in effect there is always a fire burning in the body." "Oh, I believe it, teacher," spoke up a little girl, " 'cause in winter time you can see the smoke."

BOLD

See courage, impudence.

BONE

1

During the last war many towns were under siege and food shortages became acute. In one such town, after extreme hunger had overcome their natural reluctance, a family served up their little pet dog for dinner. When they had finished, the head of the house surveyed the pile of bones on the platter sadly. "Poor Fido!" he sighed. "How he would have enjoyed these bones!"

2

The young man was very health-through-diet conscious and was forever boring people with the details. "I drink milk regularly," he informed a girl friend, "because my doctor tells me it is a great bone builder." "You'd better go easy," warned the girl. "I'm afraid your drinks are going to your head."

See also body[3], leg[1].

BOOK

1

An author and a friend were heatedly discussing a new book and found themselves at some variance as to its merits. "There's no use in your talking, Bill," said the author finally. "You never wrote a book yourself so of course you can't appreciate the fine points of one." "Oh, I don't know," retorted Bill. "I never laid an egg myself, but I can spot a bad one quicker than any hen in the country."

2

Two chorus girls were doing their Christmas shopping. "I sure don't know what to get Mamie this year," said one, referring to one of their sisters of the stage. "Why don't you get her a book?" suggested the other. "Naw," objected the first, "she's got a book."

3

The young man rushed breathlessly to the desk of the public library. "Can I get that book again that I had last week?" he demanded. "I suppose so," said the librarian. "Did you find it so fascinating?" "Heck, no, the book's lousy," replied the fellow, "but it's got my girl's phone number in it."

4

Two men were looking over the selection of popular books in a bookstore. "I wonder where the dime novel has gone to," commented the one curiously. "Humph!" snorted the other disdainfully. "It's right in front of you. It's just gone to a dollar ninety-eight."

5

The lady was examining the shelves of a bookshop. "Can I help you, madam?" asked the clerk. "I am looking for a book of synonyms," replied the lady. "Hm, let me see," pondered the clerk. "Just a moment, please, until I ask the boss. I don't believe we have any of Mr. Synonym's works."

See also appreciation[3], author[5, 7], authority, Boston[5], library[1, 2], study[4], surgery[1].

BOOKKEEPING

1

Thinking to encourage his wife to economize by making her conscious of her expenditures, the husband brought her an account book, gave her a hundred dollars, and explained, "Now, dear, on one side you write down the money you receive and on the other you put down what happened to it, and you'll always know just where you stand." Three days later he looked in the book and on one side found: "Received $100.00," and on the opposite side was written: "Spent it all."

2

The man was applying for the position of bookkeeper. "You say you are an expert accountant," said the boss, "and your references are excellent, but I'd like to know more about you from yourself." "Well, sir," replied the applicant proudly, "my wife once kept a household account book for a month, and I sat down with it one evening and in an hour managed to figure what we owed the butcher." "Hang up your hat," cried the boss instantly. "You're hired."

BOOTBLACK

1

The soldier had enormous feet, but by the time the army had fitted him with shoes according to its notion of a fit, the result was staggering, especially to the little bootblack to whom the soldier went for a shine. The little fellow went to work industriously, but soon was running short of his favorite lubricating fluid. "Say, Tom," he called to another boy, "lend me a spit, will you? I've got an army contract."

2

Two young bootblacks with neighboring stands had been feuding for some days. "I jist figgered out how to get even wit' dat guy," the one confided in a friend. "Gonna fight 'im, huh?" said the other. "Naw," replied the bootblack. "When he gits through wit' a gent's shoes, I'm gonna step right up and say, 'Shine, sir, shine?'"

BORE

1

A pretty girl was cornered by the inevitable bore at a party who inflicted hours of deadly dull conversation upon her. Finally, the girl rose to leave and the bore queried, "Who's driving you home?" "You are," she snapped, and stalked out.

2

The gentleman was partial to the sound of his own voice and had

been regaling the group for two hours with minute details of his trip to the Alps. "And there I stood," he declared impressively, "with this abyss yawning in front of me." "Excuse me," said one of the unfortunate listeners, "but was the abyss yawning before you got there?"

3

He had long-winded comments to make on any and all subjects and after enduring them for about two hours she was getting desperate. The talk turned to rural life and he said, "I read about a man who was hooked by a cow. Pretty nasty, what, being hooked to death by a cow?" "Not nearly as bad as being bored to death by a calf," she retorted.

See also classroom[2], joke[1], marriage[10], sister[2].

BORROW

1

Smith was a chronic borrower and all his friends tried to avoid him, but one day he surprised one of them on the street before he could duck. "Say, old fellow," he began, "I'm really in a jam and need money, and I haven't any idea where I'm going to get some." "I'm sure glad to hear that, Smith," replied the other. "I was afraid you might have the silly notion you could borrow some from me."

2

Two actors met and went to a restaurant. At the end of the meal one said, "I'm a little short, Jim; could you let me have ten for a week?" "Sure," said the other, handing him a bill. As they rose to go, the lender prompted the borrower, "Remember, now, that's only for a week." "You'll get your money all right," screamed the other. "Just stop hounding me!"

3

The neighborhood moocher cornered Jones in his yard one Sunday morning. "Say, Jones, are you going to use your lawnmower this afternoon?" he queried. Jones was on his guard. "I sure am," he replied. "Good!" cried the chiseler. "Then you won't be using your golf clubs, so I'll just borrow them."

See also contract[1], credit[2], lend[1], proposal[6], repay[2], sympathy[1].

BOSOM

A well-developed young lady had a slight cold. As a precaution, upon going to a dinner party, she took along two handkerchiefs, placing the extra one in the bosom of her dress. As dinner progressed she found she needed her spare handkerchief, but feeling about her dress bosom she couldn't find it. She then began to search intently, from right to left, until suddenly she realized every eye at the table was on her. Reddening, she smiled and murmured, "I *know* I had two when I left home."

BOSS

1

Two men were discussing their home life. "Honestly, now, who is really boss at your house?" asked the one. "Well, naturally," admitted the other slowly, "Mary takes complete charge of the children, the servants, the dog and cat, and the canary, but I can say just about anything I please to the goldfish."

2

"Oh, what a day!" groaned the businessman as he climbed on the 5:20 for home. "My office boy asked for the afternoon off to go to his grandmother's funeral, so I thought I'd show him up and said I'd go along." "Good idea!" grinned his friend. "How was the game?" "Game, my foot," sighed the other wearily. "It really was his grandmother's funeral."

3

The new manager had been at the plant about eight months, but he had the feeling that he still wasn't popular with the men. Calling aside one of the old employees, he asked, "What's wrong here, Bill, that the men don't seem to like me? Why when I left my last place the boys presented me with a silver teapot." "Only a silver teapot!" cried the worker. "Gee, if you'd leave here we'd make it a gold tea service."

4

The young applicant for the job was being interviewed by the boss. After the customary questions, the boss inquired, "Do you have any ambition, young man?" "Ambition!" cried the young fellow. "Why, sir, I shall never rest until I see you out of that chair and me in it."

5

The visitor looked around the office in surprise. "Your help seems all extremely happy and cheerful," he commented to the boss. "Have you given them a raise or something?" "Not on your life," answered the businessman. "To be honest, it's simply because my wife was in a little while ago and it pleases them to see someone boss me around."

See also decision[2], discharge[1], efficiency[1], search[3], suggestion[1], workman[3].

BOSTON

1

The European had found the American lady traveling abroad to be most charming and well-mannered. "I can't understand your being from Chicago," he exclaimed. "I naturally assumed you were from Boston." "What gave you that idea?" she asked. "Simply because I thought all intelligent and cultured Americans were from Boston," he replied. "Whatever made you think that?" was the natural question. "Oh, I don't know," he answered. "I think a Boston lady once told me so."

2

In a cultured Boston family the little boy came running in excitedly crying, "Mamma! Mamma! Baby has just fell out of the window!" "Bobby!" reproved mother sternly, "you mean 'has fallen,' don't you? Now never forget that. Very well, now run for the doctor quickly!"

3

The Bostonian was very democratic and tried not to show his superiority over common folk. Once in traveling he stopped over in Salt Lake City and struck up a conversation with a little Mormon girl. "I'm from Boston," he informed her kindly. "Do you know where Boston is, my girl?" "Why, certainly," replied the little girl quickly. "Our Sunday school has a missionary there."

4

The Boston lady was being very polite to the stranger seated next to her at dinner. "And where do you live, sir?" she inquired. "Out West, madam," he replied. "My home is two nights on a sleeper from Boston." "A sleeper!" exclaimed the dear lady. "How exciting! I've always wondered what they were like." "You've never been on one?" queried the Westerner. "Dear me, no," answered the lady with a pitying smile. "You see, I was born here."

5

A Boston businessman had been too busy in his youth to do much reading, but, with his fortune made, he decided to devote some time to it and began with Shakespeare. Having finished a volume of the "Collected Works," he remarked to a friend, "By Jove! That's certainly a remarkable book. I doubt if there are a dozen men in Boston who could have written it."

See also parrot[2], stop[2].

BOXING

1

The two prizefight fans were talking over the match of the previous evening. "What'd you think of the big fight last night, Joe?" asked one. "Fight!" cried Joe sneeringly. "Why, if me an' the missus would put on a bout like that on Saturday nights, the kids would boo us."

2

The prizefighter wasn't doing so well and looked pretty sick of the whole affair. "Stop those punches!" shouted his excited manager from his corner. The fighter managed to open his swollen lips enough to retort, "You don't see any of 'em gettin' past me, do you?"

3

The dizzy fighter wobbled to his corner at the end of the sixth round and was guided to his stool by his manager. As the seconds worked over him, the manager whispered into his bulging ear, "Say, Killer, I've just had a whale of an idea—the next time that guy hits you, you hit him right back."

See also confidence[1], training[1].

BOY

1

A certain town had had several earthquake shocks and the parents of a boy living there became concerned for his safety and decided to send him to live with some relatives in another locality for a while. Two days after the boy had arrived at his destination, the parents received this desperate telegram: "Am returning your boy immediately. Please send the earthquake instead."

2

A boy entered an office in response to a sign, "Boy Wanted." "What kinda boy do yer want?" he asked the manager. "Why, we want a clean, decent, and neat boy, of course," replied the manager. "One who is quiet, quick, and obedient, one who doesn't smoke, swear, whis-

tle around the office, shoot craps, or—" "Phooey!" said the boy disgustedly, turning to leave. "You don't want a boy; you want a girl."

See also appetite[3], country[1], fall[1], fight[1, 2], fun[2], perfect[1], trust[4].

BOYFRIEND

1

Father was having it out with Mabel about her boyfriend's habits about the house. "Gee, weren't you ever young yourself, father?" said Mabel. "Of course I was," admitted father, "and I'm willing to make certain allowances. I don't mind if he smokes my cigars, drinks my beer, and borrows my umbrella; but when he takes the morning papers with him when he says good night, that's too much."

2

A stenographer appeared at the office one morning wearing on her sweater two officers' silver bars. "Gee," inquired one of her coworkers, "have you got a captain for a boyfriend?" "Oh, gracious, no," was the reply, "just two lieutenants."

3

Father had been winding the clock, dropping his shoes, and stomping about for some time without getting any results from daughter's boyfriend. Finally he shouted down the stairs, "Say, there, it's two-thirty! Do you think you can stay all night?" "Well, all right, thanks," replied the boy. "But I'll have to phone home first."

See also hint[4, 7], like[1].

BRAG

See boast.

BRAINS

1

Despite his most ardent pleas, the girl continued to refuse him. At last he cried in desperation, "If you won't marry me I'll blow out my brains." "Oh, will you really?" she cooed in delight. "Please do. It will be such a joke on father who always said you didn't have any."

2

The young fellow was looking forward to the coming inter-collegiate debate in which he was to take part. "It's going to be something," he informed his bored roommate. "It will be a real battle of wits." "How brave of you," yawned the other, "to go into battle unarmed."

3

Father was giving the family a detailed account of how he had prevented a fight on his construction job. "It was just as one of the men picked up a shovel and shouted, 'I'll knock your brains out!'" he related, "that I stepped fearlessly between them." Little Junior had been listening with bated breath and now cried out, "I bet he couldn't knock any brains outta you, could he, pop?"

See also diet[5].

BRAVE

See courage.

BREAD

1

The crew of lumberjacks had been isolated in the woods for a long time subsisting on nothing but salt pork and hardtack. At last they decided they needed a change and sent one of their number on the long trip to town for some fresh victuals. After some time he returned with twelve quarts of whiskey and one medium-sized loaf of bread. As a man, the crew cried, "Now wot'n hell are we gonna do with all that bread?"

2

The commanding officer was receiving a delegation of his men who were complaining about the food and in particular about the bread that was being issued. "Soldiers shouldn't let themselves be bothered over trifles," he admonished. "Why, I'll wager that if Napoleon had had that bread when he was in Russia he'd have eaten it with gusto." "No doubt, sir," said one of the men, "it was still fairly fresh then."

See also boarding house[2], charity[4], eating[3], grace[3].

BREAKAGE

1

The exasperated mistress called her maid to her. "Bridget," she said sternly, "each month you are breaking more things than your wages amount to. Whatever can we do about it?" Bridget shrugged her shoulders and replied, "I really can't say, mum, unless you raise my wages."

2

The small boy came penitently and tearfully to his mother. "Gee, mom," he sobbed, "I'm awful sorry but I broke one of the tiles in the fireplace." "That's all right, dear," said mother soothingly, "don't worry. But how did you ever come to break it?" "Gosh, mom," replied the child, "I was just poundin' it with pop's watch."

See also reference[3].

BREAKFAST

See eating, food, meals.

BREATHING

1

The Major consulted the medical officer about a chest ailment, and deep-breathing exercises were advised. Meeting the Major again some weeks later, the medical officer asked, "Are you still taking those deep-breathing exercises every morning as I ordered, Major?" "As a matter of fact, no," admitted the Major. "I've stopped them for a while since I've been quartered directly behind the incinerator."

2

The minister was an ardent tobacco-hater and he was trying to show one inveterate old pipe smoker the error of his ways. "You expect to go to heaven, don't you, Sam?" he asked. "Yes, sir, I do," replied Sam. "But you must remember," pointed out the preacher, "that the Bible says that nothing unclean shall enter there, and the smoker's breath is unclean. What about that?" "Well, Reverend," said Sam, "when I go to heaven I figger on leavin' my breath behind."

3

The woman was a chronic ailer and a big bother to the busy doctor.

"Do you have any new aches or pains today?" he asked her. "Well, no, doctor," she admitted reluctantly, "except when I breathe. As a matter of fact, my only trouble now seems to be my breathing." "Don't worry, madam," the doctor comforted her, "I'll give you something that will soon stop that."

See also statistics[4].

BREEDING

1

The elegant lady had been seated next to an obviously low-brow person at a dinner and was trying to put him in his place. "I'm sure that all right-thinking people will agree," she observed haughtily, "that breeding is everything." "Oh, I wouldn't go quite so far as to say that," he demurred, "but I do admit, lady, that it's a helluva lot of fun."

2

"How did it happen that the new tax bill died before it ever came up for vote?" asked the green young Congressman. "Because of bad breeding, son," replied the veteran, "just a case of bad breeding." "But I don't understand?" questioned the youngster. "It was sired by the Democrats and damned by the Republicans," was the reply.

See also recruit[2].

BRIBERY

1

Little Billy was a politician's son. Also, he was afraid of the dark. One night as he was about to get into bed, his mother overheard him praying, "Dear God, if you won't let anything hurt me tonight, I'll go to church Sunday and give you some money."

2

The lawyer was determined to save his client from hanging, so just to play safe he got one of the jurors aside and said, "I'll see that you're well taken care of if you get the jury to bring in a verdict of manslaughter in the second degree." When the jury reappeared, the verdict was as desired and the prisoner got a long prison term. The lawyer later paid off the juror and thanked him. "It was sure a tough deal," said the venal juror. "They were all for acquittal, but I talked them out of it."

3

Auntie did not have much success in winning the little boy's affection. "Will you kiss me if I give you a penny?" she propositioned him. "Huh! A penny!" he grunted in disgust. "Why, I get that much for taking castor oil."

See also conscience[1], politics[8], suffrage, worm[2].

BRIDE

1

The man looked considerably the worse for wear. "Goodness! Who gave you that black eye and split lip?" cried a friend. "A fellow, just because I kissed his bride after the ceremony," replied the bruised one. "How silly!" exclaimed his friend. "Why should he object to the venerable custom?" "I don't know," said the other, "unless maybe because it was three years after the ceremony."

2

The honeymoon couple had just registered in the hotel and had been shown to their room. The new bride had been thrilled with everything, but when she saw the twin beds her face fell. "What's wrong, dear heart?" asked the solicitous bridegroom. "Oh, nothing much," said the bride sadly, "but I'd just hoped that we might get a room all to ourselves."

3

The marriage ceremony had just been concluded and the groom thrust his hand into his pocket and inquired, "What do I owe you, Reverend?" "We do not charge for this service, sir," replied the minister, "but you may pay me according to the beauty of your bride." "Okay," said the young man, and handed over a quarter. The minister raised the bride's veil, took a look, and dug into his own pocket. "Here's fifteen cents change," he said.

4

A young lady had just returned from a friend's wedding and her mother was getting the details. "And who gave the bride away?" she asked. "Her little brother—and how!" replied daughter. "Right in the middle of the ceremony he stood up in his seat and shouted, 'Hurray, Jane! You got 'im at last!'"

5

It was only a few hours after the wedding and the newlyweds had just arrived in their hotel room. "And just think, George," sighed the bride, "we're married now and don't have to pull down the shades any more."

6

The bride's girl-friend was asking her what was her biggest thrill in the whole proceedings. "Well, there were lots of thrills," said the bride thoughtfully. "First when we went to the license bureau, then when the minister pronounced us man and wife, and it was a real thrill signing the register 'Mr. and Mrs.' But by far the biggest thrill was thumbing my nose at the house detective."

See also cake[3], cookbook[2], cooking[1, 3, 6], wedding[8].

BRIDGE

See card-playing.

BRIEF

1

The editor was constantly after the young reporter to be concise and never use two words where one would suffice. His teachings bore fruit when the reporter wrote up an accident as follows: "Bill Smith struck a match to see if there was any gas in his tank. There was. Age forty-seven."

2

The housewife was in the midst of cleaning when the tramp knocked at her door and her humor was none too good. "Well, make it short," she snapped impatiently when she saw who it was. The tramp sized up the situation, took a deep breath, and blurted out, "Could you give me a drink of water, ma'am, on account of I'm so hungry that I don't know where I'm gonna sleep tonight?"

3

The cub reporter had been so

often reprimanded for his lack of brevity that when he was sent to cover a suicide and instructed to get all the details, his report read as follows: "A man was shot last night at 11 o'clock. Mr. Thos. Witless was attending a reception at Mrs. Four-flush's when he complained of feeling ill, took a cocktail, his hat, his coat, his departure, no notice of his hostess, a taxi, a revolver from his pocket, aim, and finally his life. Nice fellow. Too bad."

4

The eager reporter wired his editor: "Uncovered big political scandal. Shall I send story?" The editor wired back: "Send 600 words." This dampened the ambitious reporter a bit, and he wired again: "Story too big to be told in less than 1500 words." The reporter was further taken down when he read his editor's reply: "Story of creation of world told in 600 words. See what you can do."

5

The section foreman of a rather hazardous portion of track was always sending in lengthy reports to the manager. "Look, Mike," said the manager, "just report the condition of the track as you find it, without adding a lot of useless words." A short time later the track was flooded and the foreman sent in a one-line report: "Sir, Where the railroad was, the river is. Yours truly,—."

See also meals[2], story[2].

BROTHER

1

The small boy of the family always got the cast-off things of his elder brother—his clothes, toys, books, etc. He was at last driven to inquire, "Gee, mom, will I have to marry brother's widow when he dies?"

2

The curious old lady was always asking questions of people. At a party one evening there was a brother and sister who made a charming couple and the old lady cornered the girl. "And how many brothers do you have, my dear?" she asked in the course of her inquiry. "Four," replied the girl. Later the lady put the same question to the brother, and his answer was, "Three." "That's odd," murmured the lady, "when I asked your sister the same thing she said four."

3

The boyfriend had just surprised the girl in rather an affectionate pose and was taking her to task for it. "But I just kissed him like a brother," protested the girl. "Yeah, I know," replied the boy skeptically, "like a fraternity brother."

BUGS

See ants, flies, insects, mosquito, worms.

BUILDING

See architecture, house, tenant, real estate.

BURGLAR

1

A meek little man presented himself at the jail early one morning and sought out the jailer. "I'd like to speak to the man who was ar- rested for breaking into our house last night," he requested. "What for?" asked the jailer. "We've already got the goods on him." "Oh, it's not that," replied the man. "I just want to ask him how he got into the house without waking up my wife."

2

One burglar remained on lookout outside while the other broke into the house. When his pal re-emerged, he inquired, "How much did yuh git?" "Nuthin'," replied the other in disgust. "De guy wot lives dere is a lawyer." "Gee!" cried the first in genuine alarm. "Did yuh lose anything?"

3

The man went downstairs late one night and felt a gun in his ribs. "Quiet, or I'll shoot," threatened the burglar. "All right," said the man calmly, "but do you mind if I call my wife down?" "What're you tryin' to put over?" queried the burglar suspiciously. "Nothing at all," replied the man. "It's just that she's been expecting a burglar every night for 20 years and I'd like to have her see one."

See also Congress[2], convince[1], danger[3], minister[4], pie, robbery[1].

BURIAL

1

The rookie came up to the sergeant and asked, "What must a man be, Sarge, in order to be buried with military honors?" "He must be a Captain, or better," replied the sergeant. "Shucks!" complained the rookie. "Then I lose my bet." "Why, what did you bet?"

asked the sergeant. "I bet that he had to be dead," was the answer.

2

A funeral procession came around the corner and old Uncle Si opened his eyes wide in surprise. "Who they a-buryin' today?" he asked. "I ain't heard o' no one dyin'." "It's pore Sam White," replied a fellow whittler. "Is that a fact?" exclaimed Uncle Si. "Is old Sam dead?" "D'ya think they're rehearsin' with 'im?" snapped the other.

See also golf[1].

BUS

1

A gentleman, somewhat under the influence, boarded a two-decker bus and sat near the driver whom he pestered with endless remarks. To rid himself of the nuisance, the driver suggested that he would get more air on the upper deck. The drunk clambered up, but in a few minutes was back again. "What's the matter?" asked the driver. "Didn't you like it up there?" "'Sfine," replied the souse, "but it ain't safe—no driver!"

2

The lady was much concerned over losing her way and pestered the bus driver with many questions. "And could you tell me," she inquired, "if this bus stops at the Waldorf-Astoria?" "No, lady," answered the fed-up driver, "it can't afford it. It stays in the garage overnight."

3

The two-decker bus had made its stop and was waiting for the passengers to alight. A lady on the upper deck was taking her time to descend, fussing with her skirts and checking if she had her purse. "Come on down, lady," said the conductor at the foot of the stairs in a bored voice, "legs ain't no treat to me no more."

See also absence[1], crowd[1], fat[3], signs[1].

BUSINESS

1

Two partners in high finance found that their office boy had been pilfering from the petty cash box. One was very angry and wanted to turn the boy over to the police, but the other, taking a calmer and more sensible view, advised, "No, no; let's not forget that we began in a small way ourselves. I think we should begin grooming him for a junior partner."

2

A man bought a store from the owner who praised it highly. However, in less than six months the store had failed and the buyer was bankrupt. Meeting the original owner on the street one day, he said, "Do you remember that when you sold me that business you told me it was a going concern?" "Yes, what about it?" replied the other. "Well, you were certainly right," was the reply. "It's gone."

3

The store was so obviously poverty-stricken that the most casual observer could see it. "How do you ever manage to keep going at all and pay your help?" queried a salesman. "Well, I only have that one clerk over there," replied the storekeeper, "and I can't pay him, so in about two years he gets the store for back pay. Then I work for him, and in about two more years I get the store back."

4

The prosperous businessman was discussing his secrets of success. "The way to get on in business," he said, "is to find out what people want." "I see," interrupted a listener, "and then set about getting it to them." "No, no," the businessman shook his head in amused contempt. "The thing to do is corner it."

5

"Yes, sirree," said the hillbilly proudly, "business was shore good fer me this year. Fust I bought a pig fer nine dollar, later I traded him fer a cart, then I swapped the cart fer a calf, traded off the calf fer a bicycle, then sold thet fer nine dollar." "But, gosh, Zeke," pointed out a friend, "you didn't make nuthin' on thet." "Wall, mebbe I didn't make no money," admitted the other, "but lookit the business I done."

6

The bank president was giving some advice to his son who was going to another city to start a business. "Always remember, son," said the banker firmly, "that in business honesty is always the best policy." "Yes, father," said the boy. "And— er, harumph! You'd better study up a bit on corporation law," continued father. "You'll be surprised to find how many things you can do in a business way and still be honest."

7

The firm had started in boom

times and had made big money, but when the lean years came it was different. Looking over their accounts at the end of their worst year, one partner suggested, "The good times are definitely over. How about settling down to some regular honest business." "No, thanks," grimaced the other partner. "I never go in for experiments in business."

See also begging[3], energetic[2], finance[1], gas[1], handkerchief[3], hint[10], importance[2], interest[2, 3], morality[1], museum[3], price[5], religion[4, 5], season[1], success[2], training[2].

BUSY

See chorus girl[1].

BUTCHER

1

The neighborhood jokester went into the butchershop and, finding the butcher's wife in charge, couldn't resist the temptation to be funny. "Can you furnish me with a yard of pork, madam?" he asked. The woman never changed expression, but simply called to the boy behind the counter, "Jimmy, give this gentleman three pig's feet."

2

"And what will you have today, madam?" asked the butcher. "I'd like some nice fresh kidleys," replied the lady. "Excuse me," said the puzzled butcher, "but you said—?" "Kidleys," repeated the woman. "Ah — er — perhaps you mean 'kidneys,' madam?" queried the butcher. "Of course," snapped the woman peevishly. "Diddle I say so?"

3

"What's yours, sonny?" asked the butcher of the little boy. "Mom wants another oxtail," replied the little fellow, "an' she says that the last one you sent was so nice, to be sure an' tell you to give me another one off the same ox."

4

"That Willis dame and her cracks is gonna get my goat yet," growled the butcher to his helper. "What'd she say now?" asked the helper. "Aw, she thinks she's smart," pouted the butcher. "When she was in to buy a little piece of meat this morning she said I ought to name my scales 'Ambuscade,' and I laughed. But I just looked it up and the dictionary says it means 'to lie in wait'."

See also advice[2], price[3].

BUY

1

The little boy had a penny to spend and he'd priced about everything in the toyshop without making a selection. "Look here, sonny," cried the exasperated storekeeper finally as the lad still pondered, "what do you expect to buy for a penny—the world with a fence around it?" The boy thought for a moment, and then said cautiously, "Well, let's see it."

2

A man was asking his friend's advice on a little deal. "He seems a good enough horse to look at him," he said, "and the dealer said I could have him for a song. What do you think?" "Well," ventured the friend, "I'd say that it all depends upon your eye for horses and his ear for singing."

See also bill[3].

CADDY

1

The dub of the golf club was engaging a caddy. "Can you count, son?" he inquired. "Yes, sir," replied the boy. "Can you add well?" was the next question. "Sure can, sir," was the answer. "All right," the golfer tested him, "how many are three, six, two and five?" "Eleven, sir," said the boy promptly. "Come on, you're hired," said the dub happily.

2

The golfer was doing very badly and labored long at each hole. At the fifth hole the caddy flung himself down on the grass to wait. "You must be tired to be lying down this time of day," commented the golfer peevishly. "Oh, I ain't tired of carryin'," replied the caddy, "but I sure am tired of countin'."

See also familiar[3], mind[2].

CAKE

1

Mr. Newlywed regarded the nondescript slab on his plate dubiously. "What is it, sweet?" he asked timidly. "It's Lucifer cake, dearest," replied the bride. "But I thought you said you were going to make an angel cake?" he said. "I started to," was the reply, "but it fell."

2

It was his birthday again and the wife was reminiscent. "You've had twelve birthdays since we're married, dear," she said, "and not once have I missed baking you a cake for it, have I?" "No, darling," he replied feelingly. "I can truly look back on those cakes as milestones of my life."

3

The bride looked dejected as the meal drew to a close. "I was going to have sponge cake for dessert, dear," she explained, "but somehow it didn't come out right." "Gee, and that's my favorite cake," said the husband. "What happened to it?" "I can't imagine," replied the bride puzzledly, "unless perhaps the store sent me the wrong kind of sponges."

4

The young husband manfully tried to chew and swallow what was set before him, but with little success. "How do you like my pound cake, sweetheart?" asked the bride brightly. "Golly, is that what it is?" said the husband between laborious chews. "Are you sure you pounded it enough?"

See also tact[5].

CALIFORNIA

1

Heavy rain and sleet were being driven through Los Angeles by a stiff wind and two dyed-in-the-wool Californians stood regarding it gloomily. Finally, one of them remarked somewhat sheepishly, "Boy, oh, boy, there's sure some terrible weather blows in from Nevada, isn't there?"

2

A Californian died and in due time presented himself at the gates of Heaven. "From where do you hail?" inquired St. Peter. "From Los Angeles," was the reply. "Well, you can come in if you want to," said St. Peter dubiously, "but you won't like it."

3

Times were very bad, but the businessmen were having their convention nevertheless. One of the men asked a delegate from Los Angeles how badly the depression had hit his town. "Depression?" queried the Californian. "Why, we have no depression in Los Angeles, though I will admit we're having the poorest boom we've had in a long, long time."

See also accurate[1], pronunciation[3].

CALL

1

A minister informed his congregation that he had received a "call" to another church. One of the deacons asked him later how much more he was to receive in his new position. "I'll get $350 more," replied the preacher. "Well, I sure don't blame you for going," said the deacon, "but I'd hardly say that's a 'call'; it seems more like a 'raise' to me."

2

The little girl in the bus was a distinct nuisance circulating about, asking questions, and annoying people in general. The indulgent mother made no effort to control her, thinking her dear too cute for words. The brat finally concentrated on the gentleman behind them. He stood all he could, then leaned forward and asked the mother politely,

"Madam, what do you call this sweet little girl?" "Janie," beamed mother. "Well, for God's sake, call her!" he snapped.

See also guest[2], maid[4], salary[8].

CALLER

1

The neighborhood pest had dropped into the busy lawyer's office for a purely social chat and he later praised the lawyer to a friend. "He's sure a nice fellow," he said. "Why, I just dropped in on him to pass the time of day and I hadn't been talking with him for five minutes before he told me to come in and see him again someday."

2

The lady was doing social work simply because she felt it "the thing to do." Consequently, the busy mother in the tenement on whom she called merely endured her patiently. When the lady rose to leave, she said, "You'll excuse me if I don't return the call, but really I've got no time to spare to go slummin'."

3

The maid was new and the mistress instructed her to get cards from all callers while she was out. "Well, Bridget," said the mistress when she returned, "did you get a card from everyone who called as I told you?" "Yes, mum," replied Bridget triumphantly, "all except one feller who wouldn't give me no card, so I grabbed his hat and shoved him off the stoop—his name's on the sweatband."

See also expect[1].

CALM

1

"Bill White is certainly a level-headed, calm sort of fellow," said a man to his friend. "I wish I could be like him." "Why, what makes you say that?" asked the friend. "Golly," the other replied, "he can read a patent-medicine ad without discovering that he has even one of the symptoms of a single disease it's supposed to be good for."

2

They were having fire drill in the grammar school and the principal was giving instructions on what to do in case of fire. "And above all," he concluded, "if your clothes should catch on fire, always remember to keep cool."

3

There had been a little fracas in the school yard and when teacher arrived on the scene she found Johnny seated comfortably on a boy. "Why are you sitting on that boy, Johnny?" teacher demanded. "'Cause he hit me in the eye," growled Johnny. "But Johnny," reproved teacher, "haven't I always told you to keep calm and count to a hundred before you let your anger rise?" "That's what I'm doin'," said Johnny, "an' I'm sittin' on 'im so he'll be here when I finish countin'."

4

The young man was boasting of his calm behavior during the boating mishap. "And then when I fell into the water," he continued proudly, "I kept my head." "How lucky for you," yawned the girl, "it must have been a big help to you in staying afloat."

CANDIDATE

See election, politics[8], promise.

CANDY

The little boy with a penny entered the candy store. "Gimme an all-day sucker," he requested of the storekeeper. When he received the candy he eyed it critically for a moment, then said, "Ain't it kinda small?" "Yep, guess it is," agreed the candy man, "but you know the days are getting shorter."

CANNIBAL

1

The shipwrecked man had been captured by the cannibals and taken before their chief. "And what was your business among your own people?" he asked kindly. "I was in the newspaper game," answered the captive. "An editor?" queried the chief. "Naw," said the man modestly, "just one of the sub-editors." "Well, cheer up," encouraged the chief, "you are about to be promoted. After dinner you'll be editor-in-chief."

2

One of the hunting party had strayed in the jungle and been captured by cannibals. The man's son was nearly frantic and rushed the organization of a rescue party. "Hurry, men," he urged. "We want to try to reach father before he's scratched off the menu."

3

The cannibals decided they didn't want religion and bruskly dragged the missionary before their chief. The chief reproved them for their rudeness. "Never under any circumstances is there need to neglect politeness," he scolded them. Then turning to the missionary, he said in courteous tones, "It will give us great pleasure, sir, to have you for dinner tomorrow."

See also hereafter[5].

CAPACITY

The owner of a number of taverns was walking down the street with a friend when they passed a well-groomed, sanctimonious-looking man with rather a ruddy nose. "That's Simpkins," imparted the tavern man, "a prominent figure in local temperance movements, tavern control, and the like." "Is that so?" said the other. "What's his official capacity." "About three to four gallons on an average," was the reply.

CAR

See automobile, second-hand car, streetcar.

CARD-PLAYING

1

Two men met on the beach, both dressed for swimming. "Golly! What's happened to your shins; they're all beaten up?" remarked one. "If this were winter I'd say you'd been playing hockey." "Nope, nothing like that," replied the other. "I just led back to my wife's weak suit."

2

The beginner at bridge felt rather proud of himself because, through lack of any one else, he had been asked to fill in at a game with an expert. "Well, what do you think of my game?" he inquired brightly of the expert after a bit. "How would you have played that last hand of mine?" "Under an assumed name," grunted the expert.

See also cheat[2], fortune-telling[1], frank[1], interest[4], privilege, self-betrayal[3].

CAREFUL

See caution, foresight, precaution.

CASHIER

1

The restaurant owner scowled as he walked up to the cashier. "I've been checking up," he growled, "and I see that you're a little behind in your accounts." "Oh, but you're wrong," replied the cashier cheerily. "It's the restaurant that's behind; I'm a few bucks ahead."

2

The pretty cashier was plainly worried when she approached the boss. "I'm afraid I'll have to have a few days off for a rest," she said apologetically, "because I haven't been looking my best lately." "Nonsense!" replied the boss. "You look fine." "It's not nonsense," replied the girl; "the men are beginning to count their change."

3

When the man went up to the window of his bank, he noticed a strange face behind the desk. "You're new, aren't you?" he inquired. "Has the other cashier gone away to take a rest?" "On the contrary," answered the new cashier, "he's gone away to avoid one."

See also description, repay[5].

CAT

1

Little Junior raised puzzled eyes to mother. "When we visit grandma next week are we going to take kitty with us?" he inquired. "No, we can't, son," replied mother. "Why do you ask?" "Because," responded the boy, "I heard papa telling Mr. Brown that the mouse would have a high old time next week when the cat was away."

2

Little Johnny was being permitted to bring in the kittens when a shrill, protesting meowing and spitting was heard. "Be careful, Junior," cried his father, "so as not to hurt the kittens." "But I'm not hurtin' 'em, daddy," replied the boy. "I'm carryin' 'em real careful by the stems."

3

The little girl had been to Sunday school where she had heard the wonders of heaven detailed. On returning home she was thoughtful for a while, then asked, "Do cats go to heaven, mummy?" "Of course not," replied mother. "Animals have no soul and consequently can't go to heaven." "Well, then," demanded the girl, "where do angels get the strings for their harps?"

See also father[3], lucky[2].

CATCH

1

Junior had just seen a movie about an insane asylum and was full of questions. "Say, dad," he queried, "how do they catch crazy men?" "It's surprisingly simple, son," growled father sourly. "All it takes is a little powder and paint, a fancy hair-do, a low-cut dress, and a phony sweet and amiable expression, and the crazy men walk in and give themselves up."

2

Little Billy had played hookey to go fishing and had had a wonderful day along the brook, but, walking homeward, thoughts of consequences began to crowd in. Passing a couple of his small friends along the way, they inquired, "Catch anything, Billy?" Billy, his mind still on his misdeed, responded, "Aw, I ain't been home yet."

CATTY

1

Two women went into a restaurant. One, an inveterate gossip, immediately began to tear to bits the reputation of a third woman who happened to be a friend of her dining companion. The latter held her peace with an effort. The waiter arrived. "Give me a club sandwich and a glass of milk," ordered the gabby one. "But, my dear," interposed the other, "wouldn't you prefer the milk in a saucer?"

2

The young woman was gushing about her birthday party. "And my birthday cake was too, too, beautiful," she cooed. "It had eighteen candles—one for each year." There was an awkward silence, then one of her acquaintances spoke up, "Eighteen candles? Were you burning them at both ends?"

See also actress[2], birthday[1], common sense, dog[4], indulgent, miserable, personality[1].

CAUSE

1

The mistress was not pleased with the new maid. She called her to the living-room and pointed, "Jane, I see a spider-web in that corner! To what do you attribute it?" Jane considered the web a moment, and then said, "Why, to a spider, of course, mum."

2

The hillbilly woman was just about to go home from the hospital with her eighteenth child when her doctor came by. "Well, good-by," he said. "I'll be seeing you again in about 18 months." "Won't be a-seein' me no more, doc," asserted the woman. "Come, now," the doctor laughed skeptically, "you've been here regularly every year and a half since you're married." "I know," she agreed, "but me an' my ol' man foun' out what's a-causin' 'em."

See also hangover[2], reason[1].

CAUTION

1

The elderly man had stood for some time reading through the names in the hotel register and the clerk was growing impatient. "Just sign your name on that line, please, sir," he urged. But the old fellow glared at the clerk and snorted, "Young man, I'm old enough to have learned never to sign anything without reading it first."

2

The man was interviewing the applicant for the position of chauffeur. "Are you careful?" he asked. "I want a driver who doesn't take the slightest risks." "That's me, sir," replied the man. "May I have my salary in advance?"

3

Many of the church members had noted that a certain old lady would always bow whenever the name of Satan was mentioned. At last the minister grew sufficiently curious to ask her the reason for it. "Well, Reverend," she answered, "politeness costs nothing, and you never can tell."

4

A businessman was known for his extreme caution in all things and never going beyond the evident facts. One day in traveling through a pleasant countryside a companion, by way of idle conversation, remarked, "Those houses over there seem to be freshly painted." "Well, on this side, anyway," was the cautious reply.

5

The doctor met one of his former patients on the street. "Well, good morning," greeted the doctor. "And how are you feeling today, Mr. Black?" "First I want to know, doctor," replied Mr. Black cautiously, "will it cost me anything if I tell you?"

See also barber[1], check[3], driver[4], drugstore[4], opinion[2].

CELEBRATION

1

It was the Western town's annual three-day rodeo and folks came from miles around to join in the hilarious celebration that went with it. One old pioneer who had never missed this chance for a spree, met a friend on the street. "Hi, pardner," he greeted the old-timer. "What hotel you stayin' at?" "Hotel!" snorted the old boy. "Why, man, I'm only going to be here for three days!"

2

Hubby was sitting at the kitchen table when wifey walked in. "What's this?" she said in surprise. "Two bottles of ginger ale? You must certainly be thirsty." "It's not that," he replied. "Have you forgotten? Today's our wedding anniversary."

CEMETERY

The salesman was trying to sell a cemetery lot to a miserly old fellow, but with little success. "No use in being previous," he said, "I might not get full value out of the investment." "But you can't miss on this," the salesman protested; "every one has to die sometime." "That may be," admitted the old man shrewdly, "but suppose I should be lost at sea?"

CHANCE

See opportunity.

CHANGE

The small boy was always coming home from school talking about this or that little girl he had met. It seemed that every few days it was a different girl who was getting his attention. "It looks to me, Billy," said his mother, "that you must have a changeable nature." "Oh, no, mom," replied the boy, "it ain't me that changes; it's the girls when you get to know 'em better."

See also substitute.

CHARACTER

See clothes[8], ear, reputation.

CHARITY

1

An elderly gentleman put a nickel in the Salvation Army lassie's tambourine, then a thought struck him. "What happens to this money?" he asked. "I give it to the Lord," the girl replied. "And how old are you, miss?" the man continued. "I'm twenty-one," was the answer. "Well," remarked the old man as he retrieved his nickel, "no need for you to bother, as I'm seventy-nine and will be seeing the Lord long before you."

2

The lady was touched by the tramp's decrepit appearance. "I think you can use these old trousers," she said. "They're quite good and only need a little mending." "That'll be fine, mum," replied the tramp. "I'll call back in about an hour and you have them ready then."

3

"What have you there, Betty?" asked the minister meeting the little girl on the street. "A dime to buy ice cream soda," was the happy response. "But why don't you contribute the dime to the missions?" suggested the minister. "I thought of that," admitted Betty, "but I decided to buy the ice cream and let the drugstore man get the credit for giving it."

4

A tramp knocked at the door of a very religious household and asked for something to eat. The woman frowned, then went into the house and returned with just one piece of dry bread. "Ordinarily I do not believe in pampering idleness, my man," she said severely, "but just this once I give you this bread in the name of God, from whom all blessings flow." The bum looked at the dry bread and then asked, "Well, for Christ's sake, lady, can't you put some butter on it?"

5

"Look, mamma," cried a small boy, pointing at a nun on the other side of the street, "what's that lady dressed up like that?" "That's a Sister of Charity, son," replied mother. "Which one, mamma," asked the boy, "Faith or Hope?"

6

The collector for charity thought that the well-dressed young man in the sporty roadster should have money, so he asked him, "Pardon me, sir, but would you like to help the Poor Girls' Home?" "And how!" was the prompt and eager reply. "Where are they waiting?"

7

It was one of those restaurants where they have a pretty girl in the window making griddle cakes. A ragged little boy stood outside the window with his nose pressed intently against the glass. A kindly gentleman was touched by the sight and asked the boy, "Hungry, little fellow?" "Heck, naw!" snapped the boy in irritation. "Cripes! Can't a feller take a gander at a swell dame no more widout drawin' no crowd?"

8

The girl smiled sweetly as she approached the man. "I'd like to sell you a couple of tickets, sir," she said, "for a raffle we're holding for a poor woman." But the gentleman shook his head. "Sorry, no," he replied, "I wouldn't know what to do with a poor woman if I won her, but if you ever hold a raffle for a rich woman, let me know."

9

The missionary had given the meeting a long and piteous talk on the miseries and needs of the heathen, and ended by suggesting that all present should give something for them. A citizen noted for his caution with money rose and announced, "I have been deeply touched by this story and feel that something should be given. I move that we all give three hearty cheers for the heathen."

See also bed[3], horse racing[1], philanthropy[1, 2], sympathy[5].

CHAUFFEUR

1

The weekend visitor rushed breathlessly on the driveway. "I'm afraid I'm a little late," he panted to the waiting chauffeur. "Try not to let me miss my train." "Don't worry, sir," reassured the chauffeur. "The missus already told me that if I did I could look for another job."

2

An old gentleman was questioning an applicant for the position of chauffeur. "And I suppose that I can write one of your previous employers for a character reference?" he asked. "Sorry, sir," replied the ap-

plicant, "but all the gentlemen I've worked for have died in my service."

See also caution[2], touring.

CHEAT

1

"What's all the commotion out front?" asked the storekeeper of the crossroads village. "Jest a coupla fellers from down the road argying," replied the clerk. "They swapped mules an' now each 'un claims the other'n skinned him." "Well, why don't they swap 'em back again?" inquired the proprietor. "Dunno," said the clerk, "less'n I reckon they're skeered o' gettin' skinned agin."

2

It was a saloon in the old West and an intent crowd gathered around the card game where the stakes were growing bigger and bigger. Suddenly the dealer jumped up, flung down his cards, and whipping out his six-gun cried, "Gents, this here is a crooked game! Dapper Dan over there ain't a-playin' the hand I dealt him."

3

A couple of golfers both sliced and their balls went wild into an adjoining woods where a lady happened to be picnicking. The golfers searched and poked about in the bushes for a half-hour, and all the while the lady watched with interest and sympathy in her expression. "I don't mean to butt in on your game, gentlemen," she ventured timidly, "but would it be cheating if I gave you a hint on where the balls are?"

See also lunatic[1].

CHECK

1

A pretty young lady entered a strange bank to get a check cashed. The teller examined the check, then shook his head regretfully. "The check is unquestionably all right," he said politely, "but you are not known here. Do you have anything about you that would serve to identify you?" "Well, er," faltered the girl blushingly, "I have a birthmark on my right hip."

2

A young wife went into a bank to cash a check. "Please indorse it," requested the teller. "But my own husband gave it to me," protested the wife. "That's the point," explained the teller, "if you indorse it on the back he'll know we paid you the money for it." The woman took the check to the desk and in a short while returned with it signed on the back: "Your devoted wife, Helen."

3

"There is little faith in humanity these days," complained one traveling man, "to judge by the number of 'No Credit' signs one sees in stores and hotels." "That's nothing," replied his companion, "compared to the caution indicated in one I saw in a small hotel the other day, reading: 'No more checks cashed; not even good ones.'"

4

The farmer knew little about banking, but he was induced to open a checking account for convenience. About two months later he was loud in his praises. "By gum," he boasted, "that's a smart bank I've got, all right." "How is it any smarter than any other bank?" asked a friend. "Crackey, but it is," he insisted. "Them fellers was slick enough. They went and got all the checks I wrote back for me."

5

The young husband had started a joint account for the convenience of his wife, but the keeping of the stubs in order was beyond her. He called her to him sternly one night and said, "The bank has just returned your last check, dear." But the bride clapped her hands in joy. "Oh, fine!" she cried. "Now I can buy something else with it."

See also banking[1], job[4], speech[4].

CHEERFUL

"Grandma's feeling ill, Billy," said mother, "so you might go to her room and try cheering her up a bit." "Yes'm," replied Billy dutifully and trudged off. A short while later he was back looking discouraged. "It's no use, mom," he said discouragedly, "I tried, but she only seems to get worse." "What did you say to her, dear?" asked mother. "Gosh!" Billy answered, "I just asked if she'd like soldiers at her funeral."

CHEESE

1

The apple pie was luscious, but still the wife was full of apologies to the visitor. "I'm dreadfully sorry," she explained, "but I entirely forgot to get cheese for the pie." Junior, who had been listening, slipped away and soon returned with a cube of cheese which he placed on the visitor's plate. "Thanks, sonny," said the visitor, popping it in his mouth. "Where'd you find it?" "In the rattrap," replied the boy.

2

A dealer bought 200 pounds of limburger cheese in a distant town and in order to avoid the expense of a special car to ship it, he packed it in a coffin box and checked it on his own train as a corpse. Going to the baggage car later to see if it was all right, he met the baggage man who asked sympathetically, "A relative?" "My brother," replied the dealer in a sad voice. "Well," sighed the baggage man, "at least you can be sure he's dead."

CHEMISTRY

A farmer was visiting his son at college and, in the course of seeing the sights, was taken to the chemistry laboratory. "What they so busy about?" he asked. "Their problem is to try to find a universal solvent," he was told. "What's that?" he asked. "A liquid that would dissolve anything," was the answer. "That might be handy," conceded the farmer, "but what would you keep it in if you found it?"

CHESS

See patience.

CHEWING

An elderly man had become hard-of-hearing and was constantly worried lest the affliction progress to total deafness. Seated one day on a park bench he noted that another man on the same bench was talking rapidly, but he could not hear a sound. He groaned aloud, "I'm deaf at last! I can see you've been talking all along, but I haven't heard a word." But the other just grinned and said, "Ain't been a-talkin'— jest a-chewin'."

See also cow^2.

CHICKEN

1

Two preachers came to dinner, so the farmer's wife cooked three chickens. "Then there's sure to be plenty," she said, "and the family can eat on what's left." But when the preachers had finished, only bare bones remained. A little later the farmer was showing the two guests about the farm when an old rooster began to crow vigorously. "He seems mighty proud about something," said one. "Why shouldn't he be," growled the farmer, "he's got three of his family in the ministry."

2

The butcher's phone rang and an angry woman's voice greeted him when he picked it up. "Listen," the voice barked, "if I ever order another chicken from you, don't you dare give me any more of those special airplane fowl of yours." "Airplane fowl?" asked the puzzled butcher. "You know what I'm talking about," was the reply; "all wings and machinery and no body."

3

The boarder stabbed tentatively with his fork at the chicken served him. "This must be an incubator chicken," he observed. "Why, so it is," agreed the landlady, "but how did you guess?" "It's very simple," replied the boarder, pushing his plate back, "no chicken with a mother would be this tough."

4

The diner in the restaurant pushed his plate back in disgust. "Doesn't the chicken please you, sir?" inquired the waiter. "I suppose I can't complain because it does live up to your claim," replied the guest. "You said it was spring chicken, and it is—I just bit into one of the springs."

5

The underprivileged child from the city slums was in the country for the first time vacationing on a farm. Everything he beheld was new and wondrous to his pinched little eyes. Toward sunset of the first day he stood intently watching the farmer's wife plucking a chicken. After a bit his curiosity grew too great and he asked gravely, "Do you take off their clothes every night, lady?"

See also garden[4], grammar[3], peacock.

CHILDBIRTH

1

The little girl rushed into kindergarten late and in breathless excitement. "We just got a new baby at our house," she panted. "Why don't you come and see it, teacher?" "Thank you," replied teacher, "but I think I'd better wait until your mother gets better." "Oh, you don't have to be afraid," reassured the little girl, "it's not catching."

2

The doctor's office was empty save for his young son. "Will the doctor be back soon?" asked the patient who had stopped by. "I don't know, sir," answered the boy. "He said he was going out on an eternity case."

3

The young doctor went to a small town to start a practice. A short time later he met a friend who asked him how he was doing. "Oh, fine," replied the doctor, "I've already had a case—a birth." "And how did you make out?" inquired the friend. "Well, it's a little early to say," said the doctor, "the woman passed on and the baby died, but I still have hopes of saving the father."

4

A young naval officer was trying so desperately for a leave that finally his Commanding Officer asked him his reason. "It's because my wife is going to have a baby, sir," the young man replied. "Is that all?" grunted his superior. "Just remember this, son: you are necessary only at the keel-laying—for the launching you are entirely superfluous."

5

The nervous young husband had just brought his bulging wife to the maternity hospital and they were waiting at the desk to register the woman for immediate entrance. While the attendant was looking up the record, he paced about and fidgeted and grew no calmer. Finally, he turned to the expectant mother and asked very gravely, "Look here, dear, are you sure you want to go through with this?"

See also cause[2], facts of life[2], hospital[3], pregnancy[2], statistics[3], stork, stuttering[5], telegram, triplets[2].

CHILDREN

1

The young lady was sobbing her sad heart out in the Powder Room of the dance hall. "What's wrong, dear?" asked the kindly lady comfortingly. "Oh!" wailed the girl, "I've just found out that I'm engaged to a man who can't bear children." "There, there," consoled the kind lady, "you mustn't expect too much of a husband."

2

"Tommy," reproved mother sternly, "how do you explain the fact that this morning there were two pieces of cake in the pantry and now there's only one?" "There is?" cried Tommy in amazement. "It must have been too dark for me to see the other one."

3

The elderly man stroked the head of the smiling, golden-haired boy on his knee and sighed regretfully. "What wouldn't I give to feel like a child again," he murmured longingly. "You would!" exclaimed the boy, looking up in surprise. "Well, why don't you try gettin' mamma to spank you?"

4

The mistress was pointing out the advantages of the place to the new maid. "Not only will you find the work very light here," she said, "but also we have no children to annoy you." "As a matter of fact, mum, I'm very fond of children," replied the maid, "so don't go restrictin' yourself on my account."

5

A worn-looking woman boarded a bus followed by a long line of eleven children. "Whew!" cried the conductor. "Are those all your children, madam, or is this a picnic?" "They're my children, all right," snapped the woman, "and believe me, bud, it's no picnic."

6

The country doctor's two children were admitted to be the two prettiest little girls of the village by far. They were walking down the street one day when a stranger noticed and admired them. "Who are those two beautiful little girls?" he asked a village lad who chanced by. "Oh, they're the doctor's children," explained the boy. "He always keeps the best for himself."

NOTE: This subject has not been cross referenced because of its frequent occurrence throughout this dictionary.

CHIVALRY

1

Through the kind offices of modern dress and cosmetics, the lady who boarded the crowded bus could have been judged to be most any age. A gallant gentleman rose to offer her his seat, and she cooed, "But why should you be so kind to me?" The man made a quick appraisal, then answered tactfully, "Because, madam, I myself have a mother, wife, and daughter at home."

2

The streetcar was jammed and a number of women were standing. The conductor noticed a man sitting with his eyes closed, apparently asleep, and fearing he might miss his stop shook him and said, "Wake up, sir." "But I wasn't asleep," said the man. "You had your eyes closed," insisted the conductor. "I know," replied the man, "but it's just because I can't bear to see a woman stand."

3

A group of tourists out West encountered an Indian brave going down the road astride a pony accompanied by a heavily overburdened squaw who shuffled along beside the pony. "This hardly seems right, does it?" objected one of the tourists. "Why doesn't the squaw ride?" "Ugh!" grunted the Indian without turning his head. "Squaw gotum no pony."

4

The crowded bus stopped and, as a pretty girl climbed on, an elderly gentleman nearby rose to his feet. "No, no, don't get up, I insist," cried the girl, pushing the old man back into his seat. "I can stand just as well." "You can suit yourself about that, Miss," growled the old fellow, struggling to his feet again, "but please let me by—this is where I get off."

5

An old country couple came to town to spend the day at the Fair. They had provided an ample lunch which filled a huge basket with which the old woman struggled along painfully. As they approached the Fair, the old man said, "I'll take that," and grabbed the basket. "Thet's shore kind of ye, Hiram," sighed the woman in relief. "Kind, heck," snorted the old man, "I was afeared ye'd git lost."

See also angel[1], gallantry, modern[1].

CHOICE

1

Two grimy laborers stood looking into a jeweler's display window. "Golly, Bill," said one longingly, "How'd you like to have your pick there?" "Shucks," replied Bill disdainfully, "you can have your pick if you want it—just let me in there with my shovel."

2

It was the day before Christmas and the boss was in a generous mood. He called the office porter to him and said, "John, you've worked hard this year, so for a present I'm going to give you your choice between a ton of coal and a jug of good whisky." Without a moment's hesitation the answer came back, "I burns nuthin' but wood."

3

The girl was in a terrible temper. "And I thought Eddie loved me," she stormed, "yet when I asked him what he'd do if he had to choose between a million dollars and me, he said he'd take the million." "That doesn't mean he doesn't love you," comforted her friend. "He just knew that if he had the million, getting you would be a cinch."

See also intention[1], shrewd[4].

CHORUS GIRL

1

A friend dropped in on a theatrical producer. "Busy this morning?" he asked. "I'll say I am," responded the producer. "Why, I've just interviewed twenty chorus girls and hired twelve of them in ten minutes." "Gosh, you're sure quick at figures," commented the friend.

2

The chorus girl had been advanced to a rôle that had a small singing part and she had just finished her first rehearsal. "Well, what do you think of her?" asked the stage manager dubiously of the producer. "Oh, she's a peach all right," said the producer admiringly, "but certainly no Melba."

3

Two men were discussing the escapades of an elderly playboy. "So old Gotrocks finally married that chorus girl he'd been chasing around with," observed one. "Well, he certainly spent enough money on her." "He sure did," agreed the other. "They do say he married her for his money."

4

"What's the matter with those two comedians tonight?" asked the stage manager. "They seem awfully nervous." "Aw, it's just because they were held up by stage robbers last night," explained the electrician. "Stage robbers!" cried the incredulous manager. "How could that be in this day?" "Oh, they just took a couple of chorus girls to dinner," was the answer.

See also blackmail.

CHRISTENING

1

The revival meeting had reached the time for baptism and the elders were standing in the water performing the ceremony on one after the other. A lean old fellow, a recent convert, was brought out and the usual question was asked as to whether there was any reason baptism should not be administered. One in the crowd spoke up, "I don't want to butt in, Elder, but one dip ain't a-gonna do that old sinner much good—you'll have to anchor him out in deep water overnight."

2

The lady who had recently been baptized was walking down the street and met a small boy whose family was of the same church. "Hello, Tommy," she said, and as the boy seemed puzzled, she added, "You don't know me, do you?" "Now I remember," said the boy. "You're the lady who went swimmin' with the preacher last Sunday."

3

The Sunday school class had been studying the covenant of baptism. "Can you tell me, Billy," questioned the teacher, "what two things are necessary for baptism?" "Sure," replied Billy unhesitatingly, "water and a baby."

4

Little Willie was still sad over father's drowning the extra kittens, so to placate him they permitted him to go along to church to see the christening of his twin baby sisters. He was well-behaved until he saw them approach the christening font filled with water, when he cried out, "Say, mom, which one you gonna keep?"

See also forget[3].

CHRISTIAN

1

A traveler had been shipwrecked and after floating for days on a crate was finally cast up on an island. Fearful of cannibals, he explored cautiously, and at last detected smoke from a fire rising above the bushes. As he crawled slowly through the brush with many misgivings, he heard a voice say, "Pass that damn bottle!" and another voice shout, "Why'n hell d'ya play that card?" "Thank God!" he murmured fervently. "I'm among Christians!"

2

The church usher had served faithfully for many years, and now a younger man was taking over. The retiring usher was instructing the beginner in the little details of the office. "And always remember, my boy," he admonished, "that we have nothing but good, kind Christians in this church, until you try to put someone else in their pew."

3

An Oriental was guest at a mixed dinner party. When the meal was concluded and the men withdrew to the lounge for coffee, brandy, and cigars, the guest remained with the ladies. "But aren't you going with the gentlemen?" asked one of the women. "No, madam," he replied. "You see, I don't smoke, I don't drink, and I don't swear. But then, of course, I am not a Christian."

See also sympathy[2].

CHRISTMAS

1

The farmer had made his regular annual trip to town to do his Christmas shopping and was hurrying with his arms full of bundles toward the station to catch his train. Stumbling over a curb, a jug slipped from his arms and splintered on the walk. Surveying the large wet area ruefully, he gave a heartbroken moan and sighed. "Lookit that! Christmas has done come and gone fer this year."

2

Two old maids were making their plans for the Christmas season. "Mary," asked the younger, "do you think that one long, wide stocking would hold all you want for Christmas?" "No, May," replied the elder with a sigh, "but a pair of short socks would."

See also Florida.

CHURCH

1

Mother came into the room and found the children seated on lined-up chairs. "Whatever are you doing?" she inquired. "We're playing church," announced one boy. "But you girls on the end shouldn't be whispering in church," reproved mother. "Oh, that's all right," replied one of the girls, "we're the choir."

2

The family was on its way home from church when mother asked her little son, "What part of the church service do you like best, Danny?" "Oh, I like the part where they pass the plate of money," responded Danny with enthusiasm. "But I only got a nickel today." Then turning to his father he inquired, "How much did you get, pop?"

3

The sermon dragged on and on and little Johnny was getting restless. "Say, mom," he whispered, "if we give him the money now will he let us go?"

4

The minister encountered the village drunk on the street and, much to the sot's amazement, shook his hand warmly. "I am so happy that you have reformed and repented, William," the minister declared. "It was a real pleasure to see you at prayer meeting last night." "Prayer meeting?" mumbled the drunk puzzledly. Then his face cleared as he cried, "So *that's* where I was?"

5

The minister met one of the unregenerate on the street. "Just what do you have against coming to church?" he inquired solicitously. "Plenty!" growled the sinner. "The first time I went they threw water in my face, and the second time they tied me to a woman I've had to support ever since." "I see," observed the minister dryly. "And the next time you go they'll throw dirt on you."

6

A woman churchgoer stopped to chat with a friend outside church after services. Suddenly she remembered she had left her purse on the seat. She returned and found it gone, and on seeking out the minister found that he had picked it up. "I felt that I had better hold it," he explained. "You know, there are some in the congregation of such simple faith as to believe it might be an answer to prayer."

7

It was a custom of the church during the service for the congregation to repeat the 23rd Psalm in unison, but a certain member with a loud clear voice would always be somewhat ahead of the rest. A visitor to the church one day noted this and asked a member, "Who was that woman who was already by still waters while the rest of us were just lying down in green pastures?"

8

The church was small, but it was notable for the forthrightness of its members, one of whom was telling a friend, "Last month our church had about the best revival we've had in years." "Why, that's fine," replied the friend. "How many new members did you add to your flock?" "Oh, we didn't get any new members," explained the other with grim satisfaction, "but we got rid of four."

9

A visiting preacher was asked to conduct services at an Episcopal church and he was in the rectory getting prepared. "I suppose you'll want to wear a surplice," said the rector. "Surplice!" exclaimed the visitor. "My dear sir, I am a Methodist. What could I know about surplices? All I'm familiar with is deficits!"

10

A newly converted bum from a water front mission happened one Sunday into a very fashionable church and slipped timidly into a rear seat. As the minister's sermon grew impassioned, the convert gave vent to a loud "Amen!" as they did at the mission. The usher cautioned him, but soon he was moved again to shout, "Praise the Lord!" Again the usher cautioned him, "My man, you *must* be quiet. This is no place to praise the Lord."

See also acquaintance[8], advertising[3], attendance[2], Christian[2], circus, collect[3], convert[1], cough, devil[2], expense[2], flirt[2], janitor[1], light[1], minster[2], sermon[3], stranger[2], thankful[2], heater[6].

CIGAR

1

The husband had been rather caustic and outspoken about the Christmas cigars from his wife and the little woman was in tears. "I asked for the best," she sobbed. "The best!" exclaimed the husband. "What did you ask for?" "I just told the clerk that I wanted them for a middle-aged partly bald man who always dresses in gray."

2

A man bought a cigar on the clerk's recommendation and left. In about two minutes he dashed back with an agonized look on his face. "This cigar is simply terrible," he gasped. "You've got a nerve complaining," said the clerk haughtily, "you've got just one of them, but we've got hundreds of the lousy things."

3

"I'd like to get some cigars for my husband," said the woman entering a cigar store. "Do you want 'em fairly strong?" the clerk in-

quired. "Yes, please, the stronger the better," was the reply. "The ashes kept breaking off the last ones he had."

4

A man lit up a cigar and offered his friend one, who also lit up. "How do you like it?" the donor asked. "Not bad," conceded the other dubiously. "I think they're quite good for the price," insisted the first; "they're two for a quarter." "Is that so?" was the choking reply. "Well, I think you must have the twenty-cent one."

See also better[1], gift[3].

CIRCUS

The small boy had just been to his first circus and he returned home still dizzy with the wonder of it all. "Well, how did you like it, son?" inquired his mother. "Gee, mom," sighed the boy rapturously, "if you'd go just once to the circus, you'd never go to church again for the rest of your life."

See also clumsy, disappointment[2], elephant[2], friendship[1], museum[5], sneeze.

CITY

See Boston, Hollywood, London, New York.

CIVILIZATION

After several desperate weeks on a life raft, two weak and bedraggled shipwrecked sailors were cast up on a desolate shore with no sign of human life. Painfully they dragged themselves inland through the brush for miles, and still no life. At last one pointed excitedly ahead. There beside a burnt house stood a gibbet with a man's body swinging from it and a child with bashed-in head lying on the ground. "Thank God!" cried the other, "civilization at last!"

CLASSROOM

1

It was a glorious spring day and the small portion of the class that was present was in a dreamy state. The Professor was calling the roll in an absent-minded manner and, despite the small attendance, to each name called there sounded a "Here." But the name of Brown was followed by complete silence. "My goodness!" cried the Professor, looking up startled. "Has Mr. Brown no friends here today?"

2

The professor of mathematics had been detailing a long and involved proposition on the blackboard when, upon turning toward the class, he noted one pupil daydreaming out the window. He rapped on his desk and cried sharply, "Smith, Smith, board!" Smith started, looked at the professor, and nodded, "Yes, sir," he yawned, "very much so."

See also order², sarcasm³.

CLEAN

1

It was the hour for the hygiene class in school and the teacher was asking questions. "Johnny," she demanded, "which is more important to keep clean, your face or your teeth?" Johnny pondered for a moment, then answered hesitatingly, "Your teeth, teacher, 'cause they'll rot off, but your face won't."

2

The young kindergarten teacher was distressed by the slovenly, almost filthy appearance of one of her little pupils. So after speaking generally of the need of cleanliness and sanitation, she asked the dirty boy pointedly, "Now, Tommy, when your house gets all mussed up and dirty, what does your mother do?" "We move," replied Tommy at once.

CLERGY

See minister.

CLIMAX

The famous movie producer was no given to subtlety for achieving effect in his productions. He had decided it was time for a super-super-colossal picture and he had called his script men together to plan it. His ideas being none too clear, one of the men finally asked if he had any definite suggestion "Sure I have," he cried. "You can start off with an earthquake, and from there work up to a smash climax!"

CLOCK

1

A man waiting for his train was worried by the discrepancy between the various clocks in the station which varied from each other as much as thirty minutes. He questioned a passing porter about the matter, who puzzled over it for a few moments, then brightened and replied, "Well, sir, it really don' make no difference about them clocks no-how, 'cause the train leaves at 3:20 no matter what they say."

2

The devoted lover was sitting entranced in the parlor with his lady fair and he could hear the clock upstairs striking the hours; first nine o'clock, then ten, then eleven, and at last midnight. "Ah, how the hours fly on wingèd feet when I'm with you, my darling!" "Don't be crazy!" admonished the girl. "That's dad setting the clock."

3

The boss was angry as the clerk straggled in late. "How is it that you can never get to the office on time?" he demanded. "It's really your fault, boss," explained the clerk. "You've so impressed on me not to watch the clock at the office, that now I don't think of watching it at home either."

4

The itinerant salesman was trying to sell a farmer a new eight-day clock. After extolling its various features and refinements, he concluded, "And in addition to all that, sir, this remarkable clock will run for eight days without winding." The farmer's eyes widened in amazement. "You don't say!" he exclaimed. "And how long will it run if you wind it?"

See also funeral[8].

CLOTHES

1

The female lecturer was warming to her subject. "It is proven by statistics," she declared, "that the trend to common sense, modern design in women's clothing has cut down accidents on streetcars by 50%." A masculine voice spoke up eagerly from the rear, "Well, let's do away with accidents entirely."

2

"My, how beautiful your wife looks tonight!" exclaimed a man to a struggling author. "That dress she has on is a poem." "A poem!" cried the author. "How do you get that way? That dress happens to be three poems and a short story."

3

"Look here," cried the man angrily, bursting into the clothing store, "it's not two weeks since I bought this suit here and it's turning rusty-looking already." "Why, naturally, sir," replied the clothing man. "Didn't I guarantee when you bought that suit that it would wear like iron?"

4

Two elderly women were discussing their children. "And how is your daughter coming with her golfing?" asked one. "They tell me that she's going around in less and less every week," replied the other. "I know," said the first grimly, "I saw her yesterday. But I asked about her golf."

5

The dear ladies were having a little get-together luncheon at the house of one of their number, and, a short time before it was to start, one of the guests called the hostess and asked what would be suitable to wear. "Since it's to be simply a hen party, dear," replied the hostess, "I'd suggest that you come in something with an open throat and a back suitable for knifing."

6

The minister had been asked to present the prizes to the winners of the local dog show, but when he got there he was outraged at the dress of some of the girls. "Just look at that young person there with the cigarette, close-cut hair, and breeches," he cried to a bystander. "Is it a boy or a girl?" "It's a girl," replied the other. "She's my daughter." "Oh, forgive me, sir," apologized the preacher. "I never dreamed you were her father." "I'm not," was the dry reply. "I'm her mother."

7

"And did you notice Jane at the party last night?" gasped the old-fashioned Mrs. Simms. "She was quite décolleté, wasn't she?" "She was?" cried Mrs. Gray in shocked tones. "Why, I didn't know that she ever touched a drop."

8

The garrulous lady had cornered the famous judge. "I hear that you have quite a reputation, judge, for being able to judge a woman's character from her clothing," she cooed. "Now, what would be your verdict on my sister over there?" The judge took a look, then a good look. "Insufficient evidence," he gasped.

9

A bachelor had bought a new shirt and had found a slip pinned inside with a girl's name and address and the request: "Please write and send a photograph." Romance stirred in the bachelor's heart. He sent off a letter and a picture of himself. A few days later a letter arrived which he opened with racing heart, but it said: "Thanks, I just wondered what kind of goof would wear such a dopey shirt."

10

"How do you manage always to be dressed so well?" asked a man admiringly of an acquaintance. "Does your wife pick your clothes?" "Nope," responded the other genially. "Just the pockets."

11

The floorwalker of a department store noticed a young man looking very confused, so he went to him and asked, "Can I help you, sir? You seem puzzled about something." "So I am," admitted the young fellow. "I was supposed to buy either a camisole or a casserole, but, so help me, I can't remember which." "Perhaps I can help you," suggested the floorwalker amiably, "if you tell me what sort of chicken you intend putting in it."

12

It was the swankiest opera performance of the season and all the fashionable ladies were very décolleté in their boxes. A noted churchman who was present was looking over the audience through glasses in amazement. "Tell me, Reverend," asked one of the ladies of his party, "have you ever seen anything like this in all your life?" "Never, madam," was the grave reply, "at least, not since I was weaned."

See also corset, dress[1], Eskimo, fashion, henpecked[1], hint[10], house[1], signs[2], tree[1].

CLOUDS

1

Two Kansas farmers stood regarding critically some clouds drifting across the sky. "Guess mebbe we're gonna have some rain at last," observed one hopefully. But the other, an old railroad man, was not so optimistic. "Heck," he growled, "them's jest empties comin' back from Illinois."

2

A farmer had been moaning to a friend about adverse farming conditions until finally the friend objected, "It's not that bad, Hi. Remember, every cloud's got a silver lining." "Humph!" grunted Hiram. "It'd be better if they had an arsenic linin' then when it rained it'd spray the crops with bug-killer as well as water 'em."

CLUB

1

The doorman ran down the steps of the club to open the limousine door, but halfway down he caught his toe and rolled down the rest of the way. "For goodness' sake, be more careful," scolded the manager from the top of the steps, "or people will be thinking you're a member."

2

The married couple were quarreling because he had come home late again. "No matter what you say, at least I am a man of my word," he declared hotly. "I always call a spade a spade." "That may be, John," conceded the wife sweetly, "but you rarely call a club a club—usually you call it working late."

3

The amateur huntsmen were exchanging experiences. "I once went lion-hunting with a club," boasted one. "Hunting lions with a club!" exclaimed a listener in amazement. "But weren't you afraid?" "Oh, no," said the brave one. "You see, it was a lion-hunting club and had over two hundred members."

4

The phone rang in the men's club and a woman's voice asked, "Please ask my husband to ——." "Your husband's not here, ma'am," interrupted the attendant. "What!" cried the lady. "Don't be smart with me, young man! How do you know my husband isn't there when you didn't even get the name?" "Don't need no name, ma'am," replied the attendant smoothly. "There ain't nobody's husband ever at this club, ma'am."

CLUMSY

The stout gentleman was trying to work his way past the other people toward his seat at the circus and was having difficulty. "Excuse me, madam," he said to one woman, "but did I step on your foot?" The lady surveyed the circus arena carefully. "It's quite possible you have," she said acidly. "The elephants all seem still to be out there."

COAL

1

An irate gentleman burst into the newspaper editor's office. "You've made a terrible blunder," he cried. "I was in that amateur athletic contest last night, and you refer to me in your paper as the 'well-known lightweight champ.' " "Well, aren't you?" asked the editor. "No, I'm not," was the angry response, "and it's darned embarrassing, seeing that I'm a coal dealer."

2

A man entered a coal dealer's office. "I'd like you to send me a ton of coal," he requested. "Yes, sir," replied the dealer. "What size do you want?" "Well, if it's not asking too much," replied the man who had bought coal before, "I'd like one of those old-fashioned 2,000-pound tons."

3

A coal dealer called a friend who was an insurance agent. "Say, Bill," he said, "I'd like to get some fire insurance on my coal-yards. What's the premium on a $25,000 policy?" "What kind of coal is it?" asked the agent. "The same kind as that last load you sent me?" "That's right," replied the dealer. "Then I wouldn't waste the money insuring it," snorted the agent. "That stuff will never burn."

See also laughter[1], religion[4], right[1].

COAT

1

One man approached another as he was struggling into a coat at the cloak rack of a restaurant and asked, "Do you happen to be Ronald Duncan?" "No, I'm not," replied the other surprised. "Well, I am," declared the first icily, "and that's his coat you're putting on."

2

The doctor came down to the living-room where the husband sat.

"Your wife has a very bad cold," he announced. "How do you suppose she caught it?" "It was probably because of her coat," replied the husband. "I see," said the doctor. "Too thin for this weather?" "No, it's not that," was the grim answer. "It's last year's coat and she won't wear it at all."

COCKTAIL

1

The backwoods farmer was visiting a city friend and in the course of their sightseeing they dropped into a fashionable bar. "What'll it be, gents?" asked the bartender. "You can make mine a sidecar," ordered the sophisticated city slicker. "And you?" the bartender asked the farmer. The yokel gulped and looked confused. "Who, me?" he gasped. "Guess I'll jest have a plain horse 'n' buggy."

2

"Why is it that cocktails seem to pack more of a punch than straight liquor?" asked one drinker of another. "That's hard to say," pondered the other, "unless it's because you put liquor in to make it strong, water to make it weak, lemon to make it sour, sugar to make it sweet, ice to make it cold, and you drink it to get warmed up. Heck, it makes you dizzy just to think of it."

COFFEE

1

The boarder came down to breakfast a little late. "I'm awfully sorry," said the landlady, "but the coffee is exhausted." "I've been expecting it," growled the boarder; "it's been getting weaker and weaker every morning."

2

The doctor came out of the husband's room. "It's his nerves," he informed the wife. "He drinks too much strong coffee and you mustn't let him have it, as he gets too excited." "But, doctor," protested the wife, "you should see how much more excited he. gets when I give him weak coffee."

3

The angry diner called the waiter to his table. "What is this stuff supposed to be, tea or coffee?" he demanded indignantly. "It tastes more like turpentine." "Like turpentine?" said the waiter placatingly. "In that case, sir, I can assure you it's coffee, because our tea tastes like dishwater."

4

The customer in the restaurant loudly demanded the headwaiter and then had a vigorous talk with him, after which the headwaiter sought out the diner's waiter. "Your customer at table 3 insists on having some freshly-made coffee," he explained in a bored tone, "so just keep him waiting about ten minutes and then serve him some out of the urn."

5

The new boarder looked critically at the contents of his cup, sniffed it carefully, then resolutely set the cup down. "Well," demanded the landlady belligerently, "do you have anything to say against the coffee?" "Not a word, madam," the boarder answered politely. "You see, I never speak ill of the absent."

See also boarding house[3], restaurant[6].

COINCIDENCE

Two strangers waiting on a street corner struck up a conversation. As they talked, two women appeared in the distance down the street. "See those two women coming toward us?" asked one. "It's strange they should happen along together, for one's my wife and the other's my mistress." "Why, what a coincidence!" cried the other. "I was just going to say the same thing."

COLD

The elderly boarder was complaining to the landlady about the lack of heat in his room. "It's bad enough in the daytime when I'm up and about," he protested, "but at night it's often so bad that I'm awakened by the chattering of my teeth on the table."

See also grave.

COLLAR

A dominating woman walked into a men's wear shop and said, "I wanted to get some collars for my husband, but it seems I've forgotten the size." "Could it be thirteen and a half, madam?" suggested the clerk. "That's it," cried the woman. "How did you know?" "Very simply, madam," explained the experienced clerk. "Men who permit their wives to buy their collars for them usually wear that size."

COLLECT

1

The girls were talking about the personal affairs of their friends. "You all know Mabel, don't you?" said one. "Well, she's only twenty-four and she's already been divorced three times. And it's very odd, but her three husbands and her present boy-friend are all named William." "Is that a fact?" replied one of the listeners. "She must be a regular Bill collector."

2

The manager of a gas company had just hired a new collector. "Take this key and this list," he instructed him, "and go around and empty all the coins from the pay meters." Nothing was heard of the collector for three weeks, then he came to the office and said, "I'd like a new key. I've lost the other one." "Sure," replied the manager, "but why haven't you been in on Fridays for your pay?" "What!" cried the man, his face shining. "Do I get a salary too?"

3

The minister's son looked up from his schoolbooks puzzled. "Father," he queried, "it says here in my grammar that the verbs 'collect' and 'congregate' mean the same thing. Is that true?" "It may be true of the verbs, son," replied the minister, "but there certainly is a great difference between the nouns 'collection' and 'congregation.'"

4

The philatelist was showing a friend his large collection of postage stamps. "It's a marvelous collection," said the friend admiringly.

"It almost seems that collecting must be in your blood." "It is," replied the other. "My father was a collector." "Indeed?" said the friend, pleased at his own keenness. "What did he collect?" "Garbage," was the terse reply.

5

All the chickens had been shut up in the coop save one which paced nervously about in front of the door clucking excitedly. Little Billy watched this for a while, then ran to his mother. "Gee, mom," he cried, "that chicken out there must be a collector." "Why, whatever makes you say that, Billy?" asked mother. "Because he can't get in," was the knowing reply.

See also debt[1], dentist[1], fortune-teller[2].

COLLEGE

1

A stranger, looking for a certain college, took the wrong turn and ended up at the insane asylum. He soon discovered his mistake and the guard gave him his direction. "Well," he quipped as he left, "I suppose there isn't much difference between the two institutions after all." "That's what you think," grunted the guard who had a son in college. "In this place you've got to show improvement to get out."

2

Prexy finally had to call the indifferent student to his office. "Why did you ever come to college if you're not going to study?" he asked. "Well, I'm not really sure myself, sir," answered the boy. "Mother says it's to fit me to be

President; Uncle John says it's to sow my wild oats; my sister thinks I ought to get a rich friend for her to marry; and dad says it's to bankrupt the family."

3

At the convention for college presidents several of the delegates were discussing what they'd like to do after retirement. "I'd like to superintend an orphan asylum," said one, "so I'd never get letters from parents." "As for me," declared another, "I'd like to be warden of a penitentiary so I'd never have to welcome back the alumni." A third sighed and said, "I'd like to conduct a correspondence school so that I could blame any lack in my students' education on the mails."

4

The sporty freshman had just finished his unpacking and sauntered out on the campus to accost a glum-looking junior. "Hi, fella!" he hailed him. "What do you boys have around here in the way of a good time?" "The Dean," was the gloomy response.

5

The statistically-minded college president was conducting a survey to find out the students' reasons for attending college. Almost always the answers were full of airy and trite idealism, but one gum-chewing co-ed refused to mince words. "Jeepers!" she exclaimed when the question was put to her, "I come to be went wit'—but I ain't bin yet!"

6

Junior was home from college with little to show for it but a sheepskin and an air of bored sophistication. "What was the most difficult thing for you to learn at college, son?" questioned the proud papa. "How to open beer bottles with a quarter," replied the young hopeful.

7

"Don't you want to get a college education?" teacher asked little Johnny who wouldn't study. "Naw," replied Johnny, "me brudder ain't got none. He was t'rown outta Vassar the foist day he was dere." "Vassar!" cried teacher. "Why, that's for girls only." "I know, I know," said Johnny. "Dat's why he was t'rown out."

See also classroom[1], cooking[4], examination[6], graduation[2], language[4], letter[2], mind[1], opportunity[6], professor[3], roommate, student[1], vacation[1], vice.

COLOR

1

"I'd like some gloves, please," said the man to the haberdashery clerk. "What color would you like, sir?" queried the clerk. "I believe I'll take coffee-colored gloves," replied the customer. "Yes, sir," said the clerk. "With or without cream?"

2

The district inspector was visiting the Sunday school and was conducting a little examination. "It is most important to the soul to know yourself honestly," he said. "Now, suppose all good people were white, and all bad people were black, what color would each of you be?" Most of the answers were "White," some few brave ones answered "Black," but one little girl said timidly, "Please, sir, I'd be streaky."

3

It had been a busy day in the department store and it was just about closing time when the phone rang. "Is this the hosiery department?" inquired a bored voice. "Yes," replied the worn-out sales-girl. "Do you carry flesh-colored stockings?" continued the voice. "Yep," said the girl, her eye on the clock. "Whatcha want, lady—pink, yellow, or black?"

See also author[1], wedding[1], woman-driver[3].

COMMANDMENT

1

Teacher called little Sammy to her desk. "Do you know, Sammy," she said sternly, "that by stealing Jimmy's apple you have broken the eighth Commandment?" "I know, teacher," replied Sammy, "but I figured that I'd as well break the eighth and have the apple as to break the tenth and just covet it."

2

The Sunday school lesson for that day was the Ten Commandments. "Can any of you give me a Commandment having only four words in it?" teacher asked the class. A little hand shot up immediately. "Yes, Tommy, what is it?" said teacher. "Keep off the grass!" was the prompt reply.

3

A weather-beaten old sailor wandered into a water front mission where a preacher was holding forth in strong language on the Ten Commandments, detailing at length the many ways in which they could be broken without its being realized.

The sailor departed in a very subdued mood, but after walking a few blocks his face brightened and he squared his shoulders. "Anyhow," he muttered, "I never made no graven images."

See also musician[3].

COMMON SENSE

One girl had accused another of trying to steal her boy-friend and a bitter quarrel had ensued. "What would I want with that fellow?" cried the accused. "The man I marry must at least have common sense." "Well, he won't have," retorted the other.

COMMUTER

1

"What's that you've got there?" one commuter asked another as they waited for the evening train. "This?" said the other, holding out a package. "It's a new kind of breakfast food I bought because I was missing too many trains. The other brands all take three and a half seconds to prepare, but this one requires only one and one-half seconds."

2

"Henry," asked the commuter's wife, "which train does Mr. Black take to town in the morning?" "He takes the one twenty minutes after mine," replied the commuter. "That's ridiculous," said the wife. "If he takes a train after yours how can you know which one it is?" she questioned. "Because it's the one I always take," was the answer.

See also ambition[6].

COMPANY

1

The old bachelor had been visiting the elderly widow regularly every evening for three years. "Since you two seem to get along so well together," asked a friend, "why don't you marry her?" "I've often thought of that," admitted the bachelor, "but then where would I spend my evenings?"

2

The little boy looked up from his book. "Dad," he inquired, "it says here, 'A man is known by the company he keeps.' Is that right?" "It certainly is, son," replied father. "Well, then," insisted the boy, "if a good man and a bad man go together, is the good man bad because he keeps company with the bad man, or is the bad man good because he keeps company with the good man?"

3

It was 3 o'clock in the morning during a heavy snowstorm when the doctor was called out urgently, but examination of the patient proved it to be a trifling ailment. "You had better send for your lawyer and minister also," he told the patient as he snapped his case shut. "Oh, am I that ill, doctor?" she gasped. "No," he replied. "It's just that I don't want to be the only one dragged out of bed on such a night for nothing."

4

The jury had brought in a verdict of not guilty and the judge dismissed the defendant, but gave him a stern warning about his behavior in the future, concluding with the admonition, "From now on you want to be sure to keep away from bad company." "Yes, indeed, Your Honor," replied the man fervently, "you'll not see me here again if I can help it."

See also invitation[1].

COMPETITION

1

A social worker met a child of a family she had been working with. "Did your uncle ever find a job?" she asked. "Yep," replied the boy, "he's sellin' fly paper." "Why, it's the middle of winter!" exclaimed the woman. "What's the idea of trying to sell fly paper now?" "Aw, uncle's smart," said the boy. "He figured there wouldn't be any competition now."

2

There had been an unusually long drought and the farmer had at last begun an elaborate series of irrigation ditches to save his crops. Just as he was getting them well on to completion a heavy downpour began. "That's the heck of it," he said, flinging his shovel down in disgust, "you can't do anything nowadays without competition."

See also honest[3].

COMPLAINT

1

After trying unsuccessfully for twenty minutes to get a waiter's attention, the customer went to the cashier's desk and demanded heatedly to see the manager. "Whatcha want wit' 'im?" she asked through her chewing gum. "I have a complaint," he said. "Complaint?" retorted the cashier in high disdain. "Look, bub, this here's a restaurant, not a hospital."

2

The angry diner called the waiter to his table. "I can't eat such garbage," he exclaimed, pushing his plate back. "Call the manager." "It's no use, sir," replied the waiter sympathetically, "he won't eat it either."

3

The crew had chosen a committee to complain to the captain about their food, but they felt a little diffident about being too outspoken before him. "Ain't satisfied with the grub, huh?" growled the Skipper. "What's the matter, not enough of it?" "Oh, no, sir," said the spokesman, "there's plenty, such as it is." "What then?" barked the Captain, "not good enough?" "No, sir," was the reply, "it's quite good, what there is of it."

4

A traveler had written a very indignant letter to the railroad company as to why he had sat up all night in the club car rather than use the berth he had paid for. However, he was greatly mollified by the extremely courteous letter he received full of apologies and logical explanations, until he saw this note jotted on the margin of his own letter which had been enclosed by mistake: "Smith, send this griper the bedbug letter No. 4."

5

The farmer was a chronic complainer and never missed an opportunity to indulge in laments, but this year perfect weather had combined with his natural industry to produce a bumper crop. "Well, you couldn't ask for more this year," observed a friend. "There's certainly nothing to kick about." "Oh, I dunno," grunted the farmer gloomily, "crops like this is durned hard on the ground."

COMPLIMENT

1

The two men had just left the rather plain young lady. "How could you be so deceitful as to tell that girl she's pretty?" reproved the one. "I wasn't deceitful," replied the other. "Didn't I hear you tell her that she was actually pretty?" insisted the first. "Of course you didn't," the other answered. "What I told her was that she was as pretty as she could be."

2

The young poet had at last managed to get in to see the editor. "I do not wish to be paid for this poem, you know," he said. "I submit it entirely as a compliment." "In that case, sir," replied the editor with charming courtesy, "I insist upon returning the compliment."

3

The lady was not at all satisfied with her new cook and was trying to tell her so tactfully. "It's very odd, Mary," she observed, "but it seems that it is the worst mistresses that always get the best cooks." Mary looked down coyly and twisted her apron in her hands. "Aw, go 'long witcha, now, mum," she giggled.

4

He had just met her and they

were dancing. "You're really quite a pretty girl," he said conversationally. "Oh, come now," she smiled blushingly, "you know you'd say that even if you didn't think so." "Sure I would," he agreed readily, "because you'd think so even if I didn't say so."

5

The gallant young man took the hand of the elderly lady to whom he had been introduced and regarded her admiringly. "Madam," he said feelingly, "you look like a rare old Rembrandt." The lady jerked her hand back and sniffed. "Is that so, bud?" she snapped. "You don't look so hot yourself."

6

The amateur dramatic club had just finished rehearsal and the young man wished to compliment the lady sponsoring the project. "You played your part marvelously, madam," he said. "It suits you perfectly." "Oh, I'm afraid not," protested the pleased sponsor. "That part really calls for a young and pretty woman." "But no, madam," insisted the young fellow, "you have just so completely proved the opposite."

7

A young man was stuck with an elderly lady and he was trying desperately to think of something complimentary to say. "You certainly look young," he finally came out with. "Oh, you're just flattering me," she said coyly. The boy was confused by this response. "Well, maybe," he blurted out, "but at least you try to, anyway."

See also eating[4], praise[3].

COMPROMISE

1

Each week the boarder had promised to pay his rent next week, but each time something unexpected had come up and the payment was put off another week until at last the landlady got fed up. "Look here," she offered, "I'll meet you half-way and forget half of what you owe me." "Fine!" cried the boarder. "And I'll meet you half-way and forget the other half."

2

Two ladies in the railroad car had been arguing for some time about the ventilation problem. "Open a window, porter," demanded one, "or I shall suffocate." "If you open that window, porter," objected the other, "I shall freeze to death." The porter scratched his head and looked helplessly at a bored man who suggested, "Why don't you open the window and freeze one, porter, then close it and suffocate the other, and then we'll have some peace."

3

Two men were discussing feminine foibles. "Some women will believe anything you tell them," declared one. "You said it," agreed the other heartily. "Why, before I married my wife I told her that I would be her humble slave for life, and she believed me so implicitly that to this day she won't accept any compromise."

CONCEIT

1

The young man had just finished a full hour's recital of his own virtues and talents and concluded by saying, "Now, I hope you don't think I'm conceited." "Oh, no, no," yawned his young lady victim, "but I was just thinking how annoying your neighbors must find it to hear you cheering every time you look in the glass."

2

The quarrel was finally dwindling away and the husband observed in mock-humble tones, "Of course, I must admit that I do have my faults." "Of course," snapped the wife, "only in your eyes your worst faults are far better than other people's best virtues."

3

The girl was being granted the rare and precious privilege of dancing with the movie star and she was trying to make conversation. "Isn't it a pity," she ventured, "that handsome men are always so conceited?" "That's not always true, my girl," replied the star patronizingly. "I'm not."

See also importance[1], sarcasm[7].

CONCERN

1

The doctor had just finished examining his patient and seemed pleased. "Why, you're getting along just fine," he said. "Of course, your right hip is still badly swollen, but that doesn't bother me in the least." "I guess not," growled the patient, trying painfully to move. "If your hip were swollen it wouldn't bother me either."

2

The little boy was leaning against the fence weeping when a kindly passer-by noticed him. "What's wrong, little fellow?" the old gentleman asked sympathetically. But sobs were his only answer. "There, there, my boy," he said comfortingly, "don't mind." "I—I didn't," was the quavering reply, "an' that's what I got w-whipped for."

See also precaution[2].

CONCERT

1

It was the opening symphony concert of the season and a marvelous program had been prepared. The conductor was leading the orchestra through a thunderous and crashing overture and reached the point where there was a complete rest. In the sudden momentary silence a shrill feminine voice could be heard objecting, "But I *always* fry mine in lard."

2

The young couple had been keeping up an animated conversation throughout the concert, and finally a man behind them exclaimed, "What a pesky nuisance!" The young man turned indignantly and asked, "Were you referring to *me,* sir?" "Goodness, no," the man assured him blandly. "I meant the musicians—they're making such an infernal racket that I can't make out a word you're saying."

3

It was little Billy's first concert and he was interested in everything, especially when the orchestra accompanied the woman soloist in her number. "Mamma," he cried out, "why's that man shakin' that stick at the lady?" "Hush, child," reproved mother. "He's not shaking the stick at her." "Then why's she screamin' like that?" demanded Billy.

4

A young lady arrived late at the concert and the usher would not admit her to the auditorium until the intermission. "But I'll stand in the back and not disturb any one," she promised. "I'm especially eager to hear that new symphony they're playing." "That's just the trouble, ma'am," sighed the usher regretfully. "If I opened that door now, half the audience would rush out."

5

The Culture Club of a small town had arranged for a touring symphony orchestra to play a concert in their community. It was the first time most of the inhabitants had seen such a thing, and the comments were many around the general store stove the next day. "Well, all I got to say," ventured one old-timer, "is that it wuz a durned long ways to bring that big drum jest to whack it oncet."

6

The village band was giving their annual summer concert and had finished an extremely loud, if not especially harmonious, number and had sunk back perspiring to enjoy the enthusiastic townsfolk's applause. "What's the next number?" asked the red-faced trombonist of the leader. The leader looked at his program and replied, "Washington Post March." "Cracky!" exclaimed the musician. "I just got through playin' that!"

See also musician.

CONDITION

1

The Sunday school teacher was examining her pupils for the extent of their Bible knowledge. "Can you tell me, Tommy," she asked, "what condition the patriarch Job was in at the end of his life?" "Dead," was the prompt answer.

2

The drunken New Yorker stumbled into his apartment and was confronted by his angry wife. "William," she demanded, "what do you mean coming home in this state?" "Wha' shtate ja wan' me come home in, m'love?" asked the drunk. "Mizzuri?"

CONDUCT

See behavior.

CONDUCTOR

1

The streetcar passenger counted out his fare in pennies into the conductor's hand. "Aw, I can't take those pennies," objected the conductor. "Then give them to the company," said the passenger, turning back to his paper.

2

The passenger on a train had a quarrel with the conductor and he ended by declaring, "Well, this railroad company will never see another cent of my money." "Yeah?" sneered the conductor. "What'll you do? Walk?" "No," replied the passenger grimly, "I'll just stop buying tickets and pay my cash fare to you."

CONFESSION

The young priest was being instructed by the old experienced father in how to conduct a confession. "Here, you try your hand with this young lady coming now," he told the fledgling, "and I'll listen and correct your mistakes." The confession proved quite colorful and, after it was ended, the young priest asked how he had done. "Very well, indeed," commended the old priest, "only I'd suggest that when you hear some startling confession you'd better say simply 'tzst, tzst' instead of 'whew!'"

See also education[3], mistake[5].

CONFIDENCE

1

The coming young boxer had finally been slated to battle the champ but, as the time came for him to enter the ring on the night of his big opportunity, it was noted that he tended to hang back. "It's okay, Slugger," encouraged his manager, "just keep telling yourself, 'I'm gonna lick 'im,' and you'll win." "I'm afraid that's no good," replied the fighter dubiously, "because I know what a liar I am."

2

The flying instructor was trying a new system. When they were well up in the air, he threw his stick out of the plane, "This will show you that I have complete confidence in your ability to fly." "Thank you, sir, and I'll show you that I have complete confidence in you also," replied the student as he threw out his stick, too.

See also banking[7].

CONGRESS

1

The father had taken his small son to see the House of Representatives in session. "Who's that man, pop?" asked the boy. "That, son, is the chaplain of the House," replied father. "Does he pray for the Representatives, pop?" continued the boy. The father thought a moment, then answered grimly, "No, son, when he gets up there and looks around at the members of the House, he prays for the country."

2

The Congressman's wife shook her sleeping husband vigorously. "Wake up, John," she whispered excitedly, "there's a robber in the house." "Nonsense, my dear," was the husband's sleepy response. "In the Senate, yes, but in the House, never."

3

It was a big banquet, even for Washington, and the dining room was lavishly decorated and palms decked all the tables save a few. "Why are there no palms on those tables?" asked one of the early arrivals of the headwaiter. "Well, to tell you the truth, sir," confided the headwaiter, "those are the tables set aside for Congressmen, and if we put palms on them they'll just eat them up for celery."

See also recognize[2], statesman[2], trust[3].

CONSCIENCE

1

The inquiry into election bribery was proceeding and a witness was called. "According to your deposition," said the judge, "you received $10 to vote the Democratic ticket, and you got another $10 to vote Republican?" "That's right, Your Honor," replied the witness. "And how did you finally vote?" inquired the judge. The witness drew himself up proudly. "Your Honor," he said, "I voted according to my conscience."

2

A traveling man had been away for a number of weeks and returning late one night retired with his wife. At about 2:30 in the morning there suddenly came a loud knocking on the door. "My God!" cried the wife, starting up fearfully, "my husband's back!" "My God!" cried the husband, and jumped out of the window.

3

A man came to a psychiatrist. "I've come to you," he said, "because my conduct hasn't been of the best lately and my conscience is troubling me." "Ah, I see," said the psychiatrist, "you want me to help you strengthen your will power?" "Heck, no," cried the patient disgustedly, "I want you to try to weaken my conscience."

4

The little girl had just returned much impressed from Sunday school where she had received her first information on the voice of conscience. "If you hear somethin' right here," she told her slightly older sister, pressing her hands over her stomach, "it's your conscience whisperin' to you." "Aw, phooey!" sneered the sister, "'at's only wind on your tummie."

5

It was Sunday morning and it looked very much like rain, and old Sam sat with bait and fishing tackle on a log by the river road casting dubious glances at the sky. The minister passed by on his way to church and called to him, "Well, brother Sam, are you going to church or are you going fishing?" "Dunno yit, Reverend," answered Sam, "I'm still a-settin' here a-wrastlin' with m'conscience."

6

Two business partners were discussing the ethics of a deal which one of them opposed on the grounds that it would bother his conscience. "You make me tired," cried the other heatedly. "Why, you can't even tell me what conscience it." "But I can," replied the first bitingly. "Conscience is a deterring emotion which most people think should bother the other fellow to their advantage."

See also repent[2], worry[1].

CONSEQUENCE

A crude fellow was pouring abusive language upon a Quaker who stood enduring it meekly. But, when the vigor of the invective was doubled, he approached the other and said gently but forcefully, "Take care, my friend, lest thou runnest thy face against my fist."

CONSERVATION

The lecturer on forest conservation was loudly berating the general public for its complete indifference to the need of preserving our timber reserves. "I daresay," he cried, "that there isn't a person here tonight who has done a single thing toward conserving our timber supply." After a short but impressive silence, a meek voice spoke up timidly from the rear, "Well, I once shot a woodpecker."

CONSOLATION

1

The co-ed's football team was losing badly and tears ran down her lovely cheeks. "There, there, little girl," comforted her escort, "I'll kiss those tears away." And manfully he strove to fulfill his vow, but still they streamed on. "Will nothing stop them?" he cried at last. "I'm afraid not," she murmured. "It's asthma, but just go right ahead with the treatment."

2

The man's wife had just died and his minister was trying to console and comfort him. "I know, brother," he told him, "that your grief is great for the loss of her who was your companion and helper in life. But be consoled, brother, by the assurance that there is Another who knows your woe and would embrace you in the arms of unfailing love." The bereaved looked up eagerly through his tears and asked, "What's her name?"

CONSPICUOUS

1

A rookie was idling down a street in town when he was halted by a lieutenant. "What's the matter, soldier, don't you know that you're supposed to salute officers?" asked the lieutenant. "Oh, yes, sir," replied the rookie, "but you see I'm AWOL and I don't want to be conspicuous."

2

An American advertising man was traveling abroad and was describing to a foreigner an electric sign he had built back home. "It has over 75,000 red globes, about 20,000 blue globes, almost 35,000 green ones, and about 25,000 white ones, all flashing and forming different combinations, topped by a sunburst of about 80,000 orange globes." "It sounds very colorful," admitted the foreigner, "but isn't it a trifle conspicuous?"

CONTEMPT

1

The judge had overruled the lawyer and after a brief clash of opinions, the lawyer turned on his heel and stalked away. "Are you by any chance, sir, trying to show your contempt for the court?" demanded the judge hotly. "On the contrary," replied the lawyer evenly, "I'm trying to conceal it."

2

There had been a little conflict between the judge and lawyer. The judge had ordered the lawyer to sit down, but the lawyer was a little deaf and didn't hear him and went right on talking. "Ten dollars' fine for contempt of court," decreed the judge. "What did he say?" the lawyer asked the clerk. "He fined you $10 for contempt," explained the clerk. The lawyer eyed the judge as he pulled out his wallet. "I'll pay it now," he said, "it's a just debt."

3

A small-town judge was very

arrogant in his notions of the court's dignity, and one day he passed a young man on the street who neglected to remove his hat to him. "Young man!" thundered the judge ponderously, "I fine you $3 for contempt of court! " "Aw, you can't do that," replied the youth, "the court's not in session now." "This court's always in session," declared the judge, "and thus is always an object of contempt."

CONTRACT

1

A customer came into a little lunchstand next to a bank and asked the proprietor for a loan of "a coupla dollars till next week." "I'd sure like to help you out," said the lunch man, "if only it wasn't for my agreement with the bank." "Whatcha mean, agreement?" asked the cadger. "Why, they agreed not to sell sandwiches if I wouldn't lend money," was the reply.

2

A client was consulting a lawyer about a man's failure to fulfill his promises. "Do you have a contract with him?" asked the lawyer. "Well, I have a verbal contract," replied the client. "A verbal contract, my friend," pronounced the lawyer, shrugging his shoulders, "is not worth the paper it isn't written on."

CONTRADICT

The young man had been trying to explain something to the girl, but at every point she would correct him in some manner. "The next time you contradict me," he finally announced with pretended stern-

ness, "I'm going to kiss you." "Oh, no, you're not!" declared the girl promptly.

CONTRIBUTION

1

The speaker had finished his scheduled address to the local Culture Society and the secretary sought him out with a check. "No, no," he refused politely, "I was happy to speak to you. Why don't you contribute it to some worthy cause?" "Would you mind if we put it in our special fund?" queried the secretary. "Of course not," said the speaker. "What's the fund for?" "To help us get better lecturers next year," was the reply.

2

The committee was out collecting funds for a new church and they approached one of the town's old citizens, who refused them. "But you could give something," they insisted. "Nope," was the firm reply, "I owe too many people. Debts come before charity, you know." "But don't you think you owe God a larger debt than any one?" they pointed out. "Mebbe so," the old fellow agreed, "but He ain't a-pushin' me like my other creditors."

3

The village tightwad was tearing his hair. "I just can't understand how I did it," he wailed. "I put a silver dollar in the church basket this morning instead of my regular nickel!" The usher who took up the collection had noted it also, and he said nothing for the next nineteen Sundays when the man let the basket pass him by. But on the twentieth

Sunday he tapped him and said, "You're time's up now, Mac."

See also blind.

CONVALESCENT

1

A sturdy, weather-beaten woman applied at the back door of a house in a Western town asking for light housework. "Cain't do heavy work fer a spell yit 'cause I'm convalescin' frum typhoid," she explained. "Where've you been?" asked the mistress. "I haven't seen you around town." "Oh, I bin a-workin' on a ranch out a pieceways," replied the woman, "Diggin' postholes while I was gittin' m'strength back."

2

A rural herb-doctor was passing the house of a well-to-do family and he leaned over the fence to hail the yardman. "How's the mistress doin', Sam?" "I ain't sure," was the reply. "I heard the doctor say this mornin' she was convalescent." "Humph! Nuthin' to it," grunted the quack airily. "Why, I've cured convalescence in twenty-four hours!"

3

An untutored laborer stopped a nurse in the hospital corridor. "I'd like to see how my friend George Black is gettin' on, Miss," he said. "Why, just fine," replied the nurse. "He's convalescing now." "That's all right," responded the man, "I'll jest set down and wait."

CONVERSATION

1

A rabid golfer was seated next to a pretty girl at dinner and he re-galed her at such great length on his game that she could barely crowd in an occasional "Oh!" Toward the end of the meal he smiled apologetically and said, "Goodness! I'm afraid I've monopolized the conversation with nothing but my talk of golf." "That's quite all right," replied the girl, "but would you mind telling me, what is golf?"

2

The famous man had invited the daughter of an old friend to dinner and she was all excited at the honor. "But I'm sort of scared," she confided to her mother. "Whatever can I talk about with him?" Later she returned all smiles and happiness. "Gee, he's swell!" she exclaimed. "Why, we weren't half through with the soup before we were talking chummily about the fleas in Italian hotels."

3

"You say that Percy has proposed again!" exclaimed the girl's friend. "Gracious! How many times does that make now?" "Oh, I don't know, but it really doesn't mean anything," replied the other. "You see, he's not much of a conversationalist, and proposing is about the only thing he can manage in the way of pleasant small talk."

See also operation[1], stuttering[4], wife[3].

CONVERT

1

Miss Blodgett had been a faithful member of the Baptist church for over ten years when one day she called on the Methodist minister and told him that she was joining his church. "But why are you changing?" he asked, delighted to get a convert. "Do you find greater truth and comfort in my sermons?" "No, nothing like that," replied Miss Blodgett. "It's just that they've cindered the path at the Baptist church and it hurts my feet dreadfully."

2

One of the church's mission committee called on a member of the church. "I've called about the yearly contribution to our fund for converting the heathen," he explained. "Last year you gave a half-dollar, sir." "What!" barked the Christian, "haven't you converted them yet?"

CONVINCE

1

The wife shook her sleeping husband excitedly. "Wake up, William," she whispered. "I'm convinced that there's a burglar downstairs." "Well, m'love," replied the husband sleepily as he turned over, "I certainly hope you don't expect me to have the courage of your convictions."

2

The bum knocked on the back door and when the lady appeared he began his long story of his gradual fall from respectability and prosperity to his present low estate. The lady heard him out, then shook her head doubtfully. "I'm sorry, but your story lacks conviction," she said; "it has a hollow ring." "That, mum, is only the natural consequence of speakin' on an empty stomach," replied the bum.

COOK

1

The restaurant owner went from one pot to the next sampling the work of the new cook. "Hmm," he frowned, "you say you were an army cook during the war?" "Yes, sir," was the reply. "Cooked for officers' mess for over two years and was wounded three times." "Humph!" grunted the boss. "You're durned lucky they didn't kill you."

2

The summer-boarder trade had been picking up every year and the farmer was highly satisfied. "Guess next season we kin afford to have a chef," he told his wife. "What's a chef?" she asked. "Oh, that's jest a cook what knows enough words to give the soup a different name every day fer two weeks."

3

"Sorry to be late," said hubby sheepishly as he came home in the evening, "but I got a ticket for speeding and I have to appear in court tomorrow and get either fifteen dollars or fifteen days." "Oh, what a break, Henry!" cried wifey in huge relief. "You must take the fifteen days, because cook has just quit."

4

"Now, Maggie," inquired the mistress of the new house servant, "are you really a good cook?" "Oh, I kin cook good enough, mum," was the frank reply, "if only you'll not try to be helpin' me."

5

The new cook had been in service for about a week and the mistress of the house was making an unannounced check-up inspection, when much to her surprise she opened the pantry and found a policeman. "What's this man doing here?" she demanded sternly. "Sure, mum, and I don't know," was the innocent response, "unless maybe he's been left over from the last cook."

See also compliment[3].

COOKBOOK

1

Two old bachelors were discussing their household difficulties. "I bought me one of them big cookbooks once," confided the one, "but I gave it away." "What was the matter; too much fancy stuff in it?" asked the other. "Heck, yeah!" snorted the first in disgust. "Why, would you believe it, every one o' them blamed recipes began with, 'Take a clean dish ——.'"

2

It was the bride's first day in her new kitchen and she was trying to follow her cookbook implicitly. Finally, she called her mother in desperation. "There's something wrong with this cookbook," she wailed. "I'm trying to make a pudding and it says very distinctly, 'Bring to boil on brisk fire, stirring for two minutes, then beat it for fifteen minutes,' and when I got back it was burnt to a cinder!"

COOKING

1

"Darling," cried the bride, rushing out of the kitchen, "I've just made my first doughnuts. Now I want you to try them and be perfectly frank in telling me if you can think of anything to improve them." "Well," ventured hubby, as he hefted one in his hand, "don't you think it might be better if you made the hole bigger?"

2

"Why feed every tramp that knocks on the door?" growled the husband. "You never get a lick of work out of any of them." "I know," admitted the wife, "but it gives me a lot of satisfaction to see a man eat one of my meals without complaining about the cooking."

3

"Phew!" said the husband, with a wry face. "What makes this meat taste so funny?" "I just can't imagine what's wrong," replied the new bride with a puzzled frown, "especially when I took such good care of it, too. Why, when I burnt it a little on one side I even put sunburn oil on it right away."

4

"Gracious, what a messy kitchen, Mary!" cried the mistress as she entered. "Every pot, pan, and dish in the place is dirty and the table and floor is one big litter. What've you been doing?" "Me? Nuthin', mum," sighed the cook. "It's just that yer daughter has bin showin' me how they boil a pertater in her cookin' class in college."

5

The bride, while shopping, had seen a new spring outfit that she wanted very much, so she hurried home and prepared an elaborate meal for hubby to put him in a good mood. When the meal was over, she cuddled up to him and cooed,

"What will 'oo Babykins get if she keeps cookin' like 'at for her Snookums?" Hubby suppressed a burp as he moaned, "My life insurance."

6

The new wife could never satisfy her husband with her hot biscuits. Always he complained that they were not "like mother used to make." One morning she put a plate of biscuits before him and said, "Try those and tell me what you think." "Oh, boy!" he cried, as he bit into one, "just like mother's. How'd you do it?" "Very simply," was the reply. "I just used oleo for butter, cold storage eggs, put a little alum in the flour, and watered the milk."

7

The young wife had not been cooking very long, but she bravely tried a pie. That evening she presented it rather dubiously to hubby, remarking, "I'm afraid the pie's not very good; I must have left something out." Hubby sampled the pie gingerly, then shook his head. "No, that's not it, my dear," he declared. "Nothing you left out could make a pie taste like this. It's something you put in."

See also aviation[1], cookbook[2], egg[7], inspiration.

CORPSE

1

Mrs. Gadabout had died and was laid out in the family living room for the neighbors to come and shake their heads over before she took her one-way ride to the cemetery. "And doesn't she look simply marvelous," commented one good lady to the rather grim husband. "And why shouldn't she?" he snapped. "Didn't she spend all last winter in Florida?"

2

A small-town preacher was holding a funeral oration and was giving each and every detail of the life and accomplishments of the deceased, among which he included the startling announcement: "The corpse has been a member of this church for over twenty years."

3

A cow had been killed by a train and it fell to the lot of the section foreman to make out a report of the accident on a regular form the company supplied for that purpose. He checked all the boxes and filled in all the lines readily enough until he came to one headed: "Disposition of Carcass." The foreman scratched his head a moment, then wrote in: "Kind and gentle."

See also mouth[3].

CORRECT

See right.

CORRECTION

It was late Sunday evening when the phone in the newspaper office rang for some time before a sleepy figure took his feet down from the desk to answer it. "I'd like to speak to the religious editor," came an excited voice. "I'm it," was the yawning reply. "This is Rev. Bland," said the voice. "Do you have the notes on my sermon?" "Yep," was the answer. "Well, would you mind taking Daniel out of the fiery furnace and putting him in the lions' den?"

CORSET

A badly confused man went into a ladies' wear shop and looked about in helpless bewilderment. "May I help you, sir?" asked a salesgirl. "Yes, I'd like an—er—a corset for my wife," he replied. "What bust, sir?" queried the girl. "Oh, nothing, nothing at all," he assured her. "It just wore out."

COSMETICS

1

The minister had been loud in his denunciation of the various paths to perdition that modern youth was taking, and he inveighed in particular against cosmetics. "The greater that my experience of lipstick becomes," he thundered, "the more distasteful I find it."

2

Little Billy saw the Indians in the movies painting their faces and he asked his mother why they did it. "Indians always paint their faces when they're going on the warpath to do their scalping and killing," explained mother. Next evening while sister's boy-friend waited in the parlor with the family, Billy came tearing down the stairs. "Let's get out of here quick, folks," he cried. "Sister's goin' on the warpath."

3

A woman was confiding in her minister who had called. "I'm afraid, Reverend," she confessed, "that I have sinned through vanity. I have been painting." "Painting?" queried the minister. "Painting what?" "My face," was the sheepish answer. "Come here to the window," requested the preacher. He took a good look and shook his head and said, "Don't worry, sister, it's no sin to paint such a face."

4

She had been caught in the rain without an umbrella and was quite wet when she encountered a friend who was about to pass her by without a word, when she cried out, "What's the idea, Hazel; are you trying to snub me?" The other woman peered, then raised her brows in amazement. "Why, is that you, Georgia?" she exclaimed. "I certainly didn't recognize you without your face on."

See also beauty[1].

COST

1

A long, sleek $10,000 limousine was gliding over a country road when it overtook a small car bouncing merrily along. The owner of the big car slowed up as he passed the other car and leaned out to mock its driver. "Goodness, friend," he cried, "what makes that terrible rattling noise in your car?" "Oh, that's just my $9,500 change jingling around in my pocket," was the calm reply.

2

A young man was considering marriage and was getting some information from an older, much-married friend. "And what will be the cost of the marriage license?" he queried. "It'll be just two dollars down," growled his friend sourly, "and your total income for the rest of your life."

COUGH

The minister met one of his congregation on the street and stopped to talk. "I felt so sorry for your wife in church last Sunday," he said sympathetically, "when she had that terrible spell of coughing and every one turned to look at her." "Don't concern yourself about that," replied the husband dryly. "She had on her new spring hat."

COUNTING

1

An actor, who had a high opinion of his abilities, was on tour when he received an offer by wire of a part in a new play. He immediately wired back imperiously: "Must have double what you offer, otherwise count me out." It was not many hours later when he received the following explicit telegram: "One, two, three, four, five, six, seven, eight, nine, ten, *out*."

2

The Senator had not come out well in the recent election. "To what do you attribute your defeat at the polls, Senator?" asked a reporter. "I was made a victim," complained the politician. "A victim?" exclaimed the amazed reporter. "A victim of what?" "A victim of accurate counting," was the glum reply.

3

"Mom, oh, mom, can I have another custard?" cried the little girl. "No, dear," replied mother, "you've had yours and there's only one for each of us—cook counted noses." "Oh, darn!" pouted the girl. "Why couldn't she have counted ears?"

See also caddy[1, 2], calm[3].

COUNTRY

1

The little city boy had been invited to spend a week in the country at uncle's farm, but he steadfastly refused and no amount of coaxing and promises could swerve him. "But why don't you want to go to the country?" his mother asked him at last. "You can't get me there," he retorted. "I hear they've got thrashin' machines out there, an' it's bad enough here where they do it by hand."

2

An old farmer had been visiting relatives in New York and when he returned his neighbors were very curious to hear about his experiences. "What's the main difference between life in New York and life back here anyhow?" queried one. "Wal, main thing I noticed," observed the farmer, "is that here in the country folks go to bed feelin' all in an' git up feelin' fine, an' in the city they go to bed feelin' fine and git up feelin' all in."

See also telephone[2].

COURAGE

1

The battle was not going well and the general leaned from behind his tree to cheer the men on. "Keep a-fightin', boys, and never say die," he cried. "Don't stop till your last shot's fired, and when it's fired, then run. Of course," he amended, "seein' as how I'm a little lame and got no more bullets, I'll just start runnin' now."

2

The town gossip was avidly detailing the recent wedding scandal over the back fence. "And just think," she gloated, "it was just as the bride was coming down the aisle and was half-way to the altar that the groom suddenly turned and ran from the church and skipped town." "Guess he lost his nerve," remarked the neighbor. "Gracious, no," corrected the gossip, "he found it."

3

The bootlegger was making a sale down a dark alley. "I need something to give me a boost," said the customer, sniffing the bottle suspiciously. "I want something that'd make a rabbit slap a bulldog in the face." "Is that all!" exclaimed the bootlegger pityingly. "Why, that stuff there'll make a tenant snap his fingers under the landlord's nose."

4

A cautious man was getting prices from the dentist beforehand. "Of course, to insure painless extraction you'll have to have gas," explained the dentist, "and that'll be 75 cents extra." "Aw, the gas won't be necessary, just forget it," said the man. "Very well. You're a brave man," said the dentist admiringly. "Oh, it ain't my tooth that's comin' out," replied the brave man; "it's the wife's."

See also fear[2].

COURT

1

The backwoods court was in session and it was a gala day with everyone in town meeting old friends. The buzz of conversation in the courtroom grew louder. "We must have less noise in the court," roared the judge, rapping sharply. "There's already been a half-dozen men convicted without the court's being able to hear a word of the testimony."

2

The witness was speaking aimlessly out toward the courtroom when the judge cautioned him, "Speak to the jury, sir, to those men sitting in the box behind you." The witness turned around surprised, smiled, nodded affably to the jury, and said, "Good morning, gentlemen."

3

A young lawyer was summing up his case to the jury and for almost six hours had subjected them to the uninterrupted flow of his flowery rhetoric. When at last he finished, the opposing lawyer, a seasoned old veteran of the bar, rose and smiled slyly at the judge and said, "Your Honor, I shall take example from my learned young colleague here and submit my case without argument."

4

A rather bewildered man of the people had just taken the stand in court. "Are you the defendant in this case?" asked the prosecuting attorney. "Who, me? No, sir," replied the puzzled man in the stand. "Well, who are you, then?" he was asked. "Oh, I'm just the guy what broke into the house," was the humble response.

5

The prisoner was worried about the way his case was going and was fearful that prejudice was being exercised against him. "Justice!" he shouted. "I want justice! I demand justice!" "Silence!" thundered the judge, frowning down on him. "The defendant will please remember that he is in a courtroom."

See also company[4], contempt[1, 3], doubt, evidence[1], jury[1], lawsuit[1], lawyer[4], oath[2], preference, witness[1].

COURTESY

See chivalry, manners, polite.

COURTSHIP

1

It was a dark evening and the hired man was getting a lantern ready to go down the road to call on his girl. "Humph! Wastin' oil," growled the miserly farmer. "When I was a-courtin' I didn't take no lantern; I went in the dark." "I know," replied the hired man wryly, "and just look at what you got."

2

"How are you coming with your courting of the boss's daughter?" a young man asked his ambitious friend. "Oh, just fine now," beamed the other. "I was getting discouraged, but she gave me some encouragement last night." "Yeah? Let you kiss her or something?" queried the friend. "No, not that," replied the suitor, "but she told me she had said 'No!' for the last time."

3

The young suitor was asking the girl's father for her hand in marriage. "Humph!" grunted the old man. "Do you think you're financially able to take care of her?"

"Listen, pal," said the boy wearily, "after a guy's bought flowers and candy for a girl for two years, taken her to dinner twice a week and the theater once a week, and remembered her and her mother's birthdays and Christmases, marriage is a cinch."

NOTE: This subject has not been cross referenced because of its frequent occurrence throughout this dictionary.

COW

1

A farmer had just added a small dairy department to his farm and he wrote to the Questions and Answers column of a rural paper: "Can you tell me how long cows should be milked?" The next issue carried the answer: "They should be milked the same as short cows, of course."

2

A city boy was on his first visit to a farm and he stood at the pasture fence watching a cow chew her cud when the farmer happened by and noticed his interest. "Pretty nice cow, don't you think?" he asked. "Swell," agreed the boy. "But it sure must cost a lot to keep her in chewing gum."

3

A city girl stood watching a six-weeks-old calf nibbling the grass in a farmer's yard. "Tell me," she called to the farmer's wife sitting on the porch, "does it really pay to keep so small a cow as that?"

4

A small city boy was visiting his country cousin on his farm and the talk fell to the relative knowledge of city and country boys. "Aw," derided the rural lad, "see that cow down there in the pasture? Betcha can't even tell me if it's a Jersey cow or not." "Well, I can't tell from here," objected the city boy, "because I can't see its license plate."

5

The sweet young girl from the city was just too thrilled by everything on the farm. "Why doesn't that cow over there have any horns?" she demanded. "Wal, miss," drawled the farmer, "could be lots o' reasons. Some cows is born without horns, some loses 'em, some we cut off, an' some breeds ain't supposed to have any. But the reason that there cow ain't got horns is because she ain't a cow—she's a horse."

6

It was the city boy's first morning of his vacation on grandpa's farm, and he was up early romping about everywhere excitedly. Under a tree by the roadside where some tourists had stopped, he found several empty milk bottles in the grass. Back to the house he rushed, shouting loudly, "Hey, grandma, come quick! I've just found a cow's nest!"

See also affectionate[1], bicycle, masquerade[2].

COWARD

1

A lion-tamer was somewhat henpecked and, happening one night to stay out late, was fearful of facing the wifely wrath. So he went to the zoo, entered the cage of the most ferocious lion there, ordered the

snarling beast to lie down, and went comfortably to sleep with his head on the lion's shoulder. Next morning the wife came to the zoo looking for him, saw him in the cage, and hissed contemptuously, "You coward!"

2

"What happened at the picnic, Algy, that the girls are all sneering at you?" asked a friend. "Oh, they wanted me to climb a tree and get them a hornets' nest," said Algy, "and they called me a coward when I wouldn't." "I see," chortled the friend, "and now you're unhonored and unsung?" "That may be," conceded Algy, "but also I'm unstung."

CRAFTSMANSHIP

1

The janitor of a large bank was boasting of his professional abilities. "You should have seen that floor when I came there," he said in disgust. "No more polish to it than a sidewalk. But since I've been taking care of that floor," he continued, swelling with pride, "I've had one broken hip, one broken leg, three broken arms, a dislocated back, and any number of bruises among the customers."

2

A man wishing an especially fine pair of trousers went to a tailor recommended for his careful work. The man was duly measured, but it was six months before he was notified the trousers were ready. "It seems odd," he said coldly when he called for the garment, "that God could make the world in six days, but it takes you six months to make a pair of pants." The tailor shrugged. "All right," he said calmly, "just look at the world—then look at these pants!"

3

The American traveler was seeing the sights in Italy. "Now, this is the Leaning Tower of Pisa," recited the guide. "What was that name?" asked the traveler. "The Leaning Tower of Pisa," repeated the guide. The American shook his head. "I still can't recall the name," he said, "but it certainly looks like the work of the contractor who built my house."

4

A doctor hired a laborer to weed and trim his gravel driveway and clean up the lawn. Later when the workman came to be paid the doctor went to inspect the job and found that quite a mess had been left. He shook his head and said, "I think it's a bad job, Mike, because you left this whole walk covered with gravel and dirt." "And you should talk," exclaimed Mike, "who's had many a bad job covered with gravel and dirt."

5

Two street cleaners sat on the curb eating their lunch and discussing a fellow-worker who had died the previous day. "Well, at least you must admit that old Sam was a good street sweeper," declared one. "Um—yes," agreed the other a little reluctantly. "But just between you and me, don't you think he was a little weak around lampposts?"

6

The young lady was watching the artist at work. "You seem to take endless pains with your painting, Mr. Blotch," she observed. "Yes, I do," replied the artist proudly. "But then, you know, I enjoy the pains." "Oh, I see," quipped the girl, with a malicious smile, "you follow art for art's ache, so to speak."

CRAZY

1

The psychiatrist peered intently at the robber who was holding him up. "Don't you remember me?" he cried, as he recognized him. "I'm your benefactor. I once saved you from life imprisonment by proving you crazy." "Sure, I remember youse now," replied the thug, as he continued to go through the man's pockets. "An' kin youse t'ink o' anyt'ing crazier than stickin' up yer benefactor?"

2

A man walked into a bar, ordered a dry Martini, drank it, ate the olive, then proceeded to chew up and swallow the bowl portion of the glass until he reached the stem, which he tossed over his shoulder, and ordered another. He was on his seventh Martini when he noticed the bartender watching him intently. "'Smatter?" he demanded. "Guess you think I'm crazy, huh?" "You sure are," said the bartender, "them stems is the best part."

3

The lawyer was having trouble saving his client from the extreme penalty, so he enlisted the services of a noted psychiatrist. "Then you feel sure that you can prove my client is crazy?" he asked as they concluded their conference. "Positively," replied the psychiatrist emphatically, "and what's more, if you ever get in trouble and need my services, I'll do the same for you."

See also catch[1], deduction, farming[1], insects[1], proof[2], telephone[4].

CREDIT

1

"Gosh! You're not looking well, Bill," said Jim as they met on the street. "Is something wrong?" "There certainly is," replied Bill. "I've had to give up drinking, smoking, and playing the horses." "Gee, it *must* be serious," exclaimed Jim. "But at least it's all to your credit." "Humph! That's just where you're wrong," snapped Bill. "It's all due to my lack of credit."

2

A man had barely paid off his house when he put another mortgage against it in order to buy a car. Having the car, he went to a loan broker to try to get a mortgage on the car in order to build a garage. "But if I make you the loan," asked the broker, "how will you buy gas for the car?" "It seems to me," replied the man with dignity, "that if I own a house, car, and garage, I should be able to get credit for gas."

3

The country storekeeper had carried the sharecropper through the growing season for his groceries, but as soon as the harvest was in and the man had a little money he saw him going into his competitor's store down the street. "How come, Sam," he asked, "that after all the credit I gave you, you take your cash to the other store?" "Jeepers!"

cried the man in astonishment. "Do you sell fer cash, too?"

See also beggar[5], generous[2].

CREDITOR

1

The old man was dying and he called his family about him and through labored breaths he gave them the names of fifteen or more of his debtors and the amounts they owed him. When this was all carefully written down, a son leaned over and asked, "Now, father, who are the people to whom *you* owe money." But the old man closed his eyes and muttered, "Let them die and tell you."

2

A lawyer who was drawing up a man's will paused and asked the client, "How does it come that you've named six of your biggest creditors as pallbearers? Wouldn't it be more seemly to have some closer friends for this service?" "No, just leave it that way," instructed the client. "Those guys have carried me this far and they might as well do it the rest of the way."

3

The doctor finished his examination of the man and shook his head regretfully. "I'm sorry, but I'm afraid you have a bad case of small-pox," he announced. The patient turned weakly on his pillow and said to his wife. "If any of my creditors come pestering around now, Mary, you can tell them that I am finally in a position to give them something."

See also contribution[2], thankful[3].

CREMATION

1

At last the good man died and his hard-working wife decided to have him cremated instead of buried. The attendant at the crematory tried to show her some little decorative urns for the ashes, but she waved them aside. "Not on your life," she declared. "That bum never did a day's work in his life, so I'm puttin' his ashes in an hour glass on the mantel and from now on he'll be doin' somethin' all day long."

2

Two old maids were spending a quiet evening together, and one looked up from her newspaper to announce, "There's an item here about a woman out West who has just cremated her fifth husband." "Well, how do you like that!" cried the other. "Here you and I can't even get us one husband between us, and other women have husbands to burn."

3

The lawyer slowly shook his head. "I'm sorry, madam," he said, "but I can't see that you have any claim against the insurance company for your husband's death. He had no policy on his life, but carried insurance only against fire." "I know," cried the widow. "That's exactly why I had him cremated."

CRIME

The town loafer had been caught in some petty thievery and was appearing before the judge. "And you want to remember, my man," said the judge as he sentenced him, "that crime doesn't pay." "That may be," conceded the prisoner with a yawn, "but the hours are optional."

See also burglar, robbery, thief.

CRITIC

1

A noted critic came to the opening of a play during the second act and was stopped by the producer who said in aggrieved tones: "It's hardly fair that you with your influence should get here in the middle of the show. You won't know if the play's good or not." "Don't worry," the critic assured him, "you'll get a good review. I'm in a poker game at the club and I'm $20 ahead. I just dropped by for a program."

2

A critic had been asked his opinion of a new four-act play that was a distinct flop. "Well, when I was sent to review the show," he said, "the audience sat silent after the first act and I applauded. After the second act, the audience hissed and I sat silent. But after the third act, I went out to the box office, bought my own ticket, and came back and joined in the hissing."

3

A dramatic critic, who was noted for the vitriolic phrasing in his reviews, was approached by an admiring young reporter who asked, "How in the world do you think of all the nasty, sarcastic things you say about the shows you review?" "There's nothing to it," replied the critic. "I just sit quietly and jot down the things being said by the people who are seeing the show on passes."

See also play[1, 2], precocious[2].

CRITICISM

1

A music critic had been sent to review an amateur musicale by some of the local social élite. He suffered doubly, both from listening and not being permitted to express himself freely, but he did manage to slip into his notice the item: "One of the features of the evening was a string quartet playing Brahms. Brahms lost."

2

The critic was at a loss for words to describe the show he had just seen, but his frown changed to a smile when, in passing through the lobby, he overheard an elderly gentleman growl to his wife, "Well, you *would* come!"

3

"Daddy," asked the little boy, looking up from his books, "what do they mean by 'constructive criticism'?" "Well, son," replied father, who was a seasoned citizen, "it usually takes the form of a fancy set of resolutions drawn up with enthusiasm, adopted unanimously, heralded as the salvation of mankind, and completely forgotten by the next day."

See also belching[1], home[1].

CROPS

1

A couple of Western farmers were discussing the effect of the drought on the crops. "Well, I did manage to harvest a little wheat this year," said one, "but the dry spell sure did make it short." "Short?" cried the other. "Say, I had to lather mine to mow it!"

2

"How'd your peach crop do this year?" asked one farmer of another. "Had bad luck," replied the other. "Just when it was about ripe, comes a windstorm and blows down half the crop, and we barely get that picked up when another wind comes and knocks down the other half." "Too bad," said the first. "Manage to do anything with them?" "Oh, sure," was the reply, "my wife ate one an' I ate t'other."

3

"Crops is purty bad this year, Jed," observed Si to his neighbor. "Yep, but I seen wuss," replied Jed. "I rec'llect back in '87 that the corn crop was so durned pore that when we cooked some fer dinner one day, paw eat sixteen acres of it at one settin'!"

See also complaint[5], family tree[3], garden[1], heat[2], triplets[4].

CROSS-EYED

A cross-eyed man approached a lady seated on the sidelines at a dance and, with a gallant bow, asked, "May I have the honor of this dance with you?" But the lady gave no response or any sign, while the women seated on each side of her both said as with one voice, "It will be a pleasure."

CROWD

1

The bus was very crowded and the fat lady was trying furiously to get under her tightly-buttoned jacket to get at her fare. After a while, a man beside her said, "Will you allow me to pay your fare, madam?" "Fresh!" she snapped. "I'd slap your face if I could get my hand up." "I only made the offer, madam," the man explained wearily, "because you've already unbuttoned my suspenders three times trying to reach your own pocket."

2

Two elderly ladies stood on the church steps after services talking things over. "My, such crowding and pushing as when the people left today," complained one, "I was very nearly trampled." "And there's no need for it," said the other primly. "If every one would wait quietly in his seat until every one else is gone out, there would be none of that crowding at the doors."

See also police[7], sandwich[2].

CRUELTY

1

"Hello?" cried a shrill female voice over the phone. "Is this the Humane Society?" "Yes, madam, what can we do for you?" was the reply. "I want you to send an officer right over to 120 Main Street," demanded the voice. "Why, what's the trouble?" was asked. "There's a nasty peddler sitting in a tree out in front teasing my poor bulldog," was the reply.

2

A spy had been caught with the goods, given a quick trial, and was being led out to be shot. "You people are barbarous brutes," he snarled, "to walk me through this terrible sleet and slush." "You should com-

plain," grunted the soldier escorting him. "What about me? I've got to come back through it."

See also lonely.

CURE

"I went to the doctor to see what could be done about curing my husband of drinking," said a woman to her neighbor, "and he gave me a powder to put in my husband's coffee." "Well, did it cure him?" asked the neighbor. "Yes," responded the wife grimly, "of drinking coffee."

See also deaf[2].

CURFEW

"I thought you folks had a curfew in this village," remarked a traveling salesman to the store-keeper. "We did have, but we had to give it up," answered the other. "What was the trouble?" queried the salesman. "Well, they never rang that durned bell until 9 o'clock," explained the storekeeper, "and everybody got to complainin' because it was always a-wakin' 'em up."

CURIOUS

The girl was very interested in automobiles. "Is this the choke?" she asked, pulling it out as they sped along. "Yes, dear," replied the boy patiently, pushing the choke back. "And is this the light switch?" she continued, snapping it. "Yes, dear," he answered, swerving desperately to avoid a truck that had just pulled out. "But what on earth can this be?" she queried, pushing the accelerator with her foot. "This is heaven, dear," he replied, flitting away with his harp.

See also hereafter[7], lost[1], surgery[2].

CUSTOMARY

1

The stage director was peeved with the English actor. "Can't you drop your aitches?" he demanded. "But my part is that of an English nobleman," objected the actor. "Sure," agreed the director, "but don't all the English drop their aitches?" "My word, no!" cried the actor. The director thought it over for a moment, then said, "Well, you better go ahead and drop 'em anyway. Folks over here expect it."

2

A keeper had been on the job constantly for 35 years at a lighthouse where, in addition to the light, a warning gun was fired automatically every five minutes night and day. The keeper paid no attention to this booming, but late one night when he was sleeping soundly the gun missed fire for the first time. The old man woke up with a start and cried out in terror, "What was that?"

3

The suitor had just popped the question, but the fair lady was undecided. "If I should refuse you," she queried anxiously, "would you commit suicide?" "That," he announced magnificently, "has been my customary procedure."

CUSTOMER

1

A rather bashful man walked into a restaurant and sat down at a table, but nothing happened. Four waiters playing cards at a table in the rear looked up at him curiously, then went back to their game. A while later the boss walked in and took in the situation at a glance. "Four waiters I've got," he shouted, grabbing his hair, "and they can't even wait on one lousy customer!"

2

A salesman in a department store was fired because he had been rude to a customer. Some weeks later the store manager noticed him on the street in a police uniform. "Well, Brown, how do you like this job?" he asked him. "Like it?" was the answer. "This job is the answer to a salesman's prayers. It's the only job I know of where the customer is always wrong."

DACHSHUND

1

A prize dachshund of considerable value was run over and killed near the station house. The sergeant detailed a policeman to break the bad news to the owner. "But be sure to break the news to her gently," he instructed, "as she thinks the world of that dog." The policeman pondered this, and when the woman answered his knock, he said, "Sorry, ma'am, but part of your dog has been run over."

2

Mother was telling the family a story about a dachshund, but this word had slipped her mind. "Oh, bother!" she exclaimed in vexation, "what *do* you call those long German dogs?" Her small son looked up brightly and volunteered, "Frankfurters?"

See also dog.

DAMAGE

See breakage.

DANCING

1

Grandpa and his granddaughter were watching the modern dancers. "Pretty swell, eh, Gramps?" cried the girl, swaying with the music. "Bet you never saw dancing like this when you were a young fellow." "Yes, I did, once," replied the old man grimly, "just before the place was raided."

2

The man did not like the way his wife was dancing nor the attention she and her partner were attracting. "Hazel," he whispered as she passed near, "everybody's staring. You'd better tell your partner not to dance so close to you." "Tell him yourself, dear," she replied blithely, "I don't even know the guy."

3

A member of the polo team had cut in on the beautiful young lady's dancing partner, but soon found that his dancing was worse than he'd thought. "My dancing isn't very good this evening," he apologized. "To tell the truth, I'm a little stiff from polo." The girl maintained her air of frigid disdain and replied, "I'm not at all interested in where you come from."

4

The minister was dining with a family and was proclaiming loudly against the modern dance. "Now tell me honestly, Miss Smith," he asked the daughter of the house, "do you really think the girls who indulge in these dances are right?" "Well, they must be," reasoned the girl, "because the ones that don't are always left."

See also honor, importance[5].

DANGER

1

The girl was going down for the third time when the brave young man sprang into the water and rescued her. The girl's father was extremely grateful. "How can I ever thank you, young man?" he cried, wringing the boy's hand. "And how brave you were to face such danger to save my daughter." "Why, there was no danger, sir," replied the rescuer modestly. "You see, I'm already married."

2

The storm was growing worse and the ship was being tossed about like a chip. "Oh, Captain," cried a nervous woman passenger, "are we in much danger?" "We are in the hands of God, madam," the captain answered gravely. "Heavens!" exclaimed the woman paling, "is it as bad as that?"

3

The young reporter was interviewing inmates of the jail to get some sidelights on life. He stopped at the cell of a well-known burglar and asked, "What is the greatest danger you face in your profession?" "Having the woman mistake me for her husband when I break into a house," was the terse response.

DARK

See courtship¹, light, tunnel.

DATING

1

He was saying good-by to the young lady on her doorstep. "Then you'll call next Sunday to take me driving?" she asked. "I shall," he replied, then asked, "but suppose it rains?" "Well, if that happens," decided the girl, "we'd better make it on Saturday."

2

Grandma was tearing the younger generation apart again. "Going to the movies with a young man, are you?" she snorted to her granddaughter. "In my day no young lady would have thought of going to a show with a man unless he was her fiance." "Oh, don't let that worry you, Grandma," comforted the girl, "he's one of my fiances."

See also good⁶.

DAUGHTER

1

A bachelor struck up a conversation with the worn-looking man in the smoker on the train. "Yes, indeed," related the latter, "I have quite a family. I'm the father of seven daughters." "Well, well," observed the bachelor naively, "so you have seven mouths to feed." "Huh! That's what you think," grunted the other sourly. "I've got fourteen mouths to feed—they're all married."

2

The one and only daughter was going to be married and her father was curious as to what the wedding was going to cost him. He approached a friend who had already had this experience, and asked, "Say, Bill, you had a daughter married about four years ago, didn't you? How much did the wedding cost you?" The friend grimaced. "On an average, about five thousand dollars a year," he replied.

See also acquaintance¹, grammar⁵.

DAY

A preacher was trying to bring religion to the working classes. One day, while passing among some laborers during the lunch hour, he put his hand on the shoulder of one and asked, "Do you hear that relentless ticking of the clock? Are you aware of what day it is inevitably bringing you closer and closer to?" "Sure," replied the workman, taking half a sandwich at a bite, "payday."

DEAD

1

A man had fallen into a coma and had been taken for dead, but recovered suddenly just as they were about to bury him. "What did it feel like to be dead?" asked a friend later. "Heck!" he snorted, "I wasn't dead and I knew it, because I was hungry and my feet were cold." "But what would that prove?" he was asked. "Well," he replied, "I knew that if I were in heaven I wouldn't be hungry, and if I were in the other place my feet wouldn't be cold."

2

Two hoboes were taking a short cut through a cemetery. One was reading the inscriptions on the tombstones and came across one that said: "Not dead, but sleeping." The bum shook his head sadly and sighed, "Now look at that! That guy sure ain't foolin' nobody but himself."

See also burial[1, 2], condition[1], death, imagination, quarrel[2].

DEAF

1

The waiter who served the lady her drink was a little hard-of-hearing. "I'd like a straw with my lemonade, please," she requested. "Hey?" queried the waiter, cupping a hand to his ear. "No. I said a straw," repeated the lady, firmly.

2

An elderly man had just taken the last of a series of treatments for his hearing. "Well, how much do I owe you, doctor?" he asked the specialist as he pulled out his checkbook. "Fifteen dollars," replied the specialist rather shyly. "Fifty dollars, did you say?" inquired the man calmly. "No, no; sixty dollars," was the response, in a much louder tone.

3

Three deaf men were walking down the avenue on a blustery day. "Windy, isn't it?" observed one. "No, yesterday was Wednesday," replied a second. "It's Thursday today." "Yes, I've been thirsty all day, too," agreed the third. "Let's go somewhere and get a drink."

4

The old gentleman was getting quite deaf. One day while driving his car he crossed a bridge over a railroad track. A huge locomotive sped beneath and let out a shrill whistle. "Hm!" muttered the old man happily, "first robin I've heard this spring."

See also boarding house[4], chewing.

DEATH

1

A talkative visitor had been idling at the village store for some time and pestering the storekeeper with questions. After queries about the climate, altitude, and distances to here and there, he asked, "And what is your death rate around here?" The storekeeper, impatient, snapped, "About one per person," and moved away.

2

The young man and his sweetheart, out walking, had cut across a field when a large, vicious-looking dog suddenly ran out barking at them. They both fled, but the young man soon outdistanced the girl. "But, Bill," she protested pantingly, "I thought you said you'd face death for me?" "I would, sweet," he called back, picking up more speed, "but that dog ain't anything like dead."

See also absent-minded[2], hell[2], hereafter, moron[4], peace, reincarnation, salary[5].

DEBT

1

The chronic debtor grinned impudently at the collector. "If I don't have any money, you sure can't get any," he announced triumphantly. "You can't get blood out of a turnip, you know." "That may be true," grunted the collector sourly, "but you're not a turnip—you're a *beat*."

2

"Here's a letter from Dunn & Co. asking that we remit something on what's due," said one partner of an almost bankrupt business to another. "They enclose a stamp for a reply. What'll we do?" "Just send them back the stamp on account," answered the other.

See also owe[1], payment[7], religion[5].

DECEIVE

1

Little Helen was praying, and at the end of her routine prayer added the little amendment: "And please, dear God, send a beautiful thick, soft snow that'll last all winter, to keep the poor little flowers warm." "That was a sweet thought, Helen," said mother proudly. "Oh, I was just foolin' God," whispered Helen confidentially. "I really want the snow for my new sled."

2

The old gentleman stood puzzled watching the small boy sitting at the foot of the telegraph pole picking caterpillars from a can and placing them on the pole. "What *are* you doing?" he finally inquired. "Caterpillars climb trees to eat the leaves, don't they?" asked the boy. "Certainly," agreed the man. "Well, I'm just foolin' this bunch by lettin' 'em climb up this bare pole," was the gleeful answer.

3

Two little girls wanted to take a short cut through the pasture, but were afraid of the cow there. "Let's just walk on through as if we're not the least bit scared," suggested one. The other girl shook her head doubtfully. "But wouldn't that be deceiving the cow?" she said seriously.

See also gold digger[2].

DECISION

1

In a certain town, the quality of milk had not been of the best and a committee had been appointed to investigate the situation. After considerable but fruitless debate, the chairman arose ponderously and declared, "Gentlemen, it's very clear that what this town needs is a supply of fresh, wholesome milk, and I think it's up to the committee to take the bull by the horns and demand it."

2

Two married men were discussing who should be the head of a household. "I think the man should be," declared one. "After all, he's the breadwinner." "I think it's better settled by compromise," maintained the other. "My wife and I have agreed that I should decide on all major matters, and she on all minor ones." "And how has it worked out?" asked the first. The second smiled grimly and said, "So far, no major matters have come up."

See also practical[1].

DEDUCTION

"I shall now test your powers of deduction," said the Professor of Logic to his class. "If beans are 20¢ a pound, butter goes up a dime, 4% of next month's beer is flat, and my dog runs away, how old am I?" "You're just forty-eight, sir," promptly replied a beetle-browed youth in back. "Excellent!" cried the Professor. "Now tell us how you deduced the correct answer." "Simple," was the reply. "I've got a brother who's twenty-four and he's only half nuts."

See also logic.

DEFECT

1

They were back from the honeymoon. "Now that we're married and settled, dear," he observed, "it might be helpful if I pointed out a few of your little defects." "Don't bother, darling," replied the bride sweetly. "I know them all. They're what kept me from getting a better man."

2

A man bought a horse from another man. A few days later, angry, he brought the horse back. "You told me that horse had no faults," he cried. "That's right; and he hasn't," insisted the seller. "But that horse is nearly blind!" complained the other. "Come, now, man," said the seller in a reasoning tone, "surely you'd call that no fault of the horse —it's the poor beast's misfortune."

See also conceit[2], mother[1].

DEFINITION

1

Teacher had been giving the pupils a lesson in the classification of foods, nutrition, etc. "Now, Willie," she questioned, "tell me what sugar is." Willie pondered a moment, then announced brightly, "Sugar's that white stuff that makes oatmeal taste so bad when you don't put some on it."

2

Teacher was examining the students in elementary anatomy. "Can you tell me what the spine is, Johnny?" she queried. Johnny thought a moment, then gravely reported, "The spine is a long, limber bone that has your head settin' on one end and you settin' on the other."

3

The little girl had been pestering her mother with questions. "What's 'transcontinental' mean, mom?" she asked. "It means across the continent," replied the vexed mother. "Does 'trans-' always mean 'cross,' mom?" persisted the girl. "Yes, yes!" cried mother. "Now if you ask me anything else I'll send you to bed." The child subsided for a moment, but after a while ventured, "Then, I guess 'transparent' means a cross parent."

See also conscience[6], ethics[1], marriage[3, 7], mining[1], oyster[5], politics[11], psychology, scandal, synonym, wife[7], woman[1].

DELAY

1

The customer had been sitting patiently in the restaurant. At last he called the waiter over and asked for pen, ink, and paper. "Do you want to write a letter?" queried the waiter. "No, nothing like that," replied the customer. "It's just that I've given up all hope of seeing that dinner I ordered, so I want to draw up a will leaving it to my heirs."

2

A merchant, noted for his sharpness in money matters, took out fire insurance on his store. On the very same day the store burned to the ground. The insurance company suspected crooked work, but was unable to prove anything. However, it did write the merchant the following letter: "Dear Sir: Your policy was issued at 11:30 a.m. Your fire did not occur until 2:20 p.m. Will you kindly explain the delay?"

3

The train had been stopping frequently, but this time it seemed to have taken root at the spot. At last, when the conductor wandered idly through the car, a passenger asked, "Say, Conductor, what's wrong with the train?" "Nothing's wrong," was the reply. "We're just taking on water." "Humph!" grunted the passenger sarcastically, "don't you think they might use another teaspoon?"

See also waiting[1].

DELUSION

1

Two men sat in hazy rapture in an opium-den. "Yes, indeed," remarked one grandly in an offhand manner, "I've about decided to buy up all the gold, diamond, and ruby mines in the world." The other

puffed dreamily at his pipe for a few moments. "It would be a good deal," he conceded reflectively, "but I don't know that I care to sell."

2

A couple of marijuana smokers sat among the rubbish in a back lot puffing away at the weed. "Say, pal," asked one, "do you happen to have twelve million dollars?" The other shook his head regretfully and replied, "Yes, but not on me."

3

Two young fellows were discussing each other's girlfriend. "I certainly hope that you're not suffering from any hallucination that your girl is any great beauty," sneered one. "I certainly am," replied the other complacently, "and I'm going to keep right on hugging that illusion."

4

A man helped a friend get to his hotel room, then asked the clerk to call for a doctor. The doctor asked, "Do you see any pink elephants or green tigers?" "Nope," mumbled the patient. "No snakes or dragons?" the doctor continued. "Nope," was the answer again. "Then just sleep it off and you'll be all right," pronounced the doctor. But the helpful friend was worried. "My pal's in bad shape," he confided to the clerk. "Didja hear 'im say he couldn't see any o' them animals, when the room was full of 'em!'

See also lunatic[5], real.

DEMOCRATS

1

The politician was campaigning through the South and stopped at one cabin. "My, my, you have a fine family—eighteen boys!" he complimented the man. "All good Democrats, I suppose?" "Waal," replied the man, shaking his head sadly, "I tried to bring 'em up right, and they're all good Christians, and all but Sam, there, is Democrats—thet ornery cuss, he got to readin'."

2

The political speaker had had little success in organizing a meeting in a Southern town. "What's the matter?" he demanded in exasperation. "Can't the Democrats around here get together?" "Get together!" snorted a fellow with a black eye and swollen ear. "Why just last week it took fourteen deputies to keep them apart!"

DEMONSTRATION

A workman was put to work operating a buzz-saw for the first time. The foreman gave him lengthy instructions on how to protect himself from injury. But barely had he left, when he heard a howl. Rushing back he saw that the man had already lost a finger. "Now, how did you do that?" the foreman demanded. "Well, I was just goin' like this," illustrated the workman, "when—whoops, there goes another one!"

DENTIST

1

A dentist had gone out to collect a bill and returned home in anger. "What's the matter, didn't you get your money?" asked his wife. "No, I didn't," fumed the dentist. "And on top of that, he had the nerve to gnash my own teeth at me!"

2

The dentist was about to leave his office with his golf bag on his shoulder, when the phone rang. "Oh, doctor, I'm in great pain," whined a voice, "and I must see you at once." "Sorry," replied the dentist firmly, "but I already have an appointment to fill eighteen cavities this afternoon."

3

"How much do you charge for pulling a tooth?" inquired a prospective patient cautiously. "Five dollars," answered the dentist. "What! Five dollars for less than a minute's work?" objected the patient. "Well, I can pull it out very slowly, if you prefer," offered the dentist.

4

Despite the boy's lusty protests, the perspiring dentist finally managed to pull the boy's tooth. "That will be five dollars," he informed the mother, as he wiped his brow. "Five dollars!" she cried. "Why, I thought that you charged just a dollar for an extraction." "I do ordinarily," explained the dentist, "but this kid yelled so loudly that he frightened four other patients out of the waiting room."

5

"Did you get your tooth pulled all right?" asked mother of the boy when he returned from the dentist's. "Yep," replied the boy, "an' the doc told me when he started that if I yelled it would cost a dollar, but if I was a good boy and kept quiet it would be only a half-dollar." "Well, did you yell?" queried mother. "How could I?" reasoned the boy patiently. "You only gave me fifty cents."

See also courage[4], gangster, pain[2], threat.

DEPARTURE

1

Mother-in-law had been with daughter for a long, long visit, but now she was going home. "Do you remember when my train leaves tomorrow morning?" she asked her son-in-law. "It leaves in seventeen hours, twenty-one minutes, and thirteen seconds from now, mother, dear," was the quick response.

2

The suitor was gallant and romantic, but it was very late. "Ah, my love," he sighed, "tell me, how *can* I leave you?" "By train, plane, bus, taxi, or on foot," she yawned.

See also good[5].

DEPENDENT

A rookie from away back in the hills had inquired about dependents' allotments and was given an application blank to fill out. But when he returned the blank to the officer, the line after "Have you any dependents?" was filled in with "No." "But you're married, aren't you?" questioned the officer. "Sure am, sir," the soldier replied, "but that woman ain't a bit dependable."

See also mistake[2].

DEPTH

1

The sailor was casting the sounding lead when the captain came by.

"How deep is she here?" he asked. "Don't know, sir, can't touch bottom," replied the sailor. "Jumpin' seahorses, man!" cried the captain in exasperation, "then how close do you come to it?"

2

A stranger on horseback came to a stream which he had to cross, but there was no bridge in sight. "Is it very deep here, sonny?" he asked a boy who was fishing nearby. "Nope," was the answer. So the man rode into the water, but soon he and his horse were swimming for their lives. "Thought you said it wasn't deep," he cried to the boy. "Aw, it ain't," the boy insisted. "Grampa's ducks only go in up to their middle."

DESCRIPTION

The bank president had called in a detective. "We find that our cashier who left us suddenly was an embezzler. We need your help to find him." "Can you give me a good description of him?" asked the detective. "Well," said the president thoughtfully, "he was about five feet seven inches tall, and about eight thousand five hundred dollars short."

DESERTION

1

A neighbor tried to comfort the deserted husband. "It was a terrific shock to hear that Smithers ran away with your wife. I'd always thought he was your best friend." "He is," replied the husband with a happy smile, "only he doesn't know it yet."

2

Two women were discussing the

case of a woman down the street whose husband had abandoned her. "It must be a terrible thing," observed one. "Don't you think it would just kill you if your husband should run away with another woman?" "It might," conceded the other cynically. "Great joy is said to kill sometimes."

3

Two men were having drinks on the sidewalk terrace of a bar and one of them was acting very strangely. "Why is it that you cringe so every time you hear an auto horn?" queried the other. "Have you been run down lately, or something?" "Nothing like that," replied his companion. "It's just that a fellow ran off with my wife in a car last week, and every time I hear a horn I'm afraid he's bringing her back."

4

The lawyer was putting up a vigorous defense for his bandage-swathed client who was charged by his wife with desertion. But the case seemed to be going against him. Finally, he ordered his client to remove his bandages, thus exposing a black eye and numerous bruises. "I submit, Your Honor," said the lawyer, "that one look at this man will convince you he is not a deserter, but a refugee."

See also grief[3].

DESIRE

Two hillbillies met at the village store and got to talking. "Yore wife's a-holdin' her haid mighty high these days," observed one, "what with thet new second-hand

dress and fancy third-hand hat she's bin a-wearin'." "An' thet's the truth," agreed the other, shaking his head. "Dun't know what I'm gonna do with thet woman—next thing I know she'll be a-wantin' shoes."

See also Christmas[2].

DESTINATION

1

There was a long line before the railroad ticket window, but the man brusquely shouldered his way in at the head of it. "Gimme a ticket to Sandusky," he demanded, slapping down a half-dollar on the counter. "But you can't get to Sandusky for 50 cents," objected the ticket agent. "Well, then," asked the man, "where can I go for 50 cents?" And in no uncertain terms the whole waiting line told him where he could go.

2

A small boy was going along a road tugging manfully on the leash of a huge Great Dane. "Where are you going with that dog, sonny?" a passing man asked curiously. "W-well," came the panting response, "I-I can't t-tell until I s-see first where he wants to go."

See also wicked[1].

DESTRUCTION

See breakage.

DETAIL

The porter rushed excitedly into the manager's office. "Dere's a telegram outside from de boss in Africa what says he sendin' us some lions' tails," he announced. "Lions' tails? You're crazy, Sam," observed the manager incredulously. "Well, go read it yourself," insisted the porter. "It says plain as can be: 'Just shot three lions. Will send details by mail.'"

See also location[2].

DETERMINATION

Two old hoboes were talking things over by their campfire. "Yes, sir," announced one proudly, "when I was just a young feller of nineteen I made up my mind that nuthin' wuz gonna stop me from gettin' rich." "Yeah? But then how come yuh never got rich?" queried the other. "Oh, it was just that by the time I was almost twenty I figgered out that it wuz lots easier to change my mind."

See also energetic[3], will power[3].

DEVIL

1

The little girl had had a quarrel with her friend which had ended up in a rough fight. "Shame!" scolded her mother. "It was the Devil who put you up to pulling Mary's hair." "That could be," conceded the girl thoughtfully, then added proudly, "but kicking her in the shins was my own idea."

2

The minister sensed that the meeting was not exactly in harmony with him. "I've a feeling that Satan is present at this meeting today," he declared gravely. "Hurray!" cried a voice from the rear. "Now that you've got him cornered, lock all

the doors and windows and give him where he comes from!"

3

Two small girls were walking home from Sunday school and talking over what they had been told that day. "Do you *really* believe that there's a mean old Devil?" questioned one seriously. "Heck, no!" replied the other scornfully. "It's just like Santa Claus—it's only your father dressed up."

4

The little girl had been saying, "What the devil" quite frequently, so her mother cautioned her, "That's a word that nice people do not use, dear, and I never want to hear you say it again." Several weeks passed and the girl had obediently refrained from the word. Then, one Sunday evening the mother asked her what the Sunday school lesson had been about. "Well, it was about when—ah—," was the stammering response, "our Lord was tempted by the—ah—by the *gentleman who keeps hell!*"

See also caution[3], lawyer[5].

DEVOTION

1

"Say, I was in your home town last week," he remarked to the girl-friend. "You were? And did you think of me, Joe?" she cooed coyly. "I most certainly did," replied Joe gallantly. "I was hardly there when I said to myself, 'Why, I believe that this is the town where what's-her-name used to live.'"

2

She had just accepted his proposal and he had been kissing her rapturously for a full fifteen minutes without pause. At last he stopped, and she burst into tears. "Oh, darling, you have stopped loving me," she sobbed. "No, I haven't," he protested pantingly, "but I must breathe."

3

The wife had been watching the new neighbors down the street for several days. She reported to hubby, "They seem a most devoted couple. Every time he leaves she comes out on the porch and he hugs and kisses her. Why don't you do that?" "Me?" cried hubby in amazement. "Goodness! I haven't even been introduced to her yet."

See also affectionate[2], death[2], faithful[3], separation[2].

DIAGNOSIS

1

A pretty young girl was troubled with a pain in her right side and consulted a doctor. "Hm," he said, after he had finished his examination. "You have acute appendicitis." She blushed and looked down. "Oh, doctor!" she gurgled. "I'll bet that you tell that to all the girls."

2

A rich old fellow who was peevish and arrogant had sent for a doctor. "Well, sir, what seems to be the trouble?" began the doctor cheerily. "That's what you're being paid to find out," snapped the old grouch. "Of course," agreed the doctor reflectively. "Well, if you'll just excuse me I'll be back shortly with a veterinarian friend. He's the only one

I know who can diagnose without asking questions."

3

Despite the doctor's confidence, the patient was worried. "But are you sure it's pneumonia, doctor?" he queried anxiously. "I've heard of cases where a doctor diagnosed and treated a patient for pneumonia, and he ended up dying of typhoid fever." "Tut, tut," reassured the doctor firmly. "Sheer nonsense! When I treat a patient for pneumonia, he dies of pneumonia."

4

The case of the elderly man had his doctor puzzled. So he called in another doctor, then another, and another, until finally seven gray heads were grouped around the patient, all shaking their heads dubiously, and unable to agree on a diagnosis. Finally, the patient spoke up gently, "May I request that you gentlemen perform an autopsy on me to find out what's wrong, for I'm dying to know what ails me myself."

5

A physician, who was noted for the speed and brusqueness with which he diagnosed and prescribed for his patients, was consulted by a young man. When he finished, the young man held out his hand and said, "I came to you because my father, Alvin Gray, spoke of you so often." "What!" cried the doctor. "You're old Al's son? For God's sake, boy, throw that silly prescription away and sit down and tell me what's wrong with you."

6

Hospitals frequently use letters

to designate a disease on the diagnosis report, such as "T. B." for tuberculosis. An interne who was new at a certain hospital was puzzled by the frequent occurrence of the letters "G. O. K." on the slips in the files. "There must be an epidemic of this G. O. K. around here," he remarked to the resident physician. "What is it?" "Huh! That just means, 'God Only Knows,'" grunted the doctor.

7

The famous specialists who had been called into consultation had examined the patient and then retired to another room to discuss the diagnosis. The patient was curious and sent his small son to listen at the door. "Could you hear what they said?" he asked eagerly when the boy returned. "I listened awful hard, but I couldn't get the big words," replied the boy. "But I did hear one of them say, 'Oh, well, we'll find out at the autopsy.'"

See also right[2], sick[2], teeth[5].

DIAMOND

The farmer's hired man took his first trip to the big city, and when he returned he was sporting in his necktie a huge shiny diamond. All the village girls admired it and all the men envied it. But the farmer was a little skeptical. "Air ye sure that there diamond's real, Jed?" he inquired. "Real?" snorted Jed scornfully. "Waal, if she ain't, I bin plumb skinned outta four bits."

DICTIONARY

The admiring young student had been granted an interview with the famous lexicographer. "However did you manage to compile your great dictionary, sir?" he asked in awed tones. "Oh, it works out gradually," the great man replied in a deprecating voice. "It's just like quarreling with one's wife—one word leads to another."

DIET

1

"You seem to be getting prettier all the time," he complimented the girl. "Thank you," she replied, pleased. "I've been living on a diet of whole wheat bread and water to help my complexion." "How long do you think you could keep that up?" he inquired anxiously. "Oh, indefinitely," she declared. "In that case, let's get married, darling," he quickly proposed.

2

The food faddist was lecturing on the evils of modern diet and had become vehement about it. According to him, practically everything that most people ate or drank was little short of poison. At last he singled out a bored man in the front row and demanded, "Can you tell me, sir, what most of us eat at some time and which is the worst possible thing for us?" With no hesitation the bored man grunted, "Wedding cake!"

3

A hospital patient was ill with a stomach disorder and the doctor ordered him put on a diet of sherry and egg. "Well, how do you like your new diet?" the doctor asked him a few days later. "It wouldn't be bad at all," responded the patient weakly, "if only the sherry were as old as the egg and the egg were as new as the sherry."

4

A woman went into a shoe store and asked for a certain brand of shoe polish. "I'm sorry, madam, but we've never carried that brand," said the clerk. "However, I think that you'll find either of these quite satisfactory." "No, I must have the other," the woman insisted. "It's made especially for babies' shoes and contains vitamins, so that when the baby chews his shoes he gets his vitamins at the same time."

5

A girl who had recently been studying about diet was vacationing at a coastal fishing village. "What do the inhabitants of this village eat?" she asked the hotel proprietor. "They live mainly on nothin' but fish, ma'am," he replied. "But fish is a brain food," she objected, "and these people are about as stupid-looking as I've seen." "Mebbe," was the answer. "But think how they'd look if they didn't eat fish."

See also reducing[1].

DIFFERENCE

1

A Southerner and a Northerner were talking. "I cain't see where there's so much difference between us folks," declared the Southerner, " 'ceptin' mebbe that we-uns reckon where you-uns guess." "That's about it, brother," agreed the Northerner, "except that we can guess a danged sight better than you can reckon."

2

The young widow had money,

was pretty, and was quite a catch. The ambitious young man asked her to marry him. "Before I give you my answer," she said, "can you tell me what's the difference between Farmer Brown's cow and myself?" The young fellow puzzled a moment, then replied, "No, I don't know." "In that case," said the widow firmly, "you'd better marry the cow."

3

"What in the world made you pick out Helen for a girlfriend, Bill?" asked a friend. "It's because she's different from other girls," replied Bill. "Different? In what way?" pursued the friend. "She's the only girl who'll have me for a boyfriend," was the answer.

DIGNITY

"I certainly made that usher respect the dignity of my family last night," announced Percy proudly. "How did you manage that, old thing?" inquired Algy. "Well," said Percy, "when he threw me out of the side door for talking to the girl beside me, I said, 'See here, my man, I come from an old aristocratic family,' and he picked me up, apologized, and threw me out of the front door."

DINNER
See eating, food, meals.

DIPLOMACY
See shrewd, strategy, tact.

DIRECTION

1

There was a heavy fog on the river and the steamboat was tied up at the bank. "Why aren't we moving?" an impatient passenger asked the captain. "Can't see where we're going," he replied shortly. "But you can see the stars overhead very plainly," objected the passenger. "Sure," agreed the captain, "but unless the boilers bust, we ain't a-goin' that way."

2

A truck-driver was going along a road in such a hurry that he missed a turn, bumped over a ditch, ran through a farmyard, and crashed into the farmer's kitchen where the wife stood stirring a pot on the stove. She looked up calmly, then went back to her cooking. The driver managed somewhat sheepishly to inquire, "Can you tell me how to get to Hillsboro?" "Yep," responded the woman coolly, "jest keep on straight past the cupboard, then turn left at the pianner."

3

It was only a small town, but still the stranger couldn't find the post office, so he asked one of the whittlers in front of the store. "Well, lemme see," said the native, scratching his head. "Fust you go a block north, then two blocks east. No, wait, it's a block east, then three blocks south. Nope, that's wrong too. Let's see, now. B'gosh! I'll be switched, but ye can't git to the post office from here!"

4

A traveling revivalist preacher was strange in the city and asked a newsboy the way to the City Hall. "Keep on this street for three blocks and then go two blocks to the left," the boy directed. "Thank you," said the preacher, then added brightly, "you know, I'm holding those revival services at the Auditorium, so if you'll come down tonight I'll show you the way to heaven." "Go on!" cried the boy scornfully, "you don't even know the way to the City Hall."

5

A little girl, carrying a large package, was walking down the street looking confusedly about her. "Can I help you, my child?" asked a kindly old gentleman. "Please, sir," she asked politely, indicating a cross street, "could you tell me if this is the third turn to the right?"

See also fog^2, permission.

DIRTY

1

"Dinner is almost ready, son," scolded the provoked mother, "and I've told you three times to wash your hands, but you haven't done it yet." "But, mother," explained the boy patiently, examining his hands critically, "they aren't really dirty—just kinda blurred."

2

The overseer of a rubber plantation had been suspecting that the contents of his whisky bottle, while remaining the same in quantity, kept growing lighter in color. At last, he called his native boy to him and said accusingly, "See here, Kanaka, you've been drinking my whisky and putting dirty water in the bottle." "No, no; not true!" cried the boy indignantly. "Me always fetch clean water from cistern."

3

A flat tire forced some tourists to stop near a hillbilly cabin. The elegant lady from the car got to talking with the hillbilly woman. "My goodness!" she exclaimed, shuddering in disgust, "how dirty your hands are!" "Call thet dirty, ma'am?" cried the hillbilly, regarding her hands in amazement. "Jeepers! Ye oughtta see my feet!"

4

The janitor of the building was more cautious than tidy, and though he had placed a large sign at the entrance reading, "Please wipe your feet," he nevertheless allowed the corridors to become filthy. Things finally reached such a state that one of the tenants wrote in at the bottom of the sign, "On leaving the building."

See also feet[3], wife[2].

DISAPPOINTMENT

1

The little boy was weeping bitterly, and the kind lady paused to comfort him. "There, there," she said soothingly, "what's the trouble, little fellow?" "Mom went and drowned all the kittens," wailed the boy. "What a pity," consoled the lady, "maybe you can find yourself another one." "Aw, I d-didn't want any of 'em," sobbed the boy. "It's j-just that she promised me I could drown 'em."

2

A group of men were discussing the greatest disappointments of their lives. One said it was the loss of his sweetheart to a rival, another the bankruptcy of his business, and still another his inability to follow an artistic career. "My greatest disappointment came as a boy," announced a quiet man. "What was that?" he was asked. "It was when I'd spent an hour sneaking under a tent to see a circus only to find it was a revival meeting."

DISBELIEF

A man was telling a marvelous tale of rescue. "At 7:15 I suggested to my wife we take a sail. At 7:30 we started, but as soon as we were well out a high wind capsized the boat. We both would have drowned if a passing dolphin hadn't taken us on his back and brought us to land." One listener was smiling skeptically, so the man asked, "Don't you believe the story?" "I'll say I don't," was the derisive reply. "Trying to tell me your wife got ready in 15 minutes!"

DISCHARGE

1

The boss was going through the shipping room when he noticed a boy sitting idly on a box whistling. "What's your salary, boy?" he demanded. "Twelve dollars a week, sir," was the reply. "Well, here's a week's pay," said the boss. "Now get out; you're fired." When he saw the foreman a little later, he asked, "How long have we had that boy?" "Why, he doesn't work here," replied the foreman, "he just delivered a package."

2

Poor business was forcing the boss to lay off a man who was a good worker. To make it easier he informed the man of his discharge by mail. The man was absent for four days thereafter, but on the fifth he was back working hard. "Didn't I send you a letter telling you that you were fired?" "Yes, sir," answered the man, "the letter said I was fired, but on the envelope it said, 'Return in five days.'"

See also jury[6].

DISCOVER

See find.

DISEASE

See sick.

DISPLAY

1

The daughter of an old aristocratic but poverty-stricken Southern family was going for a visit in the North. Her scanty wardrobe was elaborated as much as possible, the old family laces and jewels were brought out, and all purses were scraped to provide traveling expenses. "Now, honey," instructed the mother as daughter was about to depart, "don't be tellin' that you're from the South—that would be like talkin' about money befo' po' folks. Fo'tunate folks mustn't parade their advantages."

2

The dear ladies at the bridge club meeting were talking about their jewelry. "My diamonds I naturally clean with ammonia," remarked one lady, "but my rubies require Moselle wine, and my emeralds need fine brandy for sparkle. My sapphires clean well with fresh milk." There was a short silence, then another spoke up, "My dear, do you *clean* your jewels? I just throw mine away when they get dirty."

DISSIPATION

1

The mild little man had been put through a rigid examination for an insurance policy and had been asked every conceivable question. Finally, the examiner inquired, "Do you drink, smoke, live fast, or dissipate excessively in any way?" The man was thoughtful for a moment, then replied hesitantly, "Well—er—ah—I sometimes chew a piece of gum."

2

The young man had been leading a gay life for sometime and his father thought it was time to speak to him about it. "My boy," he pointed out, "don't you realize that by going in for this wild sort of life, you are shortening your days?" "Could be," answered the boy coolly, "but it evens up—if I am shortening my days, think how I'm lengthening my nights."

See also longevity[3].

DISTANCE

1

The perspiring vacationist was angry when he approached the clerk at the resort hotel. "Your ads all say that this hotel is only five minutes from the station," he said, "but I've been almost an hour getting here." "Well, of course," replied the clerk haughtily, "because you've been walking. We don't cater to the pedestrian trade."

2

A tourist stopped his car and leaned out to shout at a boy trudging along the road, "Say, son, how far is it to Jonesboro?" "It's about 24,998 miles in the direction you're goin', but if you turn around and go t'other way it's only five."

3

"Which way to Piny Hollow?" asked a driver of a glum-looking man sitting on a log by the road. The fellow jerked his thumb limply to the right. "Thanks," said the tourist. "And about how far is it?" "'Tain't very fur," was the lifeless response, "an' when ye git there ye'll wish it wuz a danged sight further."

4

Inspection showed the gas tank to be empty, so the driver started walking to find a town. After having covered a long stretch of hot, dusty country road, he saw a farmer working in a field and hailed him, "Say, friend, how long is it going to take me to get to town?" The farmer looked up slowly, squinted, and drawled, "How fast you aimin' to walk?"

5

"How far to the next filling station?" a stranded tourist called to a passing farmer. "Purty near three mile as the crow flies," replied the farmer, ejecting a stream of tobacco juice. "Very interesting," barked the motorist peevishly, "but how far is it if that damned crow has to walk and roll a flat tire?"

DISTURBANCE

1

At about the middle of the sermon a baby in the congregation started to cry lustily. The mother arose and started to leave the church. "Remain, madam," called the preacher. "Your child is not disturbing me." "Well, maybe he ain't," the mother sniffed scornfully, "but you're sure disturbin' him."

2

A man had been to a party where the spirits had flowed freely. He arrived home at 2:30 in the morning in a gay and exalted mood. "Good ol' Bill," he mumbled to himself, "think I'll call 'im up an' see how he is." When a sleepy voice finally answered the phone, the drunk said brightly, "Hope I haven't disturbed you, Bill." "Oh that's all right," replied Bill patiently, "I had to get up anyway to answer the phone."

See also audience[1], concert[2], miracle[2], neighbor[1], noise[1], opportunity[3], reading[1], shouting, speaker[2].

DIVIDE

Teacher was drilling the class in fractions. "Now, Johnny," she questioned, "suppose your mother has five children to feed and has only three potatoes in the house for them and wanted to divide them so that each would get an equal share. How would she do it?" "She'd mash the potatoes," was the prompt reply.

DIVORCE

1

A young wife entered a famous divorce lawyer's office. "I came to you to find out if I have grounds for divorce," she announced. "Are you married, madam?" inquired the great man. "Yes, I am," replied the woman. "Then you most certainly have," was the firm assurance.

2

The census taker was interviewing an old maid. "Are you unmarried, madam?" he queried. "Oh, gracious, no," giggled the woman blushingly. "I've never even been married yet."

See also alimony, America[4], kind[3], punishment[5], relatives[2], remarriage[3].

DO

1

The boss was questioning the applicant for a job. "What was your last job?" he inquired. "I was a doer, sir," was the reply. "A doer?" exclaimed the boss. "What in the world is that?" "Well, you see," responded the man, "whenever the manager wanted something done, he would tell the cashier, the cashier would tell the bookkeeper, the bookkeeper the clerk, and the clerk me, and as I had no one to tell to do it, I did it."

2

The rookie policeman was being questioned by the examining board. "Now, suppose you were in a squad car and were being chased by a gang of desperate killers in a car that was making fifty miles an hour," he was asked. "What would you do?" "At least sixty," was the prompt reply.

3

The maid had just left the room with a tray heaped high with dishes when there was a loud clattering crash. "Bridget," called the mis-

tress anxiously, "what are you doing out there?" "Ain't doin' nothin', mum," came the faint reply. "It's done."

See also seasick[1], tombstone[3].

DOCTOR

1

A faculty member of a London medical school had been appointed an honorary physician to the king. In order to inform his class of his distinction he proudly wrote on the blackboard: "Prof. Jenkins wishes to inform his students that he has been appointed honorary physician to His Majesty the King." When he returned sometime later, he found written below his notice: "God save the King!"

2

There were two brothers who looked very much alike. One was a minister and the other a doctor. The medical brother was greeted on the street one day by a man who said, "I wish to compliment you on your fine sermon last Sunday, Doctor." The other shook his head and replied, "I'm sorry, but I'm not the doctor who preaches—I'm the one who practices."

3

A gravedigger was walking down the street of a small town when he noticed two of the local doctors coming along behind him. He immediately stopped and waited until they had passed, then fell in behind them. "What's all this about?" inquired one of the doctors wonderingly. The gravedigger smiled knowingly and replied, "It's just that I know my place in this procession."

4

A man met a doctor on the street and stopped him. "Doctor," he asked between violent coughs, "what should a person do when he has a bad chest cold?" The doctor had frequently been chiseled out of free advice, and was consequently on his guard when he answered, "Such a person, my dear sir, should see a good physician." "Thanks, doc," replied the man turning to go, "that's just what I'll do."

5

The man had got his ailing friend as far as the doctor's door, but there he balked. "I'm a little leery about going in there," the sick one said. "Nonsense!" scoffed the other. "This is one of the best doctors in town. What's wrong?" "It's just that I don't like the odds he offers," was the reply. "Look on his sign there—10 to 1."

6

The patient who lived away out in the suburbs was apologizing to the doctor. "I feel terrible about making you come all the way out here, doctor," he said, "but I do seem to be quite ill." "Think nothing of it, Mr. Black," reassured the doctor. "I have another call out in this direction anyway, so I'm really killing two birds with one stone."

7

The seedy-looking elderly doctor was giving the young doctor some advice. "Be very careful of the smallest details, my boy," he cautioned. "It was a small slip that brought me to my present condition." "How was that, sir?" inquired the beginner. "It was in the simple routine filling out of a death certificate,"

replied the other, "when I absent-mindedly signed my name in the space marked 'Cause of Death.'"

See also advice[6], angel[6], breathing[3], caution[5], childbirth[2, 3], children[6], company[3], craftsmanship[4], diagnosis[3], ethics[2], experience[2], expert[2], faith[1], fashionable, filling station[2], gratitude, hurry[4], inheritance[3], instructions[4], patient, progress[3], proof[1], recognize[1], recovery[1, 5], restaurant[3], right[2], sanity[2], skin, sleep[1], specialist, suitor[1], treatment[1], undertaker[1], waiting[7], whisper.

DOG

1

The lady was boasting of her dog to the neighbor. "He may not be a very fancy-looking dog or have a long pedigree," she admitted, "but just let a tramp or a peddler come to the door and he soon lets you know it." "What does he do, bark like crazy?" asked the neighbor. "No, nothing like that," said the proud owner. "He just crawls away back under the bed."

2

It was only a mangy little cur, but the boy who was playing with it was as proud as could be. "What kind of dog is it, son?" inquired a passing man. "He's a police dog," responded the boy defiantly. "A police dog?" exclaimed the man. "He certainly doesn't look like one." "Of course he doesn't," replied the youngster. "You see, he's in the secret service."

3

The dog's leash was old and weak and during the night he broke it and got into the pantry and ate all the provisions. "Did Fido eat much of the food, Mary?" asked the mistress when the maid told her the news. "He ate every single thing in the place, mum," answered the maid, "'ceptin' the dog biscuits."

4

An elegant lady had brought a little dog into a hotel dining room with her, and the animal yapped and yipped constantly while she ate. A man, at an adjoining table, endured the disturbance for a long while, but finally he leaned over and inquired of the woman, "Your first dog, madam?"

5

As the little boy's birthday drew near, he kept throwing out broader and broader hints as to the dog he would like to have for a present. "But, Georgie," objected mother, "you don't need a dog. You already have a nice pink velvet doggie." The boy shook his head. "That's not the kind I want," he insisted. "I want one with fleas."

6

"That's a funny-looking dog you have," remarked a man to his friend. "Funny-looking!" exclaimed the other. "I'll have you know I paid a hundred dollars for that dog. He's part terrier and part bull." "Oh, yeah?" returned the first. "Which part is bull?" "The part about the hundred dollars," was the frank reply.

7

The Arctic explorer was relating some of his adventures. "On and on through the polar blizzards we pushed," he said, "and we had every prospect of reaching the Pole, when our dogs gave out." "Indeed?" exclaimed a lady listener. "But I thought that those Esquimaux dogs were practically tireless." The explorer gulped, hesitated, then explained, "I was speaking, madam, in a—er—ah—culinary sense."

8

The man had been haled into court for keeping a dog without a license. Every time he tried to speak he was silenced by the court. Finally, the clerk demanded, "Is the court to understand you refuse to renew the license?" "Yes, but—" began the defendant. "No buts," snapped the clerk. "You know your old license expired on January 1st." "I know," said the man wearily, "and so did the dog."

9

The animal fancier was on his pet subject. "I say that some dogs have almost human intelligence," he maintained. "You may be right," conceded the married man. "I often think that our dog tries to curry favor with my wife by growling at me."

See also bone[1], dachshund, cruelty[1], destination[2], end[2, 3], favor[1], food[1], germs[2], grandma[2], house[5], language[2], proverb[1].

DOLL

1

The little girl stood holding her badly banged-up doll which had an arm and a leg missing, and had a cracked head, while she watched a young mother bathing her baby. "How long have you had your baby?" she inquired of the woman. "Almost five months, now," was the answer. "My goodness!" exclaimed the child. "You've certainly kept her nice!"

2

Little Janie was hugging and loving her doll and speaking lovingly to it. "You is a beau'ful dolly, very beau'ful wif your pink cheeks an' curly hair," she crooned to it as she hugged it close, "but, dolly, you is dot no brains."

DONKEY

See ass.

DOUBT

The lawyer had been bested in the cross-examination, so he turned to the judge in a dignified manner and declared, "It is my misfortune, Your Honor, to be opposed by an unprincipled rascal." "My honorable opponent," responded the other lawyer, "is such an infamous liar that—" "Come, come!" prompted the bored judge. "Counsel will please confine itself to such matters as are in dispute."

DOWRY

The young visitor seemed a likely prospect, so the father grew confidential. "I've several girls and I'd like to see them all comfortably married," he announced, "and they won't go penniless to their husbands. Jane, who is 23, will take $1,000 with her. Then there's Lizzie, who's 34, she'll take $2,500 with her. And Mary, who's 41, will take $5,000 to her husband." The young fellow thought a moment, then asked, "You don't have a daughter about 50, do you?"

DRAWL

A soldier from the North was transferred to a camp in Arkansas, and this was his first experience in the South. He returned from his first weekend leave very much elated. "I sure go for this Southern drawl down here," he declared gleefully. "All you gotta do is step up and ask any Little Rock gal for a kiss and, before she can say no, it's too late."

See also slow[1].

DREAM

1

"Hm," said the psychiatrist solemnly as he stroked his chin. "And what is this nightmare that you say you have every night?" "I always dream that I'm married," replied the patient. "Ah, ha!" cried the psychiatrist. "And to whom do you dream that you are married?" "To my wife," explained the patient disgustedly. "That's what makes it a nightmare."

2

The young man had been keeping company with the girl for over two years, but still had given no indication of serious intentions. "I had a strange dream last night," he remarked one day. "I dreamed that I proposed to you. I wonder what that's a sign of?" The girl answered, "It's a sign that you've got more sense asleep than awake."

3

A little boy came down to breakfast with his face all aglow. "Gee, mom," he cried, "wasn't that an excitin' dream I had last night?"

"Now, how should I know what your dream was about, son?" replied his mother. "Of course you know, mom," insisted the boy. "Don't you remember that you were in it?"

See also millionaire[1].

DRESS

1

The little boy was tucked in his bed when his mother came into the room wearing a very décolleté evening dress to kiss him good night. "Where ya goin' all dressed up, mummy?" asked the child. "I'm going to the opera with daddy, son," replied mother. "But, gee, mummy," queried the boy, "ain't ya scared somebody might see ya?"

2

Guests were expected and hubby was awaiting them when the wife came down in her new evening gown. Hubby examined the dress with a frown. "Don't you think that dress is a little extreme?" he suggested. "It seems a bit short at the bottom and rather low-cut at the top." "Well, what of it?" snapped the wife. "Are these people coming to see me or my dress?"

DRESSING

"How did you enjoy your vacation at that swanky resort, Bill?" asked Jones. "Oh, fair enough," replied Bill. "Was there much to do there?" continued Jones. "Well, there wasn't much for me to do," admitted Bill, "but my wife and daughters were certainly kept busy." "Guess they did a lot of riding and swimming?" supposed Jones. "No,"

explained Bill, "their time was completely taken up with dressing for meals."

See also disbelief.

DRINK

1

A red-nosed barber with a definite odor of spirits about him was shaving a minister and not making a very good job of it. Suddenly, there was a slip of the razor, and the clergyman was bleeding from a bad cut. "Now you see, Sam," reproved the preacher, "what comes from drinking too much." "Yes, sir," agreed the barber sympathetically, "drinkin' sure does make the skin tender, don't it?"

2

An old judge was having lunch in a café one hot summer day when an acquaintance stopped by his table. "You shouldn't be drinking hot coffee on a day like this, Judge," he observed. "Iced, stimulating drinks are better in this weather. Did you ever try gin and ginger ale?" "No, I haven't," snapped the judge, "but I've tried a number of fellows who have."

See also never, objection[1], sense, temperance[3], whiskey[1].

DRINKING

1

The doctor completed his examination of the elderly man and shook his head. "If you keep on drinking whisky it will surely shorten your life," he declared, "but if you stop drinking you can prolong your days." "I believe you're right about that, doc," agreed the man. "I remember once about two years ago I went twenty-four hours without a single drink, and I never endured a longer day in my life."

2

The confirmed old toper was back after having taken the cure. "Was the treatment severe?" an acquaintance asked him. "Oh, it was horrible!" cried the rounder. "Why for days and days I had to live on nothing but food and water."

3

The temperance leader was interviewing a political candidate to see if the man was worthy of his support. "One more question, sir," interrogated the dry, "do you ever drink alcoholic beverages?" "Before I answer that," replied the politician cautiously, "I'd like to know if it's in the nature of an inquiry or an invitation."

4

Father was drinking beer in a tavern one evening and his young son was with him. He was cautioning him about the evils of intemperance. "Drinking is all right, son," he declared, "but to get drunk is a disgrace." "How would I know when I'm drunk?" asked the boy. "See those two men there?" father pointed. "Well, if you saw four you'd know you were drunk." The boy looked intently. "But, father," he objected, "there's only one man there."

5

The young fellow had just popped the question to the girl of his dreams, but still she hesitated. "Before I give you my answer," she announced seriously, "I must ask you a question: Do you drink anything?" The fellow drew himself up proudly and replied promptly, "Anything!" "Darling!" cried the girl, and fell swooning into his arms.

6

A preacher, who was not averse to an occasional nip, hired a handy man to clean out his basement. In the process several boxes of empty bottles were brought out. The workman lifted each bottle to inspect it carefully. The preacher, who happened to be passing by, called, "They're all dead ones, Sam." "Yes, they are," replied Sam. "And they were lucky in that they all had the minister with them when they passed away."

7

Mary was at the bar drinking a beer when a girl acquaintance came in. "Hi, there, Mary," called the newcomer. "I see you're having one, eh?" "Don't be silly," answered Mary. "It's just the cut of this lousy coat makes me look that way."

See also cure, election[6], eyes[2], hangover[2], indulgent, magazine[3], moderate, rubbish, see[1], sick[3], Western[1].

DRIVER

1

Mother had Junior out in the car for an afternoon drive. After a period of silent, uneventful driving, the little boy asked with a puzzled frown, "Mama, where's all 'ose 'fernal idiots?" "Don't let it bother you, son," mother replied. "They're on the highway only when your father's driving."

2

Two men took the last of a long series of drinks at a roadside tavern, said good-by to their friends, and began the fifty-mile drive to town. It was their first time over this road, and after a while one of them said, "Think we're gettin' closer to the city now." "What makes you think so? See a sign?" asked the other. "Nope," was the reply. "But we're hittin' more people."

3

The new car owner was genuinely shocked. "Never, until I got an automobile did I realize that profanity was so prevalent," he exclaimed. "I suppose you do hear quite a bit of it on the highway," a friend agreed. "Goodness, yes," was the reply. "Why, almost every one I bump into swears terribly."

4

A certain young man who had a reputation for his reckless driving was at home one afternoon when he received a telephone call. A woman's voice asked if he intended to go driving soon. "No, I think not this afternoon," he replied. "Why, and who are you?" "That's immaterial," said the voice. "I just wanted to send my little girl down the street on an errand."

5

"What most impressed you on your tour of the West last summer?" asked a friend of the inveterate driver. "Oh, I saw a great deal of magnificent scenery," was the answer, "but what most took my eye was the boundless prairies, and it filled me with sadness as I looked at them and thought of all that parking space going to waste."

6

A tourist came out of a roadside cornfield with a dozen fine, plump ears of corn in his arms just as another car came down the road and stopped. A man got out. The tourist, somewhat shamefaced, asked, "How much?" "Oh, about a dollar, I guess," said the other. Receiving the dollar and shoving it into his pocket, he looked around and commented, "Sure a nice field of corn. Wonder who it belongs to?"

See also chauffeur, distance[3, 4], drunk[8], emergency[2], feeling[6], oath[3], pedestrian[1], reassurance[2], suspicion, truck-driver, woman-driver.

DROUGHT

1

A tourist stopped at an isolated filling station out West and got to talking with an old native and his son about the drought. "It's certainly been a terrible dry spell," he said, "but it looks as if we might have a little rain at last." "Shore hope so," replied the old-timer. "Don't care so much about it fer m'self as fer m'boy here—I've already seen it a-rainin'."

2

The grimy tourist tried to knock some of the dust off himself and asked for another drink of water. "Doesn't it *ever* rain in these parts?" he inquired of one of the natives. "Rain!" snorted the native. "Did you say rain? Say, stranger, there's bullfrogs in this yere town over seven year old what ain't even learned to swim yit!"

See also competition[2].

DROWNING

1

"Isn't that Mabel in there swimming?" asked one girl of another as they sat on the beach of a summer resort. "She shouldn't be going in alone. She almost drowned yesterday and Bill had to drag her out and use artificial respiration." "Humph!" sniffed the other knowingly. "You mean Mabel had to use artificial drowning."

2

It was late at night. The reporter, just coming off duty, passed along the river and heard sounds as of someone struggling in the water. "Hey, there!" he shouted. "Is someone drowning?" "Yes, I am," came a feeble voice from the river. "Dang it!" cried the reporter regretfully, "you're just too late to make the last night edition. But don't worry, you'll have a nice little paragraph all to yourself in the morning paper."

3

Smith had been having trouble at home and was looking pretty glum when he met a friend on the street. "Oh, cheer up, Smith," advised the friend, slapping him on the back, "things aren't as bad as they seem. Why don't you drown your sorrow?" "Boy! I'd sure like to," replied Smith vehemently. "But she's bigger than I am, and besides, it would be murder."

4

The lady was listening attentively to the old sailor's tale of how he had been swept overboard in a storm and almost drowned. "I suppose, of course," she observed, "that when you sank for the third time your whole previous life passed before your eyes?" "Mebbe it did, mum," the sailor conceded, "but seein's as how I had me eyes shut, I missed it."

5

The river was swift and treacherous at the ferry crossing and the boat was rickety. The woman passenger inquired anxiously of the ferryman, "Has any one ever been lost while crossing here?" "Nobudy a-tall, ma'am," stated the ferryman emphatically. "'Course, m' brother was drownded here a couple of weeks ago, but we done foun' him early next mornin'."

See also newlyrich[2], search[1].

DRUGSTORE

1

"I want a dozen canine pills," the old lady demanded of the druggist. "Just what is the trouble with the dog?" inquired the druggist. "Why, the very idea!" cried the lady indignantly. "My poor husband's burning up with a fever and you call him a dog!" The druggist reflected a moment, then proceeded to wrap up some quinine capsules in silence.

2

Two druggists were attending the funeral of one of their colleagues and were speaking of the deceased in hushed voices. "Whatever else they might say," insisted one, "he at least was a great druggist." "He was, indeed," agreed the other heartily, then added in a more confidential tone, "but, honestly now, don't you think he put a little too much salt in his tuna salad?"

3

"Does that lunch counter really pay for all the trouble it causes and the extra help you have to hire?" a friend inquired of the druggist. "Well, to tell the truth, I just about break even on the lunch counter," admitted the druggist, "but man, oh man, how it's boomed the sale of indigestion tablets!"

4

An elderly lady went into a drugstore and peered suspiciously at the young clerk. "You look a little young to be a registered pharmacist," she stated. "But I am, madam," the clerk said. "And you have passed all your examinations?" she continued. "With high grades," was the answer. "Well, I guess it's all right, then," decided the lady, still a little dubious. "Give me a nickel box of cough drops."

5

A man wanted an empty bottle so he went into a drugstore for it. After selecting one, he asked the price. "If you want just the empty bottle," said the druggist, "it'll cost you a dime, but if you take something in it you may have it for nothing." "That's satisfactory with me," agreed the man. "I'll take a cork in it."

See also handwriting[3], insects[5], memory[2], pill[1, 3], revenge[2].

DRUNK

1

A policeman saw a drunk crawling about in the gutter under a lamppost and asked him what he was doing. "Lookin' for a quarter I losh," replied the drunk. "Where'd you lose it?" inquired the cop. "'Bout a block down th' shtreet," was the answer. "Then why look here?" insisted the officer. "'Cause there's lotsh more light here," explained the drunk, continuing his search.

2

He was a chronic toper and a regular visitor to the police station. "Hiya, Judgie!" he cried when the officer brought him in. The judge frowned and announced severely, "George Brown, you are charged with habitual drunkenness. Do you have any excuse to offer in your defense?" "Sure do, Judgie," replied the sot. "Habitual thirst."

3

An inebriated old fellow stopped a man on the street and inquired, "Shay, bud, whish's th' other side the street, huh?" "Why, over there, of course," replied the man, pointing. "'Sfunny," pondered the drunk puzzledly. "Was jus' over there and a gen'lman shaid it was over here."

4

The judge eyed the well-dressed prisoner dubiously. "Are you certain this man was drunk when you arrested him?" he asked the officer. "Indeed I am," was the reply. "What makes you so positive?" insisted the judge. The officer shrugged his shoulders and said, "Well, he was dropping pennies in a mailbox on Main Street and looking at the clock on the City Hall tower and saying, 'Golly, I've lost eighteen pounds.'"

5

It was the Christmas season and Mrs. Jones was provoked with hubby because he didn't take more interest in its celebration. "I don't see why we can't have a cheery Christmas like the Blacks," she pouted, looking out the window. "See, they're carrying in a Yule log." Hubby came over and took a look. "Yule log, my eye!" he snorted. "That's Black."

6

It had been a big night at the club, and Brown approached his house very unsteadily. A solitary tree stood on the lawn, but Brown, of course, saw it as two. Cautiously he attempted to pass between the two, but banged into the tree and was knocked down. Again and again he tried, with the same result. At last he sat on the ground and tearfully cried, "Losht, hopelessly losht in an impen'trable foresht!"

7

It was very late but the drunk finally managed to corner the elusive keyhole. He got into the house and was fumbling about in the dark for the stairs when his wife was awakened by a loud crash. "That you, William?" she called down. "What *are* you doing?" After a moment's silence came the reply, "Teachin' your damn' goldfish not to snap at me."

8

Some of the most vitriolic cussing that the policeman had ever heard was coming from a parked car. So he walked over to it and demanded, "What's wrong in there?" A befuddled face appeared at a window and said, "Some dirty, lousy so-and-so swiped my steering wheel!" "Take it easy," cautioned the officer. "Just quiet down and get up in the front seat where you belong."

9

A drunk was hobbling along a street with one foot in the gutter and the other on the curb, and weeping. A policeman, puzzled, followed him around the block, then said, "You'd better keep that foot out of the gutter, buddy, or a car might come along and hit you." The drunk looked down, then smiled up through his tears. "Thank God!" he exclaimed. "Thought I wash a hopelesh cripple."

10

Papa hog had been down to the corner mud wallow talking with the boys. On the way home to his sty he passed a brewery where there was a big puddle of sour beer that had been thrown out. Papa hog drank and drank. When he reached home he was staggering badly and trying to squeal "Sweet Adeline." Mamma hog rushed to tuck the little piggies in their wallow, then came back to scold papa: "For shame, Henry Hog, to go make such a human of yourself before the children!"

11

A drunk had just stumbled aboard a bus and was stopped by another in the same condition who asked, "Wha'sha time, friend?" The first drunk pulled out a pocket comb, stared at it, then announced, "Ish June 3rd." "Golly," exclaimed the other in distress, "then I shoulda got off lash shtop."

12

A drunk entered a phone booth, dropped in a nickel, waited a moment, then started to bang and twist everything on the instrument. Finally, the voice of central came through the receiver asking, "Number, please?" "Number, hell!" cried the drunk heatedly. "I want my peanuts!"

See also acquaintance[6], better[4], bus[1], church[4], club[1], condition[2], delusion[4], driver[2], elevator[3], fish[2], grave, hanging[2], horse[1], hurry[2], joke[2], location[2], moon[3], moving, pronunciation[4], puzzle[2], real, search[1], sleep[2], stand[1], taxi[4], telephone[1], thrift[3], waiting[3], weight[1], wrong[2].

DRY

See drought, thirst.

DUET

A hobo paused outside an elaborate mansion as he noted a colleague shuffling from the door. "Any luck, 'bo?" he inquired as the other reached the gate. "No use goin' in there, pal," declared the other disgustedly. "Why, that dump's so poverty-stricken that there's a couple o' wimmin in there tryin' to play on one bloomin' pianner at the same time!"

DUST

1

The ardent suitor sank to his knees before his ladylove. "Just see how I grovel here in the dust at your tiny feet," he cried flinging wide his arms. "Dust! Well, I like that, you insulting creature!" exclaimed the girl angrily. "And after I spent the whole afternoon cleaning this room!"

2

The mistress called the new maid into the living room. "Look there!" she commanded reprovingly, pointing at the piano. "I wrote your name in the dust on the piano this morning." "I saw it, mum, and I've been meanin' to speak to you about it," replied the maid. "You've got it spelled wrong."

See also patriotism[3].

DUTY

See wound.

DYING

1

The mince pie at the social had been so good that the minister had eaten too much. As a result he was now ill indeed. A brother clergyman visited him and, in the course of their conversation, inquired if he would be afraid to die. "Not just to die," groaned the suffering preacher, "but I should certainly be ashamed to die from eating too much."

2

They were rehearsing the big scene of the play where the hero was dying nobly, but the director was far from satisfied. "For the love of Pete!" he cried, "can't you put a little more life into your dying?"

3

She was not pleased with things this evening and was taking it out on her meek boyfriend. "But, darling," objected the boy reproachfully, "how can you say such mean things to me when I'd gladly die for your sake?" "I know, I know," she snapped. "You're always saying that, but you never do it."

4

The new reporter had been sent out to investigate a case of sudden death. Sometime later he strolled in casually. "Well, what happened?" demanded the city editor. "Why didn't you phone in a story?" "Aw, there wasn't anything to it," replied the reporter. "A fellow was just walking along the street when all of a sudden he threw up his hands and said, 'I'm going to die.' Then he just leaned up against a building and made good."

See also economy[5], expert[2], faithful[3], name[3], patriotism[1], spurned[4], thrift[4], will[1], willing.

EAR

"I can read a person's character by his ears," insisted one man to another. "For example, small, thin ears are an indication of a weak character." Just then an ex-prize-fighter passed by, and the other fellow laughingly pointed at him and asked, "And what are those big, thick ears a sign of?" "A weak defense," was the prompt reply.

EARLY

1

Two men were traveling together. The first morning out one of them was up bright and early. "Come, come," he said, prodding the other. "Don't you know that it's the early bird that catches the worm?" "Well, it serves the worm right for being up so early," mumbled the other as he turned over, "and my wife says that I'm a worm."

2

The new hired man was sleeping soundly when the farmer went to awaken him at four in the morning. "Come, get up," he called, "we're going to cut oats today." "Are they wild oats?" asked the helper sleepily. "No, of course not," replied the farmer. "Then why do we have to sneak up on them in the dark?" inquired the hand.

3

The farmer was an early riser himself and because of this had trouble keeping a hired hand. So he decided to be more lenient with his new man. The first morning he waited until the late hour of four to awaken him. "Better git out here quick if ye want somethin' to eat," he called in to the man. "Thanks a lot," replied the new hand, turning over, "but I never eat just before going to sleep."

See also pregnancy[1].

EARN

1

The judge glared down at the ragged individual who had been dragged into court on a vagrancy charge. "Have you ever earned a dollar in your life?" he asked scornfully. "Yes I have, Your Honor, twice," replied the prisoner. "One for each time I voted for you in the last election."

2

An indignant clerk confronted the professor of a course on How to Be a Success in Business. "Remember when you said that if I took your course I'd soon be earning fifty dollars a week?" said the complainant. "Well, I'm only making twenty-five." "But my dear fellow," replied the professor, "don't you really feel that you're earning fifty dollars? Most clerks think that they earn twice what they get."

EARTHQUAKE

The Newlyriches had returned from a trip abroad and Mrs. Newlyrich was describing her husband's experience with an earthquake while he was in the Orient. "It was *ter*rible," she declared. "When John went to bed everything was as quiet as could be, then suddenly he woke up in the middle of the night and there beside him was a yawning abbess!"

See also boy[1].

EASTER

A religious gentleman met a friend on Easter Sunday. "A beautiful Easter," he observed. "And what did you give up during Lent?" The other made a wry face and replied with a sigh, "Forty-five bucks for the wife's new Easter bonnet."

EASY

See simple.

EATING

1

In a lumbering town up North they held an annual eating contest to find out who could eat the most food. This year the winner took the lead at the start and held it easily, putting away a three-pound roast, a thick steak, two pounds of sausages, and a big meat pie, wth all the trimmings. As he was about to leave with his prize, he cautioned the others, "Say, fellows, don't say anything about this to the wife, will you, or she won't give me any dinner."

2

The tourists had had lunch in the valley, and then drove on up the mountain. As they went over the summit and started down the other side, the woman, who had been looking back at the lovely valley, remarked, "My, what a beautiful gorge that was!" "Yes, wasn't it," agreed her more prosaic husband, "but personally I could have used another piece of that peach pie."

3

Despite father's protests, Junior ate only the centers of his slices of bread. "When I was a boy I always ate my crusts," stated daddy virtuously. "Didja like 'em, pop?" asked Junior. "Like them? Why I loved them," lied father blandly. "Well, here then, pop, you kin have mine," said the young son.

4

She was a vision in her new dress and the most beautiful girl at the cocktail party. He had imbibed enough to appreciate her. "How heavenly you are!" he sighed rapturously. "You look sweet enough to eat." "I do eat," she retorted. "Where shall we go?"

5

A paunchy, middle-aged man wasn't feeling well. So he went to see a stomach specialist. "What did you have for lunch?" inquired the doctor. "Let's see," replied the patient reflectively, "some green turtle soup, lobster Newburg, a club sandwich, nut salad, ice cream on mince pie, and cheese and crackers." "You don't need a stomach specialist," stated the doctor, "you need a brain specialist."

6

The maid was none too bright, but the man needed someone to care for his pet parrot while he was abroad. All the way over he worried about his pet, and immediately upon arrival cabled: "Be sure to feed parrot." The next day he received the following cable: "Have fed him, but he's hungry again. What shall I do now?"

7

Mother frowned as the little boy reached for the pie plate. "Why do you always reach for the largest piece of pie, Sammy?" she reproved. "Don't you think your big brother ought to have it?" "I should say not," declared Sammy as he scooped up the piece in question. "He was eatin' pie five years before I was born."

See also appetite[1], dying[1], face[2, 4], glutton[1], insects[2], manners[4], starve, thin[3].

ECHO

1

Two married men were visiting an art museum. They paused before a large painting of a beautiful female figure entitled "Echo." "I suppose the artist thinks it appropriate to show Echo as a woman because she always has the last word," mused one. "That might be," conceded the other, "but on the other hand, an echo speaks *only* when spoken to."

2

An American was visiting in the Alps, and a native, wishing to show off his country, took him to a certain spot, gave a loud cry, and waited. After about three minutes the echo came back clearly. "I guess you don't have anything like that in your country?" he said triumphantly. "Oh, I don't know," replied the American coolly. "At my summer place in the Rockies I just lean out the window before going to bed and yell, 'Hey, wake up!' and eight hours later the echo wakes me."

See also telephone[1].

ECONOMY

1

"Say, Bill," said one commuter to another as they met on the train. "Did you ever lay down the law to your wife about economizing like you said you were going to?" "Yes, I did it last week," was the response. "Well, did it bring any results?" asked the first. "I'll say it did," sighed Bill regretfully. "I've got to give up smoking and playing poker."

2

It was the day of the school picnic and father gave his son a dollar for spending money. "Now be careful with this, son," he cautioned, as he handed it over reluctantly, "and make it go as far as you can." "I sure will, dad," said the boy emphatically, "I'll make it go so far you'll never see any of it again."

3

It was the efficiency expert's first sea voyage, and a rough one. He was suffering. As he lay groaning in his bunk, his wife came in and asked, "Shall I have the steward bring you some lunch, John? It's all paid for, you know." "I've been thinking of that, dear," was the weak reply. "Suppose you just have him carry it up and throw it over the rail for me."

4

Smith was known throughout the neighborhood for his extreme thrift, so when he suddenly appeared in a complete new wardrobe it occasioned some surprise. "Why the glad rags?" asked one. "Haven't you heard the news?" grunted Smith sourly. "I've had triplets!" "But what's the connection?" asked the puzzled neighbor. "Humph!" snorted Smith. "What the heck good does it do to try to be economical?"

5

The man was surely dying and the doctor had given up hope, but his friend sat beside him trying to give him medicine. "It tastes terrible, Jack," objected the dying man weakly, "and there's no use in my taking it now." "But you must, my friend," insisted Jack through his tears. "You can't die and leave all this expensive medicine go to waste."

6

Hubby had been scolding the wife on her wastefulness. "You're not the least bit economical," he told her. "That's what you think," snapped the wife scornfully. "If a woman who saves her wedding dress for a possible second marriage isn't economical, I'd like to know what she is."

See also magazine[1], practice[1], stingy, thrift.

EDITOR

1

The female poet was provoked by the number of editorial restrictions on her work. "I don't see the point in insisting that I write on only one side of the paper," she pouted. "That, madam, is in the nature of a compromise," explained the editor. "Compromise? What do you mean?" inquired the poetess. "Well," replied the editor cynically, "if we could have our way you wouldn't be writing on either side."

2

"Is the editor in?" inquired the man of the office boy. "Guess he's around," said the boy. "Who wants to see him?" "Just a friend," stated the visitor. "Do you live in town?" questioned the boy dubiously. "No, I'm from out-of-town," was the reply. "Okay, I'll tell him you're here," said the boy in more friendly tones. "He says he ain't got no friends in this town."

3

The new girl reporter was very pretty. The editor invited her to lunch. "How did you enjoy it, dearie?" asked one of the office girls. "Oh, all right; but I'll never again go out to eat with an editor," was the firm response. "Why, did he make a pass atcha?" asked the girl. "Oh, no," said the pretty one, "but he blue-penciled about three-fourths of my order."

4

The Hollywood movie mogul was branching out and had bought a large newspaper. On his tour of inspection with the managing editor he spotted the exchange editor at his desk. "Who's that guy in the corner?" he asked. "He's the exchange editor," he was told. "Well, fire him," ordered the new owner. "All he ever does is sit there and read papers."

See also cannibal[1], publisher.

EDUCATION

1

The mountaineer took his young son to the schoolhouse to enter him in class. "What'll the boy larn here, ma'am?" asked pappy after the formalities had been completed. "Oh, we teach grammar, spelling, trigonometry, arithmetic, and the like," explained the teacher. "Waal, better give him lots o' thet there triggernometry," advised pappy, "on account o' he's the worst durned shot in the family."

2

Mother was entering her boy in school and was very anxious about his education. "I want Ronald to have a completely modern and up-to-date education, including Latin," insisted the mother. "To be sure, madam," said the principal, "though you know, of course, that Latin is a dead language." "That's quite all right," replied the lady. "Ronald's to be an undertaker."

3

The farm had been mortgaged and their life's savings had gone to give daughter a college education. Paw was driving the truck to the station to call for her after graduation. She climbed in beside him,

slipped an arm through his, and whispered, "I want to confess something, Paw: I ain't a virgin any more." Paw dropped his face in his hands and wept bitter tears. "After all the sacrifices Maw an' me made for your education," he sobbed, "you still say 'ain't.'"

See also answer[2], preparation[1], self-made[2], simple.

EFFICIENCY

1

The business magnate had been famous for his efficiency. At almost any time he could visit some department of his plant, look over the situation, and advise the foreman to lay off several men. Finally, he died and as his body was being carried from the funeral chapel, he rose up in his coffin and asked, "How many men are carrying me?" "Six, sir," someone answered. "Hm. Better lay off two," he ordered as he sank back again.

2

"What does your husband work at?" one woman asked of another. "He's an efficiency expert in a big office downtown," replied the other. "Efficiency expert? What are his duties?" was the next query. "It's hard to say exactly," explained the second woman, "but if we women did it, they'd call it nagging."

3

It was in the malarial district of Arkansas. A farmer's son one morning withdrew his knife with the fried egg still perched on it from his mouth, and announced with a weary sigh, "Pappy, m'chill's a-comin' on agin." "Be it?" said the farmer, rising hurriedly. "Waal, jest hold 'er back fer a bit till I git thet churn ready fer ye."

4

An important railroad bridge in the mountains had burned down, and the bridge-engineer's office had been ordered to replace it with all speed. Three days later the division superintendent alighted from his private car and sought out the foreman on the job. "This bridge must go up in a hurry, George, as every hour is costing us money," he declared. "Got the engineer's plans, yet?" "Don't know if the picture's drawed yet or not," replied the old fellow, "but the bridge is done up and trains is goin' over it."

See also brief[5], system.

EGG

1

The speaker was stressing the logic of cause and effect. "We all know," he pointed out, "that you can't get eggs without hens, and that—" "My pop kin," interrupted a small voice from the rear. "Nonsense!" declared the speaker. "How could he?" "He keeps ducks," replied the boyish voice.

2

"How much are eggs today?" inquired a woman of the storekeeper. "Sixty cents a dozen, madam," was the reply. "What!" exclaimed the woman. "Why, that's a nickel for each egg!" "I know, madam," agreed the storekeeper. "But don't forget that an egg is a whole day's work for a hen."

3

The political speaker had not been well received in the last town. "No more had I arisen to speak," he related, "than someone threw a base, cowardly egg which hit me on the forehead." "What in the world kind of egg is that?" inquired a listener. "A base, cowardly egg," explained the victim, "is an egg that hits you and runs."

4

"My goodness, but these eggs are small," complained the young bride to the grocer. "That may be," conceded the grocer, "but they came directly from the farm this morning." "I suppose it's all the fault of the greedy farmers," fumed the bride, "who're so eager to sell their eggs that they take them out of the nest too soon."

5

A romantically inclined bachelor was breakfasting in a restaurant on a soft-boiled egg which he noted bore the inscription: "Should some young man see this who wishes to marry a pretty farmer's daughter of 19, write to . . ." The bachelor promptly wrote, and a few days later received a note saying: "Sorry, but your offer came too late. I have been twice married, once divorced, and have five children."

6

"And are these good eggs?" queried the customer dubiously of the grocer. "Why, madam, these are some of the best eggs we've had for years," was the enthusiastic reply. "That's quite possible," declared the customer, "but I'd like some that you haven't had for so long."

7

The ragged, hungry-looking man

who entered the lunchroom counted his change carefully, then ordered two eggs. "How d'ya want 'em cooked?" asked the counterman. "Is there any difference in price?" inquired the customer cautiously. "Nope, same price any way you take 'em," was the reply. "Good!" cried the man eagerly. "Then I'd like them cooked with a slice of ham."

See also waitress[3].

EGOTISM

See conceit, pessimist[1], sarcasm[4, 6].

ELECTION

1

The politician burst into the living room excitedly. "Congratulate me, dear," he cried to his wife, "I've just won the nomination." The wife looked up in surprise and responded, "Have you, honestly?" The politician frowned. "Now, why in heck do you have to bring up that point?" he demanded.

2

The political candidate was being interviewed. "And what will you do if you're elected?" he was asked. The politician's mind had been wandering a bit, and the question startled him into sudden honesty. "Good gracious!" he exclaimed, "what in the world will I do if I'm not?"

3

A member of the losing party was grumbling to one of the opposing side. "Your mayor simply stole that last election," he accused. "He did no such thing," defended the other.

"But everyone knows he did," insisted the first. "Well, it's a lie," was the indignant response. "He paid spot cash for it."

4

It was the morning after election and two party workers were talking it over. "That election was crooked," declared one. "Why, when I went into the voting booth I saw Bill and Slim stuffing the ballot box." "I was with you and didn't see anything," objected the other. "Oh, that was the first time," was the explanation. "I saw them when I went in to vote the third time."

5

The village storekeeper had recently been elected mayor and the traveling salesman was congratulating him. "I suppose your victory was due to the fact that you've always dealt fairly with your customers?" he observed. "Could be that," admitted the mayor, "but I think it was more because I was the only one a-runnin'."

6

An election was held in a town noted for its many breweries. One of the issues was local option, and at the end of the day the poll attendants were counting results. "Wet, wet, wet, wet, wet. . . ." one was calling off from the ballots, then paused and cried in amazement, "Good night! Here's one 'Dry'!" Then he continued, "Wet, wet, wet . . . when his eyes opened yet wider. "Well, I'll be . . ." he gasped. "That son-of-a-gun repeated!"

7

The defeated candidate was gloomy and a friend was trying to cheer him up. "I just *can't* understand it," declared the friend. "I thought this election would be a walkover." "It was," replied the ex-candidate morosely, "and I was the doorstep."

See also counting[2], politics[8].

ELECTRICITY

1

A self-made man was being modest at a party for the benefit of a pretty young thing. "I sometimes feel that in my struggle for success I have permitted myself to remain too ignorant of modern science," he observed. "For example, there's the electric light—I haven't the slightest idea of how it works." The girl gave him a pitying smile. "It's really quite simple," she explained, "you just snap a switch, and there's the light."

2

Returning home from work one evening, an electrician was met by his small son who had one hand bandaged. "What happened, son?" he queried. "Did you cut your hand?" "Oh, no, pop," said the boy. "I just happened to pick up a pretty fuzzy little fly, and one end of it wasn't insulated."

3

The student in the science class had been dozing and inattentive, so the professor suddenly asked him, "Mr. Smith, will you tell us what electricity is?" Smith squirmed and ah'd for a bit, then said, "I did know, professor, but I'm afraid I've forgotten." The professor heaved a heavy sigh, then said, "What a loss to science! You are the only man who ever lived who knew what electricity is, Mr. Smith, and you had to forget."

4

The family had moved to another town and the father was taking the boy to school to enroll him. As they entered the building they saw some electricians at work. "What are those men doing?" inquired the boy. "Putting in an electric switch," replied father. The boy turned to leave. "Then, I quit," he declared. "I won't put up with any school where they do their licking by electricity."

See also lightning[1].

ELEGANCE

The lady who had just moved into a new neighborhood was attending her first meeting of the local sewing circle. "And what does your husband do, Mrs. Brown?" she was asked. "He's manager of a pail factory," replied the new member. "Pail factory?" queried the other. "I didn't know we had one. Where is it?" "Well, my husband calls it a bucket shop," answered Mrs. Brown, "but I think pail factory sounds much more elegant."

ELEPHANT

1

Teacher was examining the pupils in natural history. "Now, Georgie," she said, "you tell me where the elephant is found." Georgie pondered and squirmed for a moment, then his face cleared. "Well, teacher," he replied, "the elephant is such a big animal that it's hardly ever lost."

2

In traveling through the country, a small circus was overtaken by a violent storm which wrecked some of the cages. A few of the animals escaped. Early next morning the policeman of a nearby village got a phone call. "Come out here at once," demanded an excited woman's voice. "There's a huge animal of some sort out in my garden a-pullin' up my cabbages with his tail." "There is?" said the policeman. "What's he doin' with 'em?" "Humph!" snorted the woman. "You wouldn't believe me if I told you."

See also clumsy, grief[1], zoo[1].

ELEVATOR

1

A little girl had been with mother on a shopping tour in a large store and had had her first ride on an elevator. "How did you like the elevator?" her father asked her that evening. "Oh, all right, but it's the funniest thing you ever saw," replied the little girl. "You just get into a small house with other people and the upstairs comes down to you."

2

A real estate man, with offices high up in a skyscraper, had an appointment with a farmer who was long overdue. At last the man arrived, an hour late, panting and breathless. "Sorry I'm late," gasped the farmer, "but it's a long climb up fifty flights of stairs." "Why in the world didn't you take the elevator?" inquired the businessman. "I shore wanted to," replied

the farmer, "but I jest missed the durned thing."

3

Two well-liquored gentlemen wandered into a dance hall and asked for the cloakroom. They were told to take the second door to the left and go down two steps. But the first took the second door to the right, stepped into the elevator shaft, and fell three stories to the basement. The second drunk stuck his head in the door and called, "Hey, wha'cha doin' there?" "Hanging up m'hat," came the faint response. "But watch that first step—it's a lulu."

See also imitation[4], necessity[3], reading[4], skyscraper[1].

ELOPEMENT

1

It was midnight and, as prearranged, the romantic young lover climbed the ladder and rapped at his fair lady's window. As she raised the window cautiously, he inquired, "Are you ready, dear?" "Ssh! Be quiet!" she whispered. "Do you want father to catch us?" "Oh, don't worry about that," said the boy. "He's down there holding the ladder."

2

The young couple had eloped and had now been married for some months, when the husband one day met a friend on the street. "That was quite an elopement you two pulled," commented the friend. "But what about her father—did he ever catch you?" "I'll say he did," was the gloomy reply, "and the old boy is still living with us."

ELOQUENCE

1

Whatever might be said against the way the cruel father treated his family, he was dead now and the family hired a famous orator to conduct the funeral oration. As the speaker warmed to his subject, he said, "O noble spirit! We hail and acclaim thee as you start your glorious journey to the regions of eternal truth and light . . ." The widow, standing to one side, nudged her son and said, "George, go over and see if that's your father who is in the coffin."

2

The young preacher was dwelling eloquently upon the selfishness of certain men who spent all their evenings away from home in pursuit of pleasure. "Just picture, my friends," he said in a shaking voice, "the poor neglected wife sitting alone in the gloomy house, rocking the cradle of her sleeping infant with one foot while she wipes away her tears with the other!"

EMERGENCY

1

The doctor's phone rang and when he answered it a man's voice spoke urgently, "Please come quickly, doctor, my little boy just swallowed my fountain pen." "Of course, I'll be right there," replied the doctor hastily. "But what are you doing in the meanwhile?" "Oh, I'm getting along," was the answer, "I'm using a pencil."

2

Junior had been pleading to drive the family car, so father was examining him on his presence of mind in an emergency. "And what would you do if the brakes on the car failed?" he questioned. "Pick out something cheap to hit," was Junior's prompt reply.

3

A man's servant habitually indulged in sprees on which he spent all his money. His employer finally gave him a talk on the necessity of saving for a rainy day, and the man promised to do better. About two weeks later the master asked, "Well, Simpkins, have you profited by my talk?" "Oh, yes, very much, sir," replied the servant, "but it happened that it rained all day yesterday, sir, and my money's all gone again."

See also fainting[2].

EMOTION

A woman's husband had gone off alone for a weekend again, and a neighbor was comforting her. "You must miss him a great deal," she observed. "Well, I just can't think of him without a choking sensation," said the wife. "My, my," said the other sympathetically. "Yes," continued the wife savagely, "every time I think of him I want to choke him!"

See also luggage[1], musician[1].

EMPTY

"Mamma, I've got a stomach-ache," complained a little girl. "That's just because your stomach's empty, dear," explained mother. "You'll feel better after lunch when you get something in it." That afternoon the minister called and in the course of the conversation he observed that he'd had a headache all day. "Oh, that's just 'cause it's empty," spoke up the girl. "You'd feel better if you had something in it."

ENCOURAGEMENT

1

"How are you getting along with your courting of that widow?" asked a man of a bachelor friend. "Has she given you any encouragement?" "She certainly has," replied the bachelor. "Why, last night she even asked me if I snored."

2

The ardent lover was not at all pleased with the progress he was making. "I sometimes feel that it's all so hopeless," he sighed to his girl friend. "If only you'd give me the least encouragement I would—" "Goodness!" interrupted the girl callously, "I've certainly given you the least I ever gave any man."

See also courtship[2], pull[1].

END

1

The beggar became impudent when he was refused alms and the old gentleman was angry. "I can tell you one thing for certain," he cried, pointing his cane at him, "that there's a scoundrel at the end of this stick." "Oh, yeah?" retorted the beggar sneeringly. "And which end do you mean?"

2

A tourist's pedigreed bulldog had viciously attacked a farmer in a field. The farmer defended himself with a pitchfork and ended by killing the dog. "Did you have to kill him?" demanded the distressed owner. "Why didn't you use the other end of the fork and just beat him off?" "I would have done that," replied the farmer firmly, "if your dog had also come at me with the other end."

3

Two slightly tipsy men were at a dog show and stopped before an exceptionally woolly Skye terrier. They regarded the dog and were puzzled. Then one asked, "Which end is the head of that thing, Bill?" "I'm switched if I know," replied Bill, shaking his head. "Here, I'll just stick a pin in it and you watch to see which end barks."

See also teacher[4].

ENEMY

The young minister was talking to an aged member of his flock on the beauties of brotherly love, and the old man proudly announced, "Well, Reverend, I'll be 95 next month and I can truthfully say that I haven't an enemy in the world." "That's a great credit to you, sir," approved the preacher. "How did you manage it?" "Simply enough," was the reply. "I just outlived 'em all."

ENERGETIC

1

The lady of the house was a very energetic worker, but this morning she was quite discouraged and said to her maid, "Just look, Mary, here it is Monday morning again, and tomorrow will be Tuesday, and after that will come Wednesday—and there's a good half of the week gone already and we don't have anything done yet!"

2

The boss called the ambitious young clerk to his office. "I've been watching you, Smith," he said, "and of all my employees you are by far the most hard-working, the most interested in your work, and watch the clock least." "Yes, sir?" responded Smith with eager expectation. "So I'm afraid I'll have to fire you," continued the boss, "as it's young men like you that learn here and then go out and start rival businesses."

3

The self-made man was detailing the secret of his business success at great length to an acquaintance. "The reason that I never miss," he explained pompously, "is that I throw myself into everything I do." "I see," replied the other wearily. "Now, why don't you go out and dig a very deep well?"

4

A prosperous tourist stopped at a little crossroads filling station down South tended by a boy who was reclining in the shade. "Here, boy, get going! I want some gas!" demanded the motorist. "Get some push about you! Push is what got me where I am." "Well, mister," said the boy without moving, "reckon as how you'll have to push some more, 'cause we ain't got a speck o' gas in the place."

See also early[1].

ENGAGEMENT

1

He had just asked her and she had coyly accepted. After their first kiss she grew thoughtful for a moment, then asked, "Tell me, dearest, am I the only girl—" "Now please don't ask me if you're the only girl I've ever loved, sweet," he interrupted. "You certainly must know that—" "No, no!" she interposed. "I was only going to ask you if I was the only girl who'd have you."

2

Uncle was horrified when his nephew told him of his latest engagement. "That makes six girls you're now engaged to!" he exploded. "Just how do you explain this, young man?" "Oh, I don't know, uncle," replied the nephew vaguely, "unless maybe it's because Cupid shot at me with a machine gun."

3

It was a summer-resort engagement and the young man had heard rumors that led him to ask the girl, "Is it a fact, dear, that since you've been here you've become engaged to Sam, Bill, Dan, John, and George, as well as to me?" "And what's it to you if I have?" retorted the girl haughtily. "Oh, nothing," replied the boy amiably, "except that if it's true I thought we could all chip in together on a ring."

See also acquaintance[4], ring[1, 3], twins[1].

ENOUGH

1

A young man was seeking advice of a sour old bachelor. "Don't you think," he inquired, "that after a fellow's bought a girl flowers and candy, taken her to dinner, a show, and dancing afterward, and brought her home in a taxi, she ought to let him kiss her good night?" "Humph! I don't know," snorted the old boy grumpily. "It seems to me that he's already done more than enough for her."

2

Junior was passing his plate for his fourth helping of pie when mother cautioned him, "Be careful, dear, there once was a boy who ate too much pie and burst." Junior thought a moment, then replied, "Couldn't be. No such thing as too much pie." "But there must be," reasoned mother, "else why did the boy burst?" Junior passed his plate again and announced, "Just not enough boy."

ENTERTAINMENT

"How are you and the folks getting along in your new place?" asked a friend of Mr. Newlyrich. "Did you entertain much during the social season?" "Well, that's a matter of opinion," said the self-made man. "My wife and daughters didn't think so much of me as an entertainer, but I overheard some of the company sayin' that I was the most amusin' guy that ever crashed a party."

ERROR

See mistake, wrong.

ESCAPE

The nephew was prodding his old rake of an uncle for some of his experiences. "Go on, Uncle Bill, and tell me about some of the narrow escapes you've had from women," he pleaded. "Listen, m'boy," responded uncle with a lewd cackle, "you can bet that if there were any narrow escapes the women had 'em."

ESKIMO

An Arctic explorer encountered an Eskimo who appeared worried. "What's the matter?" he asked. "Hunting no good?" "Not that," replied the Eskimo. "Wife says I must match piece dress goods for her." "Well, that shouldn't be hard," comforted the explorer. "Huh! Says you!" grunted the Eskimo. "Wants me to match polar bearskin dress she's wearing."

ETHICS

1

The merchant's son looked up puzzled from his schoolbook. "Papa," he queried, "what do they mean by ethics?" "Well, son, I'll explain," answered the merchant. "Suppose a customer comes into the store, buys a lot of goods, puts down ten dollars too much, and leaves. Now ethics is: should I or shouldn't I tell my partner about that ten?"

2

The professional-looking gentleman approached the reporter at the scene of the accident. "By the way," he said, offering his card, "you might mention that the victim was expertly attended by Dr. Smith, with offices in the Front Building, or some such thing." "Oh, yes," said the reporter, "you're right next to Dr. Brown, aren't you?" "Yes," was the disdainful reply, "but we ethical doctors do not recognize him —he advertises."

3

"Man's code of ethics puzzles me," remarked one young lady to another. "Puzzles you? In what way?" queried the other. "Well," was the reply, "they think nothing of taking another man's last dollar on any cock-and-bull story, but regard it as an unforgivable breach of honor to take his last cigarette."

ETIQUETTE

See chivalry, manners, polite.

EVIDENCE

1

Bill's wife was suing for divorce. She was telling the court horrible tales of brutal beatings and almost unbelievable cruelty. Finally, the judge turned to Bill and inquired sternly, "And what do you have to say to this, my man?" Bill waved the evidence aside. "You can't believe a word of it, judge," he declared. "She's punch-drunk."

2

"Shall I leave a light in the hall for the master, ma'am?" asked the maid as she was about to retire. "No, don't," replied the mistress. "I know he won't be home before daylight because he kissed me good-by when he left and gave me twenty-five dollars for a new hat."

See also clothes[8], guilt[4], jury[1].

EVOLUTION

1

The family was sitting quietly in the living room. Junior looked up from his schoolbooks. "Mamma," he said, "Teacher was talking today about something she called evolution. Is it true that I'm descended from monkeys?" Mother cast a look in father's direction. "I really can't say, son," she replied. "I haven't seen your father's people."

2

The Sunday-school teacher was relating the Biblical story of the creation of man, when little Willie interrupted to remark, "But my father says we are descended from the apes." Teacher impatiently replied, "Your private family matters are of no concern to me or the class."

3

The married couple had quarreled, and now they sat quietly, not speaking. The husband, trying to smooth matters over, looked up from his paper to remark, "I see here that they have more proof that we all sprang from monkeys." "Well, don't be so proud about it," retorted the wife, "you certainly didn't spring very far."

EXAGGERATION

1

The little boy ran excitedly into the house. "Mamma, mamma!" he cried, "a truck just went by that was bigger'n a house!" "There you go again, Johnny, with your exaggerating," reproved mother. "I've told you a hundred billion times not to exaggerate, but it just doesn't seem to do any good."

2

Little Georgie came running breathlessly into the house. "Oh, mother!" he panted, "there's about a thousand big dogs fightin' out in our yard." "Now, now," cautioned mother, "how many dogs?" "Well, maybe it's five hundred dogs," conceded Georgie. "How many dogs?" pursued mother. "All right," agreed the boy, disheartened, "there was our dog, the Smith's dog, and that big black dog from down the block —and I won't come down another single dog."

3

The lady was looking over some field glasses. "Are you certain this is a high-powered pair?" she inquired of the salesman. "Madam," was the suave assurance she received, "if you should look at anything less than ten miles away with those glasses it will appear to be behind you."

EXAMINATION

1

Just before the Christmas holidays the professor gave an examination, one question of which was: "Where did life originate?" In answer to this, one of the students wrote: "God knows! I don't. Merry Christmas!" When this paper was returned it bore the notation: "God gets 100. You get zero. Happy New Year!"

2

The examination in economic geography carried a question which read: "State the tonnage of coal shipped from the United States in any given year." A struggling student knit his brows long over this one, but finally his expression cleared and he wrote in a firm hand: "1492—none."

3

The examination period was ended and the professor rapped for attention. "Now, gentlemen," he requested, "you'll kindly pass your papers all to the aisle, and may I request the man there to insert a piece of carbon paper beneath each sheet so that I can correct all the papers at once."

4

It was the last lecture of the semester. The professor was going over some things with the class before the final examination. "I advise you all to study well in the meantime," he urged. "The examination papers are already at the printer's. Now, are there any questions?" There was a short silence, broken by a plaintive voice from the rear asking, "Who's the printer?"

5

The professor was correcting the examination papers when he came across one which bore none of the statements, figures, or other data in answer to the questions. Instead it had only a sketch of a grave and tombstone with an inscription reading: "Sacred to the memory of the memory which always dies a sudden death on these occasions."

6

The examination was proceeding quietly and the professor was working on a set of questions for the next class. He wrinkled his brow, then looked over the classroom and said, "Would one of you gentlemen who isn't using his textbook for the moment be so kind as to lend it to me for a few minutes?"

7

It was an examination in com-

EXAMPLE   158   EXCUSE

position, and the students had been told to write a brief but fully descriptive account of a baseball game. All the students were busily writing on this, except one. He sat chewing his pencil until just before time to turn in the papers, when he suddenly got to work and wrote: "Rain —no game."

8

Two farmers were discussing their boys' progress in school. "However'd your boy manage to pass those examinations, Si?" asked one, "they were sure tough." "Don't know," replied Si, "but I reckon it must've been when nobody was lookin'."

See also answer[3], grades[3], professor[3], question[3], shaving[3], sweating.

EXAMPLE

1

"Hiram," the farmer said to the hired man, "I'd shore appreciate it if you'd eat off by yourself instead of at the same table with the summer boarders." "Humph!" snorted Hiram. "And why ain't I good enough to eat with them?" "Oh, it ain't that," explained the farmer. "You're plenty good enough—it's jest that your appetite sets them such a terrible example."

2

"I'd like to bring Bill home to dinner tonight," said the married man to his wife. "To dinner tonight!" screamed the wife. "You idiot, you know that cook's just left, I've got a cold, baby's cutting his teeth, the furnace is broken, and the butcher won't give us any more meat until we pay up, and—" "I

know," he interrupted quietly. "That's why I want to bring him. I like Bill, and the young fool's thinking of getting married."

See also crowd[2].

EXCITEMENT

Father was visiting his son in college and to entertain him the boy took him to a football game. "Well, dad," he declared, as they got into their seats, "you're about to see more excitement for two dollars than you ever did before." "Oh, I don't know, son," grunted the father. "Two dollars is all I paid for the license to marry your mother."

See also coffee[2].

EXCUSE

1

It was the wee hours when the son came home, but father was waiting for him. "What's the meaning of your getting home at such an hour?" he thundered. The boy was nonplussed, but soon had a happy thought. "Oh, I meant to tell you, dad, but forgot," he explained. "I was sitting up with the sick son of that sick man you are always telling mother you were sitting up with."

2

The Commanding Officer shook his head as the soldier ended his request. "Look, Johnson," he objected, "you've already had leave to help your wife move, to go to your mother-in-law's funeral, to be at your boy's christening, and to be with your little girl when she had her tonsils out. What reason have you now?" "Well, sir," replied the soldier calmly, "it's just that I wanted to get married."

3

A businessman in St. Louis received a wire from an associate to meet him in Chicago. Remembering some unfulfilled obligations, the man wired back: "Sorry can't get there. Washout on line." Shortly the St. Louis man got another wire saying: "Don't let little thing like that stop you. Buy a new shirt and come on."

4

Little Billy had been playing hookey frequently and his teacher said, "The next time you're absent, Billy, you'll have to bring an excuse from your father." "Oh, but I don't want to do that," objected Billy. "Why not?" asked teacher. "Because mother says father isn't any good at making excuses," explained the boy.

See also clock[3], dentist[2], drunk[2], hangover[3], hint[11], indispensable[1], repay[1], rude[1], stenographer[4], truckdriver[2].

EXERCISE

1

The drill officer was putting a group of soldiers through some exercises during which he ordered them to lie on their backs, raise their legs, and then to move them as if riding a bicycle. He noticed one man holding his legs motionless, and shouted at him, "Hey, Brown! What's the idea of stopping?" "Oh, I'm just coasting down a hill," replied Brown.

2

A group of soldiers in line were being given some exercises. "All right," commanded the sergeant, "everybody raise his left leg and hold it out at right angles from the body." One rookie got confused and raised his left leg instead, and the sergeant, looking down the line, saw two legs out together. "Hey, there!" he shouted. "Who's that raising both legs?"

3

"Yes," commented Smith to a neighbor, "the doctor said that both the wife and I need exercise, so I bought myself a set of golf clubs." "But what did you get your wife?" inquired the neighbor. "Oh," replied Smith, "I bought her a lawn mower and a set of washtubs."

4

The man with arthritis was describing his sufferings to a friend. "My worst pain," he declared, "is when I bend over, put my hands down below my knees, then straighten up and bring them up above my waist." "Well, why take such silly exercises then?" observed the friend. "Exercise, my eye!" he cried. "I have to do that to get my pants on."

5

"Calisthenics is the secret of health, dad," a young girl just home from college stated enthusiastically. "Look! To develop the arms and shoulders I have only to take this wand at either end, hold it vertically before me, and swing the lower end rhythmically from side to side." "Well, what won't science discover next!" marveled father. "Why, if that wand had straw at the lower end, you'd be sweeping."

6

An elderly lady was visiting an army camp. She saw a line of soldiers first squatting on their heels, then rising again to a standing position. "What are those men doing?" she asked her guide. "Oh, they're going through their setting-up exercises," was the explanation. "Humph!" observed the lady. "Looks more to me like setting-down exercises."

See also muscle.

EXPECT

1

As the boyfriend reached the girl's house he was met by her little brother. "Hello, Johnny," he said cheerily, "is your sister expecting me?" "She sure is," he responded. "She is? How do you know?" asked the swain. "Because she hurried up and went out," stated little brother.

2

The butler was new in the house. He stopped the gentleman caller firmly at the door to ask, "Is Mrs. Smythe expecting you, sir?" "Look, my good man," explained the caller impatiently, "Mrs. Smythe was expecting me before I was born—she's my mother."

3

The small-town child had been taken to New York for her first visit there. On her return a neighbor asked her about the trip. "And I suppose you found the city much bigger than you expected?" observed the lady brightly. "Oh, no," replied the child, "on account of I went there expecting to find it lots bigger'n I expected."

EXPENSE

1

The young wife was boasting of her family. "And you can depend upon it that when father gives you something it's always something expensive," she stated. "Yes, I know," agreed the husband glumly. "I discovered that when he gave me you."

2

The preacher paused in his sermon to catch his breath and a deacon behind him leaned forward to whisper, "Don't forget that you were going to say something about the rising cost of living." "I know, I know," replied the parson under his breath, "but I won't speak of that until after the collection has been taken up."

3

The judge had passed sentence on the prisoner for stealing. He was now giving him a bit of advice. "Always remember," he said ponderously, "that if you wish to succeed in the world you must keep straight. Do you understand?" "I'm afraid not," replied the prisoner, "unless Your Honor can tell me how a man is going to keep straight when he's trying to make both ends meet."

See also daughter[2], face[5], hotel[4], necessity[1], vacation[2].

EXPERIENCE

1

An artist was watching a fishmonger draw a fish in chalk on the pavement before his stall, and he asked, "What kind of fish is that?" "A shark," replied the man, looking up. "But you've never seen a shark, have you?" objected the artist. "That's right," agreed the man on his knees, "but don't some of you artist fellows draw angels, and green shadows, and things like that?"

2

A man had long been a sufferer from asthma, so he tried a new doctor. "I've tried a lot of doctors and none could help me," explained the patient, "so my friend insisted I see you. I suppose you've had a great deal of experience with this ailment?" "Indeed I have," declared the doctor. "Why, I've had it myself for the past twenty years."

3

Baby pulled his five-year-old brother's hair so hard that the boy yelled in pain. "There, there," soothed mother, "baby doesn't know how it hurts." A short while later mother heard the frantic howling of baby. "Gracious, what's wrong with him?" asked mother. "Nothing's wrong," replied the boy, "'ceptin' now he knows how it hurts."

4

The old man had been in ill health for years and was always changing doctors. One day he called on a young doctor, described his ailments, and declared that he had symptoms of heart trouble. "Oh, not necessarily," said the young doctor. The old man frowned. "It's hardly fitting," he observed, "for a young doctor just out of college to disagree with an old experienced invalid like me."

5

The woman-driver had struck a pedestrian and was arguing with him. "If you hadn't been walking so carelessly I'm sure this wouldn't have happened," she declared. "I'm a careful and experienced driver and have been driving a car for six years." "That may be, madam," conceded the man, brushing himself off, "but as for me, I've been walking for fifty-seven years."

See also marriage[12], newspaper[5], reporter[1].

EXPERT

1

A little boy sat on the curb crying. A passer-by stopped to ask what was wrong. "My pop just gave me a lickin'," sobbed the boy. "Well, you must take it in good spirit," said the man. "All fathers must punish their sons at times." "Yeah, but my pop ain't like other kids' fathers," sniffled the lad. "He plays bass drum in a band."

2

The doctor finished examining the sick man and shook his head. "I'm sorry, but I'm afraid I can't offer you much hope for his recovery," he told the man's wife. The patient protested weakly, "Here, here! What're you talking about? I ain't gonna kick the bucket." "Now, now, be quiet, dear," said the wife soothingly. "The doctor knows best."

EXPLANATION

1

Mr. Newlyrich was describing his South American trip to a fellow racketeer. "We came around a bend in the river," he related, "and there was a whole bunch of gladiators swimming around." "No, no," corrected the other, "you mean navigators—something like crocodiles." "Well, then, what *are* gladiators?" questioned the first. "Oh, they're some sort of flower that grows up from bulbs," was the reply.

2

The city machine had put the politician in as mayor, but hadn't taught him manners. At a public function, he rudely cut in front of another man, brushing him aside and stepping on his toes. "Well," said the man, very much annoyed, "you might at least excuse yourself." "Who, me? I'll have you know I'm the mayor," was the pompous response. "Ah, I see," replied the man. "That certainly is hardly an apology, but it *is* a complete explanation."

See also poetry[2].

EXPLOSION

1

It was about 2:30 in the morning when Smith was suddenly awakened by a tremendous uproar in the Browns' house next door. Meeting Brown the next morning, he asked, "Say, what was the cause of that big explosion in your house last night?" Brown grinned and replied, "Just a little powder on my coat sleeve."

2

A gas leak had developed in a barber shop overnight. When the barber opened up next morning and struck a match to light the heater, there was a terrific explosion and the barber landed in the street. A passer-by rushed up to help him, and inquired, "Hurt much, Sam?" The barber gazed into his now burning shop and shook his head. "Nope, ain't hurt none," he replied, "but I sure got out just in time."

3

A visitor approached a stone quarry shortly after there had been an accidental explosion and inquired, "Is Bill here?" "He was, but he's gone," replied one of the workmen. "For good?" asked the visitor. "Well, sir, he was headin' in that direction when last I saw him," was the reply.

4

John was rather careless with the dynamite in the quarry and let a stick drop. The whole box went up, taking John with it. A short time later the foreman came by and asked, "Where's John?" "He's gone," answered a fellow-worker. "When'll he be back?" queried the foreman. "Well, sir," responded the other, "if he comes back as fast as he left, he'll be back day before yesterday."

5

There had been a bad explosion in the powder mill and the manager was investigating. "What caused it?" he asked the foreman. "One of the men went into the mixing-room," was the answer, "and he must've forgot himself and struck a match." "Struck a match!" exclaimed the amazed manager. "I'd think that would be the last thing on earth he'd do." "It was, sir," said the foreman.

See also spots[1].

EXPOSURE

A bum knocked at the door of a house. When the woman appeared, he announced sadly, "Lady, I'm dying from exposure." "How very interesting," observed the woman. "Are you a tramp, politician, financier, or bathing beauty?"

EYES

1

The proofreader was telling a friend about the terrific strain his eyes were subject to. "It's so bad," he said, "that I don't open my evening paper until I get home and into a dark room." "What! You read the paper in the dark?" asked the friend. "Sure. It rests my eyes," was the reply. "But how can you see the print?" continued the friend. "I can't," said the proofreader. "That's how it rests my eyes."

2

An old man, a heavy drinker, was having trouble with his eyes and went to an oculist. "You're going blind because of your drinking," announced the doctor after examining him. "Either stop drinking or lose your eyesight—it's up to you to choose." The man was silent for a moment, then replied, "Well, doctor, I'm quite an old man now and I've been thinking that I've just about seen everything worth seeing."

See also accurate[3], spots[2].

FACE

1

Little brother stood staring at sister's boyfriend until he grew embarrassed. "Is there anything wrong?" he asked the youngster. "No," replied the boy. "I was just wondering if your face hurt much." "Of course not, Willie, what made you think so?" said the boyfriend. "Oh, I heard Sis tell Mom that you were painfully homely," answered the little fellow.

2

"Johnny," said teacher sternly, "you ought to wash your face before coming to school in the morning. Why, I can see what you had for breakfast this morning." "You can? What was it?" asked Johnny. "You had eggs," was the reply. "Oh, no, teacher, you're wrong," retorted Johnny. "The eggs were yesterday morning."

3

The middle-aged lady shook her head dubiously. "I'm not sure that I care for these photos," she declared. "The face seems rather indistinct on them." "That might well be, madam," admitted the photographer shrewdly, "but you must remember that your face is not at all plain."

4

"Broke again," announced a young man, "and all because of my girlfriend. I've put a fortune into her face." "You have?" said a friend. "In expensive beauty treatments, or have you been paying for a plastic operation?" "Neither one," sighed the young man. "I've just been feeding her in swanky restaurants."

5

The flashily-dressed matron went to the plastic surgeon. "And what will the face-lifting operation cost, doctor?" she asked. "My fee will be five thousand dollars, madam," said the specialist. "Why, that's ridiculous!" exclaimed the woman. "Isn't there something less expensive I could try?" "You might try wearing a veil," suggested the surgeon.

See also absence[4], America[3], clean[1], cosmetics[3], mask, teacher[4], ugly.

FACTS OF LIFE

1

The soldier had returned after a long period overseas shortly before his wedding. He had scarcely seen his bride before the ceremony. Therefore, when the time for the kiss arrived, it was a long and lingering one. A sympathetic hush prevailed throughout the church until it was broken by a clear childish voice asking, "Mummy, is he spreading the pollen on the bride now?"

2

The little girl was puzzled as to her origin. "How'd I get here, mummy?" she inquired. "God sent you, dear," answered mother, using the well-worn evasion. "And did God send you, too, mummy?" was the next question. "Yes, dear," said mother. "And grandma and great-grandma, too?" Again the answer was yes. The child shook her head dubiously. "Then you mean to tell me, mummy, that there have been no sex relations in this family for over 200 years?"

3

Father felt that the time had come to tell his young son some of the simple truths of biology. So after much internal struggle, he one eve-

ning called the boy into the living room and closed the door. After some evasion and hesitation, he said, "My boy, I'd like to discuss some of the facts of life with you." "Why, fine, dad," replied the boy calmly. "Just what is it you'd like to know?"

See also cause[2].

FAIL

1

Two self-made men were discussing their lack of formal education and their success in spite of it. "Yes," said the one, "I left school before I was ten. I got discouraged and quit because I failed in everything except geography." "How come you didn't fail in that?" asked the other. "Because I didn't take geography," replied the first.

2

The businessman was trying to teach his son some of the fundamentals of shrewd business. "Look, John," he instructed, "you can figure it like this: Two bankruptcies just about equal one failure, two failures equal one good fire, two fires . . ." "Papa," interrupted John, whose mind had been wandering, "is marriage a failure?" Papa considered a moment, then declared, "If the woman's got money, son, marriage is almost as good as a failure."

See also business[2].

FAINTING

1

A man rushed excitedly into the smoking-car of a train. "A lady has just fainted in the next car," he cried. "Has anybody got any whisky?" Immediately several flasks were brought out. He seized the nearest one, tilted it back, took a drink, and returned it, saying, "Thanks a lot. It always did make me feel sick to see a lady faint."

2

A naval hospital orderly was up for advancement in rating and he was being examined by a medical officer. "Suppose the captain fainted on the bridge," asked the officer, "what would you do?" "I'd bring him to," answered the orderly. "And then what would you do?" was the next question. "Why, I'd bring him two more," was the reply.

See also first aid[1].

FAITH

1

The sick man was an unwilling patient. "I may as well tell you, doctor," he warned, "that I come to you only because my family insisted. Personally, I haven't any faith in medical science." "That's quite all right," replied the doctor smoothly. "You know, the mule has no faith in the veterinary surgeon, but he nevertheless cures the ailing animal."

2

The managing editor of the tabloid paced the floor in distress. "Good Heavens, Jim," he groaned to the city editor, "what're we going to do for our front page? Nothing scandalous has happened in town for almost twenty-four hours!" "Take it easy, Bill," comforted the other. "Something'll happen. Be like me and have more faith in human nature."

See also watch[4].

FAITHFUL

1

"Anything unusual happen at lodge meeting last night, John?" asked the wife at breakfast. "Well, the boys were talking about being true to one's wife," replied John. "The president offered a red robe to any man who could stand up and truthfully say he'd never kissed any woman but his wife during his married life—and do you know, not a man stood up." "Why didn't you stand, John?" demanded his wife. "Well, ah, you see," stammered John, "you know I look like hell in red."

2

The young man had just proposed to the broker's daughter, but she was undecided. "Will you be true to me?" she questioned. "I'll be true as steel," he declared ardently. "Common or preferred?" she asked.

3

The dying man was trying desperately to say something, and his friend bent over to catch the last feeble words. "I know I'm dying," the poor fellow gasped, "so after I'm gone—I want you—to go to Mabel—tell her—I died with her—name on my lips. Then go to— Susie—and Margie—and Tillie— and tell them the same thing."

See also widower[1].

FALL

1

The little boy caught his toe and went sprawling on the pavement. "Upsa-daisy," cried a dear old lady brightly who chanced to be nearby. "Upsa-daisy, hell," said the little fellow, rubbing his knee, "I'm hurt."

2

A judge was leaving his bench when his foot slipped and he bumped heavily down several steps and landed on the floor. "I hope Your Honor is not hurt," cried a clerk solicitously, running up. "My honor is quite intact," the judge assured him, rubbing his rear, "but my seat is damnably bruised."

3

"Gee, mom, there's a crazy man across the street," cried the little boy, running into the house. "What makes you think he's crazy, son?" asked mother. "He must be," declared the boy. "He's sittin' there on the sidewalk talkin' to a banana peel."

4

A man slipped at the top of a long flight of stairs leading to a subway station and started sliding down. About midway he upset a lady who fell backwards into his lap and finished the trip with him. Reaching the bottom, the woman was too dazed to get up. Somewhat embarrassed, the man spoke up politely, "Madam, would you mind getting off now? This is as far as I go."

See also accident[4], hanging[3], optimist[1], sarcasm[10], sin[3].

FAME

1

The author was describing some of the troubles of his career to a friend. "To make a long story short," he summed up, "it took me twelve years of work to discover that I had absolutely no talent for writing." "What a pity!" said the friend. "Then you gave it up, I suppose?" "Oh, dear, no," replied the popular author. "By that time I was much too famous."

2

He had left town broke ten years before. Now he was coming home, a successful businessman. He expected something of a welcome from the townsfolk, but the station platform was empty when his train pulled in. Disappointed, he sought out the stationmaster, a boyhood friend, and was about to greet him heartily when the man asked, "What you doin' at the station, Sam; goin' some place?"

3

The fond mother took her young hopeful into the fortune-teller's booth to have his future told. The seeress looked into her crystal, then took a good look at the boy. "Your son will be very famous, madam," she predicted, "if only he lives long enough." "He will?" said the delighted mother. "And what will he be famous for?" "His old age," was the reply.

See also author[6], future[1].

FAMILIAR

1

The lawyer was examining the witness in court. "Have you ever been arrested or in court before?" he demanded. "No, sir," replied the witness vehemently. "Humph! Are you sure?" questioned the lawyer dubiously. "Your face certainly looks familiar; I've seen it some place before." "That's quite possible," agreed the witness. "I'm the bartender in the saloon across the street."

2

The tailor was up before the judge for a traffic violation. "Haven't I seen you somewhere before, my man?" asked the judge suspiciously. "That may be, Your Honor," conceded the tailor, "but so many men owe me money that I can't remember all their faces."

3

The rabid golfer was eating a late dinner and talking with his wife as she served him. "Junior was telling me that he caddied for you this afternoon," she informed him. Junior's father pondered a moment, then his expression cleared. "That explains it," he cried. "You know, I thought that I'd seen that boy somewhere before."

See also widow.

FAMILY

1

The family quarreled a great deal, and the maidservant finally gave notice that she was leaving. The mistress was much upset, as the girl was a good worker. "Why, Mary, what's wrong?" she questioned. "Haven't we always treated you like one of the family?" "That you have, mum," agreed Mary grimly, "and I've stood all of it that I can."

2

Some men were boasting of the size of their families. One came from a family of twelve, another from one of fourteen. "Well," declared a man who hadn't been heard from, "there were ten of us boys in my family and each of us had a sister." "Whew!" exclaimed one. "Guess you win. So you had twenty in your family?" "Oh, no," was the grinning reply. "Just eleven."

See also ancestors[2], evolution[1, 2], support[8].

FAMILY TREE

1

"I've got a little job I'm dreading," remarked a genealogist to a friend. "Rich Mrs. Williams engaged me to look up her family tree and I find that one of her forebears was electrocuted for murder." "Aw, don't let that bother you," comforted the friend. "Just describe the man as 'having occupied the chair of applied electricity at one of our large public institutions.'"

2

Several men were bragging about their family tree. After listening quietly for a while, one gentleman spoke up modestly, "My family is quite old, too. I can't say just how far back it runs, but its history is detailed in seven large volumes, and along toward the end of the fourth volume there is a footnote stating: 'At about this time the world was created.'"

3

The college boy had been in a series of escapades and the dean had called him to his office and was scolding him. Finally the student said in self-defense, "I'll have you know, sir, that our family tree is second to none." "The tree may be all right," retorted the dean, "but the crop is certainly a failure."

See also ancestors[1], breeding[1], recruit[2].

FAREWELL

1

The boy was very proud of his French, so when he left the girlfriend he said, "Au revoir, my sweet." "I don't get it," declared the matter-of-fact girl. "Oh, that's just good-by in French," explained the boy. "Well, carbolic acid," said the girl. "What's that?" queried the fellow. "That's good-by in any language."

2

Smith was famous for the yearly birthday party he gave at which liquor was served without limit. Bill was one of the guests who never failed to take full advantage of it. Therefore, it was quite surprising to see Bill, before the party was half over, going around bidding everyone a fond farewell. "You're not going yet?" cried the host. "The party's just begun." "Heck, no," replied Bill vehemently. "I'm just tellin' everybody good-by while I still know 'em."

See also good night[1], sermon[8].

FARM

1

The city visitor looked over the New England farm and shook his head. "I've never seen such a poor farm," he announced. "Nothing but rocks, rocks everywhere. I don't see how you make a living." "Humph! I ain't as poor as you might think," retorted the farmer. "At least I don't own this durned farm."

2

The doctor was examining the pupils in a little country school. He finished with a thin, peaked little fellow and asked, "Don't you drink much milk, sonny?" "Don't drink none," answered the boy. "What!" exclaimed the doctor. "You live on a farm and don't drink any milk?" "Nope," said the boy. "Ain't hardly got 'nuff fer the hogs."

See also summer boarder[1].

FARMER

1

The city man was frank about his ignorance of farming. "Just what's the difference between these theoretical and practical farmers that I'm hearing about?" "Waal," replied the old weather-beaten farmer, "a theoretical farmer is a fool what insists on tryin' to make a living by farmin' the place, while a practical farmer is got sense enough to take in summer-boarders and start a hot-dog stand."

2

The city man said enviously to the farmer, "You certainly have a cinch —all your own eggs, milk, butter, meat and vegetables. Plenty to eat and a place to sleep—what more could you want?" "Sure, I know," agreed the farmer, "but you jest come 'round about nine or ten months from now and you'll see the sleekest, fattest, nakedest farmer you ever did see."

3

The city folks had spent Sunday in the country and their car was filled with plunder—the farmer's fruit, flowers, vegetables, etc. Pointing to a diverging road, the driver asked of the farmer, "Could I take this road back to town?" "You might as well," snorted the farmer sarcastically. "You took about everything else."

4

The city man had made money and moved his family to the country. He was to become a "gentleman farmer." But they were still conscious of their high position. A neighboring farm woman, trying to be friendly, asked the daughter, "Are your hens laying any eggs?" "They can, of course," replied the girl haughtily. "But in our position, you know, they don't really have to."

5

"Is this your farm?" asked a tourist of a middle-aged farmer. "Nope, it's pappy's," replied the man. "Pappy's ninety, was born here and bin here all his life." "Ninety?" exclaimed the tourist. "How is his health?" "Was sound all his life, but he's bin ailin' last few months," was the answer. "What seems to be the trouble?" questioned the tourist. "Dunno," said the farmer. "Sometimes I git to thinkin' that farmin' don't agree with 'im."

See also complaint[5], crops, driver[6], heat[2], meals[1], misfortune[1], shrewd[1], skyscraper[2].

FARMING

1

A farmer was delivering produce to an insane asylum when one of the inmates approached him and said, "Say, I used to be a farmer, too." "Is that so?" replied the farmer soothingly. "Yep," declared the other. "Say, friend, did you ever try bein' crazy?" "No, I never did," responded the farmer, moving away nervously. "Well, you oughta try it," called the ex-farmer. "It's got farmin' beat all hollow."

2

A farmer's wife was in court testifying for her son. "You say your son worked on a farm all his life?" questioned the lawyer. "Ever since he was born," stated the woman. "Hm. And what did he do the first year of his life?" was the lawyer's sly question. "He milked," replied the mother.

3

A high-pressure salesman was traveling through the country selling a ten-volume set on scientific agriculture. He tried to sell one to an old farmer. The old fellow paged through the books and said, "Nope, don't want 'em." "But you ought to have them," insisted the salesman. "They'll teach you to farm twice as well as you do now." "Hell, son," snorted the farmer, "I don't farm half as good now as I know how."

4

The farmer's son was staying with his city aunt and was attending school in town. "Now, John," the teacher asked him, "if a farmer has 6,000 bushels of corn and corn is bringing 35 cents a bushel, what will the farmer get?" "A government loan," replied the farm boy promptly.

5

The tourist was looking over the farmer's offerings at his roadside stand. "Farm produce certainly costs more than it used to," remarked the city man. "That's right," agreed the farmer. "You see, we just used to raise crops, but now we've got to know the botanical name for what we're raisin', the entomological name of the bug that eats it, and the chemical name of what kills it, and somebody's got to pay."

6

"How's crops this year?" asked the city motorist of the farmer. "Waal, so-so," replied the farmer reflectively. "The hot-dog stand an' the fillin' station has fell off a bit lately, but they're a-gonna hold 'Othello' over fer another week in my barn."

See also ability[2, 3], crops[1], early[2, 3], fruit[1], garden[1], help[5], opportunity[2], Providence, work[5].

FASHION

The author had struggled for years but at last his work was being recognized and one after another of his books were best sellers. "Now, my dear," he sighed happily to his wife, "I can afford to buy you some decent clothes." "You'll do nothing of the sort," she snapped. "I want the same kind that other women are wearing."

See also feet[2].

FASHIONABLE

An elderly physician called on a young doctor. "I wish you'd look after my office while I'm on vacation," he asked the younger man. "I'd certainly like to, doctor," said the boy, "but I'm barely out of college and have no experience." "Tut, tut, my boy," the veteran reassured him. "My practice is strictly fashionable. Just tell the men to play more golf and advise the women to take a long trip somewhere."

See also church[10], garbage, sick[2].

FAST

See speed.

FAT

1

"How does it happen, George," a man asked a stout friend, "that you fat fellows are always so good-natured?" "We have to be in self-protection," responded the pudgy one. "You see, we can't fight and we can't run."

2

A fat lady was trying to board a streetcar, but she couldn't manage it. A male passenger watching her, suddenly burst out laughing. This annoyed the woman very much. "If you were half a man you'd help me on." "And if you, madam," retorted the man, "were half a woman, you wouldn't need any help."

3

A stout woman was trying to get on a bus, but the narrow door wouldn't accommodate her. "Why not try sideways, madam?" suggested the driver. "Because I ain't got no sideways," she snapped.

4

The man was exceptionally stout. He approached a weighing machine that bore the sign: "I speak your weight," stepped on the platform, and dropped a coin in the slot. At once, a groan issued from the machine and a voice requested, "One at a time, please."

5

"How does your father look?" asked one schoolboy of another. "Why, he's so fat," replied the other, "that when he stands there in his shorts he looks like a bureau." "A bureau, how do you mean?" questioned the first. "Oh, just a big thing with drawers," was the reply.

See also polite[4], thin[1].

FATHER

1

"Oh, Willie," cried mother in exasperation, "will you please be a good boy?" "I'll be good for a penny, mom," offered the brat. "Oh, dear," sighed mother, "why can't you be like your father? He's good for nothing."

2

Chancing by the nursery, the wife noticed her husband standing by the crib of his sleeping son in rapt contemplation. Silently she watched him for a while, wondering what thoughts raced through his mind as he looked at his own flesh and blood. At last she tenderly slipped her arm through his and asked, "What are you thinking of, John?" "Huh?" he came to with a start. "Oh, I was just wondering how the heck they can make a crib like that for three ninety-eight!"

3

Little Mary was observing, for the first time, a mother cat carrying one of her kittens by the scruff of the neck. She was horrified by what she thought was such rough treatment. "Shame, Tabby," she scolded. "You ain't fit to be a mother. Why, you ain't hardly fit to be a father!"

4

It was the first day of school and teacher asked one of the little girls what her father's name was. "Daddy," replied the little girl brightly. "No, no," said teacher. "I mean his name. What does your mother call him?" "She don't call him nuffin," retorted the child. "She likes him."

5

A Protestant clergyman was walking down the street dressed in ministerial black when he met two Catholic boys. One of the boys drawing conclusions from the garb, raised his hat and said, "Good morning, Father." The other boy nudged him and whispered, "Quiet, stupid, he ain't no father; he's got a wife and three kids."

6

Father was easy-going with the children and mother had to discipline them. But now mother was sick and the children were getting out of hand, so father found it necessary to correct his little daughter. "Behave yourself at once, Joan," he ordered sternly, "or I'll take you from the table and punish you." But

Joan only giggled behind her hand and snickered, "Gee, Billy, listen to father trying to talk like mother."

7

The man had been so busy with his work that he'd given no time to his family. One night, however, he consented to stay in with the children while mother went out. "Did you have any trouble?" she asked him next morning. "No," he replied proudly, "except with that little red-headed girl. I had to lick her before she'd go to bed." "Heavens!" gasped the wife. "That's the little girl from across the street!"

See also artist[4], elopement[2], excuse[4], greeting, ignore, intelligence[1], proverb[2], revenge[1], son[5], teacher[1, 2], weather.

FATHER-IN-LAW

1

She waited nervously on the porch while her sweetheart went into father's den to ask for her hand. He came out looking a bit dazed. "What did he say?" inquired the girl eagerly. "He asked me how I was fixed for money, and I told him I had $3,500 in the bank," replied the boy. "What did he say to that?" the girl wanted to know. "Nothing," answered the boy. "He just borrowed it."

2

The young wife was showing a friend her house and other possessions, including a gleaming roadster. "That's a nice car," commented the friend. "I suppose your father got it for you?" "Indeed not!" protested the bride indignantly. "William would never accept such a thing. All dad does is pay the rent, the household expenses, and my clothing bill."

See also expense[1].

FAULT

See blame, defect, guilt.

FAVOR

1

A man entered a store and looked about. "Have you seen my dog?" he asked the storekeeper. "Have I!" exploded the grocer. "He ran in here, upset a pickle barrel, bit me in the leg, tripped a customer into an egg crate, and ran out with half a ham." "My, my, is that so?" said the man calmly. "I wonder if you'd do me a favor and put this 'Lost' sign in your window?"

2

The stranger's clothing was worn, but gratitude shone in his face as he entered the man's office. "You did me a favor ten years ago, and I've never forgotten it," he stated. "Is that so?" said his benefactor expectantly. "And now you've come back to repay me?" "Well, no," replied the stranger. "I've just hit town and I need another favor, so I thought of you at once."

FEAR

1

The couple had been to a party and the husband had drunk more than his share. On the way home he started to abuse his wife, beginning with slighting remarks, then slapping her, and finally punching her vigorously. At this stage the frightened woman began to shout, "Help! Help!" The man stopped punching long enough to pat her on the shoulder and say, "Don't be frightened, dear, I'm with you."

2

Father was giving his easily-frightened little daughter a talk on being brave. After he finished, the girl asked, "But ain't you 'fraid o' cows an' horses?" "Of course not," asserted father. "An' ain't you 'fraid o' bees an' thunder'n'lightnin'," continued the child. "Most certainly not," was the reply. "Gee, pop," came the admiring observation, "guess you ain't 'fraid o' nothin' in the world but mamma."

See also deceive[3], wedding[7].

FEE

1

There was a famous surgeon who was known for both his outspokenness and his high fees. A rich businessman who needed a delicate operation consulted him and, asking what the price would be, was told the charge would be a thousand dollars. "But that's outrageous!" cried the rich man. "Then I suggest you go to Dr. Smith," said the surgeon. "His fee will be half of mine and you won't have to pay it— your heirs will."

2

A farmer was sued for $450 and he engaged the best lawyer in the county to defend him, and won his case. Going to town with his wife later, he left the woman outside while he went into the lawyer's office. "What do I owe you?" he asked. "Well," said the lawyer,

"seein' that I know you since you were a boy and knew your pappy, I guess $400 will be about right." The dazed farmer went out to his wife. "Cracky!" he gasped. "I'm durned glad he didn't know grandpappy, too."

3

A man was giving evidence in a lawsuit and the defendant's lawyer asked him, "Didn't you tell the defendant that you would testify for him if he would pay you better?" "That I did," admitted the man. "And let me ask you, wouldn't you be on the other side yourself if they'd offered you a bigger fee?"

4

The lawyer was talking. "I'll always remember the case when I had the least chance of getting a fee," he related. "A client came to me and his only possession was a watch without any works in it." The other, who knew the lawyer well, said, "So I suppose you took the case?"

5

The boy looked up from a book he was reading. "What's a retainer, pop?" he asked. "Oh, that's money you pay a lawyer before he does any work for you," explained the father. The boy pondered this a moment, then said, "I see. It's like the quarter you put in the gas meter before you get any gas."

See also advice[2], dentist[4], lawsuit[6], singer[2].

FEELING

1

"You'd better wear your gloves if you're going out; it's chilly," a young man cautioned his roommate. "Oh, I never wear gloves when I go to see my girl," declared the other. "You don't? Why not?" he was asked. "Because I feel better without them," he answered.

2

Hubby came home from the office shaking his head. "I'm beginning to feel my new stenographer—" he began. "What's that!" exclaimed wifey sharply. "I was just about to say," he repeated patiently, "that I'm beginning to feel my new stenographer will have to go."

3

Two Southern gentlemen who had spent a convivial evening together, met on the street at about 10 o'clock the next morning. "An' how do you-all feel this mawnin', Cunnel?" inquired the one politely. "Ah feel like the very devil, Cunnel," roared the other genially, "just as any Suthen gentleman should at this ungodly hour of the mawnin', suh."

4

The little boy came to mother with a doleful face. "I don't feel good, mamma," he announced. "That's a pity, dear," said mother kindly. "Where do you feel worst?" "In school, mamma," replied the boy.

5

It was at dinner that the décolleté young lady let out a cry. "My necklace just came loose and slithered down the back of my dress, and it tickles," she explained to the young man next to her. "Would you mind getting it for me?" The young man started fishing, but as the necklace continued to elude him he grew embarrassed. "I feel a perfect ass," he confessed. "Never mind your compliments," she retorted. "Get that necklace!"

6

Two drivers were comparing experiences. "I've never had a bad accident," stated one, "but I imagine it must give you a terrible feeling to run over a man." "Well, if it's a real large man," declared the other, "it does give you a pretty bad jolt."

See also children[3], hash[3].

FEET

1

Two women were quarreling and one said, "Well, all I can say is that I'd certainly hate to be in your shoes." "Don't let that worry you, dearie," retorted the other, "you could never get into them."

2

The shoe clerk was trying his best to sell a gentleman a certain pair of shoes. "But these shoes are too narrow and too pointed," objected the customer. "But they're all wearing narrow, pointed shoes this season," the clerk informed him. "Maybe so," conceded the man, "but I'm still wearing last season's feet."

3

Extensive repairs had been completed and the woman once more had the house clean and tidy, when the carpenter called. "I'd like to look around to be sure everything's all right," he told the woman. "Very well," said the housewife, then thinking of her clean floors, "but are your feet dirty?" "Well, yes, ma'am," admitted the carpenter, "but I've got my shoes on."

4

An elegant, domineering lady boarded a crowded bus and, taking her stand by a tired workman, began loudly airing her views to a companion about men who didn't give women their seats. Finally, the workman touched her arm and asked, "Madam, would you mind getting off my foot?" "Why don't you put your big foot where it belongs," she snarled. "Just don't tempt me, madam," replied the man grimly, "don't tempt me."

See also dirty[4], tough[1], wealth[3].

FENCE

The lawyer grinned as he felt he had the witness cornered. "Now, you say that this fence between you and the accident was eight feet high and you were standing on the ground?" he asked. "That's right," said the witness. "Then perhaps you'll explain," continued the lawyer triumphantly, "how you, a man barely five feet tall, could see what happened on the other side?" "There was a hole in the fence," responded the witness calmly.

FERTILIZER

1

A farmer was driving by an insane asylum with a load of fertilizer when one of the inmates hailed him from the wall to ask, "Hey, there! What're you gonna do with all that fertilizer?" "Take it home and put it on my strawberries," explained the farmer. "Humph! We put cream and sugar on ours in

here," retorted the nut, "and still they say *we're* crazy!"

2

The city lady wrinkled her dainty nose in disgust. "Whatever is that awful odor coming from that field?" she asked the farmer. "That's fertilizer, ma'am," explained the farmer. "Oh, for the land's sake!" exclaimed the lady. "That's right, ma'am," replied the farmer.

See also growth[2].

FICKLE

The gentleman at the party sighed as he spoke to a guest who chanced to be beside him. "Women are certainly fickle," he observed. "See that pretty woman over by the palm? Well, she's been smiling and flirting with me for the past quarter-hour, but now she's cold as ice." "I didn't notice as I've just arrived," replied the other man, "but that woman is my wife."

See also change.

FIDELITY

See faithful, loyalty, unfaithful.

FIGHT

1

The boy had a fight and he'd gotten a black eye. He met the minister. "My, my," clucked the preacher in horror. "I'll return home, my boy, and pray that you may never fight again and that you may never get another black eye." "Shucks," retorted the boy scornfully, "you'd better go home and

FIGURE   176   FILLING STATION

pray for your own kid—I just gave him two black eyes."

2

The slightly-battered boy went in to see his father. "Pop, me an' Billy Brown had a fight today," he confessed. "I know," confirmed the father gravely. "Mr. Brown has already been to see me about it." The boy's face lighted with great excitement. "He has?" he cried. "Gee whiz, pop, I hope you made out as good as I did!"

3

The judge peered down sternly at the two disarrayed men. "This officer states that he found you two fighting in the middle of the street," he said accusingly. "Oh, no, Your Honor, the officer is mistaken," declared one of the men. "By the time he arrived we were trying to separate each other."

See also apology[4], boxing[1], identify[2], quarrel, separation[2], sportsmanship[1], word[5].

FIGURE

1

"George, dear," cried the wife when he returned home one evening, "I'm going to be in that amateur benefit show. I wonder what people will say when they see me in tights?" "They'll probably say that I married you for your money," grunted hubby.

2

A workman in a steel mill asked the manager for a day off to get married. "Why, certainly, John," agreed the boss, then asked, "what kind of a bride are you getting— tall, short, thin, or plump?" The bridegroom-to-be pondered, then answered gravely, "Well, I must admit that if I'd had the rollin' of her, I believe I would've given her three or four more passes."

See also chorus girl[1], fat, moron[1], reducing, thin.

FILLING STATION

1

The motorist had his gasoline and now was patiently enduring the filling station man's service routine. "Check the oil, sir?" "No, it's all right." "Water in the radiator?" "No, thanks." "Check your battery?" "It's in good shape." The attendant scratched his head and inquired, "Well, anything else at all, sir?" The weary motorist sighed, "You might stick out your tongue so I can seal this letter."

2

The helper rushed into the filling station. "Say, boss," he cried, "your doctor's out here with a flat tire." "Good!" exclaimed the boss gleefully. "Diagnose the trouble as puncture wounds resulting in prolapsus of the perimeter and prescribe plastic surgery followed by the administration of violent flatulents, and charge him accordingly. That's the way he does it."

3

"Papa," asked Junior as they drove away from the filling station, "what do they sell there besides gasoline?" "Besides!" growled father as he nursed his coughing motor along. "You mean 'instead of,' son."

See also America[2], energetic[4].

FINANCE

1

The big businessman was sneering at his struggling little competitor. "I don't know what your trouble is," he said disdainfully, "as there are thousands of ways to make money." "But only one honest way," declared the other. "Yes? And what way is that?" demanded the financier. "I didn't think you'd know," was the sly reply.

2

The financier had been in an auto accident and a piece of glass had penetrated deeply into his thigh. He was taken unconscious to a hospital where the doctors examined him. "We'll have to probe," decided one. The patient came to just in time to hear this, and with a groan he said, "If it's a surgical operation, go ahead; but if it's another congressional investigation, please give me an anesthetic."

FIND

The waiter in the swanky restaurant hovered over the customer. "And how did you find your steak, sir?" he inquired. "It was sheer luck," sighed the hungry man glumly. "I just happened to knock that little piece of potato aside, and here it was."

See also elephant[1], husband[4], mosquito[3].

FIRE

1

"Hey, there, your house is on fire!" cried a passing motorist to the Arkansas hillbilly reclining under a tree. "Done know it, stranger," replied the man without moving. "Well, why don't you do something about it?" demanded the motorist excitedly. "Doin' it now," declared the hillbilly. "Bin a-prayin' fer rain ever since she started."

2

One merchant met another in the street. "How'ya, Jack," he greeted him. "How was that fire in your store last week?" "Shush!" cautioned Jack in a nervous whisper. "It was next week."

3

The soft-spoken insurance adjuster was investigating a recent fire in the neighborhood and was interviewing a hard-of-hearing old fellow. "How does the consensus of neighborhood opinion run concerning the Jones' fire," he asked, "that it resulted from some natural cause or had an incendiary origin?" "Hey?" said the old boy. "He jest wants to know, paw," shouted the wife in his ear, "was the Jones' fire ketched or sot."

See also calm[2], delay[2], insurance[2], moron[5], opposite[3], pajamas[2], speeding[2].

FIREMAN

1

"How did you do on that examination?" asked one applicant for a position on the New York Fire Department of another. "I did all right except for that question: 'What piece of fire apparatus can't go up a one-way street?'" answered the other. "That stumped me." "Why that was easy," declared the first. "The answer is: 'A fireboat.'"

2

Two women watched the fire trucks go dashing by. "I can never see why they have a man steering from the rear of the ladder truck," said one whose husband had no car. "I suppose it's necessary," observed the other, whose husband did have a car, "but I must say that I don't feel that it's a man's work."

3

"I can easily understand," said a taxpayer to a fireman, "why you fellows rush like you do to get to a fire, but what I can't see is why you rush back from it in the same way." "Oh, that's so we don't forget what's trump," he explained.

4

The village fire brigade was suddenly called out one very dark night. When they reached the scene of the fire they found the building emitting dense clouds of smoke, but no trace of flame could be seen. The chief settled back and lit his pipe. "Better leave her burn a bit, boys," he ordered, "so's we kin see what we're doin'."

See also wife[5].

FIRST AID

1

It was examination time for the first aid class and one sweet young thing was asked, "What would you do, Miss Williams, if you found a man in a fainting condition?" "I'd give him a nice drink of brandy," replied the girl promptly. "And if you had no brandy?" continued the questioner. "Oh, then I'd promise him some," she said.

2

A woman had just got her certificate for the completion of her first aid course. On her way home she saw a man lying face down in the street. Amazed at the indifference of the passers-by, she flung herself upon the man and began applying artificial respiration. After awhile, the man raised his head and, in a patient voice, said, "Lady, I don't know what *you're* tryin' to do, but me, *I'm* tryin' to fish a wire down this manhole."

FISH

1

"What the heck *is* this leathery stuff?" demanded a diner of the waiter. "That, sir, is filet of sole," explained the waiter. "In that case you may take it away," ordered the diner, "and see if you can get me a nice tender piece from the upper part of the boot."

2

A drunk wandered into the Museum of Natural History and paused before a case containing a huge stuffed tarpon. He stared in unsteady amazement at this for a while, then shook his head. "The—hic—feller who caught that," he muttered, "is a—hic—liar!"

3

The woman shopping in the fish market turned up her nose disdainfully. "I certainly don't like the looks of that codfish," she told the man behind the counter. "Lady, if it's looks you want," retorted the man, "why don't you go buy a gold fish?"

4

The woman eyed the fish on th

platter critically. "Maggie," she demanded of the cook, "did you wash this fish carefully before baking it?" "Lordy, no, mum," was the amazed response. "Why wash a fish what's lived all its life in the water?"

5

"There's a boy at the door with a package, mum," announced the maid. "What is it, Mary?" inquired the mistress. "It's from the fish-market, mum, and it's marked C.O.D.," replied the maid. "Well, have him take it back at once," the lady commanded testily. "I distinctly ordered salmon."

See also fresh.

FISHING

1

A fisherman sat on the bank trying every trick he knew for over five hours without getting even a nibble. A woman and a small boy chanced by. "Oh, mister," the boy cried out, "lemme see you catch a fish!" The mother frowned and said to the angler, "Now, don't you catch a single fish for him until he says 'Please!' "

2

"Gosh, I forgot the bait!" said one fisherman to his companion. "What!" screamed the other. "Why, you thick-headed half-witted dumb-bell, how in blazes—" "Well, what was the matter with your remembering it?" said the first hotly. "You saw me put the can of worms down when—" "Oh, the worms," the other sighed in relief. "I thought you meant the bottle."

3

"Is there any fishing around here, sonny?" the sportsman asked the barefoot lad. "Some down at the creek," he answered. "What do you catch there?" the man wanted to know. "Oh, that's different," said the boy. "You said 'fishin',' not 'ketchin'.' "

4

All the villagers of the little resort town assured the visitor that the fish were biting like mad at a certain spot along the river. There he went, and after several fruitless hours he returned disheartened to his hotel. "Fish bitin'?" the desk clerk asked him. "They may be," replied the disappointed fisherman, "but if they are, they're biting each other."

5

The wife was checking over a pile of supplies on the kitchen table. "Let's see, John," she said, "do you have everything you'll need for your fishing trip tomorrow?" "Not by a jugful," he replied as he put on his hat and headed for town.

6

A man had been fishing in a pond for a while and the whole time he was there a local boy had been watching him from a distance. Finally, the lad approached and asked, "How many fish you ketch, mister." "None yet, sonny," replied the fisherman. "Well, you ain't doin' so bad," said the boy. "I know a feller who fished here fer two weeks an' he didn't get no more fish than you didn't get in only a half hour."

See also amount[2], catch[2], lucky[5], lunatic[3], Sunday[1, 3], swearing[2] truthful[2], weight[4].

FIX

See repair.

FLATTERY

The judge, about to pass sentence on the convicted thief, frowned severely upon the defendant and remarked, "This robbery was carried out in a clever and expert manner." The prisoner blushed and looked down shyly. "Oh, come now, Your Honor," he said coyly, "no flattery, please."

FLIES

The minister was dining with Johnny's family and was using the occasion to give the boy a little instruction. "Yes, Johnny," he stated, "everything in this world has a use. Now take flies, you wouldn't think they had a use but—" "Oh, I know what flies are good for," interrupted Johnny. "Pop says that they're the only thing that keeps him awake while you're preaching."

See also behavior[5], lazy[4].

FLIRT

1

The businessman's wife was complaining over the back fence to her neighbor. "I just can't trust my husband anywhere, he's such a flirt," she said. "I wouldn't worry," comforted the neighbor, "he's probably only reverting to type." "Oh, no," corrected the wife. "He's reverting to typists."

2

Just before the plate was passed, the minister addressed the congregation, saying, "There's a certain man in this gathering who is flirting with another man's wife, and unless he puts five dollars in the collection, his name will be read aloud next Sunday." When the collection was counted, twenty-one five-dollar bills were found in it and a two-dollar bill with a note pinned to it saying: "Will send other three on payday."

3

A middle-aged woman came up to a policeman and declared, "Officer, a man has been following me and flirting with me. I think he must be drunk." The cop scrutinized the woman for a moment. "Yes," he assented, "I think he must be!"

See also annoyance, fickle, worry[1].

FLORIDA

Two rabid Californians were at it again. "You sure couldn't pay me to live in Florida," said one. "They never have Christmas there." "No? How come?" asked the second. "Oh, haven't you seen those signs in the travel offices saying: 'It's always June in Miami'?"

FLOWERS

1

Mrs. Newlyrich had been attracted by some salvia she had seen in another's garden, and she was giving her own gardener directions for the planting of some. "Now this bed," she instructed, "I want you to plant completely in salvias. What do you think we ought to put in the next bed?" "Well, madam," replied the gardener, "it might be a good idea to put some spittoonias there."

2

The ardent horticulturist was showing a dear old lady some of the slips and seedlings he was nursing along. "That plant in the green pot," he explained, "belongs to the gardenia family." "I see," cooed the lady, "and you're minding it for them while they're away on a trip?"

3

A milling magnate was walking through a blooming woodland with a girl who found some new beauty to admire at every step. "One seems lovelier than the other," she cried. "What's your favorite flower?" The serious businessman considered a moment, then replied, "By and large, I believe I like whole-wheat best."

See also gift².

FOG

1

The fog was thick and the officer on the ship's bridge was very nervous. Suddenly, there was a momentary rift in the fog and dead ahead a short distance he saw a figure leaning over a rail. "Hey!" he bellowed. "Where you tryin' to take your ship? Don't you know the rules of the road?" "This ain't no ship, mister," came a voice. "This here's a lighthouse."

2

The fog was bad, so thick that the gentleman couldn't see his hand before his face. He was lost, and grew alarmed when he found himself in a slimy alley. Hearing footsteps approaching, he called out anxiously, "Where am I heading, please?" From the gloom a voice replied, "Into the river; I've only just come out."

3

Two much-traveled men were comparing notes. "London is by far the foggiest place in the world," declared one. "Oh, no," objected the other. "I've been in a place that's much foggier than London." "Yes? Where was that?" asked the first. "I haven't the slightest idea," confessed the second. "It was much too foggy to see."

See also London².

FOOD

1

A traveler was telling some of his experiences. "And finally," he said dramatically, "we came to the point where we ate our last dog." "Oh, how terrible!" shuddered the pretty young lady. "Yes, it was," admitted the sufferer, "for they had neither mustard nor relish to put on it, and it was at least twenty-five miles to the next stand."

2

Mother was trying out a new dish on the children, but her little daughter pushed her plate away, declaring, "I don't like it." "Oh, you mustn't say that," cautioned her brother, "'cause the more you don't like sumpin' the gooder it is for you."

3

Little Janie was visiting her aunt the day after Thanksgiving. She was offered some leftovers from the previous day and she refused. "But I thought you liked turkey, dear," said her aunt. "I do, but only when it's new," said Janie.

4

The captain burst into the mess-room while the crew were eating. "What's this complaining I hear about the food?" he demanded. "Here, let me try it." He dipped a spoon into a pot and sampled the contents. "Can't see anything wrong with that," he declared. "Seems like very good tea to me." "Yes, sir," ventured one sailor, "but they keep tellin' us it's soup."

5

It was the first lesson in the cooking class. The teacher was questioning her little pupils. "Who can tell me what a waffle is?" she asked. One little girl spoke up proudly, "I can, teacher; it's a pancake with a non-skid tread."

See also alphabet[3], army[5, 10], bet[1], bread[1], complaint[3], eating[5], hospital[2], meals[2], restaurant[8], sandwich[3], sick[3], tramp[2].

FOOL

1

They were quarreling again, and the husband said, "And you mean to say that several men proposed to you?" "That's right," replied the wife complacently. "Well, I wish you'd married the first fool who proposed to you," declared hubby. "Oh, but I did," she returned.

2

She was very pretty and he was a little bashful. "Are you married?" he asked timidly. "Of course not," she tossed her head. "I'm nobody's fool." "Oh, good," he cried, relieved. "Will you be mine, then?"

3

For the sermon, a preacher took for his text the quotation: "The fool hath said in his heart, there is no God." He later asked a member of the congregation how he'd liked it. "Well, sir," replied the man thoughtfully, "I thought the sermon was right good, but I can't say that I agree with you—I think that maybe there might be a God after all."

4

The Professor of Logic was becoming irritated with one of his dumb students, so one day he asked him, "How would you discover a fool, Brown?" "By the questions he'd ask," was the unexpected retort.

5

The judge peered down at the two men before him. "Did you really call this gentleman an old fool last night?" he demanded of one of them. The accused thought for a moment, took a long look at the other man, shrugged his shoulders, and answered. "Well, I really can't remember, Your Honor, but the more I look at him, the more likely it seems that I must have."

See also moron, speaker[1], suitor[3], thrift[2].

FOOLISH

The husband shook his head sadly over his wife's latest purchase. "It takes a woman to do foolish things," he observed. "That may be," conceded the wife, "but you never saw a woman buy a bottle of hair-restorer from a bald barber."

See also absent-minded, crazy, drunk, moron.

FOOTBALL

1

A man bought a couple of football tickets. He asked the agent, "Are those fifty-cent seats very far from the field?" "Oh, no, not so very far," replied the agent, "and in addition they're right across the street from a radio store that will have the game on their loud-speaker system."

2

Little Willie had been taken to see his first football game and the noise, cheering, and general excitement had impressed him. That night, as mother entered his room to hear his prayers, she saw him standing in bed swinging his arms from side to side and crying, "God bless papa! God bless mamma! God bless sister! Rah! Rah! Rah"

See also help[4], lose[2], Republicans[4], Western[2].

FORCE

The married couple were selling some property and they were at the lawyer's signing the papers. "Do you sign this deed of your own free will, madam?" asked the lawyer routinely, then added as the woman looked puzzled, "I mean, there's been no compulsion from your husband, has there?" "Who, him?" snorted the woman. "I'd just like to see the likes of him try to compulse *me!*"

FOREIGNER

1

The ladies' Kozy Kulture Klub was profoundly discussing world politics when the subject of the fiasco of the League of Nations was brought up. "Well, it might have been a good idea to start with," declared one woman, "but I knew it couldn't help being a failure when they went and let all those foreigners in it."

2

"Who was the first man, Billy?" asked the Sunday-school teacher. "It was George Washington," answered Billy promptly. "He was first in war, first in peace, an' first—" "No, no," corrected the teacher, "it was Adam, remember?" "Oh, that one," said Billy. "I didn't know you were gonna count foreigners."

3

A young American-born boy of an immigrant family informed his teacher one day, "If my father tries to whip me again, I'll run away." "But, Tony," objected the teacher, "your father has the right to punish you if you are bad." The boy threw back his head proudly. "I'm a citizen of the United States," he declared, "an' no dam' foreigner's gonna lick *me,* you bet!"

See also America[3, 7].

FORESIGHT

1

There was a picture to be hung and the butler stood waiting with the ladder and hammer. The master thought it should be hung on the north wall, the mistress on the east wall. The butler finally drove a nail where the master wished it, but when they'd left the room he drove another on the east wall. "There," he said to himself, "I won't have to bring this ladder up tomorrow again when he comes around to seeing it her way."

2

The muskrats were endangering the mill dam so the company hired old Sam to sit there all day and shoot them when he saw them. A friend paused to chat with Sam one day. "So the muskrats are undermining the dam?" he remarked. "That's right," agreed Sam. "Hey, there goes one now!" cried the friend, pointing. "Why don't you shoot?" Sam slowly spat before he replied, "Shoot, heck! Think I want to lose my job?"

3

The Queen was attending a children's pageant and as she passed one of the little flower-girls the tot put up a wee rosy mouth to be kissed. The Queen kissed her. Later, her mother scolded her. "What made you do such a thing, Anne," she cried. "Oh, I dest fought it'd be awful int'restin' to tell my gran'children," explained the little one sweetly.

See also tombstone[2].

FORGET

1

A lady came up to a famous man and offered her hand which he took politely. "Now confess," said the lady coyly, "that you've forgotten me entirely." The man searched his memory in vain. He bowed low and replied tactfully, "Of course, madam, as I have made it a major business of my life to try to forget you."

2

The jilted young man was dejected and a friend was trying to console him. "Don't worry about it, Jack," he advised. "You'll soon forget all about May and be happy again." "Oh, no, I won't," he insisted. "I bought her too many presents on time payments."

3

The minister announced that the time had come for the candidates for baptism to be presented at the font. At this, a woman in the congregation gasped and turned to her husband. "Oh, my!" she said in a distressed whisper. "I just knew we'd forget something. You run right home, George, and fetch the baby quickly."

4

The man had been telling the minister of his grievances against his hated neighbor. "No, no, my friend," reproved the minister sternly, "you must hold no hatred against your neighbor. If he does you an injury, you must forget it." "Oh, but I do forget it," insisted the man, "but my memory's so durned bad that I keep forgettin' that I forgot it."

5

The couple were on their vacation when the wife suddenly cried out, "Oh, John! I just remembered that I forgot to turn off the electric iron." "Don't worry, nothing'll burn," comforted John. "I just remembered that I forgot to turn off the shower-bath."

See also compromise[1].

FORGIVE

1

The Sunday-school teacher was speaking about forgiveness. "We must all learn to forgive those who harm us," she declared. "Do you think, Danny, that you could forgive a boy if he called you names and hit you?" "Well—I *think* I could," replied Danny, then added more positively, "I *know* I could if he was a lot bigger'n me."

2

An old employee asked the boss for a day off. "Why, certainly," he said. "What are you going to do with it?" "Reckon I'll go to my wife's funeral," was the drawling reply. "She up an' died t'other day." Two weeks later he asked for another day off. "What are you going to do this time?" asked the boss. "Reckon I'll get married," was the slow response. "What! So soon after burying your wife?" The old fellow smiled and explained, "Waal, you see I was never one to hold a grudge."

See also sin[1].

FORM

See figure, shape.

FORTUNATE

See lucky.

FORTUNE

See money, newlyrich, rich, wealth.

FORTUNE-TELLING

1

"Do you know anything about palmistry, Joe?" she asked the boy-friend. "Well," he replied, "just last night I happened to look at a man's hand. I at once predicted that he would shortly come into some money, and before the evening was over he was handed a tidy little sum." "And you were able to tell that from his hand?" she marveled. "Sure," he said. "You see, it had four aces in it."

2

A young man entered the palmist's room. "Madam," he began, "I've come to—" "Sit down, my boy," said the woman, seizing his hand. "I can see that you have known disappointment, that what you have striven for has escaped you, but your goal is now in sight. Success is assured." "Good!" cried the young man, bringing forth a paper. "I've come six times about this bill, and I'm glad to know that I'm going to get my money at last."

See also fame[3], restaurant[7].

FOUNTAIN PEN

1

"What do you consider your greatest discovery, sir?" asked an admiring young man of a famous scientist. "My greatest was made quite by accident," confessed the scientist. "I found that by keeping a bottle of ink handy at all times, one can use a fountain pen as easily as an ordinary pen, without all the mess and bother of filling it."

2

A man stood watching another writing with a fountain pen. "Wonder why they call 'em fountain pens?" said the onlooker. "I think 'reservoir-pen' would be better, because a reservoir contains liquids while a fountain throws 'em around." The writer crumpled up his sheet of paper and reached for another. "The fountain pen," he declared grimly, "is correctly named."

See also emergency[1].

FRANK

1

The tourist out West was defending the virtues of the Easterners. "Perhaps we're not as strong and healthy as you," he conceded, "but we do always call a spade a spade." "Thet's a right good idee, stranger," approved a cowboy. "There wuz a feller shot in a game here just last week fer tryin' to call a spade a club."

2

The wife came home quite pleased with herself. "Well, I was certainly outspoken at the Club today," she informed her husband. "You were, my dear?" said hubby in amazement. "Who in the world outspoke you?"

3

Mabel had on a new dress and was eagerly fishing for compliments from her best friend. "I know I look a perfect fright in this, don't I?" she asked coyly. But the friend's mind was elsewhere, and she answered in absent-minded agreement, "Yes, dear, you certainly do." "Oh, you horrid creature!" cried Mabel. "Never speak to me again!"

4

The woman who was getting on in years, said to a friend, "Mae is certainly careless with her talk.

Why, yesterday she told me that I was a hopeless old maid." "That was certainly being frank," said the friend. "Yes, and in very bad taste," added the first. "It was rude," agreed the friend, "but at that it's better than having her going around telling lies about you."

See also club[2], kiss[2], wrong[1].

FRATERNITY

1

"You say that the water here at the fraternity house is unsafe to drink?" asked the visitor. "That's right," said one of the boys. "Well, what precautions do you take with it?" queried the stranger. "First we filter it," replied the loafer, "then we boil it, and then we chlorinate it." "Yes?" prompted the visitor. "Then we throw it away and drink beer."

2

He held her tenderly in his arms as he inquired, "Darling, am I the first man you've ever loved?" "Yes, my sweet," she cooed. "All the rest were fraternity boys."

See also brother[3].

FREEDOM

1

"Why did the Puritans come to this country?" questioned a history professor of one of his students. "So that they would be free to worship in their own way," was the reply, "and make other people do the same."

2

The loud-mouthed man had been

thundering his opinions on different subjects for over an hour. One of his involuntary listeners at last cried, "Aw, pipe down!" "Sir!" said the speaker with great dignity, "I believe in free speech!" "Well, so do I," admitted the other, "but sometimes it kinda reminds me of the old free lunch where you hated to see a man make a pig of himself just because it was free."

See also talk[8].

FRESH

The woman shopper in the fish market looked at the fish being offered her. "Are you sure it's fresh?" she asked the dealer. "Fresh, did you say, lady!" he cried indignantly. "Why, this fish breathed its last just as you walked in the door." The woman wrinkled her nose. "And what a breath it had!" she snapped as she walked out.

See also egg[6], small.

FRIEND

The little boy stood leaning against a tree. He was the picture of dejected loneliness, his hands in his pockets and digging his toe in the earth. "Don't you have anyone to play with, little boy?" asked a kindly woman. The boy shook his head as he replied, "Well, ma'am, I've got one friend—but I hate him."

See also desertion[1], editor[2].

FRIENDSHIP

1

A man met an animal trainer on the street and asked him how he was doing. "I've got a swell act now in the circus," the trainer informed him. "It's a 'Friendship of the Lion and the Lamb' act." "Sounds good," admitted the man, "but aren't there quarrels between them?" "Well, yes, they do have their little quarrels at times," conceded the circus man, "but then we just buy a new lamb."

2

The very poor man had died and the rich, stingy old Squire was deeply affected. "You must have thought a great deal of him," observed one of the townspeople. "Indeed I did; I held him in high esteem," replied the Squire. "Never had a man a truer friend. Why, to the day of his death he never asked me to lend him a cent, though I knew full well he was starving to death."

FRIGHT

The army was holding maneuvers and some visitors were out to watch. Suddenly a number of rifles were fired and a pretty girl gave a little shriek and stumbled backwards into the arms of a young man. "Oh, pardon me," she said blushingly, "the rifles frightened me." "It's quite all right," said the young man as he took her arm. "Let's go over and watch the heavy artillery."

FRUIT

1

The young man, just out of agricultural college, shook his head disapprovingly as he informed an old, grizzled farmer, "Your methods of farming are entirely out-of-date. Why, I'd be surprised if you got as much as fifteen pounds of apples from that tree there." "So would I, sonny," replied the farmer dryly. "That there's a peach tree."

2

The little city girl was interested in Nature. "What do the li'l birdies eat, mamma?" she asked. "Oh, fruit," replied mother vaguely from behind her book. The girl considered this for a moment, then inquired further, "But how do they get the cans open?"

3

The fruit dealer was trying to help out the young bride. "Any limes, pomegranates, or honeydews?" he suggested. "No, thank you," said the young wife. "I've got some fine alligator pears," he persisted. "Oh, you silly!" giggled the bride. "We don't even keep a goldfish."

4

"I'd like a dozen limes, please," asked a man of a girl clerk at a large store. The girl looked puzzled, disappeared in the back, and returned with twelve lima beans. "No, no," said the customer, "I want limes. They're a fruit. Green lemons." The girl drew herself up with dignity and, with touching loyalty to the firm, declared, "Sorry, sir, we handle nothing but ripe lemons."

5

The doctor arrived to find his patient in tears. "There, there, cheer up, old fellow," he said encouragingly. "We'll pull you through all right." "It's not that, doc," sobbed the man. "I've just been thinking of all the money I've wasted buying apples to keep you away."

See also tree³.

FUN

1

An old maid was very fond of her faithful she-cat, and before she left on a cruise, she instructed her sister, "Now feed Tabby well, and whatever you do, *don't* let her out nights!" After a few weeks, the sister received a card, reading: "Having more darned fun. Met a peach of a man on the boat. . . . P.S.: Let the cat out tonight."

2

Cousin Billy, who was nine, came to visit Sammy, who was eleven. "Go out and play with Sammy and his friends, Billy," said Sammy's mother, "and be sure to have lots of fun." When the boys returned some time later, Sammy looked very happy, but Billy was decidedly downcast. "Did you have lots of fun?" mother inquired. "I'll say!" replied Sammy. "But Billy looks unhappy," objected mother. "Well, you see," explained Sammy, "the rest of us had our fun with Billy."

See also limit.

FUNERAL

1

The florist was away when the phone rang, so the new assistant took and filled the order. "Be sure the wreath is large," came the order, "and put on a wide ribbon with 'Rest In Peace' on both sides, and if there is room, 'We Shall Meet In Heaven.'" When the wreath arrived it caused quite a flurry, for there on a wide ribbon was the inscription: "Rest in peace on both sides, and, if there is room, we shall meet in heaven."

2

A veteran reporter had served long at fire headquarters and had become quite a favorite with the firemen. When he died the men raised some money for a floral offering and gave it to a florist with instructions that he work up something appropriate. When the offering arrived it proved to be a huge fire badge made entirely of flowers and bearing in red carnations the inscription: "Admit within fire lines."

3

The tired man sat in the barber's chair. The barber began a cheery conversation. "I just got back from a funeral," he informed the customer brightly as he lathered away. The victim sputtered half a mugful of soap out of his mouth and responded wearily, "You certainly ought to be glad to get back—there are a great many who never do."

4

"Your friend Brown is burying his fourth wife today, isn't he?" asked Mrs. Smith of her husband. "Aren't you going to the funeral?" "Nope," replied Smith. "But you went to the funerals of his other three wives," objected the woman. "That's just it," explained Smith, "I feel a little cheap about always accepting his invitations and never having anything of the same sort to invite him back to."

5

It was the young minister's first funeral and he was a little unfamiliar with the proceedings. Having concluded his sermon, he announced, "The friends of the deceased will now pass around his bier for the last time."

6

The doctor and the undertaker were whispering together in the corner just before rich Farmer Brown's funeral was to start. "How come Mrs. Brown wasn't with him when he passed away?" asked the undertaker. "Oh, she'd hitched up and driven to town to get her mourning outfit at the time," explained the doctor. The undertaker smiled and went about his duties. "Hey! Where's that other pallbearer?" he demanded. "He's upstairs," volunteered another pallbearer. "It's his turn to propose to the widow."

7

"Excuse me, mum," said the maid to the mistress one Monday afternoon, "but I'd like to get off Thursday to go to me intended's funeral." "Why, of course, Mary," said the mistress sympathetically. "But why aren't you wearing mourning?" "Oh, it's too early, mum," explained the maid. "You see, the hangin' ain't till Thursday."

8

The farmhouse was quite small and the many friends and relatives who had come from miles around for old Sam's funeral crowded it. One woman who hadn't been there for some time looked around the room curiously. "Why, Jane," she exclaimed, pointing to a corner of the room, "when did you get the new grandfather's clock?" "That ain't no clock," explained the widow. "That's Sam. We stood his coffin on end to make more room."

See also corpse[1, 2], creditor[2], eloquence[1], mouth[3], praise[4].

FUR

1

The sweet young thing was being shown around an extensive fox farm and was oohing and ahing over the beautiful animals. "And how many times can a fox be skinned for his fur?" she inquired of her guide. "Usually not more than three times, madam," replied the guide with a straight face. "Any more times is likely to spoil his disposition."

2

The wife's new fur coat had just been delivered and she was in transports of delight admiring it. But suddenly a look of sadness replaced her happy expression. "What's the matter?" asked her husband. "Aren't you satisfied with it?" "Oh, yes," she replied, "but I just can't help feeling sorry for the poor creature that was skinned for it." "Thanks," replied hubby.

3

Her Christmas gift from her husband was a magnificent skunk coat, and as she unwrapped it Christmas morning she bubbled over with delight. "Isn't it marvelous!" she cried. "I just can't believe that such a beautiful coat can come from such a foul-smelling beast." At this the husband bridled. "I hardly expected gratitude, my dear," he said angrily, "but I would like a little respect."

4

As a long-suffering husband entered Heaven he noticed quite a group of animals—beavers, foxes, otters, seals, etc.—who were shivering in smooth skins, looking at him intently. "Why are you so interested in me?" he asked them. "It's just that we're the animals who were skinned for your wife's furs," explained one seal. "Oh, I see," said the man. "Mind if I join you?" And they spent Eternity together.

FURNITURE

A lady entered a furniture store and looked around. "May I help you, madam?" asked a clerk. "I'm looking for an easy chair for my husband," said the woman. "Morris?" inquired the clerk. "No, Henry," replied the woman. "Morris died."

See also premium, realism[2].

FUTURE

1

Two train travelers got to talking about the uncertainty of life. "Ah, yes," sighed one, "how little we know what the future holds for us." "How true, how true," agreed the other. "Little did I think, for example," continued the first, "when some forty years ago I used to rise before dawn in the log cabin in which I was born, milk the cows, and trudge eight miles to school, that someday I should grow up and fail to become famous."

2

"Buck up, Jack!" encouraged Bill. "What's making you look so downhearted?" "My future," replied Jack glumly. "Nonsense! What makes your future seem so hopeless?" asked Bill. "My past," explained Jack.

3

Father decided it was time to

have a talk with rather irresponsible Junior. "Son," he began gravely, "you're growing up now and it's time you were taking life more seriously and giving a little thought to the future. Just suppose I should die suddenly—where would you be?" "That's easy: I'd be here," replied Junior. "The question is, pop, where'd you be?"

See also ambition[4].

GALLANTRY

After something of a struggle, the plump, middle-aged woman managed to get on the streetcar alone while her husband stood back and watched. "You might have helped me, George," she rebuked him gently. "You're not as gallant as you were when I was a gal." "That may be," he retorted, "but don't forget, you're not as buoyant as you were when I was a boy."

See also chivalry[1].

GAMBLING

1

The lieutenant called to a corporal. "Go break up that crap-game behind the mess-hall," he ordered. It was almost an hour before the corporal was again seen. "Did you break up that game?" questioned the officer. "I certainly did, sir," replied the man. "What in blazes took you so long?" the lieutenant wanted to know. "Well, sir," explained the non-com, "I only had two-bits to start with."

2

The minister chanced upon a juvenile crap-game behind a bill-board, and all managed to scamper off but one lad whom he caught by the arm. "My boy," scolded the preacher, "don't you know that it's sinful to gamble?" "I guess you're right, sir," agreed the boy, "and, believe me, I've sure been paying for my sins."

3

Little Billy came running in with a handful of bright marbles. "Look, mom," he cried, "I won all these from Ronnie Jones." "Shame, Billy," frowned mother. "Don't you know it's wicked to play for 'keeps'? Run give them all back to Ronnie." "Yes'm," said Billy despondently, then as an afterthought added, "and shall I take back that teapot you won at his mother's card party?"

See also doctor[5], privilege.

GAMES

A man walked in on a tennis tournament when a game was in progress. He sat down on a bench between two girls. "Whose game?" he inquired generally. The girl on his left looked at him and murmured, "I am."

See also patience.

GANGSTER

A gangster left his bodyguard in the outer office, and sat down in the dentist's chair. "Me tooth's killin' me," he said. "Pull it!" "Which tooth is it, sir?" inquired the dentist. "Find it fer yerself," snarled the gangster, "I'm no stool pigeon."

See also gun[3], robbery[4].

GARBAGE

The mistress of the house walked into the kitchen and found her maid making a bundle of empty grapefruit rinds. "What in the world are you going to do with those old rinds, Maggie?" she asked. "They're not good for anything." "I know, mum," admitted the maid, "but I likes to take 'em on account o' they makes my garbage look so stylish."

See also collect[4], complaint[2].

GARDEN

1

It was late fall, and two backyard gardeners were discussing their crops. "How did your potatoes turn out?" inquired one. "Oh, splendidly," replied the other. "I got a few as big as marbles—they're my baking size—some about the size of peas, and of course quite a lot of little ones."

2

The little boy sat watching his father dig tin cans and broken brick out of his backyard garden. "Papa," he asked, "why do they put such pretty pictures on the seed envelopes?" "They have to, son," grunted pop as he straightened his back with an effort, "so the people can see what the seeds they plant would look like if they'd ever come up."

3

A young woman had advertised for a gardener, and two men applied at the same time. As she was interviewing the men, she noticed her mother making motions to indicate that she should choose the smaller. "Why did you want me to take the little man?" she asked when they were alone. "The taller had much the better face." "Look at the trousers, not the face, in picking a gardener," advised the mother, "and pick the one who has patches on his knees, not the seat."

4

The neighbor looked suspiciously over the fence at Williams who was busily digging. "What are you burying there, Williams?" he inquired. "I'm just replanting some of my seeds," he replied. "Seeds!" cried the neighbor. "It looks to me like one of my chickens." "That's right," agreed the other. "The seeds are inside."

GAS

1

The president of the gas company was making an address at a public function and was extolling the virtues of his company. "The gas company," he declared, "has played an integral part in all developments of the community. I might well say, to make a pun, 'Honor the Light Brigade!'" To this, a long-suffering customer shouted, "Oh, what a charge they made!"

2

The detective was congratulating the housewife on her part in bringing a notorious sneak-thief to justice. "Oh, I spotted him for a crook the moment he spoke," she said. "I don't see how you did it," marveled the detective, "he's one of the cleverest in the business." "It was simple," she replied. "I knew he was a fake when he said the gas company had sent him to examine our meter and see if we were entitled to a refund."

3

In response to a complaint, the gas company had sent a man out to check the customer's meter. But the man declared it to be in good order. "What!" cried the outraged customer. "Do you mean to tell me that this meter measures the amount of gas we burn?" "I have no intention of starting an argument with you, sir," replied the inspector with dignity, "but merely state that the meter measures the amount of gas you'll have to pay for."

See also collect[2], lawyer[1].

GENEROUS

1

The country swain was taking his sweetheart around the county fair when they passed a popcorn stand. "That's sure nice, ain't it, Hiram?" observed the girl suggestively. "What's nice?" asked the boy. "That popcorn; don't it smell grand?" replied the girl. The boy sniffed appreciatively for a moment. "Sure does," he agreed. "Here, I'll walk you a little closer so's you kin git a better smell."

2

The older wife was complaining to the young bride. "My husband is getting stingier all the time," she said, "always fussing about the bills and where he's going to get the money for them." "Oh, my husband is just the opposite," boasted the bride. "He's the most generous man I've ever seen. Why, he'll give me anything credit can buy."

GENIUS

The father was talking to little Willie about the necessity of developing some talent to aid in his livelihood later. "Say, pop," queried the boy, "what's the difference between talent and genius?" "Well, son," replied the old man, "the most important difference is that talent gets paid every Saturday."

GENTLEMAN

1

A man dropped into his tailor's. "I'd like to know what I owe you," he said. "You've never sent me a bill." "Of course not; I never ask a gentleman for money," declared the tailor. "Is that so?" said the customer. "How do you ever get your money if a man doesn't come in to pay?" "Well, ah, you see," stammered the tailor, "if he doesn't pay after a certain time, I decide he's no gentleman and I demand my money."

2

A young lawyer, trying his first case, got a little confused and kept addressing the court as "gentlemen." During a recess an associate told him that he should use "Your Honors." As soon as court reconvened he arose to apologize, saying, "If it please the court, through oversight I called Your Honors 'gentlemen.' I apologize for my mistake, Your Honors."

3

The landlady sternly called to her girl roomer as she was ascending the stairs. "Miss Williams," she said severely, "I thought I saw you taking a gentleman up to your room last night." "You did?" replied Miss Williams. "You know, I made the same mistake myself."

See also judge[1].

GEOGRAPHY

1

Teacher was giving a quiz on geography. "Now, Willie," she asked, "can you tell us why the sun never sets on the British flag?" The boy thought a moment, then replied, "I guess maybe it's 'cause they take it in at nights."

2

It was the hour for the geography lesson and the teacher was pointing to a large wall map. "Now, Robert," she questioned, "if you stand here in Europe and face north, you have on your right hand the continent of Asia. What do you have on your left hand?" "It's a wart, teacher," confessed Robert, "but I can't help it."

3

Teacher was trying to give her pupils some idea of the relative size of countries. "Cambodia is just about as large as Siam," she informed the class. In a written quiz a few days later one of the questions was: "How large is Cambodia?" Three of the papers came back with the answer: "As large as you are, teacher."

4

Little Daniel, for the first time, went with his parents to a summer cottage in Maine. As they were being driven from the station to the cottage, the boy looked upon the countryside in some confusion. "Are you sure this is Maine, mummy?" he asked. "Why, certainly, Danny," mother assured him. "Why do you ask?" "Well," said the boy, still puzzled, "on my map it's red."

GERMS

1

The old farmer was in his nineties and still hale and hearty. "How do you account for your unusual health?" asked a visitor. "Waal," said the old man, "reckon mebbe it's because I got a good start on most people by bein' born afore them there germs was discovered an' not havin' so much to worry myself sick about."

2

The mother was very hygienic and was constantly warning her little daughter against the dangers of bacteria. One day the little girl ran in and announced, "Oh, mummy! I ain't never gonna play with my puppy no more 'cause he's got germs on him." "Nonsense!" said mother. "That little puppy doesn't have any germs." "Oh, yes, he has," insisted the child, " 'cause I saw one hop."

See also salary[3], sanitary[3].

GET

1

The poor but honest young fellow was paying court to the college girl, and she was trying to discourage him. "Inevitable considerations of a seemly subsistence force me, however regretfully, to forego all consideration of a marital connection with a man of little pecuniary resource," she pointed out kindly. "Huh!" said the boy, his eyes popping. "I don't get you." "That's right," she agreed.

2

Grandpa was telling off the younger generation again. "You

young fellows of today expect entirely too much," he informed his bored grandson. "Do you know what I was gettin' when I married your grandmother?" "No, Grandpa," replied the boy, yawning and preparing to leave, "and I'll bet you didn't, either."

GHOST

1

"Oh, doctor!" cried a wild-eyed farmer, "I don't know what's the matter with me. Every night after sundown the ghosts of all my dead relatives come and perch on the tops of my fence-posts and just keep sittin' there waitin' an' waitin'. What'll I do, doc?" "Humph!" grunted the doctor. "I'd put spikes on the tops of the fence-posts."

2

It was a bad night for haunting in the old graveyard and two ghosts sat upon an overturned tombstone to talk shop. "By the way, pal," spoke up one ghost curiously, "do you believe in human beings?"

3

Two small-town boys were having an argument about ghosts. "I don't care what you say," insisted one stoutly, "but comin' through the woods last night I saw a ghost." "Aw, go on!" said the other. "What was this ghost doin' when you saw him last?" "He was losing ground fast," was the reply.

See also spiritualism, unusual.

GIFT

1

Two men were discussing human nature. "I have always insisted," declared the younger, "that fundamentally no two people in the world think alike." "Humph! Just wait until you're married," advised the other, "and you'll change your mind when you look over your wedding presents."

2

She opened the box and gasped at the sight of the lovely flowers. "Why, they're perfectly gorgeous!" she exclaimed. "And so fresh looking. There's still a little dew on them." "Well, er, yes, a little," he admitted stammeringly. "But I'll clear that up Saturday night."

3

"What are you giving your husband for his birthday?" asked one woman of another. "A hundred cigars," replied the other. "What did you have to pay for them?" queried the first. "Oh, nothing at all," responded the second. "I just take one from his box every day for several months. He never notices it and compliments me for getting his favorite brand."

4

Little Willie stopped sister's boyfriend on the porch. "Say, thanks for that mouth-organ you gave me for my birthday," he said gratefully. "It's the best present I got." "That's fine," replied the young man. "Can you play it?" "Oh, I don't play it," explained Willie. "Mom gives me a dime a week not to play it during the day, and pop gives me a quarter not to play it nights."

5

"You're not very attentive any more," pouted the wife. "Before we were married you used to send me a bouquet every week." "That was a cinch," grunted the husband from behind his paper. "This week so far I've sent you two chickens, a roast, three boxes of groceries, and two tons of coal."

See also appropriate[1], choice[2], expense[1], silver[1], surprise[1].

GIRL

1

The social worker patted the poor little girl on the head. "What's your name?" she inquired. "Feemollie," was the prompt answer. "Feemollie!" exclaimed the woman. "That's certainly an unusual name. How do you spell it?" "Just like the doctor put it down on the paper he gave maw when I was borned," explained the girl, "F-e-m-a-l-e."

2

"How do you stand in your class, son?" inquired father one evening. "I'm second from the top, dad," replied the boy. "There's just one girl ahead of me." "What!" cried the old man. "Surely you're not going to let a mere girl get the better of you!" The boy looked at his father. "What you don't seem to realize, dad," he explained condescendingly, "is that girls aren't nearly so mere as they used to be."

See also blush, change, charity[6].

GIVE

1

It was the holiday season and a kindly neighbor halted little Tommy on the street to inquire, "And what are you going to give your little baby brother for Christmas, Tommy?" "I dunno," replied the boy. "I gave him the measles last Christmas."

2

In order to test his little son, a father one Sunday morning gave the boy a dime and a quarter and told him to put one of the coins in the collection plate in church and keep the other. "Which coin did you put in the plate, son?" he asked later. "Well, pop," explained the lad, "I thought I oughta put in the quarter, but then I remembered what you say, that 'The Lord loveth a cheerful giver,' an' I knew I could give the dime more cheerfully. So I did."

See also hopeless.

GLASSES

1

"Well, Billy, do you find that glasses help your eyes?" inquired teacher. "Oh, yes, ma'am," replied Billy decidedly. "I don't get my eyes blacked nearly as much now as I used to."

2

"Why do you need three pairs of spectacles, Professor?" inquired a student. "Well, I need a pair for close work and a pair for distant vision," he replied. "I understand that," said the student, "but why the third pair?" "Oh, I wear that to look for the other two," was the explanation.

3

A sweet young thing came into the oculist's very much distressed. "Oh, doctor," she cried, "I've broken my glasses. Now will I have to be examined all over again?" Unfortunately, no, my dear," sighed the doctor regretfully. "Just your eyes."

4

A shrewd businessman thought he hadn't got enough for his money, so he dropped into his oculist's to complain that his new glasses weren't nearly as strong as he'd like them to be. "But they're No. 2 power," objected the oculist. "Well, what's the next stronger kind?" asked the customer. "No. 1 power," was the reply. "And after that?" insisted the man. "After that, sir," declared the doctor grimly, "you buy a dog."

See also reading[3], spots[2].

GLOVES

"Will you please bring my gloves, John," called the wife to her husband. "Your cloth gloves?" he asked. "No, my white goats," she specified. "What do you mean, your goats?" he asked. "You used to call those your kids." "I know," she said pointedly, "but they're getting so old I hate to call them kids any longer."

See also feeling[1].

GLUTTON

1

A group of men were boasting of their accomplishments, and one of them spoke up, "I once ate forty-nine hard-boiled eggs at one sitting." "Forty-nine?" said one of the others. "Why didn't you eat one more and make it an even fifty?" "What!" cried the egg-eater indignantly. "I should make a hog of myself for just one egg?"

2

It was the morning after a big party and one woman who was very proud of her jewelry met another of the guests on the street. "It was a lovely party, wasn't it?" gushed the first. "And did you see my sunburst?" "Gee, no, I'm sorry I missed that," replied the other. "But I was certainly expecting it the way he was eating."

GO

1

A bashful young man was driving with his girlfriend in the country and reached a lonely, wooded spot where he parked. "How does this place look to you?" he asked. "Oh, fine," she said. "You can go as far as you like." Whereupon the young man started his motor and drove on deeper into the country.

2

It was the rush season and the office boy had had to work overtime for three consecutive nights. On the third night he complained to the boss, "Say, this is the third night in a row you've worked me and I'm tired out. I ain't no machine, you know; I can't go forever." "That's just where you're wrong, my boy," said the boss grimly. "You go forever next Saturday."

See also school[1].

GOD

1

Ronnie was bent over his desk. "What are you so busy with, Ronnie?" teacher inquired. "I'm drawing a picture of God," replied Ronnie without looking up. "But

Ronnie, you can't do that," objected teacher. "No one knows how God looks." "Well, they will when I get finished with this picture," declared the boy.

2

The Sunday-school teacher was trying to put across the idea of God's omnipresence, so she asked, "Now, Willie, where do you think God is this morning?" "In our bathroom at home," was the unhesitating reply. "Whatever makes you say that?" cried the amazed teacher. " 'Cause just before I left I saw pop poundin' on the door an' hollerin', 'Good Lord! How long are you going to stay in there?' "

3

The little girl came in from the garden weeping. "God doesn't love me any more," she wailed. "Nonsense! Of course God loves you," comforted mother. "What makes you think He doesn't?" "I know He doesn't," insisted the child. "I just tried Him with a daisy."

See also charity[1], contribution[2], danger[2], deceive[1], examination[1], fool[3], lunatic[2], medicine[5], religion[2], South[1].

GOLD DIGGER

1

A gold digger had died and her possessions were being auctioned off to pay her debts. And among them was a parrot. "What am I offered for this lovely bird?" said the auctioneer. "One dollar," came a bid. "Two dollars," came another. "Aw, make it five, daddy, and I'll be specially nice to you," squawked the parrot in wheedling tones.

2

Two gold diggers were talking. "I think it's a horrid shame the way poor Mabel was deceived when she married that old man," declared one indignantly. "Why, didn't he have the money she thought he had?" asked the other. "Oh, he's got plenty of money," said the first. "It's just that he's ten years younger than he told her he was."

GOLDFISH

1

A lady stopped in a pet shop and asked the clerk, "Can I get a small live shark here?" "A live shark!" exclaimed the clerk. "Why, madam, what would you do with a live shark?" "The neighbor's cat has been eating the goldfish from my pool," she explained grimly, "and I want to teach it a lesson."

2

"Bridget!" called the mistress to her maid. "Have you given the goldfish fresh water today?" "There's no need to, mum," replied the maid, "they ain't finished the water I gave them yesterday."

See also drunk[7].

GOLF

1

A minister had been playing golf with one of his flock. This man was much older than the minister and played a better game and beat him badly. Returning to the clubhouse, the preacher was so glum that the other tried to cheer him up by saying, "Don't be sad, Reverend. Remember, you'll win in the end, for you'll probably be burying me one of these days." The minister, still unhappy, answered, "Even then it will be your hole."

2

It was his first time on a golf links. He hit the ball a wallop, and by some miracle the ball landed right in the cup. He teed off for the second hole, swung again, and by some even greater miracle the ball wavered for a moment on the edge of the cup, and then fell in. "Phew!" sighed the man in relief. "I thought sure I'd missed it that time."

3

Some laborers working near a golf course had never seen the game played before, and they were watching the efforts of a dub with interest. First the ball landed in a rut, then behind a rock, and then in a sand trap, from each of which the man had much trouble in getting the ball out. Finally, he got a clear shot and sank the ball in the cup. "Oh-oh!" called one of the watchers sympathetically, "now you *are* in a hell of a fix, mister."

4

He had never played in a golf tournament before. He tried his best to appear unconcerned despite the large crowd. He stepped up to the ball, swung, and missed. He tried again, and missed again. A third time it was the same story. He looked up at the spectators, smiled cheerily, and remarked, "Tough course, isn't it?"

5

The golf club secretary walked out to see how the amateur tournament was getting along and found one of the players about to swing at a ball a full foot in front of the teeing mark. "Hey, you're disqualified!" the secretary cried. "You're teeing off in front of the mark." The golfer looked at him and said, "Aw, go on back to the clubhouse. I'm playing my third stroke."

See also caddy[1], cheat[3], clothes[4], conversation[1], dentist[2], familiar[3], learn, mind[2], moon[2], mother-in-law[5], reward[1], score, spitting[2], worse[1].

GOOD

1

"How many are three and four, Billy?" questioned teacher. "Three and four are seven," replied Billy. "Right! That's very good, Billy," approved teacher. "Good!" echoed Billy. "Hell, teacher, that's perfect!"

2

"Have you anything to say for yourself before I pass sentence?" the judge frowned at the pickpocket. "Just what good have you ever done for mankind?" "Well, Your Honor," ventured the prisoner, "I've kept four or five detectives working regularly and I've helped several reporters, prison guards, and you keep their jobs."

3

"What are your intentions in the coming election?" asked the young reporter of the political boss. "I'm out of politics for good, son," replied the boss blandly. "Whose?" queried the reporter.

4

Mother smiled at her little son in his new Boy Scout uniform. "Well, Jimmie, have you done your good deed for today?" she inquired. "I sure did," answered the boy. "I taught that little girl next door not to stick out her tongue at Boy Scouts."

5

"Miss Johnson, that cute stenographer, is leaving," the bill clerk informed the bookkeeper. "For good?" the latter wanted to know. "No," replied the clerk, "for better or worse—she's getting married."

6

"When are you going out with me, Babe?" he asked for the fifth time. "Don't rush me, Big Boy," she cautioned him. "I'll make a date with you when I'm good and ready." "Well, maybe I'll wait until you're ready, Toots," he retorted, "but I sure can't wait until you're good."

See also behavior[6], explosion[3], father[1], numbers[3].

GOOD-BY

See farewell, good night.

GOOD NIGHT

1

He lingered on her doorstep, and then he lingered some more. "Ah, my life!" he murmured, "must we say good night?" "Heck, no!" snarled a voice from the top of the stairs. "Wait about ten minutes and say 'good morning.'"

2

Mrs. Smith had guests in for cards. As nine o'clock approached, the patter of bare feet could be heard at the top of the stairs. "Quiet, please," she said. "The children are

about to give their good night message. I always get a sentimental thrill out of hearing them." After a momentary silence, a shrill voice cried, "Mamma! Mamma! Tony found a bedbug!"

GOSSIP

1

Two gossips were talking about some recent marital strife. "And what do they say is the reason that the Browns separated?" asked one eagerly. "Nobody knows," replied the other. "Oh, how terrible!" cried the first.

2

She was giving the new maid instructions as to her conduct. "I expect you to be neat and clean at all times, Mary," she said, "but above all you must be reticent." "Oh, yes'm," replied the maid, then leaning forward she inquired in a hoarse whisper, "And what's there to be reticent about, ma'am?"

See also catty[1], clothes[5], rumor[1, 3], secret[2], talk[1], truth[4].

GOVERNESS

See nursemaid.

GOVERNMENT

1

A group of tourists stood spellbound looking into the depths of the Grand Canyon. "And this wonder is all the more impressive," the guide droned on, "when you realize that it took millions and millions of years to carve out this great abyss." "Well, well!" exclaimed a plain citizen. "I'd never have suspected that this was a government project."

2

A lazy worker on a government job was being bawled out by the foreman. "I know your kind," said the foreman in disgust. "You'd like a job where you could lie in bed all day and get everything done by pushing buttons." "Not me," said the lazy one. "You wouldn't catch me pushing buttons all day."

3

An immigrant farmer had decided to become a citizen and he appeared for his naturalization papers. "Do you like this country?" the official asked him. "Yah, sure," replied the applicant. "And does our government here suit you in every way?" was the next question. "Vell, yah, pretty much," was the hesitating answer, "only I like maybe to see a little more rain."

4

After two days of chasing around from clerk to petty official, an elderly lady was at last shown into the office of a high official in the Department of Agriculture. "But you won't do," she objected. "I want to see the Secretary of Agriculture himself." "But he's out of town just now," replied the assistant. "Can't you tell me what you want?" "Well, maybe," conceded the lady. "It's about a geranium I have that isn't doing at all well."

5

The aristocratic foreigner was sneering at the American democratic government. "It must be frightfully unpleasant to be governed by people that you wouldn't care to invite to dinner," he observed scornfully. "Oh, I don't know," retorted the American bluntly. "I don't see that it's any worse than being governed by people who wouldn't invite *you* to dinner."

See also Congress[1], hole.

GRACE

1

A radio announcer and his family were invited out to dinner and the hostess asked his young daughter to say grace. The child cleared her throat, gave a quick glance at the clock, and said, "This food, friends, is coming to you through the courtesy of and as a service of Almighty God."

2

It was Monday evening and they were having hash made from the remains of Sunday's roast. As father was about to say grace before the meal, little John remarked, "I don't see why you have to ask another blessing tonight, pop, because you did it yesterday, and it's the same old stuff."

3

Little Molly was having lunch at a friend's house and she was puzzled as she saw the family bow their heads to say grace. "What are you doing?" she inquired. "Why, we're giving thanks for our daily bread, Molly," she was informed. "Don't you do that at home?" "Of course not," said Molly in a superior tone. "We pay for our bread."

4

A well-known writer was present one evening as a guest at a large dinner. When the meal was about to begin, it was suddenly discovered that there was no clergyman present though several had been invited. The master of ceremonies turned to the writer and asked, "Mr. Black, since there is no clergyman here, will you say grace, please?" The man arose, bowed his head, and with deep feeling said, "There being no clergyman present, let us thank God!"

5

The family was having a special dinner for the young son who had been confirmed that day. He was exceptionally hungry. Father wanted his son to say grace, but the boy was impatient to start eating. However, the father insisted, so at last the lad bowed his head, folded his hands, and said simply, "O Lord, have mercy on these victuals. Amen!"

6

A boy whose family was not in the habit of saying grace was visiting a relative who always observed the practice. Sitting down to his first meal there, the boy began immediately to eat without waiting for the others. "Billy," said his aunt, "we usually say something before we eat." "Go ahead, say all you want," replied the boy, continuing to eat, "you can't turn my stomach!"

See also prayer.

GRADES

1

Father's frown kept deepening as he read through Willie's report card. "Hm!" he growled. "Grammar, poor; spelling, very poor; arithmetic, poor; penmanship, fair. What've you got to say to this?" "I know it looks bad that far, dad," admitted the boy, "but just read down there." And he pointed to a line near the bottom reading: "Health—Excellent."

2

Junior's grades were all low, and stayed that way despite mother's pleading and scolding. At last she promised him a quarter if he would get a high grade in something. The next day he came running home crying, "Gimme the quarter, mom, I got 100 in two things today!" "You did?" said mother. "What were they?" "Spelling an' 'rithmetic," replied the scholar. "Got 55 in one an' 45 in the other."

3

The college boy had flunked his examination and he went in to complain about it to the professor. "I don't think this quite fair," he asserted. "I don't believe I deserve a zero on this exam." "Nor do I, my boy," agreed the professor readily, "but there's no lower mark I can give you."

4

Little Tommy had been getting good grades for the past month, to the delight of his parents. But suddenly they fell off. "What's wrong son?" asked father. "Aw, it's all teacher's fault," declared Tommy. "How could it be her fault?" asked father. "She went an' moved that smart little girl that sat next to me," explained the boy.

5

Dad scowled over the boy's report card. "Why are your grades so much lower for January than for December?" he demanded. "Why, dad, I'm surprised at you," said the boy in an aggrieved tone. "Don't you know that everything is marked down after the holidays?"

See also examination[1], parents[1].

GRADUATION

1

The chancellor of the university was delivering his commencement address. In very flowery language he was telling the class that now they must leave these hallowed halls to go out into the world and use their vast knowledge for its improvement, etc., etc. A foreign couple in the audience was a bit puzzled by his language. "What da beeg fella in black dress saying?" asked the woman. "Not much," replied the man. "He joost say dat school is out."

2

Two fathers were discussing the education of their sons. "What's your boy going to be when he gets out of college?" inquired the one. "An octogenarian, the way it looks," replied the other sadly.

3

"Well, my boy finally made it and got his A.B. last week," declared a man to a friend. "Good! I suppose now he'll be looking for a Ph.D.," observed the friend. "No, indeed!" replied the father grimly. "He'll now be looking for a J-O-B."

4

"Did your son get what he deserved when he graduated from college?" asked one man of another.

"I suppose he did," sighed the father. "At any rate, they gave him a black sheepskin."

GRAMMAR

1

It was Bobby's first day in school, and he walked up to teacher's desk and announced, "Say, I ain't got no pencil!" "Oh, Bobby!" corrected teacher, "I have no pencil." "Gee, ain't you neither, teacher?" said the boy. "We're both in the same fix, ain't we?"

2

The tramp knocked at the back door and asked for something to eat. "Did you see that big pile of wood in back?" asked the lady. "Yep, I seen it," replied the bum without enthusiasm. "Such grammar!" snorted the woman. "You should say you saw it." "Oh, I don't know, lady," was the answer. "You saw me see it, but you sure ain't seen me saw it."

3

The farmer's two schoolboy sons were arguing about a point of grammar. "I'll betcha it's right to say a hen is 'sitting,'" declared one hotly. "And I'll bet it should be 'setting,'" insisted the other. At this point the farmer spoke up. "All that don't amount to a durn, boys," he advised. "What I want to know is, when a hen cackles be she layin' or lyin'."

4

Mother had taken her young son to the zoo and they were looking at the hippopotamus. "Gee, mom," remarked the boy, "ain't that the damnedest ugliest thing you ever saw?" "John!" reproved mother severely. "Haven't I told you never to say 'ain't.'"

5

It was a warm midsummer afternoon and a number of mother's friends had gathered on the porch, and the small talk flew thick and fast. Daughter, home for the summer from college, squirmed uncomfortably for a while, then abruptly rose and went into the house. "What's the matter, is your daughter suffering from the heat?" asked one caller. "Oh, no," said mother. "She's just suffering from the family grammar."

See also stenographer², stop², weapon.

GRANDMA

1

The firelight's flicker cast a warm glow over the cozy scene as grandma sat in her rocker knitting. It caught bright reflections from the steel bows of her spectacles and from the gleaming, flashing needles. Little Joan sat watching, and finally asked, "Why do you knit so much, grandma?" "Oh," replied the old lady with a smile, "just for the hell of it."

2

"What's wrong, little fellow?" inquired a kindly man of a weeping boy. "My dog's dead," was the sobbing answer. "Well, you mustn't carry on too much about it," advised the man. "Just look, my grandmother died last week, and you don't see me crying." "No," admitted the boy, "but you didn't raise her from a pup."

3

"Did you hear that old lady Williams cut off her little grandson in her will without a cent because of a social error?" said the lawyer to a friend. "Why, the child's only four," objected the other. "How could he make a social error?" "Well, perhaps it was the parents' fault," admitted the lawyer. "They allowed the child to address the old lady as 'Grandma' at a debutante's tea."

See also wisdom.

GRASS

For his text one Sunday morning, a minister took the quotation, "In each blade of grass there is a sermon," and proceeded to preach a lengthy sermon on it. On the following afternoon the minister was cutting his front lawn, when one of his congregation passed by. "Ah, Reverend," said the man, "I'm glad to see that you're cutting your sermons short."

See also sympathy⁴.

GRATITUDE

The newly-graduated physician had been giving his father some advice about his health, but the old man was not taking it. "This is a fine reward for me!" he stormed. "For years I've scraped and saved and denied myself to send you through medical school—and what happens? The first thing you do is to tell me to cut out smoking and drinking!"

See also favor².

GRAVE

A gravedigger got so absorbed in his work that he didn't notice how far he had gone until he had the grave so deep that he couldn't get out. As the chill of night descended he got very uncomfortable and began to shout for help. At last a passing drunk heard him. "Get me out of here, I'm cold," cried the prisoner. The drunk looked at the gravedigger for a moment, then grabbed a shovel and said, "No wonder you're cold, poor fellow, you ain't got any dirt on you."

See also mourn[1].

GREEDY

Two little girls were playing in the yard when the mother of one called out, "You girls may have those two apples in the kitchen." The tots scampered in and looked at the apples in the plate. One was large and one was small. "Is 'oo a gweedy dirl?" finally inquired the daughter of the house. "Oh, no, I'se not a bit gweedy," said the guest. "Aw wight," said her hostess grandly, "then 'oo choose."

GREETING

"Hi'ya, dad, old sock," greeted sonny, slapping the old man on the back. "How are things here in the old sweatshop? Just passing by and thought I'd drop in and say hello." "That's great, son, but it's no use," said father. "Your mother and sister already dropped in to say hello and got all I had."

See also waitress[1].

GRIEF

1

A woman visiting the zoo passed two of the attendants who were crying. "What's troubling you fellows?" she asked sympathetically. "The elephant died," sobbed one. "What a pity!" said the woman. "You fellows must have loved the big creature dearly to weep so for it." "Love 'im, hell, lady!" cried the other. "The boss just told us we've gotta dig his grave."

2

A dear old lady sat at the train window watching the lingering farewells of a young couple on the platform. As the train pulled out with the girl, she burst into tears and stumbled to a seat near the old lady. "There, there, my girl," said the lady going over to comfort her. "Are you crying so because you have to leave your husband?" "No," was the tearful response, "because I have to go back to him."

3

"Well, if your wife's left you, why don't you go home and drown your sorrows in drink," suggested a friend. "I'm afraid that's impossible," objected the deserted one. "How so? No liquor?" asked the friend. "Oh, no," was the response. "No sorrow."

See also drowning[3], mourn[2], weeping[2].

GROCER

1

"Do you ever have any nice butter?" inquired a customer. "I get a fresh supply in every day," declared the grocer. "Then why in blazes don't you sell some of it once in a while?" snapped the customer.

2

The store was crowded when the little boy came in and said, "My mom says she wants two pounds of butter exactly like that you sent her last week, but it's gotta be *exactly* like it." The grocer beamed on his other customers as he remarked, "I always say that quality goods makes customers very particular. Just a moment, boy." "Now be sure it's the same kind," cautioned the boy. "Dad's relatives are visiting and Mom doesn't want them to come again."

See also egg[2], fruit[4], store[1], substitute[2].

GROWTH

1

"My, my, Billy," remarked an uncle who hadn't seen him in a long time, "you're certainly getting quite big, aren't you?" "Yep," replied Billy, "pop says I'm growin' like the public debt."

2

The Sunday-school teacher was illustrating the miracle of life and growth with the example of the Easter lily. "Now, children," she asked, "who can tell me what makes this beautiful flower come from this drab-looking little bulb?" "God does it," spoke up one little girl promptly. A small country lad nodded knowingly and said, "Fertilizer helps."

3

Little Danny's mother was ob-

sessed with the notion of cleanliness for children, and despite the lad's weary protests she bathed, washed, and scrubbed him. As he walked down the street one day a neighbor exclaimed, "Goodness, Danny, how you are growing!" "What do you expect," growled Danny, "the way mom keeps waterin' me?"

See also tree[2].

GUESS

1

The romantic young man crept slyly behind the pretty girl, slipped his hands over her eyes, and announced, "If you can't tell who this is in three guesses, I'm going to kiss you." "Let's see," said the girl, "could it be Charlemagne, Alexander the Great, or Jack the Ripper?"

2

"Hey, Pat," called a breezy young man to a policeman, "how do I get to the post office?" "How'd you know my name was 'Pat'?" asked the copper, coldly. "Oh, I just guessed it," replied the fellow. "You did, did you?" retorted the officer. "Well, now guess your way to the post office."

See also difference[1].

GUEST

1

Hubby's friend hesitated before he entered the house. "You're quite sure that your wife knows you're bringing me home to dinner?" he inquired cautiously. "Knows it! Well, I should hope!" declared his host vigorously. "Why, man, I argued with her for almost an hour about it this morning!"

2

Mrs. Bland was having a swank reception and she was giving her maid some final instructions. "Now, Mary," she ordered, "during the first part of the evening I want you to stand at the door and call the guests' names as they come in." "Gee, thank you, mum," replied the maid. "I've been dyin' to do that to some of your friends for the past 15 years."

3

It was late when the guest finally rose to go. "Please don't bother to see me to the door," he urged. "Really, it's no bother at all," insisted his host, stifling a yawn; "it's a pleasure."

See also chauffeur[1], hint[8], invention[1], party, singer[2].

GUIDE

See direction.

GUILT

1

The judge peered over his spectacles at the man accused of stealing chickens. "Guilty or not guilty?" he demanded. "Well, judge, I think mebbe I'm guilty," replied the prisoner, "but I'd rather be tried an' make sure."

2

Law and order had finally come to Bloody Creek and its first jury trial was in progress. The evidence had been heard and the jury had been out arguing for hours. Finally, they straggled back and the foreman stood up to announce the verdict. "We reckon as how he didn't do it," he drawled, "on accountta we 'low he warn't there, but we think he'd a-done it sure if'n he'd had the chancst."

3

The prisoner called at the warden's office. "I'd like permission to write the Governor asking for a pardon," he requested. "What grounds do you have for a pardon?" asked the warden. "Well, sir, I'm afraid of corrupting the other inmates," explained the man. "It seems that I'm the only guilty man in this prison."

4

Little Billy was having fun with his new air rifle. Suddenly there was the sound of shattering glass, and an angry woman's face appeared. She yelled, "Did you break my window, you brat?" "Did you see me do it?" asked the boy. "Well, no," admitted the woman, "but —" "Then I didn't do it," declared Billy.

See also conscience[2].

GUN

1

A woman customer was inspecting a case of revolvers. "Here's a very nice pistol, madam," recommended the clerk, "it shoots eight times." "Say, what do you think I am," demanded the woman haughtily, "a polygamist?"

2

The mountaineer came into town

for one of his rare visits. He paused before the new movie theater which bore a large sign reading: "Children in Arms not Admitted." "Gawsh A'mighty!" he exclaimed in amazement. "Since when has even the kids took to totin' shootin iron!"

3

The nervous gentleman almost fainted when the highwayman pointed a long, nasty-looking gun at him. "For g-goodness' s-sakes," he pleaded, "b-be careful. T-that g-gun might g-go off." "So what?" said the robber indifferently. "I can easily reload it."

See also army[6], robbery[4].

HABIT

1

"So this isn't your wife's first marriage, eh?" asked an acquaintance. "Are you her second husband?" "No, I'm her fifth husband," was the reply. "Heavens, man!" gasped the other. "You're not a husband; you're a habit."

2

Teacher was giving the class a lecture on "Bad Habits" and in trying to make things clear she asked, "Now, children, what is it we find so easy to get into and so hard to get out of?" After a momentary pause, one little fellow raised his hand and volunteered, "Bed."

3

"For almost fifteen years," boasted an elderly man to a group of listeners, "my habits were as regular as clockwork. I got up at quarter of six, had breakfast at six-fifteen, was working at seven-thirty, had lunch at twelve-thirty, dinner at six-thirty, and was in bed at ten sharp." "My, my," commented a listener sympathetically, "and what were you in for?"

See also punishment[8].

HAIR

1

It was fall and Mrs. Johnson was airing her husband's clothes. "Henry," she called sternly, "what are these blonde hairs doing on your last winter's coat?" "You should ask!" retorted hubby. "You were a blonde last winter, weren't you?"

2

The romantic young suitor drew the girl's little brother aside. "How'd you like to make a quarter, Tommy?" he asked. "Sure," replied the boy. "What do you want me to do?" "Do you think you can get me a lock of your sister's hair?" he requested. "It's a cinch," declared Tommy. "For a buck I'll get you the whole wig."

3

A worried man entered the doctor's office. "My hair's coming out pretty fast, doc," he announced. "Can you give me something to keep it in?" "Why, certainly," replied the doctor obligingly. "Here, take this large pillbox."

4

"Can you give me some medicine for my hair?" a patient asked a dermatologist. "It's beginning to worry me." "Oh, don't let it worry you, old fellow," comforted the specialist. "It'll all come out all right."

See also bald[2], memento[3], photography[3].

HAIRCUT

1

"Just a shave," ordered the customer as he sat in the barber's chair. "Your hair wants cutting badly," hinted the barber, as he shook out the apron. "No it doesn't," snapped the customer. "It wants cutting nicely. You cut it badly last time, so that's why I'm going down the street for my haircut."

2

"How would you like your hair cut, sir?" asked the barber, eager to please. "Off," replied the customer, heading off all further attempts at conversation.

3

"Where have you been?" demanded the boss of a workman caught walking in the door in mid-afternoon. "Out getting my hair cut," replied the man. "But you can't get your hair cut on my time," objected the boss. "Why not? It grew on your time," the man pointed out.

4

The man who had been vacationing in the woods for the entire summer, dropped into a barber shop with a very heavy crop of hair. "Haircut?" inquired the barber, as he adjusted the chair. "Of course not," replied the customer sarcastically. "I just dropped in for an estimate."

5

The little fellow climbed into the barber's chair and settled himself. "Well, my little man," said the barber, "how do you want your hair cut today?" "I want 'em cut like daddy's," insisted the boy, "with a hole on top."

See also baby[5].

HALF

1

"I can't sleep good with brother, mom," declared little Jimmy wearily one morning. "Why not, son?" asked mother. "Well, the bed's pretty hard," explained the boy, "but mainly because brother takes up half of the bed." "But why shouldn't he have half of the bed?" objected mother. "It'd be all right," said the boy, "only he wants his half out of the middle."

2

The aviator climbed and climbed until the airport was just a small patch below. Then he cut his motor and began gliding. "Know what?" he cried to his only passenger. "I'll bet half those people on the field down there think we're going to fall and crash." "They've got nothing on us up here," gulped the passenger weakly. "Half of us do, too."

See also bill[2], deduction, fat[2], like[2], sister[3].

HANDKERCHIEF

1

A ragged little boy sat beside the elegant lady on a streetcar and began to sniffle. The lady endured it for a while, but then, turning to the boy, demanded haughtily, "Do you have a handkerchief?" "Sure I do," replied the boy, "but I never lend it to strangers."

2

Two housemaids were talking shop on their afternoon off. "My missus is all right, but her husband is an old grouch," remarked one. "That's too bad," said the other, "but there's not much you can do about it but quit." "Oh, I don't know," replied the first, with a gleam in her eye. "Every time he scolds me, I starch his handkerchiefs."

3

"How's things?" asked one man of another. "Well, everybody's putting his nose in my business this winter," replied the other. "Cheer up," comforted the first. "That's one of those things you just have to put up with." "Oh, I'm not complaining," the other assured him. "You see, I manufacture handkerchiefs."

See also bosom.

HANDS

1

The nursemaid had called to bring little Margie home from the party and as they crossed the street she took the little girl's hand to help her. "Goodness! How sticky your hands are, Margie!" exclaimed the nurse. "Well, so would yours be," replied the child calmly, "if you had a piece of chiffon pie, a cream puff, and a chocolate éclair in your muff."

2

A witness, who was left-handed, was being sworn in before testifyin in court. "Raise your right hand, ordered the clerk. Up went th man's left hand. "No, no," said th judge sharply. "Raise your *righ* hand." "That's what I'm doin Your Honor," insisted the witnes "only me right hand's on me lef hand side."

See also dirty[1, 3], fortune-telling[1].

HANDWRITING

1

The new guest put down the pe and was about to turn away whe the hotel clerk asked, "What's you name, please, sir?" "Name!" crie the man indignantly. "Don't you se my signature right there on th register?" "Yes, I do, sir," replie the clerk. "That's what aroused m curiosity."

2

A newspaper had, as one of it features, a column conducted by handwriting expert. A girl reade sent in to this column one of he sweetheart's letters with the request "Enclosed is a specimen of my boy friend's handwriting. Can you tel me if he will make a good hu band?" Soon came a reply: "I'r afraid not, as he's been a rotten on to me for five years. Thanks for th evidence."

3

A woman who was giving dinner had sent an invitation to doctor. In reply she received a lette in such bad writing that sh couldn't read it. Wishing to know i he'd accepted or refused, she tool it to one familiar with doctors' per manship—her corner druggist. Th druggist gave the letter one glance and, before she could explain her purpose, disappeared into the back room. Soon he came out with a bottle which he handed her, saying, "That'll be 75 cents, please."

4

A student came up to the professor with his returned examination paper. "What is this notation you've put on my paper, sir?" he inquired. The professor studied the scrawl for a moment, then said, "Oh, yes, I remember now. I told you to write plainer."

HANGING

1

It was to be a public hanging and as the prisoner was being escorted to the gallows he noticed a crowd of people rushing on ahead. "There's no need to hurry, folks," he advised them. "I can guarantee you that there will positively be nothing done until *I* get there."

2

A dirty, ragged man was up in court on a charge of drunkenness. Just as the judge was about to pass sentence on him, his old belt snapped and his trousers sagged to his knees. "Take this man out in back and get some rope," the judge commanded a nearby bailiff. "Holy Smokes!" whispered a waiting prisoner in alarm to his lawyer. "Can they hang a man for that?"

3

A young man was applying for a part in a new play. "Were any of your ancestors ever on the stage?" inquired the director. "Well," hesitated the applicant, "I had an uncle who once was the leading character at a public exhibition, but just after he mounted the platform it fell." "Did he fall to the floor?" asked the director, "Oh, no," was the reply, "the rope stopped him."

See also funeral[7], murder, suicide[1].

HANGOVER

1

"You are charged with drunkenness," the judge informed the prisoner before him. "Do you have anything to say?" "But I've never been drunk in my life, Your Honor," protested the prisoner, "and what's more I don't ever intend to be, because it always makes me feel so terrible the next morning."

2

It was the morning after, and hubby sat groaning and holding his head. "Well, if you hadn't drunk so much last night you wouldn't feel so bad now," commented the wife tartly. "My drinking had nothing to do with it," answered the man. "I went to bed feeling wonderful and woke up feeling awful—it was the sleep that did it."

3

He had been to a party the evening before, and when he awoke the next morning with an oversized head he knew he was in no condition for work. Calling his boss at his home, he said lamely, "I'm sorry, but I'm afraid I won't be able to get to the office today. I've taken a bad cold and—" "That's too bad," said the boss, "but you needn't have bothered to call—this is Sunday."

See also feeling[3].

HAPPY

1

A friend came up and pressed the future bridegroom's hand warmly. "I want to congratulate you, Bob," he said, "on this, one of the happiest days of your life." "But I'm not getting married until tomorrow," objected the other. "I know," replied the friend. "That's what makes this one of your happiest days."

2

Two women met and got to talking about old friends. "Well, well," remarked one, "so Clara finally got married. Is she happily married?" "Happily married?" replied the other. "Well, I should hope she is! Why, she's so happy that she has to go to the movies for a good cry."

3

"Remember what I told you last Sunday, children, that you should all try to make some one happy during the week?" asked the Sunday-school teacher. "Well, how many of you did so?" "I did, teacher," volunteered one child brightly. "That's fine," approved teacher. "What did you do?" "I went to see Aunt May," replied the boy, "an' she's always happy when I go home."

4

It was little Tommy's custom to recommend most of his relatives to God in his prayers, but on this evening he had failed to mention a favorite aunt. "Why, Tommy," said his mother, "why didn't you say 'God bless Aunt Bessie and make her happy,' as you always do?" "Don't have to no more, mom," explained the boy. "Aunt Bessie's engaged now."

See also boss[5], old maid[4], spiritualism, vanity.

HARD

One man approached another in a saloon. "I'll bet you five bucks that I've got the hardest name of anybody here," he said. "I'll take you," said the other. "What's your name?" "Stone," replied the first triumphantly. "Pay me," said the other. "My name's Harder."

HASH

1

The customer in the hole-in-the-wall restaurant looked over the stained menu. "Guess I'll have some hash," he told the waiter. "Gent wants to take a chance," he called back to the kitchen. "Guess I'll take hash, too," said the first man's companion. "Another sport," yelled the waiter.

2

It was the natural history lesson and the teacher was explaining the different types of life. "Now, Bill," she questioned, "can you think of anything that belongs to both the animal and the vegetable kingdoms?" Bill knit his brows, then ventured, "How about hash, teacher?"

3

The lunch hour was over and the two men reported back to work. "Well, how do you feel now, Bill?" queried one. "Oh, I had hash for lunch," replied Bill, "and now I feel like everything."

See also grace[2], soup[2].

HAT

1

Mrs. Williams was proudly showing her husband a new lampshade she had just bought. "Isn't it pretty, dear?" she asked. "And it only cost a dollar ninety-eight." Williams took one look at it and said, "There's a limit to everything, and this is it! If you step out of the house with that thing on your head, I get a divorce."

2

A woman was looking over hats in a shop, and the saleswoman showed her a very simple model. "Here is a very nice hat, madam, for only $75," she said. "What!" gasped the customer. "Why, there isn't anything at all on the hat!" "That's just it," explained the saleswoman quietly. "You must pay for the restraint."

3

"How do you like my new hat, William?" asked the wife, as she walked into the room with it on her head, Hubby drew a deep breath. "Well, dear," he began, "to tell you the truth—" "Stop right there, you wretch!" interrupted the wife, angrily, "If that's the way you're going to talk about my hat, I won't hear a word!"

4

"Oh, madam, come quickly!" cried the maid excitedly, bursting into the room. "Your husband's lying unconscious in the hall beside a large box with a piece of paper clutched in his hand!" "Oh, goody!" exclaimed the mistress in delight. "My new hat's come."

See also bet[2], **cough**, modesty[2], own[2].

HEAD

1

"Are you sure the laundry sent back the right shirts?" gasped hubby as he struggled to get into a clean garment. "This one's so tight I can scarcely breathe." "It's your shirt, all right," said the wife. "You've just got your head through a buttonhole."

2

The Sunday-school teacher had been telling her class the rewards that would go to the holy in heaven. "Now, who can tell me," she concluded, "who will get the biggest crown in heaven?" "I ain't sure, teacher," ventured one little fellow, "but I think it would be him with the biggest head."

3

"I can't understand it," said one college student to another in the gymnasium. "When I stand on my head, the blood rushes to my head; but when I stand on my feet the blood doesn't rush to my feet." "That's easy," explained the other. "Your feet aren't empty."

4

A quarryman had been hurt by a falling rock. He sued for damages and an uneducated fellow worker was called on to testify. He was asked about the size of the rock in question, but he couldn't describe it. "Well, was it as big as my fist?" asked the lawyer. "Oh, bigger," was the reply. "As big as my two fists?" "Bigger," was the reply again. "Was it as big as my head?" cried the lawyer. "Well, about as long, but not so thick," he answered.

See also art[5], calm[4], sarcasm[1].

HEALTH

1

A neighbor met Smith on the street. "What's this I hear about your wife going to Florida for her health?" he asked. "What did she have?" "Eleven hundred dollars she inherited from an uncle," replied Smith.

2

Mr. Johnson had been sick for some time, and he finally called in the doctor. The doctor examined him thoroughly, then declared, "There is some chronic evil possessing you that is ruining your health and happiness." "Shh, doctor! For pity sakes speak softly!" whispered the patient fearfully. "She's sitting right in the next room."

3

"Not much of a town," observed a tourist as he looked over a miserable little settlement. "Nope, but it sure is healthy," replied a native. "Why, would you believe it, when I first came here I hadn't the strength to speak a word or walk. I had to be carried everywhere, and I didn't have a hair on my head." "Marvelous!" exclaimed the tourist. "How long have you lived here?" "Born here," chuckled the native.

See also appetite[1], caution[5], farmer[5], germs[1], London[3], old[1], oyster[2], weak[2].

HEAR

A young man from the country suddenly halted on Broadway in New York and declared, "I hear a cricket!" "Nonsense! You couldn't in this traffic noise," said his com-panion. But the lad walked over to a nearby window-box and pointed out the insect. "Marvelous!" exclaimed his friend, "How'd you do it?" The boy took a quarter from his pocket and dropped it to the pavement. At the clink of its dropping, a dozen New Yorkers dived for the coin. "See," said the boy, "you can always hear what you're listening for."

See also audience[1], music[2], prayer[2], speaker[2].

HEART

1

The doctor shook his head and again applied his stethoscope to the young man. "I don't like your heart action," he declared. "You've had some trouble with angina pectoris, haven't you?" "You're right about the trouble," admitted the young fellow sheepishly, "only you've got the wrong name."

2

"Haven't seen you around lately," one man greeted another. "Oh, I've been in the hospital with a high fever," replied the other. "Gee, too bad! What did they give you to slow down your heart action?" asked the first. "An elderly nurse," he answered.

3

The doctor entered the sickroom with a brisk, businesslike manner. "Good morning," he greeted the pretty nurse. "And how is our patient's heart action this fine morning?" "Oh, excellent, doctor," replied the nurse, blushing. "He's already proposed to me three times."

HEARTBREAK

1

"What's wrong, Anne?" inquired a friend as she walked in to find the girl weeping. "I—it's Elmer," sobbed Anne, "he's b-broken my heart." "The cad!" said her friend fiercely. "A-and that's n-not all," Anne wailed on. "H-he played cards w-with dad and broke him, too."

2

It was a coroner's inquest and the dead man's wife was being questioned. "Then it is your belief," said the coroner, "that your husband died of a broken heart?" "Beyond a doubt," declared the woman positively. "If the brute hadn't broken my heart, I wouldn't have shot him."

3

"What was your last case?" one lawyer asked another. "Breach of promise," replied the second. "My client claimed the man broke her heart, and she was awarded $10,000. What was your case?" "Accident," said the first. "Man hit a woman with his car and broke an arm and two ribs. She was awarded $375." "Hmm!" mused the first lawyer. "It seems advisable in fooling with women to break their bones rather than their hearts."

HEAT

1

A New Yorker was grumbling about the summer heat and a Southerner in New York for a visit overheard him. "Do you folks here call this weather hot!" he asked, amazed. "Why, shucks, the day I left the South it was so hot that I saw a dog chasin' a rabbit, and they were both walkin'."

2

"Shore is hot," said a farmer in front of the general store, mopping his brow, "but it's good fer the crops." "Is the heat really good for the crops?" inquired a tourist of another farmer. "Well, stranger, I'll tell ye," replied that farmer, "in some real hot spell a long time ago some durned fool said so, an' 'twas too hot at the time fer anybody to deny it, an' that's how the damned idea got started."

HEAVEN

1

The sick man had been delirious with fever for days. But now he regained consciousness and became aware of his comfortable bed and the gentle assurance of cool, loving hands. "Where am I?" he asked weakly. "In heaven?" "No, dear," said his wife soothingly. "I'm still with you."

2

"But you must say your prayers, son," insisted the father to his offspring, "or you won't go to heaven." "But I don't want to go to heaven," replied the boy; "I want to go with you an' mom."

3

A talkative drunk climbed aboard a streetcar and sat next to a clergyman. "Humph!" snorted the drunk in a loud tone. "I don't believe in a heaven." The minister merely nodded and went on reading his paper. "D'ya hear?" cried the drunk more loudly. "I don't believe there *is* a heaven." "Very well, my friend," replied the minister pleasantly, "go to hell, then, but please don't make such a fuss."

4

A Sunday-school teacher was trying to enlist her class in the cause of righteousness. "Will all who wish to go to heaven please stand," she requested. All save one small boy immediately stood up. "Why, Jimmie!" cried the teacher aghast. "Do you mean you don't want to go to heaven?" "No, *ma'am,*" replied the boy, "not if that bunch is goin', I don't."

See also breathing[2], California[2], cat[3], dead[1], direction[4], hereafter[5], homesick[3], lying[4], minister[3], spiritualism, wife[9].

HEIGHT

See size.

HELL

1

A meek-looking man arrived in hell. But strangely enough he immediately began conducting himself with considerable arrogance. "Hey, you!" cried Satan, not at all pleased with his bluster. "You act as if you owned the dump." "Well, I sort of figure I do," replied the new arrival; "my wife, my boss, and my neighbor certainly gave it to me often enough."

2

The revivalist was proclaiming hotly against the sins of the modern world and foretelling their future punishment. "Hell, my friends," he shouted, "is filled with liquor, cigarettes, dance halls, short skirts, and one-piece bathing suits. It is—" "Oh, Death, where is thy sting?" cried a voice from the rear.

See also authority, dead[1], place[2].

HELP

1

Cries for help were heard, and Jones ran around the corner to find a large man beating up a much smaller man. His sportsmanship offended, Jones stepped in and with one well-aimed blow knocked out the big fellow. "Gee, thanks," said the little man gratefully, getting up. "I sure appreciate your help. Here, you take half of this forty bucks I just took off him."

2

The housewife had her hands in the dough, and she was annoyed to find that the knock at the door was that of a tramp. "Please, lady," whined the bum, "could you help a poor man out of his troubles?" "Gladly," snapped the woman. "Would you rather be shot, poisoned, or hit with an axe?"

3

A little boy was trying hard to get his heavily-laden cart up the curb. But he couldn't manage it. A kindly old gentleman who was passing laid down his bundles and gave him a hand. "Goodness, son," puffed the old fellow, "I don't see how you ever get that cart over the crossings." "I can't," admitted the boy, "but there's always some nosey gook standin' 'round who does it for me."

4

The old grad was back at his

college on a visit. He was bemoaning the poor quality of present-day football players to the captain of the team. "When I was in college," he boasted, "I helped Harvard beat Yale for three years running." "Indeed, sir?" said the young man politely. "Which team did you say you were on?"

5

A farmer had got a new hired man, but the fellow was not especially satisfactory. "How's that there new hand o' yourn?" asked a friend whom he met in town. "Hand!" snorted the farmer in disgust. "That critter ain't no hand—he's a sore thumb!"

6

A passer-by stood watching the struggles of a truck-driver trying to get a large box from one truck to another as they stood backed together. "Here, let me help you," he volunteered, and taking opposite sides of the box the two puffed, grunted, and struggled for some time without result. "Afraid it's no use," panted the helper, "we'll never get it off." "Off!" cried the driver. "I'm trying to get it on."

7

"May I be of any help?" inquired a passing motorist of a red-faced man who was struggling with a flat tire while his wife stood by. "You sure can, pal," answered the other. "My wife here has very decided views on driving, so if you'll just let her tell you all about it until I get this tire changed, I'll be ever so much obliged."

See also charity[6], conservation, glasses[1], housekeeping, lazy[6], maid, medicine[4], mother-in-law[3], playing, reference, rescue, servant, serving, workman[2].

HEN

See chicken.

HENPECKED

1

A woman was helping her husband pick out a new suit, but the two disagreed over the one to be chosen. "Oh, very well," cried the woman finally, "go ahead and please yourself. After all, I guess you're the one who'll wear the suit." "Well, dear," said the man meekly, "I did figure that I'd probably be wearing the coat and vest anyway."

2

The doctor answered his phone and heard a meek voice which said, "This is Mr. Williams, doctor. My wife has just dislocated her jaw." "That's too bad," replied the doctor. "I'll be right over." "Oh, no hurry, doctor," the voice hastened to assure him. "Any time in the next few weeks will do."

3

The husband had spoken sharply to his fat wife, and the outraged woman had chased him all over the house with a broom. Finally, the man sought refuge under a low bed. She couldn't follow him because of her plumpness. "Come out from there at once, Henry, do you hear!" she panted in fury, poking him with the broom handle. "I shall not!" he declared stoutly, warding off the broom. "I *will* be master in my own home!"

See also boss[1], collar, health[2], listen.

HEREAFTER

1

Brown opened his paper at breakfast one morning and was surprised to see a notice of his own death. Highly amused, he called up a friend and said, "Say, Bill, did you see the announcement of my death in the paper?" There was a gasp, and a pause. "Yes, I did," replied Bill uncertainly, then added, "Say, Brown, where are you calling from?"

2

A farmer called to a neighbor's hired man who was passing by, "Say, Josh, I hear your boss has been sick with a fever. How's his temperature today?" The hired man thought for a moment, then decided not to take a chance. " 'Tain't really fittin' fer me to say," he replied. "The old man died last night."

3

Little Betty had been rummaging through an old dresser drawer when she suddenly exclaimed, "Oh, dear, poor grandpa!" "What makes you say that, Betty?" asked mother. "Well, look," said the girl, holding up a case, "grandpa's gone off to heaven without his glasses."

4

The small-town businessman had been such a pillar of the church that when he passed away the minister posted a sorrowing notice on the church door, reading: "Deacon Brown has left us. He departed for his future home in heaven at 10:30 this morning." Some time later the following was added mysteriously to the notice: "HEAVEN, 4 P.M. Great

anxiety and confusion exists here! Deacon Brown long overdue! No news of him yet!"

5

"Teacher," asked Johnny in Sunday school, "do cannibals go to heaven?" "Of course not," replied teacher. "Cannibals are wicked and always go to hell." "Well, do missionaries go to heaven?" persisted Johnny. "Why, certainly," asserted teacher. "Well, then," inquired Johnny, much puzzled, "what happens to a missionary when he's inside a cannibal?"

6

A member of the congregation had been out of town and didn't know that Deacon Brown had died the week before. Meeting the minister on the street, he inquired, "When do you expect to see Deacon Brown again, Reverend?" "Alas, never again!" declared the preacher mournfully. "The deacon is in heaven."

7

The Sunday-school teacher was talking about the rewards and punishments of the hereafter. She spoke at length upon the glories and wonders of heaven and the horrors and frightfulness of hell. "Now, Helen," he concluded, "would you rather go to heaven or hell?" Little Helen, who had been listening raptly, replied thoughtfully, "Well, teacher, I'd kinda like to see both places."

8

"Now, children," said the Sunday-school teacher, winding up the lesson on the hereafter, "we've learned that if we're good here on earth, when we die we go to a place of everlasting bliss. Who can tell what happens if we're bad?" "In that case, teacher," spoke up a small boy promptly, "we go to a place of everlasting blister."

See also dead[1], future[3], operation[2], spiritualism, teeth[3].

HEREDITY

Two men were discussing modern psychology. "Do you believe in heredity?" asked one. "I'll say I do," declared the other heartily. "That's how I got all my money."

See also breeding[1], collect[4].

HILLBILLY

1

A hillbilly came to town and wandered into a first-class restaurant, bringing a lot of mud in with him. "Look here, my man," barked the head-waiter, "don't you know enough to wipe the mud off your shoes before you come in here?" The hillbilly looked down and around, then asked, "Gawsh A'mighty, mister, *what* shoes?"

2

The fact that the hillbilly hadn't bathed in a long time didn't bother his family in the least. But one day the man had an encounter with a skunk. Then, despite his vigorous protests, they set out to bathe him. Pinning him down, they managed to remove his outer garments and then his long underwear, under which, to their surprise, they discovered a sweater. "Waal, I swan," drawled the victim, "here I bin a-lookin' ev'ry place fer that sweater fer nigh on three year!"

See also ignore, lazy, linen[1], mirror, tough[1].

HINT

1

"How are you getting along with those relatives that show up every Sunday, eat a big dinner, and never invite you in return?" a friend one day asked Jones. "Oh, they stopped coming," replied Jones. "They finally took the hint." "Hint? How did you manage to give them a hint that worked?" inquired the friend. "We just took to serving them sponge cake every time," was the reply.

2

A customer entered a swanky restaurant, sat down, and tied his napkin firmly under his chin. "Outrageous!" gasped the owner to a waiter. "Go over and hint, tactfully, that such things aren't done here." The waiter walked over to the man and asked politely, "Pardon me, sir, but do you want a shave or haircut?"

3

It was getting late and the young couple in the porch swing had not spoken for a half-hour. "Suppose you had money, Frank," asked the girl, breaking the silence at last, "what would you do?" The boy flung his head back, looked far into the distance, and announced grandly, "I'd travel." He felt her warm, soft hand slip into his—then suddenly she was gone. He looked down, and there in his hand was a dime!

4

It was past midnight and still the young man hung around at the front door bidding the girl a lingering good night. Suddenly a loud crash from upstairs broke the silence. "Gracious!" cried the startled lad. "What was that?" "Oh, that was just daddy dropping a hint," replied the girl sweetly.

5

After much pleading, little Jane had been allowed to sit at the dinner table with the guests on condition that she behave. No hitch occurred until the dessert was served, when, by some mischance, Jane's plate was overlooked. Remembering her promise, she sat quietly for a while, until finally she inquired brightly, "Would any one care for a clean plate?"

6

The boyfriend had been keeping company with the girl for two years without showing any signs of serious intentions. One evening he had been boasting of his knowledge of parliamentary law. The girl asked, "What's that phrase the presiding officer uses when he wants to call for a vote?" The boy at once responded proudly, "Are you ready for the question?" "Yes, dear," said the girl coyly, "go right ahead."

7

Father entered the living room where daughter and her boyfriend were sitting. It was past midnight. "Did you want something, daddy?" inquired daughter. Father held out an umbrella he was carrying. "I just wanted to give this to Jack," he explained. "It looks as if it might rain before morning."

8

A country relative came to visit a city couple. He enjoyed his visit so much that he stayed on and on. The couple became impatient over his extended visit. Finally, the young husband one day hinted broadly, "Say, Josh, don't you think that your wife and children must be missing you?" "Gee, thanks for reminding me," said Josh gratefully. "I'll send for 'em right away."

9

The bashful young man one day took his sweetheart on an outing to the zoo. "Isn't it wonderful," he remarked as they walked around the cages, "the lessons we can learn from the poor dumb animals?" "Yes, indeed," agreed the girl heartily, "and especially from the bear." "Why from the bear particularly?" asked the boy. "Because he's so accomplished at hugging, you know," replied the girl.

10

They had been engaged, but he'd never got to the point of setting a date for the wedding. Looking at the paper together one evening, he remarked, "Look, dear, there's a suit for only twenty-one dollars." "Is it a wedding suit?" she inquired. "No, only a business suit," he replied. "Well, I meant business," she declared bluntly.

11

The girl was explaining her actions to a fresh young man. "When I don't want to be bothered any further with a man," she stated, "I always tell him that I live in the suburbs when he asks me where I live." "Very clever, indeed," said the young fellow. "And where do you really live, Miss Brown?" "In the suburbs," was the reply.

See also dream², handkerchief¹, hospitality¹, tipping².

HISTORY

1

"Say, pop," inquired Junior, looking up from his history book, "who was it said, 'We haven't begun to fight yet.'" "I'm not sure, son," answered father, "but it must have been a couple on the first day of their honeymoon."

2

Teacher had been telling the pupils the story of Columbus' discovery of America. She ended with, "And just think, children, all this took place over 400 years ago." "Gosh, teacher," cried a little boy who had been listening with open mouth, "what a memory you've got!"

3

Teacher was conducting a little examination in medieval history. "What happened in 1483?" she questioned. "Luther was born," replied the bright boy of the class. "Correct. Now, Billy," she asked the class's backward member, "what happened in 1488?" Billy thought for a moment before he answered, "Luther was five years old."

4

Little Joan was weak on history, so when teacher asked her, "Who followed Edward VI?" she didn't know. "Don't you remember, Joan?" prompted teacher. "It was Mary. Now, can you tell me who followed Mary?" "I know," cried

Joan proudly. "It was her little lamb."

See also stock market³, war¹.

HOBO

See beggar, tramp.

HOLE

A foreman decided to play a trick on one of his dumb workers. "Tell you what you do," said the foreman. "You go over there and dig a good-size hole and then fill it in again. That'll keep you busy for a while." Later the workman reported, "I did what you said, but there's some dirt left over." The foreman had a ready answer. He said, "Guess you'll have to do it over, but this time dig the hole deeper for the extra dirt."

See also fence.

HOLIDAY

It was the Christmas season when all children should be joyous, but the little girl went along the street weeping. "What's wrong, my child?" asked a kindly lady. "M-my brother's got holidays for Christmas," sobbed the girl, "b-but I d-don't get any." "That's strange," observed the lady. "Why don't you?" "B-because I don't go to school yet," replied the girl.

See also forgive².

HOLLYWOOD

1

A man entered a pet shop and asked the clerk, "Do you have any good talking parrots?" "Yes, we have, sir," replied the clerk. "Now here's a fine bird that for years was kept in the office of a big movie producer—weren't you, Polly?" "Yes, *sir!*" cried the parrot shrilly. "Yes, yes, oh, yes, sir! Yes, indeed! Positively, sir, you're *so* right! Yes, sir!"

2

"That was quite a reception Mrs. Brown gave to the Hollywood stars," remarked one extra to another. "Yes, but she wasn't taking any chances on its being overcrowded," replied the other. "Why, what do you mean?" she was asked. "Well, she sent invitations that read, 'Admit Bearer and One Wife or Husband.'"

3

A Hollywood star was applying for a passport and the clerk was asking her questions as he filled out the form. "Occupation?" "Movie actress," she replied. "Married?" was the next question. "Off and on," was the answer.

4

A movie producer had an afternoon appointment with a well-known writer about a new scenario. But he lunched and drank so long and was so late in returning that the writer was awaiting him in his office and had the manuscript already lying on his desk. "Well, let's see what we have here," he sighed, but he picked up the telephone directory by mistake. "Not a bad little story," he approved, paging through, "but I'm afraid you'll have to cut down the number of characters a little."

5

A man who was engaged to a movie star was rushing a business trip so he could get to Hollywood in time for their wedding. However, he found himself late, so he sent his intended bride a wire, reading: "Delayed three hours. Don't marry any one till I get there."

See also movies, playwright[2].

HOME

1

A wealthy man had made a hobby of painting. He had more enthusiasm than talent. Encouraged, finally, by the praise of some parasitic hangers-on, he invited several critics to view his work. They regarded the daubs silently until at last one paused before a canvas to remark, "Here's one you ought to call 'Home.'" "Why?" asked the amateur eagerly. "Because there's no place like it," said the critic grimly.

2

"Congratulations, Jack," said Bill as he met his friend for the first time in several years, "I hear you married a very talented wife." "Oh, yes, she's quite accomplished," replied Jack. "She's perfectly at home in art, at home in science, quite at home in music and in literature; in fact, she's at home everywhere but at—well—" "Well, but where?" prompted Bill. "Everywhere but at home," answered Jack.

3

"Is your mother at home, sonny?" asked the peddler of a small boy playing in the yard. "Yep," said the boy, continuing his game. The peddler rang the bell a number of times, but got no reply. "Say, are you tryin' to kid me, tellin' me your mother's home?" demanded the peddler sharply. "Well, she is," replied the boy coolly; "but we don't live here."

4

It was late when hubby stumbled in and flung himself into a chair opposite his wife who had been waiting up for him. "So you finally decided to come back, did you?" she said. "I guess you found that home is the best place after all." "Humph!" grunted the unsteady one. "It's the only place open this time of night."

5

A lawyer's wife was complaining to him about their home. "We need furniture, draperies, carpets, and everything," she insisted. "If you'll be patient, dear, I'll take care of it," he promised. "I'm working on a divorce case for a woman now whose husband has plenty of money, and just as soon as I finish breaking up their home, we can fix up ours."

6

"We'll take good care of you, Mr. White," declared the hotel clerk genially to the man who had just registered. "We'll do everything we can to make you feel at home." "If you don't mind, I'd rather you didn't," requested White. "I came away from home to get a change, and what I want is to feel like I'm at a hotel."

See also parents[3].

HOMESICK

1

A company of soldiers was on a long march through the hot, dry desert. They found the well dry at which they'd expected to refill their canteens, so they had to march back without water. During a rest period one of the rookies sat with his head in his hands. "What's wrong with him?" asked the sergeant of another. "Homesick," said the soldier. "So are we all," declared the sergeant. "But it's worse with him," explained the other; "his father owns a saloon."

2

A gloomy-looking man sat down in a restaurant and told the waitress, "Please bring me two eggs fried until they're like rubber, two pieces of dry toast burnt black, and some weak, lukewarm coffee in a greasy cup with sour cream." "Are you kiddin'?" said the waitress. "No, I mean it," insisted the man. When the waitress brought the order she asked, "Anything else?" "Now please sit down and nag me while I eat," requested the man. "I'm homesick."

3

"Hey, rookie, back on the firing line!" commanded the sergeant of a soldier who was trying to slip away during battle. "What if you do get killed—heaven's your home, ain't it?" "That may be," admitted the boy, returning reluctantly, "but right this minute, sarge, I ain't homesick."

4

"Boy, I'm sure homesick," declared Jim to Joe as they were walking down the street. "But wasn't that your home we just passed?" queried Joe. "Yep, that's my home," replied Jim emphatically. "And am I sick of it!"

HOMEWORK

1

"Well, Willie," asked father as he settled down with his evening paper, "are you going to need any help with your homework tonight?" "No, thanks, dad," replied Willie. "I might as well get it wrong all by myself."

2

"Do you think it's right, teacher," asked Johnny earnestly of his teacher, "to punish people for something they haven't done?" "Of course not, Johnny," replied teacher. "That would be most unjust." "I'm sure glad to hear that," Johnny sighed with relief, " 'cause I didn't do my homework."

See also ignorance[1].

HONEST

1

A man was applying for the position of cashier, and he gave the name of one of the clerks of the establishment as reference. The manager sought out this clerk and asked him, "Is this man Williams perfectly honest?" "Honest!" exclaimed the clerk. "Well, I should say! Why, to my own knowledge he's been arrested for stealing eleven times, and acquitted each time."

2

A party of tourists wished to see some Indian ruins in a desolate section of the West. In order to get to them they had to leave their car and walk some distance. When well on their way, one suddenly cried, "Gracious, I forgot to lock the car!" "Don't worry, it's all right," the Indian guide comforted him. "There isn't a white man within fifty miles of this place."

3

Two friends who hadn't met since their school days bumped into each other on the street. "What're you doing these days?" inquired one. "Just trying to earn an honest living," replied the other cheerily. "Well," commented the first, who was in business for himself, "you certainly shouldn't have much competition."

See also business[6, 7], ethics[1], expense[3], finance[1], New York[1], trust[2].

HONEYMOON

1

The newly-married couple stood in their hotel room alone for the first time since the mad bustle of the ceremony and congratulations. "At last, my love," sighed the groom ecstatically, "we are truly one!" "Yes, dear," agreed the bride in a matter-of-fact tone, "but from a practical point of view I think it would be better to order dinner for two."

2

After long and impatient waiting, the soldier finally got his ten-day furlough, rushed home and married his dream girl, and went on a honeymoon. On the ninth day, he wired his commanding officer: "On honeymoon. It's wonderful here. Request five days extension. Answer collect." His commander wired back at once: "It's wonderful any place. Report back to camp at once."

3

It was the first morning after

the honeymoon and they were in their own home. The groom quietly arose early, slipped down to the kitchen, and soon returned with a tasty breakfast for his bride in bed, much to her delight. "Well, did you notice how I fixed it all?" he asked. "Yes, dear, every little detail," she replied lovingly. "Good," he declared. "That's how I want my breakfast served every morning."

4

The newlyweds were touring the West on their honeymoon and halted at a little wayside restaurant in the mountains one afternoon for lunch. After the food had been served, the groom beckoned to the waiter and said, "Waiter, we want a spoon." "Well, go right ahead," replied the waiter, "no one here cares, and they all do it."

See also boat[3], history[1].

HONOR

A middle-aged maiden, while traveling abroad, was invited to an elegant ball at which some royalty was present. In the course of the evening she danced with a Prince. She was overwhelmed when later he asked her to dance a second time. "Oh, Your Highness does me too much honor," she cooed coyly. "Not at all, madam," replied the Prince coldly. "It's just that my physician has ordered me to perspire."

See also fall[2].

HOPE

The doctor had left the man's sickroom and was met at the door by the patient's trembling wife. "Tell me, doctor," she pleaded, "is there no hope that my husband will—" "Go on, madam," prompted the doctor as the woman paused. "Is there no hope, doctor; is there no hope?" the woman repeated. "That all depends, madam," said the doctor, "upon what you are hoping for."

See also seasick[3].

HOPELESS

Two old cronies were known for their stinginess. One of them, who was leaving on a trip, was being seen off at the station by the other. "Well, Bob," observed the traveler, "if you'll lend me a dollar I'll set us up to a farewell drink." "Sorry, Sam," said Bob, "but I give all my spare cash to my old mother." "Go on," replied Sam, "your mother said you never give her anything." "There you are," declared Bob. "If I don't give my poor old mother anything, what chance do you think you have?"

HORSE

1

A farmer had stayed in town drinking quite freely with his friends and was a bit unsteady when he started to drive his mule and wagon home. As they were going along, the mule stumbled and fell, and despite the farmer's shouts and whackings refused to get up. "Come on, git up, durn ye," he cried at last, exasperated, "or I'll drive smack on over ye!"

2

A farmer was trying to sell his

old horse and was pointing out his good points to the unimpressed buyer. "Trot 'er around a bit," the man requested. The farmer did so and, returning with the nag, asked, "Don't you think he has a fine coat?" "Coat's all right," grunted the other, "but I sure don't like his pants."

3

A man walking along a road noticed a farmer driving a horse which every now and then stopped unexpectedly and was started again only with difficulty. "What's the matter, horse sick?" inquired the pedestrian. "Nope," replied the farmer. "Balky?" continued the man. "Well, I'll tell you, mister," explained the farmer. "This horse is so durned afraid I'll say 'Whoa' an' he won't hear me, that he stops every once in a while to listen."

4

Two men met at the races and got to discussing their experiences with horses. "I remember once a horse ran away with me," related the one, "and I wasn't out and around for five weeks." "That's nothing," declared the other. "I once ran away with a horse, and I wasn't out and around for five years."

See also accurate[2], automobile[4, 5], blacksmith[2], defect[2], meat[3], necessity[3], workman[3].

HORSEBACK-RIDING

1

A foreigner was visiting on a Western ranch and decided to go horseback riding. "D'ya want an English saddle or a Western saddle, mister?" asked the cowboy who was

to go with him. "What the difference is?" inquired the foreigner. "Well, the Western saddle's got a horn," explained the cowboy. "She will not be necessary, I think," said the guest. "I intend not to ride in the heavy traffic."

2

The city boy visiting out West decided to learn to ride. The boys thought it a great joke to give him a high-stepping, bucking horse for his first attempt. By some miracle the city boy stuck on though the animal twisted and turned in every direction. Finally, in one of his leaps, the horse caught a foot in a stirrup. "Okay, okay," yelled the beginner in disgust. "If you're gonna get on, I'll get off."

HORSEMANSHIP

1

A city boy sat on the corral fence watching the feats of the cowboys. Suddenly he decided that he'd like to ride, so he borrowed a horse. But barely was he mounted before he found himself sprawling in the dust. "Boy! That horse can sure buck!" declared the city boy. "Buck!" snorted the cowboy. "She only coughed."

2

A new pupil at a riding academy was about to mount a certain horse when the instructor rushed up and warned him, "You'd better choose a different horse; that one has never been ridden." "Oh, that's all right," said the beginner. "I've never ridden on a horse before either, so we'll start off even."

HORSE RACING

1

A Christian lady of very charitable temperament one day noticed an ill-dressed and despondent-looking man standing on a street corner. Her pity aroused, she came near, slipped a dollar into his hand, and whispered, "There's hope." A week later she passed the same man and he handed her ten dollars. "I don't understand," exclaimed the woman. "Why, 'There's Hope' won the third at 9 to 1," the man explained.

2

A man was in court contesting his wife's divorce action. "It's no use, judge," said the woman despairingly; "all he has on his mind is horse racing. Why, he doesn't even remember the day of our wedding." "That's a dirty lie, judge," screamed the man indignantly. "I remember perfectly well that we were married on the day Twenty Grand won the Wood Memorial."

3

"Say, you!" cried a man accusingly to an acquaintance he met on the street. "I put everything I had on that horse you gave me the tip on, and the nag lost." "Lost! Why, I can't believe it!" exclaimed the wise guy. "That horse should have won in a walk." "Well, he sure couldn't," retorted the loser, "but he tried it that way."

HOSPITAL

1

"How does it happen, doctor," demanded the elderly physician of a young interne, "that with the hospital as crowded as it is you ordered a private room for that chorus girl with her trifling ailment?" "Well, er, doctor, you, ah, see," stammered the young fellow, "I thought she was just too cute for wards."

2

A puzzled hospital orderly entered a room carrying a tray on which was a small, thin red object. "I don't get it, but this tray has your number on it," he said to the patient. "Did you order a two-cent stamp?" "Set it down, my boy," said the patient wearily. "It's probably the mutton chop rare that I ordered yesterday."

3

The expectant mother who was being rushed to the hospital didn't quite make it, but instead gave birth to her baby on the hospital lawn. Later, the father received a bill listing: "Delivery room and maternity ward—$150." Greatly angered, he wrote the hospital authorities and explained the circumstances. A short time later he received a corrected bill reading: "Green fees—$110."

See also convalescent[3], diet[3], heart[2], nurse[2, 4], smile[1].

HOSPITALITY

1

Little Tommy was playing in Danny's yard and when it was time for him to go home it began to rain. So Danny's mother gave him a raincoat and galoshes. "Oh, you shouldn't take so much trouble," protested Tommy. "Oh, I'm sure your mother would do as much for Danny," replied Danny's mother.

"Mother'd do more," declared Tommy. "She'd ask Danny to stay for supper."

2

"We ought to have the Jacksons over some evening, dear," suggested hubby. "The Jacksons! Well, I should say not," said the wife emphatically. "Why not, dear?" asked hubby. "Because I entertained her over three months ago," was the reply, "and she never has recuperated."

3

Old Uncle John was the soul of hospitality and always tried his best to make any visitor to the farm feel at home. They had a guest to dinner one day who had already eaten heartily, but still Uncle John asked him to have more. "Oh, come on, have some more," he insisted cordially, passing the platter again; "we're going to throw it to the hogs anyway."

See also mouth[1].

HOST

1

The party was very dull, and a guest who had retired behind a palm to yawn found an equally weary-looking man already there. "Gosh, this affair is an awful bore, isn't it?" said the first. "Let's slip down to the bar on the corner and get a couple of drinks." "Gee, I'd sure like to, but I can't," replied the other. "You see, I'm the host."

2

A minister received a pair of opera tickets from one of his congregation, but upon consulting his calendar he found that he was already engaged for that evening. He called up some friends and said, "I wonder if you could use a couple of opera tickets tonight, as an unfortunate engagement prevents me from going." "We'd be most happy to have them," was the reply, "but we're your unfortunate hosts."

3

The hostess had spared no trouble or expense to prepare the Thanksgiving feast for her guests. She had managed to get a huge turkey, tender and delicious. But as the maid was bringing in the giant bird she stumbled and the turkey skidded to the floor. "Never mind, Mary," said the hostess in kindly tones. "Just take that back to the kitchen and bring in the other turkey."

HOT

See heat.

HOTEL

1

Nightfall forced two tourists to stop at a little wayside hotel where they were shown to a dingy room. "Oh, my!" said the one, turning up his nose disdainfully. "And what does this pigsty cost?" Without a moment's hesitation the proprietor answered, "For one pig, two dollars; for two pigs, three dollars."

2

The country boy who had made good in the big city invited his mother to visit him in town. He installed her in one of the best hotels, in a room with private bath. The morning after her first night he met her and asked, "Did you rest well, mother?" "Not so well, son," replied the old lady. "The room and bed were fine, but I couldn't sleep for fear some one would want to take a bath and the only door to the bathroom was through my room."

3

The train was nearing a small town. A passenger preparing to get off asked his seat-mate, "Say, friend, if you know this town perhaps you can suggest a hotel for me?" "Try the Howes House," advised the other. "Have you stopped there often?" asked the first. "No, never," was the answer, "but I've tried all the rest."

4

A guest at a swanky hotel had just paid his bill and was about to leave when he noticed a sign behind the desk reading: "Have you left anything?" "Humph!" he grunted, turning back to the clerk. "You folks've got that sign all wrong. It should be: 'Have you anything left?'"

5

A guest was about to sign the register of a small-town hotel when he noticed a bedbug crawl over the desk and across the page. "I'll be durned!" he cried, throwing down the pen. "I've been bitten by every kind of insect in hotels all over the country, but this is the first time a bug has ever stopped to get my room number from the register before going to work on me!"

6

The lady tourist was displeased with the looks of the dingy little hotel. "Of course, my man, you've hot and cold running water in this hotel?" she said. "Of course, madam," replied the clerk. "It's hot in summer and cold in winter."

7

"Where've you been lately, Sam?" asked Jones of his friend on the street. "Oh, I went to a hotel for a change and rest," explained Sam. "And how did you make out?" queried Jones. "Well," responded Sam, "the bellhop got the change, and the hotel got the rest."

8

The wife was staying at an expensive resort hotel. At the end of the first week she wrote her husband a letter, saying: "Dear Jack, I am enclosing the hotel bill." A few days later she received a reply, stating: "Dear Jill, I am enclosing a check for the bill, but please don't buy any more hotels at that price—they're robbing you!"

See also bed[1], best[3], caution[1], celebration[1], distance[1], home[6], Indian[1], luggage[1], meals[1], noise[1], room[1, 3], towel[1], view[2].

HOUSE

1

"How many closets are there in our new house, dear?" asked the bride of her husband. "Fifteen, my sweet," was the answer. "But will that be enough, John?" asked the bride anxiously. "Enough!" cried John. "Surely, fifteen closets ought to be enough to hold your clothes." "Well, yes, I think so," admitted the wife. "But you'll probably be wanting part of one closet for your clothes, won't you, dear?"

2

"You dirty robber!" cried an indignant man, bursting into the real-estate office. "When you sold me that dump of a house a short time ago you said I wouldn't part with it in three months for $25,000." "That's right," agreed the realtor calmly. "And you haven't, have you?"

3

A real-estate agent took a client to inspect some low-priced houses. Leaving the customer in one room, he went into the next room and asked in a low voice, "Can you hear me?" "Yes, I can, faintly," replied the client. "Hmm," observed the agent, nonplussed for a moment. "Well, can you see me?" "No, I can't," was the answer. "There you are!" cried the agent triumphantly. "Them's walls for you, ain't they?"

4

Three young boys were boasting about their parents' accomplishments. "My pop's gonna build a swell house with a flagpole on it," bragged one. "That's nothin'," declared the second. "Mine's gonna build a big house with a tower on it." "Oh, pooh!" said the third. "My dad's gonna build a house with a mortgage on it."

5

Mrs. Brown frowned when she opened the door to a caller with a dog on a leash. "I'd much rather you didn't bring your dog into the house," she requested! "it's full of fleas." "Goodness! I'll certainly not bring the little pet in then," was the shocked answer. "I had no idea

you let your house get in such condition."

See also architecture[2], moron[8], tenant[1, 2].

HOUSEKEEPING

"My wife does all her own cooking, canning, mending, washing, and ironing," boasted Smith. "She must be quite a hard worker," observed his friend. "Don't you ever help her with any of the work?" "Oh, sure, I do," replied Smith. "On Mondays I usually wash the dishes for her, on Wednesdays I help her clean the furniture, and on Saturday nights I mop the floor with her."

See also cookbook[1], dust[2], exercise[5], neat[2], recovery[6].

HUMANE

The cultured woman got a cat from the Humane Society. A few days later she called the Society to complain, "I'm afraid I'll have to ask you to come and take your cat back as I find the inhuman beast makes a practice of killing birds in my garden." As an afterthought she added, "I'm sorry for the trouble I'm causing you, and I'll have my husband make you a contribution as soon as he returns from the North where he went to shoot deer."

HUMBLE

The bashful boyfriend one day approached the girl and asked, "I was wondering, Ethel, if you'd like to have a puppy?" "Why, you sweet boy!" gurgled the girl delightedly.

"How delightfully humble of you! Of course, dear, I accept."

See also photography[4], walking[3].

HUNTING

1

It was dusk when George returned to camp from a day's hunting. He met Joe out gathering wood. "All the rest of the boys back?" he asked anxiously. "Yep. All back," replied Joe. "All eight of them, all safe and sound?" persisted George. "Yep," said Joe again, "all of 'em, safe and sound. Why?" "Well, in that case," announced George proudly, "I've shot a deer."

2

A group of hunters from the city, loaded down with all the modern equipment, were tramping through the woods when they met a barefoot boy armed with only a slingshot. "What are you hunting for, sonny?" queried one of the men smilingly. "Dunno," replied the boy. "Ain't seen it yit."

3

Two hunters had been out since dawn and now it was getting dark. A growing uneasiness in the breast of one suddenly blossomed into panic. "We're lost, Bill, we're lost!" he cried. "What'll we do?" "Aw, take it easy," cautioned Bill calmly. "Just shoot an extra deer and the game warden'll be here in about two minutes."

4

A city man visited a farmer friend to do some hunting. Early the next morning the hunter went forth, supplied with five fine hunting dogs by the farmer, but he was back within the hour. "Back so soon?" questioned the farmer. "Yeah," replied the hunter, "I need more dogs." "More dogs!" cried the farmer. "Why, those I gave you were some of the best." "I know," replied the other, "but I've shot all those already."

5

He was showing her his trophies and boasting of his hunting adventures. "This Polar bear I shot in the Arctic," he said, pointing to a skin rug. "Believe me, it was a tight squeeze; it was a case of me or the bear." "I believe you decided wisely," agreed the girl thoughtfully; "the bear definitely makes the better rug."

6

Algy was visiting a friend who lived in a wild part of India. One day borrowing a gun, he announced that he was going tiger hunting. Some time later his friend heard a distant rifle-shot and, going to a window, saw Algy in the distance running like mad with a large tiger in hot pursuit. As Algy neared the house, he shouted with his remaining breath, "I say, open the door quickly! I'm bringing him back alive!"

7

Two city men went hunting one day and, after they had been out a while, one heard a shot and cried to the other, "Whatcha get?" "A pheasant," was the proud reply. The first came up to take a look at the game, and snorted, "A pheasant, my eye! That's a screech owl." "Well, what's the difference?" retorted the other. "When I eat a bird

I eat its meat, and I don't care what kind of voice it's got."

8

A musician once went hunting with a group of experienced hunters and horsemen. But he found the going too strenuous, and a friend came across him a little later sitting contentedly by a high gate while his horse stood grazing nearby. "What's wrong?" asked the friend. "Were they calling too fast a tune for you?" "That's right. And this," the musician nodded toward the gate, "is my five-bar rest."

See also club[3], detail, humane, moron[10], odor[3], shooting[1, 3], sportsmanship[2].

HURRY

1

A moron raced into a barber shop and shouted, "Gimme a haircut, quick." "Sure," said the barber. "Just take off your hat and coat and sit down." "No, no," he objected. "I'll keep them on and stand." "But why?" queried the barber. "Because I'm in a hurry," explained the moron.

2

A drunk hailed a taxi and fell into the back seat. "Jush drive 'roun' block a hunert times," he ordered. The driver looked amazed, but set about carrying out his request. On the seventy-third circuit of the block the drunk leaned forward and tapped the driver on the shoulder. "Shay, shake it up, can'sha, buddy?" he requested. "I'm in a hurry."

3

The ferry was about four feet away from the dock when an excited young man rushed up, gave a big leap that carried him across the water and onto the deck of the boat. "Well," he observed as he got up painfully and brushed himself off, "I made it, anyway." "What's your rush, mate?" asked a deckhand. "The boat's comin' in."

4

"Where's my hat?" cried the doctor as he hung up the phone. "I've got to hurry over to the White's—their boy's sick." "Is it that serious?" asked his wife, handing him his hat. "It sure is," said the doctor, rushing for the door. "I don't know what's wrong with the boy, but she's got one of those books on 'What to do before the doctor comes,' and I must get there before she does it."

5

A lady rushed into a little hardware store near the railroad station and clamored for attention. "Clerk, clerk, quickly, please!" she cried. "Give me a mousetrap right away, please, because I want to catch a train."

See also efficiency[4], firemen[3], punctual[4], punishment[6], speeding[2, 3], teeth[6].

HURT

See injury, pain, wound.

HUSBAND

1

There had been another family quarrel, and the man observed, "A man's a fool to get married. A husband leads a dog's life." "You said it!" agreed the wife heartily. "He growls all day and snores all night."

2

A man looked up from his paper on the 5:20 and observed to his seat-mate, "It says here that they occasionally find earthworms in Australia that are ten feet long." "Is that so?" grunted the old married man. "Well, we don't have 'em that long here, but we have 'plenty between five and six feet who work themselves to a frazzle trying to make enough money for their families to keep up with the Joneses."

3

The preacher (an unmarried man) had been giving a sermon on unnecessary domestic strife, and he concluded by saying, "Now, all you husbands be honest and let each of you who has trouble at home stand up." All but one man immediately arose. "Ah, sir!" cried the minister, "You are one in a million!" "Heck, it ain't that," growled the seated one. "It's just that I'm paralyzed and can't get up."

4

A tearful woman entered a police station with a picture in her hand, which she showed to the desk sergeant and sobbed, "This is a picture of my missing husband. I wish you'd find him for me." The sergeant eyed the picture, then inquired, "Why?"

5

"How does it happen that you've never married?" asked an acquaintance of an old maid. "Pooh!" retorted the spinster. "I have a dog that growls over everything he eats, a parrot that swears whenever it opens its mouth, a fireplace that smokes and scatters ashes on the rug, and a cat that stays out all night. What need do I have for a husband?"

6

A woman who was getting a divorce was complaining to a widowed friend about all the bother she was subjected to with her lawyers. "Oh, you don't have to tell me anything about these legal tangles," declared her friend. "I tell you, I've had so much trouble over my property that, I swear, I actually sometimes wish my husband hadn't died."

7

"Henry, you blasted idiot!" roared the wife sternly. "Take your big feet off that table, don't tilt back your chair, and stop smoking this instant!" "See here, Annie," spoke up the man angrily, "there's only one person in the world I permit to talk to me like that." "And who is that?" thundered the wife, approaching threateningly. "You, dear," was the meek reply.

8

An acquaintance stopped by to offer his condolences to the widow. "Your husband," he said earnestly, "was a man of exceptionally fine qualities." "Yes," agreed the widow with a sigh, "he must have been a very good man, as every one says so. Personally, of course, I wasn't very well acquainted with him. You see, he belonged to a half-dozen lodges, a number of clubs, and two bowling leagues."

9

It was the day before Washington's Birthday and teacher was telling of the many virtues of the Father of Our Country, emphasizing his bravery, resourcefulness, honesty, sincerity, perseverance, and kindliness. "And now, children," concluded teacher, "for what high position in the nation do you think such a man would be fitted?" A little girl in the rear raised her hand and answered, "He'd make a very nice husband."

NOTE: This subject has not been cross referenced because of its frequent occurrence throughout this dictionary.

ICE

1

The professor was lecturing the science class on the states of matter. "Now, can you tell us, Mr. Jones," he questioned, "what is the biggest change that occurs when water becomes ice?" Jones looked up through sleepy eyes and mumbled, "The price, sir."

2

The bride proudly announced to her husband, "I told you I was going to be a help to you, dear. I made a deal today that's going to save you a lot of money." "What did you do?" asked the husband. "I made arrangements to get our ice from a new iceman," she explained, "and he's promised to give us colder ice for the same money."

3

The thirsty passenger stuck his head out from his berth in the Pullman and demanded, "Porter, get me another glass of ice water, please." "Sorry, sir, but I'm afraid I can't," replied the porter. "You

see, if I take any more ice off'n that corpse in the baggage car it ain't gonna keep."

IDEA

"Good morning, sir," said the ambitious young man as he burst into the boss's office. "I'm Smith who sent you those ideas on how to increase your business. Did you carry any of them out?" "Did you notice that office boy with the waste basket who passed you just as you were coming in?" asked the boss. "Yes, sir, I did," was the reply. "Well," said the boss, "he was carrying out your ideas."

IDEAL

"It is very important for people to have ideals," insisted a young lady. "Yes, I once had an ideal," confessed the elderly woman. "And what happened to it?" queried the other. "I married him," was the bitter reply.

IDENTIFY

1

A stranger called at the village post office for a registered letter, but the clerk said, "You'll have to offer some proof of your identity. The stranger drew a photograph from his pocket and handed it to the clerk who looked at it and then the man for a moment, and said, "Yep. That's you, all right. Here's your letter."

2

"What's this I hear, Tommy," scolded mother, "about your fighting with one of those two new boys who moved in next door?" "Yes'm, but it wasn't really fightin'," Tommy explained. "You see, the two of 'em are twins and I just gave one of 'em a black eye so's I could tell 'em apart."

3

"You dirty shyster!" said one lawyer to another in court. "Before this case is over I'll show you cheap chisler up for the mangy gorilla you are." "Why, you crumby donkey!" cried the other. "A cheating liar and lousy half-wit like you won't show up anybody!" "Come, come," interrupted the judge. "Now that learned counsel have identified each other, let the case proceed."

4

The lady presented a check to the paying teller, but he shook his head regretfully. "Sorry, madam," he explained, "but before I can cash that check you'll have to get someone to introduce you." "Sir," said the lady haughtily, "I'll have you know that I'm here on business, not to make a social call; and besides, I'm not sure that I care to know you."

See also check[1], marks.

IDENTITY

1

Two hillbillies knocked on a cabin door and, when the knock was answered, said, "Howdy, Jake. Me'n Tom jist found a dead feller over in th' holler and we thought mebbe 'twas you'uns." "What'd he look like?" asked Jake. "Oh, he was 'bout your size an'—" "Have on a flannel shirt?" interrupted Jake." "Yep." "With red checks?" continued Jake. "No; this'n was gray

with—" Jake turned to close the door, saying, "Nope, 'tweren't me."

2

The young lady walked up to the elderly woman who appeared to be the hall supervisor in the hospital, and said, "I wish to see Mr. James Brown, please." "And who are you, may I ask?" said the woman politely. "I'm his sister," declared the girl. "Well, I'm certainly glad to meet you, my dear," said the woman warmly. "I'm his mother."

3

A very stout woman in bizarre clothes got on a crowded bus and made her way to the only vacant seat. A small boy across from her looked at her then turning to his mother said in loud tones, "Mummy, it's a lady." "Hush, I know," cautioned mother. "But, mummy," objected the puzzled boy, "I just heard you ask daddy when she got on, 'What in the world's this object getting on?'"

4

Special services were being held in Westminster Abbey on Armistice Day and many notables were there. But out of the throng stepped a woman who tried to force her way into the midst of things. "Let me pass," she insisted to a policeman who halted her. "But who are you, madam?" asked the policeman doubtfully. "Who am I!" cried the woman indignantly. "I, my man, am the widow of the Unknown Soldier."

5

A small boy was taking his first railroad journey to grandma's alone.

His mother, fearful lest he get lost, told him to write his name and address on a card and keep it in his pocket in case anything went wrong. So the boy wrote: "In case of accident, this was Sammy Brown, from Hillsboro."

See also coat[1], pants[2], statue[5].

IDLE

It was a hot day and the sweating farmer straightened up from his work to greet a passing neighbor. "Shore is hot, ain't it, Zeb?" he observed, wiping his brow. "Yuh know, I sometimes kinda envy them idle rich." "Shucks, why envy them?" asked the neighbor. "I know fellers what ain't got a dollar who kin be as idle as anybody."

IGNORANCE

1

Junior looked up from his homework to ask, "How far is it to the nearest star, pop?" "I'm sure I don't know that one," confessed the father. "Humph!" sniffed Junior with a frown. "Well, all I can say is that I hope you'll feel sorry tomorrow when I'm being punished for your ignorance."

2

Teacher was testing the general information of her class and she asked, "In what part of the country are the most ignorant people found?" Without hesitation a small boy volunteered, "In New York." "Why, where did you ever get such information?" gasped the teacher. "Out of my geography," replied the boy. "It says that in New York the population is densest."

3

The man who was nursing a painful bruise observed to a friend, "Whenever I get hurt like this I always envy you." "Why, in what way?" asked the friend. "Well, you know the old saying, what you don't know doesn't hurt you?" asked the first. "Of course," said the other. "So, you lucky dog," declared the bruised one, "you're invulnerable."

4

A lady who was seated next to a noted scholar at dinner chatted with the learned man so amiably and readily that he complimented her, saying, "You appear well-informed on a number of subjects, madam." "Oh, nonsense," she replied modestly. "I've just been concealing my ignorance." "Not at all, madam," insisted the great man. "Quite the contrary, I assure you."

See also fool, law[4], moron, sarcasm[7].

IGNORE

"Fetch me thet axe, son," commanded a hillbilly of a boy, but the lad went on sitting and ignoring the old man. "Didn't you hear your father speak to you, boy?" asked a tourist who happened by at that moment. "Oh, sure, I heerd 'im," admitted the boy lazily, "but I don't pay the old feller no mind. Neither does maw ner sis, and 'tween us'uns all we jest about got the dawg so he don't."

ILL

See sick.

IMAGINATION

"How's your father feeling, Mary?" inquired a woman of a little girl on the street. "Oh, he's feeling pretty sick," replied Mary. "Nonsense," declared the woman with optimism. "He only imagines he's sick." A few days later she met the girl again and repeated the question. "Well," answered the girl hesitatingly, "today pop imagines he's dead."

See also scenery².

IMITATION

1

"I hope, Mrs. Smith," the neighbor spoke up indignantly, "that you have spoken to your boy about mimicking me on the street." "I certainly have, Mr. Brown," replied the woman. "I told him not to go around acting like a fool in public."

2

It was approaching midnight, but still the young man had not exhausted his bag of parlor tricks. "And did you know," he asked brightly, "that I can imitate any bird you care to mention?" "Indeed?" she said, wearily. "Can you imitate a homing pigeon?"

3

The young fellow entertained the company with his impersonations of people, and at a party one evening he undertook to imitate a certain famous actor who was present. "What did you think of my performance?" he asked the actor later. "Well, one thing is certain," observed the actor, "one of us is terrible."

4

The public-speaking class was studying appropriate gestures, and the professor was calling on one after the other to go to the platform and give a performance. When it came the turn of one not-too-bright student, he went to the platform and stood still. "Well, what are you supposed to represent?" asked the prof. "I'm imitating a man going up in an elevator," was the reply.

5

A lady was walking through the park when two ragged little urchins approached her and one said, "Fer a nickel, lady, me brudder'll do an imitation of a chicken fer ya." "And what will he do?" questioned the lady, searching for a coin. "Crow?" "Naw. Dat's old stuff," declared the lad witheringly. "He'll eat a worm."

IMPERSONAL

A gangster rushed into a bar waving and firing his gun at random and shouting, "All youse dirty, lousy skunks get outta here." Within a minute the patrons had fled in panic, dodging bullets as they ran, all save one meek-looking little fellow who stood at the bar finishing his drink. "Well?" barked the gangster menacingly, waving his smoking gun. "Goodness," observed the little man, "there were certainly a lot of them, weren't there?"

IMPORTANCE

1

The successful businessman was so proud of his rise from nothing that he presumed everyone knew of his fame. He stopped at a small country hotel one night, and as he entered the dining room next morning the only other occupant in the room arose from his table. "Tut,

tut!" said the great man condescendingly. "Sit down, sit down!" "Why the heck should I?" asked the other, surprised. "I want to get that jelly from the next table."

2

The fellow had never amounted to anything but, when oil was struck on his land, he suddenly became very pompous and important. Rushing into the railroad station one day, he pushed ahead of the other people, flung down a fifty-dollar bill, and said, "Gimme a ticket, quick." "But to where?" asked the puzzled agent. "Any place," replied the important man. "I got business all over."

3

Teacher had been lecturing her class on some of the great modern inventions, and now she questioned, "Who can tell what there is of great importance today that did not exist forty years ago?" A bright little fellow promptly raised his hand and answered modestly, "Me."

4

A young wife was boasting to a friend about what a great man her husband was, but the friend was skeptical. "I guess he's a greater man than Edison or Ford," said the friend. "Well, I should hope so," said the wife. "Why, he's greater than any President we've ever had." "Is he greater than God?" sneered the friend. "Well, perhaps not," admitted the wife reluctantly; "but he's still young."

5

Miss Williams, a young Hollywood starlet, was quite certain that she was one of the world's most important people. So when at a dance one evening a strange young man brusquely cut in on her, she asked coldly, "Do you know with whom you're dancing?" "Nope," was the reply. "I," she announced impressively, "am Gloria Williams." "And do you know with whom you are dancing?" asked the boy. "I do not," she said. "Nobody," he replied, walking away and leaving her alone.

6

"The man speaks very well," observed one in the audience at a lecture, "but does he have any prominence?" "Say, that speaker comes from one of the most prominent families in this section," replied his companion. "Why, on the day his grandfather passed away all the stores in town closed, and on the day after his father went away, all the banks in town closed."

7

A newly-elected Congressman took his little daughter on a tour of the Capitol. After she had seen the splendors of the chambers, assembly rooms, etc., she grew quiet and thoughtful. "What's troubling you, dear?" asked father. "Well, daddy, I was just thinking," she said in somewhat dejected tones, "that you're such a big man in our house, but you're not very much around here."

8

"That new bookkeeper of yours seems to be a very important man in your office," observed a caller to the boss. "That's right," agreed the boss. "Ah, then he is important?" asked the caller. "No, no," said the boss strongly. "You were right the first time—he just seems important."

See also asylum[1], better[3], boast[2], conceit, dignity, fame[2], impudence, indispensable, success[4].

IMPRESSION

The psychology professor had been lecturing on the mental states. "Now, gentlemen, in looking on you as a group I get an impression," he said, tapping his head with his forefinger. "Who of you can tell me what an impression is?" There was a long pause before one of the students ventured, "I know, professor. An impression is a dent in a soft place."

See also lesson.

IMPROVEMENT

He was a good father but he would never have won a beauty prize. He was sitting one evening near a mirror with his young daughter on his lap, and the girl was looking at herself in the glass. "Papa, did God make you?" she asked. "Yes, dear," replied father. "And did He make me, too?" continued the girl. "Of course," said father. The girl took another look in the mirror, then observed, "Seems to me that He's doing better work lately."

IMPUDENCE

A man entered a restaurant with two children. When the waiter came he ordered three plates and three glasses of water, then taking some sandwiches from his pocket he unwrapped them and they began to eat. The astounded manager ap-

proached and said, "You know, sir, this is not a—" "Who are you?" interrupted the man. "I'm the manager," was the reply. "Good, I was just going to send for you," said the man. "Why the heck ain't the orchestra playing?"

See also diagnosis[1].

INCOME

"John finally said he loves me, dad," she confessed blushingly. "Does he want to marry you?" asked father. "Oh, yes," replied the maiden. "Well, what's his income?" grunted the old man. "Now, that's a coincidence!" she cried, surprised. "John asked me the very same question about you."

INDEPENDENT

1

"Mamma," said the little girl coming into the kitchen, "please button my dress." "I'm sorry, dear," said mother, her hands in dough, "but I can't. You'll have to do it yourself." "Oh, dear!" sighed the child, struggling with the buttons. "I dest don't know what I'd do wifout myself."

2

"And now," said teacher ponderously, concluding a stirring little lecture on ambition and self-reliance, "who can tell me why we should strive to rise by our own efforts?" "I know," cried little Willie eagerly. "Because you don't know when something might happen to the alarm clock."

See also devil[1].

INDIAN

1

A buck Indian, schooled in the ways of the white man, once took a friend who had never been off the Reservation on a visit to the big city. They arrived late and went at once to a modern hotel where they engaged a room and private bath. In the stillness of the night, a war-whoop suddenly rent the air, and rushing to the Indians' room the manager found the sophisticated buck lying on the bathroom floor with an arrow through his heart. The other Indian looked up in outraged dignity and declared simply, "Him foul spring!"

2

The class had just had a lesson on the American Indian, and now the teacher was asking, "What are the leaders of the tribes called?" One bright little girl immediately volunteered, "Chiefs." "Correct," said teacher. "And what are the women called?" After a brief pause, a boy ventured, "Mis-chiefs."

3

A teacher in an Oklahoma school one day remarked, "I wonder if any of you children have some Indian blood." "I have, teacher," replied Tommy. "That's quite interesting," observed teacher. "What tribe?" "Well, I don't think it was exactly a tribe," said Tommy, "it was just a wandering Indian."

See also bigamy[1], chivalry[3], honest[2], lost[2], medicine[2].

INDIFFERENT

The sergeant had been drilling rookies for a long time, but this one was the worst he'd ever seen. The more he shouted and cursed, the less concerned the rookie appeared to be. "Don't anything I say make no difference to you?" the exhausted sergeant finally asked. "Not in the least," replied the rookie cheerfully. "You see, in civilian life I was a baseball umpire."

INDISPENSABLE

1

A foreman of a big shop who was called up for jury duty was trying to get excused. "We're awfully busy at the shop," he explained to the judge, "and I ought to be there." "Humph!" grunted the judge. "Guess you're one of those fellows who think the company can't get along without him." "Oh, no," replied the foreman quickly, "I know darned well they can, but I don't want them to find it out." "Excused," said the judge promptly.

2

A friend called by a businessman's office to go to lunch with him and inquired, "How's your new office boy coming along?" "Oh, just fine," replied the other. "He certainly knows his job—he's got everything so mixed up now that I just can't get along without him."

See also hanging[1].

INDULGENT

Mrs. Johnson was consoling a neighbor whose husband's brutal treatment of her was neighborhood talk. "I can feel for you, my dear," she said in mock sympathy, "especially as my own husband is so indulgent." "Oh, yes, we all know that," purred the other. "It's just a pity that he often indulges too much!"

INHERITANCE

1

"Why so sad about your aunt's death?" asked a man of his dejected friend. "You never appeared overly fond of the old lady before." "No, I never cared much about her," agreed the melancholy one, "but it's just that it was through my efforts that she was kept in a lunatic asylum for the past eight years, and now she's gone and willed me all her money and I've got to prove that she was of sound mind!"

2

"I'll have you understand," declared the wealthy young man, "that all the money I've got I got through hard work." "Aw, go on!" said his friend scornfully. "I happen to know that it was all left to you by your rich uncle." "Sure it was," agreed the other. "But don't you ever think it wasn't tough work getting it away from the lawyers."

3

"Thanks, doc," said the patient, rising to go. "Since you and I have been pals from our schooldays, I wouldn't dream of insulting you by offering you money. But I want you to know that I've remembered you generously in my will." "That's sure nice of you, old fellow," replied the doctor thoughtfully. "By the way, let me see that prescription again, will you—there's a little correction I'd like to make in it."

4

A friend of the family stopped by to console a woman whose husband had died. "Your husband was a fine man and a good provider," he commented. "I suppose he left you quite a bit?" The woman smiled grimly. "Practically every night," she replied.

5

"Say, uncle," requested little Junior one evening, "would you mind makin' a noise like a frog?" "Now, why in the world do you want me to make a noise like a frog, Junior?" asked uncle. "Well, there's an awful lot of things I want," explained Junior, "an' whenever I ask pop to get me any of 'em he always says, 'Just wait until your uncle croaks, son.'"

See also heredity, medicine[4].

INJURY

1

A couple of old fellows sat at the club swapping experiences. "I recall the time in the Zulu War," related the retired colonel, "when a Zulu threw a spear and pinned me to the ground with it, and there I lay for three days." "Goodness, it must have hurt!" exclaimed the other. "Oh, it wasn't so bad," said the colonel, "except when I laughed."

2

With screeching brakes a car skidded in a wide circle, struck a pedestrian standing at a crossing, and flung him about thirty feet. "Are you hurt, sir?" asked a kindly passer-by who rushed to help him up and dust him off. "Well," replied the victim, gingerly bending one joint after another, "it's a cinch it ain't done me any good."

3

A soldier sat in a hospital. His entire head was wrapped in bandages except for two tiny eye holes. "Oh, you poor fellow!" cried a lady visitor sympathetically. "Were you wounded in the head?" "Oh, no ma'am," replied the soldier gravely. "It was me ankle where I was hit, but me bandages has slipped."

See also demonstration, smoking[2].

INJUSTICE

Two boys who had been disorderly in school were told by the teacher to remain after school and to write their names 500 times as punishment. After they had been busy writing for about twenty minutes, one boy started weeping and said to the teacher, "You ain't bein' fair to me! His name's Bly an' mine's Heatheringston!"

See also mother-in-law[2].

IN-LAWS

See father-in-law, mother-in-law, relatives.

INNOCENCE

She was dining with her boyfriend's family for the first time, and the sweet, unspoiled innocence of her face was a joy. "Wouldn't you like a Scotch and soda before dinner?" suggested the boy's father devilishly. "Oh, sir, I've never tried liquor," she protested blushingly. "Well, try one now and see if you like it," the old man insisted. Daintily she raised her glass to taste, then her smooth brow clouded.

"What's the idea!" she cried. "You gave me Irish whiskey!"

INSANITY

A famous psychiatrist was called in by the supervisor of an asylum to see what he could do for one of the inmates. "This man is most insistent that he's a king," said the supervisor as he showed the specialist to the man's cell. "I *am* a king," said the man. "Satan told me so." At this an angry voice from the next cell broke in, "He lies, gentlemen; I told him nothing of the sort!"

See also interest[1], jury[2], President[1], wife[1].

INSECTS

1

A farmer got on a train and noticed across the aisle a sheriff with a handcuffed man next to him. "What's he done, Sheriff?" inquired the farmer. "Bugs," replied the sheriff, pointing significantly to his head. "He's crazy." "Well," cried the farmer. "Bugs in his head and his hands tied! No wonder he's crazy!"

2

"Are caterpillars good to eat, pop?" asked little Billy at the dinner table. "Goodness! Of course not!" exclaimed father. "Why must you ask such things when we're eating?" "Oh, I was just wonderin'," replied Billy calmly, "'cause there was just one on your lettuce, but he's gone now."

3

Mother glanced from the window

and saw her little son standing quiet and thoughtful before a blackberry bush. "Is anything wrong, son?" she called. "Do blackberries ever have legs, mom?" he asked. "Why, of course not, dear," replied mother. At this the boy looked more thoughtful than ever. "Guess, then, it *was* a caterpillar I swallowed," he decided.

4

A government crop inspector was going through a rather primitive part of Kentucky and stopped to talk with one of the natives. "Are you folks around here ever troubled with insects getting into your corn?" he asked. "Shucks, yes, mister," was the reply. "But we-uns jest fishes 'em out an' drinks it down anyway."

5

A woman from the poorer section of town entered a drug store. "Gimme a penny's worth of insect powder," she ordered when the clerk came up. "But that's hardly enough to be worth wrapping up," objected the clerk. "Who the heck asked you to wrap it up?" replied the woman scornfully. "Here, jist blow it down me back."

6

Little Sally was interested in watching the gardener putting bands around the fruit tree trunks. "What's that for?" she inquired. "That's to keep insects from crawling up the tree," explained the gardener. A few days later when Sally was in town with her mother they passed a gentleman with a mourning band around his left sleeve. "Oh, mamma," cried the little girl excitedly, "what keeps 'em from crawlin' up his other arm?"

See also ants, coward[2], deceive[2], flies, hotel[5], mosquito.

INSOMNIA

1

A wan-looking man entered a drug store. "Can you give me something for my insomnia?" he requested. "The least noise keeps me awake. Even a cat on the back fence stops my sleeping." The druggist disappeared into the rear and soon returned with a small packet. "This powder ought to do the trick," he said. "Good! When do I take it?" asked the customer. "You don't," explained the druggist. "Just give it to the cat in milk any time."

2

A man from the audience came to the platform at the end of the lecture and shook the hand of the speaker warmly. "I'm certainly happy that I attended your lecture on insomnia, doctor," he said. "Did you find it that interesting?" asked the doctor. "Heck, no," replied the other happily, "but it sure did cure my insomnia."

3

The rabid lodge and club member, very much upset, called on his doctor. "It's about my wife, doc," he explained. "She suffers from insomnia so badly that sometimes she remains awake until after two in the morning. What can I do for her?" The doctor, who had known the man and his habits for years, merely grunted, "Go home earlier."

4

"Looks like you're still suffering from insomnia," observed a man to a gaunt, hollow-eyed friend he met on the street. "What are you taking for it now?" "I take a large glass of whiskey every thirty minutes," replied the sleepless one. "Does that make you sleep?" asked the first. "Oh, no," answered the other, "but it makes me content to stay awake."

INSPIRATION

The landlady was telling the new boarder interesting facts about her life as he ate. "Then there was my second husband, poor fellow, who was an artist," she related. "He insisted that he found inspiration in my cooking." The boarder tried once more to cut his pie crust, then laid the bent fork aside. "He was a sculptor, I presume," he said glumly.

INSTRUCTIONS

1

A housewife decided to go shopping, so she locked up the house and for the benefit of the grocer left a note on the door, reading: "Gone for the day. Don't leave anything." On her return that evening, she found the house had been broken into and ransacked, all of her valuables gone, and an addition to her note which read: "Thanks a lot! We didn't leave much."

2

The blacksmith had hired a new and inexperienced helper and was instructing him in his duties. "Now, I'll bring the hot shoe from the forge and lay it on the anvil," he directed, "and then when I nod my head you hit it with this hammer." The helper did exactly as he had been told, but the first thing the blacksmith did when he got out of the hospital was to fire him.

3

The boss had given the new office boy explicit instructions, so the lad halted the caller in the outer office and demanded, "Are you a salesman, a bill-collector, or just a friend of the boss?" The caller smiled and responded, "I'm all three." The boy was puzzled. But he said, "Well, in that case, he's in conference; he's out of town; and hop right in and see him."

4

"My instructions to you, madam," directed the doctor as he finished his examination, "is to bathe frequently, get enough fresh air, and dress in cool, loose clothing." "What'd the doctor say?" inquired the woman's husband when she came home. "He said that I must get to Atlantic City for awhile, and then to the mountains," replied the wife, "and that I must have some new light dresses at once."

5

"Have you given your husband this medicine according to directions, madam?" asked the doctor. "I've done me best, doc, but somethin' musta went wrong," said the woman despondently. "You said to give Bill one o' them pills three times a day until gone, an' here I've done run outta pills an' he ain't gone yit."

See also ants[2], medicine[3], singing[1].

INSULT

1

A beggar who had just been refused by a gentleman on the street, asked, "How many chiselin' skinflints do you figure live on this street besides you?" "Besides me!" exploded the gentleman angrily. "Do you mean to insult me, my man?" "All right, all right," said the bum. "Then how many do you figure there are includin' you?"

2

Hubby came home and found his young wife in tears. "I won't stand for it," she wailed. "Your mother's insulted me!" "But Marge, dear," he protested, "mother lives over fifty miles away. How could she insult you?" "Well, a letter for you came from her this morning, and I opened it," she explained. "Yes?" prompted hubby. "Oh, just look at that postscript!" she sobbed. "It says: 'Dear Marge, be sure to give this letter to Jim when you've finished with it.'"

3

"What do you mean insulting me in that yellow sheet of yours?" roared the politician at the editor. "Now, just a minute," cautioned the editor. "Didn't we print that item exactly as you gave it to us, to the effect that you'd resigned as city treasurer?" "You printed it correctly enough," conceded the grafter, then bellowed, "but look where you put it—in the column headed 'Public Improvements!'"

4

A traveling salesman was on his first trip, and got to chatting one evening with an old veteran of the road who asked him how he was doing. "Not so good," admitted the beginner. "Every place I go I get insulted." "That's odd," said the old-timer, looking puzzled. "I've been on the road for over forty years and I'll admit I've had my

samples pitched out the door, been thrown out, kicked down stairs, and have even been punched a few times—but insulted, never!"

See also ass[5], mouth[2], offense.

INSURANCE

1

The insurance agent called on the widow and handed her a check. "This is the full amount your husband was insured for, Mrs. Smith," he said. "Why don't you take out a policy on yourself with our company?" The woman pondered a moment, then replied, "I think I shall, since my husband had such good luck with his."

2

"Suppose this building should burn down tonight," asked the man as he picked up his new policy on the structure, "what would I get?" The agent looked grim. "About ten years, at least, I should estimate," he said.

3

"You blasted idiot!" cried the manager to his new insurance agent. "What in thunder ever made you write a policy on a man ninety-nine years old?" "It seemed a very good risk," explained the agent. "I looked up the statistics and found that there are surprisingly few people of that age in the whole country who die each year."

4

The little boy ran up to his mother who sat reading on the beach and asked, "Mummy, can I go in swimmin'?" "Certainly not, dear," answered mother. "It's much too deep and there's a bad current." "But daddy's in swimmin'," the boy pointed out. "That's different," replied mother, returning to her book. "Daddy's insured."

5

An insurance salesman wrote a policy on the head of a backwoods, uneducated family, and for over five years the premiums were mailed in promptly. But suddenly these payments stopped coming in, and, after sending several notices, the company received an explanation: "Dere Sires, Pleas excuis us that we kant pay no more insurence on Sam because he died last April. Yours Truely —."

6

The agent had been patiently explaining the details of a fire insurance policy to a woman. "Then if I pay you five dollars now," she asked, "you'll pay me a thousand if my house burns down? But do you ask questions about how the fire started?" "Naturally, we always make a thorough investigation," replied the agent. "I thought so," said the woman in disgust, "I knew there was a catch to it."

7

A woman was telling her lawyer why she wanted a divorce. "And the latest thing he's done," she said, summing up her grievances, "is to insure his life for ten thousand dollars." "But, madam," pointed out the lawyer, "insurance is for your protection." "Humph! You don't know that man," cried the woman. "He took that insurance with no intention of dying. He just took it to tantalize me, that's all!"

8

The insurance salesman was trying his best to sell a man a policy on his life, but for every argument he advanced the client had an objection. "But insurance is a great thing," the agent insisted. "No man should be without it. Why, I carry a $50,000 policy payable to my wife." "Too much," grunted the prospect. "What excuse can you give her for living?"

9

The agent brought the lady's fire insurance policy, and suggested politely that she might like to make the first payment on it at once. "How much is that?" asked the woman. "About $75," replied the agent. "Just a moment, I'll give you the exact figure." "Oh, why bother with all this nonsense!" cried the woman impatiently. "Just tell the company to let it go and deduct it from what it will owe me when my house burns down."

See also coal[3], cremation[3], delay[2], fire[2, 3], selfish[1], selling, soul, testimonial[2].

INTELLIGENCE

1

"This is a very interesting article, dear," commented the man to his wife, looking up from his paper. "It tells how the cleverness of the father often proves a stumbling-block to the progress of the son." "Well, thank heavens," said the wife with a sigh of relief, "Junior won't have anything to fall over."

2

The lawyer had been trying to browbeat and trick the witness into making certain admissions, but he had been outwitted. "You seem to have plenty of intelligence for a man of your position," said the lawyer finally with a sneer. "I'd be most happy to return the compliment," said the witness, "if only I weren't under oath."

See also diet[5], opposite[2].

INTENTION

1

A hillbilly youth had been calling on his girl for over a year. One evening the girl's pappy stopped him and asked, "Lookee here, son, you bin a-seein' Nell fer a good year now, and what I wanna know is what's yer intentions—be they honorable or dishonorable?" The boy's face lit up. "Yuh mean ter say thet I got a choice!" he cried delightedly.

2

Father cornered the young man on the porch one evening before he could ring the bell. "See here, my boy," he said, "you've been keeping company with Susie for over two years. Now, tell me, man to man, what're your intentions?" "My intentions, sir," declared the boy, "are honorable, but remote."

See also wooing[4].

INTEREST

1

The sophisticated youth turned to his dinner companion and inquired in a bored tone, "Who is that odd-looking man across the table who keeps staring at me so intently?" "Oh, that's Doctor Brown," the girl informed him. "Haven't you read about him, the famous authority on insanity?"

2

The specialist finished his examination of the pale-looking man and said, "You're suffering from melancholia caused by boredom. You should take more interest in your business." "I'd certainly like to," replied the patient. "Well, why don't you?" asked the doctor. "The law won't allow it," was the answer. "I'm a pawnbroker."

3

"I've got to spend more time at the office somehow," declared Williams to Jones. "Do you suppose that if a man got a good-looking stenographer it would help him take more interest in his business?" "Well, I don't know if *he'd* take more interest in his business," replied Jones dubiously, "but I'm sure his wife would."

4

"You certainly made a nuisance of yourself at the game tonight," said the man to his wife as they came home from the bridge party. "What's wrong with your memory? You must have asked what was trump at least twenty times." "Why, dear, I knew what was trump all the time," protested the wife. "I only kept asking to show that I was taking an interest in the game."

See also author[4].

INTERRUPT

In the course of the court proceedings, the defendant admitted that he hadn't spoken to his wife in almost seven years. "And what possible explanation can you give," demanded the judge severely, "for not speaking to your wife all that time?" "Simply the fact, Your Honor," explained the man, "that I'd been taught never to interrupt a lady."

See also speaker[1].

INTOXICATED

See drunk.

INVENTION

1

A famous inventor was proudly showing off all the clever labor-saving devices and gadgets of his own design that he had in his summer cottage. But they were all puzzled by a turnstile that could be moved only with difficulty on leaving. "Why," they asked, "in such a house do you have that cumbersome thing?" "Oh, that," replied the inventor with a grin, "pumps five gallons of water up into a tank every time it's turned around."

2

"Here's an odd invention," said the girl, looking up from her paper. "It's a contraption for keeping girls from falling out of rumble seats. Do you think it's practical?" "I don't like the idea at all," said the boyfriend. "It's just another example of the replacement of man by machinery."

See also newlyrich[1], spots[1], tobacco[2].

INVITATION

1

A lady living near an army post wished to do her bit to help morale.

So she sent an invitation reading: "Mr. and Mrs. Smythe request the pleasure of Captain Small's company at dinner next Sunday." A few days later she received an answer which stated: "With the exception of six men on leave and two on sick call, Captain Small's company will be most happy to take dinner with you Sunday."

2

The wife looked up from her morning mail with an unhappy face. "Do you remember that couple we took such a fancy to on that cruise last year, John?" she asked. "You know, that couple we kept insisting should come to visit us any time." "Good heavens!" cried John. "You don't mean —" "Yes, I do," said the wife. "The idiots are actually coming!"

3

Two debutantes, who were social climbers, were having tea together. "Are you going to the big reception tomorrow night?" inquired one. "Well, I really should, but unfortunately I'll have to be out-of-town tomorrow night," replied the other. "I know," said the first. "I didn't get an invitation either."

See also walking[2].

ISLAND

See shipwreck[2], world[2].

JAIL

See prison, prisoner.

JANITOR

1

An elderly man was testifying in court and was asked his occupation. "Well, sir, I work at the Episcopal church," he replied, "but I ain't right sure just what I am. I used to be the janitor, but that was years ago. Then we had a parson who named me the sextant. Later came a fancy college man who called me a virgin. And the young preacher we got now says I'm a sacrilege."

2

The country boy came to town and got a job as janitor in a girls' boarding school. He was given, along with his cleaning equipment, a passkey that fitted every room in the building. After he'd been there a week the dean one day met him in the corridor and asked, "Why didn't you come in last Friday for your pay?" "What!" gasped the man. "Do I get wages, too?"

JAZZ

"Hot diggitey!" cried daughter ecstatically as she put the latest swing record on the phonograph. "Did you ever hear anything like it?" "No, not exactly," admitted father with a wry face; "but the nearest thing to it I ever did hear was when a truck loaded with empty milk cans ran into another truck loaded with pigs."

JEALOUSY

The mistress of the house was much upset. "Do you know," she said to her maid, "I suspect that my husband is having an affair with his stenographer." "Oh, madam!" answered the maid. "You're just saying that to make me jealous."

JOB

1

"Well, pop's workin' again," reported little Billy when he came to school. "That's fine," approved teacher. "What is he doing?" "He's got a pretty tough job," said Billy. "He's got to watch six watchmen."

2

The employment manager looked over his references and shook his head. "Sorry," he said, "but we want a single man for this job." "What!" yelled the little fellow. "When I was in here yesterday you wanted a married man." "Sorry," repeated the manager. "Must be a mistake." "Mistake!" moaned the applicant. "I went right out yesterday and got married!"

3

"Yes," replied the storekeeper to the boy looking for a job, "I can use a bright, energetic boy to be partly indoors and partly outdoors." "Well, I guess that'd be all right," said the boy. "Only what happens to me when the door slams shut?"

4

"I guess your boyfriend's all right," conceded father, "but does he have a job?" "Not just now," admitted daughter, "but he's going to get one that pays $25,000 a year." "Fine!" approved father. "What will he be doing?" "Well," explained the girl, "he read about some man to whom the Bankers' Association pays $50,000 a year not to forge checks, and he's going to do it for half that amount."

5

"What are you going to raise

your youngest son, George, to be?" inquired a friend. "Well," replied George's father, "I made a lawyer of Jim, a doctor of John, a minister of Charles, Tom turned out to be a writer, and Bill became an artist. So I guess I'll bring George up to be a laboring man—I want one of the boys to have a little money of his own."

See also blacksmith[1], capacity, competition[1], do[1], elegance, foresight[2], movies[4], work.

JOKE

1

The host at the Christmas party was feeling quite jovial and kept telling a lot of stale jokes. "You know, Bill," sighed one of the guests at last, "it's hard to believe, but I actually envy that turkey there on the platter." "You do? How come?" asked Bill in surprise. "Well," explained the guest, "he isn't stuffed with chestnuts until after he's dead."

2

A lone man stood drinking at the bar and mumbling to himself. Every once in a while he would chuckle, but occasionally he would frown and say, "Phooey!" "Hey! What goes on here?" asked another patron who'd been watching him. "Oh, I'm just telling myself jokes and laughing at them," explained the drunk. "But why the 'Phooey's'?" the other asked. "Aw, that's when I've heard 'em before," was the reply.

3

The vaudeville comedian was playing to a rural audience that was

cold and unreceptive. In desperation he pulled what he considered one of his high-power gags, only to be met with stony silence. "Well," he sneered, "I suppose you folks'll laugh at that one next summer." "Nope," came a voice from the audience, "it was summer before last."

4

"Is it true," the judge said to the prisoner, "that you stole this man's hammer?" "Why, no, Your Honor," protested the defendant. "I just took it as a joke." "How far did you take it?" queried the judge. "From the job to my house—about four miles," was the reply. "Thirty days!" barked the judge. "That's carrying a joke entirely too far."

JOURNEY

"Well, good-by," said Jack to Bill, holding out his hand. "I'm leaving on my trip tomorrow." "But tomorrow's Friday!" exclaimed Bill. "I'd certainly never start a journey on a Friday." "Aw, that's just a silly superstition," declared Jack. "Not with me it isn't," insisted Bill. "Saturday's my payday."

JUDGE

1

"So you insist that the defendant insulted you," said the lawyer to the plaintiff. "Repeat the words he used." "Well, er, I'd rather not," the plaintiff hesitated. "You see, the words aren't fit for a gentleman's ears." "Very well," conceded the lawyer. "In that case you may just whisper them to the judge."

2

A new judge was trying his first

case. He was so impressed by the eloquent appeal of counsel for the plaintiff that he stopped the proceedings to say, "No need to hear the defendant's side. Plaintiff wins." "But, Your Honor," objected the defendant's lawyer, "at least let me present my case." "All right, go ahead," agreed the judge. But when this lawyer had finished, the judge was even more astounded. "Now don't that beat all!" he gasped. "Now defendant wins."

3

A well-known judge was taking an ocean voyage and there was some rough weather. Walking along the deck one day he saw a lawyer whom he knew leaning over the rail in the miseries of seasickness. "Can I do anything for you, Sam?" asked the judge kindly. "I'll say," was the weak response. "Your Honor can overrule this motion."

4

"You say the prisoner had been drinking?" asked the judge of the officer. "What had he been drinking?" "Whiskey, I guess, Your Honor," replied the officer. "You guess!" cried the judge very angry. "Don't you know the smell of whiskey? Aren't you a judge?" "No, Your Honor," was the humble answer; "just a policeman."

See also banking[2], court[1], drink[2], earn[1], fall[2], gentleman[2], justice[4], plumber[4], self-betrayal[1].

JUDGMENT

1

The domestic quarrel was quite violent. "Next thing you'll be telling me you have just as good judg-

ment as I," shouted the husband in a rage. "Well, no, I'm afraid not," admitted the wife meekly. "Just the one fact of our choices of partners for life proves that my judgment is not to be compared with yours."

2

A bachelor friend had been trying to advise a married man about his domestic troubles. The married man got impatient and cried, "Aw, what do you know about it? You're not even married." "That's quite true," agreed the bachelor. "But then, I'm no hen either, and I consider myself to be a far better judge of a good egg than any hen in the country."

JUMP

1

The boat bound for the ship was several feet from the dock when a sailor came running up, gave a mighty leap, and landed in a heap on the deck, knocking his head against a seat. He lay there stunned for a few minutes. When he revived the boat was a couple of hundred feet from the dock. "Man, oh, man!" marveled the sailor. "I sure can jump!"

2

Two henpecked husbands were discussing marriage. "I wish I could be more like Tom White," said one wistfully. "He says that whenever he speaks his wife jumps." "She sure does," answered the other derisively, "all over him."

See also opportunity[5], puzzle[1].

JUNK

See rubbish.

JURY

1

"Am I correct in believing, Your Honor," inquired the foreman of the jury, "that this attractive young lady is suing that old gentleman for $10,000 for a stolen kiss?" "That's right," said the judge; "and you must decide if it was worth it." "That's just it, Your Honor," continued the foreman; "how can we decide the value of a thing without a sample?"

2

It was a hearing to investigate a case of suicide. The jury had heard the evidence and had retired to deliberate. When they filed back in, the foreman arose and gave the verdict: "The jury is all of one mind —temporarily insane."

3

The lawyer was cross-examining the witness. "Do you know any of the men on the jury?" he questioned. "Oh, yes," replied the witness; "more than half of them." "Are you willing to swear that you know more than half the jury?" persisted the lawyer. "Well, if you come right down to it," said the witness, "I'd be willing to swear that I know more than the whole bunch of 'em."

4

The whole county had turned out to see Slim the Rustler hanged, but the townfolk had insisted on the formality of a jury trial first. The jury had been sworn in and the judge was about to open proceedings, when he noticed only eleven jurors in the box. "Where'n heck's that twelfth juror?" he demanded.

"Please, jedge," spoke up one of the jury, "hit's m'brother who had to git back to tendin' bar. But he's done left his verdic' with me."

5

A country boy was in court for the first time to testify. He spoke in such a low voice that the examining lawyer, gesturing toward the jury, said, "Speak up, please, so these gentlemen can hear you." "Land sakes!" cried the lad in surprise. "Are those men interested in this case, too?"

6

The judge finally got so provoked with the irregularities of the trial that he cried, "I discharge this jury!" A tall, rugged-looking member of the jury rose and protested, "See here, jedge, you-uns cain't discharge *me!*" "And why not?" roared the judge. "Waal, becuz," the objector replied, pointing to the defense counsel, "it wuz thet guy over there what hired me in the fust place."

7

When the jury filed into the box it was found that they numbered thirteen men. "What is your name?" the judge asked the man left standing after the others sat down. "George W. Braynes," he replied. "Mr. Bailiff," instructed the judge, "take this man back to the commissioners and tell them that we don't need him, as we already have twelve men without Braynes."

8

"Your Honor," cried the prisoner in piteous tones as he eyed the jury box, "do I have to be tried by that lady jury?" "Be quiet, you fool!" whispered his lawyer. "I won't be quiet!" whimpered the prisoner. "It's no use, judge. I can't even fool my own wife, let alone twelve strange women. I'm guilty!"

See also bribery[2], court[2], guilt[2], law[1], numbers[2], prejudice, repay[1], stubborn[3], tailor[3], witness[4].

JUSTICE

1

A man was on trial for horse stealing in an old Western town. As he took the stand to testify in his own behalf, the judge hitched his six-guns forward and cautioned, "Somepin I wantta tell yuh, prisoner, before yer swore on the Book. There's Somebody here bigger'n you or me. There's a Divine Justice and a Eternal Providence above an' beyond this 'yere courtroom, an', so he'p me, He ain't a-gonna be took in by no lyin' hoss thief."

2

A businessman had to leave town before a lawsuit brought against him by a competitor was ended. So he told his lawyer to wire him the outcome as soon as it was over. Several days later he received a telegram: "Justice has triumphed." He hastened to wire back immediately: "Appeal at once!"

3

"Do you think I'll get justice in this court?" asked a criminal anxiously of his lawyer. "No, I don't think you will," replied the lawyer calmly, looking around the courtroom. "I see three men on the jury who I know are opposed to hanging."

4

The judge, who had very little legal training but got his appointment through politics, sat sleepily while the plaintiff's counsel made a presentation of his case. When the lawyer for the defense arose, the judge asked, "Now, what're you gonna do?" "Present our side of the case, of course," explained the surprised lawyer. "Don't wantta hear both sides," declared His Honor flatly. "It has a tendency to confuse the court."

See also court[5], jury[4].

KANGAROO

A guide was conducting an elderly lady through the zoo and pointing out the exhibits. "Now, here, madam," he said, pausing before the kangaroo's pen, "we have a native of faraway Australia." "Good heavens!" cried the lady with a shudder. "And to think my sister went down there and married one of those!"

See also zoo[1].

KANSAS

The drought had been long and the Kansas farmer was out of food and money, so he stopped by a bank in town to try to get a loan on his farm. "Maybe I can arrange it," said the banker. "I'll just drive on out to your farm with you and appraise it now." As they stepped outside, the farmer saw a large cloud of dust rolling up the road. "No need to bother," he called to the banker. "Here comes the farm now."

See also clouds[1], wind[2].

KILL

1

An ignorant boy was in court for murder. "Do you mean to tell me," cried the judge aghast, "that you killed a man for the miserable sum of five dollars!" "Reckon it don't seem much to you, jedge," replied the boy, shrugging his shoulders, "but you'd be s'prised how five dollars here an' five dollars there mounts up."

2

A talkative old fellow boarded a transport plane and immediately began telling the other passengers of his flying experiences. "It really takes a good deal of courage for me to fly now," he declared, "as I was almost killed three times in an airplane." "Once would have been quite sufficient," observed a bored listener.

3

A minister was having tea with one of his parishioners in her garden, when up rushed her young son holding a rat by the tail. "Oh, don't be afraid, it's dead, mom," he reassured his mother. "Me an' Tommy hit 'im with rocks and whacked and beat 'im with sticks until —" the boy paused, catching his first glimpse of the minister, then added in a lower voice, "—until God called him home."

KIND

1

He was a lonely stranger in the big town, and when he entered a restaurant a gum-chewing waitress came up and demanded briefly, "Well, whatcha want?" "Two eggs, a cup of coffee, and a kind word," he requested. The waitress brought his order and was about to move away, when he asked her, "How about that kind word?" "Okay," she replied, and leaning over, whispered, "Don't eat them eggs."

2

Hubby got to thinking one afternoon of his wife's many virtues. So he bought some flowers and candy and rushed home, kissed her, and said, "You've been looking worn-out, darling. Come on, slip on your best dress and we'll go out to dinner and a show." Wifey burst into tears. "It was bad enough when baby fell down the steps and I broke my best platter and burned my hand," she wailed. "And now you come home drunk!"

3

"I think I have the kindest and most considerate husband in the world," said a woman ecstatically. "What's up? Did he buy you a new car or a fur coat?" inquired her friend. "Oh, nothing like that," said the other. "He's going to let me get a divorce on grounds of extreme cruelty."

4

Junior in college felt that his father hadn't been sending him enough money. So he wrote an indignant letter: "I don't know how you can call yourself a 'kind father' when you haven't sent me a check in over two weeks. What sort of kindness do you call that, anyhow?" In his next letter father wrote: "In answer to your question, son, I wish to inform you that it is unremitting kindness."

See also chivalry[5], marriage[9], virtue[3].

KING

A well-known English wit and jokester always boasted that he could make a pun on any subject. When he was master of ceremonies at a banquet one evening, some one asked, "How about these puns of yours that you're always bragging about?" "Certainly," agreed the jokesmith. "Name a subject." "The king," replied the other promptly. Quick as a flash the punster replied, "The king is not a subject."

See also doctor[1].

KISS

1

A famous man once visited a large city and was greeted by a huge crowd. He was kissed by two thousand girls within two hours. When questioned later as to how he had enjoyed the experience, he replied, with twinkling eyes, "Oh, it was all right. But I'd much rather had my pick of the two thousand girls and kissed her exclusively for two hours."

2

"I think I ought to be frank with you," declared the young fellow as he relaxed his embrace, "and tell you that you're not the first girl I've kissed." "In that case, I'll be frank with you, too," replied the girl, "and tell you that you've got a heck of a lot to learn."

3

The roadster slid around the corner on two wheels, glanced off a lamppost, took the front porch off of a house, hit two parked cars, bounced through an excavation, and came to a shuddering halt against a stone fence. A dreamy-eyed girl stepped happily from the wreck. "Oh, darling," she exclaimed, "that's what I call a *kiss!*"

4

"Do you know, Priscilla," said John poetically, "that they say kisses are the language of love?" "Well," said Priscilla practically, "speak for yourself, John."

5

"Mrs. Williams must certainly love her husband," said a woman to her neighbor over the back fence. "She never fails to kiss him every time he comes home." "Humph! Of course she doesn't," said the other, "but that's only to see if he's been drinking."

6

A group of seasoned travelers gathered in the lounge of the ocean liner one evening and over their cigars discussed the respective charms of women of various nationalities. "I've seen most of the world," declared one elderly man, "and I've kissed charming girls in France, Spain, Holland, India, Italy, and practically any country you can name, but I find my wife's lips the sweetest of all." A bronzed young fellow in the group slapped his knee and exclaimed, "By Jove! and that's the truth, sir!"

See also acquaintance[7], bribery[3], bride[1], brother[3], consolation[1], contradict, devotion[2], enough[1], facts of life[1], guess[1], lucky[1], oath[1], payment[1], sister[1], suffer[2], teaching[2], waste, wooing[5].

KNOWLEDGE

1

"But you positively need this Book of Universal Knowledge, sir," insisted the salesman, his foot in the door. "It will tell you everything you ought to know." "Can't use it," growled the man of the house. "My wife tells me all that—and a lot more to boot."

2

"Why, I am, too, smart," insisted the little fellow despite the jibes of his fellows. "I betcha my daddy'n' me between us know everything in the world." "Aw, gawn!" mocked one of the others. "Betcha don't know where Ethiopia is." "No, *I* don't," admitted the boy readily, "on account o' that's one my daddy knows."

3

Little Tommy had spent his first day in school, and that evening his father asked him how he'd liked it. "Oh, all right," replied Tommy. "Well, how's your teacher?" persisted father. "Is she smart?" "Well," admitted Tommy, "she knows more than I do."

4

"And that, dear," said hubby, concluding a long, learned lecture, "sums up the main points of the theory of money, values, and economic security and prosperity." "You're marvelous, darling," approved his wife. "But what seems even more wonderful to me is how anybody can know as much as you about money without having any of it."

5

The Colonel frowned as he surveyed a huge barricade of sandbags that had collapsed into a tangled heap. "Does the sergeant know about this?" he queried. "He ought to, sir," replied a private; "he's underneath."

6

Ronnie had learned to spell a certain word the wrong way, and every time he came to that word in his spelling lesson he misspelled it. "Just be patient, Ronnie," said teacher sympathetically. "I know it's hard to know all these things and get them straight." "Sure," agreed Ronnie, "but it's a lot harder to unknow 'em after you get 'em crooked!"

7

Little Bobby had heard talk among the family about his sister's new boyfriend, but he didn't quite understand it all. One evening as the young man sat in the parlor, Bobby approached him, opened his hand, and demanded, "What's them?" "Why, they're beans, sonny," replied the young fellow. "See, mom," shouted Bobby triumphantly as he ran into the next room, "he *does* know 'em."

See also electricity[1, 3], explanation[1], teaching[4], unconscious[1].

LABOR

See job, work.

LABORER

See workman.

LADY

1

A young woman traveler missed train connections and found herself stranded for the night in a little village. "Where can I spend the night?" she asked an old fellow hanging around the station. "Waal, there ain't no hotel in town," replied the old man, "but you could sleep with the station agent." "Sir!" she cried indignantly. "I'll have you know I'm a lady!" "So's the station agent," said the old boy with a chuckle.

2

As the streetcar lurched, a man lost his balance and stepped down hard on a woman's foot. He immediately made apologies but the woman listened impatiently, and then replied, "Sure, sure! Walk all over a person with your big clumsy feet, an' then yap yer big ugly mouth off about how sorry ya be. Yer jist lucky I'm a perfect lady or I'd whack yer dirty face fer ya!"

3

A little girl came home thrilled about her new teacher. "She's wonderful, and a perfect lady," she cried enthusiastically. "But how can you tell yet, dear?" asked mother. "You've only had her for two days." "Aw, it's easy to tell," replied the child. "I know she's a perfect lady because she makes you feel polite all the time."

4

Two modern young girls boarded a bus that stood at the terminal. One pulled out a pack of cigarettes. "It's all right if we smoke, isn't it, pop?" inquired one of the driver. "Go right ahead, it won't bother me," replied the driver amiably; "but you'll have to stop if any ladies get on."

5

Two women were quarreling.

"Well, all I can say," observed one haughtily, "is that you're certainly no lady." "Ha! So you say!" cried the other. "Let me tell you, if it wasn't that I was a lady, maybe I'd be able to tell you what kinda lady you ain't."

LAND

See America, geography, real estate.

LANDLORD

1

"Are you sure you have no children?" questioned the landlord, his pen ready to sign the lease. "Oh, yes, I have children," replied the woman sadly; "eight of them—all in the cemetery." "That's where children should be," growled the landlord, and signed the lease. When he had gone, the woman turned to her husband and said, "Take the car and get the children, John; they're playing in the cemetery."

2

The judge frowned at the man brought before him, but the man stood defiant. "What's the idea of kicking your landlord downstairs?" demanded the judge. "Do you think that's part of a tenant's privilege?" "Look, judge," replied the man, suppressed anger in his voice, "I'll show you my lease, and I think you'll agree that anything they've forgot to forbid in it, I've got a perfect right to do."

3

The client sat patiently while the landlord's agent read the provisions of the lease to him; then he picked up his hat to leave. "Look, bud," he said in a weary voice, "I haven't been able to keep the Ten Commandments in order to get a mansion in heaven, and if you think I'm gonna tackle about three hundred of 'em just to get a three-room cottage on Main Street, you're crazy."

4

A big, husky man called at the minister's house and asked to see the minister's wife, who was well known for her charitable work. "Madam," said the man in an anguished voice, "I wish to call your attention to the terrible plight of a poor family in town. The father is dead, the mother too sick to work, eight small children starving, and they're about to be put on the street because they owe $60 in rent." "Horrible!" cried the lady. "And who are you?" "I, madam," sobbed the man, "am the landlord."

See also courage[3].

LANGUAGE

1

A tramp was brought into court on a charge of vagrancy. "What excuse do you have, my man?" asked the judge. "My God!" cried the tramp. "I ain't had no chance to git a damn job." "Hey, there! What kind of language is that to use before the judge!" exclaimed the bailiff, jumping up. "Not only did you use a double negative, but I'm sure you must know that 'ain't' is incorrect."

2

A dear old lady went into a pet shop to price some dogs. "You can have that small bitch over there for $25," said the clerk, pointing, "or that large bitch in the corner for $35." The lady frowned as the man spoke. "Why, madam," asked the clerk, "aren't you familiar with the term 'bitch'?" "Why, certainly," replied the lady haughtily, "but never before have I heard it applied to dogs."

3

The Blacks had adopted a little five-months-old French girl orphaned by the war. One evening a friend dropped in and found the couple studying an "Easy French at Home" course. "Why in the world do you two want to learn French?" inquired the friend. "Are you kidding or just dumb?" said Black. "Little Marie will soon start talking, and don't you think we want to know what she's saying?"

4

Junior was home from college on a visit and father asked him, "Well, son, what language have you decided to study next year?" "I've about made up my mind to take Pictish, dad," replied the boy. "Pictish!" cried father, amazed. "Why in heaven Pictish?" "Because only five words of it remain," explained Junior.

5

An American traveling abroad saw a restaurant with a sign in the window stating: "Here all languages are spoken." He entered, and in conversing with the manager remarked, "You must employ quite a variety of interpreters." "I don't have a single one," was the answer. "Well, then, who speaks all the languages?" asked the American. "The customers," replied the manager.

See also education[2], parrot[2].

LARGE

See size.

LATE

1

It was a terrible snowstorm and the Commuters' Special floundered valiantly through the drifts, but finally, after many halts, it stalled for good. Toward dawn, one of the passengers, numb with cold, fought his way through the snow to a nearby telegraph office and wired his boss: "Won't be at office today. Not home yesterday yet."

2

The stranger poked his head in the ticket window in a small-town station and said, "I'd like to return to the city tonight on a late train. What do you suggest?" "Waal," replied the agent reflectively, "reckon you kin take No. 9. She's usually 'bout as late as any of 'em."

3

"You're late, Billy," scolded teacher. "Well, it was late when I left home," said Billy. "Why didn't you start earlier?" demanded teacher. "Because, ma'am," explained the boy, "it was too late when I left to start early."

4

"Say, what's the idea?" demanded hubby of the new maid. "Why did you have to tell my wife what time I came in last night?" "Oh, but I didn't, sir," protested the maid. "When she asked me what time you'd got in, I simply told her that I was too busy cooking breakfast at the time to look at the clock."

5

It was well past the customary supper hour when a neighbor, in a hurry to get home himself, spied little Danny leisurely playing marbles with some other boys. "You'd better rush on home, Danny," suggested the man, "or you'll be late for supper." "Oh, no, I won't be late," replied Danny. "I've got the meat."

6

"Why are you late for school this morning, Georgie?" demanded teacher of the boy straggling in. "On account of the bell rang before I got here," explained Georgie patiently.

See also boyfriend[3], clock[3], commuter[2], excuse[1], good night[1], hint[7], imitation[2], office[2], punctual[1], train[3].

LAUGHTER

1

Little Johnny ran sobbing to his mother. "What's wrong, dear?" inquired mother. "I was watching daddy fix the furnace," explained the boy tearfully, "an' he dropped a big lump of coal on his toe." "Well, that's nothing to cry about, son," said mother; "you should laugh at that." "I did," wailed Johnny.

2

"Timmy!" reproved teacher, rapping her desk, "you shouldn't laugh out loud in the classroom." "I'm sorry, teacher, I didn't mean to," apologized Timmy; "I was just smilin', an' the smile busted."

See also salary[5].

LAUNDRY

"My brother's out of work again," complained a girl to her chum. "I might be able to get him a job at the Model Laundry," offered her friend. "Well, I don't know if he could handle that," replied the first doubtfully. "I don't think he's had any experience at washing models."

LAW

1

It had been a long case and the man had served on the jury for several weeks. A friend who met him said, "You must have heard so much law in the past few weeks that you're almost a lawyer yourself." "You're not kiddin'," said the juror. "I'm so full of law that it's going to be hard for me to keep from cheating people when I get back to my business."

2

It was in the early days when the regulations concerning admission to the bar were more liberal. "What is law?" was one of the questions a young man was asked at his examination. "Law is an unjust application of justice," he replied promptly. "And what is equity?" was the second question. "A damned imposition on common sense!" he responded. And he was welcomed into the brotherhood forthwith.

3

The Debating Society at the village store was bemoaning the times. "Somethin's gotta be done soon," declared one forcefully; "there's laws bein' busted every day of the month." "Waal, I wouldn't worry," reassured another, " 'cuz I reckon they're makin' new ones jest about as fast as the old ones is busted."

4

The judge interrupted proceed-

ings to observe, "Ignorance of the law is no excuse in the eyes of the law." "I should like to ask, Your Honor," inquired the prosecuting attorney, "if your remarks are addressed to the defendant or to his lawyer?"

5

The big business magnate entered the famous lawyer's office wearing a worried frown. "That law I spoke to you about is stopping a big deal of mine," he said, "and I'd like to know if you can prove it unconstitutional?" "Very easily," declared the lawyer. "All right; then get busy and familiarize yourself with the law," he was instructed. "No need to," replied the lawyer. "It's that same law you had me prove constitutional a couple of years ago."

See also business[6].

LAWN MOWER

A man entered a hardware store with a determined air. "I'd like to have three lawn mowers," he announced. "Three lawn mowers!" echoed the amazed clerk. "You must have a very large estate." "No, just an ordinary yard," growled the customer; "but I have two neighbors."

See also borrow[3].

LAWSUIT

1

A man met a friend hobbling along the street on crutches. "What the heck happened to you?" he inquired. "Got hit by a streetcar," replied the other. "It happened a little over two months ago." "And you're still using crutches?" asked his friend. "Well, it's like this," explained the crippled one; "my doctor said I could get along without them a month ago, but my lawyer says I still need them."

2

A famous lawyer made his will in which he stated: "After all just debts have been satisfied, the residue of my estate I leave to fools and madmen." When asked his reason for this unusual bequest, he replied simply, "It was from such that I got my money, so it is only just that to such I give it back."

3

An old lawyer had retired and left his practice to his son who had just graduated from law school. "Congratulate me, dad," cried the boy proudly several weeks after he had taken over. "I've settled that old equity suit you've had pending for so many years." "Settled it!" exclaimed the old man in outraged tones. "Why, I left you that suit as an annuity for life!"

4

"Without a doubt," declared the lawyer, nodding his head sagely as his client finished his story, "you've one of the best and surest cases I've ever encountered." "Thanks," said the client, grabbing his hat. "I'll settle this case out of court." "But I said it's the best I've heard," cried the astonished lawyer. "I know," replied the other; "but I've just told you the other fellow's side of it."

5

Two old fellows got into a dispute over a small matter and ended by taking their quarrel before the local magistrate. The loser, however, did not take the court's decision kindly. "I ain't through with ye," he warned. "I'll law ye to th' Circuit Court." "I'll be thar," replied his opponent. "An' I'll law ye to th' Supreme Court," the first promised. "I'll be thar," was the response. "An' I'll law ye to hell!" was the final threat. "My lawyer'll be thar," said the other coolly.

6

A man who'd been gravely injured by a fall into an open sewer engaged a lawyer to sue the city for $5,000. After several lengthy appeals, they won the case and the city paid damages. The lawyer then sent for his client and handed him a dollar bill, explaining, "That's your damages, after deducting my fee, all costs and expenses." The man looked the bill over very carefully, then inquired, "What's wrong with this dollar—is it counterfeit?"

LAWYER

1

The dean of the law school was busy when the telephone interrupted him. "Is this the gas works?" inquired a woman's voice when he picked up the instrument. "It is not, madam," he roared peevishly. "This is the law school." "So sorry," replied the voice sweetly; "but I didn't miss it so far, after all, did I."

2

The judge halted proceedings and leaned forward from the bench. "Look here, my man," he said to the defendant, "I granted you the right to plead your own case, but you're lying so clumsily that I really think you ought to get a lawyer."

3

A poor man who had been struck by an auto went to see a lawyer. "I'd like to engage you," said the man, "but I haven't any money." "Well, I might take your case on a contingent fee," suggested the lawyer. "What's that?" asked the man. "A contingent fee means in effect," explained the lawyer, "that if I don't win your case I don't get anything, and if I do win you don't get anything."

4

A friend of the judge dropped in for a visit one morning before court opened and looked around. "Goodness, you certainly have a tough-looking bunch of jailbirds and scoundrels to try this morning, haven't you?" he observed. "Oh, not so bad," grunted the judge. "You're just looking at the wrong bunch—those are the lawyers."

5

A client was consulting a lawyer about collecting a debt long due. "Did you present this man a bill?" asked the lawyer. "I sure did," was the reply. "What did he say to that?" was the next question. "He told me to go to the devil," responded the client. "Then what did you do?" continued the lawyer. "Why, I came to you, of course," was the answer.

6

There was a strong case against the man accused of bank robbery, but so strong and eloquent was the plea put up by his lawyer, that the man was acquitted. Later, when alone in his office with the man, the lawyer asked, "Now just between us, Jim, you did rob that bank, didn't you?" "Well, sir, I'd kinda figgered I had," admitted Jim, "but since hearin' you talk, I'm beginnin' to doubt it."

7

A man strolling through a cemetery suddenly paused in amazement before a tombstone bearing the inscription: "Here lies a lawyer and an honest man." "My goodness!" marveled the man. "You'd certainly never think there was room for two men in that one little grave!"

8

"Pardon me," said the stranger in town to the old native, "but I'm looking for a criminal lawyer and I wonder if you could tell me whether you have any in this town?" "Waal, stranger," replied the old fellow, "there's three of 'em we're purty durned sure about, but we ain't been able to prove nuthin' on 'em yit."

9

The lawyer was new in the court and his persistent disregard for the formalities irritated the judge who beckoned to the opposing counsel and asked, "Who did you say that attorney is?" "Sunavich," was the reply. "Sure, I know that," declared the judge impatiently; "but I said who, not what."

See also advice[1, 2], answer[2], burglar[2], divorce[1], doubt, familiar[1], fee[3, 5], home[5], identify[3], inheritance[2], law[4], lawsuit[2, 5, 6], necessity[2], payment[3], pleasure[3], Republicans[2], salary[4], tailor[2], think[2], truth[5, 6], wicked[1], witness[1].

LAZY

1

A man approached a group of bums lounging under a tree and

said, "I'll give a dollar to the laziest man here." Most of them sprang up with outstretched hands; two of them remained seated and held out their hand; and one remained lying on the ground without moving. "I guess you win," said the man to the prone figure, holding out the dollar. "Aw, roll me over an' put it in me pocket," was the reply.

2

A number of hoboes got together and arranged a track meet. When it was in progress, a spectator arrived and saw eight men in track suits walking leisurely down the race course. "That's certainly the slowest walking race I ever saw," he observed. "Walking race, my eye!" snorted another onlooker; "that's the hundred-yard dash!"

3

A hillbilly was complaining about hard times to a tourist. "But, man," objected the latter, "you should be able to make a lot of money now raising and shipping green corn north." "Mebbe I could," said the yokel. "Well, you've got the land and could get the seed, couldn't you?" asked the tourist. "Reckon so," was the reply. "Then, why don't you?" asked the other. "Becuz," explained the hillbilly indignantly, "the ole woman's too durn lazy to do the plowin' an' plantin'."

4

In traveling through the backwoods country, a tourist one day noticed a woman dousing with pails of water, at regular intervals, three ragged and bearded men who lay under a tree. "Is something wrong?" cried the tourist, leaping from his car. "Have these men been hurt?"

"Nope," replied the woman placidly; "jest a-keepin' the flies off'n 'em."

5

A man was engaged in his favorite, customary occupation, that of lying in the shade of a tree. His wife came out and started to scold him. "Loafing, always loafing!" she cried. "All you ever do is loaf!" "Maybe so," said the man, not moving, "but it's better than doing nothing, ain't it?"

6

The plumber was not one to expect too much from a helper, but the extreme laziness of his new man finally got on his nerves. "My goodness, Sam, you bother me standing there with both hands in your pockets all the time," he cried. "For Pete's sake, take one of them out, will you?"

7

"Now, if there's anything wrong with me, doc, don't scare me to death by giving it a fancy scientific name," pleaded the patient anxiously. "Just tell me in plain English." "Well, to be quite frank," replied the doctor, "you're just plain lazy." "Gee, thanks, doc," sighed the patient in relief. "Now give me a fancy scientific name for it so that I can tell it to the wife."

8

Old Zeb lived pretty far up the mountain side, and one day word got to him that there was a letter for him in the village in the valley. So Zeb started out leisurely down the slope to fetch it. At a place where several of his pals were lolling in the shade, the slope became steep enough to force him into a trot.

"Lookee there at Zeb," observed one of the loafers sneeringly; "too durned lazy to hold back."

9

Old Pappy was sitting in his rocking chair on the porch, facing north and rocking gently. Nearby in his rocker sat Sonny, a wisp of a boy of about 45, facing west and also rocking. Soon Pappy heaved a sigh and spoke up slowly. "Look here, son, they ain't a mite o' sense in you a-wearin' yo'se'f to a frazzle thetaway," he cautioned gently. "Allus rock with the grain, boy, an' save yore stren'th."

10

The studious but indolent man closed his book on history with a thoughtful look. "If I'd been in Napoleon's place, Jane," he observed, "do you know what I would have done?" "I sure do," snapped his hustling wife. "You'd have settled right down on a farm in Corsica and let it grow up in weeds."

See also ambition[5], cremation[1], crime, fire[1], painting[3], regret, shoes[2].

LEAF

The meek little man was making a long complaint, so the judge cut him short to say, "All right, we can pass up the small details. Just tell us how your quarrel with your wife ended." "Well, sir," said the man, "it ended when she picked up an oak leaf and hit me over the head with it." "She certainly couldn't have hurt you much with a leaf," observed the judge. "Oh, no?" retorted the other. "It was an oak leaf from the dining-room table!"

LEARN

A sporting-goods house hired a golf professional to give golf lessons to the customers. When on duty one day he was approached by two women. "Do you want to learn to play golf, madam?" he inquired politely of one. "Oh, no, it's my friend here who wants to learn," was the reply. "I learned yesterday."

See also love[1], Sunday school[3], swearing[1].

LECTURE

1

A clergyman was asked to address a luncheon meeting of the Ladies' Culture Club. He was specifically asked to speak on China and Chinese art, religion, and philosophy. This puzzled him as he knew very little about the subject. He spent several weeks in research studying for the lecture. "Why, madam," he asked the chairman just before the luncheon, "did you ask me to speak on China?" "Oh, we wanted the talk to be appropriate," she explained brightly. "You see, it's a chow mein luncheon."

2

"I certainly enjoyed your lecture last night, sir," said the young man enthusiastically, shaking the speaker's hand. "Thank you, but I didn't see you there," replied the lecturer. "Oh, I wasn't," admitted the boy. "Then how in the world could you enjoy it?" questioned the puzzled man. "Why, I bought tickets for my girlfriend's parents and they both went," was the explanation.

3

The business affairs of the club

had taken almost all the time of the meeting, so the chairman whispered to the speaker of the day, "We're running a little short of time and I'm afraid we can only spare you about ten minutes for your talk. What's your subject?" "Time, Space, and Life," replied the speaker dryly.

4

The sweet young thing was finding the lecture far above her and she soon lost interest. "What's that tiresome old gook talking about, anyway?" she at last asked of the woman next to her. "Progressive Peru," replied the other. "Oh, is that so?" said the girl with re-awakened interest. "And how do you play it?"

5

It had started to rain during the lecture, so the speaker felt he should cut his talk short. Having reached a suitable place in his address, he said, "And here I shall conclude my talk for this evening. I'm afraid I've already kept you too long." "Oh, keep right on," encouraged a voice from the audience. "It's still raining and a lot of us don't have umbrellas."

See also insomnia[2], pastime, South[3].

LEG

1

The village baseball team was playing their Sunday game in a pasture. A very thin fielder was annoyed by the attentions of a small but lively dog. "Will the one who owns this dog please call him off," he finally requested of the nearby spectators. "Come here, Skipper," called a voice from the crowd.

"Them ain't bones, boy—them's legs."

2

"My uncle had to stay in yesterday," little Jimmie volunteered to a neighbor. "What was wrong with him?" asked the woman. "His wooden leg hurt him," replied the boy. "Now, how could a wooden leg hurt any one?" asked the neighbor. "Well, it sure hurt him," explained Jimmie, "when auntie hit him over the head with it."

See also argument[2], waitress[2].

LEGACY

See inheritance, will.

LEND

A sultan's jester was approached by a neighbor who wished to borrow his camel's-hair rope. "I'm sorry, but it's in use," said the jester. "At the moment I have fifteen gallons of water tied up in it." "Oh, come, now," scoffed the neighbor. "How can you tie up water in a rope?" "Allah is mighty, my friend," replied the jester, "and permits us to do marvelous things with a rope when we do not wish to lend it."

LESSON

It had been a hectic day at school and little Ronald returned home in a thoughtful mood. "Well, Ronnie?" asked father that evening, "what lesson did the teacher most forcefully drive home to you today?" "That I need a thicker pair of pants," was the grave reply.

See also homework.

LETTER

1

"What's the idea of asking for your letters back?" demanded the girl who had just returned his ring. "Surely you don't think that I'd ever take them to court!" "Oh, no, I'm not worried about that," answered the young fellow. "It's just that I paid an expert good money to write them for me, and I may want to use them again some day."

2

Two men with sons in college were talking things over. "My boy's certainly getting smart," boasted one; "his letters always send me to the dictionary." "You're lucky," growled the other. "My boy's letters always send me to the bank."

See also blackmail, complaint[4], discharge[2], insult[2].

LIBERTY

See freedom.

LIBRARY

1

A distinguished visitor to a royal court was inspecting the palace library. He started to talk with the librarian and found him to be a very ignorant man. Later, in speaking to the king, he said, "I suggest that Your Majesty make your librarian the administrator of your finances." "What makes you say that?" asked the king. "Because he never makes use of the treasures entrusted to him," was the reply.

2

A small boy stood in line in the public library clutching a worn, ragged, soiled volume, awaiting his turn to return it. The librarian finally reached for the book, looked at it, looked at the size of the boy, then remarked, "This book's rather technical, isn't it?" "Maybe it is, ma'am," said the boy defiantly, "but it was that way when I got it."

See also book[3].

LIE

See lying, truth, truthful.

LIFE

See longevity.

LIGHT

1

It was a little church and it had difficulty in meeting its expenses. At an evening service the preacher was reading from the Book of Job: "Yea, the light of the wicked shall be put out," when suddenly the church was plunged into total darkness. With very little hesitation, the preacher continued, "Brethren, in view of this unexpected fulfillment of the prophecy, we will all spend a few minutes in silent prayer for the electric company."

2

"You're quite a little man, aren't you," observed a visitor, patting a small boy on the head. "And when did you first see the light of day?" "About two years ago," was the reply. "But you're much older than two," objected the visitor. "Oh, sure," said the boy; "but for the first four years we lived in Pittsburgh."

See also tombstone[1].

LIGHTNING

1

The physics teacher was quizzing the class on their knowledge of electricity. "Now, Johnson," he said, "you may tell us what is the chief difference between electricity and lightning." "Well," replied Johnson, "you don't have to pay for lightning."

2

"Why did you run and hide in the basement during the storm, Danny?" asked mother. "I was afraid of the lightning and I wanted to protect myself," explained the boy. "Nonsense!" scoffed mother. "If the lightning's going to hit you, it'll hit you wherever you are." "Maybe so," answered the boy; "but if it's gonna hit me, let it look for me."

3

The woman was very religious, of strong but simple faith, and she was also deathly afraid of lightning. One evening, while addressing a church meeting, a thunderstorm suddenly broke with much electrical display. Above the crash of thunder the woman could be heard praying, "O Lord, shelter us beneath Thy protecting wings, for Thou knowest that feathers are splendid non-conductors."

4

Teacher was giving a lesson on the wonders and powers of nature, and in the course of it she questioned, "Now, Tommy, can you tell us why it is that lightning never strikes twice in the same place?" "I'll say," replied Tommy. "It's 'cause after it strikes once the same place ain't there any more."

See also remind[4].

LIKE

1

"Look here, daughter," scolded father as the girl came in, "I can't say that I especially like that young fellow you're going out with lately." "Aw, that's okay, pops," retorted daughter breezily; "you're poison to him, too."

2

"How do you like your new governess, Margy?" inquired a neighbor of a small girl. "Oh, she's all right, I guess," replied the girl. "I half like her an' I half don't like her, but I guess I half don't like her most."

3

The little girl stood before the counter of twenty-five-cent framed prints studying them with an eye toward a gift for mother. "Would your mother like this one of the vase of flowers?" asked the clerk. "Nope," was the reply. "Would she like this one of a tree, or this boatful of children?" persisted the clerk. Again, "Nope." "Well, what *does* your mother like?" asked the clerk. "Men!" declared the child.

4

The new minister had finished the funeral service of the elderly farm woman, and now he was driving back with the bereaved husband. Thinking to comfort the man, he sighed and observed sympathetically, "Forty-three years is quite a long time for a man and wife to live together." "Yep, an' Marthy made me a right good wife," replied the old farmer; "but d'ya know, Reverend, somehow I never *did* like that woman."

See also food[2], objection[2].

LIMIT

"You're charged with assault and battery," declared the judge severely. "But, judge, I was only swinging my arms in fun and my hand hit his nose," protested the prisoner. "I've got a right to swing my arms, ain't I?" "That's true," agreed the judge; "but your right to swing your arms stops where the other man's nose begins."

See also moderate.

LINEN

1

A tourist whose car broke down in the backwoods was forced to spend the night at a hillbilly's cabin. Early in the morning he was awakened by the young son of the house, who declared, "Maw's a-puttin' on the dawg 'cause we got company fer breakfast an' she wants to know will ya please git up, mister, on accounta she wants the sheet for a tablecloth."

2

Smith was to attend a banquet with a bachelor friend. As it grew late without the friend appearing, he dropped by the other's home and found him standing before a mirror holding a dress shirt in his hands. "Don't you know it's late, Bill?" he cried. "What's wrong?" "Aw, it's this blasted shirt," replied the bachelor disgustedly; "it's much too dirty to wear, and it's not quite dirty enough for the laundry, and I can't make up my mind."

LION

See coward[1].

LIQUOR

1

The man had bought a bottle of liquor guaranteed to be "good stuff." But he found it too corrosive for even his cast-iron system, so he gave it to the janitor. "How'd you like the liquor, Sam?" he inquired a few days later. "It was just right," was the reply. "What do you mean 'just right'?" asked the donor. "Well," explained the victim, "if it'd been any better you'd have drunk it yourself, an' if it'd been any worse it woulda killed me."

2

Two moonshiners were boasting of the powers of their respective products. "M'likker's so durned strong," declared one, "thet when yuh drink it yuh kin smell th' cornfield where the corn cum frum." "Shucks, thet's nuthin'," replied the other. "I spilled a few drops on th' bed where m'wife had planted pansies, an' durned if they didn't cum up tiger lilies!"

See also cocktail[1], courage[3], drinking[2], innocence, insects[4], necessity[1], opportunity[1], preparation[2], Prohibition[1], temperance[1, 2].

LISPING

1

"What's wrong, Jane?" asked auntie as she noted a lisp in the child's speech. "Oh, I loth another toof," explained the girl, "an' now I limp when I talk."

2

An archeologist was relating some of his adventures to a sweet young thing. "And it was in an old bath at

Rome," he said, "that I one day happened upon a wonderful myth." "Why, you sly old dog, you!" giggled the girl. "And I suppose you begged her pardon and then kept right on staring."

3

The kindergarten teacher was trying to give the tots some elementary instruction in natural history. "Can you tell me, Jane, what a panther is?" she asked. "Oh, yeth, ma'am," she replied proudly. "A panther ith a man who makth panth."

LISTEN

"But why are you angry with me, dear?" protested the henpecked husband. "You've been talking for almost an hour and I've sat here quietly without saying a word." "Oh, I know you haven't said anything," barked the woman, "but, Henry Brown, you've been sitting there listening in a most aggravating manner, and I simply won't put up with it, do you hear!"

See also tired[2].

LITERAL

"Now, children, I want each of you to write a short essay on any subject," directed the teacher of the composition class, "but I want you to pay especial attention to literalness; that is, do not be imaginative, but write just what's in you." One small lad turned in a brief essay reading: "In me is my heart, stumick, liver, lungs, an apple, two cookies, and my breakfast."

LITERATURE

See author, book, poetry, publisher.

LITTLE

See small.

LOAD

A farmer driving his wagon along a road overtook a peddler walking with a heavy pack on his back. He offered him a ride and it was gratefully accepted. After a while, the farmer noticed that the man still had his pack in place and asked, "Why don't you ease that load off your back and put that pack back in the wagon?" "Well, I would," replied the peddler, "only your horse doesn't seem very strong, so I thought it better to take some of the load myself."

LOCATION

1

The shapely and quite décolleté young lady was seated at dinner next to an admiring young man. "I've had a miserable week," she confided in him. "I was vaccinated last Monday and it has become sore and painful." The young man gazed curiously at her bare arms and shoulders but saw no mark. "Why, where were you vaccinated?" he asked. She smiled sweetly and replied, "In Chicago."

2

A drunk hung himself upon a policeman's shoulder and inquired, "Shay, offisher, 'scuse me, but where am I?" "You're on the corner of Third and Main Streets," replied the officer as he steadied the inebriate. "Aw, n-mind the details," said the drunk; "jush what town am I in?"

3

"Where did the automobile strike the deceased?" asked the coroner of the doctor at the inquest. "At the junction of the lumbar and dorsal vertebrae," was the reply. "Oh, but that's wrong," objected the policeman in the case. "It was at the corner of Twelfth and Pine. And besides, I've been on the force thirty years now and I've never heard of those other two streets before."

4

Two yokels were on a fishing expedition and after rowing about the lake half the day without success, they finally struck a spot where there were many fish. "We'd better mark this spot so's we can come back tomorrow," suggested one. When they got back to the dock, this same one asked, "Did you mark that spot, Pete?" "Sure," replied Pete; "I put a chalk mark on the side of the boat." "You dumbbell!" cried the other in disgust. "How do you know we'll get the same boat tomorrow?"

5

The aviator had been flying blind for some time in a fog. When a momentary rift in the cloud enabled him to land in a field, he had no idea as to where he was. "Say, bud," he asked one of the country boys who had come running up, "can you tell me where I am?" "Sure, mister," was the ready response. "You're in Squire Peters's south pasture."

6

The man of the house returned home early from the office one evening, but found his wife nowhere around. So he asked the maid, "Maggie, do you know anything of my wife's whereabouts?" "No, I don't, sir," Maggie answered, "but maybe they're in the wash."

See also boat[1], future[3], meeting[3], search[2], tattoo[3].

LOGIC

Two small boys were playing together on the corner lot when one, noticing that it was getting dark, remarked, "Wonder what time it is?" "I don't know," said the other, "but it can't be four o'clock yet." "Why can't it?" inquired the first. "Because," replied the other with cold logic, "my mother told me I positively had to be home by four o'clock—and I'm not."

See also deduction.

LONDON

1

"And how did you find the weather in London, old fellow?" inquired a friend of the traveler who had just returned from abroad. "Humph! You don't have to find the weather in London," snorted the other; "it bumps into you every time you turn around."

2

"How was the weather in London?" asked a man of his neighbor who had recently returned from England. "I really couldn't say," responded the traveler. "It was so darned foggy I couldn't tell."

3

"The sun," declared an American

doctor to an English visitor, "is the greatest physician in the world." "That may well be," conceded the Englishman, "but the greatest difficulty in London is to get an appointment."

See also fog², violin².

LONELY

"Why, you nasty cruel boy!" said a lady to a boy on the street. "Whatever made you cut that poor defenseless little worm in two?" "I don't know, ma'am," replied the lad, with the look of a humble but righteous Christian, "but it somehow just seemed so lonely."

LONGEVITY

1

The medicine-show quack was loud in his claims for his Rejuvenation Elixir. "If you don't believe the label, just look at me," he shouted, "I take it, and I'm 350 years old." "Is he really that old?" asked a skeptical listener of the doc's youthful helper. "I really couldn't say," replied the other with disarming frankness. "You see, I've only been with him for 120 years."

2

It was the old fellow's hundredth birthday, and a reporter had been sent to interview him. "To what do you attribute your great age?" asked the newshound. "To clean living," replied the old man positively. "I never drank, smoked, overate, or stayed up past nine o'clock." "But my grandfather did the same," objected the reporter, "and he only lived to be eighty-two." "His trouble was that he didn't keep it up

long enough," was the calm explanation.

3

The vigorous centenarian was just concluding his interview with the newsreel men. "My vigor and age is due solely to my sane and wholesome living habits," he declared. "I never use liquor, tobacco or meat and I always go to bed early." Just then a great clatter broke out in the next room. "What's that?" asked one of the interviewers. "I'm afraid that's my old father coming home," was the answer. "He *will* go out dissipating every night."

4

"To what do you attribute your exceptionally long life, Uncle Zeke?" queried the newspaper reporter of the white-haired old native. "Well, sir," replied the old fellow, sucking thoughtfully on his pipe, "I reckon it must be becuz I wuz bo'n sech a long ways back."

See also drinking¹, source².

LOOKS

See also appearance, beauty.

LOSE

1

The girl was rich and the boy was poor, and he had been especially attentive to her this evening. "You're worth a million dollars, aren't you?" he asked. "That's right," confirmed the girl. "Will you marry me?" continued the boy. "No," was the answer. "I thought not," said the young fellow calmly. "Then why did you ask me?" she questioned. "Oh, I just wanted to see how it felt to lose a million dollars."

2

It had been a terrible season for the local football team, and a friend was trying to cheer up the coach. "At least you have taught the boys fine sportsmanship," he comforted; "they're certainly good losers." "Good?" growled the coach. "Why, they're perfect!"

3

A young reporter had been sent to write up the story of a man who had been murdered by burglars, and the last paragraph of his account read: "The deceased had been very fortunate in that just the day before he had put all his money and other valuables in the bank and safety vault, so that he lost practically nothing but his life."

4

There had been a lot of hogs missing in a certain locality and every one had strong suspicions of a certain individual, but could prove nothing on him. A farmer who one day got in a large shipment of hogs sent for this character and said, "Look, Sam, I'll give you your pick of any two of these hogs if you'll promise to leave the rest alone." "Well, all right," agreed the other reluctantly; "but I'm gonna lose a lotta good meat on this deal."

5

A bass drummer was on the train for an engagement in another city, but he had celebrated too much before leaving. So when the conductor came around for the fares he couldn't find his ticket. The conductor stood patiently by while the drunk searched every pocket, and finally observed politely, "Surely you couldn't have lost something like a ticket." "The heck I couldn't!" was the indignant retort. "Why, once I lost a bass drum."

6

A boy ran breathlessly up to a man on the street and inquired, "Have you lost a half-dollar, mister?" "Why, er, yes, I believe I have," replied the man hesitantly, feeling in his pockets. "Have you found one, sonny?" "Oh, no," replied the boy, making a notation in a notebook; "I just wanted to see how many had been lost today, and yours makes sixty-three."

See also sportsmanship[3].

LOST

1

A one-armed man entered a lunchroom, sat at the counter, ordered food, and began eating expertly with his one hand. The man next to him watched curiously for awhile, then remarked, "I beg your pardon, sir, but I see you've lost an arm." The other laid down his fork, picked up his empty sleeve with his one hand, peered intently into it, and replied in great surprise, "Well, bless me, if I don't believe you're right!"

2

An Indian had strayed away from camp and got lost. He asked some tourists he met to point the way back. "What's the matter, Indian, are you lost?" they asked. "Ugh, no, Injun not lost," he declared scornfully; "wigwam lost. Injun," he explained, striking his chest, "here!"

3

The wife came running excitedly into hubby's office one morning. "Oh, John," she wailed, "I've lost my diamond ring. It must have slipped off my finger somewhere and I can't find it any place." "Don't worry, May," said hubby; "I came across it a little while ago right here in my wallet pocket."

4

Little Junior came running in one evening with a fine penknife in his hand. "Look, daddy," he cried, "see the swell knife I found!" "Are you sure this knife was lost, son?" asked father. "Of course it was lost," declared Junior. "I know it was lost because I saw the man hunting for it."

5

Little Billy returned from Sunday school with the news that he had lost the penny that had been given him for the collection. "But, Billy," protested mother, "this is four Sundays in a row that you've lost your penny." "I know, mummy," replied the boy gravely, "but I've just *gotta* win soon."

6

A passenger who had just come to the rear of the bus stood and picked up a coin, while four other nearby passengers eyed him. The man looked at the coin in his hand, and asked, "Did any of you gentlemen drop a half-dollar?" "I did," clamored the four in unison. "Well," said the finder, handing the coin to the nearest man, "here's a nickel of it."

See also beggar[7], drowning[5], hunting[3], property, wife[5].

LOUD

A department manager who had a very loud voice was using the telephone one morning when the general manager happened to be in the outer office. "What's all that noise and shouting in Smith's office?" he inquired of a stenographer. "Mr. Smith is talking to Chicago, sir," was the reply. "Well, why in the world doesn't he use the telephone?" commented the big boss.

LOVE

1

"Ah, my sweet," sighed the romantic young man, "don't you think that you might learn to love me?" "Well, I might," conceded the girl dubiously. "After all, I did learn to eat spinach."

2

"There's love for you," declared Mrs. Brown, looking up from her newspaper. "This tells about a man who got to be forty years old without learning to read or write. Then he fell in love with a cultured woman and he made a scholar of himself in two years." "That's nothing," grunted Brown. "I know of a man who was a great scholar at forty, and then he fell for a chorus girl and made a fool of himself in two days."

3

"But, daughter," protested father angrily, "you can't marry that young nitwit. Why, he only makes $40 a month." "I know, daddy," replied the girl dreamily; "but a month flies by so fast when you're in love with each other."

4

Her fiancé slouched despondently into the room and slumped into a chair. "I've lost all my money, darling," he announced, sadly. "I haven't a cent left in the world." "That won't make the slightest bit of difference, sweetheart," declared the girl warmly. "I'll love you just as much as ever—even if I never see you again."

5

"You're never affectionate to me any more," sobbed wifey. "I sometimes think that you loved me more when we were only engaged." "That may well be," admitted hubby thoughtfully. "To tell you the truth, my dear, I never did care very much for married women."

6

A young minister, thinking to be facetious, took his host's small daughter on his knee and gravely declared, "I don't love you, Sally." Every one present laughed, save Sally who frowned and said, "But you've gotta love me. You've *gotta!*" "And why must I?" questioned the smiling minister. "Because," explained Sally, "the Bible says you've gotta love them that hate you—an' I sure do hate you!"

See also affectionate[2], alike[2], devotion[1], dying[3], God[3], kiss[5], marriage[9], reason[3], suitor[3], sweetheart[1], waiting[5].

LOVELORN

"Do you know what I did, mother?" reported daughter gleefully. "I advertised under an assumed name that a beautiful young girl would like to make the ac-quaintance of a refined gentleman." "Oh, Hazel, how terrible!" gasped mother, horrified. "Did you get any replies?" "Only one," chuckled Hazel; "it was from father."

See also handwriting[2].

LOYALTY

It was almost midnight and hubby, who was to have been home for dinner, had not been heard from. So the worried wife sent wires to six of his lodge brothers, reading: "Am worried about Jim. Is he spending night with you?" About an hour later hubby arrived home, and a short while after six telegrams were delivered, each saying: "Don't worry. Jim spending night with me."

LUCKY

1

"Gosh, sis sure is lucky," commented a young boy to his pal. "What's she lucky about?" asked the pal. "Well," explained the first boy, "she was at a party last night where they played a game that made the fellows either kiss a certain girl or give her a box of chocolates." "But how was she lucky?" insisted the other. "Why, sis came home with fourteen boxes of chocolates," was the answer.

2

"Pop, oh, pop!" cried Leslie excitedly, running into the living room just before dinner. "There's a big black cat in the dining room." "Never mind," mumbled father. "Black cats are lucky." "Well, this one sure is," declared Leslie; "he's just had your dinner."

3

The editor of the little country paper returned home jubilant. "What're you so happy about?" inquired his wife. "Did you have some good luck today?" "I'll say I've had luck!" cried the editor gleefully. "You know old Deacon Brown who hasn't paid for his paper in over twelve years? Well, he came in today and canceled his subscription."

4

The laborer was an extreme optimist to whom all things worked for good. One morning, after he had walked four miles to the job, he suddenly exclaimed to a fellow workman, "Good gosh! I forgot to bring my lunch along today!" But in a moment he regained his customary composure and smiled happily. "And a mighty good thing it is, too, because I also left my teeth at home."

5

"Hi, there, Jones," called a neighbor. "I saw you leaving early yesterday morning on a fishing trip. Did you have any luck?" "I'll say I had luck!" declared Jones emphatically. "While I was away four bill collectors came by."

See also lose[3].

LUGGAGE

1

The hotel manager eyed the new arrival critically, then said, "I'm afraid I'll have to ask you to pay in advance as your luggage is too, ah, shall we say, emotional." "What do you mean, emotional?" demanded the guest. "Ah—too easily moved," was the reply.

2

It was to be only a one-week vacation, but by the time the wife had packed all her clothes, poor hubby was bent nearly double under the luggage as they arrived at the station. "Maybe we should have brought the piano along," he murmured as the train pulled in. "Don't be sarcastic," snapped the wife coldly. "But I'm not, dear," he insisted. "It's just that I left the tickets there."

See also newlyweds[1].

LUNATIC

1

An inmate of a mental hospital sat in his cell playing solitaire and another stood watching. "Hey!" cried the kibitzer. "You're cheating yourself!" "Ssh!" whispered the player. "Don't say anything. I've been cheating on myself at solitaire for years." "Is that so?" said the spectator, amazed. "And don't you ever catch yourself at it?" "Nope," was the proud reply. "I'm too clever at it."

2

"That man over there," explained the guide to a group of visitors in an asylum, "thinks he's God." One of the visitors, thinking to get a laugh, approached the man and asked, "Is it true, Lord, that you made the world in seven days?" The man gave him a withering glance and said scornfully, "I'm not in the mood to talk shop!"

3

An inmate of a mental hospital sat holding a fishing pole with the line dangling in a flower bed. "What are you fishing for, my man?" inquired a visitor. "Suckers," replied the fisherman without looking up. "Catch any yet?" continued the visitor. "You're the eleventh today," responded the inmate calmly.

4

The woman who consulted the psychiatrist wore a worried frown. "I'm here at the insistence of my family, doctor," she explained. "They think something's wrong with me because I like waffles." "Why, there's nothing wrong about liking waffles," declared the doctor. "I like them myself." "You do, doctor?" cried the woman delightedly. "Then you must come up some time. I have nine trunks full of them."

5

It was a visitor's second trip through the mental hospital, and he paused to ask an inmate his name. "George Washington," was the response. "But the last time I was here," objected the puzzled visitor, "you were Napoleon." "I know," replied the inmate sadly, "but that was by my first wife."

6

Every Sunday night the asylum permitted the patients to dress in their best and attend a formal dinner with the staff. At one of these affairs one of the nurses passed the potatoes to an elderly, dignified-looking lady, and was amazed to see her start taking them from the bowl and piling them on her head. "My dear," chided the nurse gently, "why are you putting the potatoes on your head?" "Goodness, I must be crazy!" cried the lady, embar-

rassed. "I thought it was the spinach."

See also fertilizer[1], sanity[1], smoking[1].

LUXURY

See army[8], desire, suicide[3].

LYING

1

Smith had been scolding his wife and he ended by saying, "And in addition, dear, I believe that you fib a little at times." "But I mean well," retorted the wife meekly, "as I think it's a wife's duty to speak well of her husband occasionally."

2

Teacher had been telling her pupils an elaborate story about Santa Claus. Little Tommy began to chuckle, then to laugh out loud. "Tommy," reproved teacher, "what did I whip you for yesterday?" "For lyin', teacher," replied Tommy through guffaws, "an' I was just wonderin' who's gonna whip you."

3

A group of sailors on leave were being shown through an English cathedral. "Under that altar," the guide droned on, "lies Richard the Lion-Hearted, and to that side of it lies Henry the Eighth, and in the churchyard outside lies Mary Queen of Scots. Now, who do you think," he asked, stepping on an unmarked stone, "is lyin' here?" "I don't know for sure," grunted one of the sailors, "but I sure got my suspicions."

4

Little Willie had just returned

from Sunday school where he had been told that liars do not go to heaven. "Does pop ever lie, mom?" he asked. "I imagine so," replied mother. "Well, do you, an' Uncle Bill, an' Aunt Betty ever lie?" "I guess we all do occasionally," admitted mother. "Gosh, it must be awful lonesome in heaven," declared Willie, "with nobody around but God and George Washington."

5

The instructor of the adult Bible class opened his book and announced, "Today I shall talk on liars. How many of you have read the twenty-seventh chapter of our textbook?" Almost everyone present raised his hand. "Obviously, this is the group to whom I should address myself," declared the instructor. "The book has only twenty-five chapters, ladies and gentlemen."

6

"Say, what do you know!" exclaimed a commuter to his seatmate. "I've just been reading here in the paper about some professor who's invented a new device that can tell whether or not a man is telling the truth." "What's so wonderful or new about that?" snorted the other. "I've been married to one of those things for years."

See also lawyer[2], marriage[11], politics[2], progress[2], truth[4].

MAGAZINE

1

"You know, you can save some money by subscribing to several magazines on one of these club lists," Jones told his neighbor. "If you take three you get them at a discount. My wife and I are trying to pick out three now." "Have you made your choice yet?" asked the neighbor. "Practically," said Jones. "We can get one I don't want, and one she doesn't want, and one neither of us want for only $2.15."

2

"Gosh, I'm bored," yawned hubby. "Why don't you settle down and read something?" suggested his wife. "I'd like to," he answered, "but there's nothing around to read except some old next month's magazines!"

3

The new minister was making his first round of his parishioners and was trying to get some idea of their interests. "Do you take any periodicals?" he asked one woman. "Well, no, Reverend, I don't personally," she replied; "but my husband does, an' I've been tryin' my best to get him to sign the pledge."

MAID

1

"I hate to complain," said the new maid blushingly to her mistress, "but every time your husband sees me he tries to kiss me, and wants me to sit on his lap, and—" "That's enough, Susie," interrupted the mistress. "When he does that, you just go right on with your work and pay no attention to him. He used to try the very same thing with me!"

2

He was returning home from a long business trip and his ring was answered by a new maid who had been hired in his absence. He handed her a large bunch of flowers and said, "Please give these to Mrs. Smith and tell her I'd like to see her at once." "Well, okay," conceded the maid. "But you'd better make it snappy, buddy, because she's expecting the old man any minute now."

3

The new maid had been relating her many adventures in service, so the mistress finally remarked, "You seem to have had a good many places. Just how many different mistresses have you had, all told?" "Seventeen, all told, ma'am," replied the maid promptly, "an' all told exactly what I thought of 'em, ma'am."

4

Mrs. Williams was giving her new maid her general instructions. "And by the way, Mary," she added, "do you have to be called in the morning?" "Well, I don't really *have* to be, mum," explained Mary, "unless you just happen to need me."

See also angel[2], caller[3], cause[1], dust[2], family[1], gossip[2], jealousy, penny[1], realism[1].

MAIL

As a reward for his services to the political party, a farmer was appointed postmaster of a little backwoods town. As time went by, the postal department began getting complaints that no mail was going out from this office, so they sent an inspector to investigate. The inspector asked the postmaster why no mail had been sent out, whereupon that official pointed to a large mailbag hanging in the corner and replied, "Heck, thet bag ain't near full yit."

MAKE-UP

See cosmetics.

MAN

1

"Gracious!" exclaimed hubby as he closed a volume on "The Marvels and Immensity of Nature." "When I read a book like this on the grandeurs of nature it makes me think what a poor insignificant thing is man." "Humph!" grunted the wife. "You never saw a woman who had to wade through five hundred pages of stuff just to discover that obvious fact."

2

A visiting minister was addressing a Sunday school and speaking on the human nature of Christ. "Now let me ask you, children," he concluded, "was He not a man like myself?" "Oh, no, sir," spoke up a bright little boy. "He was a good man."

See also fraternity[2], woman[3].

MANAGEMENT

A farmer with two children came up to the ticket-window of a circus and asked for three seats. "Sorry, but we're sold out," said the ticket-seller. "What!" cried the farmer. "You mean to tell me you don't even have three seats left you can sell me?" "That's about the size of it," was the answer. "Well, all I kin say," growled the old fellow, turning away, "is thet I calls thet durned poor management."

MANNERS

1

"Did you deliver my note to the mayor?" inquired the politician of his hireling. "Sure did, boss," replied the thug; "but dere ain't no use sendin' dat guy notes—he's stone blind." "Nonsense! The mayor's not blind," protested the grafter. " 'Course he is," insisted the other. "Why, t'ree times while I was dere he asks me where is me hat, see, an' de whole time it's dere in plain sight on me head."

2

Little Timmy had gone with mother to dinner at a friend's house and been warned to remember his manners. When it came time for the dessert, the hostess said, "I have a choice of desserts today, Timmy. Will you have pie or ice cream?" "Oh, boy! Ice cream!" cried Timmy with shining eyes. "What did I tell you, Timmy?" mother reproved. "Ice cream, what?" "Ice cream, first," was the prompt reply.

3

A tourist stopped at a little lunch counter out West and asked for coffee and rolls. She was surprised to find the coffee served in a cup without a saucer. "Where's the saucer?" she demanded of the girl behind the counter. "We don't put out saucers no more, ma'am," was the explanation. "We found that there's allus some lowbrow what'll drink outa them, an' thet's bad fer the trade in a swell dump like this'n."

4

It was one of those stuffy little summer resorts. The main course had just ended and there was a clatter and a banging as the tables were being cleared. Suddenly the cook, in a dirty apron, stuck his head through the door and shouted, "Keep your knives, everybody; we're gonna have pie for dessert."

See also abnormal, explanation[2], hint[2], lady[2], tact[2].

MARKS

An immigrant farmer had one of his calves stolen. He had one of his neighbors arrested as the thief. When the case came up in court, the defendant's lawyer questioned the plaintiff, "Could you positively identify your calf? Did it have any earmarks?" The farmer scratched his head reflectively, then replied, "Vell, der only earmarks vot I remember vas dot his tail vas cut off."

See also grades[1].

MARKSMANSHIP

See shooting.

MARRIAGE

1

"Well, I've decided to accept old William's proposal and marry him," announced Mamie to Marge. "Say, he's a wild one," observed Marge. "You can bet he'll lead a double life." "Very likely," admitted Mamie. "But if I don't marry him I'll lead a single life, and that'd be worse."

2

She had accepted him, and now they were talking over plans for their life together. "You believe in allowances for married women, don't you?" she asked eagerly. "I certainly do," he replied. "I think a husband must make allowances for a lot of things."

3

A minister was examining a confirmation class and he asked one of the boys to define matrimony. "Matrimony," recited the lad, "is a place of punishment where some weak souls must suffer for a while before they can go to heaven." "Hmm!" mused the minister, a married man. "That's not quite what I had in mind, but it'll do very well."

4

"Well, how do you like married life?" inquired a friend of a young bride. "Oh, I can't see much difference from before," replied the new wife. "I used to stay up half the night waiting for Bill to go home, and now I stay up half the night waiting for him to come home."

5

"Goodness!" exclaimed wifey with a shudder, looking up from a magazine article. "I think all this talk about trial marriage is simply awful." "Oh, I dunno," replied hubby glumly. "What! You don't mean to say that you believe in it?" demanded the wife indignantly. "How can I help it?" asked hubby sadly. "If you can show me any marriage that ain't a trial, I'd like to see it."

6

"Hiya, Jim!" cried Sam, meeting an old crony of his for the first time in years. "By the way, Jim, did you ever marry that girl you were going with, or do you still do your own cooking and darning?" "Yes," was Jim's reply.

7

"Now, Tommy," ordered teacher during the spelling lesson, "spell 'matrimony.'" "M-a-t-r-i-m-o-n-y," spelled Tommy. "Very good," approved teacher. "Now define the word." "Well, I don't know exactly what it means," said the boy, "but I do know that it's something that mother says she sure has plenty of."

8

The bride tottered down the aisle, her thin gray hair neatly dressed and her sunken, withered cheeks cracked in smiles. She approached her bald, toothless groom standing waiting on two stout crutches and supported by the best man. "How come such old people ever fell for each other?" whispered a spectator. "Oh, they've been engaged since they were nineteen," replied another, "but they just waited until they could afford to get married."

9

"When people get married, mom," asked a five-year-old boy, "what do they say?" "Oh, they don't say very much, son," replied mother uncertainly. "They just promise to love and be kind to each other." "Oh!" said the boy. Then after pondering this a moment, he remarked, "You're not *always* married, are you, mom?"

10

A maid who had left three months before to get married, dropped in one day to visit her former mistress. "Well, Tillie, how do you like being married?" asked the lady. "Oh, gettin' married's just fine, ma'am," replied the maid enthusiastically, and then in a more thoughtful tone added, "but, Lord, ma'am, ain't it tedious!"

11

"You ought to get married, Bill," a married man said to a bachelor friend. "It's swell having a quiet, comfortable home waiting for you every night; a loving wife there with your pipe and slippers and a good hot meal; the fun of taking care of a garden and lawn; and children are a pure joy and practically no trouble." "I might get married at that," replied Bill thoughtfully, "if I could lie like you."

12

The archbishop had delivered an inspiring sermon on the beauties of married life, its joys and rewards. Two toil-worn women left the service in rather an introspective mood. "That was a beautiful sermon his reverence gave us this morning," observed one. "It was indeed," agreed the other. "I just wish I knew as little about the subject as he does."

NOTE: This subject has not been cross referenced because of its frequent occurrence throughout this dictionary.

MASK

A curate was being reprimanded by his bishop for having attended a ball. "But, my lord," protested the curate, "I wore a mask." "Umm, I see," responded the bishop. "Well, that puts a new face on the matter."

MASQUERADE

1

The masquerade was strictly for children and a policeman had been stationed at the door to keep out all adults. An excited woman came up and demanded entrance, but the policeman refused. "But I *must* get in," exclaimed the woman; "my child's there dressed as a butterfly, and she's forgotten her wings." "Sorry, ma'am," said the officer, "but I guess she'll just have to remain a caterpillar."

2

Two country boys had been invited to a masquerade in the village, and they arranged a cow-skin so that they could get inside and imitate the live animal. They got into the skin at home and started for the village. But in going across a pasture the boy in front suddenly started to run, and the one in back could only follow. At last the one in front gasped, "It's no use, Zeke. Better brace yourself—here comes the bull!"

MATCHMAKING

Two college girls were having tea together. "Goodness, Sue," remarked one, "why do you always refer to your mother as 'the mater'? It's only in corny college movies they do that." "But the term means something with my mother," explained the other. "You see, she's managed to get husbands for all of my eight sisters."

MEALS

1

A farmer went to the big city to see the sights and engaged a room at a hotel. "What time d'ye have yore meals around here?" he asked the clerk. "Breakfast is from 7 to 11, lunch from 12 to 3:30, and dinner from 5:30 to 8:30," replied the clerk. "Well," exclaimed the farmer, "when the heck am I gonna get time to see the town?"

2

The hungry tourist stopped in a little restaurant out West and sat expectantly at a table. "Howdy, stranger," greeted the waiter, coming up. "Do yuh like creamed chipped beef on toast?" "Gracious, no!" exclaimed the customer with a shudder. "I never touch the filthy stuff!" "Waal, then," remarked the waiter, moving away, "dinner's over."

3

The rich business magnate was seated in an elegant restaurant eating milk and crackers. "Why eat that stuff?" inquired an acquaintance. "Got dyspepsia," grunted the big shot. "I suppose you don't enjoy your meals, then," ventured the other. "Enjoy my meals!" cried the dyspeptic. "Say, all that meals are to me are guideposts for taking medicine before and after!"

See also hint[5], late[5], medicine[6], polite[1], South[4].

MEANING

Helen sat reading a book on the meaning of names. Her mother sat looking at her and reflecting on what a sweet girl she was. "It says here, mother," said Helen, looking up, "that Philip means lover of horses, and that James means beloved. I wonder what Bill means?"

"I hope, darling," said mother fondly, "that Bill means business."

See also collect[3].

MEAT

1

A little boy was having dinner at a playmate's house and was making a manful attempt to handle his knife and fork properly. After watching his struggles, his hostess asked, "Are you sure you can cut your meat, Frankie?" "Oh, yes, ma'am," answered the boy politely. "We often have meat as tough as this at home."

2

"Isn't it a pity," observed the landlady sentimentally as she served the roast, "that this poor little lamb had to be slaughtered in the full bloom of its youth just to satisfy our appetites?" "I'll say," agreed a boarder, stabbing at his piece; "it's sure tough."

3

Two Americans were dining in a Parisian restaurant. "I think this is horse meat," declared one suspiciously. "Oh, I don't think so," said the other. "I'll bet you," offered the first. "No, thanks," the second refused. "I never won a bet on a horse in my life."

See also automobile[4].

MEDICINE

1

"Got any medicine, mister?" inquired the farm boy as he entered the village drug store. "Sure, lots of it. What kind do you want?" replied the druggist. "Oh, reckon it don't make much difference," said the boy, "'long as it's somethin' good an' strong. Pappy's ailin' powerful bad."

2

When an Indian reappeared in a Western drug store for the fourth time and asked for a half-dozen bottles of a certain cough medicine, the druggist grew curious. "Somebody in the family sick?" he asked. "Nope, no sick," grunted the Indian. "Then what in the world are you doing with all this cough syrup?" persisted the druggist. "Ugh!" responded the Indian. "Me likeum on pancakes."

3

The doctor smiled complacently as he entered the sickroom. "Ah, I see you're looking much better," he observed. "That medicine of mine must be doing the work." "I think it must be because I followed the directions to the letter," stated the patient. "What were they?" asked the doctor. "'Keep this bottle tightly corked,'" was the reply.

4

"Gee, doc, I sure want to thank you for that medicine you gave me," cried a man gratefully as he met his physician. "It fixed up all my troubles." "Well, I always do my best for my patients," replied the doctor modestly. "How many bottles of it did you take?" "Oh, I didn't take any of it," explained the grateful one. "My rich uncle took one bottle, and I'm his sole heir."

5

Little Johnny was sick, but refused to take his medicine. "But it's good for you, Johnny," insisted mother patiently, "and God wants you to take it." "Humph! I don't believe He does," declared the youngster. "Just a minute an' I'll ask Him." The boy buried his head beneath the bedclothes, from whence after a moment issued a hoarse voice saying, "Why, no, of course not!"

6

A tramp knocked at the back door and, when the lady answered, said, "Please, mum, I'm a sick man an' a doctor gimme this medicine, but I need somethin' to take it with." "Why, you poor man!" cried the lady sympathetically. "I'll fetch you a spoon and a glass of water." "Oh, it's not that, mum," interrupted the tramp. "It says on the bottle that it hasta be took after meals. Do ya happen to have a meal handy?"

7

Father threw down his paper in disgust. "The price of everything is increasing these days," he growled. "It says there that even castor oil is going up." "Well, that sure doesn't worry me," declared the young son with a shrug. "The only time castor oil bothers me is when it's going down."

See also beer, instructions[5], meals[3], patent medicine, refusal, will power[3].

MEDIUM

See spiritualism.

MEEK

See henpecked, yield.

MEETING

1

A group of married men had drunk themselves into a romantic mood and each was telling, as poetically as he was able, the circumstances of his first meeting with his wife. Finally, one turned to a meek little man who had been sitting quietly in the corner, and asked, "And how did you meet your wife, sir?" "I didn't meet her, gentlemen," was the grave reply; "she overtook me."

2

"Were you an' daddy born here, mom?" asked a young lad of his mother. "No, son," she answered. "You're the only one of the family who was born here in Missouri. Daddy was born in Maine, I was born in Kentucky, and your sister was born in Ohio." The boy considered this for a moment, then asked, "Gosh, mom, how'd we all get together?"

MELODY

See music, musician, singer.

MEMENTO

1

An angry neighbor went to the Smiths'. "Mrs. Smith," she said heatedly, "your little son Algy has just thrown a rock through my front window!" "He has?" said Algy's mother with a fond smile. "I wonder, would you mind bringing me that rock? You see, we're keeping all such little mementos of his boyish pranks."

2

"Look what I found in the Bible, mom!" cried little Betty excitedly, running in with a pressed, dried leaf from a tree. "Gee, do you think it belonged to Eve?"

3

"That's a lovely locket you have," remarked one woman to another. "I suppose you keep some kind of memento in it?" "Oh, yes; a lock of my husband's hair," was the reply. "But your husband's still alive," objected the first. "Yes, I know," said the other; "but his hair's gone."

MEMORY

1

"I don't know what I'm going to do about my wife," declared Brown to a pal. "She has the worst memory I've ever encountered." "Forgets everything, I suppose?" asked the pal. "Heck, no!" cried Brown. "She remembers everything."

2

The absent-minded professor entered a drug store and said to the druggist, "Would you please give me a package of prepared tablets of the monacetic-acidester of salicylic acid." "I suppose it's aspirin you want?" inquired the puzzled druggist. "That's it!" cried the professor, greatly relieved; "I never *can* remember that name."

3

"I've been having so much trouble lately," confided the Senator, "that I've about decided to take a course to train my memory." "What system will you use?" asked a friend. "That's just it; I can't find one to suit me," replied the Senator. "I'm looking for one that will help me, while being interviewed, to remember what to forget."

4

"It embarrasses me," the new boarder informed an old-timer, "that I can never remember the landlady's name." "Why, that's a cinch," replied the other. "Her name's Womack, and that rhymes with stomach. Well, here's where you get your stomach filled, so, Womack—stomach. Get it?" "Gee, thanks," said the new boarder gratefully. Next morning when he came down to breakfast, he called out confidently, "Good morning, Mrs. Kelly."

See also examination[5], history[2], statue[4].

MENU

1

The waitress came up and set a glass of water before the customer. "We have everything on the menu today, sir," she announced. "So I've been noticing," replied the customer in distaste. "How about a clean one?"

2

The sweet young thing studied the menu, then said, "I think I'll have an order of Spimoni Vermatelli." "What!" cried the boyfriend. "Where do you see that?" "Right here on the menu," retorted the girl, pointing. The fellow looked, then snorted, "Try again, babe; that's the name of the owner of the restaurant."

See also cannibal[2].

MIDGET

1

A circus midget had to take an overnight train trip and all he could get was an upper berth. He had dinner late and drank two large cups of coffee with it. Around midnight, the man in the berth below the midget rang for the porter and complained, "Porter, I can't get to sleep. Someone is pacing about overhead."

2

A side show to a circus had a big poster advertising a dwarf five feet tall. "Shucks, I don't see anything so wonderful about that," commented a farmer. "I've seen dwarfs a lot smaller than that." "Ah, my friend, but that's just what makes this one so remarkable," declared the barker. "He's the tallest dwarf in the world."

3

A man went to a lawyer to get a divorce. "We were happily married for almost two years," he explained, "and then a little stranger arrived." "But that's good," said the lawyer. "A baby should have made you all the happier." "But it wasn't a baby," growled the client. "It was my wife's uncle—he's a midget—and he's been with us ever since."

MILK

1

The old farmer was ill in bed and his sons were running the farm. "How're the cows doin', Jake?" he inquired of his eldest son one day. "Not so bad," reported Jake. "We're gettin' about twelve gallons a day." "How much skimmed milk ye sellin'?" asked the old man. "About ten gallons." "An' how much cream an' whole milk?" "About three gallons each." The farmer frowned suspiciously and demanded, "What'n hell ye doin' with the rest?"

2

"Where'd you spend your vacation, Jack?" asked Tom. "At a watering place," replied Jack. "But I thought Jim told me you were spending it on a farm?" objected Tom. "That's right," confirmed Jack; "a dairy farm."

3

A city boy visiting in the country, saw a cow being milked for the first time. "Well, sonny, now you know where milk comes from, don't you?" smiled the farmer. "I sure do!" affirmed the boy. "You just give the cow some breakfast food and water and then drain the crankcase."

4

"It looks like rain today, doesn't it?" observed the milkman sociably as he delivered the housewife's daily quart of milk. "I'll say it does!" agreed the woman, regarding the bluish fluid scornfully. "But then it always does."

5

"Do you keep any calves?" inquired the new mother anxiously of the milkman. "Why, yes, ma'am, I do," was the reply. "Ah, good," the young mother heaved a relieved sigh. "Then please bring me a pint of calf's milk every day. I'm afraid cow's milk is a little too strong for baby."

See also cow[6], decision[1], farm[2].

MILLIONAIRE

1

Two men were discussing the little peculiarities of their wives. "My wife tells me," remarked one, "that almost every night she dreams that she's married to a millionaire." "Boy, you're lucky!" exclaimed the other enviously. "My wife thinks that during the daytime."

2

"Now, children," instructed the teacher, "I want each of you to write an essay on what you'd do if you had a million dollars." All of the pupils began writing industriously, but one little boy just sat twiddling his thumbs. When the papers were collected he handed in a blank sheet. "How's this, Ronnie?" asked teacher. "You've done nothing at all." "Well," replied Ronnie, "that's what I'd do if I had a million."

See also amount[4].

MIND

1

The high-school teacher was acting as adviser to some of the senior students. "Do you know," said one of the students, "I've got half a mind to go to college." "Well, why don't you?" encouraged the teacher. "That's as good as most who go."

2

"If you don't keep your big mouth shut," cried the irritable lady golfer to the caddy, "you'll drive me out of my mind!" "That ain't no drive, lady," snickered the caddy impudently; "that's a putt."

3

"Frankly, I'm alarmed, doctor,"

the lady confided. "My husband seems to be wandering in his mind lately." "I wouldn't be worried, madam," comforted the physician. "I know your husband, and I assure you he can't wander far."

MINING

1

A group of men were discussing mining, and one of them said, "I've never understood exactly what the term 'bonanza' means. Who can tell me?" "I can," volunteered a man gloomily who had bought stock. "A bonanza is a hole in the ground owned by a champion liar!"

2

The warden of a jail called one of his prisoners to his office. "I understand, Jones," he said, "that you're here because of a mining deal in which you wrote a prospectus so glowing that it snared the suckers by the hundred." "That's right, sir," admitted the prisoner; "I was a bit optimistic." "Well, the governor wants a report on conditions in the jail," the warden went on, "and I'd like you to write it."

MINISTER

1

A group of soldiers and a chaplain were sitting at a restaurant table when a waitress, hurrying up, slipped and spilled a bowl of hot soup all over the chaplain. "Well, I'll be—, I mean, of all the—," spluttered the clergyman, struggling for self-control. "Oh, come, one of you sinful comrades, say something appropriate!"

2

"Can I be a preacher when I get big, mom?" pleaded a young lad. "Of course, dear, if you wish," agreed mother; "but what gave you the idea?" "Well, if I've got to be goin' to church all my life anyway," explained the boy, "it'll be a lot easier if I can stand up and holler instead of sittin' quiet all the time."

3

"You do so much good in our community," gushed one of the Ladies' Aid to the parson's wife, "that I think there ought to be a special place in heaven for ministers' wives." "That's kind of you to say so," murmured the other modestly; "but I'd much prefer to go with my husband."

4

A minister suddenly awakened in the dead of night to discover that there was a burglar in the room. "You're a dead duck if you squawk, buddy," threatened the thug. "I'm lookin' fer your money." "If you'll just let me get up, my good man," offered the preacher calmly, "I'll turn on the light and we'll both search."

See also call[1], chicken[1], day, doctor[2], drinking[6], father[5], fight[1], fool[3], funeral[5], golf[1], grace[4], nothing[3], opportunity[3], practical[1], practice[2, 3], prayer[6], pronunciation[5], save, sermon, silence[2], sin[3], source[1], swearing[2].

MIRACLE

1

An elderly woman was crossing the frontier and when asked at customs if she had anything to declare, replied in the negative. "But what's in this bottle?" inquired the official.

"Just holy water from Lourdes," answered the woman piously. The official pulled the cork and sniffed. "This is whiskey," he stated. "Glory to God!" cried the woman, throwing up her arms. "A miracle!"

2

Two young fellows dropped into a revival meeting being conducted by a very sturdy man, and began to heckle the speaker in a noisy manner. "Why did you boys come here if you can't behave?" asked the preacher. "Aw, we came to see miracles performed," said one impudently. The revivalist walked up to them, took them both by the collars and, as he ejected them, remarked coolly, "We don't perform miracles here, but we do cast out devils."

See also ass[2].

MIRROR

A hillbilly one day found in the road a mirror that had been lost by a tourist. "By crackey!" he exclaimed looking into it. "If'n it ain't a pitcher o' my old pappy!" He took it home and tried to hide it in the back of a closet, but his suspicious wife saw him and dug it out as soon as he was gone. "Ah-ha!" she cried as she looked into it. "So thet's the old hag he's bin a-chasin' after!"

See also mistake[5], portrait, reform[4].

MISERABLE

"Oh, dear," sighed the coquettish young girl as she preened herself before a mirror, "I can't help wondering just how many men will be made miserable when I get married." "I'll tell you in a minute," volunteered her chum, "if you'll just tell me how many men you're going to marry."

MISFORTUNE

1

The old farmer stood gloomily surveying the damage the flood had done to his place. "Say, Si," called a neighbor from the road, "yore pigs was all washed down the river." "How about Wilkins' pigs?" asked the farmer. "They're all gone, too," was the answer. "An' Sander's?" "All gone." "Waal," declared the farmer more cheerfully, "tain't as bad as I thought it was."

2

A lawyer, whose business called him into the slum section of town, dropped into a cheap restaurant in the neighborhood. He was surprised and shocked to find an old friend of his working there as a waiter. "Heavens, Dan!" he gasped. "You, a waiter in this dump!" "Yes, I am," answered the other with dignity; "but I don't eat here."

3

"I'm disgusted with marriage," declared a man to a friend. "I've been married twice and had bad luck both times." "What happened?" inquired the friend. "Well, my first wife ran away with another fellow," explained the complainer. "And the second?" prompted the curious friend. "She didn't," was the answer.

See also pessimist[1].

MISS

1

Two old sailors were sitting in what had been their favorite saloon. The new management had remodeled it into a modern, elegant tavern. "Guess it's all right, but I liked the old place better," observed one. "I miss the old spittoon." "That's nothin'," remarked the other; "you always did, Bill."

2

A rather caustic editor received from a lady contributor some verses written on perfumed paper and tied with a pink ribbon, bearing the title, "I wonder will he miss me?" The editor twice tried to read them, swallowed hard, and returned them with a note saying: "Dear Madam, If he does, he should never again be trusted with firearms."

See also sarcasm[8].

MISTAKE

1

A doctor was praising another physician very highly to a man. "It seems very odd that you should speak so well of him," observed the other, "as he says that you're a quack." "Is that so?" replied the doctor. "Well, it's quite possible that we're both mistaken."

2

A businessman turned in his income tax form on which he had entered himself as a bachelor, but had listed a son as a dependent. In looking over the return, the clerk noted this and observed, "This must be a stenographic error." The businessman grunted, "You're telling me!"

3

It was the young sailor's first voyage and he was very excited when he cried, "Man overboard!" With much confusion and clanging of bells the ship was finally stopped. Looking rather sheepish, the young sailor stepped up to the captain and said, "Sorry, sir, but I made a mistake when I shouted 'Man overboard.'" "Thank heavens!" exclaimed the captain. "Full speed ahead!" "Yes, sir," explained the sailor; "it was a dame."

4

"Have you ever made a serious mistake in treating a patient, doctor?" inquired a friend of a famous surgeon. "Only once," confessed the surgeon, "and that was when I was young and inexperienced." "Did it prove fatal?" questioned the friend. "No; but recovery was difficult," said the surgeon. "I charged a man $80 for an operation and later learned that he had over $300."

5

"I'm guilty of the grievous sin of vanity," admitted the woman to her confessor. "Only this morning I looked into my mirror and yielded to the temptation of thinking myself beautiful." "Is that all, my daughter?" asked the priest. "Yes, father," was the reply. "Then go in peace, my daughter," instructed the confessor, "for to be mistaken is not to sin."

6

The bank's new president was going around talking to the employees about their work. "And how long have you been with us?" he inquired of one elderly cashier. "Over forty years, sir," replied the man, then with modest pride added, "and in all that time, sir, I have made only one slight error." "That's fine," congratulated the president; "but in the future please be more careful."

See also job[2], pronunciation[5], watch[3].

MODEL

1

The model blushed as she freed herself from the artist's arms. "And you say I'm the first model you ever kissed?" she asked. "That's right," said the artist. "Well, how many models have you had before me?" asked the model coyly. "Six," was the reply. "An orange, two bananas, a vase of flowers, a shawl, and a table."

2

"Gee, Mame, dese artist guys is sure queer, ain't they?" observed a model through her chewing gum. "Howya mean, Myrt?" asked Mame. "Aw, dey's a'ways doin' things the other way 'round," declared Myrt. "Now, when I goes to get me pitcher took, I puts on all me best clothes, but when dey wants to paint me pitcher, I has to take 'em all off."

See also laundry.

MODERATE

The old fellow had been a hard drinker all his life, and now he was at the point where he saw snakes and dragons at times. His wife was worried. One day she came to him with a bottle of medicine and said, "John, you know you're getting worse and on one of your drunks you'll be passing away. Now I want you to drink this whole bottle, and after that you'll never want another drink for the rest of your life." The old boy looked at the bottle, then said, "Couldn't you maybe get me something not quite so strong?"

MODERN

1

The young man was romantic in an old-fashioned way. He held her hand tenderly and asked, "Darling, may I kiss your hand?" "Okay, bud, help yourself," consented the modern miss breezily, "but be careful you don't burn your nose on my cigarette."

2

Wifey had been rather disdainful since the quarrel. "Why don't you come down off your high horse?" growled hubby. "That's your big trouble, John, you're so old-fashioned," retorted the modern wife. "Why don't you learn to motorize your thinking?"

3

"I just can't get used to these modern times," sighed Jones. "Why, what's happened now?" asked Smith. "Oh, I was at a little family party last night," explained Jones, "and the women were all talking politics while the men got off in a corner and exchanged recipes and household hints."

See also clothes[6], dating[2], farming[5], pregnancy[3].

MODESTY

1

Four-year-old Betty was in the nursery for the night when her little brother wanted to come in, but found the door locked. "You tan't tum in, Jimmy," the girl called, "'cause I'se in my nightie an' nursie says little boys shouldn't see little dirls in their nighties." The boy was puzzling this over, when Betty called out again, "It's aw wight, Jimmy, you tan tum in now; I tooked my nightie off."

2

The hillbilly woman was in town wearing a new hat, when suddenly it started to rain. The woman immediately pulled up her skirts to cover her precious hat. "Laws, Mandy, put down them skirts," protested her husband disgustedly; "yore a-showin' yore anatomy." "Shucks, man," retorted the woman, "I've had thet anatomy fer nigh on forty-five year, but this yere hat's plumb new."

3

A man whose son was just graduating from college was speaking to a friend who was head of a big business to try to get his son a position. "If I do say it myself," declared the father proudly, "he's an honest, intelligent, modest young man." "Humph!" snorted the big shot. "What's he ever done to be modest about?"

MONEY

1

Two young fellows were discussing the ethics of marriage. "You wouldn't marry a girl just because she had money, would you?" asked one innocent boy. "Well, no," admitted the other. "But on the other hand, I couldn't be so cruel as to let her die an old maid just because she had money, could I?"

2

"I don't entirely approve of Hazel's engagement to that rich Mr. Johnson," observed Hazel's mother to father. "I believe that she might be happier with a man who had less money." "Don't let that worry you," growled father. "After they're married, Hazel will take care of that little detail."

3

The politician climbed out of the taxi and began thumbing through his wallet for a new dollar bill. "I suppose that like a lot of other folks these days," he remarked pleasantly to the driver, "you would rather have clean money?" "Just gimme my dough, bud," said the driver, holding out his hand; "I don't give a hoot how *you* make it."

4

"I think these men who marry for money are low creatures," stated the sweet young thing. "You wouldn't marry me for money, would you, Bill?" "No, indeed," declared Bill, who hadn't proposed, "I wouldn't marry you for all the money in the world." "What!" cried the girl, outraged. "You horrid wretch!"

5

A man looked up from a newspaper account of the most recent daring robbery. "You know, Jim," he remarked, "it's getting to be dangerous to carry around a large roll of money." "I don't know how dangerous it is," Jim answered, "but personally I find it impossible."

See also acquaintance[1], advice[5], economy[2], finance[1], hint[3], kind[4], knowledge[4], love[4], New York[2], playwright[2], satisfaction[2], stingy[3], thrift[2].

MONTH

See Florida, pronunciation[3], season, weather.

MOON

1

Wifey lowered her magazine to remark, "Here's an article, John, that says that too much moonlight tends to make people crazy. I don't believe it, do you?" "Oh, I don't know," retorted hubby, remaining well hidden behind his newspaper. "After all, it was in the moonlight that I proposed to you, you know."

2

An amateur astronomer was entertaining a friend who was a rabid golfer. After dinner, he took his friend to his observatory and let him take a look at the moon through his telescope. "Well, what do you think of it?" he asked. "I guess it's all right," replied the golfer, "but it's got an awful lot of bunkers."

3

A drunk was on his way home and as he crossed a high bridge he happened to look down and was amazed to see the bright reflection of the moon in the still water below. "Whassat down there?" he asked a pedestrian who happened to pass. "Why, that's the moon," was the reply. The drunk scratched his head. "Now how'n heck did I get up here?" he muttered.

MORALITY

1

A lawyer was cross-examining a woman witness for the opposing side and, seeking to discredit her testimony, asked, "Mrs. Smith, are you promiscuous?" "That's my own business," snarled the witness. The lawyer considered this a moment, then inquired gently, "Well, madam, do you have any other business?"

2

A woman of profound religious sentiments was shocked when one Sunday morning the new neighbors sent their maid over to borrow the lawn mower. "How horrible!" cried the lady to her maid. "Why, the idea of cutting grass on the Sabbath! It's positively shameful! I should say they can't have the mower. Tell them we don't own a lawn mower."

MORE

Little Mary Jane had been visiting at the home of one of her small friends, and when it came time for her to go home the friend's mother said cordially, "Good-by, now, Mary Jane, and come again soon. We'd like very much to see more of you." The girl looked puzzled at this. "But there isn't any more of me," she protested.

MORON

1

Two morons were hiding in the bushes spying on a nudist camp. A naked young woman came into view and one moron nudged the other and said, "Oh, boy, some shape, huh?" "She's all right," conceded the other. "But, man, I'd sure like to see her in a sweater."

2

Two morons were trying to hang

a picture. One was trying to drive a nail into the wall with a hammer, but was having no success because he was holding the nail head-first to the wall. "The sap who made this nail was crazy," he exclaimed irritably; "he put the point on the wrong end." "No, the nail's all right," insisted the other, "but you're wrong. That nail's meant to go in the opposite wall."

3

A man was sitting in a streetcar slowly rocking his head from side to side like a metronome. Another man watched him, then asked him why he was doing it. "So I can tell the time," was the reply. "Well, what time is it?" asked the man. "Four-fifty," declared the head-shaker. "But you're wrong. It's five-ten," objected the other. "It is?" said the moron, rocking his head faster. "I must be slow."

4

A moron who had once heard a doctor discuss the process of death, stood by sympathetically while one of his relatives breathed his last. As soon as the man had died, the moron slipped from the room and soon returned with a chair. "What's the chair for?" some one inquired. "Oh, that," explained the moron, "is for Rigor Mortis to set in."

5

Two morons were discussing the death of another of their fraternity. "How did Willie die?" asked one. "He froze to death in his basement," replied the other. "How did he do that?" asked the first. "Well, he went down to feed the furnace," related the second, "and he thought he'd bargain with it, so he took a shovel of coal, opened the fire door, and said to the furnace, 'Now give me some heat, and I'll give you this coal.'"

6

A moron was walking awkwardly along the street hampered by a cane that was several inches too long for comfort. "Why don't you cut a few inches off the bottom?" a friend suggested. "That wouldn't help," replied the moron; "it's the upper end that's too high."

7

A moron got off the train looking a bit green about the gills. "What's wrong?" asked a friend who met him. "Train sickness," was the reply. "It always nauseates me terribly to ride backwards on a train." "Why didn't you ask the person sitting across from you to change with you?" asked the friend. "Oh, I thought of that," declared the moron, "only there wasn't anybody sitting there."

8

A moron bought one of those mail-order houses that come in sections, and shortly after it was assembled a friend passed and asked, "Well, how's the house?" "Aw, I don't like it very much," confessed the moron. "No wonder!" cried the friend, taking a look. "You've got it together upside down!" "Darned if I haven't!" agreed the moron. "Say, I'll bet that's why I always keep falling off the porch."

9

"Whoever thought of putting shoe polish in those collapsible metal tubes was crazy," declared the moron. "Why?" he was asked.

"Why, they're not going to fool anybody that way," said the moron. "I could tell the difference the minute I got the stuff in my mouth."

10

Two morons were out hunting. Suddenly, one of them raised his gun to take aim. "Hey, don't shoot," cried the other. "Your gun's not loaded." "Can't be helped," said the first. "No time to load it now—that rabbit won't wait."

See also fool, hurry[1].

MOSQUITO

1

The summer boarder slapped his neck and looked accusingly at the farmer. "I thought you told me you didn't have any mosquitoes," he said. "So I haven't," maintained the farmer. "Those you see have come over from Hi Simms' place— they ain't mine."

2

A man from New Jersey was spending his summer vacation in the Vermont hills. In the middle of his first night, four chickens roosting in a tree outside his window were disturbed by a cat and flew into his room. Half asleep, the guest batted wildly with a pillow until the fowls found their way out. Next morning he declared enthusiastically, "Had a swell sleep. Think I'll spend all my vacations here. Only saw four mosquitoes all night, and they were just little ones."

3

Brown was just back from a vacation in the country and was being greeted by a neighbor. "Well, how'd you find the mosquitoes?" inquired the neighbor. "We didn't have to," grunted Brown; "they found us."

See also angel[4].

MOTHER

1

"I don't understand how Mrs. Johnson can never see any of her children's faults," remarked Mrs. White impatiently. "Oh, well," White smiled indulgently, "mothers never can, you know." "What a silly thing to say!" exclaimed the woman. "And just like a man. Why, you know perfectly well, John, that I'd be quick to see any faults in our children—if they had any."

2

Mother, in a mellow mood, was relating anecdotes of the time when she had been a small girl—how she had hidden in the haystack, waded in the brook, slid down cellar doors, ridden a pony, etc. Her young son listened, heaved a wistful sigh and said, "Gee, mom, I sure wish I had met you earlier."

See also birthplace[2], like·, matchmaking, museum[2], nursemaid[1], pregnancy[1], proposal[4].

MOTHER-IN-LAW

1

He was a bashful boy and had been calling on the girl regularly for a year. One day he stammered, "Jane, I, er, I'd like to ask you an important question." "Oh, William, this is so sudden!" lied the girl. "I hardly know—" "No, no," interrupted the fellow; "what I want to ask is, what date have you and your mother set for our wedding?"

2

The domestic quarrel was increasing in acrimony, and wifey declared, "I wish to heaven I had taken mother's advice and never married you." Hubby's jaw dropped in amazement. "Do you mean to say that your mother tried to keep you from marrying me?" he demanded. "She certainly did," was the reply. "Merciful heavens!" exclaimed hubby remorsefully. "How I've wronged that woman!"

3

"Henry, dear," said the wife in a wheedling tone, "I've just had a letter from mother. She wants to visit us, but it's an expensive trip for poor little mother, and I was wondering if we mightn't help her a bit." "Why, certainly we can," agreed Henry generously. "You write and tell her that I'll be only too glad to buy her return ticket any time she's ready to go home."

4

"Say, Bill," anxiously asked the young man about to be married, "what did you call your mother-in-law after you were married?" "Well, that sort of took care of itself," explained Bill. "For the first year I got by simply by addressing her as 'Say,' and from then on we just called her 'Grandma.'"

5

He was so proud of his skill at golf that he had brought his mother-in-law along to watch him perform. He stationed her at a suitable spot to observe. As he teed off for the first hole, he remarked to his opponent, "I especially want to make a terrific drive today. That's my wife's mother standing down there."

The other looked, and shook his head. "Afraid it's hopeless," he declared. "You can't expect to hit her at two hundred and fifty yards."

See also departure[1].

MOTORING

See automobile, second-hand car, touring.

MOTORIST

See chauffeur, driver, woman-driver.

MOURN

1

A man stood before a grave weeping and saying over and over, "You shouldn't have died! You shouldn't have died!" A passer-by noticed him and came up to inquire sympathetically, "One of your parents, I suppose?" "Oh, no, nothing like that," wailed the man. "It's my wife's first husband."

2

A hillbilly woman was sitting in her cabin door eating pig's feet when a neighbor hurried up to tell her that her husband had just been killed in a saloon brawl. The new widow continued calmly to munch away while the tragic news was being related. "Well, you certainly take it cool," observed the neighbor at last. "Humph!" she grunted through mouthfuls. "Jest you wait'll I finish this-yere pig's trotter, an' ye'll be a-hearin' some hollerin' as is hollerin'."

3

At his wife's wake, the bereaved husband's sorrow reached such excesses that he had to be restrained by friends from trying to throw himself into the open coffin. The day after the funeral, a man who had been at the wake met the widower and commented sympathetically on his display of grief. "Were you at the cemetery for the buryin'?" inquired the bereaved eagerly. "No, I wasn't," was the answer. "Boy, you missed it," he declared proudly. "I *really* cut up there."

4

The day after the big quarrel, the husband came home with a mourning band on his sleeve. "Why, James, why the mourning?" exclaimed the wife. "Did one of your family die?" "No," replied the man. "I'm wearing it for your first husband—I'm sure sorry he died."

See also insects[6].

MOUTH

1

"Won't you have a little more of the dessert, Miss Smith?" insisted the hostess. "Well, a little," Miss Smith gave in; "but only a mouthful." "Mary," the hostess ordered the maid, "fill Miss Smith's plate, please."

2

"I'm sure never going back to that church after the way I've been insulted," declared Brown angrily. "What happened?" asked a friend. "Aw, it was when I stood up in meeting to relate my experience," explained Brown, "and as soon as I opened my mouth the Deacon in front got up and said, 'Will some brother please close that window, and keep it closed!'"

3

A rich young man whose father had been missing called at an undertaker's to see if an unidentified body there was his father. He said it was and ordered an elaborate funeral. Just as he was leaving, he took a last look and noticed that the lower jaw had dropped, exposing a set of false teeth. "Oh, that's not my father," he said, and left. The undertaker disgustedly yanked the corpse from the expensive coffin and snarled, "You durned fool! If you'd kept your mouth shut you'd have got a classy funeral."

MOVIES

1

"Well, Bridget," inquired the mistress as her maid returned from the movies, "did you enjoy the show?" "Oh, yes, ma'am, it was swell," declared the maid heartily. "What was the picture?" asked the mistress. The maid thought a moment, then replied, "Well, now, I don't believe I know, ma'am. You see, I went with my boyfriend."

2

The manager of the movie house was very angry when he sent for his assistant. "Is there anything wrong?" asked the helper anxiously. "Wrong!" roared the manager. "Well, I should say there is! Just look at that ad you put in the papers for next week's show: 'Smiling Eyes—with a strong cast!'"

3

The movie had been a very bad one, and the two men who left the theater were silent. "You know," one at last remarked, "it's marvelous how movies have progressed in these past few years." "How do you mean?" asked the other. "Well," explained the first, "at first they were silent and just moved, then they talked, and now this one we just saw smells!"

4

A boy applied at a big movie theater for a job as an usher and was accepted, fitted with a uniform, and put to work. Less than an hour later he appeared at the manager's office and announced, "I want to resign." "But why?" protested the manager. "You've only just started." "I know," said the boy, "but I've seen this picture."

5

A Hollywood writer got a big idea for a story and immediately phoned one of the noted producers. "Not only is it a great comedy and just suited for your star," asserted the writer, "but it also has a message." "A message?" snorted the producer contemptuously. "Listen, just write me a good comedy. Messages are for Western Union."

See also America[2], audience[1], climax, Hollywood[1, 4], salary[8].

MOVING

The Johnsons were moving just a couple of blocks down the street, and not wanting to trust some of their precious heirlooms to the moving men, Mr. Johnson personally carried some of them to the new house. He was carrying a valuable grandfather clock late at night when he met a drunk. The stew gazed in amazement, then remarked, "Shay, ol' fella, doncha think it'd be han'ier to carry a watch?"

See also clean[2].

MUD

A labor gang was building a cement wall along some mud flats by a river, when suddenly one of the workmen shouted, "Hey! Quick! Bring picks and shovels! Bill's stuck in the mud." "How far is he in?" yelled the foreman. "Up to his knees," was the reply. "Aw, let him walk out," ordered the foreman. "But he can't," insisted the other excitedly. "He's in wrong end up!"

MULE

1

A farmer, after trying patiently to get two mules to pull together, lost his temper and was expressing himself freely when his parson passed by. "Here, Zeb," admonished the preacher, "you shouldn't speak to those animals like that." "You're jest the man I bin a-wantin' to see, Parson," said the farmer, wiping his brow. "Tell me, how did Noah ever git two o' these critters into the ark?"

2

"I see that your mule has 'U. S.' branded on his hindquarters," observed a tourist to a hillbilly. "Was he an army mule before you got him?" "No, suh, not thet there mule," said the hillbilly. "Thet U. S. don't stand for 'United States' —it jes' means 'unsafe.'"

3

A shipment of army mules were being unloaded, and one rookie made the mistake of getting too close to the rear end of one of them. His comrades caught him on the bounce, placed him on a stretcher, and started for the hospital with him. On the way he regained consciousness. He saw the blue sky overhead and felt the swaying motion of the stretcher. "Good gosh!" he groaned. "I ain't even hit ground yet!"

See also stubborn[2].

MURDER

It was the day after the trial of little Willie's brother for murdering a man, and an inquisitive neighbor stopped the boy to inquire, "Well, Willie, how did your brother come out?" "They're gonna put him in jail for a month," replied Willie. "A month!" was the amazed exclamation. "That's certainly a light sentence for a cold-blooded murder." "Oh, I don't know," said the boy. "You see, at the end of the month they're gonna hang him."

See also alibi[1], lose[3].

MUSCLE

A sweet young thing who had been working in a factory during wartime greeted a friend with a sigh of relief. "I certainly feel better since I saw that doctor," she confided. "What did he do for you?" asked the other. "Do you remember those hard lumps in my arms that I was worried about?" said the first. "Well, he looked at them and told me that they were just muscles."

MUSEUM

1

Two men walking through a museum came to a halt before a case containing an Egyptian mummy over which hung a sign: "B. C.

1229." "What do you make of that, Bill?" asked one, much mystified. "I don't know," replied Bill, equally puzzled, "unless it's the number of the automobile that killed him."

2

Auntie was taking little Joan through the museum and they finally got into the Egyptian room. "What's that, Auntie?" asked Joan, pointing at a mummy. "Why, that's someone's mummy, dear," explained the aunt. "Gee!" cried the girl. "I'm sure glad my mummy's not like that!"

3

The grain broker was relaxing from money-grubbing by taking a little tour of the museum. "We have a mummy here," declared the guide, "that has some wheat in its hand since the days of the Pharaohs." "Hmm," said the broker thoughtfully. "Well, I'd advise him not to hold it any longer—wheat'll never be higher."

4

"I can't say much for the completeness of this museum's collection," sniffed Mrs. Williams on a visit to the local museum. "Why, they don't even have a skull of Cromwell. There is an excellent one in the Oxford Museum in England."

5

A teacher one day took her class of small pupils through the museum of natural history to see the mounted animals and birds. "Well, how was school today?" asked one of the boys' mothers that evening. "Gee, it was swell!" declared the lad joyfully. "Teacher took us to see a dead circus."

MUSIC

1

The pretty young lady was idly drumming on the piano and humming a tune. The young man listened for awhile, then inquired, "Do you sing and play much?" "Not much," the girl informed him. "I just do it to kill time." "Well, you've certainly chosen an excellent weapon," said the fellow.

2

A lady and her caller sat on the veranda listening to a chimes recital from the carillon of a nearby church. "Beautiful, aren't they?" observed the lady. "What did you say?" asked the guest, cupping his ear. "I said, aren't the chimes beautiful?" repeated the lady more loudly. "I'm sorry," shouted the other, "but I can't hear a word you say because of those damned chimes."

3

Two chorus girls took a night off and went to the opera. "Beautiful, ain't it?" commented one dreamily during the show. "Gosh, yeah," agreed the other in like manner. "Gee, if you just close your eyes you can imagine you're home listening to the radio."

4

"How come you're advertising your cornet for sale?" inquired a friend of the amateur musician. "I thought that you got a lot of fun out of it." "I did," sighed the other regretfully. "But I figured I had better get rid of it when I saw my neighbor in the hardware store yesterday buying a shotgun."

5

The culture-conscious young man was a little puzzled. "I try to appreciate good music," he confided in an older friend, "but I have trouble telling the classical music from some of the popular kind." "It's quite simple," explained the other. "When a piece seems every minute to threaten to become a tune but always disappoints you, you can be pretty sure it's classical."

6

A pretty young lady entered a music shop and went to the counter where a new clerk was sorting out sheet music. "Pardon me," she said, "but have you 'Kissed Me in the Park One Night?'" The clerk looked at her startled and blushed. "S-sorry, Miss," he stammered, "but it must have been the clerk at the other counter. I've only been here a week."

See also appreciation[4], criticism[1], pessimist[2], pleasure[2], police[4], tactless.

MUSICIAN

1

It was a cozy musical evening, and as the anemic-looking lady plaintively rendered, "Carry Me Back to Old Virginee," an old man in the corner bowed his head and wept quietly. The hostess tiptoed over and asked him, "Pardon me, sir, but are you a Virginian?" "No, madam," moaned the man through his tears. "I'm a musician."

2

The circus band was playing in the backwoods village square and the inhabitants had clustered around to watch. They had seen most of the musical instruments before, but the slide trombone was a complete novelty to all of them. After watching, fascinated, one hillbilly cautioned his young son, "Don't be took in by thet feller, boy. There's a trick to it—he ain't really a-swallerin' thet horn."

3

A wandering musician was stranded in a little village on Sunday morning. As he stood on a street-corner playing his fiddle and waiting for alms, the local preacher came up and sternly demanded, "Do you know the Fourth Commandment, my good fellow?" The fiddler scratched his head with his bow. "Can't say that I do, sir," he replied; "but if you'll just whistle the chorus over once, I think I can make it."

4

An old fellow was applying for admission to a charitable home for the aged. "What was your occupation?" he was asked. "I was a musician," the old man replied. "I was an organist up until a few months ago." "Why did you give it up?" was the next question. "Because my monkey died," was the old man's response.

5

A child prodigy, a boy violinist, was performing at an intimate little musicale. He was playing a difficult concerto which contained several long rests for the soloist. During one of these a kindly old lady leaned forward and whispered loudly, "Oh, why don't you just play something you know, little boy?"

See also concert[6], hunting[8].

MUSIC LESSONS

1

The new arrival had scarcely entered heaven when St. Peter stepped up and presented him with a beautiful golden trumpet. "But, I can't play this instrument," protested the newcomer. "I never practiced while I was on earth." "I know you didn't," chuckled St. Peter. "That's why you're here."

2

"Does my practicing the cornet make you nervous?" inquired the man of the fellow next door. "Well, it did at first when I heard the other neighbors discussing it," admitted the other; "but it's got me to the point now that I don't give a hoot what happens to you."

NAKED

"Mamma, mamma, come quick!" cried little sister. "Goodness! What's wrong?" cried mother. "Jimmy's takin' off all his clothes, mamma," said the little girl, "an' soon he'll be barefoot all over!"

See also birthplace[1], moron[1], nudist.

NAME

1

Adam and Eve were strolling through the Garden of Eden naming the various animals, when they saw a rhinoceros. "Just look at that beast," exclaimed Adam. "What in the world can we name that?" "Let's call it a rhinoceros," suggested Eve. "But why that name?" asked Adam. "Because," declared Eve, "it certainly looks a lot more like a rhinoceros than anything we've come across yet."

2

The motorist had been in a minor automobile accident and the cop on the beat was asking his name. "John Smith," was the reply. "Come on, come on," said the policeman scornfully; "let's have your right name." "All right," answered the motorist pleasantly. "Just put me down as Ralph Waldo Emerson." "That's better," declared the officer, writing it down. "You didn't think you could kid me with that Smith stuff, did you?"

3

The Russian soldier on furlough sought out his fallen comrade's sweetheart, Olga Grigorevna Aleksandrovskaya, to tell her the tragic news. "So poor Ivan died in battle!" sobbed the girl. "And you say that he died with my name on his lips?" "Part of it," replied the soldier softly, "part of it."

4

"After we're married, dear," declared the girl with social aspirations, "I think it would be much smarter if we were to have a hyphenated name. Let's see, now, what would go well with Eaton?" At this her kid brother broke in with the suggestion, "How about 'Moth'?"

5

The young couple were trying to select a name for their first baby. "We'll call her Eurythmia," announced the mother. The father didn't care for this at all, but being wise he didn't object, saying only, "That's fine, dear. The first girl I ever loved was called Eurythmia and the name will awaken pleasant memories." There was a short silence, after which the wife said firmly, "I've decided to name her Jane, after my mother."

6

It was the first day of school and teacher was making a list of her new pupils. "And what's your name?" she asked one little fellow. "Jackie," was the brief reply. "Jackie what?" prompted teacher. "Aw, that's all right," said the boy, "just call me Jackie."

7

A young lady and two young men traveling on a train happened to be seated in the same compartment. They decided they might as well become better acquainted. "My name's Paul," announced one fellow, "but I'm no apostle." "Well, my name's Peter," declared the other fellow, "but I'm no saint." "My name's Mary," said the girl hesitantly, "and I don't know what to say."

8

When oil was discovered on the poor, uneducated farmer's land, he suddenly had more money than he'd ever dreamed of. He deposited it in the bank, started a checking account, and arranged with the banker that his signature should be two crosses. After a few months, a check came through signed with three crosses, and the banker called the farmer for an explanation. "Aw, it's my wife, she's a-gittin' inter sassiety now," said the farmer, "an' she thinks I oughta have a middle name."

9

The manager of a neighborhood show halted the performance to announce, "If Mr. Smith is in the audience, I wish him to know that I've just been informed his house is on fire." At once forty-three men sprang excitedly to their feet. "Just a moment," cautioned the manager, looking at a slip of paper. "It's the house of Mr. John Smith." "Thank God!" exclaimed one of the men fervently, dropping back into his seat.

See also father[4], girl[1], guest[2], hard, lawyer[9], lazy[7], memory[4], publisher, training[1].

NATION

See America, foreigner.

NAVY

1

The deck was deserted when a naval officer fell overboard, but a sailor on watch saw him and rescued him. "You've saved my life," said the officer gratefully. "Is there any special way in which I can reward you?" "What I'd appreciate most of all, sir," replied the sailor, glancing anxiously about, "is if you'd just say nothing about it. If the other fellows learn I pulled you out, they'll chuck *me* in."

2

An admiral was watching a newly-enlisted sailor at work, willingly but clumsily, on the quarterdeck, and asked kindly, "How long've you been in the Navy, son?" "Three weeks," replied the boy. "How long you been in, bud?" The admiral was somewhat startled, but answered good-naturedly, "Thirty

years." The youngster shook his head sympathetically and sighed, "It's hell, ain't it?"

See also complaint[3], food[4], sailor.

NEAR-SIGHTED

A near-sighted man was taking a stroll in the country when a sudden gust of wind blew his hat from his head. He was chasing it when a woman from a nearby farmhouse cried, "Hey, there! What are you trying to do?" "I'm trying to get my hat, madam," replied the man with dignity. "Your hat?" snorted the woman. "That's my little black hen you're chasing."

See also bald[3].

NEAT

1

Despite mother's scoldings, little Junior was careless with his clothing. One evening after he was in bed, mother entered his room and, finding his clothing scattered about, sternly inquired, "Who was it that didn't hang up his clothes when he went to bed?" From beneath the covers came the muffled reply, "Adam."

2

The housewife had such a mania for neatness that even her husband caught some of it. "Have you wiped the sink dry yet, Mary?" he asked one evening. "Yes, Sam, I have," she replied. "Why do you ask?" "Oh, that's too bad," he replied regretfully. "I did want a drink, but I reckon I can get along 'til morning."

See also reading[6].

NECESSITY

1

A tourist was talking to a hillbilly in a backwoods region. "I suppose," remarked the tourist, "that even in these remote regions the necessities of life have increased in price." "Right ye be, stranger," agreed the man from the hills glumly; "an' when ye do get it the durned stuff ain't wuth drinkin'."

2

The trial had been proceeding for some time and every one was amused by one lawyer's consistently referring to the opposing lawyer as "Mr. Necessity." After awhile, the judge inquired, "May I ask, Mr. Jackson, why you always refer to learned counsel as 'Mr. Necessity'?" "Simply, Your Honor," was the reply, "because he knows no law."

3

A man came into a large department store leading a horse and attempted to get the animal on the elevator. "You can't bring that horse in here, sir," objected the operator. "Oh, but I *must*," insisted the man. "I positively have to." "What do you mean, you 'must'?" asked the operator. "Poor fellow," explained the man, patting the horse sympathetically, "he always gets sick on the escalator."

See also childbirth[4], christening[3], praise[1].

NECK

1

"Oh, mamma!" cried little Willie, running in excitedly. "Do you know Tommy Smith's neck?" Mother paid no attention to such an irrelevant question, so Willie repeated, "I said, mamma, do you know Tommy Smith's neck?" "Yes, yes, I suppose so," replied mother. "What of it?" "Well," said Willie, "it's just that he fell into the lake up to it."

2

The class had been studying natural history and the manner in which Nature adapted animals to the conditions under which they had to live. "Now who can tell me," questioned teacher, "why the giraffe has such a long neck?" "I can, teacher," volunteered a small boy. "It's because his head is so far from his body."

NECKTIE

A man stood at the counter selecting neckties. He passed over many, chose a few, and occasionally encountered a terrible specimen which he would fling aside contemptuously. These latter the clerk would pick up and place in a separate tray. "What're you going to do, burn 'em?" asked the man scornfully. "Oh, no," explained the clerk. "We save these for the women who come in to buy ties for men."

NEIGHBOR

1

The party was still on although the hour was late. The hostess decided to ask one of her guests, a noted singer with a powerful voice, to sing a song for them. "I'm afraid it's too late," protested the singer. "It would disturb the neighbors." "Don't let that bother you," declared the lady. "Those on one side poisoned our dog last week, and those on the other broke our lawn mower."

2

"How do you get along with your neighbor?" inquired Mrs. Black. "Do you have a speaking acquaintance with her?" "A speaking acquaintance?" said Mrs. White scornfully. "Why, I know that woman so well that we don't speak at all."

3

The minister tried to stop a quarrel between two neighbors. "Tut, tut, my friends," he implored, raising his hands in pious horror. "You must remember that the Bible tells you to love your neighbor." "That's true, Reverend," agreed one, glaring savagely at the other; "but don't forget that the Bible was written in days when your neighbor didn't live so danged close to you."

4

The boring young man at the summer resort insisted on being attentive to the young lady. "I'm quite a close neighbor of yours now, you know," he said. "I'm in the cottage just across the lake from you." "Indeed?" she yawned. "I hope you'll drop in some day."

See also borrow³, devotion³, lawn mower.

NERVES

The small girl had been ill-tempered all day and her older sister was putting her to bed early as punishment and scolding her for her behavior. "Aw, it sure ain't fair," at last complained the younger girl; "when it's me it's just plain temper, but when it's you it's nerves."

NEVER

"Gosh, my doctor's strict with me," complained one old fellow. "Why, so help me, I never had a drink in the last three years." "What!" chorused his cronies. "Never?" "Oh, well," conceded the sufferer, "I guess maybe it just seems like never."

NEWLYRICH

1

Mr. Williams had told the landscape artist to go the limit in laying out his formal garden, and now he was inspecting the finished job. "What's this?" he asked, puzzled, as he came across a sundial. "That's a sundial," explained the artist. "The vane casts a shadow from the sun on the dial and tells you the time." "My, my, I just can't keep up with these modern inventions," marveled the other. "What won't you fellows think of next!"

2

The self-important old fellow came puffing and panting to the beach where two lifeguards were working over his only child. "What're you doing to my daughter?" he demanded. "She almost just drowned, and we're giving her artificial respiration," explained one guard. "You'll do nothing of the sort!" declared the old boy indignantly. "My daughter's going to get nothing artificial. You give her the genuine article—I can afford it."

3

Mrs. Newlyrich was telling her friend about her trip around the world. "Yes, indeed. And while in Egypt, of course, we visited the pyramids," she said proudly. "Some of them were literally covered with hieroglyphics, my dear." "Goodness!" her friend shuddered. "And wasn't you afraid some of them horrid things would get on you?"

See also beggar[2], entertainment, name[8], singer[1], violin[1].

NEWLYWEDS

1

The newlyweds had just got off the train and the blushing bride was a bit self-conscious because of all the people about. "Henry, dear," she whispered, "let's try to make these people think that we've been married a long time." "Sure thing, sweet," agreed hubby heartily. "Here, you carry the suitcases."

2

The couple had gone directly from the wedding to the photographer's for pictures, and he promised to send them proofs in a few days. When a large envelop arrived, it was opened by the newlyweds eagerly. Inside were several views of a chubby baby lying kicking on a rug, bearing a notation on the back reading: "Please state clearly what size you wish, and how many."

See also praise[1], premature.

NEWS

1

The man dropped in at a little lunch counter for breakfast. "Quite a rainy spell, isn't it?" he remarked conversationally to his neighbor. "Almost like the flood." "Flood? What flood?" grunted the other, fishing a doughnut from his coffee.

"Why, *the* flood—you know, Noah and the Ark and Mount Ararat," explained the first. "Nope," said the second. "Ain't seen the mornin' paper yet."

2

The train was late and the waiting clergyman was very impatient. He kept pestering the ticket agent for news of the over-due train. At last, he came up again to inquire, "Are there any tidings from the belated train?" "No, sir," replied the agent, irritably. "Not a damned tiding!"

See also faith[2].

NEWSPAPER

1

An angry man entered a newspaper office and demanded of the office boy, "I want to see the scoundrel, Jim Williams, who wrote that libelous article about me yesterday. I demand satisfaction!" "I'm afraid you'll have to sit down and be patient, sir," replied the boy. "He's out attending the funeral of a man who called to get satisfaction a couple of days ago."

2

A kindly old gentleman smiled sympathetically at a small newsboy who was staggering under a load of newspapers. "Goodness, my boy," he said, "don't all those papers make you tired?" "Naw," replied the lad. "I don't read 'em."

3

The reporter came yawning back from the political speech he had been assigned to cover. "Well, what did our noble senator have to say?"

inquired the editor. "Nothin'," grunted the reporter. "In that case," instructed the editor, "keep it down to a column."

4

The editor was interviewing an applicant for the position of proof-reader. "I suppose you're aware of the responsibility attached to this job?" he questioned. "Oh, yes," replied the applicant. "I know that when you make a mistake, I take the blame."

5

An editor was questioning an applicant for a job on the paper. "I suppose you know all about how a newspaper should be run," he remarked sourly. "Well, no, sir," was the answer; "I don't know the first thing about it." The editor brightened. "Good! I'll try you," he cried. "You talk like a man of experience."

6

Without warning, the building housing a Chicago newspaper shook to a dull, rumbling roar and all the windows were crashed from the concussion. "Great!" cried the editor, springing excitedly to his feet. "I knew that new gossip column would be a big success."

See also apology[2], brief[4], drowning[2], editor[4], faith[2], lucky[3], politics[2], reporter[2].

NEW YORK

1

Diogenes had spent a long day searching New York for an honest man, and was wearily wending his way homeward. "Well, what luck?" asked an acquaintance, passing by. "Surprisingly good, everything considered," reported Diogenes brightly. "I still have my lantern."

2

A visitor from the West was walking down a dark street in New York one night when he was stopped. "Hand over your money, or I'll blow out your brains!" the bandit threatened, waving a gun. "Blow away!" said the Westerner calmly. "You can live in New York easy without brains, but you shore can't live here without money."

3

A small boy from New York was being taken for a trip into the country by his aunt. He was thrilled by the country sights. "Lookit, Auntie!" he cried out excitedly. "Dere's a boid!" "No, no, dear, not a 'boid,'" corrected the aunt. "It's a 'bird.'" "Chee!" said the kid in wonder. "It sure choips like a boid, don't it?"

4

The old desert rat who had been in on the rise and fall of many Western boom towns, finally struck it rich. He came to New York for the first time, stayed at the Waldorf, and took in all the sights. "Whatcha think o' the town, Zeb?" an old crony asked on his return home. "Waal, sir," Zeb replied thoughtfully, "she looks to me like mebbe she was a-gonna be a permanent camp."

5

A distinguished foreign visitor on his first trip to New York was taken to view the wonders of Broadway at night. After the visitor had read many of the dazzling, multicolored, flashing and leaping signs, he was asked by the New Yorker what he thought of it. "It's very unusual," replied the foreigner reflectively; "but how much more wonderful it would be for a man who couldn't read."

6

A small businessman from the Middle West was in New York for a few days, and while there someone asked him how he liked the big town. "To be honest, I don't care so much for it," he replied. "Just stop to think, now, if you lived in New York and wanted to go fishing—where in heck would you go to dig a can of worms?"

See also country[2], hear, ignorance[2], religion[1].

NOISE

1

A bunch of boys were holding an all-night poker party in a hotel room. As it progressed the revelry increased. Finally, at about 3 A.M. a weary guest in the next room started to pound on the wall. "Well, I must say," shouted one of the merrymakers indignantly, "that this is certainly a hell of a time to be hanging pictures!"

2

The landlord was interviewing the prospective tenant. "Before I give you a lease," he warned, "I want you to know that we keep it very quiet here. Do you have any children, animals, parrots, canaries, or the like?" "Oh, no," was the meek reply. "Well, do you have a piano, radio, or phonograph, play any musical instruments, or have any noisy hobbies?" "No," said the tenant, then added hesitantly, "but I do have a fountain pen that scratches like hell once in awhile."

3

In a large repair shop all the men were friendly and happy and constantly whistling, singing, and shouting pleasantries at each other. "Goodness!" exclaimed a new man on his first day there. "This is the noisiest place I've ever worked in." "It's plenty noisy," agreed an old-timer. "In fact, the only time it's quiet here is when somebody starts the trip-hammer and drowns out the noise."

4

The professor stuck his head out of his study door and demanded irritably, "What's all that noise out there?" "One of the children just fell down the stairs," explained his wife as she rushed by excitedly. "Well, tell them that if they can't be more quiet about it they'll have to stop it," commanded the professor.

See also cost[1], customary[2].

NOSE

1

The man had a long nose and was complaining about its disadvantages. "Only last week its end was frostbitten and it was damn painful." "You should have rubbed it," advised a friend helpfully. "I did," replied the other; "as far as I could reach."

2

An inveterate old toper with the bright-red nose of his trade got a job in a boiler works. A few hours after he'd started he presented himself to the company doctor with the tip of his nose terribly smashed. "Goodness, man, how did that ever happen to your nose?" cried the amazed doctor. "Aw, I was workin' inside a boiler," was the explanation, "an' I stuck my nose out of a hole for a breath of air, and the man outside thought it was a hot rivet, and whang!"

See also limit, odor[4].

NOTHING

1

The elderly lady felt that she was being cheated on the fare and was arguing with the driver. "Don't try to tell *me, my good fellow,"* she declared loftily. "You know, I haven't been riding in taxis for ten years for nothing." "Maybe not," replied the taxi-driver sarcastically; "but I'll bet it wasn't because you didn't try."

2

A stingy farmer had been elected to the school board, and he had dropped into the village school to inspect it. Thinking to test the intelligence of the pupils, he asked, "Can anyone here tell me what nothing is?" After a short silence, a small boy in the rear arose. "It's what you gave me the other day for helping you carry those big bundles," he said.

3

The wealthy old skinflint was very indignant. "I have no patience with people who are forever criticizing young ministers for their lack of experience," he declared. "Now as for me, I have nothing but praise for our young preacher; nothing but

praise." "So I've often noticed," was the comment from the deacon who took up the collection.

See also fishing[6].

NUDE

See naked.

NUDIST

1

"I understand that you spent the summer at a nudist colony," said the girl curiously. "How did you like it?" "Oh, it was all right," replied the boy, "but it certainly reminded me of my first ride in an airplane." "How do you mean?" she asked. "Man, oh, man!" he said feelingly. "I'll never forget that first take-off!"

2

The fellow who had recently joined a nudist club was describing his experiences. "When I arrived," he related, "they were all completely nude; even the butler who took my hat and bag." "But if they had no clothes on," objected a listener, "how did you know it was the butler?" "I knew damned well it wasn't the maid," snapped the other.

See also moron[1].

NUISANCE

1

The punster had been drunk and disorderly, and he was haled into court. "You're guilty of no grave offense," said the judge; "but you are a nuisance and I must commit you." "Look here! Even if you are a judge," declared the drunk stoutly, "you have no right to commit a nuisance."

2

"What I can't understand," remarked a plain citizen, "is if this Congressman is as unpopular and obnoxious to every one as the newspapers claim, how he can get so many concessions from the House." "That's easy," replied another. "Suppose you're in business and have a lot of important things to do, and a man comes in and sits down by you and begins to file a saw—wouldn't you give him what he wanted?"

See also call[2].

NUMBERS

1

The professor stepped to the blackboard and wrote on it: "LXXX." Looking over the class, he picked out a pretty girl in front and asked, "Miss Jones, can you tell me what that means?" "Sure thing," replied the girl promptly. "It means, 'Love and kisses.'"

2

A young lawyer was presenting his first case in court. It was a simple damage suit of a farmer against a railroad company whose train had killed twenty-four of his hogs, but the youngster was trying to dramatize it. "Just think of it, gentlemen, twenty-four hogs!" he declaimed impressively. "Twenty-four! That's twice the number there are on the jury!"

3

Two politicians were talking shop. "Just what do you consider to be the chief object of legislation, Sam?" asked one. "The greatest good for the greatest number," responded Sam pompously. "And what do you consider the greatest number?" continued the first. "Number one," was the prompt reply.

NURSE

1

The doctor looked over the patient, then turned to the pretty new nurse on the case to inquire, "Have you kept a chart of this patient's progress, nurse?" "Well, no, doctor, I haven't," replied the nurse. "But I can let you look at my diary."

2

Two friends of the sick man met on the street. "Well, I'm afraid that Bill will be in the hospital for some time," observed one. "Why, did you see his doctor?" asked the other. "No," replied the first, "but I saw his nurse."

3

The vain young man had been in the hospital for quite awhile and had been well cared for by the pretty nurse. "Ah, nurse," he sighed one morning. "I'm in love with you. I don't want to get well." "Don't worry, you won't," replied the nurse cheerily. "The doctor's in love with me, too, and he saw you trying to kiss me yesterday."

4

"Goodness," said the nurse, "that new patient in 511 is certainly a good-looking fellow, isn't he?" "Yes, he is," agreed the supervisor of nurses; "but don't wash his face—he's already had that done by five different nurses this morning."

See also heart[2, 3], temperature[4].

NURSEMAID

1

Two nursemaids met in the park with their small charges. "Well, I guess you'll be at the dance tomorrow afternoon, since you're so crazy about dancing," remarked one. "No, I'm afraid I won't be there," said the other. "Can't you get the afternoon off?" asked the first. "It's not that," explained the second. "It's just that I'm afraid to leave the baby with its mother."

2

Mr. Williams was leaving for the employment agency when his wife cautioned him, "Now be sure that you engage a good-looking nursemaid for Junior." "But why?" he asked. "Oh, I just want to be sure that Junior has ample police protection," replied Mrs. Williams.

OATH

1

An impetuous young fellow once tried to kiss a pretty Quaker maid. "No, friend," she objected, "thee must not." "Oh, by Jove! but I must!" declared the mad youth. "Well, friend," conceded the Quakeress meekly, "as thee hast *sworn* to, thee may do so, but thee must not make a practice of it."

2

The witness about to give testimony in court did not appear to be any too bright, so the judge thought it best to impress on him the solemnity of the proceedings. "Do you know what it means when you take that oath?" he inquired. "I sure do, judge," replied the witness with assurance. "That oath means that if I swear to a lie I gotta stick to it no matter what."

3

The attorney for the defense leveled a finger at the plaintiff who was on the stand. "Do you still maintain," he demanded, "that this is the person who knocked you down with his automobile? Could you swear to the man?" "I not only could," declared the plaintiff eagerly, "but I did—but he only swore back at me and drove away."

See also actor[4], intelligence[2].

OBEDIENCE

1

Father was trying to read his paper, but Junior kept romping about the room creating quite a disturbance. At last the old man commanded sharply, "Sit down!" "Aw, I won't do it," replied the young hopeful impudently. "Very well, then, stand up," ordered father. "I *will* be obeyed!"

2

"Henry, dear," said the bride-to-be to her intended, "mother wanted me to insist on the word 'obey' being left out of the ceremony." "And what did you tell her?" inquired Henry. "I said to let it go and not worry," replied the girl. "I told her that you could take a joke as well as any man."

See also ignore.

OBJECTION

1

The young man was calling at his sweetheart's home for the first time, and he seemed to be making a good impression on the family. "Well, my boy," invited the girl's father, "do you have any objection to a whiskey-and-soda?" "Well," said the boy, "I've never had one before." "What!" exclaimed the amazed father. "Never had a whiskey-and-soda?" "Oh, no," explained the young fellow. "Never had an objection."

2

"My girl's old man certainly doesn't like me," complained Jim to a pal. "He doesn't?" said the friend. "On what grounds does he object to you?" "Humph!" snorted Jim. "On any grounds within five miles of the house."

See also war[1].

OBSTINATE

See stubborn.

OCCUPATION

See job, work.

OCEAN

1

The honeymooners were strolling along the seashore when the bridegroom was suddenly seized by a poetic mood and began to recite, "Roll on, thou deep and dark blue ocean, roll." His bride gazed at the water for a moment, then in awed admiration gasped, "Oh, John, you wonderful man! It's doing it!"

2

Two young soldiers, fresh from the farm where they had never seen more water than was in the meadow brook, were on a transport in the middle of the ocean with nothing but water in all directions. "Golly!" said one. "I knew the ocean was big, but I never thought it was this big." "And that ain't all," said the other with a shudder. "You're just a-lookin' at the top of it."

3

A small girl had gone with her mother to visit some friends in their seaside cottage. At breakfast the next morning the hostess asked her small guest, "Well, Jane, did you sleep well last night?" "No, ma'am, I didn't," replied the girl. "The snoring of the ocean kept me awake almost all night."

4

The ocean liner had run into bad weather, and two passengers stood at the rail watching the water. "It's frightfully rough, isn't it?" remarked one to the other. "Waal," observed the second, who happened to be a farmer, "it wouldn't be so bad if only the cap'n would jest keep in th' furrows."

See also seasick.

ODOR

1

The unkempt Arab rug peddler was making his way down a Parisian boulevard trying to sell his wares. "Will you buy a carpet, monsieur?" he pleaded to a passing tourist. "No, no!" snapped the tourist, drawing back. "They stink!" The Arab drew himself up in proud indignation. "How dare you say that!" he cried. "I'll have you know, monsieur, that my carpets do not stink! It's me!"

2

As the train coming into Chicago drew near the big stockyards, a lady passenger opened her bottle of smelling salts. The train came still closer to the yards, and soon the horrible animal odor permeated the car. A farmer on board endured it as long as he could, but finally cried out, "Gosh, lady, would ye mind puttin' thet cork back in th' bottle?"

3

"When I was hunting the other day," related an amateur sportsman, "my dogs scared up a skunk, but they finally gave up the chase." "Did they lose the scent?" asked his friend. "No, they gave up the skunk," explained the hunter, "but I don't think they'll *ever* lose the scent."

4

Little Mary Anne had a bad cold. After sniffing at a rose, she held it to her mother's nose and asked, "Does the flower smell good, mummy?" "It's very sweet, dear," replied mother. "Can't you smell it?" "No, mummy," said the girl; "my nose is deaf."

See also breathing[1].

OFFENSE

"Mrs. Black, our neighbor, must be offended at something I said or did," remarked the woman to her husband. "She hasn't been over for almost a week now." "Well, when she does come over be sure to find out what it was," instructed the husband, "and we'll try it on her again."

See also insult[1], newspaper[1].

OFFICE

1

"Why do you insist upon having married men work for you in your office?" asked the businessman's friend. "Do you find that they're better workers than the bachelors?" "No, it's not that," said the boss. "It's just that they're more used to taking orders and don't get so upset when I yell at them."

2

"You're late this morning, Smith," frowned the boss as the clerk straggled in. "Do you have an excuse?" "I'm sorry, sir, but I overslept," replied the employee. "What!" cried the boss. "Do you mean to tell me that you sleep at home, too!"

3

There was a persistent bore at a businessmen's convention who insisted upon going around and talking shop with every one. He approached a man who sat quietly in a corner smoking his cigar, and led off by inquiring, "And, my dear sir, how many people work in your office?" "Well, offhand," replied the quiet man, rising to move away, "I should say about half of them."

See also boss[5], do[1], payment[2], stenographer[3], system[2].

OFFICE BOY

1

The boss frowned at the applicant for the position of office boy. "Look here, son," he said, "weren't you here a week ago for this job?" "Yes, sir," was the reply. "And didn't I tell you then that I wanted an older boy?" asked the employer. "You did, sir," answered the boy. "That's why I'm back—I'm older now."

2

A tall, husky man came into the outer office and gruffly instructed the frail office boy, "Tell your boss I want to see him. My name's Williams." "So you're Mr. Williams," said the boy, looking up at the towering figure in awe. "That makes it something of a problem." "What do you mean, a problem?" growled Williams. "Well, you see," explained the boy, "I've got orders to throw you out on your ear."

See also boss[2], business[1], indispensable[2], instructions[3], promotion[1], realism[5], salary[4].

OFFICER

1

"Yes, sirree," declared an old battle-scarred veteran in describing one of his big battles to a small boy, "the rifle fire was so heavy that a fly couldn't have gone through it and lived." "But why didn't you get behind a tree?" asked the lad. "Tree!" snorted the old soldier. "Heck, son, there wasn't enough trees for even the officers."

2

A general and a colonel were walking down a street and they met many privates, all of whom, of course, saluted them. The officers returned the salutes, but each time he did so, the colonel would mutter under his breath, "The same to you." Finally, the general inquired, "Why do you say that each time?" "You must remember, General," explained the other, "that I was once

a private myself and I know what they're thinking."

3

It was a dark night in camp and as a private passed another figure in uniform he called out, "Hey, buddy, give us a match." As the match flared to his cigarette and he raised his eyes to thank the other, the soldier almost dropped when he saw the stars of a general. "P-pardon me, sir," he stammered. "I c-couldn't see you was a general." "That's all right, buddy," replied the general kindly, "but just thank your stars I wasn't a second lieutenant."

4

A muddy, unshaven soldier went into a recreation hut a short distance behind the front line and slumped into a front seat to watch the entertainment. Immediately an attendant bustled up and said to him, "Sorry, buddy, but the entire front section is reserved for officers." "Okay," said the soldier as he got wearily to his feet, "but the front section I just got back from wasn't."

See also boyfriend[2], navy.

OIL

1

It was in the old days when whale oil was used in lamps, that the man of the house looked up from his paper to remark, "It says here, my dear, that it will not be long before oil from petroleum will have entirely replaced whale oil for lighting." "Dear, dear," said the wife sympathetically, "whatever will the poor whales do then?"

2

"What's this story I hear, Si,"

asked Hi, "about you havin' an oil well on your farm?" "Waal, there's some truth to it, Hi," admitted Si; "I've got the well."

OLD

1

"Johnny," instructed mother, "I want you to run across the street and ask how old Mrs. Smith is this morning." "All right," replied Johnny dutifully. He was back in a few minutes looking a little downcast and said, "I asked her, mom, but she said it's none of your durned business how old she is."

2

Little Betty sat upon grandpa's knee looking at his snowy hair and long white beard. Suddenly she questioned, "Grandpa, were you on the Ark with Noah?" "Why, of course not, dear," replied the old man, somewhat startled. "Then why weren't you drowned?" demanded the girl.

3

Grandma was visiting the family, and when little Sally was preparing for bed that night mother cautioned her, "Now don't forget to include grandma in your prayers, dear, and ask God to bless her and let her live to be very, very old." "Hm, I think she's old enough," objected Sally. "I think it would be better to pray God to make her young."

OLD MAID

1

The woman next door was talking with the maiden lady. "I hardly ever go to town to shop any more," she said. "I find you can get anything you want from the mail-order houses." "Yes, I suppose so," sighed the old maid; "anything but a male."

2

The old bachelor was smitten with Jane who was an old maid. But he could never get up enough courage to pop the question, so he decided to do it by telephone. "Miss Smith?" he inquired when he'd got her number. "This is she speaking," was the reply. "Will, er, you, ah, marry me?" he stammered. "Why, of course," replied Jane promptly. "Who is this, please?"

3

It was a friendly little church, and toward the end of the services the minister inquired, "Is there any one who would like the prayers of the congregation for a relative or friend?" A woman in the rear arose to say, "I'd like the congregation to pray for my husband." "But, sister Martha," objected the preacher, "you don't have a husband yet." "I know," was the reply. "That's why I'd like you all to pitch in and pray for one for me."

4

A wedding announcement received by her middle-aged but still single mistress prompted the maid to inquire, "When you gonna get married, Miss?" "I really don't know, Mary," sighed the mistress sadly. "I sometimes think I'll never get married." "Shucks, don't let it worry you, Miss," urged the maid in a kindly attempt to comfort her. "They do say that old maids is the happiest kind once they quits strugglin'."

See also annoyance, Christmas[2],

frank[4], fun[1], husband[5], please, rumor[1], suggestion[2], virtue[4].

OPERATION

1

A woman called upon a surgeon and said, "I'd like to have you do an operation on me, doctor." "An operation for what, madam?" inquired the surgeon. "Oh, anything you're good at," replied the patient. "You see, I go to so many women's bridge parties and as I've never had an operation I simply can't enter into the conversation."

2

A patient came out of the ether after an operation to find that the blinds in his room had been drawn. "What's the idea of closing those blinds?" he protested weakly. "I like light." "It was just a precaution," explained the doctor. "There's a big fire burning across the alley, and I didn't want you to come to and think the operation had been a failure."

3

Little Margie had to go to the hospital for a minor operation. As she had been begging for a kitten, her mother promised that if she behaved well at the hospital she could have one. The operation went well, but as the girl was coming out of the anesthetic the nurse was puzzled to hear her mumble, "It's a lousy way to get a cat."

4

"I hear your Aunt Betty's in the hospital," commented a neighbor to a small boy. "Yep," replied the boy. "She had her appendix taken out the other day." "Did they give her anything for it?" asked the neighbor. "Course not," said the boy scornfully. "It wasn't worth anything."

5

The boy was seriously ill and the doctor advised an operation, but the mother objected. "I don't believe in operations," she declared; "and, besides, the Bible is against 'em." "Nonsense!" said the doctor. "The Bible says nothing about it." "Oh, yes it does," insisted the woman. "Don't it say plain as can be: 'What God hath joined together, let not man put asunder'?"

See also bargain[1].

OPINION

1

"Your opinions in this matter have undergone some changes, haven't they, Senator?" asked one of the constituents. "Not at all," replied the Senator. "But your views as I saw them expressed some time ago were quite different," objected the other. "But those, sir, were not my views," explained the Senator; "they were my interviews."

2

A man sat down in a San Antonio barber shop and called for a shave. As the Mexican barber stropped his razor he inquired, "And what is your opinion on this Mexican situation, sir?" "Why, ah, it's the same as yours," replied the customer. "But how do you know what mine is?" objected the barber. "Doesn't matter," was the response. "You've got the razor."

3

"I'm surprised at your stand on public opinion, Senator," cried the average citizen. "Do you mean to say that you ever doubt the wisdom of the majority?" "But just what is a majority?" questioned the Senator. "In many cases it is merely a large number of people who got tired of trying to think for themselves and decided it was easier to take over somebody else's opinion."

See also agreement[5], judgment[2].

OPPORTUNITY

1

"Where are you rushing to?" asked the wife as her husband was dashing from the house. "Jim White just telephoned to ask to borrow a corkscrew, and I'm taking it over," explained the husband. "But couldn't you send it over with Junior?" inquired the wife. "My dear," said the man in tones of heavy scorn, "your question shows me clearly why women are not fit to lead armies or make quick decisions in big deals— when the psychological moment arrives they muff it."

2

"You come well recommended, so I'll give you a try, son," said the farmer to the boy who was applying for a job. "Thank you, sir," answered the lad, "but is there any chance to rise here?" "Indeed there is," answered the farmer. "You'll rise every morning at three-thirty sharp."

3

A group of young people were cutting up toward the rear of the church, and the disturbance got so bad that the minister finally halted his sermon to glare at them. "There are some godless young men back in that corner having fun with the girls," he declared, pointing his finger accusingly, "and when they get done perhaps they'll give me a chance."

4

The old gentleman was strolling along the pier enjoying the evening breeze and his cigar, when suddenly cries for help floated up from below. Leaning over the edge, he saw a young man struggling in the water. "What's wrong down there?" he inquired calmly. "Help!" spluttered the young fellow. "I can't swim!" "Every one should be able to swim," observed the old man. "But since you can't, this is your chance to learn."

5

A meek young man approached the big business magnate shyly and ventured, "May I ask you, sir, the secret of success?" "There's no clear-cut secret, my boy," was the reply. "You must just jump at your opportunity." "But how can I tell when my opportunity has come, sir?" inquired the boy. "That's just it, you can't," barked the big man; "so you've got to keep on jumping."

6

It was the day after graduation and the college graduate swaggered confidently into the big corporation and asked to see the president. He was told to wait in the anteroom, and while there he noticed a gum-chewing boy also waiting. "Maybe you could tell me, son," he inquired importantly, "if there is an opening for a college graduate here?" "There will be, bud," replied the boy, "if they don't come across with that five-dollar raise I'm gonna ask for."

See also accident[4].

OPPOSITE

1

Teacher was examining the class on their knowledge of antonyms. "What is the opposite of white, children?" she questioned. "Black," came the reply. "And the opposite of pleasure?" "Pain," chorused the class. "And the opposite of woe?" continued teacher. There was a pause, then a small boy in front ventured timidly, "Giddap?"

2

"I've determined that I won't marry," declared Algy firmly, "until I meet a woman who is my exact opposite." "Well, what's stopping you, Algy?" asked Jane. "There are quite a few intelligent girls right in this neighborhood."

3

The young writer eagerly sought the editor's advice. "Do you think I should put more fire into my articles?" he asked. "No, no," replied the editor wearily. "I recommend just the opposite."

OPTIMIST

1

"Too bad about Smith's death, wasn't it?" remarked one man to another. "Yes, it was a pity," agreed the second. "But he was an optimist to the end." "How do you mean?" asked the first. "Well, as you know, he fell from the top of a skyscraper," explained the other, "and as he passed the third floor some one in the window there heard him murmur, 'So far, so good!'"

2

"I hear all this talk about optimists," said Bill, "but I'm not sure that I know just what one is." "Well, an optimist could be defined in various ways," replied Jim. "But I know of no finer example than the old fellow who got married at the tender age of 85 and started at once to look for a large house close to a school."

See also lucky[4].

ORATORY

See speaker, speech.

ORDER

1

The sweet young thing had led a sheltered life, and it was her first date. She had never been in a café before and knew nothing about what or how to order. So when the waiter came to the table she watched the boy closely so that she could follow his example. "Two beers," ordered the boy of the waiter. "That's good enough for me," said the girl demurely. "Bring me two beers, too."

2

The classroom was in an uproar when the professor entered, so he rapped sharply on the desk and shouted, "Gentlemen! Order, please!" With one accord, the class promptly yelled back, "Beer!"

3

The manager had one of his salesmen in his office and was giving him a thorough dressing down. The salesman listened to the manager, then finally protested, "Say, you can't talk to me that way. I'll have you know, I take orders from no man!" "Good! Now you're talking," approved the manager. "That's just what I've been raising hell about."

4

A merchant received the first shipment of a large order of goods. But upon finding the quality not up to that of the samples, hastily wired the wholesaler: "Cancel my order immediately." A short time later he received an answering telegram that stated: "Regret cannot cancel order immediately as very busy. You will have to wait your turn."

OSTRICH

1

Two women were being shown through the zoo, and their guide halted before the ostriches to explain, "Now this, ladies, is a very unusual bird. It can see very little and can digest practically anything." "Goodness!" exclaimed one of the women. "Wouldn't it make an ideal husband?"

2

A group of ostriches were quietly feeding when suddenly they heard the sound of some one approaching. They immediately hid their heads in the sand. The intruder, however, proved to be only an adventuresome buck ostrich who had been taking a little jaunt about the nearby country. He came to a stop at the home feeding-grounds, looked around, and exclaimed, "Gosh! Wonder where everybody is!"

OWE

1

Two actors were walking down the street when they met an elderly, toil-worn woman. One of them removed his hat and made an elaborate and respectful bow. "Why all the ceremony for the old dame?" asked the other. "I'll have you know, my boy," replied the first, "that I owe practically everything to that lady." "Oh, is she your mother?" asked the second. "No," was the answer. "My landlady."

2

The office boy came into the business partners' office. "There's a Mr. Johnson outside," he reported. "Shall I show him in?" "No, no!" cried the junior partner hastily. "I owe him fifteen dollars." "Show him in," ordered the senior partner authoritatively. "He owes me forty dollars."

See also gift[2].

OWN

1

An old gentleman stood watching a delivery boy who sat on a doorstep with a sandwich in its opened wrapper lying on his knees. The boy had the top piece of bread removed and was delicately picking out and eating a bit of chicken here, and a piece of lettuce there. "Why don't you just eat the sandwich right down, son?" the old man finally asked. "Gosh, I don't dare!" was the reply. " 'Tain't mine."

2

The old fellow in charge of the cloakroom of a large hotel was noted for his memory. He never used checks or marks of any sort to help him return hats to their rightful owners. Thinking to test him, a well-known judge one day asked him as he received his headgear, "How do you know this is my hat, Sam?" "I don't, sir," was the calm response. "Then why did you give it to me?" cried the puzzled judge. "Because," said Sam, "it's the one you gave me, sir."

See also farm[1].

OYSTER

1

"I think it's so exciting eating oyster stew," observed the conversational waiter to the diner. "There's always the chance that you may find a pearl." "Humph!" growled the customer, poking about his bowl with the spoon. "I'll settle for an oyster."

2

The woman studied the menu. "Do you think raw oysters are healthy?" she finally inquired of the waiter. "They probably are, madam," was the reply. "I've never heard of one complaining."

3

The innocent young lady oyster was back in her oyster bed after her first date with a lobster, and she was telling her younger sister all about it. "He's just too wonderful," she sighed rapturously. "First he took my hand and gazed deeply into my eyes. Next he put his arm around my shoulders, and then—" She stopped, and a panicky look came into her face. "Heavens!" she screamed, clutching her throat. "My pearls!"

4

Teacher had been explaining that different classes of animals had characteristic coverings, such as feathers on birds, scales on snakes, wool on sheep, etc. "Now, children," she questioned, "who can tell me what oysters have?" "I can, teacher," volunteered one little girl. "Crackers!"

5

"Now which of you," asked teacher of her natural history class, "can tell me what an oyster is?" A small hand was raised. "Yes, Robert," said teacher. "An oyster," defined Robert proudly, "is a fish built like a nut."

See also small.

PAIN

1

A man was bending over to tune his radio when he felt a sudden twinge of pain in his back. "I do believe I'm getting lumbago," he observed to his wife. "What good will it do you?" she answered. "You won't be able to understand a word they say."

2

The boy had been nursing a bad tooth for some time, afraid to go to the dentist. After much persuasion his mother finally got him into the dental chair. Scarcely, however, had the dentist touched the tooth than the boy began to scream. "Take it easy, son," the man advised. "Don't you know I'm a 'painless dentist'?" "Maybe *you* are," whined the boy, "but I'm not."

See also empty, exercise[4], injury[1], leg[2], razor[1].

PAINTING

1

"How much will you charge to paint my shed?" inquired the house owner of a painter. "Fourteen dollars a day," was the reply. "What!" cried the man. "Why, I wouldn't pay Michelangelo that price." "Say," protested the painter indignantly, "if that guy's offerin' to do the job fer any less, he ain't no union man."

2

The artist gazed entranced at the picturesque bewhiskered old hillbilly, then said, "I'll give you five dollars if you'll let me paint you." The man scratched his head and shifted from one leg to the other. "It's easy money," urged the artist. "Oh, I hain't a-denyin' thet," replied the hillbilly, "but I wuz jest a-wonderin' how in thunder I'd be gittin' the paint off arterwards."

3

A woman had engaged a handyman to paint the sheds and fences and he got leisurely to work. She watched the awkward, slow, left-handed strokes he was making with the brush, then asked, "Do you always paint with your left hand?" "Laws, no'm, not always," drawled the man; "but today I got m'hat in t'other hand."

See also picture.

PAJAMAS

1

A hillbilly from away back in the woods had come to town and he stood in the general store watching the clerk arrange some gaily patterned men's pajamas on a shelf. "What's them?" he asked. "Pajamas," replied the clerk. "What's pajamers fer?" continued the puzzled man. "You wear them at night," explained the clerk. "Want some?" "No, sirree," refused the hillbilly. "I don't go no place nights 'ceptin' to bed."

2

The host was telling of his love for good coffee. "The fresher it is the better," he insisted, "and in order to have it good and fresh every morning, I get up early and build a fire in my pajamas." "That must be a darn warm business in the summertime," observed the guest. "And what are your pajamas made of—asbestos?"

PANTS

1

A pretty young teacher was explaining to her class in composition the difference between the words "concrete" and "abstract." "Concrete," she explained, "means something you can see; whereas abstract means something you can't see. Now, who can give me an illustration?" A lad in the front row volunteered. "My pants are concrete, teacher," he said, "but yours are abstract."

2

"Oh, mamma!" called Johnny up the stairs. "I just tore my pants." "I'm busy right now," replied mother; "but get them off and I'll be down to mend them in a few minutes." When she came downstairs a little later, she found the pants on a chair, but no sign of Johnny. Hearing a noise in the basement, she called down, "Say, are you running around down there without your pants?" There was a pause, then a deep voice answered, "No, ma'am. I'm just gonna read the gas meter."

3

Mother had little Willie all dressed in a white summer suit for a party. "Now be careful," she warned as she got ready to dress herself, "and don't get the suit dirty." Willie was an obedient boy, but after awhile he grew tired, so he called to his mother, "Please, mom, may I sit on my pants?"

See also appeal[1], craftsmanship[2], exercise[4], hanging[2], tailor[1].

PARACHUTE

1

The class in aviation was being lectured on the use of the parachute. "But what if the parachute doesn't open?" asked one of the students. "If that should happen, gentlemen," replied the instructor, "you'd find yourselves doing what is known as 'jumping to a conclusion.'"

2

"Goodness, this parachute-jumping certainly looks hazardous to me," gushed the sweet young thing to the aviator. "You must've had some terrible experiences." "Yes, miss, some terrible ones," agreed the aviator gravely. "Why, one time I came down on a lawn where there was a 'Keep off the Grass' sign!"

3

The dear old lady was asking the parachute-jumper innumerable questions. "And what would you do if your parachute didn't open after you

jumped?" she asked. "When that happens, madam," replied the aviator wearily, "we just take it back to the hangar and fix it."

See also aviator[1], wind[1].

PARENTS

1

Father frowned as he looked over Junior's report card. "Well, gee, pop," said Junior, "all the fellows in school got low grades this time." "All of them?" asked father. "How about the little Smith boy across the street?" "Well, yes, he did get high marks," admitted Junior reluctantly. "But, you see, he's different —he's got bright parents."

2

The young man clasped her in his arms. "My darling, I want to marry you," he declared ardently. "But have you seen father and mother?" questioned the girl. "Yes, often," replied the boy grandly. "But that makes no difference; I still love you and want to marry you."

3

It was almost 8 o'clock and still both parents sat comfortably in their armchairs. At last, little Betty asked with a puzzled air, "Is 'oo an' daddy both gonna stay home t'night, mamma?" "Yes, dear, we are," answered mother. The little girl looked at them, then asked, "What's th' matter, mamma?"

See also definition[3].

PARKING

"Hey! What's the idea of stopping there?" a policeman shouted at a woman who had halted her car at a busy intersection. "Parking my car, of course," replied the woman calmly. "It seemed an ideal place as the sign there says: 'Safety Zone.'"

See also driver[5].

PARROT

1

An indignant old lady entered the pet shop. "That parrot you sold me yesterday," she said to the clerk, "uses violent language." "Well, maybe he does swear a little, lady," admitted the clerk, "but you ought to be thankful that he doesn't drink, smoke, chew, or gamble."

2

It was a Boston pet shop and the dignified-looking lady had just instructed the clerk to call the manager. "Your complaint, I understand, madam," began the manager placatingly as he came up, "is that the parrot you got here uses improper language?" "Its language is intolerable," declared the lady haughtily. "Only yesterday I distinctly heard him split an infinitive!"

3

A hunter had promised a friend that he would bring him a parrot from South America. But as he neared home he remembered that he'd forgotten all about it. More or less in jest, he caught an owl, dyed it green, and presented it to his friend. Meeting him again sometime later, the hunter asked slyly, "Well, does your parrot talk yet?" "No, he doesn't talk," the other replied, "but he sure thinks a lot."

4

A man came across an unusually clever talking parrot which he bought and sent home. On the same day his wife went out to order a chicken and left orders with the cook to start roasting the bird as soon as it was delivered. The parrot arrived first, and ended its career in the roasting-pan. When the man learned what had happened, he flew into a rage. "That parrot could speak ten languages!" he shouted at the cook. "Humph!" she snorted. "Then why didn't the stupid thing say something?"

See also gold digger[1], Hollywood[1], teaching[1].

PARTNER

1

"How did you make your money, sir?" inquired the ambitious young man of the rich businessman. "I went into partnership with a rich man, my boy," explained the big shot. "He had the money and I had the experience." "And how did it work out?" the boy continued. "Just as I'd figured it would," replied the other. "Now he has the experience and I have the money."

2

The partners of a brokerage office were attending a banquet at one of the big hotels. Halfway through the meal one of the members of the firm became nervous and worried. "What's bothering you?" whispered one of his partners. "I just remembered that I forgot to lock the office safe before I left," was the reply. "Well, why worry?" put in another partner. "We're all here."

See also banking[5], engagement[3].

PARTY

The maid was cleaning the house the morning after a big party. Halfway up the stairs to the second floor she found one of the solid silver teaspoons. "My goodness," she murmured as she picked it up, "one of the guests had a hole in his pocket."

See also bath[2], farewell[2], host[1], pleasure[1], self, surprise[2].

PASTIME

A lecturer noticed that the attention of some of his listeners was lagging shortly after he had begun to speak. So he startled the gathering by announcing, "Ladies and gentlemen, we shall now have a twenty-minute intermission." The audience looked rather confused, then after a moment the speaker continued, "Meanwhile, in order to pass the time, we shall proceed with the lecture."

See also music[1].

PASTRY

See bread, cake, pie.

PATENT MEDICINE

The itinerant quack was telling about his "famous herb tonic, good for man and beast" and exhorting the crowd to take advantage of his special offer. "I have been selling this tonic for over twenty years, gentlemen, without ever hearing a word of complaint," he declared. "Now, what does that prove?" "That dead men tell no tales," cried a voice from the crowd.

See also calm[1], longevity[1], medicine, testimonial[1].

PATIENCE

Ever since the game had started, a fellow had been looking over the chess expert's shoulder and watching him play. "I say," cried the expert finally, irritated, "you've been watching me for over four hours now. Why don't you try playing a game yourself?" "Shucks," drawled the onlooker, "I ain't got the patience."

PATIENT

A doctor was checking over his books one day, comparing the lists of patients for various years. "I can't understand it, but I had a great many more patients last year than I have this year," he remarked to his wife. "I wonder where they've all gone?" "Well, there's no use in worrying, dear," consoled the wife. "All we can do is hope for the best."

See also experience[4].

PATRIOTISM

1

The elderly lady was gushing over the soldier lately returned from war. "So you're one of those wonderful heroes who went over to die for your country!" she exclaimed ecstatically. "The hell I did, ma'am," the soldier corrected her. "I went over to make some other guy die for his."

2

The Congressman was delivering a windy speech of welcome to some soldiers back from the war. "We are really one, my friends," he declared pompously, "in that we all love our country dearly and are willing to shed our last drop of blood for it." "Did you ever notice," whispered one soldier to another, "that those who are always shouting about shedding their last drop of blood are damned particular about shedding the first?"

3

While the regiment was out on maneuvers a bad dust storm blew up suddenly and one of the soldiers took shelter in the cook-tent. Noticing that the lid on the soup kettle was half off, allowing much dust to blow in, he told the cook, "If you'd put that lid on tight we wouldn't get so much dust in our soup." "Look, my lad," said the cook peevishly, "your business is to serve your country." "To serve it, yes," retorted the soldier, "but not to eat it."

4

All day the troops had been marching through chill rain and mud. Toward evening a skidding gun-carriage had thrown one of the soldiers headlong into a deep puddle, from which he emerged uninjured but soaked with mud and very disgusted. "Are you hurt, man?" cried the captain anxiously, hurrying up. "No, sir," was the reply; "but if ever I love a country again, you can *kick* me!"

5

The captain had been lecturing for a full hour on "A Soldier's Duties," and most of his men had tried hard to stay awake. "Now, Private Smith," he addressed one sleeping figure, "why should a soldier be ready to die for his country?"

Smith fidgeted and thought, then smiled, and said, "You're quite right, sir, why should he?"

See also war[2].

PAYMENT

1

A pretty six-year-old girl entered the village store and said, "I'd like some cloth for a dress for my dolly." The storekeeper found a piece of goods, wrapped it, and handed it to the child. "How much is it?" she asked. "Just one sweet kiss," was the smiling reply. "All right," said the girl, turning to go. "Grandma said to tell you she'd come in tomorrow and pay you."

2

The boss came into the office unexpectedly early one morning and surprised the bookkeeper in the act of kissing the pretty stenographer. "Do I pay you to do this?" he demanded. "No, you don't," replied the bookkeeper calmly. "I do this free of charge."

3

"Here's my bill for services," said the lawyer to his client. "You can pay $100 down and $20 a week for the next fifteen weeks." "Hmm," said the client. "Sounds like buying an automobile." "I am," was the simple and frank reply.

4

"But our easy-payment plan makes it simple to own a car," insisted the auto salesman to the prospect. "Just give me one good reason that you can't buy a new car." "I'll tell you why," replied the other. "It's because I'm still paying instalments on the car I swapped for the car I traded in as down-payment on the car I've got now."

5

"I hate to bother you," said the jeweler to a customer, "but you're two instalments behind on that watch you bought." "That makes it about even," answered the customer. "That watch is about two months slow by this time."

6

The doctor had arranged time-payments for Mrs. Jones for his fee for delivering her baby, and now she was in his office making the final payment. "And how is the baby, Mrs. Jones?" asked the doctor, writing out a receipt. "Oh, he's just fine," beamed the lady. "He's getting married next month."

7

The grocer knew that his dead-beat customer was moving out of the neighborhood, so he said to him, "Look here, Smith, I know you'll never pay me your account, and it's not worth suing you, so here's a paid-in-full receipt." "Gee, thanks," said Smith, but continued to linger. "Did you want something else?" asked the grocer. "Well, gosh," said Smith, "ain't it customary to give a feller a cigar when his account's settled?"

8

A retailer wrote to a wholesaler to order a carload of goods, but the firm immediately wired back: "Sorry, but cannot ship your order until last consignment is paid for." Without delay, the retailer sent the following telegram to the whole-saler: "Cannot wait that long. Cancel order."

See also bride[3], gentleman[1].

PEACE

The poor husband had been terribly henpecked, but now that he was dead the widow was wan with grief. She even spent a part of the insurance money for a modest headstone upon which she had engraved a most fitting inscription: "At peace, until we meet again."

PEACOCK

The little city girl was visiting grandma in the country. Walking in the garden, she saw a peacock, a bird she had never before seen. She gazed in admiration at it, then ran into the house crying excitedly, "Oh, grandma! Come quick! One of your chickens is in bloom!"

PECULIARITY

"Do you have to stutter like that?" asked a man impatiently of another. "S-sure," was the reply. "I-it's my p-p-peculiarity. Everybody's g-got some p-peculiarity." "Well, I haven't," maintained the first stoutly. "D-don't you s-stir your t-tea with your r-right hand?" asked the stutterer. "I do," agreed the other. "Well, that's y-your p-peculiarity," was the explanation; "m-most people u-use a s-spoon."

PEDESTRIAN

1

"Goodness!" gasped the passenger to the reckless motorist. "You just missed that pedestrian back there!"

"Can't be helped," grunted the driver as he neatly took a fender off a parked car; "I don't have time today to go back and try again."

2

The Sunday-school teacher paused in her reading of a text to ask, "Who can tell me the difference between the quick and the dead?" One little fellow, whose dad owned a car, waved his hand eagerly. "The quick," he explained, "are the pedestrians who jump out of the way of automobiles in time, and the dead are those who don't."

3

The motorist was in court for having struck a pedestrian. "Don't you know that it's your duty to do everything you can to avoid hitting a pedestrian?" asked the judge severely. "Yes, sir," was the answer. "Then why didn't you zigzag your car and miss him?" demanded the judge. "I tried that, Your Honor," said the motorist, "but he was zig-zagging, too, and zagged when I thought he was going to zig."

See also automobile[2], experience[5], museum[1], walking[1].

PEN

See fountain pen, handwriting.

PENNY

1

The mistress of the house was trying to make exact change for a delivery and found that she lacked three pennies. She went to the rear and called to the cook in the kitchen, "Mary, do you have three coppers in there?" "Well—ah—no, ma'am,"

came the reply, "there's only two here, and they're both me cousins."

2

"Such ingratitude!" fumed the benevolent old lady. "I just gave a beggar a penny and I didn't even get thanks for it." "That's to be expected," consoled a friend. "You can't get anything for a penny these days."

See also buy[1], robbery[2].

PERFECT

1

Little Junior was being sent to bed early as punishment. "Aw, I can't help it if I'm not perfect," he pouted. "There was only one perfect boy in the world that I know of, anyway." "Whom do you mean?" asked mother curiously. "George Washington?" "No, not him," said Junior scornfully. "It was papa when he was a boy."

2

The man had been sitting around the house out of work for a month. "You're a shiftless, lazy, worthless lout!" his wife cried angrily. "And in the bargain, you're a mean, ill-tempered brute and a thorough liar!" "Now, dear," pleaded the husband, "you know that no man's perfect."

3

The evangelist had himself worked up to a lather. "We're all sinners and far from perfect," he shouted. "Do any of you know of a perfect man?" A meek, nervous little man stood up in the rear and declared, "I do, sir." "What!" cried the astonished evangelist. "Do you mean to say that you know of a perfect man?" "Yes, sir, I know all about him," insisted the little man stoutly. "He's my wife's first husband."

4

The judge peered down at the middle-aged woman charged with shoplifting. "It appears from your record, Maggie," he said sternly, "that you've already been convicted forty-one times for stealing." "I guess maybe that's right, judge," admitted Maggie; "but you must remember, no woman's perfect."

See also good[1].

PERFUME

A woman waved a small, ornate bottle under her husband's nose. "How do you like my new perfume?" she asked. "Now what did you pay for that trash?" he scowled. "Only twenty-seven dollars," she said happily. "What!" he cried. "Did you really pay twenty-seven dollars for that little bottle of junk?" "Oh, don't get excited," answered the woman impatiently. "They told me they'd give me a nickel back on the bottle."

PERMISSION

It was the farmer's first visit to New York. As he stepped from the bustle of Grand Central into the confusion of Forty-second Street he stopped, hopelessly bewildered. Spying a policeman, he said to him, "Officer, I want to go to Central Park." The policeman thought this over. "Well, all right," he consented grudgingly. "You can go just this once, but don't ever, ever ask me again."

PERSEVERANCE

1

The energetic salesman was trying to get in to see the big boss toward the end of a busy day. By various means he at last got past the numerous secretaries and reached the magnate. "A salesman, huh?" snorted the big shot contemptuously. "Do you know that I've already had fifteen salesmen thrown out of here today?" "I'm perfectly aware of that, sir," replied the salesman amiably. "I'm them."

2

A millionaire was scolding his son for his indolence and lack of ambition. "Why, do you know," he said, "that when I was your age I worked ten hours a day carrying water on a construction job, and worked five hours at night washing dishes in a restaurant." "And I'm proud of you for it, father," approved the boy warmly. "Why, if it hadn't been for your pluck and perseverance, I might have to do something like that myself."

3

"How did you like my speech?" inquired the speaker of a listener at the end of the oration. "Oh, fine, fine," said the other. "What part struck you most?" persisted the speaker. "Well, sir," answered the listener, "what impressed me most of all was your perseverance—the way you went over the same thing again and again was remarkable!"

See also truck-driver[1].

PERSONALITY

1

"You seem to think a great deal of Marge," observed one woman to another. "Who could help it?" re-plied the second. "She has a mag-netic personality." "And well she might have," was the catty retort. "She never has a thing on her that isn't charged."

2

"What was wrong with that pa-tient who just left here in such a hurry?" inquired the nurse of the psychiatrist. "Well, instead of let-ting me diagnose his case, he kept insisting that he had a split per-sonality," answered the doctor. "What did you advise for him?" asked the nurse. "Oh, I just told him to go chase himself."

PESSIMIST

1

The pessimist shook his head mournfully and moaned, "Good gosh! It's only to me that these un-lucky things happen!" "Why, what's wrong now?" inquired his friend, looking around in bewilderment. "What's wrong!" barked the pessi-mist. "Gracious, man, can't you see that it's raining?"

2

A caller was congratulating the man of the house warmly. "Your family is certainly talented," he gushed. "Your wife plays the harp, one son the trumpet, another the banjo and drums, your daughters the piano and accordion, and the rest of your children the ukulele. As father of all those musical geniuses, you must be something yourself." "I certainly am," was the grim re-sponse. "I'm a pessimist."

See also identity[5], prophet.

PHARMACY

See drug store.

PHILANTHROPY

1

"I hear that Mrs. Williams, with all her fine airs and big house, hasn't paid her servants any wages for months and months," a gossip in-formed a friend. "Well, why in the world does she keep so many of them then?" inquired the other. "Oh," was the answer, "she always tells everybody that she thinks it her duty to employ as many as possible during these hard times."

2

A solicitor called upon the stingy rich man. "I am seeking contribu-tions for a worthy charity, Mr. John-son," he began. "Our goal is $100,000, and a well-known philan-thropist has already promised to do-nate a quarter of that." "That's fine," approved the tightwad hastily. "And I'll give another quarter. Got change for a dollar?"

PHOTOGRAPHY

1

The customer threw down the proofs in disgust. "I certainly don't like these photos of me at all," he declared. "I look like an ape." The photographer gave him a withering glance. "That may be, sir," he ad-mitted. "But you should have thought of that before you had them taken."

2

A man entered a photoshop. "Do you make life-size enlargements of snapshots?" he inquired. "That, sir, is our specialty," the proprietor assured him. "Good," said the customer, holding out a small negative. "Here's a shot I took of the Grand Canyon."

3

"Can you enlarge this picture of my son?" asked the woman of the clerk in the photoshop. "We can, madam," was the reply. "And could you remove his hat in the enlargement?" she wanted to know. "That can be done, madam," said the clerk. "But how is his hair—is it parted, straight back, or curly?" "Don't be silly!" snapped the lady. "You can see that for yourself when you get the hat off!"

4

An old lady, who had never had her picture taken, finally gave in to her family and visited the photographer. When the proofs arrived, however, she was far from pleased. She went to the photographer's at once. "Is this me?" she demanded, holding out the picture. "It is, madam," was the reply. "Is it a good likeness?" she wanted to know. "It is, indeed," she was assured. The old lady regarded the photo and grew thoughtful. "It's a humblin' sight, ain't it?" she remarked.

5

"Did the photographer send your pictures yet, grandma?" asked the grandson. "Yes, but I sent 'em right back," said the old lady in disgust. "But why did you do that?" the grandson inquired. "I'll have none of his impertinence!" snorted grandma. "On the back of each photo that brazen young man had stamped: 'The original of this is carefully preserved.' "

See also face[3], newlyweds[2].

PHYSICIAN

See doctor.

PICNIC

See ants[1], children[5].

PICTURE

1

It was in the art class. Teacher said to her small pupils, "Now, children, I want you to draw a picture of what you want to be when you grow up." All set to work industriously except one little girl who sat chewing her pencil. "What's the matter, Jane, don't you know what you want to be when you grow up?" asked teacher. "Oh, sure, but I don't know how to draw it," replied the girl. "I want to be married."

2

The young minister was making a call. While sitting in the living room he noticed that the young daughter of the house was busy with paper and pencil and giving him many an intent look. "What are you doing, dear?" he asked. "I'm drawing your picture," she informed him. The young fellow sat still to help her but, after a short time, the girl shook her head in disapproval. "Don't like it," she announced. "Guess I'll put a tail on it and make it a dog."

See also God[1], foresight[1], painting[2], photography, son[3].

PIE

"George, wake up," whispered the wife excitedly in the middle of the night. "There are burglars in the kitchen and they're eating all my pies!" "Aw, what do we care," grunted George, turning over; "just so they don't die in the house."

See also cooking[7], eating[7], manners[4], praise[5].

PIG

1

Father frowned disapprovingly as he watched his young son reach for the last piece of cake. "Tommy, you're a pig," he declared. "Do you know what a pig is?" "Yes," mumbled Tommy, his mouth full of cake. "A pig is a hog's little boy."

2

A college professor was touring through the country and noticed an old farmer dumping a tub of spotted fruit and vegetables to the hogs. "You should cook those," advised the professor, "and then they could digest them in half the time." The farmer thought this over for a moment. "What the heck if they could!" he answered. "What's time to a hog?"

See also drunk[10], summer boarder[1].

PILL

1

"I'd like to have two dozen cold pills," asked a customer of the druggist. "Yes, sir," said the druggist, counting them out. "Shall I put them in a box?" "Why, of course not," replied the customer sarcastically. "I'll just roll them home."

2

The farmer had been having stomach trouble, but none of the usual medicines seemed to help him. One day the doctor came to him with a large black pill. "Here, this is a new treatment," he said. "If you can keep this pill on your stomach it ought to cure you." When the doctor called the next day he asked, "Well, how did you make out with the pill?" "All right as long as I stayed awake," replied the farmer, "but everytime I fell asleep it rolled off."

3

"A friend recommended that I try your special laxative pills," said a customer to the druggist. "Let me have a box, and make 'em double strength." "Here you are, sir. Forty cents, please," and the druggist handed over the package. The man offered him a dollar bill, but when he got his change he exclaimed, "Hey! Why give me all my change in nickels?" "With those pills," explained the druggist grimly, "you'll need the nickels."

See also wine.

PLACE

1

The preacher had got very involved in his sermon. He had devoted an hour and a half to the major prophets, and after an additional twenty minutes wasn't even a third of the way through the minor prophets. He made an impressive pause, then asked academically, "And Habakkuk—where shall we place him?" A man in back arose and answered, "He can have my seat, Reverend."

2

A man halted a minister on the street. "Your face looks damned familiar but I can't place it," he said. "Where in hell have I seen you, anyway?" "From whereabouts in hell do you come, my friend?" asked the clergyman.

See also doctor[3].

PLAN

See idea, system.

PLANT

See flowers, garden, tree.

PLAY

1

The new play was obviously a flop. After the first act a number of the spectators got up and walked out, but after the second act almost all those remaining arose to leave. "Wait!" cried one of the more caustic critics, raising his arms for attention. "Women and children first!"

2

About midway in the second act the critic had had all he could stand of the new play and got up to leave. "Don't go yet," pleaded the manager, trying to stop him. "I guarantee that there's a terrific kick in the next act." "Swell," retorted the critic. "Just give it to the author."

3

Several persons were discussing a new play. "Gosh, I think that was about the dullest play I've ever seen," remarked one. "Well, perhaps," admitted another, who was trying to defend the production; "but at least you'll agree that it wasn't hissed." "That's true," conceded the first, "but for the simple reason that one can't hiss and yawn at the same time."

See also critic[1, 2], criticism[2].

PLAYING

"Mamma," cried the small boy, running into the kitchen, "Danny an' me are gonna play elephants at the zoo an' we wantcha to help us!" "But, goodness, Robert," said mother, surprised, "what in the world can I do to help?" "Gee, you can help lots," insisted the boy. "You can be the nice lady who comes and gives the elephants peanuts and candy."

PLAYWRIGHT

1

"I suppose you've noticed the complete lack of any comment on my last play," remarked the young playwright irritably. "It seems plain that I'm the victim of a conspiracy of silence. What do you advise me to do about it?" "If I were you," suggested his best friend, "I'd join it."

2

A playwright who had been enticed to Hollywood decided to return to Broadway. He gave his producer notice to that effect. "Don't do it," pleaded the movie magnate. "You can't make any money on the stage. Take your last play—how much did that make?" "Eighty thousand," replied the playwright, with a certain amount of pride. The producer turned up his hands and shrugged his shoulders. "See?" he said.

3

The new play had just ended and the theater was in an uproar. "They're calling for the author," said the manager, trying to push the reluctant young playwright onto the stage. "Go on out." "But I can't make a speech," objected the author. "Aw, that's all right," urged the manager, giving a final shove. "Just go out front and tell 'em you're sorry."

See also precocious[2].

PLEASE

All of the girl's friends had married and they were chiding her about her single state. "Oh, lay off!" she snapped at last. "I'll have you know that I can marry anybody I please." "Oh, yeah?" retorted one of the others. "Why don't you, then?" "Because," said the spinster, "I don't seem to please anybody."

PLEASURE

1

Little Willie had been invited to a friend's birthday party the day before, but his chum Danny had not. "Well, how was the party?" inquired Danny. "Did you have a good time?" "Did I have a good time!" echoed Willie. "Say, I ain't hungry yet!"

2

The music teacher was giving a recital for her class. After a lengthy musical program, ice cream, cake, and soda water were served. One of the students had brought her little brother along as a guest. As they were leaving, the teacher asked the youngster, "Well, Jimmy, did you enjoy the recital?" "I sure did," answered Jimmy; "that is, all but the music."

3

The young lawyer had been delivering a long and wearisome dissertation on the merits of his case when, noting an apparent lack of interest on the part of the judge, he paused to ask, "Is it the pleasure of the court that I continue?" The judge heaved a heavy sigh and replied, "Pleasure, my dear sir, has now long been out of question; but you may proceed."

See also ants[1], college[4], fun[2], self.

PLUMBER

1

A young fellow was applying for a position as plumber's helper. "Got any references?" asked the plumber, looking him over. "Yep," yawned the applicant, "but I left 'em at home. I'll go get 'em." "Never mind," said the plumber. "You'll do."

2

The soldier was being court-martialed for cowardice in battle and things looked black indeed for him. Then the officer appointed to defend him arose and said, "Gentlemen, I admit that appearances are against this man. But I propose to show that in civil life this man was a plumber, and consequently was only going back for his bayonet." "Acquitted!" cried the court.

3

The plumber was leisurely engaged, at two dollars an hour, in repairing the kitchen sink. He was not averse to filling in some of the time with a little pleasant banter with the cook. When finally he picked up his tools to leave, the cook hinted, "Thursday's my evening off. Maybe we could go to a movie?" "What!" snorted the plumber. "On me own time?"

4

"Prisoner at the bar," intoned the judge sonorously, "do you choose to be tried by judge or jury?" "By jury," replied the prisoner positively. "I'm takin' no chances on you." "What!" thundered Hizzoner. "Do you mean to imply that I—" "I don't mean nuttin'," declared the prisoner, "but I jist ain't takin' no chances, seein' as I done some plumbin' fer you last year."

See also revenge[2].

PLURAL

1

Teacher was examining the class in grammar. "Can you tell me, Georgie," she questioned, "what the plural of man is?" "Men," was the prompt reply. "Good. And the plural of child?" was the next question. Georgie thought for a moment, then ventured hesitantly, "Twins?"

2

The proprietor of a pet shop had an order for a mongoose, and wishing one for his shop also, he wrote a dealer: "Dear Sir, Please send me two mongeese." That didn't look right to him, so he tore it up and wrote: "Dear Sir, Please send me two mongooses." That looked no better, so he tried a third time: "Dear Sir, Please send me a mongoose. Yours truly, Smith's Pet Shop. P.S.: Please send me another mongoose."

POET

1

The editor squinted at the young poet's offerings. "Goodness," he complained, "this handwriting's so bad I can hardly read it. Why didn't you type out these poems before you submitted them?" "Type 'em!" gasped the embryo poet. "Do you think for a minute that if I could type I'd be wasting my time trying to write poetry?"

2

A man decided to call upon a friend who was a noted poet. As he was about to push the bell the poet's wife hastily opened the door and prevented him. "Sssh!" she cautioned. "Don't make any noise. Jim's upstairs having a poem."

3

The girl had consented to be his and he was clasping her tenderly in his arms. "I wonder what your folks will say," he said. "Do they know that I write poetry?" "Not yet, dear," she replied. "I've told them about your drinking and gambling, but I thought it best not to tell them everything at once."

4

"I made a mistake last night," confessed a yegg to his pal, "and stuck up a poet." "Haw, haw," laughed the pal. "The joke was sure on you." "Joke, my eye," scowled the first. "His dinner alone cost me a buck and a half, besides what he talked me out of for a new suit."

5

"Ah, me," sighed a woman ecstatically to her companion in a bus, "my husband is *so* poetic." "I wouldn't let it worry me, mum," advised an elderly lady who had overheard. "I can give you me grandmother's recipe for a liniment to rub his j'ints that'll have 'im fixed up in a jiffy."

See also editor[1].

POETRY

1

The elegant lady was having a struggling young poet in to tea. "Ah, poetry is such a romantic pursuit," she sighed. "My husband is a mere manufacturer of waste baskets, and it's such a mundane occupation." "Oh, I don't know," replied the undiscovered genius grimly. "There's really quite a bit of poetry in waste baskets."

2

The woman sat with her nose in a book of poetry and a moony expression on her face. "Please read me the poem you're reading, mother," pleaded her small daughter. "Oh, I'm afraid it's too old for you, dear," objected mother. "I don't think you'd be able to understand it." "But I would, mother," insisted the girl, "if you just didn't try to explain it to me."

See also compliment[2], miss[2], shorthand[1], verse.

POLICE

1

A reckless motorist had just been stopped for careless driving and as the policeman made out the report he kept moistening his pencil-tip in his mouth. "Why do you have to keep moistening your pencil?" inquired the motorist finally. "To make your case look blacker," was the answer.

2

In driving only one block, the sweet young thing had violated six traffic ordinances. "Well, miss," said the cop who stopped her, "I suppose you know why I halted you?" "Oh, don't tell me; let me guess," she replied. "I know! You're lonely!"

3

The police of a large city wanted a certain criminal, so they sent to police chiefs in the country circulars with pictures of the man in six different poses. A few days later a letter was received from a small-town police chief, reading: "I have your circular with the pictures of the six crooks you want, and I wish to inform you that I already have five of them under arrest and have my eye on the sixth."

4

The policeman's son had started to study music. One evening he asked his father, "Can you tell me how many beats there are to the bar in this piece, dad?" The mother, sitting sewing across the room, tossed her head and said, "Humph! What a question to ask a policeman! Now if you'd asked your father how many bars there are to his beat, he could have given you some information."

5

A weary, sweating policeman emerged from an inner room of the station. "Well, did you give that thug the third degree?" asked the captain. "Yeah. Six of us kept screaming and shouting and badgering him with questions for over four hours," was the tired reply. "And what did you get out of him?" asked the captain eagerly. "Nothing," said the policeman disgustedly. "All he did was doze off and from time to time murmur, 'Yes, dear. You're right, dear.'"

6

It was the rush hour at the busiest intersection in town when the perspiring officer directing traffic noticed an elderly lady at the curb beckoning to him. With superhuman effort he managed to halt a half-hundred cars, trucks, and taxis and made his way to her side. "What is it, madam?" he asked politely. The old girl smiled sweetly and patted his shoulder. "I just wanted you to know," she said, "that your badge number is the same as the number of my favorite hymn."

7

The man who believed in large families was taking his wife and sixteen children on an outing. He stepped off the bus, followed by his mate and offspring, but had not gone far when a policeman grabbed him and commanded, "Come along!" "What have I done?" gasped the man. "I dunno," said the copper, pulling him along, "but after I get you locked up I'll come back and find out why that crowd's followin' you."

8

"Oh, captain!" called the desk sergeant. "There's a man on the phone who wants a policeman right away because a burglar's cleaning out his house." "Let's see," said the captain reflectively. "We've got two men out censoring periodicals on newsstands, three censoring plays, two inspecting bathing suits at the city pool, and five supervising dancing at different halls. Tell him we might spare him a man in about two hours."

See also ass[4], cook[5], customer[2], do[2], name[2], nursemaid[2].

POLITE

1

Little Grace was having dinner at a friend's house, and as she finished her dessert the hostess asked, "Will you have another helping of ice cream, Grace?" "No, thank you," the girl refused politely. "Oh, do have some more," urged the woman. "Well, I don't know," the girl hesitated. "Mummy told me to be polite and say, 'No, thank you,' but I don't think she knew how small the first helping would be."

2

The streetcar was crowded, so the gallant gentleman arose and offered his seat to a young lady. "Oh, thank you very much, sir, you're extremely kind," replied the girl warmly. "Don't pay no mind to what she says, mister," advised a stony-faced matron accompanying her. "I'm takin' her to a mental hospital."

3

"Thank you, sir," said a lady

to a workman who had just given her his seat in a bus; "you are very gallant." "Aw, t'ink nuthin' of it, lady," responded the man heartily. "Some guys never gives up their seats 'less'n a dame's young an' pretty, but wit' me it don't make no difference, see?"

4

"I think that Jim is the most polite man I've ever seen," declared a girl to her friend. "What! Do you mean that big, red-headed man?" exclaimed the other. "Why, he must weigh at least three hundred and fifty pounds. What makes him so polite?" "Well, I saw him on the streetcar one day," explained the first, "and he got up and gave his seat to three women."

5

"I'm ashamed of you, Robert," said father when his young son came into the house. "I saw you kick your little friend. Why did you do that?" "Aw, I was tired of playin' with 'im an' wanted him to go home," explained the boy. "Then why didn't you just ask him to go home?" asked father. "Why, daddy!" cried the boy in shocked tones. "That wouldn't have been polite."

See also caller[1], cannibal[3], caution[3], chivalry[4], fishing[1], lady[3], thanks[5], waiter[2].

POLITICS

1

It was early evening when six political job-holders walked into an undertaker's carrying a man who had been killed on the job. "What's the idea in waiting so long?" cried the undertaker. "It was before three when you phoned you were bringing him in, and now it's after six." "Sorry," apologized one of the men, "but you see we had to wait until after the whistle blew to find out which one was dead."

2

A politician burst angrily into the newspaper-editor's office. "You've got your nerve!" he roared. "What's the big idea in printing lies about me in your paper?" "Humph!" grunted the editor, unperturbed. "You should complain! What would you do if we printed the truth about you?"

3

"It's pretty evident that baby's going to be a great politician," observed father, proudly regarding his three-month-old offspring. "Now how could you possibly tell that?" asked the mother. "It's quite obvious," explained father. "That child can say more things that sound good and mean absolutely nothing than any kid I've ever seen."

4

A Congressional committee was in conference. "Gentlemen," announced the chairman, "we have 150 million dollars to spend which, if handled right, will get us thousands of votes." "Let's build a bridge across the Mississippi," suggested one. "But that will take only a few million," objected the chairman. "Not the way I mean," said the other. "Let's build it lengthwise to the river."

5

In the club lounge after a sumptuous dinner, a surgeon, an engineer, and a politician were arguing as to whose profession was the oldest. "The first woman was made from Adam's rib," maintained the surgeon, "and that was surely a surgical operation." "But before that," insisted the engineer, "order was made out of chaos, and that was an engineering job." The politician puffed smugly at his cigar. "And who do you think, gentlemen," he demanded, "created the chaos first?"

6

A politician was on his way to address a meeting. He was late and was rushing to get there when he was accosted by a reporter who asked, "Well, sir, what do you think of the political situation these days?" "Don't bother me now!" he cried, brushing the reporter aside. "I have to talk. This is no time to think."

7

A young lawyer from the East wished to establish himself in Chicago. Before going he asked a local big-shot politician for some help in getting started. A little dubious as to the young man's honesty, the politician said, "I'll do what I can to help you in Chicago, if only you'll promise not to steal when you get there." "Sir," said the lawyer with dignity, "I'll go to Chicago entirely unpledged, or I'll not go at all."

8

The politician returned from his big campaign speech looking a little sad. "Well, how'd it go?" inquired his campaign manager. "How did the audience receive your statement that you'd never bought a vote?" "Well, a few of them cheered," was the response, "but the majority seemed to lose interest, and some even got up and walked out."

9

Father was busy reading the latest political news in the evening paper. His young son came over to him and pleaded, "Please, daddy, tell me that story about the Forty Thieves." Father, his mind still on what he'd been reading, shook his head and said, "No, son; maybe when you're a little older. You're still too young to understand politics."

10

"I've often wondered why there are two political parties in this country," remarked a plain citizen, puzzled. "I suppose it's because there are two sides to every political question." "Oh, no, that's not it," said the experienced man, smiling. "It's because there are two sides to every political office—inside and outside."

11

"Now, gentlemen," said the professor to his English class, "can any of you give me a clear, concise definition of a politician?" "I can, sir," volunteered the son of a Congressman, "if you'll just tell me to which party you refer."

See also agreement[3], breeding[2], Democrats[1], election[1, 3], good[3], government[5], insult[3], memory[3], money[3], numbers[3], opinion[1], promise, relatives[5], Republicans[1], shrewd[2], Socialist, spitting[4], statesman[1], triplets[3].

POLYGAMY

See bigamy.

POOR

The man left the saloon where he'd been spending the evening with some friends and started home. On the way he passed a men's-wear shop in the window of which was a dummy wearing an out-of-style hat bearing a label: "Reduced to 39¢." "Poor fellow!" murmured the man, tears of sympathy in his eyes. "I've often been reduced to that myself."

See also duet, farm[1], support[2].

POPULAR

The professor asked one of his female students to remain after class. "It's about Mary Smith," he began. "She seems to be one of the prettiest, sweetest girls in the college, yet you all seem to dislike her. Why is she so unpopular?" "Don't you know?" was the surprised reply. "It's because she won the popularity contest last year."

See also boss[3].

PORTRAIT

A near-sighted man and his wife were looking over an art exhibit. "Goodness!" cried the man in disgust, pausing before an ornate frame and squinting critically. "That is without a doubt the ugliest portrait I've ever seen." "Come along, you old fool!" urged the wife, pulling his sleeve. "That's a mirror."

See also banking[6], realism[3].

POSITION

See job, posture.

POSTAGE

1

A lady entered a post office and bought a stamp. "Must I stick it on myself?" she asked the clerk. "I wouldn't recommend it, madam," he replied. "It will accomplish much more if you stick it on the letter."

2

The absent-minded professor stopped in at his doctor's one day on his way to class. "I'm afraid I feel a cold coming on, doctor," he said. The doctor took his pulse, then said, "Now let me see your tongue, please." The professor stuck out his tongue and the doctor looked at it in amazement. "Why the postage stamp on it?" he asked. "Ah, thank you, doctor," said the professor in grateful relief. "I was wondering where I'd left it."

3

"I want twenty cents' worth of stamps," requested the farmer at the village post office. "What denomination, sir?" asked the clerk. "Waal, I happen to be Baptist, an' proud of it," replied the farmer, "but I don't know's it's any o' your durned business, young feller."

POSTURE

A pompous village banker out driving one morning met an aging farmer along the road. "Good morning, Zeke," he boomed affably. "My goodness, man, you're certainly getting bent. Why don't you stand up straight like I do?" "D'ye see thet field o' corn yonder?" asked the old fellow. "Certainly," responded the banker. "Waal," observed the old boy, "ye'll notice thet it's the full heads thet hang over an' the empty ones that stand up straight."

POVERTY

See poor.

POWER

See ability[2], force, strength.

PRACTICAL

1

The pastor of a small church had received a call from a larger church at a substantial increase in salary. He said that he would retire to pray for guidance and give his answer later. "Well, Wilbur," someone asked the pastor's son about an hour later, "has your father decided to accept?" "I don't know about pop," the boy replied; "he's still prayin', but ma, she's got everything packed."

2

The clergyman was talking to a policeman noted for his severity with anyone getting into trouble. "Remember, my friend," he admonished, "that the wicked flee when no man pursueth." "Maybe so," admitted the policeman, "but they make better time out of town when somebody's after 'em."

See also farmer[1], honeymoon[1].

PRACTICE

1

An old family friend dropped in to see a young lawyer who was trying to establish a practice. "Well, well, Elmer," he remarked amiably, "so you're now practicing law." "I'd hardly say just that," corrected the young fellow. "What I'm really practicing is economy."

2

A young clergyman roomed in a house near his church. He would practice next Sunday's sermon in his room with full oratorical effects. He was roaring and ranting mightily one day when his landlady had a visitor. "Goodness!" exclaimed the caller. "What is that racket?" "Oh, don't mind it," advised the woman. "It's only the young minister practicing what he preaches."

3

"I understand, Deacon, that you told Brother Jones that I don't practice what I preach!" declared the minister indignantly. "That I did, Reverend, and it's true," maintained the deacon. "For over three years, now, you've been preaching resignation, but you sure haven't resigned yet."

See also music lessons[2].

PRAISE

1

"Well," said the young husband as he bit into his bride's pastry, "I *must* say these are fine biscuits." Later the bride's mother stopped him in the hall and asked in a whisper, "Goodness, John, how could you say that those were fine biscuits?" "But I didn't say they were fine," he pointed out. "I merely said I *must* say so."

2

The small-town banker was known for being a close-fisted businessman and severe creditor. But when he died the whole town nevertheless turned out for his funeral. No one being able to think of any honest tribute to pay the man, all were silent. But coming back from the cemetery one old fellow made a feeble effort at praise by saying, "Well, there's one thing you can say for Sam: he wasn't always as mean as he sometimes was."

3

"The way that new office manager looks at us, Marge," remarked Mame through her chewing gum, "I got a feelin' he don't think we're so hot." "Oh, no? Why, he just thinks we're swell," declared Marge. "Just yesterday I heard him tell the bookkeeper that we were perfect nonentities!"

4

Old Dead-Eye Dugan, the bad man of Devil's Gulch, was finally killed in a saloon fight after a life of crime. After they'd buried him, all stood around the grave waiting for someone to speak a few good words for the deceased. Finally, old Cactus Joe stepped forward. "Friends," he said feelingly, "I've known Dead-Eye man an' boy, an' I must say he shot a danged good game o' marbles as a kid."

5

It so happened that on the day the wife had baked the worst pie of her career her husband brought home an unexpected guest. Having no other dessert, she was forced to serve the pie. Much to her surprise, the guest praised the pie profusely. A few weeks later he was in again, but this time the pie was excellent and he said nothing. "How come

you praised that bad pie of mine," asked the puzzled woman, "and don't mention this fine one?" "Well, madam," he replied, "that first pie needed praising."

6

Two actors were talking over their work. One was downcast because his performances had not been well received of late. "Oh, well," he remarked, "people will praise my work after I'm dead." "You may be right," conceded the other, "but don't you feel that such a sacrifice is a little extreme for a little praise?"

See also mistake[1], nothing[3].

PRAYER

1

The boat was sinking fast and the captain shouted out, "Does anyone here know how to pray?" A man spoke up in a confident tone, "Yes, Captain, I do." "Good!" cried the captain. "You'd better get to your praying while the rest of us put on these life belts—we're one short."

2

The little boy was kneeling by his bed saying his prayers in a very low voice. "I can't hear what you're saying, dear," his mother said. "Well, mother," retorted the boy, "I wasn't talking to you, you know."

3

"Now, dear," mother reminded the little tot as she knelt by the bed to pray, "don't forget to ask God's blessing on everyone dear to you." "Yes, Mummy," replied the child, and after she had concluded her "Now I lay me," she added, "And

Dod bless mummy, an' daddy, an' bruvver, an' auntie. An' by the way, Dod, take good care of yourself."

4

Mother had taken her young daughter to an Episcopal church service for the first time, and as things progressed the child was amazed to see the entire congregation suddenly kneel. "What they doin', mamma?" cried out the girl shrilly. "Hush, dear!" cautioned mother. "They're going to pray." "What! Wif all their clothes on?"

5

Two ministers traveling by auto in winter were forced by a snowstorm to seek shelter for the night at a farmhouse. The only spare room was unheated. The elderly cleric was on his knees but a short time before crawling under the covers, but the younger one performed his usual elaborate and lengthy devotions despite the chill. "You didn't pray very long, brother," remarked the younger as he slipped into bed. "No," said the elder; "I keep prayed up."

6

The little backwoods church had a new preacher. His sermon was eloquent and his prayer was marvelous for the completeness with which its requests covered the entire list of human wants. After services, two hillbillies were talking over the new pastor. "Thet preacher shore kin pray," remarked one admiringly. "He shore kin," agreed the other. "Why, he asked th' good Lo'd fo' things th' otha preachah didn't even know He had!"

7

A revivalist was trying to carry on his work back in the hill country, but his meetings were very poorly attended. Meeting one of the local hillbillies one day he inquired, "Why weren't you at our revival last night, Jed?" "Oh, I dunno," was the vague reply. "Well, don't you ever pray?" demanded the preacher. The hillbilly shook his head. "No, suh," he replied. "I jest carries a rabbit's foot."

8

A gentle, kindly old minister accepted a call to a Kentucky church. Soon after he arrived, he was asked by one of the deacons to invite the prayers of the congregation for one Lilly Jones. This he gladly did for four Sundays. On the fifth the deacon told him, "Never mind asking those prayers any more, Reverend." "Why, did she die?" asked the minister anxiously. "Oh, no," he was reassured; "but she won the steeplechase."

See also behavior[2], bribery[1], church[6], Congress[1], football[2], grace, happy[4], lightning[3], old maid[3], radio[2, 3], remind[4], study[2], swearing[3].

PREACHER

See minister.

PREACHING

See sermon.

PRECAUTION

1

A man walked into the village store and said, "I'd like to have all the rotten eggs you have in the place." "What do you want 'em for?" asked the amazed clerk. "Are you goin' to see the new comedian down to the Opera House tonight?" "Sssh!" cautioned the customer nervously. "I *am* the new comedian."

2

The family was on a picnic and father stood near the edge of a high cliff admiring the wild sea dashing on the rocks below. His young son came up and said, "Mother says it's not safe here, and you're either to stand back farther or give me the sandwiches."

3

The ferryboat was a rickety one. It had just got well out when a bad storm blew up. The ferryman and his helper held a worried consultation, then the former turned to the passengers, concern in his face. "The wind's gettin' worse an' there's no tellin' what might happen," he informed them, "so we're thinkin' we'd best collect your fares now."

See also chivalry[5], expense[2], farewell[2], fraternity[1], fruit[5].

PRECOCIOUS

1

"Now, children," questioned the Sunday-school teacher, "who can tell me what happened to Lot's wife when she turned to look back at the burning cities?" "It is said," responded the serious-looking lad, "that she was transmuted into chloride of sodium."

2

The playwright sat at the club's bar with his head dejectedly in his hands. "What's wrong, old man?" inquired a critic friend, slapping him on the shoulder. "Oh, I've suf-

fered a terrible calamity," moaned the playwright. "My little son got hold of my new play and tore it all to bits." "Well, cheer up," comforted the critic. "Obviously your boy is destined to become a critic, but I'm surprised he can read so young."

PREFERENCE

The dead-beat was being sued for a debt and the judge was familiarizing himself with the case. "And is it you," he inquired of the creditor, "who preferred charges against the man?" "Not me, Your Honor," denied the other quickly. "I always prefer the cash if I can get it."

PREGNANCY

1

An air raid was in progress and an air-raid warden was checking on the precautions. He stuck his head into a crowded shelter and shouted at the woman in charge, "Are there any expectant mothers down there?" Before the woman could reply, a voice from the darkness answered, "Not yet. We've just got down here."

2

A bride entered a drug store and asked anxiously of the clerk, "Does that baby tonic you advertise really make babies bigger and stronger?" "We've had no complaints on it, madam, and we sell a lot of it," declared the clerk. "I'll take a bottle," said the woman, then in a whisper asked, "Who takes this tonic—me or my husband?"

3

A modern mother believed in

frankness in the education of children and in teaching them the facts of life. She became a bit dubious about the wisdom of it, however, when one day boarding a crowded streetcar with her young daughter, the little girl looked around at the seated men, then shrilled indignantly, "Is there no gentleman present who'll give my poor pregnant mother a seat?"

See also drinking[7].

PREJUDICE

The case had seemed quite simple and clear-cut, but the jury had been out all afternoon. As time for adjournment approached, the judge sent for the jury and asked the foreman, "Do you gentlemen require any further instruction to reach a verdict?" "We don't need no more instruction, Your Honor," replied the foreman irritably. "The trouble is that there's eleven prejudiced and unreasonable men on this jury who won't agree to nothin'!"

PREMATURE

A young lady was out canvassing the neighborhood to get new pupils for her Sunday school. She called at the home of some newlyweds. "I'm trying to get more members for our Sunday school," she explained. "Won't you please send your children?" "But we've just been married," said the bride blushingly, "and have no children." "Well, then," urged the young lady brightly, "will you please send them when you get them?"

PREMIUM

The bride-to-be was all thrilled. "I just saw an ad saying that you could furnish your home with soap premiums," she said to a married woman. "You get a coupon with each cake of soap. Do you think I can furnish my home that way?" "I have a friend who did it," replied the woman. "She furnished a six-room house. But she only needed furniture for one room—the other five were filled with soap."

PREPARATION

1

"This is a tough world and you have to be able to take care of yourself in it," said the practical man, "so I'm giving my son boxing lessons to teach him to fight if he has to." "But suppose he comes up against a bigger fellow who has also been taught to fight," objected a friend. "I've thought of that," replied the practical man, "so I'm teaching him how to run, too."

2

An old desert rat had been to town and had hung on the bar in the saloon until thoroughly saturated with alcohol. Fearing to become thirsty on his way home in the desert, he put a bottle in each pocket and started. As he stumbled through the cactus, he took frequent nips. At last he kicked against a huge rattler which at once coiled to strike. "Bite, dern ye, bite!" said the old fellow, wavering about. "I was never better prepared in me life."

PRESENT

See gift.

PRESIDENT

1

A lawyer had called in a psychiatrist for expert testimony as to his client's sanity, and the doctor was conducting his examination. "Who was our first President?" he asked. "Washington," was the prompt reply. "Right. And our second?" was the next question. "John Adams," he promptly answered. The psychiatrist hesitated, and the lawyer whisperingly prompted, "He's doing fine. Go on!" But the learned man whispered back, "I'm not so sure myself who the third President was."

2

"Gee," said a rabid young radio fan to her girl chum, "do you know that some of those radio singers get $75,000 a year?" "Gosh, do they?" exclaimed her friend. "Why, that's what the President of the United States gets." "Yeah, can you imagine!" cried the first in disgust. "And the President can't sing a note."

See also Socialist.

PRESS

See book, magazine, newspaper.

PRETTY

See beauty.

PRICE

1

"And see this lovely jar?" said the collector, holding up his treasure proudly. "It cost me sixty dollars." "Hmm. Sixty dollars?" said his friend, viewing the object critically. "I suppose they threw in the marmalade."

2

"Howdy, Jake," the storekeeper greeted the farmer as he entered. "What'll ye hev today?" "How much be sugar?" asked the farmer cautiously. "Six cents a pound," he was told. "Golly!" exclaimed the customer. "Shore has went up, ain't it?" "Why, what did ye pay last time?" asked the storekeeper. "Five an' three-quarters cents." "Waal, how much did ye want?" the storekeeper inquired. "Kinda figgered on gittin' 'bout a pound," was the answer.

3

"How much is hamburger?" inquired the young wife. "Twenty-seven cents a pound," the butcher answered. "That's outrageous," she exclaimed. "Why, down at the corner store they have it for thirteen cents." "Well, why don't you buy it there?" asked the butcher. "Because they haven't any," she answered. "I see," said the butcher. "Well, when I don't have any I sell it for ten cents a pound."

4

"I don't mind paying a fair price," declared a lady to her grocer, "but you sold my neighbor apples for less than you charged me." "Oh, no, Mrs. Smith, that ain't so," answered the grocer. "I've got only one price here and I assure you that you get the lowest."

5

The purchasing-agent was sick and a specialist was called in. "Yes, I'm quite sure I can cure you," declared the specialist after making an examination. "What will it cost, doc?" asked the patient weakly. "My fee," said the physician, making a quick calculation, "will be ninety-seven dollars." "I'm afraid you'll have to shade that a little, doc," gasped the buyer; "I've got a better price from the undertaker."

See also deaf[2], hat[2], medicine[7], perfume, student[3], value[2].

PRIDE

1

Mrs. Murphy waved a letter at her neighbor. "My boy has just written me from jail," she shouted, "and he tells me they're gonna cut six months off his sentence for good behavior." "My, my," beamed the neighbor. "You must be proud to have a son that does you so much credit."

2

Two thugs held up a man on a lonely street, but he put up a terrific fight. They finally overcame him, but a search revealed only a nickel in his possession. "Why put up a fight like that for a lousy nickel? We almost had to kill you," said one of the thugs. "Well, to tell the truth," explained the victim sheepishly, "I didn't want my financial condition exposed."

See also boast[2].

PRISON

1

A social worker was paying a visit to a penitentiary and she noticed one man who appeared unusually gloomy. "Well, my poor fellow," she said sympathetically, "what's the length of your term?" "Depends on politics, lady," was the morose answer. "I'm the warden."

2

"I suggest a resolution," said a member of the Uplift Society, "for the immediate reform of conditions in our prisons." "I quite agree," cried an elegant lady, springing up. "Nowadays, there are so many of our very best people who are being indicted, convicted, and sent to prison for long terms, that we really must make their surroundings more pleasant and refined."

See also cook[3], mining[2].

PRISONER

1

"I suppose it will be your happiest day when your sentence is finally over," observed a lady visitor cheerily to a prisoner. "Well, I dunno, ma'am," he said sadly, "but I doubt it." "You doubt it!" exclaimed the lady. "And why?" "Because I'm in for life," was the reply.

2

A reporter was trying to telephone his story of an execution from Sing Sing, but the hammering of a convict tacking some linoleum on the floor was disturbing him. "Would you mind stopping that for a few minutes, friend?" he requested pleasantly. "Not at all," was the amiable response. "Just take your time—I've got twenty years to finish this job."

See also absent-minded[1], advice[1], guilt[3], police[5], pride[1].

PRIVILEGE

A tenderfoot was standing in a saloon in a rough-neck mining town out West watching a poker game for big stakes. Suddenly, he was horrified to see the dealer give himself four aces from the bottom of the deck. "That man's dealing from the bottom of the deck," he informed a nearby native in a shocked whisper. "Waal, what of it?" drawled the other, astonished. "It's his deal, ain't it?"

PRIZE

1

It was the last day of school and prizes were awarded for certain talents and accomplishments. One of the boys returned home to find that his mother had callers. "Well, Jimmy," asked one of the guests, "did you get a prize today?" "No, ma'am," replied the boy, "but I did get horrible mention."

2

"Where did you get the new book, Danny?" inquired mother as the boy came in with the volume under his arm. "It's a prize from school," replied Danny. "A prize for what, dear?" asked mother. "For natural history," was the answer. "Teacher asked how many legs an ostrich had, and I told her three." "But an ostrich has two legs," objected mother. "I know that now," agreed the boy. "But I was closest—all the rest of them said four."

PRIZE FIGHTING

See boxing.

PROFESSOR

1

The professor stepped to the edge of the platform and asked, "If there are any dumbbells present, please stand up." There was a lengthy pause, then a solitary freshman arose. "So you consider yourself a dumbbell, do you?" asked the professor. "Not exactly, sir," was the reply; "but I just felt sorry for you seeing you standing all alone."

2

A college student was being scolded by his professor. "Your last theme was almost impossible to read," he declared. "Your work should be written in such a manner that even the most ignorant can understand it." "Yes, sir," replied the student meekly. "Which part was it you couldn't get?"

3

The president of the university came down to breakfast looking haggard and sunken-eyed. "Are you ill, dear?" asked his wife. "No, no. It's just that I had a horrible dream last night," explained prexy, trembling. "I d-dreamed that t-the trustees had suddenly d-decided t-that I—" he gulped, "—that I s-should p-pass the freshman admission examination!"

See also absent-minded, punishment[2].

PROFIT

The garage owner was trying to figure his income tax, but the arithmetic had him stumped. "Look, Junior," he said to his college student son, "if it costs me fifty-five cents to repair a man's car and I charge him seventeen dollars for it, what percent profit do I make?" "I'm afraid I can't help you, pop," replied the son. "You'll have to go to someone who knows the rules of grand larceny for that. The rules of simple percentage won't do."

See also church[9].

PROGRESS

1

Two little girls were comparing their progress in catechism. "I've come to original sin," announced one proudly. "How far are you?" "Me?" said the other. "Oh, I'm already 'way beyond redemption."

2

"The trouble with this country is that we're at a standstill," fretted the pessimist; "we're not making any real progress." "Oh, I don't know," countered the optimist. "Just look, at the beginning George Washington couldn't tell a lie, and now almost everybody can."

3

"My indigestion still keeps me awake nights, doc," complained the patient. "The thing for you to do," advised the doctor, "is to eat a hearty meal at night and not bother about it." "But the last time I was here you told me that I should eat only a very light supper in the evening," objected the sufferer. "There you are," said the physician, "just see the progress medicine is making."

See also movies[3], nurse[1], son[2].

PROHIBITION

1

"Speaking of dry towns," said the traveling salesman, "the worst I've ever struck was Leavenworth, Kansas." "Can't you get any liquor there at all?" asked a listener. "Only if you've been bitten by a snake," was the reply. "When I was there they had only one snake in town, and after I'd stood in line for four hours,

the snake was too worn-out to bite any more."

2

"It's a wonderful thing," declared the prohibitionist from a dry state, "to be able to walk the streets without seeing a saloon on every corner." "I suppose so," replied the man with a red nose; "but it's a great comfort to know that they're there even if you can't see them."

See also election[6], water.

PROMISE

The city election was coming up and the politician was out canvassing for votes. "I hope I'll be able to count upon your support," he said to one merchant he had called on. "I'm afraid not," was the reply. "You see, I've already promised my support to your opponent." The politician laughed. "In politics," he stated, "promising and doing are two different things." "Well, in that case," declared the merchant affably, "I'll be happy to give you my promise."

See also success[2].

PROMOTION

1

"You've been with us a year now," said the boss grandly to the office boy, "and I'm going to promote you to junior clerk. There will be, of course, a small increase in salary." Instead of the thanks the boss expected, the boy considered the matter gravely. "If it's all the same to you," he concluded finally, "I'd rather go on at my present salary and keep on taking care of the stamp drawer and petty cash box."

2

The boss called his faithful old clerk into his office. "Jones," he began, "you've been working for me for fifteen years and in all that time you've never failed me." "Yes, sir," said the clerk expectantly. "So in order to show my appreciation," the boss continued, "you will henceforward be addressed here as *Mr.* Jones."

See also cannibal[1].

PRONUNCIATION

1

There was a town along a railroad named Eurelia. There was much dispute concerning its pronunciation. Each brakeman who would call the station had his own version. As a train one day neared this station, a brakeman stuck his head in one end of a coach and shouted, "You're a liar!" which he thought correct. Almost at once, a dissident brakeman put his head in the other end of the car and called, "You really are!"

2

Grandma and her little grandson were taking a train trip and the old lady was dozing. As the train was pulling into a station, the old lady awakened with a start and asked the boy, "What station did the conductor call?" "He didn't call any station," the boy replied. "He just put his head in the door and sneezed." "Quick, get your bundles," cried the old lady. "We get off here at Oshkosh."

3

A woman traveler on her way to California got to talking with a native of that state. "I've already been to San Jose once," she informed him. "You pronounce that wrong, madam," said the man. "It's San Hosay. In California all J's are pronounced as H's. When were you there?" The woman considered a moment, then responded cautiously, "Last Hune and Huly."

4

Wifey returned home and called to her husband. "Henry," she said sternly, "when you came in last night you told me that you'd been to the Grand Inn with Mr. Brown. But I just met Mr. Brown and he said that you were at the Trocadero Tropical Paradise. Why did you lie, Henry?" "I didn't lie, dear," explained Henry. "I was in no condition last night to say Trocadero Tropical Paradise."

5

The culture-conscious lady was lavish in her praise of the minister of their church. "He has the most perfect pronunciation I've ever heard," she declared to her husband. "In fact, I can't recall that he's ever made a mistake in pronunciation." "Well, I can," grunted hubby, "and that was when he pronounced us man and wife."

6

The foreigner looked up from the English novel he was laboriously reading. "How is it, my friend," he inquired, "that you pronounce the word 'pneumonia'?" His American friend gave him the desired information. "That is odd," replied the foreigner. "It says in this book that the doctor pronounced it fatal."

See also New York[3].

PROOF

1

A doctor was presenting his bill to the executor of the estate of a deceased patient. "Would you prefer that I have this bill sworn to?" he asked. "No, that's not necessary," replied the executor. "The mere fact of the death of the deceased is ample proof that you attended him professionally."

2

Two politicians got into a heated argument and one at last shouted angrily, "Aw, you're crazy!" "I'm not crazy," the other answered. "You are crazy!" insisted the first. "I'm not crazy," maintained the second. "I can prove I'm not, and I'll bet that's more than you can do." "All right," agreed the first, "I'll take that bet. Let's see you prove it." Whereupon the other took out his discharge papers from the state asylum.

3

"Now, William," questioned teacher during the geography lesson, "how do you know that the world is round and hangs unsupported in space? How can you prove it?" "Hell, teacher, I don't have to prove it," replied William. "I never said it was."

4

Two men sat fishing on a river bank when suddenly one dropped his line and jumped to his feet. "Did you see that, Bill?" he cried excitedly. "A fellow just fell off that cliff over there into the river!" "Don't get worked up," advised Bill. "Maybe it was just a movie-stunt man making a picture." "But how can we tell?" inquired the first. "Well," decided Bill, "if he drowns, he ain't."

See also asylum[6], gas[2], honest[1], patent medicine.

PROPERTY

"Look here, officer," said a man indignantly, halting a policeman in front of his house, "this dead cat has been lying here for over three days now. What am I to do with it?" "Well, you can take it down to headquarters," suggested the cop calmly, "and if nobody claims it within a reasonable time, it's your property."

PROPHET

Robert Fulton was just ready to make his trial run with his steamboat "Clermont" and among the many spectators lining the bank was a farmer and his son. "They'll never start that danged contraption," he predicted gloomily to the boy. As the boat moved away and picked up speed, the son looked curiously at the farmer. The man spat, and in the same gloomy tone said, "They'll never stop that danged contraption."

See also science[1].

PROPOSAL

1

Jim had taken his girl to lunch and he noticed her smile and nod at an elderly gentleman at the next table. "Do you know that man?" he inquired. "Yes, I do," she replied. "Then I guess I might as well ask him to join us," decided the young man. "Oh, Jim, this is so sudden!" said the girl. "Huh? What do you mean, sudden?" asked Jim. "Why, that man is our minister," answered the girl.

2

A fellow and girl were sitting in the porch swing when the girl spoke up in firm tones. "I know what's in your mind," she announced, "and why you keep coming here every night, taking up my time and keeping other men away. You want me to marry you." "I-I d-do!" stuttered the amazed young man. "I thought so," replied the girl triumphantly. "Very well, I'll do it."

3

The girl had just refused him, but she showed concern. "Now don't be downhearted," she pleaded. "It pains me very much to have to cause you grief." He looked up and gave a hearty laugh of relief. "Oh, don't worry about it," he said. "My proposal was only an election bet."

4

"I love you!" he whispered fiercely, holding her close. "Will you be mine? Answer me!" "Oh, Dan, this is so sudden!" was her original response. "Well, take your time," he told her gently. "Shall I ask your mother first?" "No, no!" she answered in alarm, throwing her arms around his neck. "Mother's a widow, and I want you for myself!"

5

Life held little for the broken-down old bum, but he found a certain solace in the company of an equally battered old woman. Sitting glumly together one evening in a saloon, the bum was suddenly struck by an idea. "Say," he suggested, "mebbe we'd be better off if we got married." "Aw, I thought o' that," replied the old girl, "but who'n hell ud have us?"

6

The bashful young man had had a cut in pay and this, with increased expenses, became apparent when he took out his girl. "Gee, Sally," he said hesitantly one evening, "you know how I've always counted on you, and I thought maybe—well, that is, could you—aw, gee, will you marry me?" "Golly!" sighed Sally in relief. "You had me scared. I thought you wanted to borrow some money."

7

"Looks like you're going to be an old maid, Jane," remarked a woman cattily to her friend. "Humph!" sniffed Jane, with a toss of her head. "I'll have you know that I've been asked to get married plenty of times." "Yeah? Who asked you?" inquired the friend. "Oh, pa and ma," was the answer.

8

The young man's love-making was passionate, but had a simple, childlike quality. First he knelt and put his head upon her knee, then climbed upon her lap and put his head on her shoulder. "Will ooo be my wittle bittleums wifey?" he pleaded. "Your wife?" gasped the girl. "Good gosh, from the way you were going on I thought that you wanted me for a mother!"

See also acquaintance[3], advertising[2], bashful[3, 4], boarding house[5], conversation[3], courtship[2], diet[1], difference[2], dream[2], fool[1, 5], hint[6], humble, lose[1], moon[1], mother-in-law[1], old maid[2], spurned[2], stenographer[1], support[2], talk[5], warning[3], word[4].

PROTECTION

There was an old superstition that the wearing of a turquoise would protect the wearer from injury through falling. An ancient king who wore a turquoise ring once asked his jester, "What do you think would happen if I were to jump from the castle tower with this ring on my finger?" "I think, Your Highness," replied the jester readily, "that the ring would not be hurt."

See also fear[1], silver[2].

PROUD

See conceit, pride.

PROVERB

1

A delivery boy was trying to enter a yard with some bundles but stopped at the gate because of a vicious, barking dog on the other side. "Oh, come on in," encouraged the owner from a window. "You know the old proverb: 'A barking dog never bites.'" "Yeah, I know the proverb," admitted the boy, "and you know the proverb. But what worries me is, does the dog know the proverb?"

2

Hubby was very fond of quoting proverbs. So one evening as he sat idly watching his wife trying to put the fretful baby to sleep, he remarked cheerily, "Don't get annoyed, dear. Just remember that, 'The hand that rocks the cradle rules the world.'" "That's wonderful," said the wife wearily. "Suppose you step over here and rule the world awhile and let me rest."

PROVIDENCE

The old farmer was complaining bitterly to his minister about the poor crops, bad weather, and the like. "Now, Hiram, you shouldn't talk like that," reproved the preacher gently. "There's always much for us to be grateful for. Never forget that Providence watches out for every creature. Even the birds are fed daily." "I'll say they are," growled the farmer wryly; "and Providence uses my corn to do it!"

See also cook[3], justice[1].

PSYCHIATRY

1

A man on trial for murder was being examined by a group of alienists to determine his sanity, or lack of it. One of the examiners suddenly leveled his finger at the accused and barked, "Quickly, now, how many feet does a centipede have?" The defendant looked at him scornfully and then shook his head. "Good Lord," he sighed, "is that all you've got to worry about?"

2

Two psychiatrists met on the street and stopped to greet each other. "Well, well, Dr. Williams," observed one, "you're certainly fine today. How am I?"

See also crazy[3], lunatic[4], personality[2]

PSYCHOLOGY

"Father," asked the son, looking up from a periodical he was reading, "what is psychology?" "Psychology, my son," explained the old man, "is a word of four syllables that you throw into a discussion to distract attention when you've got yourself cornered and can't explain your way out."

PUBLICITY

1

"How's your new publicity agent making out?" inquired a friend of the movie actress. "Oh, he's wonderful!" exclaimed the actress. "I've had him less than a month and already my house has caught fire once, I've been robbed twice, been in an auto accident, had three suicide notes from admirers, and I've been threatened by kidnapers."

2

One of the less talented actors was complaining to the manager about the lack of publicity he was getting. He wanted to be billed on the marquee in front of the theater. "There's plenty of room at the bottom for one more name in lights," he pointed out. "You could easily add my name and put 'with' in front of it." "What do you mean, 'with'?" cried the manager. "Why not 'in spite of'?"

3

The big businessman was dying and his lawyer was at his bedside drawing up his will. "I think it would be nice to remember my employees," he said weakly. "Better put in a clause to the effect that to each man who has worked for me over twenty-five years I bequeath $100,-000." "But you've been in business only fifteen years," objected the lawyer. "I know it," agreed the man; "but just think of the publicity!"

PUBLIC SPEAKING

See speaker, speech.

PUBLISHER

A struggling young author called to see a publisher with whom he'd left a manuscript some time before. "Your stuff isn't at all bad," admitted the publisher grudgingly, "but it's a policy of my firm to publish only the work of writers with well-known names." "Say, that's swell!" exclaimed the young fellow in great excitement. "My name's Smith!"

PULL

1

A motorist driving down a lonely road passed a car that apparently was stalled. He stopped and got out to see if he could be of any help. To his amazement, he found the driver down in front of the car in the act of hitching a pair of kittens to the front axle. "For Pete's sake, man!" he exclaimed. "You're surely not going to try to pull that car with those kittens?" "And why not?" asked the man impatiently. "I've got a whip."

2

Mother heard a terrible spitting

and meowing on the back porch and looked out to see what little Junior was doing to the cat. "You naughty boy!" she scolded. "Stop pulling that cat's tail!" "But I'm not pulling it, mamma," protested Junior innocently. "I'm just holding it. It's the cat that's doing the pulling."

PUNCTUAL

1

"Ye know, Zeke, it's shore funny," observed the farmer to one of his hired hands, "but you're allus late of a mornin' an' ye live right here on the farm, while Sam who lives two miles away is allus on time." "Don't see nuthin' funny 'bout thet," retorted Zeke. "If Sam's late of a mornin' he kin hurry a bit, but if I'm late, I'm here."

2

"The man who's always punctual," declared the chairman to a director who was tardy for a board meeting, "never loses anything by it." "Oh, no?" replied the director scornfully. "Only about a half-hour waiting for the other fellows to show up."

3

A dealer in garden produce hired a boy to be at his shop every morning at three o'clock in order to deal with the farmers when they brought their truck in. The boss himself came in about nine. Being on a late party one night, the boss thought he'd check up and dropped by the shop at about 2:30. Three o'clock arrived, but no boy; 3:05, but still no boy. At 3:06 the boy rushed in. "Ah, ha!" shouted the boss, outraged. "Bankers' hours, huh?"

4

The big boss had died, and on the day of his burial one of his clerks was seen dashing madly down the street. "What the heck's the big hurry?" inquired a friend who saw him. "Your office is closed today, isn't it?" "I know," replied the clerk hastily; "but I'm going to my boss's funeral, and there's nothing he hates more than tardiness."

PUNISHMENT

1

"What's wrong, son?" asked mother anxiously as little Willie came home weeping. "Teacher hit me for bein' bad in school," sobbed the boy. "The idea!" cried mother indignantly, and sat down and penned teacher the following note: "Dear Teacher, You must not strike Willie in school as he is a delicate child and not used to it. At home we never hit him, except in self-defense."

2

The professor was trying to illustrate the different degrees of punishment. "Now, if I were whipped," he questioned, "what would that be?" About half the class responded in unison, "That would be corporal punishment." "And if I were beheaded?" continued the professor. This time the entire class joined in an enthusiastic roar, "Oh, that would be capital."

3

A farmer had been called up for jury duty and was being examined. "Do you believe in capital punishment?" asked the prosecutor. The farmer scratched his head and stroked his beard, and finally stammered, "Well, ah, yes, sir, er, I guess so; that is, if it ain't too severe."

4

The doting mother was enrolling her little boy in school. She was giving the teacher a long list of directions as to how to treat her darling. "And I want you to remember that my Percy is much too delicate for physical punishment," she instructed. "If he should misbehave, just slap the boy next to him soundly —that will frighten Percy."

5

A woman suing for divorce was telling her side of it. "This man is a brute, judge," she insisted. "He wants to keep some of his pay, smokes two cigars a day, takes a drink on Saturday, stays out late on his birthday, reads the paper when I'm talking to him, and is unkind to my relatives." "Then, you want this man punished?" asked the judge. "I most certainly do," declared the woman. "Very well," agreed the judge. "I won't divorce you from him."

6

A small boy dashed madly around a corner and collided with an elderly gentleman. "Sorry, sir," the boy gasped, "but I gotta get home so's my mom can spank me." "Bless me," cried the old man, "I've never seen a boy hurrying to get spanked before." "But I gotta hurry," explained the lad, " 'cause if I don't get home before six o'clock my pop'll be there to do it."

7

A man had a dog that was very vicious. One day, after an especially evil act, the man decided to kill the animal. So he took a club and killed the dog with a blow on the head, but he then continued to beat it. "No need to strike any more," protested a friend; "the dog's dead." "I know," replied the other, "but I believe in punishment after death."

8

"This is the fifth time this week I've had to punish you, Donald," said teacher wearily. "Don't you wonder why?" "Heck, no," replied Donald. "I just figure that you've got the habit, that's all."

See also America[1], artist[2], expert[1], goldfish[1], homework[2], injustice, lying[2], murder.

PURE

See innocence, modesty[1], virtue[4].

PURPOSE

The miserly rich man stepped into the village drug store. "I want to get a quarter's worth of arsenic," he said. "That's a poison, sir," explained the clerk politely. "What do you want it for?" "About fifteen cents," was the prompt reply.

See also truck-driver[1].

PUZZLE

1

"Can any one name an animal," asked the life of the party, "with legs that cannot walk, eyes that cannot see, and that can jump as high as the Empire State Building?" After much guessing, all gave up. "It's a wooden horse," explained the bright boy. "Its eyes don't see and its legs don't walk." "But it certainly can't jump as high as the Empire State Building," objected some one. "Of course it can," was the reply. "That building can't jump either."

2

Two drunks were wending their way homeward after a big evening. "Shay, Bill," asked one, "wha'sh it tha's got a purple body, pink horns, a long pointed green tail, carries a pitchfork, an's got shmoke comin' out its nose?" "Give up. Don' know," replied the other drunk. "Neither do I," whispered the first confidentially, "but it's been followin' us for th' lasht three blocks."

3

"That's a good one!" roared Black, slapping his knee as his friend explained the conundrum. "Wait till I tell the wife!" He rushed home and burst into the kitchen. "Say, dear," he began, "do you know why I'm like a mule?" "Well, no," she replied thoughtfully. "I know that you *are,* but I can't say that I know *why.*"

See also volcano[2].

QUARREL

1

Two truck drivers locked bumpers at a busy intersection and both got off their trucks. "Yuh big, lousy ape!" yelled one angrily. "Are dem dopey eyes too bleary to see where you're goin', or is dose clodhopper feet too big to git 'em on de brakes?" "Aw, shucks, bud," replied the other, smiling sweetly, "you're cute, too."

2

The young married couple were having their first quarrel. "Oh, I wish I were dead!" cried the wife despondently. "And I wish I were dead, too," echoed the husband glumly. "Oh, well," put in the wife quickly, "in that case I don't wish I were." And the squabble got off to a new start.

3

"My wife is the darnedest woman," complained a man at the club. "As soon as we start quarreling she always becomes historical." "No, no," corrected a listener, "you mean hysterical." "No, I don't. I mean historical," insisted the first. "She always goes into the past."

4

"Why did you leave your last position?" inquired the lady of the handy man who had applied for some work. "Well, mum," was the answer, "it was just that I couldn't stand the way me boss and his wife wuz always a-quarrelin'." "I can imagine that was very disagreeable," sympathized the lady. "It sure was, mum, an' they wuz always at it," said the man. "When it wuzn't him an' me, it wuz me an' her."

5

The lady had been away on an extended trip, and when she returned she inquired of her charwoman, "Mandy, do you and your husband still have those terrible quarrels?" "No'm, not no more," she was told. "We ain't quarreled for two months, ma'am." "That's fine," approved the lady warmly. "And how did you come to stop quarreling?" "Couldn't help it, ma'am," replied Mandy. "He ups an' died."

6

The old minister had been talking

eloquently of the beauties of perfect love and understanding in marriage, and many eyes in the congregation were moist. "I know," he concluded, "that you've all heard of the man and wife who traveled side by side through fifty troublous years of marriage without a cross word or a difference. How do you account for this?" After an impressive pause, he lowered his voice to a confidential tone and said, "They were simply lying about it."

7

"When my husband and I patched up our first quarrel," related a lady at the sewing circle, "we planted a tree in the yard in memory of it and as a reminder to be more tolerant." "That's an excellent idea that we might all well follow," exclaimed one of the others. "I don't like the idea," objected a third. "I'd be afraid coming home late at night if I had to go through a forest."

See also boat[3], dictionary, friendship[1], lady[5], mother-in-law[2], selfish[2], separation[1, 4].

QUESTION

1

Two travelers from the West had a wager about the alleged peculiarity of New Englanders in always answering one question with another. To prove his point, the one who insisted they did said to a native, "I want you to give me a straight answer to a plain question." "All right, mister," agreed the Yankee. "Then why is it," asked the better, "that New Englanders always answer a question by asking one?" "Do they?" was the calm reply.

2

"I've never seen such a boy for asking questions!" cried father impatiently to his young son. "I wonder what would have happened if I had asked as many questions when I was a boy." "Maybe," suggested the lad, "you'd be able to answer some of mine now."

3

During an examination, the professor paused by a student who was puzzling over one of the questions. "Does this question trouble you?" he inquired kindly. "Not at all," replied the student. "The question is quite clear—it's the answer that bothers me!"

4

The speaker had gone on and on, and the speech was dull and tiresome. At last he said, "Whenever I reach this point in a discussion, my friends, I ask myself some questions." "If you do," cried a voice from the audience, "you must get some damned long and stupid answers!"

5

A man leaped into the first taxi at hand, then discovered it was being driven by a woman. "Well, how do you like this job?" he ventured conversationally. "Fine," was the answer. "Do men get fresh with you?" was his next question. "Not so far," answered the girl. "What questions do passengers usually ask you?" was his third, and he was told, "'How do you like this job?' 'Do men get fresh with you?' and 'What questions do passengers usually ask you?'"

6

A group of men, whiling away a

dull evening, decided on a game in which any one who asked a question that he could not himself answer would have to forfeit a dollar. The first man asked, "Why doesn't a ground squirrel leave any dirt at the top of his hole when he digs it?" After many guesses, the group called upon him to answer his own question. "He starts at the bottom," was his explanation. "But how does he get to the bottom?" asked another. "Ah, that's *your* question," he was told.

See also examination[4], fool[4], statesman[1].

QUIET

See silence.

RADIO

1

A thunderstorm was raging. The young parents thought their small son would be frightened, so they tiptoed into the nursery. The boy was a little restless in his bed, and opened his eyes for a moment, looked at his mother sleepily and asked, "What's daddy doin' with the radio now, mom?" and went back to sleep.

2

Little Betty was a radio fan and rarely missed anything that came over the air. One night as she concluded her prayers and was about to rise, a thought struck her and she lingered on her knees long enough to announce, "Listen in tomorrow night at the same time, God, for another prayer."

3

A small radio station opened its early morning program with a 15-minute religious transcription that started with a brief prayer. It was the custom of the announcer to put this record on and then dash out for his morning coffee. One morning he returned to find the phone ringing madly and one woman declared, "It's blasphemous!" Another said, "I've reported this to the police!" The bewildered announcer made a quick check-up and found that the transcription had stuck and had for 10 minutes been repeating the close of the prayer— ". . . for Christ's sake, Amen."

4

"Maybe I'm stupid," said a woman in tones that lacked conviction, "but I sure can't understand how the radio works." "Why, there's nothing to it," explained another. "It works just like the telephone, only they use the air instead of wires." "Oh, I know that," declared the first, "but how do they fasten the air to the poles?"

See also grace[1], music[3], pain[1], simple.

RAILROAD

1

"Say, fellow," asked the traveling salesman of the driver of the small town's one and only taxi, "why in heck did they put the station so far from the town?" "Kain't say fer sure, stranger," was the reply, "but I kinder expect 'twuz becuz they wanted to hev the station close as they could to th' railroad."

2

"Here's something odd," remarked Brown, looking up from his paper. "It's about a fellow who's been employed in this country for over eight years and can't speak a word of English." "Why, that's not possible!" objected Black. "What does he work at?" "He's a train announcer at the Union Station," was the answer.

3

A railroad had just been laid through a backwoods section, and as the first train was being taken over the line it overtook a boy on a horse. The engineer whistled and the boy whipped up his horse but stayed on the track. The train was finally forced to creep along at the horse's heels. "You durned fool," shouted the engineer, "why don't you git offen the track?" "No, sirree!" yelled the boy. "Ye'd ketch me in a jiffy on thet-thar plowed ground."

4

The roadbed of a little jerk-water line was very rough. The passengers on the train were thrown about so much that they found conversation impossible. At last they struck a stretch where they could keep their seats and be heard. "The going's a little smoother here," yelled one. "Yes, it is," agreed another. "Guess the old thing's off the track."

5

A reporter who was first to reach the scene of a train wreck rushed up to a badly bruised and battered man lying in the ditch and asked, "How many were hurt?" "Haven't heard of any one getting hurt," grunted the man, rising painfully. "What caused the wreck?" the reporter next asked. "Wreck? Haven't heard of any wreck," insisted the other. "You haven't!" cried the amazed reporter. "Say, who are you?" "Oh, I'm the claim agent for this line," was the response.

See also excuse[3], speed[1], timetable, witness[3].

RAIN

1

"Let's see," said the weatherman to his assistant, "you'd better put down rain as positive for this afternoon." "But what makes you so certain?" asked the assistant, looking at the blue sky. "It's a cinch," replied the weatherman. "I've a date for golf, I've lost my umbrella, my kids are going on a picnic, and the wife is giving a lawn party."

2

"Can you tell me, Jones," asked the physics professor, "if rain after it falls ever rises again?" "Well, er, ah, yes, sir," stammered Jones uncertainly. "When?" was the professor's next question. "Well, ah, sir," Jones tried again, "in due time—" "That's fine, Jones," congratulated the prof. "You may sit down."

3

A traveler reached a strange city in the midst of a heavy downpour and made his way hastily to the hotel. After several days had passed and the rain showed no signs of slackening, he went out to purchase an umbrella. "Quite a rain," he observed to the clerk. "Been raining here long?" "Can't say for certain, sir," replied the clerk disgustedly. "You see, I've only lived here a year."

See also clouds, dating[1], drought[1], lecture[5], news[1].

RAT

"I'm being bothered something terrible with rats," remarked the boarding-house landlady to her neighbor. "Why don't you buy some rat biscuits for them?" suggested the other. "What kind of place do you think I run—the Waldorf?" cried the landlady indignantly. "If the beasts can't eat what the rest of the boarders do, they can go hungry!"

RAZOR

1

"How is the razor, sir, does it hurt?" inquired the barber of his squirming customer. "I can't answer for the razor," replied the victim, "but my face sure does."

2

The language issuing from the bathroom was explicit and forceful if not genteel. "What's wrong, William?" called wifey sweetly. "It's this double-dashed razor!" roared William. "It doesn't cut at all." "Oh, don't be silly," answered wifey. "Your beard can't be tougher than linoleum."

3

"Did it annoy you that I sharpened a pencil with your razor, dear?" asked the pretty young wife. "Only twice, darling," replied the doting husband patiently. "But you've only tried to shave with it once since, my sweet," she pointed out. "I know, my pet," he agreed. "But later I tried to write with the pencil."

See also barber, shaving.

READING

1

A bunch of the boys were having a party in a hotel room and they created such a disturbance that the bellboy was sent to quiet them. "I'm sorry, gentlemen, but you'll have to make less noise," he informed them. "The man in the next room says he can't read." "You tell him he oughtta be 'shamed o' himself," cried one of the boys. "Why, I could read 'fore I was six!"

2

A benevolent old lady was concerned because one of the villagers couldn't read or write. So she persuaded the schoolmaster to coach him in the evenings. Meeting the old fellow a few months later, she remarked, "Well, Sam, I suppose you can read the Bible fairly well now?" "Lord, ma'am," he replied scornfully, "I bin outta the Bible an' into the sports page for over a week!"

3

The man who was having his eyes examined by an oculist inquired anxiously, "Say, doc, will I be able to read after I get my glasses?" "You most certainly will," the doctor assured him. "Gosh, that's swell, doc!" cried the patient. "I never could before."

4

The lady waited impatiently for a few moments, but when the elevator boy showed no signs of putting down his book, she exclaimed, "I say, my boy, how often does this elevator go up?" Without lifting his nose from the volume, the boy answered calmly, "It goes up at the end of each chapter, lady."

5

It was the reading lesson, and the passage little Billy had to read contained the word "barque." When the boy reached this he stumbled over it, saying, "B-b-ba, b-b-bar—" "Barque," the teacher prompted. Billy looked more confused than ever, and the teacher repeated, more sharply, "Barque, *barque!*" Poor Billy shrugged his shoulders helplessly and gave vent to a lusty, "Bow-wow-wow!"

6

The caller glanced at the scattered heap of books and magazines on the floor and observed to the maid, "Mr. Williams must be quite literary." "Yes'm, he sure is literary, that man," agreed the maid heartily. "He jest litters that stuff all over th' house all th' time."

See also eyes[1], magazine[2], study[2].

READY

See preparation.

REAL

It had been a big night in the saloon down at Snaky Gulch. When old Cactus Gus opened his bleary eyes the next morning in his shack he was startled to see a huge, hideous ape perched on the foot of his bunk looking at him owlishly. Slowly reaching for his .45, Gus took careful if wavering aim. "If yore a real monkey," he remarked grimly, "yore in a damned bad fix. But if you ain't—*I* am!"

See also diamond.

REAL ESTATE

1

An eloquent real-estate salesman was trying to sell an Eastern prospect some property in west Texas. "Why, all that country needs to become the garden spot of the world," he declared enthusiastically, "is good people and water." "Humph!" grunted the prospect skeptically. "That's all Hell needs."

2

"Goodness, Henry," cried the bride as she looked at the desolate country surrounding their new home, "whatever induced you to buy a house in this God-forsaken region?" "One of the best men in the business," murmured Henry sheepishly.

See also advertising[4], house[2], tenant[1].

REALISM

1

"Speaking of realism," said a critic to his wife, "I once heard of an artist who painted a cobweb in the corner of a ceiling so realistically that the maid spent an hour trying to get it down." "That I doubt," declared the wife skeptically. "But why, dear?" asked the critic. "Artists have been known to do such things." "Certainly they have," agreed the woman; "but not maids."

2

"I must see that new play," declared the young lady. "They say it's very realistic." "Nonsense! It's far from realistic," said the man scornfully. "Why, the first act is set in the living room of a young married couple; and the second act, which is supposed to be a year later, shows this same room with the furniture arranged in exactly the same way!"

3

The man was consulting an artist before giving him a commission. "And are you certain that you can get a good likeness in my wife's portrait?" he questioned. "Absolutely, sir," asserted the artist. "I can make it so lifelike that you'll jump every time you see it."

4

The artist had just completed "The Oaks at Daybreak," a picture of a millionaire client's mansion at dawn, and was showing it to the man. "It's very good," decided the client critically, "except for one important detail." "And what's that?" asked the artist anxiously. "To be complete," said the rich man, "it should show my son trying to get his key into the front door."

5

The businessman was busy when an old friend sent in his card. Much as he regretted it, he couldn't spare the time to see him. "Look here," he instructed the office boy, "I simply can't see this man, but I don't want to offend him, so you'll have to tell him I'm out. Now try your best to convince him I'm really out." "Yes, sir," replied the boy; "but don't you think it might be more convincing if I went out smoking one of your best cigars?"

6

A young reporter was sent to write up a charity ball, but his copy was turned in late and it was sloppily written. "You young idiot!" cried the editor, looking it over. "You say here, 'Among the most beautiful girls was Alderman Smith.' You half-wit! Smith's no girl! He was one of the sponsors of the ball." "I can't help it," insisted the reporter stubbornly, "that's where he was."

See also son[3].

REASON

1

Teacher was trying to drive home the lesson of foresight and preparedness. "Now, Robert," she asked, "can you tell me why your father takes out the screens every fall and puts the storm sash in their place?" "Sure," answered the boy. "It's just because mom keeps after him and nags him until he does it."

2

The principal of the school was checking on the progress of the students in one room. Wishing to test their powers of observation and deduction, he asked, "Tell me, children, what kind of arm does the blacksmith have?" "Big and strong," chorused the class. "Fine," beamed the principal. "And why is his arm bigger and stronger than mine?" "Because he works," they all shouted.

3

The young suitor had just asked the girl's father for her hand. "Ahem!" said the old man. "And what's your reason for wishing to marry my daughter?" "I have no reason, sir," replied the boy. "I'm in love with her."

See also college[2].

REASSURANCE

1

The timid lady passenger approached the captain of the ship and anxiously inquired, "What would happen, Captain, if the ship should strike an iceberg?" "The iceberg, madam, would go on just as if nothing had happened," replied the captain. "Oh, thank you," replied the lady; "that's a big load off my mind."

2

A tourist who was traveling through the West with his wife underwent a series of annoying mishaps along the way. His wife noticed that after every breakdown he carefully examined his driver's license before going on. "Why do you keep looking at your license?" she asked him finally. "For reassurance, my dear," he explained. "It states on my license that I am competent to operate an automobile."

RECOGNIZE

1

A seriously-ill man had been unconscious and delirious, and by his bed anxiously stood his wife, his doctor, and his lawyer. Suddenly the patient began to shout wildly, "Get out of here you evil ones, you cruel enemies! Get out you frauds, you liars, you fourflushers! Get out, go away . . ." "Ah, that's better. It looks like he's coming to," the doctor comforted the wife. "He's beginning to recognize us."

2

Two tourists were visiting Washington and they decided to visit Congress while it was in session. Seating themselves in the gallery, they looked over the Representatives in hope of seeing the Congressman from their district. "It's no use," said one at last, "I can't distinguish him." "Small wonder," retorted the other quickly; "he can't even distinguish himself."

See also cosmetics[4].

RECORD

The college athletic star called on his girl the day after the track meet, which she had attended. She was lyrical in her praise of his skill. "My, didn't they cheer when you broke that record!" she cried ecstatically. "Humph!" said little brother, "pop didn't cheer when I broke one last week. He licked me."

See also aviator[1], temperature[2].

RECOVERY

1

"I'm feeling well again, doctor," said the patient, "and I'd like to have your bill." "Don't be hasty, sir," cautioned the doctor. "Be calm and take good care of yourself. You're not nearly strong enough yet for anything like that."

2

"How is your husband, Mandy," asked the lady of her charwoman. "Oh, poor Ned's worse, ma'am," was the troubled reply. "But I thought that yesterday the doctor said he was getting better?" objected the lady. "He did, ma'am," confirmed Mandy; "but today he said that poor Ned's done gone and got the convalescence."

3

"Tell me frankly, doctor," asked the sick patient, "just what are my chances of recovery?" "The best in the world! In fact, one hundred per cent!" exclaimed the doctor enthusiastically. "You see, medical statistics show that eleven out of every twelve having your disease die. Well, yours is my twelfth case, and since the other eleven all died, you can't miss!"

4

A submarine had been out on a long stretch of sea duty, but at last it put in at magic Hawaii and the eager crewmen were given shore leave. Later, in the soft tropical night, the commander encountered one of his men and asked, "How you doing, son?" "Oh, fine, sir," replied the man happily, and added, "But ain't it funny, sir, how far behind on women you can get, and how quick you can catch up again?"

5

"You've been a very sick man, sir," said the doctor to his convalescent patient. "In fact, I might safely say that it was only your iron constitution that pulled you through." "That's wonderful," replied the patient, "and I just hope you don't forget that when you get to making out your bill."

6

"Is your wife getting better?" inquired one man of another. "Well, yes and no," was the uncertain response. "What do you mean 'yes and no'?" protested the first. "Either she's getting better or she isn't." "Not necessarily," maintained the other. "She's quite well enough to go shopping, but still much too sick for her household work."

See also lawsuit[1], nurse[3], sick[4].

RECRUIT

1

The rookie had been in the army for about a week and his sergeant asked him, "Well, soldier, what do you think of the army this far?" "Maybe I'll get to like it after awhile," was the reply, "but I kinda feel that there's too much drillin' an' fussin' around between meals."

2

"Do you have any special qualifications?" asked the recruiting sergeant of the man enlisting in the army. "Well, I come from a very old family," boasted the fellow. "I'm descended from Henry Clay on my father's side, and from Peter Stuyvesant on my mother's side, and one aunt was a Vanderbilt, and another—" "Wait a minute," growled the sergeant. "We want you for fighting, not breeding!"

3

A rookie passed a captain but failed to salute him. The officer turned and overtook the rookie, demanding, "Don't you recognize this uniform, soldier?" "Yes, sir," replied the rookie, feeling of the material critically, "that's really a swell uniform. Look at this lousy thing they issued me."

4

A sergeant was drilling a group of rookies, one of whom was consistently out of step. Drawing near to this man as they marched, the sergeant remarked sarcastically,

"Have you noticed that they're all out of step except you?" "Well, you're in charge," retorted the rookie sharply, "you tell 'em."

5

A well-dressed, important-looking young fellow entered a recruiting office and announced that he wished to enlist. "I suppose you'll want a commission?" said the sergeant, looking him over. "No, thanks," replied the applicant. "I'm such a poor shot that I think I'll do better on a straight salary."

See also indifferent.

REDUCING

A pudgy, obviously self-indulgent woman puffed her way into a doctor's office. "I want to reduce, doctor," she wheezed. "What diet do you think best?" "I've experimented with them all, from the 18-Day and the 16 Formula Diets to the Daily Dozen and Two Meals a Day Diets, but for cases like you I've found the 4-Word Diet most effective." "What is the 4-Word Diet?" asked the woman eagerly. "No more, thank you," was the reply.

See also size[1].

REFERENCE

1

"Do you have any references, Maude?" inquired the woman of the applicant for the position of maid. "Yes, mum, here it is," said Maude, showing a letter proudly which stated: "The bearer, Maude Jepson, is leaving after a month in my employ. I am quite satisfied."

2

"You say you've worked as a maid for years," said the lady, frowning, "but yet you have no references. How do you explain that?" "Oh, it's quite natural, mum," replied the prospective maid. "You see, mum, I always kept me positions until all of the family died."

3

A woman who was discharging her cook wrote her the following reference: "Mary Meyer has been in my employ for one month. She is an excellent cook, but I am leaving her go as I can afford her services no longer." In looking this over, the husband remarked, "That last clause is hardly true, dear." "But it is," insisted the wife. "Why, just the dishes she broke cost me over twice her wages."

4

"Why you havin' so much trouble gettin' a new job, Bill?" asked an acquaintance. "I dunno," replied Bill vaguely. "Everything's always all right until they look at the reference me last boss give me, an' then they don't want me." "Is it a bad reference?" he was asked. "Naw, it's a swell one," insisted Bill. "It says that I'm one of the best men the firm had ever turned out."

5

"I suppose you have references?" said the lady to the applicant for the maid's job. "Yes, mum, heaps o' them," was the response. "Then why didn't you bring some with you?" asked the woman. "Because to tell the truth, mum, they're like me photographs," explained the applicant: "none o' them does me justice."

See also plumber[1].

REFORM

1

"I hope, my poor fellow," said the lady visitor to the jail, "that your stay here will give you a chance to consider the error of your ways and make you resolve to correct your faults." "That it has, ma'am," declared the prisoner emphatically. "Believe me, the next job this baby pulls, he wears gloves!"

2

"You say that Betty persuaded you to give up smoking, Bill?" inquired Jim. "That's right," replied Bill. "And then she got you to stop drinking?" Jim went on. "Yep." "And I hear that she even talked you into giving up gambling, dancing, and running around nights?" Jim added. "She sure did," affirmed Bill. "Gosh, then why didn't you marry the girl?" marveled Jim. "Heck!" snorted Bill. "By the time she had me worked over I could do better!"

3

The village ne'er-do-well had eked out a scanty living by petty thievery until he was converted at a camp-meeting. Later, the elder was receiving testimonials from the mourners' bench and he called on his new convert, "Now, Brother, will you tell us what the Lord has done for you?" The ex-thief stumbled to his feet and in a bitter tone mumbled, "I ain't quite sure, but it kinda looks like the Lord done ruint me."

4

A young woman sat before her mirror gazing long and earnestly at her image. She held her head at various angles, twisted her features about, fluffed out and then smoothed down her hair, raised and lowered her eyebrows, etc. At last she turned away despondently. "It's no use," she sighed wearily to herself. "I'll just be some kind of reformer."

REFUSAL

The more that mother tried to persuade Junior to take the medicine the doctor had ordered, the more stubbornly Junior refused. "Oh, dear!" mother finally said tearfully. "My darling boy will surely die!" "Now don't go worrying, mother," comforted the boy gently. "Papa will soon be home and he'll make me take it, you bet."

See also spurned.

REGRET

The hard-working wife was out mowing the lawn in a blazing sun when a passing neighbor paused to inquire, "Well, is your husband still taking things as easy as ever?" "My husband has only two regrets in life," was the weary reply: "one is that he has to wake up to eat, and the other is that he has to stop eating to sleep."

REINCARNATION

"After a day like this," groaned the shopgirl wearily as she returned home from work, "I certainly hope there's something to this reincarnation business." "You do? Why?" asked her sister. "Just so I could come back to earth as a mattress," said the girl. "But why a mattress?" asked the amazed sister. "So I could lie in bed all day," was the answer.

REJUVENATION

1

A rejuvenation operation was being performed on an old man, and as it was nearing its conclusion he became very impatient. "Come, come, don't get restless," cautioned the doctor. But the patient paid no heed and began to moan and sob. "Take it easy and the pain will soon disappear," advised the doctor. "It's not the pain," wailed the old boy. "I'm afraid of being late for school."

2

A despondent-looking elderly woman was walking down the street pushing a baby carriage in which howled a husky infant. "What a darling baby, Mrs. Jones!" exclaimed a friend. "But whose is it? I know you don't have any children." "That's what you think, my dear," replied the other sadly. "This is, or was, my husband. He got to fooling around with a rejuvenation remedy and went too far!"

RELATIVES

1

"It's certainly hard," morosely observed the gentleman with the mourning band, "to lose one's relatives." "What do you mean, hard?" snorted the rich man. "It's impossible!"

2

A worn-looking man sat in his lawyer's office. "So you want a divorce from your wife, do you?" said the lawyer. "What's the matter, aren't your relations pleasant?" "Well, mine are," declared the client, "but hers are positively awful!"

3

"What's the excitement, Jimmy?" inquired the man of the little boy dashing madly up the street. "I'm goin' up to my sister's. She's got twins," announced the boy breathlessly. "One's a boy an' one's a girl, so I'm both a uncle an' a aunt!"

4

Two men had met on the train and got to talking. "Well, well, so you're Sam Balder from Chicago, are you?" exclaimed one. "I once knew a Tom Balder from Chicago. Are you related?" "He's a distant relation," explained Sam. "He was my mother's first child, and I'm her fifteenth."

5

"Too bad you were defeated," a friend consoled the losing candidate after the election. "Oh, I think maybe it's a good thing," declared the loser philosophically. "That's the way to take it!" approved the friend warmly. "Yes," agreed the other. "According to one of my old aunts who keeps track of these things, I have almost five hundred living relatives, and I couldn't possibly have given more than half of them jobs."

RELIGION

1

A New Yorker on a business trip to Salt Lake City was strolling along the streets there and made the acquaintance of a little Mormon girl.

"I've come quite a distance; all the way from New York," he told her. "I don't suppose you know where New York is, do you?" "Oh, but I do!" insisted the girl eagerly. "Our Sunday school has a missionary there."

2

The village religious fanatic one day passed an old farmer on the road and shouted at him, "Brother, have you made your peace with God?" "Huh? What ye say?" asked the farmer, cupping his ear. "I said," he repeated more loudly, "have you made your peace with God?" "Waal," replied the farmer dryly, "we ain't come to no open break yet."

3

One Sunday morning little Janie knocked at the front door of the village store, but got no answer. After several more knocks a window was opened and the storekeeper's little daughter stuck her head out. "It's no use, Janie," said the girl, "because we've all been to meetin' an' got converted. So now when you want milk on Sunday you'll have to come round to the back door."

4

Two brothers ran a coal business in a small town, and one of them attended a revival meeting and got converted. Thereafter he kept urging his brother to do likewise. "Come on, John," he insisted, "why don't you get religion and join a church like I did?" "Look, George," John pointed out, "if you want to join the church it's fine, but if I joined, too, who'd weigh the coal?"

5

A hillbilly came up to a revivalist and informed him that he had "got religion." "That's fine, Brother," approved the preacher, "but are you sure you're going to put aside all sin?" "Yes, sir," he insisted. "I already done that." "And are you going to pay up all your debts?" continued the preacher. "Now wait a minute, Parson," cautioned the other, "you ain't a-talkin' religion now—you're a-talkin' business."

6

An old Fundamentalist minister, who was known for his firm and unalterable faith in hellfire and damnation, was asked his opinion of the Universalists. After making several rather slighting observations on that group, he added, "And they, of course, expect everybody will be saved, whereas we look for better things."

7

A recent convert at a camp meeting was filled with zeal for the good work and was eager to give his service in the cause. He stood up in prayer meeting and declared devoutly, "I am willing and ready to do anything the Lord asks of me—so long, of course, as it's honorable."

See also army[7], convert[2], freedom[1], kill[3].

REMARK

1

After Sam, one of the laborers, had dropped a heavy casting on his foot the foreman was required to fill out a blank for workman's compensation. He filled in all the lines and spaces readily enough until he reached the last, which was headed "Remarks." Greatly puzzled, he took it in to the manager and asked, "What do they want here—Sam's remarks or mine?"

2

After an elaborate introduction from the toastmaster, the speaker of the evening rose pompously to his feet, cleared his throat, and said, "Now, gentlemen, I should like to make a few remarks before I say anything."

REMARRIAGE

1

After much mourning for his wife, a widower decided to marry again. But everything reminded him of his first spouse, and whatever the second wife said or did would be the occasion for an ardent eulogy of the first. Finally, his wife told him with deep feeling, "I certainly sympathize with you, dear, and you may rest assured that no one regrets her loss more than I do."

2

A widow was planning to marry a grass widower and the change in circumstances was a little difficult for her young daughter to grasp. "What I'd like to know, mamma," inquired the child curiously, "is whether you're gonna get this daddy cheaper because he's second hand?"

3

The gay divorcee was chatting with a friend as the train sped along. "You know," she confided, "I've been thinking of getting married again." "What, again!" exclaimed the friend, leaning forward. "Who is it this time?" "I'm not quite sure," was the reply, "but I've been thinking of trying to get back one

of my former husbands. It's such a chore breaking in a new one."

See also collect[1], forgive[2], mourn[1, 4], perfect[3], tombstone[1].

REMEMBER

See memory.

REMIND

1

"Don't you remember, dear," prompted the absent-minded professor's wife gently, "that it was just twenty-five years ago today that we became engaged?" "Bless me, is that a fact?" exclaimed the professor in amazement. "Well, well, twenty-five years! You should have reminded me sooner, dear. It's high time we got married."

2

The absent-minded professor one evening dropped in on his doctor, who was also an old friend. The two got to chatting so amiably that, before they noticed, a couple of hours had slipped by. As the professor rose to go, the doctor inquired, "Family's all well, I suppose?" "Good Lord! That reminds me," gasped the professor. "My wife's having a fit!"

3

"Do you know," murmured the coed softly to the fraternity boy, "that every time I look at you I'm reminded of a famous man?" "Aw, you're just saying that," said the fellow coyly. "Who was he?" "Darwin," was the reply.

4

Little Ronnie, a minister's son,

was afraid of thunder. One afternoon it looked like a thunderstorm was on its way. His father saw him running desperately for home and noticed that his lips were moving as he ran. "What were you saying while you were running, Ronnie?" asked father after the boy had reached the house. "Oh," replied Ronnie, shivering, "I was just remindin' God that I'm a minister's son."

REMORSE

See repent.

RENT

1

"I'm sorry," said the roomer to the landlady when she came around for the rent, "but I'm afraid I can't pay this month." "That's what you said last month," answered the landlady. "Well, see there," replied the roomer, "I keep my word, don't I?"

2

The man looked disdainfully at the dingy room in which his friend lived. "Why don't you move to more comfortable, pleasant quarters, Bill?" he asked. "Say, I can't even pay the rent on this lousy dump," exclaimed Bill. "All the more reason, then," insisted the other. "As long as you're not going to pay the rent anyway, why not get the best?"

See also artist[1], compromise[1].

REPAIR

A millionaire with an imported automobile was touring and his car broke down in a backwoods section. The village jack-of-all-trades was recommended to him for repairs, but the rich man was a little dubious. "Do you think you can fix it?" he asked the repairman. "Well, a man made it," was the brief reply.

REPAY

1

"Please, Your Honor, I'd like to be excused from duty," pleaded an anxious-looking juryman. "You see, there's a man to whom I owe twenty dollars and he's leaving in a few hours for a post abroad. He'll be there for years and I want to catch him before he leaves as it may be my last chance to repay him." "You're excused," stated the judge coldly. "We don't want anyone on the jury who can lie like that."

2

"Now, let's see," said the ever-needy one as he stopped an acquaintance, "do I owe you anything?" "Not a cent, sir," was the cordial response. "What're you doing, going around settling up all your little debts?" "Oh, no," answered the dead-beat. "I'm just checking up to see if I've missed anybody. How about letting me have five until Friday?"

3

"George, dear," said wifey sweetly, "when are you going to pay back that dollar you borrowed from me last week?" "But, Helen," protested George, "I've already paid that back to you three times! Surely, you can't expect me to pay it again!" "Oh, very well," replied Helen contemptuously, "just let it go if you're going to be that mean about it!"

4

Two friends were sitting together

in a train when suddenly it was halted and several holdup men entered. They started through, taking the money and valuables of the passengers as they went. One of the friends grew increasingly nervous and when the robbers were only a few seats away he quickly pulled a bill from his pocket and gave it to his friend, saying, "Here, Jack, is that ten I owe you."

5

A young cashier had embezzled a large sum from the firm and lost it all gambling. The boss, being a kind-hearted man, didn't want him arrested, but was uncertain what to do. "I'd keep him on the job," advised a friend, "and deduct what he owes you from his salary." "But the amount is large and his pay is small," answered the boss. "He could never make it up." The friend thought a moment, then said, "How about increasing his salary?"

See also borrow[2].

REPEAT

A new father phoned the local newspaper proudly to report the birth of twins. As there was considerable noise in the newspaper office, the girl on the phone was forced to ask, "Will you repeat that, please?" "Not if I can help it," came the grim response.

REPENT

1

Two shipwrecked men had been drifting in mid-ocean on a raft for many days and things looked very bad for them. At last, one of them became frightened and began to pray, "O, Lord! I've been a miserable sinner all my life. I've been a hard drinker, a cheating gambler, and a louse with women, but if You spare me I promise never to—" "Hey, wait, Bill," cautioned the other. "Don't go too far. I think I see smoke from a ship."

2

A man had had his house broken into and a sum of money taken, but the thief had never been caught. A few years later he received a letter containing a five-dollar bill and the following note: "Dere Ser, Sum yeres ago I stold sum muny frum you. Remorse is gnawin at me so I send you sum bak. If it gnaws me agin, I'll send sum more."

See also reform[1].

REPLACE

1

A motorist, in going down a country road, accidentally killed a pig. No sooner had he stopped than an angry farmer came running up. "Don't get excited," said the motorist, "I'll replace your pig." "Ye cain't," growled the farmer; "ye ain't near fat enough."

2

An officer of the governor's staff had died. Immediately, a number of men who wanted his job began to show an indecent impatience. While the colonel was still awaiting burial, one of the bolder men managed to buttonhole the governor and ask, "Have you any objection to my taking the colonel's place?" "I'd be happy to have you do so," replied the governor, "if you can arrange it with the undertaker."

REPLY

See answer.

REPORTER

1

The editor called the new reporter into his office one morning. "I've an assignment for you, Mr. Williams," he said. "Are you married?" "No, sir," was the answer. "I thought not," returned the editor. "Well, go out and get married at once, and let me have three columns for the afternoon edition on how to manage a wife to achieve domestic bliss."

2

The reporter was picking his way through the train wreck and came across a badly injured passenger. "I can't last much longer," announced the victim weakly. "Aw, cheer up, my brave man!" encouraged the reporter. "Now, how do you spell your name, and do you happen to have one of your pictures on you?"

See also brief[1, 3], funeral[2], opposite[3], realism[6].

REPUBLICANS

1

A Republican canvasser was trying to persuade a voter to support his party. "I'm sorry," said the voter, "but my father was a Democrat and his father before him, so I won't vote anything but the Democratic ticket." "That's a poor argument," said the canvasser. "Suppose your father and grandfather had been horse thieves—would that make you a horse thief?" "No,"

was the reply, "that would make me a Republican."

2

A young lawyer from the North decided to set up a practice in a Southern state. So he wrote to a friend there asking him what the chances would be for "an honest young lawyer and Republican." In answer the friend wrote: "If you are an honest lawyer, you will have absolutely no competition here. As for being a Republican, the game laws will protect you."

3

During a Democratic convention in Baltimore a banquet had been given. The morning after the function a well-known Republican met one of the Democrats and said, "I understand there were some Republicans at your banquet last night." "Yes, there were," replied the Democrat amiably. "One waited on me."

4

The football team from North Carolina was not so good that year and they were about to play the Harvard team. The coach was desperate, but suddenly an idea struck him. "Now, boys," he pleaded just before his team went out, "I want you all to get out there and fight for good old N. C.—and don't forget that every man on that Harvard team is a Republican."

REPUTATION

A big businessman fell hopelessly in love with an actress and decided to marry her. To safeguard himself against the possibility of scandal attaching to his reputation, he hired a private detective to investigate her past. When the report came in it read: "The lady is of excellent reputation; her past is without blemish; her friends are all most worthy. Only one breath of scandal has touched her, and this is that of late she has been seen a great deal in the company of a businessman of doubtful repute."

RESCUE

1

The ragged man had a desperate gleam in his eye as he said to the prosperous-looking lady. "Unless I get a little help, madam, I'm afraid that I'll have to resort to something that horrifies me to think about." The lady shuddered and quickly handed over a five-dollar bill. "Tell me, my poor fellow," she asked, "from what terrible fate have I saved you?" "Work, madam," was the reply.

2

A boat, containing two men, overturned some distance from shore. One man immediately started swimming for shore, but the other floundered helplessly in the water. As soon as the first had reached shore, he turned and dashed madly back into the water. "Hey, what's the idea?" cried a spectator. "I'm going back to save Bill," shouted the swimmer. "I had to save myself first, you know."

See also danger[1], drowning[1].

RESEMBLANCE

1

A girl was dancing with a young man to whom she had just been introduced. By way of making conversation she remarked to him, "Goodness, I wonder who that ugly man is over there?" The other looked, then replied, "That's my brother." "Oh, I'm so sorry!" cried the girl in embarrassment. "I really hadn't noticed the resemblance."

2

"It looks like rain, doesn't it?" remarked the landlady conversationally as she passed a bowl of soup to one of her boarders. "Yes, it does," agreed the boarder, sniffing critically at the bowl, "but it smells just a wee bit like soup."

3

"The truth of the matter is," declared the defendant's lawyer sarcastically to the plaintiff, "that you were so frightened at the time that you didn't know whether it was an automobile or something resembling an automobile that hit you." "Well, I'll say it sure resembled one," maintained the plaintiff. "In fact, I was forcibly struck by the resemblance."

RESOURCEFUL

"The most resourceful and adaptable man I've ever known," remarked a fellow, "was a piano-tuner I once met in a wild and unsettled section of the West. 'Surely you can't make much of a living at piano-tuning out here,' I said to him, 'for there are very few pianos in this forsaken region.' 'That's true,' the fellow replied, 'but I make a nice income tightening up barbed-wire fences.'"

REST

1

Teacher was trying to illustrate the meaning of the word "recuperate." "Now, Billy," she said, "when your father comes home from work in the evening he's tired and worn out, isn't he?" "Yes'm," replied Billy. "Then when evening comes and his work is through," continued teacher, "what does he do at night?" "That's just what mom always wants to know," said Billy.

2

"Oh, my dear," gushed the lady parishioner to the minister's wife, "didn't you think your husband's sermon on the Sabbath, 'One Day's Rest in Seven,' was simply inspired?" "I can't say because I didn't hear it," replied the preacher's spouse. "I had to get his dinner."

See also cashier[3], eyes[1].

RESTAURANT

1

A man rushed into a quick-service restaurant and said, "Gimme a cheese sandwich, please." "Yes, sir," said the counter-man, reaching for one. "Will you eat it or take it with you?" "Both," replied the customer impatiently.

2

The manager of the restaurant called his waitresses together. "Now, girls," he instructed them, "I want you all to look your very best today. Put on a little extra make-up and fix your hair becomingly." "What's up?" asked one of the waitresses. "Some big shot coming in?" "No, not that," explained the manager. "The beef's tough."

3

A doctor was called to a small town on a case, and missed his return train. He was forced to put up at the town's one hotel. Next morning at breakfast a sallow, anemic waitress approached him and announced in a colorless voice, "Boiled tongue, stewed kidneys, fried liver." "The devil with your symptoms!" cried the doctor. "Bring me something to eat!"

4

"This inn looks old enough to go back to Revolutionary times," remarked a tourist in the dining room of a New England hotel. "It is very old, sir," replied the proprietor. "Would you care to hear some of the stories connected with it?" "Indeed, yes," replied the tourist. "You might start with the legend I'm sure must be connected with that curious old pie the waiter just carried in."

5

"Let's see," said the customer, looking over the menu, "guess I'll have some chicken salad." "Yes, sir," replied the waitress. "Will you have the 35-cent or the 50-cent salad?" "What's the difference?" inquired the diner. "Well," explained the waitress, "the 35-cent salad is made of rabbit, and the 50-cent one is made of tuna."

6

A motorist entered a little all-night restaurant late one night and ordered a cup of coffee. "Without cream," he added, after the waitress had taken his order. In a short while the waitress was back smiling apologetically. "I'm sorry, sir, but we're out of cream," she said. "Do you mind taking it without milk?"

7

"Hey, what does this mean?" cried

a diner in a cheap eatery. "There's a cockroach in the bottom of my teacup!" "How should I know, bud," growled the waiter. "If youse wantcher fortune told, go see a Gypsy!"

8

"What a dump!" complained a truck-driver to his companion at a lunchroom. "This butter's strong enough to walk across the table and say howdy to the coffee." "Well, if it did," responded the other, "the coffee's too weak to answer."

9

When the waiter served the steak he'd ordered, the customer eyed it critically and then inquired, "Is this all I get?" "You got no kick. That's a pretty good piece," insisted the waiter. "Humph!" snorted the diner. "I usually leave more than that."

10

The diner, who was waiting for his food, called the restaurant manager. "How long has this place been open?" he inquired. "Almost three months," replied the manager. "I should have come here then," growled the customer. "They might be about ready to serve me by now."

See also coffee[3, 4], complaint[1, 2], customer[1], delay[1], egg[5], fish[1], honeymoon[4], impudence, manners[3], menu[1, 2], misfortune[2], sandwich[2], soup[1], steak[1], waiting[1, 2], waitress[3].

REVENGE

1

"Just wait until I'm a man," sobbed little Timmie after a stormy session with father; "I'll get even!" "What'll you do, son?" asked

mother. "I'll name my boy after papa," declared the lad, "and man! how I'll spank him!"

2

The druggist came into his back room and started dancing around gleefully. "What's the matter, are you drunk?" asked the clerk. "Nothing like that," said the druggist. "But do you remember when all my water pipes froze in the middle of last winter?" "Sure," replied the clerk, "but what does—" "Well," interrupted the druggist, "the plumber who fixed them has just come in to have a prescription filled."

3

The manager of a new resort hotel was a former army captain. "All of our help," he was explaining to a visitor, "are former servicemen. The chef was a mess-sergeant, the house doctor was a medical officer, the waiters were all non-coms, the house detective was in intelligence, and so on." "Don't you have any former M.P.'s?" asked the man. "Oh, yes," was the joyous reply. "We put them to cleaning the windows on the outside on the tenth floor when there's a good stiff wind!"

See also bootblack[2], handkerchief[2], neighbor[1], train[7], will[1].

REVERSE

See opposite.

REWARD

1

A young man happened to be nearby when the millionaire's daughter's boat upset and he saved the girl from drowning. The father was very grateful and despite the boy's protests insisted upon rewarding him in some manner. "Well, if you insist," the fellow said, "just give me a golf club." A week later he received a wire: "Have bought you the Eastshire Golf Club and am now negotiating for the Shadybrook Links."

2

"Now, if you expect to get any of the things you want, son," warned mother, "you'll have to be a good boy." The child considered this for a few moments, then inquired, "If I'm a *real* good boy, mamma, an' die an' go to heaven, will God give me a nice wittle devil to play wif?"

See also head[2], navy[1], prize[1], worm[2].

RICH

After much persistence, the caller managed to get into the boss's office. "I'm a very busy man," declared the boss impatiently. "What's your proposition?" "I'm about to offer you something, sir, that will make you a rich man," announced the visitor impressively. "Well, leave your scheme here and I'll look it over later," said the boss, turning back to his desk. "Right now I'm working on a deal that I expect to make me eight dollars in real money."

See also idle, thrift[1].

RIGHT

1

"Now, Willie," said teacher, "if coal is selling at $7 a ton and you pay the dealer $35, how much coal will he bring you?" "Just barely four tons, ma'am," responded Willie without hesitation. "But, Willie, that isn't right," objected teacher. "I know it isn't," agreed the boy; "but they all do it."

2

"I don't want to tell you your business, doctor," said the patient, "but all the other doctors differ from you in their diagnosis of my case." "I know they do," replied the doctor cheerily, "but just wait, the post-mortem will prove I'm right."

See also dancing[4].

RING

1

A young man entered a jeweler's and handed him a ring with the shy request, "I'd like some names engraved on this ring, please." "What names?" asked the jeweler. "From Fred to Jane," replied the boy. The jeweler smiled. "Take my advice, son," he suggested in a kindly tone, "and have it engraved simply, 'From Fred.'"

2

The boy took his fiancee's hand and gazed proudly at the ring he had placed there a few days before. "Did all your girlfriends admire it?" he asked fondly. "They did better than that," she responded. "Three of them recognized it."

3

The engagement had been short and it ended in a bitter quarrel. "Very well," he said icily, "since you've decided you don't want to marry me after all, perhaps you'll be good enough to return my ring." "I'd be glad to," replied the girl, "but your jeweler has already called for it."

See also engagement[3].

RIVER

1

The hired girl had been sent down to the river to fetch a pail of water. But when she got to the bank she stood there lost in thought. "What is that girl doing?" asked her mistress impatiently, watching from the porch. "I couldn't say," replied the husband, "unless maybe she hasn't seen a pailful she likes yet."

2

There had been a dry spell and the river was low, and a Missouri river steamboat laboring upstream had become lodged on a sandbar. While the engines were puffing and snorting to back the boat off into deep water, a woodsman came to the bank and dipped up a bucket of water. The captain of the boat glared angrily at him. "Hey, you!" he shouted indignantly, "Put that back!"

See also depth[2].

ROAD

1

A foreigner had traveled across country to California by automobile and was much pleased by the trip. "How were the roads, John?" inquired an acquaintance after he had arrived. "Vell, zat guy Lincoln vas ze vunderful engineer," replied the traveler, "but zat Frenchman De Tour—phooey! vot a punk road-builder he vas!"

"How are the roads in this part of the county?" inquired a tourist of a farmer. "Just fine," replied the farmer. "We've done away with all the bad roads around here." "Golly, that must have been a big job," marveled the tourist. "Not at all," explained the farmer. "Wherever the going's 'specially bad we jest don't call it a 'road'—we call it a 'detour.'"

3

The farther they went the rougher the going became until the jolting became so severe that the occupants were almost thrown from the car. At last, the passenger in back leaned forward to inquire of the driver, "Are you sure we've taken the best road?" "I'm sure we haven't," grunted the driver between bumps, "and I'm also pretty sure someone else has—and a heck of a thing they've left in its place!"

4

A tourist passing through a back-woods section became slightly confused when he came to a fork in the road and didn't know which to take. Seeing a man reclining on the porch of a nearby shack, he called out, "Say, friend, can you tell me where this road goes?" "Waal, suh," replied the hillbilly, not troubling himself to move, "hit goes fust one place an' then 'nothah."

See also farmer[3].

ROBBER

See burglar, thief.

ROBBERY

1

Two burglars had broken into a

clothing store and were sorting out some merchandise when one came across a man's suit marked at $149.50. "Golly! Look at this price, Bill!" he cried indignantly to the other. "Why, that's downright robbery!"

2

It was late and the street was dark and deserted as meek little Henry Brown walked nervously along. He gave a start as two burly figures suddenly confronted him. "Pardon me, sir," requested one politely, "but could you lend me a penny?" "Why, er, I think so," stammered Brown, relieved. "What do you want with it?" "Aw, me an' my pal wants to toss it," explained the other, "to see who gets your watch an' who gets your wallet."

3

A young lady had been visiting her aunt one Friday evening and the woman had given the girl her paycheck to deposit in the bank for her the next day. On her way home she was held up, and her cries soon brought a policeman. "Oh, I've been robbed!" she cried. "Someone has taken my aunt's pay!" "Come on, now," urged the copper. "Cut out the pig-latin and tell me what happened."

4

The highwayman jabbed a gun in the man's ribs and growled, "Money or your life!" The victim gave it a moment's thought, then decided, "Better take my life. I'm saving my money for my old age."

See also gun[3], help[1], instructions[1], pride[2], repay[4].

ROCK

See stone.

ROMANTIC

See clothes[9], departure[2], hair[2].

ROOM

1

The hotel guest from the country stopped and protested loudly to the bellboy conducting him, "You call that a room! If you think that jest 'cause I'm from the country you kin get my money for a measly little room like that with a foldin' bed, you're crazy. Why, I—" "Aw, get in, get in!" replied the boy in disgust, "This ain't your room; it's only the elevator."

2

A student, who had returned to college after classes had started, had trouble in finding a room. One landlady showed him a dingy, little room and remarked, "Don't you think, that as a whole this is a very nice room?" "That could be," replied the student disgustedly; "but as a room it's a lousy hole!"

3

"Do you call this a room?" cried the outraged guest, looking about the cubicle the hotel manager was showing him. "Why, it's so cramped there's hardly room enough to swing a cat." "But that makes no difference," the manager calmly pointed out. "You see, we don't allow animals."

ROOMMATE

Two college roommates encountered each other on the campus.

"Say," cried one indignantly, "you've got a lot of nerve wearing my raincoat." "Well, I'm doing it for your sake," replied the other. "You wouldn't want your new suit to get wet, would you?"

RUBBISH

"Any rags? Any old iron?" cried the junkman, knocking at the door. The door was flung open by the man of the house himself. "Go away, don't bother me!" he ordered. "There's nothing here for you—my wife's away." "Ah, ha!" replied the junkman knowingly. "Any empty bottles?"

RUDE

1

At an elaborate Hollywood party a movie actress was being rude to some of the other guests. At last, her escort said in excuse to her most recent victim, "I'm sure you'll excuse my friend's boorish behavior. You see, she's being herself tonight."

2

Little Jane returned home very provoked from a visit with her small friend Helen. "I just don't know what was wrong with Helen today, mother!" she said. "She was rude and cross all afternoon and kept quarreling the whole time!" "I should think that you'd have come right home in that case," observed mother. "Well, I didn't," replied Jane. "I just slapped her face and stayed."

RUMOR

1

The reporter was questioning the prominent man's unmarried daughter who was getting along in years. "Is what I hear true, Miss Smith," he asked, "that you're soon to be married?" "No, it isn't," she responded, "but I'm most grateful for the rumor."

2

The hillbilly had been convicted of and jailed for feuding. He and his friends were working hard for his pardon, but the opposing clan was doing everything possible to prevent it by spreading false reports. So the prisoner wrote a letter to the governor protesting: "Dere guvner, if you-al's bin a-hearin what i'se heered yous heered you-all's heered a lie."

3

"But you're not sure of that," protested a man to his friend. "What you say is just an idle rumor." "Well, my wife brought it home from her bridge club," declared the other, "and when those ladies get hold of an idle rumor, they soon put it to work."

RUNNING

"Mamma," cried the little girl, entering the living room, "I was just in the kitchen an' there's something running across the floor but it doesn't have any legs. What do you think it is?" "Goodness, I don't know, child," replied mother. "How can anything run without legs?" "But it can," insisted the girl. "It's water."

RURAL

See country, farm, farmer, farming, hillbilly.

SACRIFICE

See credit[1], Easter, praise[6].

SAD

See grief, mourning.

SAFE

See danger, escape, parking, protection.

SAILOR

1

A sailor's term of enlistment was about to expire and a friend remarked, "I guess you love the sea too much to leave it." "Humph! I'll tell you how much I love the sea," replied the sailor. "I love it so much that when I get out I'm going to put an oar over my shoulder and start walking inland. And I'm going to keep walking until someone asks me what that thing is—and there I'll settle down for the rest of my life!"

2

Two sailors, retired from the navy, pooled their money and bought a saloon in a small town. They immediately closed it and began to paint and fix it up inside and out. A few days after repairs had been completed and there was no sign of its opening, a thirsty crowd began to gather outside. One of the crowd knocked on the door and, when a head appeared at the window, inquired, "Say, when you gonna open up?" "Open up, hell!" growled the sailor. "We bought this place for ourselves!"

See also argument[2], conspicuous[1], navy, recovery[4], salt[1], shipwreck[2], soup[4], tattoo[1].

SALARY

1

A farmer who needed some extra hands approached one of the village loafers with an offer of a job. "What'll ye pay?" asked the idler. "I'll pay ye what yore wuth," replied the farmer. The loafer thought this over, then shook his head. "Shucks, no," he refused. "Be durned if I'd work fer thet!"

2

A business firm had printed on its salary receipt forms the following caution: "Your salary is your personal affair, and should not be divulged to any one." In signing the receipt, a new employee added to the above the following: "Don't worry, I won't mention it to anybody. I'm just as much ashamed of it as you are."

3

"I'm sorry about these bills," apologized the bank teller as he passed out some soiled currency in cashing a school teacher's paycheck; "I hope you're not afraid of microbes." "Don't let it bother you," replied the teacher. "A microbe couldn't live on my salary."

4

A lawyer who was always lecturing his office boy about one thing or another, one day overheard the lad talking with the boy from the next office. "How much do you get from him?" asked the other boy. "Oh, he gives me about $6,000 a year," was the reply; "nine dollars a week of it is in cash, and the rest is in legal advice."

5

"This is outrageous!" yelled the stage manager to the actor. "What was the idea of laughing in that last scene when you were supposed to be dying?" "At my salary," explained the actor, "death is greeted with laughter and cheers, not tears."

6

The grocer advertised for an errand boy for the summer and little nine-year-old Billy applied. Wishing to test his intelligence, the grocer asked, "Tell me, my boy, what would you do with a million dollars?" "Gee, I don't know," replied the astonished boy; "I wasn't expecting that much to start."

7

The young man was asking the girl's father for his daughter's hand. "How much money do you make, my boy?" asked the father. "A hundred dollars a month," replied the boy proudly. "Hmm, that's not too much," mused the father, "but with the seventy-five dollars a month allowance I give my daughter you can—" "Oh," interrupted the boy, "I've already figured that in."

8

"And now about salary," said the movie star after the other details had been concluded. "Well," suggested the producer, "suppose we call it $10,000 a week?" "All right," agreed the actor. "Of course you understand," warned the producer, "that $10,000 is merely what we'll call it—what you'll actually get is $350."

See also audacity, breakage[1], love[3], repay[5], satisfaction[1], store[3].

SALESMAN

1

"Mr. Black," said the sales manager sternly to the young salesman, "I notice that a considerable item of your expense account is for meals and night clubs." "Well, er, you see, sir," stammered Black, "I've done a good deal of entertaining of buyers and prospective customers." "That's necessary and I'm not complaining," the manager assured him; "but I hope you'll remember that we sell rock crushers, and chorus girls have rarely been known to buy a rock crusher."

2

One traveling salesman met another in a restaurant and stared in surprise at his plate. "What's the idea of eating milk and crackers?" he asked. "Got stomach trouble or on a diet?" "Nope," replied the other, "I'm on a commission."

3

A tourist stopped at a dinky crossroads store and was amazed at the amount of salt about the place. Sacks, boxes, and barrels of salt were stacked high all about the store. "Good heavens, man!" exclaimed the tourist. "You must certainly sell a lot of salt!" "Nope, I don't sell so much," replied the storekeeper. "But you shoulda seen that salesman what come by here last week—that guy could *really* sell salt."

4

A high-pressure, super-salesman was about to commit suicide by jumping off a bridge, when a policeman ran up and stopped him, saying, "Hey, there! You can't do that!" "And what makes you think I can't?" challenged the super-sales-man. Then he proceeded to give the policeman a serious talking-to. After about ten minutes, the police-man shook hands with him and they both jumped in.

5

After a severe battering by the storm, the ship split in two and flung all the passengers into the water. Two salesmen happened to find themselves clinging to the same crate, where they stuck for two days. Suddenly one cried out, "Jack, I see a ship!" "Aw, what good does that do us?" replied Jack. "Ain't we lost all our samples?"

6

"Papa," asked the merchant's young son, looking up from his newspaper, "it talks here about 'scientific salesmanship'—what does that mean?" "That could be defined many ways, my son," replied papa, "but what it really means is selling a dress suit with all the trimmings to a man who came in for a pair of work gloves."

See also insult[4], order[3], persever-ance[1], real estate[2], selling.

SALOON

1

The temperance lecturer had a stern face but a red nose and baggy eyes. "All my life I've lived in this town," he declared virtuously. "And in this town there are sixty-three saloons and taverns; yet in all that time I've never been in one of them!" "And which one was that?" asked a voice from the rear.

2

A lady of the reforming type shook her head sadly as she saw a man coming out of a saloon. "I'm certainly sorry to see you come out of that place," she stated sorrow-fully. "Heck, lady," retorted the other, "you don't think I could stay in there all night, do you?"

3

The man at the bar finished his third glass of beer, walked up to the manager standing at the end of the bar, and inquired, "How many kegs of beer do you sell here a week?" "About forty," replied the manager with some pride. "Well, I can tell you how to sell eighty a week," offered the customer. "How?" asked the manager eagerly. "It's easy," was the reply. "Just fill the glasses."

See also crazy[2], homesick[1], Prohibi-tion[2], sailor[2].

SALT

1

A sailor just in from a long stretch at sea was at a recreation center and happened to complain of a sore throat to one of the hostesses. "Have you ever tried gargling with salt water?" she suggested sweetly. "Are you kidding?" cried the sailor. "Lis-ten, sister, I've been torpedoed four times!"

2

"Would ye pass me the salt, Jimmy?" asked the hired man of the farmer's young son. The boy leaned over toward his mother. "Should I let 'im have it, ma?" he whispered. "I heered paw say he warn't worth it."

See also salesman[3].

SAME

See alike.

SANDWICH

1

The man sat down at the lunch-counter and ordered a ham sandwich. When it was set before him, he lifted the top piece of bread and looked at the ham critically. "Did you slice this ham?" he inquired of the counter-man. "I sure did," he assured him. "Humph!" snorted the diner. "You damned near missed it!"

2

A customer elbowed his way into a crowded lunchroom and managed to reach the counter. "What'll you have?" asked the waitress when she got around to him. "Well, I feel like a sandwich," he told her. "Look, bud, I'm busy, so just give me your order," she snapped. "It's not my fault this place is jammed."

3

"This ain't no sandwich," protested a tramp after he had got the handout he requested at the back door. "It ain't got nothin' in it." "Sure it's a sandwich," insisted the cook. "It's a Western sandwich—two pieces of bread with wide open spaces between 'em."

See also own[1].

SANITARY

1

An epidemic was raging in the village and the doctor was doing what he could to check it. Calling on one family, he inquired, "Are you folks doing everything you can to prevent the spread of infection?" "We shore air, doc," the head of the house assured him. "Why, I even bought one o' them-there sanitary drinkin' cups an' we all don't drink outta nothin' but it."

2

The city man eyed the farmer's house with disapproval. "It isn't very sanitary to have your house built over the hog pen like that, is it?" "Oh, I dunno," replied the farmer. "We ain't lost a hog in over twelve years."

3

Father was sick with the flu, so after each meal mother would sterilize the dishes he'd used. "Why do you do that, mom?" inquired little Ronnie as he watched her one day. "Because, dear," explained mother, "daddy has germs, and some of the germs get on his dishes, so I boil the dishes to kill the nasty germs." "Oh," said Ronnie. He thought this over, then asked, "Say, mom, why don't you just boil daddy?"

SANITY

1

A visitor at a mental hospital stopped to watch an inmate who was pushing a wheelbarrow around upside down. "What's the idea of that?" he asked. "Why don't you wheel that barrow right side up?" "Do you think I'm crazy?" demanded the other. "I did that yesterday and they kept filling it up with bricks."

2

A doctor examined a man who

was mentally ill as a result of emotional and mental strain. "Your husband is in a serious condition," said the doctor to the man's wife. "You should have called me sooner." "I wanted to," replied the wife, "but as long as he was in his right mind he wouldn't have a doctor."

See also asylum[5], inheritance[1], sermon[1].

SARCASM

1

The lawyer was making a long and eloquent speech, when at last the judge leaned forward and brusquely cut him off, saying, "That will be enough from you. Everything you say goes in one ear and out the other." "Naturally," retorted the lawyer sharply. "What's to stop it?"

2

The president of the corporation called in his office manager. "My stenographer is quite capable and efficient," he said, "but she's so darned beautiful that every one stops to visit with her and wastes a lot of time. Get me a plain stenographer." The next morning when the president buzzed, a thin, sour, wrinkled, elderly stenographer answered. The president took one look and went out to the manager. "I know," he said, "that I asked for a plain stenographer, but why get sarcastic about it?"

3

The class had been even more stupid than usual and at last the professor lost patience. "It's no use today. Class dismissed," he said in exasperation, then added, "And please don't flap your ears as you file out."

4

During the cruise an egotistical young man had been noisily showing off to the other passengers, to the annoyance of the boatman. Suddenly the boat struck a snag and sprang a leak. The boatman hastened to supply all the passengers except this fellow with life belts. "Where's mine?" cried the show-off in terror. "Don't worry, you don't need none," snorted the boatman. "Any feller with a head as holler as your'n can't sink."

5

The young man had lost the girl to a rival. About a year later he visited the home of his former sweetheart after her marriage. "And you must see baby," she cried after she had welcomed him. She took him to the nursery and said, "Isn't he just the picture of his daddy?" "Well, yes," admitted the fellow, then added, "but you shouldn't worry about it as long as he stays healthy."

6

Hubby was trying to make up the quarrel of the previous day as he held out the package he'd brought home tantalizingly. "Guess you're wondering what's in here?" he said to his wife. "Not especially," she replied. "It's something for the one I love best in the whole world," he hinted. "Humph!" sniffed the wife. "Maybe it's that new muffler you've been needing."

7

There was one student in the class whose conceit and egotism were matched only by his ignorance. One day, after a particularly vain display, the professor inquired quietly, "Mr. Smith, do you have a visiting card?" "Yes, sir, I have," was the reply. "Well, Mr. Smith," instructed the professor acidly, "for tomorrow I'd like you to write all you know on your visiting card and bring it to me."

8

The fat man dashed madly after a departing train, reaching desperately for the rear platform which kept eluding his grasp. As he returned discouraged and perspiring, the gateman observed, "Just missed her, eh?" "Why, no," gasped the corpulent one. "I was only chasing it out of the station."

9

They thought that they had made every arrangement to insure the success of the meeting, but the speaker on surveying the platform beckoned to the chairman and asked if he could have a glass of water on the table. "Do you want it to drink?" queried the chairman none too brightly. "Not at all," retorted the speaker. "It is my unfailing custom after speaking a half-hour to do a high dive into it."

10

A pedestrian had fallen into an open manhole and his cries finally attracted the attention of a passer-by. "Gracious!" said this gentleman sympathetically. "Have you fallen into that manhole?" "Don't be silly," replied the victim disgustedly. "I just happened to be here and they built the pavement up around me."

See also bore[3], delay[3], taxi[3].

SATISFACTION

1

"I hate to mention it," said the clerk to the boss, "but didn't you promise me a raise after I'd been with you a year?" "Yes, I did," agreed the boss; "but you'll remember that I promised it on condition that you give me satisfaction." "But in what way, sir, haven't I given you satisfaction?" protested the clerk. "Do you think for a minute," demanded the boss, "that you satisfy me by asking for a raise?"

2

"Here's that suit I bought from you last week," said a customer angrily, flinging down a bundle, "and I want to remind you that you promised to return my money if it was not satisfactory." "So I did," confirmed the tailor politely. "But I'm happy to say that I found the money quite satisfactory."

See also taste[1].

SAVE

The girl was so frivolous and irresponsible that mother decided to have the minister over to talk to her. After the preacher had spoken to the young lady for some time, she inquired during a pause in his rhetoric, "You say everybody should have a mission in life. What's yours?" "My mission," declared the parson pompously, "is saving young men." "Oh, good!" cried the girl gleefully. "I wish you'd save one for me."

See also emergency[3], thrift.

SCANDAL

It was the hour for the spelling lesson and the word "scandal" had just been spelled. "Now who can tell me what the word means?" asked teacher. A little girl in front volunteered, and explained, "It means that nobody's done nothin' and everybody goes every place tellin' everybody else all about it."

SCENERY

1

Mrs. Williams stood at the window of the resort hotel and clasped her hands in ecstasy. "Isn't this just the most heavenly scenery you've ever seen!" she exclaimed. "Aw, what's so great about it?" growled her husband. "Take away those mountains and that river and lake and forest, and what've you got?"

2

The artist was painting the distant mountain scene while an old farmer looked on curiously. "Ah, you have lived close to nature, my friend," observed the artist, "so perhaps you, too, have seen her ever-changing pageant. Have you seen her lambent flames of dawn, her sulphurous cloud-isles in a sea of fire at sunset, and her raven-black winged storm demons prowling the sky?" "Nope," replied the farmer, "not since I signed the pledge."

See also eating[2], view[1].

SCHOOL

1

The kindly old gentleman beamed at the small boy trudging along the street with an armful of books.

"Do you go to school, my little man?" he asked. "Naw," replied the little man; "I'm sent."

2

Little Jane had just returned home from her first day at school and mother smiled at her and asked, "Well, dear, what did they teach you in school?" "Not much," was the reply. "I've got to go again tomorrow."

3

Little Billy was back home after his first day in school. "Well, son," asked mother, "what happened in school?" "Oh, nothin' much," replied the boy nonchalantly. "A woman wanted to know how to spell dog, and I told her."

4

Teacher was trying to explain some of the elements of science to her class. "Sir Isaac Newton was sitting under a tree looking up into it when an apple fell on his head, and from that he discovered the law of gravity. Wasn't that wonderful?" "Yes'm, it sure was," ventured a voice from the rear; "an' if he'd have been in school looking at his books he wouldn't have discovered nothin'."

5

Summer vacation was over and the small boy was protesting against returning to school. "But don't you want to go to school and learn things?" asked his father. "Oh, sure; but not that school," answered the boy. "And why not that school?" asked father. "Because they're wastin' my time," explained the lad; "they keep wantin' to teach me a lot of things I don't know anything about."

6

A young boy had been going to school about a week. One morning he announced, "I'm tired of school, pop; I think I'll stop." "But why don't you like school?" asked the amazed father. "Oh, it's all right," conceded the boy, "only it breaks up your day so."

7

The principal called one of the young girl pupils to his office and sternly said to her, "You've been very negligent in your schoolwork lately, Mary, and you must remain with me for an hour after school today." "Okay," said Mary, shrugging her shoulders indifferently. "If your wife doesn't mind it, I'm sure I don't."

See also alphabet[2], arithmetic[1], attention, education[1], electricity[4], examination[7], fail[1], feeling[4], grades[1], holiday, homework, lesson, parents[1], truant, world[3].

SCIENCE

1

A distinguished scientist sat in an observatory peering at the heavens through the huge telescope. "Hmm," he at last remarked impressively to a fellow scientist, keeping his eye glued to the instrument, "it's going to rain." "How can you tell?" inquired the other scientist. "Because," said the learned one, still studying the heavens, "my corns hurt!"

2

It was the hour for the lesson in elementary science and teacher was lecturing her small pupils on gravity. "So you see, children," she concluded, "it is the law of gravity that keeps us all on the earth." "But, teacher," inquired one puzzled child, "how did we manage to stick on before the law was passed?"

See also body[3, 4], electricity[3].

SCORE

An old golfer encountered a beginner on the links and paused to ask pleasantly, "What's your score today?" "Sixty-nine," was the proud reply. "Sixty-nine!" exclaimed the first. "Say, that's pretty good!" "Yes, it's not bad," agreed the beginner. "And I'm hoping to do even better on the second hole."

See also baseball[1].

SCULPTURE

See statue.

SEAMAN

See sailor.

SEARCH

1

A drunk, staggering along the water front, noticed several policemen hard at work at the water's edge. "Whashya doin', men?" he mumbled genially. "We're looking for a drowned man," they told him. "F'goo'ness sakes!" exclaimed the drunk. "Whashya want one for?"

2

Mother had vainly searched the whole house for her young son, starting with the first floor, then the second, and going finally to the attic without finding the boy. Standing at the trap door to the roof, she called out, "Jimmy, are you out there?" A voice answered her clearly, "No, mother, I'm not; but have you looked in the basement?"

3

It was the middle of a hot afternoon and the factory workman decided to slip up to the corner saloon for a glass of beer. But just as he was about to step out of the door, he ran into the foreman. "Hi, there!" said that person. "Were you looking for me?" "I sure was," replied the workman, "but I didn't want to see you."

See also drunk[1].

SEASICK

1

"My husband is very susceptible to seasickness," a woman informed the captain at the start of a voyage. "Quite a few people have that trouble," said the captain. "Could you tell him what to do in case of an attack?" inquired the woman. "Don't worry, madam," the skipper assured her, "he'll do it."

2

A man was taking his first ocean voyage and was dreadfully seasick. He called his wife to him and said between groans, "Mary, my will is in the bank vault and leaves everything to you. Also, my stocks and bonds are there. And, Mary," he pleaded as the boat gave another roll, "please bury me on the other side. I couldn't stand this trip over again, dead or alive."

3

"Don't be too disheartened, sir," said the steward to the seasick passenger. "You know, no one's ever died of seasickness." "Oh, don't say that, man," groaned the sufferer. "It's only the hope of dying that's kept me alive this long."

4

It was a bad storm and the ship was rolling and pitching violently. As the captain walked along the deck he noticed a sailor leaning over the rail. "Here, here!" said the captain sternly. "You can't be sick here, my man." The sailor regarded the captain for a moment, then suggested, "Watch!"

5

The ocean was only mildly rough, but yet several passengers hung miserably over the rail. A kindly old gentleman paused to comfort one of the more wretched of them, and observed, "You must have a weak stomach, sir." "What do you mean, weak!" gasped the sufferer. "Guess I'm throwin' it as far as anybody around here, ain't I!"

6

The seasoned globe-trotter was waxing philosophical. "I always say," he declared, "that if there's anything in a man, travel will bring it out." And the amateur traveler who was just back from a rough crossing, added bitterly, "Especially ocean travel."

7

It was daughter's first ocean voyage and mother was very solicitous. "Are you seasick, darling?" she inquired. "No, mother, I think not," was the reply; "but I'd certainly hate to yawn right now."

See also economy[3], judge[3].

SEASON

1

Teacher called upon the daughter of a merchant. "Mary," she questioned, "can you tell me how many seasons there are in the year?" "There's two, teacher," responded Mary promptly. "Two?" said the puzzled teacher. "What are they?" "Slack and busy," was the answer.

2

Teacher had been talking for a half-hour on what each season meant to the world—how spring brought new life to all plants, summer brought their maturity, fall their decline, and so on. "Now, Bill," she asked, as she ended, "what do we find in the spring?" "Well, ma'am," replied Bill, "there's a frog, two fish, a snake, an' a dead cat. But I didn't put the cat there— it was another fellow."

SECOND-HAND CAR

1

The old jalopy puffed up and came to a rattling halt at the toll-bridge. "Sixty-five cents," said the bridge-keeper. "Sold!" cried the driver, jumping out.

2

The motorist had been working on his broken-down old car while a farmer stood watching him. "Well what're you looking at?" snapped the irritated motorist. "Is this the first automobile you ever saw?" "No, I don't think so," replied the farmer dryly; "but it sure looks a lot like it."

3

A man bought a used car and was driving it home. He was beginning to have doubts as to his bargain, when a policeman shouted at him, "Hey, there! You're blocking traffic. Can't you go any faster?" "Of course I can, officer," said the man, "but I don't want to leave the car here to litter up the street."

4

A minister brought his flivver to a halt on the used-car lot and climbed out. "You sold me this car last week," he told the dealer, "but I've decided to bring it back as it is a little too stubborn and contrary." "What's the matter?" asked the dealer. "Can't you run it?" "Not and stay in the ministry," was the response.

5

"Why didn't you stop when I signaled?" roared the traffic cop at the man in the wheezy car. "Well, it's this way, officer," explained the motorist. "It took me over two hours to get this old jalopy started, and it seemed a shame to stop it just for a little thing like avoiding arrest."

SECRET

1

A middle-aged parson was driving along a country road when he saw a pretty young woman. He recognized her as the hired girl of a farm he would pass on his way. So he pulled up and offered her a lift, which was gladly accepted. As she got off at her gate, she said gratefully, "Thank you, sir." "Oh, don't mention it, Susan, don't mention it," replied the preacher politely. "Don't worry, sir," whispered Susan, "I won't breathe a word."

2

Myrt and Mame were having lunch together and became quite confidential. "Gertie told me that you told her that secret I told you not to tell her," informed Myrt. "Why, that nasty thing!" cried Mame. "And after I especially told her not to tell you!" "Oh, well," comforted Myrt, "I told her I wouldn't tell you she told me—so now don't you tell her I did."

SEE

1

The recently-married couple were just back from a honeymoon trip around the world. They were entertaining the husband's elder brother, the black sheep of the family. "My goodness," gushed the woman enthusiastically, "we've been everywhere and seen everything." "Have you ever had delirium tremens?" inquired the brother politely. "Why, of course not!" was the shocked answer. "Well, then, my dear," said the other, "you've never been *anywhere* and you haven't seen *anything*."

2

An experienced hunter took an amateur hunter on an expedition in the woods and agreed to let him have the first shot. As they walked along, a rabbit suddenly jumped from the grass at their feet, ran through the bushes, and disappeared. But the amateur failed to fire. "Why didn't you shoot?" demanded the other. "Gosh!" said the beginner. "It was so sudden that I didn't see him until he was out of sight."

See also eyes, near-sighted.

SEED

See garden[2, 4].

SELECT

See choice.

SELF

The party was becoming hilarious. One of the guests who was in a very jolly mood approached the hostess's husband, who stood quietly to one side, slapped him on the back, and inquired genially, "Well, old man, enjoying yourself?" "Yes, I am," replied the husband; "but it's about the only thing I am enjoying!"

See also man[2], odor[1], portrait, question[4], rude[1].

SELF-BETRAYAL

1

The bartender had been a hard worker for the political party, so he was rewarded by being appointed police magistrate. "What's the charge?" he asked impressively when his first case came up. "Drunk, Your Honor," said the clerk. "Guilty or not guilty?" he asked of the defendant. "But I never drink a drop," declared the accused. "Well, then," said the judge, "take a cigar."

2

Little Bessie at times had naughty days, and this was one of her worst. At last, her mother, in exasperation, exclaimed, "Goodness, Bessie, you should behave better. Don't you know that if you keep on being so naughty your children will be naughty, too?" "See, mother," cried

Bessie, "if I'm so naughty it must be your fault!"

3

The parson ended his sermon and in a soft voice requested, "Deacon Brown, will you lead us in prayer?" There was no response, so he repeated a little more loudly, "Deacon Brown, will you lead us?" It now became evident that the deacon was dozing, so in a loud voice the preacher said, "Deacon Brown, will you lead?" The deacon came to with a start and blurted out, "Lead yourself—I dealt!"

4

"Sammy," said mother sadly to her disobedient son, "every time you act naughty you give mother another gray hair." "Oh, mother!" cried Sammy. "In that case, you must have been terrible! Just look at poor grandma's hair!"

See also weeping[3].

SELFISH

1

"I have a surprise for you, my love," said hubby. "I've just had my life insured for $10,000." "Why, you dirty, selfish brute!" cried his wife. "Always thinking of yourself!"

2

An old couple quarreled habitually, but this time the conflict was exceptionally bitter. "Ah, me," sighed the old lady at last, "I wish I was in heaven!" "Well, I wish I was in a nice peaceful saloon!" snarled her husband. "See, there you go again!" said the wife tearfully. "Always picking the best for yourself!"

SELF-MADE

1

The visitor that father was entertaining in the living room was dumpy and fat and rather ugly, and little Junior stood looking at him intently. "Why do you stare at me, my boy?" asked the visitor finally. "Because daddy said you were a self-made man an' I wanted to see what you looked like," was the reply. "That's right," confirmed the man, "I *am* a self-made man." "But, gee!" said Junior, "why did you make yourself like that?"

2

Despite his lack of education, the ambition and perseverance of a local businessman had carried him to success. Because of his fame, he had been asked to award the annual prizes at school. "Now, boys," he began his introductory speech, "always remember there's nothing like education. Now take arithmetic. It teaches us that twice two makes four, three threes make nine, seven sevens make, ah, well—and then there's geography."

3

"You ought to be ashamed that you haven't accomplished more with your life," the lady reprimanded the tramp who knocked at her door. "But, lady, I'm a self-made man," protested the tramp proudly. "I started out without a rag on my back, and now I'm all rags."

4

One man was praising to another the success of a noted financial wizard. "And in the bargain, he's the architect of his own fortune," he declared, "entirely the architect of his own fortune." "Well, all I can say," retorted the other, "is that he was darned lucky the building inspector didn't come around while the construction was going on."

SELLING

A farmer decided to make his living in town and selling insurance appeared to him an easy way to do so. But as he had no license, it was not long before he was haled before the insurance commissioner. "What's the idea?" demanded the commissioner. "Don't you know that you can't sell insurance in this town without a license?" "So thet's what's the matter!" cried the farmer. "I shore found out I couldn't sell none, but I'm danged if I knew why 'til ye tol' me."

See also salesman.

SENSE

"You can say what you want about my uncle," stoutly maintained the nephew of the town's ne'er-do-well, "but you'll have to admit he's got a lot of horse sense." "I'll say he has!" agreed another heartily. "You can lead him to water, but you can't make him drink it."

SENTIMENT

1

A thief was being booked in the warden's office. His pockets were being emptied, each article examined, and then carefully tagged and marked. Among these was a badly tarnished silver dollar. "Would you let me keep that with me?" pleaded the prisoner. "Why? You can't

spend it here," replied the warden. "It's just sentiment," confessed the crook. "It's the first dollar I ever stole."

2

"Perhaps you could tell me, my good friend," pompously asked the touring politician of one of the natives, "what public sentiment is in these parts?" "Oh, 'bout the same as any other place, I reckon," answered the local boy: "mainly huggin', squeezin', kissin', an' spoonin' around."

SEPARATION

1

"Oh, you heartless brute! You don't love me any more!" she whimpered as they paused for breath in their quarreling. "I'm going back to mother." "Now don't make yourself that trouble, dear," he protested gallantly. "I'll just go back to my wife."

2

"What's this I hear about your sister and her husband splitting up?" asked the neighborhood gossip. "Why, I understood that they were inseparable." "Yes, that's about right," agreed the other. "Ordinarily it takes about eight people and a cop to pull them apart."

3

"So your mistress is not home?" inquired the caller of the maid. "No, ma'am," replied the servant. "She went abroad two months ago, the day before the master returned from England." "How is it," asked the visitor, "that when your mistress is home your master's abroad, and vice versa? Is there trouble between them?" "Not at all, ma'am," declared the maid. "They've just agreed between them that they can live together better when they're apart."

4

The quarrel had reached a violent climax at which hubby had announced dramatically, "This is the end—the positive end! I'm going to leave you this very minute! Forever!" "I'm afraid you can't, darling," retorted the wife. "Your pants haven't come back from the cleaner's yet."

See also departure[2].

SERMON

1

A minister was conducting services in a mental institution, and in the midst of his long and involved sermon one of the inmates suddenly shouted out, "Say, how much more of this humbug do we have to listen to?" The startled minister turned to the keeper and asked, "Shall I stop?" "No, keep right on," encouraged the keeper. "It won't happen again—that man has only one sane moment every five years."

2

The minister was noted for his lengthy, complex sermons. After having spoken for over an hour, he paused for breath and remarked, "And now, what shall I say next?" Without hesitation, a voice from the rear suggested, "Amen!"

3

The preacher was very proud of his sermons. One day after services he asked one of his elderly parishioners, "Well, how did you like my sermon today?" "There was one part I especially liked," replied the old fellow, "and that was a passage at the end." "Which was that?" asked the preacher eagerly. "The one from the pulpit to the vestry," explained the old man.

4

A clergyman sat by the fire telling his family a marvelous tale of escape from danger and subsequent good fortune that he'd heard. His small daughter sat listening, then finally asked, "Now, pop, is that story really true, or is it just preaching?"

5

A stranger entered a church after the sermon had begun and sat down in the rear. As the sermon went on and on, he began to fidget, and finally he leaned forward and asked an elderly man, "Say, friend, how long has he been preaching?" "Oh, thirty-five to forty years, I reckon," was the reply. The stranger sat back. "Guess I'll wait then," he muttered. "He ought to be nearly through."

6

A famous judge was on vacation in a small town. He went one Sunday to a local church whose preacher was known for the dullness and the length of his sermons. After services, the parson came up to the judge and asked, "Well, Your Honor, how did you like my sermon?" "Very remarkable in that I found it like the peace of God," said the jurist, "for it passed all understanding, and like His mercy in that it seemed to endure forever."

7

A young married couple were good church members, the husband officiating as an usher. One Sunday as the service droned on, the wife became worried lest the roast at home in the oven be burnt, so she sent a note to her husband by another usher. This usher, thinking the note was for the preacher, went down and laid it on the pulpit. The preacher paused in his sermon, opened the note, and was amazed to read: "Please go home and turn off the gas."

The preacher had quarreled with his congregation, but now he was leaving and had just preached his farewell sermon. "What a beautiful and appropriate farewell sermon!" remarked a visitor to one of the deacons. "Think so?" grunted the deacon. "Yes, indeed," insisted the other. "And such a suitable text: 'In my Father's house are many mansions . . . I go to prepare a place for you.' By the way, where is he going?" The deacon smiled. "He's to be chaplain of the state penitentiary."

9

The minister's son was thought old enough to hear his father preach, so he was taken to church for the first time. During the service a stray dog happened in and got upon the platform, and it was put out as gracefully as possible. When the boy was later asked how he'd liked his father's sermon, he replied, "It was pretty good, pop; but I thought that part was swell where you put the dog out."

10

A clergyman was suddenly called out of town and he asked his new curate to conduct services on Sunday. When he returned, he asked his wife how the curate had done. "Not so well," she reported. "It was the poorest sermon I'd ever heard— nothing to it at all." Meeting his curate later, the rector asked him how he'd managed. "Very well, sir," replied the curate. "As I didn't have time to prepare anything myself, I just used one of your sermons."

11

"Services were excellent today!" gushed one of the minister's admirers. "The sermon was very fine, and so well-timed, too!" "Yes, it certainly was well-timed," agreed the minister. "I noticed that over half the congregation had their watches out."

12

A minister was entertaining several fellow clergymen at dinner and his guests were praising his sermon of the previous Sunday. Finally, one of them turned to his host's young son, who was at the table, and asked, "And you, my lad, what did you think of your father's sermon?" "Oh, I guess it was all right," conceded the boy, "only he passed up three real good places where he could have stopped."

See also apology[1], church[3], correction, disturbance[1], flies, grass[2], place[1], rest[2], source[1], truth[1], wicked[2].

SERVANT

1

An elegant-looking lady stopped in at a household employment agency. "I want an odd-jobs man around the house," she explained to the attendant. "One who will run all errands, clean the yard, and who will always do my bidding and never answer back." "You're not looking for a servant, madam," she was told. "What you need is a husband."

2

"Goodness!" exclaimed the neighbor in great surprise. "You say you've had the same servant for over two years? How did you manage it?" "It wasn't so much my doing as the servant's," confessed the other. "She says she doesn't believe in changing after she's gone to all the trouble of breaking a family into her ways."

See also breakage[1], children[4], guest[2], handkerchief[2], help[5], philanthropy[1], reference[1], river[1], serving[1], spots[3].

SERVICE

An elderly lady rushed to the nearest police station to report the loss of her purse. "There, there, don't you worry," comforted the desk sergeant, touched by her evident concern; "we'll leave no stone unturned to find your purse, madam." As she left by a side door, she noticed a gang of laborers beginning to tear up the street for a new sewer. "Well, that's service," she said happily. "They certainly didn't waste any time getting to it."

See also filling station[1].

SERVING

1

"And are you able to serve company at table?" asked the lady of the prospective new servant. "Yes,

mum," was the reply; "both ways." "What do you mean, both ways?" asked the lady. "Why, either so they'll come again, or stay away," answered the girl.

2

A lady was instructing her new maid in the technique of serving at table. "Now you must be careful at dinner, Susan," she said, "always to remember to serve each person from the left and to take the soiled plates away from the right. Is that clear?" "Oh, sure, ma'am," replied the servant. "But what's the idea—superstitious or something?"

3

A woman was interviewing a prospective housemaid and settling certain details. "There's one more thing, mum," said the servant, "do you do your own stretchin'?" "Stretching?" cried the woman. "I don't understand." "Stretchin', mum," repeated the girl. "I mean do you put the stuff on the table an' do your own stretchin' for it, or do I have to shuffle it around for you?"

SEWING

A young wife was seated in the sun room with her husband's coat in her lap, and needle and thread in hand when he came in. "Really, John," she observed, "I think you ought to change tailors. The careless way he sewed this button on is a shame! This is the eighth time I've had to sew it back on for you."

SEX

1

The lady visitor to the zoo was making a nuisance of herself with her silly questions. At last she stopped before the tank containing the hippopotamus and asked, "Is this animal male or female?" "Now, after all, madam," remarked the attendant, "what difference does it really make—unless you happen to be another hippopotamus?"

2

An elderly lady at the zoo stood before the ostriches and asked the keeper innumerable questions. "What I can't see," she said at last, "is how you can tell whether these queer birds are male or female." "It's quite simple, madam," replied the keeper. "You just tell it a joke, and if he laughs, it's a male—and if *she* laughs, it's a female."

3

A large factory, employing a number of workers, had a detailed form that all applicants for jobs had to fill out. One not-too-bright girl was laboring over one of these, slowly filling in the lines labeled, "Height," "Weight," "Age," etc. At last she reached a line headed "Sex." She filled this in without hesitation: "About three times a week."

See also banking[8], facts of life[2], star[2].

SHAPE

1

A tourist entered the village general store and inquired of the proprietor, "Do you happen to have anything in the shape of automobile tires?" "Yep, quite a few things," he was told. "We've got life-preservers, invalid cushions, funeral wreaths, doughnuts, an' sich like."

2

Mother was trying to give little Willie a lesson in elementary geography by showing him a globe atlas and pointing out various countries with their odd and different shapes. "Now, Willie," she asked, "what is the shape of the world?" The boy looked confused, but soon his face brightened. "Oh, I remember," he cried. "I heard daddy say it was in a hell of a shape."

SHARE

Mother gave little Danny two apples, one large and one small, and told him to give one of them to his sister. She watched him do so, then said with a sad sigh, "Danny, if I'd been dividing those apples, I'd have kept the small one and given you the large one." "So what?" replied Danny. "I've got it, haven't I?"

See also eating[7].

SHAVING

1

The barber held the razor and asked the man in the chair, "Shall I go over your face again, sir?" "Well, all right if you go *over* it," replied the victim, "but please don't go *under* it like you did the first time."

2

"Oh, George, dear," cried wifey as she drew back from his embrace, "you didn't shave this evening." "No, I didn't," admitted George. "I shaved this morning, and it makes my face sore if I shave twice a day." "Well," said the wife, "it makes *my* face sore if you shave only once."

3

Bill came to the office one morning with a badly nicked and bruised face. "What in the world happened to you?" cried the stenographer. "You look like you got your face caught in a meat grinder." "Aw, I just went to the barber college to get shaved," explained Bill, "and one of the students flunked his examination on me."

See also barber, razor.

SHIP

1

The sweet young lady stopped the steward. "Could you tell me where the captain is?" she inquired. "The captain's forward, Miss," replied the steward. "Oh, that's all right; I still want to find him," insisted the young thing. "This is a pleasure trip."

2

The captain and the chief engineer had argued for years as to which of their jobs was the more important. Finally, they decided to trade jobs for a day and the engineer took his place on the bridge while the captain disappeared into the engine room. After a time, the oil-covered captain appeared on deck and called, "You'd better come down here, chief, I can't seem to make her go." "Wouldn't do you any good if you could," replied the engineer. "She's ashore."

See also fog[1], mistake[3], ocean[4], reassurance[1].

SHIPWRECK

1

The lady stood gazing in great concern at the ship foundering off-shore in the storm. "Can't anything be done for that ship in distress," she inquired of a coast guardsman. "Don't worry, ma'am," he reassured her. "We've already sent her a line to come ashore." "My goodness!" cried the lady. "Do they need a formal invitation at a time like this?"

2

A sailor, who for over nine years had been cast away on a desert island, awoke one morning to see a scantily attired young woman on a barrel floating toward the beach. After the barrel had drifted in, the girl approached the sailor and asked, "Hi, there, sailor! How long you been here?" "Purty near ten year," was the reply. "Gosh!" said the girl. "Then I'll give you something you haven't had in a long time." "Blow me down!" cried the sailor. "Don't tell me you got beer in that barrel?"

See also aviation[3], prayer[1], repent[1], salesman[5], world[2].

SHOES

1

"How about a new pair of shoes?" requested the soldier of the supply sergeant. "Naw," growled the sergeant. "Ya can't have a new pair until the ones ya got is wore out." "Worn out!" cried the soldier. "Say, sarge, I can step on a dime in these shoes and tell whether it's heads or tails."

2

The town loafer returned late one night from a coon hunt and tumbled right into bed as he was, shoes and all. "Get up, you lazy lout!" ordered his wife, shaking him. "You've got your shoes on." "Aw, that's all right, Mary," he mumbled sleepily, "they ain't my good ones."

3

The lady customer had looked at all the shoes in the shop, but still she wasn't pleased. "I don't like this pair either," she complained; "the soles are too thick." "Is that your only objection, madam?" asked the clerk. "Yes, it is," she admitted. "Then take them, madam," advised the clerk, "and I assure you that the objection will gradually wear away."

See also athletics, belief[1], bootblack[1], diet[4], feet[1, 2], hillbilly[1].

SHOOTING

1

Toward the end of a long, weary day of hunting, the amateur huntsman pulled the trigger and shouted excitedly, "At last, a quail!" But the man he'd hired to carry his bag only grunted disgustedly, "Serves the fool bird right for flyin' in front of your gun!"

2

It was the rookie's first time at target practice and with the very first shot he scored a center bull's-eye. His next nine shots, however, left no mark on the target. "How could you ever make nine complete misses?" snarled the sergeant. "That first one must've been beginner's luck." "Oh, I'm sorry, sergeant," apologized the rookie. "I thought I had to get all the bullets through the same hole."

3

A traveler in India hired a na-

tive boy to attend him on a hunt, but he was a very poor shot and the entire day yielded not a single bag. "Well, my shooting isn't very much, I guess," he remarked as they headed home. "Oh, the young sahib shot very well indeed," insisted the Hindu lad tactfully, "only God was very merciful to the birds."

4

A sergeant had a squad of rookies out for target practice. He had them kneel and fire at 250 yards, but the targets were untouched. He moved them up to 200 yards, but still the targets escaped damage. At 100 yards it was the same story. " 'Ten-shun!" ordered the sergeant dryly. "Fix bayonets! Charge! It's our last chance, men."

5

"Good Lord, man, where are all your shots going?" exclaimed the sergeant to the rookie at target practice. "Not a one has hit the target." "I dunno, sarge," replied the rookie, "they all left here okay."

6

The sergeant was drilling a squad of rookies in the use of the rifle. After some preliminary instruction, he distributed ammunition, ordered them to load their pieces, and then stand at "ready." "Attention, men!" he commanded. "Fire at will!" All began shooting, save the rookie on the end who looked puzzled and asked, "Say, sarge, which one is Will?"

7

"You know, soldier," said the sergeant to the rookie, "your shooting reminds me of lightning." "How's that, sarge?" asked the rookie innocently. "Because it never strikes twice in the same place," was the answer.

See also education[1], South[6], star[1].

SHOPPING

1

A lady shopper in a large department store had pestered the clerks for several hours, seeing everything but buying nothing. At last, one clerk ventured timidly, "Pardon me, madam, but are you shopping?" "Of course I'm shopping," answered the lady. "What do you think I'm doing?" "I thought perhaps you were taking inventory," was the reply.

2

"I'd like to see some blankets," said the lady to the clerk. The clerk showed her the stock and soon every blanket was off the shelves and on the counter. "Thank you," said the lady, turning to leave, "but I'm just looking for a friend." "Well, madam," offered the clerk obligingly, "if you think your friend is among these blankets I'll be glad to go through them again."

See also recovery[6], store.

SHORT

See midget.

SHORTHAND

1

The instructor in shorthand was enthusiastic about his subject and he was extolling its wonders to a new class. "It is recorded," he said, "that it took the poet Gray seven years to write his famous poem, 'Elegy in a Country Churchyard.' Now had Gray known shorthand," beamed the instructor, "he could have written it in seven minutes— some of my students have written it in that length of time."

2

A hillbilly was testifying in court, and he soon noticed that everything he was saying was being taken down by the court stenographer. He began talking faster and still faster, until finally even with the help of shorthand the stenographer was obliged to rush to keep up with him. At last the hillbilly cried out, "Land sakes, man, don't write so fast—I can't keep up with you!"

SHOUTING

"See here," demanded a voice over the superintendent's phone, "I want you to quiet that woman on the fourth floor who's shouting at her husband." "I'll do my best, sir," promised the superintendent. "Who is she?" "My wife," was the answer.

SHREWD

1

"Poor old Si shore had hard luck up in New York," commented one farmer to another as they met in the store. "Somebody sell him a gold brick?" asked the other. "Naw, he's too smart fer that," replied the first. "He went up there an' wuz gonna fool some o' the city folks. So he starts to sell a feller the Brooklyn Bridge, an' be danged if he didn't pick the feller who owned it, an' he hadda give 'im a hundred dollars so's he wouldn't call the police."

2

"Here I have a new dollar," said the politician who was talking to a group of boys, "and it's going to the lad with common sense enough to belong to the same party I do." Turning to a bright-eyed lad, he inquired, "What's your politics, son?" The youngster gave him a look and asked, "What's yours, mister?"

3

A Vermont farmer's son had gone West to make his fortune, and now he was back home telling of his adventures. "And another time," he related, "I bought a phoney silver mine for $4,000." "Gosh, wuz you dumb, buyin' a humbug mine!" jeered the farmer. "Oh, I did all right," replied the son. "I formed a company and sold half the stock to a Vermont man for $9,000." "What!" gasped the farmer, paling. "Say, I'll bet I'm the one who bought it!"

4

A boy who was the village half-wit furnished the natives much amusement. They would offer him his choice between a penny and a dime, and he would invariably take the penny. A stranger watched this one day and then asked the lad, "Why do you always take the penny? Because it seems a little larger than the dime?" "Nope," replied the boy. "It's 'cause if'n I took the dime, they'd stop offerin' me."

5

It was shortly before Christmas, and the well-dressed gentleman eyed the boys standing by a large pile of snowballs. "What're you going to do with those snowballs?" he demanded. "We're selling them, sir, three for a penny," replied one of the boys. "But those who can't afford to buy 'em gets 'em for nothin'." "I see," said the gentleman. "I guess I'll purchase the lot of them."

See also available, fright, greedy, spots[4], strategy[1].

SHY

See bashful.

SICK

1

Father had been ill in bed for some time, but now he was recovered enough for little Junior to pay him a visit. The boy was quiet throughout his stay, and when the time came to leave he approached the bed and asked, "I've been a good boy, ain't I, pop?" "Yes, son, you have," replied father weakly. "Well, then, pop," pleaded the boy, "kin I please see the baby?"

2

The fashionable doctor walked in breezily and nodded familiarly at one of his regular patients. "Well, here I am, Mrs. Williams," he announced. "And what do you think is wrong with you this morning?" "I hardly know what to think, doctor," the elegant lady murmured. "What's new?"

3

The lady had been very ill, but now she was around again and her neighbor greeted her and inquired as to her health. "I was so deathly sick I almost died," she explained. "I had ptomaine-poisoning from some chicken salad." "What a pity," sympathized the man. "You know, ma'am, what with that and the delirium tremens, a body don't know what he dare eat or drink these days."

4

The farmer's wife was seriously ill, and when he was at the store in the village the storekeeper asked about her. The farmer spat reflectively. "Oh, I don't know," he answered in dejected tones, "Marthy's failin' so all-fired slow that danged if I don't sometimes wish she'd git well or somethin'."

5

A man who was coming down with an infectious fever warned off his young son when the boy approached to greet him. "No, no, son, you mustn't hug me, or you'll catch the fever." The lad stood back and looked at his father, then asked, "Why, daddy, who did you hug?"

6

"It says here," said the wife, looking up from her paper, "that some doctors recommend that people with colds be quarantined. I suppose that's to keep them from giving it to other people." "No, of course not," growled her husband; "it's simply to protect them from the advice of other people on how to cure them."

7

"I'm sorry to hear that your mother's ill," said teacher sympathetically to one of her small pupils. "Is she sick a-bed?" "Well, no,

not exactly," said the child. "So far she's just sick a-sofa."

See also affectionate[4], army[1], coat[2], diagnosis[6], fruit[5], imagination, right[2], stock market[2], temperature[1], weak[1], workman[5].

SIGHT

See blind, eyes, near-sighted, see.

SIGNS

1

"Will this bus take me to the football game?" inquired the girl of the driver as she boarded a bus. "No, miss," he replied. "But," objected the girl, "you have an announcement of the game on the front of the bus." "I know, miss," he admitted, "and if you look back in the car you'll see signs about Boston baked beans, but this bus doesn't go to Boston!"

2

Two farmers in town on a hot afternoon had been watching the people strolling along the streets. The eye of one was caught by a sign in a dry-goods store window, reading: "Ladies Ready To Wear Clothes." "Well, it's danged near time they wuz," he observed to the other, "but I cain't notice thet they've started yit!"

3

Noticing that a shop window had for some time displayed a sign stating: "Fishing Tickle," a passerby at last went in to call it to the proprietor's attention. He ended by asking, "Hasn't any one mentioned it before?" "Oh, sure, hundreds of them," replied the merchant. "But when they drop in to tell me they almost always buy something, so I just leave the sign be."

4

A surveyor was sent to inspect a certain section that had had frequent floods. He was to post warning signs for the protection of traffic. At the side of a road where it began to dip into a small valley, he erected the sign: "Notice is hereby given that when this signboard is under water the road ahead is impassable."

5

A man who had spent time and money on the grounds of his estate had posted a number of warning signs all about. One evening he met a pair of lovers strolling moonily about his grounds, and he demanded of them, "Can't you read that sign there?" "Oh, sure," said the young fellow. "It says, 'Private,' and that's just why we came in here."

See also stupid.

SILENCE

1

"Now, children," teacher warned the class, "I want you all to be very quiet—so quiet that you can hear a pin drop." The noise in the room gradually subsided and for a minute all was still. Finally, a small boy in the rear, unable any longer to endure the tension, shrieked out, "Let 'er drop!"

2

A clergyman and one of his parishioners were playing golf, and it was a very close match. On the last hole the clergyman teed up, ad-

dressed the ball carefully, and swung mightily. But the ball merely rolled a few feet in front of the tee. The preacher knit his brow, glared at the ball, bit his lip, but said nothing. His companion regarded him for a moment, then observed, "I must say, Reverend, that yours is the most profane silence I've ever witnessed."

3

"You're silent tonight," remarked the young man to the girl. "You've spoken scarcely a word in over fifteen minutes." "I just don't have anything to say," explained the girl simply. "What!" cried the fellow. "Don't you ever talk when you don't have anything to say?" "No, of course not," was the reply. "Darling," pleaded the boy, "will you be my wife?"

See also customary[2], playwright[1].

SILVER

1

"Those spoons Aunt Kate sent us for a wedding present are quite pretty, but they're not real silver," declared the bride. "How can you tell?" asked the groom. "Do you know good silver?" "No, I don't," admitted the bride; "but I know Aunt Kate."

2

The woman was about to buy a silver service, but she hesitated. "Naturally, I believe you when you say it's solid silver," she said, "but somehow it just doesn't look like it." "But that's its greatest advantage, madam," insisted the clerk. "This is one service that can be left out in plain sight without worrying, as no burglar would even look at it twice."

See also party.

SIMILAR

See alike.

SIMPLE

A young philosophy student was trying to impress the pretty young thing with the broadness of his outlook. "A great drawback of modern life is that we're too specialized and narrow," he spouted learnedly. "Now I, for example, though well-grounded in the arts, haven't the slightest idea of how the radio works." "Gosh, you're dumb!" exclaimed the sweet thing. "It's awful simple; you just turn the knobs and it plays."

SIN

1

"Now, Billy," questioned the Sunday-school teacher, "can you tell us what we must do before we can expect forgiveness of sin?" "Sure," replied the boy readily. "First we gotta sin."

2

The minister was passing through the Sunday school and he paused to question one bright-faced little girl. "Can you tell me, my dear," he asked, "what are the sins of omission?" The child thought, then ventured, "Aren't they the sins we should have committed, but didn't?"

3

A minister was walking with one of his elderly parishioners on a win-

try day, when suddenly the latter slipped and fell flat on his back. After assuring himself that his companion wasn't hurt, the clergyman observed, laughing, "My friend, sinners stand on slippery places." The old man took a good look at the upright preacher, then retorted, "So I see; but *I* can't."

4

The old squire was a conscience-less skinflint, but he nevertheless tried to assume a holy and saintly air. Talking with some of the old boys around the village store one day, he remarked, "Ya know, I read t'other day as how there's only seven deadly sins, an' I swear I ain't committed one of 'em." A voice inquired dryly, "Which one was that, Squire?"

See also cosmetics[3], gambling[2], mistake[5].

SINGER

1

Mrs. Johnson was going to give a musicale and she was engaging some talent from an agent who said, "I can get Madame Turner for you that evening." "Is she good?" asked the lady. "She's known to be a great virtuosa," the agent assured her. "I care nothing about her morals," asserted the lady. "Can she sing?"

2

A lady of recent wealth was giving her first formal dinner and, in order to make it a success, she was engaging the services of a well-known singer. "My fee," the artist informed her, "will be $100." "That's quite all right," agreed the lady; "but you understand, of course, that you'll not be introduced to or mingle with my guests?" "Oh, in that case," replied the singer, "I'll sing for $25."

3

The vocalist had just concluded a long, screeching solo, and, while the applause was going on, the host remarked to one of the guests, "I think she's a finished singer, don't you?" "I certainly hope so," was the reply, "but I'm afraid she's going to sing again."

See also concert[3], neighbor[1], President[2], revenge[1].

SINGING

1

The young lady vocalist was being auditioned, and as her song progressed the listener squirmed in his chair. "How much of the song have you sung?" he inquired during a momentary lull. "Down to where it says 'refrain,'" she replied. "Ah, then, my dear," he remarked, "I suggest that you follow that direction."

2

It was an amateur concert, and just before one young lady vocalist began her performance she apologized for a slight cold. Then she began her song: "I'll hang my harp on a willow tree-e-e-ah. Ahem!" She tried again: "On a willow tree-e-e-awk. Oh!" Three more times she tried the high note, but each time her voice broke. "I say, Miss," cried a voice from the audience, "try hanging it on a lower branch!"

See also boast[1], chorus girl[2], story[3], voice.

SISTER

1

The young fellow had been telling his pal about the ecstasy of kissing the girl friend. "Aw, heck," declared the other. "What's the difference between kissing your sweetie and kissing your sister?" "Oh, about forty-five seconds, I'd say," estimated the first.

2

Little Junior approached mother and inquired, "Say, mom, ain't I gonna have a little sister some day?" "Why, dear, would you like one?" asked the surprised mother. "Yes, mom, I kinda would," replied Junior. "It gets awful tiresome just teasin' the cat."

3

"Gee, teacher," cried little Betty as she came to school, "I've got a new little sister!" "Why, how nice," replied teacher. "Yes, but she's only a half-sister," said Betty. "Well, does that make any difference?" asked teacher. "No, I guess not," said the child, "but I can't understand where the other half is."

See also charity[5], family[2], identity[2].

SITTING

"Thus we see," summed up the physiology professor, "that sedentary work tends to lessen the endurance." "In other words," interrupted the student, "the more one sits, the less one can stand." "Precisely," retorted the professor. "And if one lies very much, one's standing is lost entirely."

See also ambition[5], skating[1].

SIZE

1

"Now tell me, little girl," said the dear lady caller sweetly, "what will you do when you're as big as your mother?" "Diet," replied the child.

2

A talkative old man stopped to watch some boys at play. "How old are you, sonny?" he inquired of one. "I'm six," declared the boy. "Six?" echoed the old man. "Why, you're not even as tall as my cane." "Well," asked the boy, drawing himself up to his full stature, "how old is your cane?"

3

The applicant for the job of lifeguard at the city pool was about six-feet-nine-inches tall. After some incidental questions, the man asked him, "You can swim, I suppose?" "Well, no, I can't," admitted the applicant; "but I can sure wade to beat hell."

See also coal[2], expect[3], geography[3], growth[1], head[4], moron[6], ocean[2].

SKATING

1

A young woman boarded a crowded bus with a pair of skates slung across her shoulder. A gallant gentleman arose and said, "Won't you have my seat, miss?" "Thank you, no, sir," replied the girl. "You see, I've been skating all afternoon, and I'm tired of sitting down."

2

Despite the thinness of the ice, a man insisted upon skating. He soon found himself standing in about four feet of freezing water cursing the treacherous ice. "Gracious, sir," called an old lady sympathetically from the bank, "what made you come to fall in like that?" "I did not come to fall in, madam," snarled the man. "I came to skate."

SKIN

"Was there any special reason," inquired a friend of the dermatologist, "that you chose to specialize on diseases of the skin?" "There were three very good reasons," responded the specialist: "my patients never get me out of bed at night; they never die; and they never get well."

See also body[2], drink[1].

SKUNK

See odor[3].

SKYSCRAPER

1

A farmer took his young son for his first visit to New York. They got into one of the express elevators of the Empire State Building, and after they were shot up some thirty stories at breathless speed, the little fellow gasped, "Gee, pop, does God know we're comin'?"

2

Two young farmers were in New York for the first time and they wanted to see the Empire State Building. Having been directed how to reach it by subway, they emerged from the underground station and caught their first glimpse of the building. "Crackey!" gasped one, as soon as he could catch his breath. "Wouldn't she hold a lot o' hay!"

See also elevator².

SLEEP

1

It was early morning when the ringing of the telephone aroused the doctor from a deep sleep. When he picked up the receiver, a plaintive voice whined in his ear, "I can't sleep, doctor." "Well, just hold the wire," said the doctor, "and I'll sing you a lullaby."

2

"Hate to think of goin' home," declared one drunk to another. "Always takesh me 'nhour or more to go to shleep when I go home drunk." "'Sfunny," replied the other. "I alwaysh go shleep soon's I hit th' bed." "Me too," agreed the first; "but it takesh me 'nhour or sho to hit the bed."

See also awaken, beggar³, curfew, hangover², insomnia¹, storm¹.

SLEEPWALKING

1

The night clerk of a hotel was startled to see one of the guests parading through the lobby in his pajamas. "Hey, there, what do you think you're doing?" he demanded. The guest gave a jump and looked about. "Oh, I'm sorry," he apologized. "I'm a somnambulist." "Is that so?" sneered the clerk. "Well, it makes no difference what your religion is. You can't walk around here like that."

2

"I know I'm old, but I love you madly," declared aged Mr. Smith ardently, "and if you'll only have me I'll leave you my entire fortune when I die." "Do you have any bad habits?" asked the chorus girl thoughtfully. "Only walking in my sleep, if you call that a bad habit," was the reply. "Why, you old dear, of course I'll marry you," cried the girl. "And we'll spend our honeymoon on the top floor of some tall hotel, won't we?"

SLOW

1

Two old friends met after a few years and greeted each other warmly. "By the way, Joe," asked one, "do you still talk as slowly as you used to?" "We-ell, if—you—think—I—talk — slow — you — ought — to — hear — my — stenographer," replied Joe. "She — had —a—date—the— other — night — and — the—guy— parked — on — the — way — home —and—before—she—could—say,— 'I'm—not—that—kind—of—girl,'— she—was!"

2

"Are you a messenger boy, son?" asked the near-sighted man of a boy wearing an odd-looking cap. "I certainly am not!" declared the lad indignantly. "It's just a sore toe that makes me walk this slow."

See also speed, train².

SMALL

The diner in the sea-food restaurant called the waiter to his table. "These are certainly small oysters, waiter," he complained. "Yes, aren't they," agreed the waiter indifferently. "And not only that," continued the customer, "but they don't seem very fresh." "Golly, it's sure lucky they're small then, ain't it, sir?" observed the waiter.

See also room³, weak¹.

SMELL

See odor.

SMILE

1

The minister visiting at the hospital paused to speak a few words of cheer to the wan-looking bandaged young man. "You'll soon be all right again," he comforted him. "Just keep smiling." "I'll never smile again," declared the patient. "Nonsense!" scoffed the preacher. "It's not nonsense," insisted the fellow. "It was smiling at another guy's girl that put me here."

2

"What's happened, dearest?" sighed the young lover sadly. "It doesn't seem like the same old smile you used to give me." "As a matter of fact, this is quite a new one," she stated. "I've been taking some lessons at a school of dramatic art, and I've also changed my lip make-up."

3

"Come, my child, smile for me," urged an old gentleman of a serious-faced little girl. When her expression did not change, the old fellow questioned, "Do you know what a smile is, child?" "Yes, sir," replied the girl, still looking grave, "it's the whisper of a laugh."

See also laughter², tax².

SMOKING

1

A visitor at a mental hospital was watching an inmate who, in smoking a cigarette, kept putting the lighted end into his mouth. At last he could stand it no longer and asked, "What's the idea of putting a lighted cigarette in your mouth?" The fellow shrugged his shoulders and sighed, "It's the best I can do; I can't afford a cigar."

2

A man visited a doctor and complained of pain in his ankle. "Goodness, man!" cried the doctor, after a brief examination, "how long has it hurt?" "About three weeks," was the reply. "Why, this ankle is broken," declared the doctor. "Why didn't you come to me right away?" "Well, I sort of hesitated," explained the sufferer, "because every time I say anything is wrong with me, my wife insists that I stop smoking."

3

Hubby arrived home just in time to discover his four-year-old son lighting up a cigarette. He rushed to the kitchen where his wife was preparing dinner, and gasped, "Mary, this is terrible! I just found Junior lighting a cigarette!" The mother gave a little shriek. "I'll soon stop that," she declared. "He's much too young to be playing with matches!"

4

"What's wrong with your hand?" asked a hobo as he spied his fellow hobo with a bandaged hand. "Aw, it's me smokin'," he answered. "Guess I'll have to give up me after-dinner seegar." "Why give up smokin'?" he asked, puzzled. "It's too dangerous," he explained. "Twice this week, now, while pickin' up me evenin' smoke I've had fellers step on me hand."

5

A tourist was passing through a small town one morning and wanted to smoke. But he found himself out of cigarettes and it was too early for any stores to be open. Seeing a young fellow pass with a cigarette in his mouth, he asked, "Say, buddy, got another cigarette?" "Nope, but I got the makin's," was the reply. "Fine," said the tourist, "but I can't roll 'em. Will you do it?" The boy obliged. Then searching his pockets, the tourist said, "Don't believe I've got a match." "Say," remarked the boy, producing a match, "you don't have anything but the habit, do you?"

6

The bus was crowded, so the elegant lady took one of the rear seats reserved for smokers. Soon a man sat beside her and began to fill a grimy-looking pipe. "My good man," said the lady, "smoking always makes me feel sick." "Does it now?" remarked the fellow sympathetically, touching a match to the pipe. "Then take my advice, lady, and don't smoke."

See also lady[4], statistics[5].

SNEEZE

The bookkeeper had a peculiar and annoying manner of sneezing. It always began with a series of elaborate, terrifying facial convulsions that led at last to a most dis-appointing puny snort. "Your sneeze," observed the stenographer as she watched him one day, "is a regular circus." "How come?" asked the bookkeeper. "Because," she rejoined, "the performance never comes up to the advance notices."

SNOW

1

A little girl from California was on a visit North, and she awakened one morning to see it snowing for the first time. "Oh, mother, what is that?" she cried excitedly. "Why, that's snow, dear," responded mother. "What did you think it was?" "Snow!" marveled the child. "Gee, it looks like popped rain!"

2

The snowstorm had been getting worse and worse and the young couple had been trudging for hours trying to find their way back home. But they were lost. "Oh, look, Jack!" cried the girl happily. "We must be near a farm because there's a chicken sitting on the snow." "Chicken, my eye!" growled Jack. "That's the weathercock on the village church steeple."

See also deceive[1].

SOAP

A reporter was interviewing a wealthy soap manufacturer. "It's quite well-known, Mr. Smith," he remarked, "that you've made your entire fortune out of soap. Now to just what, sir, do you attribute your great success?" "To clean living, my boy, just clean living," was the response.

SOCIALIST

"Are you studying hard in school, Johnny?" asked Aunty. "No, I'm not," admitted the boy. "But if you don't study hard," Aunty pointed out, "you'll never become President of the United States." "Aw, I don't expect to anyhow," declared Johnny. "You see, I'm a Socialist."

SOCIETY

1

"How do you like our new neighbor down the street?" asked Mrs. Brown of Mrs. Black. "I really know very little about her," replied Mrs. Black; "but I do know that she's never moved in good society." "But how can you be so sure of that?" questioned Mrs. Brown. "Very simply," was the reply: "she shakes hands as if she really meant it."

2

A woman stopped a flower peddler as he drove by in his wagon and examined his wares. "Your flowers are lovely," she declared. "I do hope you'll be by next Thursday as I'll want some then for my daughter as she's coming out on that day." "She shall have the best in the market, ma'am," said the peddler sympathetically. "What's she been in for?"

See also name[8].

SOLDIER

1

Two old soldiers were boasting to each other of their respective former outfits. "Why, our bunch was so well drilled," declared one, "that when they presented arms all you could hear was slap, slap, click." "That was good," conceded the other, "but when my company presented arms you'd just hear slap, slap, jingle." "What was the jingle?" was the puzzled question. "Oh, just our medals," was the reply.

2

"And there, my son," said father complacently, concluding a two-hour discourse, "you have the story of your old dad in the last war." "But, daddy," asked the boy wonderingly, "what did they need with all the other soldiers?"

3

Diogenes wearily halted the veteran and in a patient, bored voice inquired, "What were you in the last war?" "Who, me?" said the veteran. "Oh, I was just a private." Poor Diogenes gasped, reeled back a step, and stood stunned for a moment. Then he blew out his lantern and went home.

See also army, battle[1], cruelty[2], patriotism[3, 4, 5], plumber[2], recruit, shooting[6].

SON

1

The doorbell rang and little five-year-old Junior opened the door and stared at the gentleman outside. "I'd like to see Mr. Brown," announced the caller. "I'm Mr. Brown," stated Junior, then as an after-thought added, "But perhaps you wish to see old Mr. Brown?"

2

Two friends who hadn't seen each other for several years met. "Well, well," remarked one, "I suppose your son Bob is getting on by now." "Indeed he is," answered the other. "Just a couple of years ago he used to wear my old suits—now I wear his."

3

A man took his oldest son to the photographer's so that they could have their pictures taken together. In trying to pose them suitably, the photographer suggested to the young fellow, "It would make a better picture if you stood with your hand on your father's shoulder." "Humph!" snorted the old man. "It would make a more natural picture if he stood with it in my pocket."

4

The father lined up his eight strapping sons for the visitor to inspect. "Now ain't they fine boys?" he demanded proudly. "They surely are," agreed the visitor; "and well-mannered, too." "That's because they've been brought up right," boasted the father. "I've never laid violent hands on any of 'em, except in self-defense, of course."

5

"Laws, what a mis'able, contrary, nasty li'l cuss thet boy o' yourn is, Maggie," commented the hillbilly to his wife. "But one thing sartin, he don't git none o' his orneriness fum me!" "No, reckon he don't," admitted Maggie, " 'cause you shore ain't lost none o' yourn."

See also family tree[3], glutton[2], intelligence[1], perseverance[2], realism[4], support[1].

SONG

"Who was it," asked the man of a poetic turn, "who said that if he could make the songs of a people he wouldn't care who made the laws?" "I don't know," replied the music-lover whose entire family were radio addicts, "but if he's the guy who's making the songs of the people these days, I'd certainly like to have the making of the laws for just a little while."

SORROW

See grief, mourning, weeping.

SORRY

See grief, repent.

SOUL

The general manager of an insurance company was testing the intelligence of an applicant for the position of office boy. "Suppose," he questioned, "a person came in and asked you if he could have his immortal soul insured. What would you tell him?" "I wouldn't know what to tell him," replied the boy, "so I'd just direct him to the manager of the fire insurance department."

SOUND

See noise.

SOUP

1

"Some guys would kick about anything," growled the proprietor of a restaurant as he sampled a liquid. "I sure can't see what they all got to complain about with this soup." "Aw, it wouldn't be de soup dey was grouchin' about, boss," explained the waiter, "if only de cook would admit it's soup instead of insistin' it's coffee."

2

"Ve got fine zoop today, sir," declared the waiter in the beanery. "You like zoop, mebbe?" "Zoop?" asked the puzzled customer. "What's zoop?" "You don't know what is zoop!" exclaimed the waiter. "You know what is hash, yes? Vell, zoop is same t'ing, only looser."

3

An angry diner called the waiter to his table. "Would you be so good as to tell me what this stuff is?" he asked, indicating the contents of his plate. "That's bean soup, sir," replied the waiter. "I don't give a hang what it's *been*," snarled the customer. "I want to know what it is now!"

4

Arriving in port after a long voyage and hungering for a change of diet, the captain and his mate went ashore to a restaurant where they ordered some soup. After it was served, the captain examined it, then called out, "Hey, waiter, what's this?" "That's soup, sir," replied the waiter. "Well, blow me down, Bill," marveled the captain, turning to the mate. "Here we've been sailin' on soup all our lives an' didn't know it!"

See also alphabet[3], resemblance[2].

SOURCE

1

A hillbilly was entertaining his pastor at dinner, and the preacher was lavish in his praise of the fat, juicy goose that was served. "It's a wonderful bird," he asserted to his host. "Wherever did you get such a fine goose?" "Look, now, parson," protested the host, "when you preaches a good sermon, do I ask you where you got it? So you oughtta have the same consideration fer me."

2

She was a dear old lady, going on a hundred, and she was noted in the village for her unfailing cheerfulness and serenity. The new preacher called on her and eagerly inquired, "What has been the chief source of your strength and power all these years? Tell me, dear lady, that I may impart it to others." The old lady raised her faded eyes, and murmured softly, "Victuals."

SOUTH

1

A foreigner who had become quite friendly with a Kentucky Colonel living in New York, decided to spend the winter in the South. After a week there he wrote his friend a letter in which he enthusiastically declared: "You never told me the South was like this. Why, man, it's God's country!" Promptly the Colonel wired back: "Of course it is. You didn't think God was a damned Yankee, did you?"

2

A Southerner had attended a banquet at which all parts of the country had been well represented. The next day a friend asked him who'd been there, and he answered, "Let's see now. There was a fine gentleman from Virginia, a gentleman from Kentucky, a man from Ohio, a bounder from Chicago, a fellow from New York, and a galoot from Maine."

3

A professor of ancient history, while traveling in Georgia, stopped over in one town to give a lecture on the Medes and the Persians. After it was over, he was approached by an elegant lady who informed him with animation, "My deah Professah, youahs was a most delightful discou'se. Ah found it most enjoyable because, you see, mah mothah was a Meade."

4

A Southern Colonel entered the dining room of a large resort hotel and commanded the waiter, "You-all kin bring me a Kaintucky breakfast." "What's that, sir?" asked the confused waiter. The Colonel gave him a withering glance. "That means," he explained, "that you-all kin bring me a big steak, a bulldog, an' a quart o' Bourbon whiskey." "But why the bulldog?" asked the waiter. "To eat the steak, suh!" thundered the Colonel.

5

A New Yorker went to the Canadian woods for some hunting and found the chilly nights uncomfortable. "Golly," he remarked shiveringly to his guide, "it must sure get cold here in winter." "Goes to about forty-five below," stated the guide. "How do you stand it?" marveled the other. "Oh, I go South for the winter," he was informed. "I see," said the New Yorker. "Where do you go?" "Down to Grand Rapids," was the reply.

6

A rabid Southerner who was in Washington on a visit happened to sit next to a schoolteacher on the bus. The teacher was "doing" Washington on a weekend excursion. As the bus passed the huge United States Pension Building, she addressed her seat-mate to ask, "Pardon me, sir, but can you tell me what that large building is?" "I shore kin, lady," replied the other. "Thet's a monument to Southern marksmanship."

See also display[1], drawl[1], feeling[3], Republicans[2, 4].

SPANKING

See punishment.

SPEAKER

1

There had been much heckling from the audience and at last the speaker lost patience. "We seem to have so many fools here tonight," he snapped, "that it might be advisable to hear them one at a time." "A good idea," came a voice from the crowd. "Go ahead with your speech."

2

As the hubbub continued, the speaker turned disgustedly and said, "Mr. Chairman, I've been on my feet for over ten minutes and during that time there's been so much noise and interruption that I can scarcely hear myself speak." "Cheer up," came a voice from the audience, "you ain't missin' much."

3

The great statesman had begun his address in flowery diction delivered in a deeply sonorous voice.

But after almost two hours of steady speaking he was getting increasingly hoarse. A man in the audience, a job-holder of the same party, whispered to his small son, "Isn't he wonderful? What do you think of him?" "I think he needs a new needle," commented the boy sleepily.

4

A weary-looking farmer stood on the steps of the town hall wherein a political address was in progress. "Do you know who's talking?" inquired a late-comer of him. "Or are you just going in?" "Nope. Jest come out," replied the farmer. "Congressman Smith's talking." "What's he talking about?" asked the other. "Thet's jest it," said the rustic, "he didn't say."

5

The statesman with the aggressive foreign policy was delivering an inspired address at an army camp. "How proudly our Flag of the Free waves over this beautiful camp!" he shouted. "And so it should wave over all oppressed lands! Why doesn't it wave over Kattagutsi, Zukeraminit, or the Islands of Whooziss? Tell me why—" "It could be," ventured a bored voice from the rear, "that they ain't gettin' as much wind there as we are in this here camp."

6

As the speaker droned on, small groups gradually slipped out until at last the audience had dwindled to a single man in the front row. "I wish to pause here, my dear sir," said the speaker to this lonely one, "to express my gratitude for your courtesy in remaining to hear my speech out." "Oh, that's all right," said the other. "I don't deserve any thanks—I'm the next speaker."

See also audience[4], contribution[1], perseverance[3], question[4], remark[2], time[1].

SPECIALIST

A young man had been away to a large university studying medicine, and in returning to his home town for a visit he called upon the old general practitioner of the community. "Well, my boy," remarked the old fellow, "I suppose you intend to specialize?" "Yes, indeed," said the youth, "on the nose alone, for I find that the diseases of the ears and throat are too complex to be combined with those of the nose for study and treatment." "I see," replied the old physician. "And have you picked out which nostril yet?"

SPECTACLES

See glasses.

SPEECH

1

The politician's speech went on and on and still it showed no signs of ending. "And I address myself not only to you, my friends," he bellowed, "but I am also speaking for the benefit of posterity." "It sure looks like it," said a man in the front row, picking up his hat to leave, "so I'll just be getting along and leave my seat for one of them."

2

"As ever, I'm the champion of the poor people," declaimed the politician to the plain citizen he had buttonholed on the street. "Have you heard my last speech?" "I sincerely hope so," replied the other, prying himself loose.

3

One of the audience slipped out of the auditorium and stood inhaling the fresh, clear air of the foyer. "Has the speaker finished his speech yet?" one of the ushers asked him. "Yes, he has," sighed the other. "He finished it a few minutes after he'd started, but he's still talking."

4

The coffee cups were being taken off the banquet tables and the toastmaster got on his feet. "Oh, gosh!" moaned one of the diners to his companion. "Now they'll all get up and spout. Did you ever hear a really good after-dinner speech?" "Only once," admitted the other. "That was when a friend of mine said: 'Waiter, bring us another drink and me the check.'"

See also politics[6], tired[2].

SPEED

1

A gentleman who had just returned from a trip through the South was being questioned about the country by a young lady. One of her questions was, "And what sort of plant is the Virginia creeper?" "That's not a plant," was the response. "It's a railroad."

2

Uncle Zeke drove into the city for one of his rare visits. Old Bess could pull the buggy at about five miles an hour comfortably, but anything more than that made her sweat and heave. Approaching town, he saw a sign: "CITY LIMITS. Speed 15 Miles per Hour." "To heck with their durned fool laws!" snorted Uncle Zeke. "I ain't a-pushin' old Bess to try fer no sich speed even if their danged law does require it!"

See also second-hand car[3].

SPEEDING

1

The sweet young thing was zipping down the village main street in her car when the motorcycle cop overtook her. "Now what have I done?" she asked. "You were going forty-five miles an hour, miss," said the policeman, taking out his book. "Don't be silly!" she scoffed. "I've only been out twenty minutes." The copper scratched his head, then said, "I know there's a trick to it somewhere, but go ahead."

2

"Goin' to a fire, bud?" said the copper with heavy sarcasm as he halted the hurrying motorist. "N-not exactly," stammered the meek little driver. "I was just trying to prevent one." "Oh, yeah?" retorted the policeman. "And how wuz you gonna do that?" "Well, my boss said that's what he'd do if I was late again," explained the other, "and I was just rushing to get to the office on time."

3

A motorist was driving through a sleepy little village at moderate speed when he was picked up by the local officer and taken before the justice. "Ten dollars fine for speeding!" pronounced His Honor with scant ceremony. The man took a bill from his wallet, placed it on the desk, and turned to leave. "Hey, wait!" cried the judge. "This is twenty dollars." "Just keep it," said the motorist. "I intend to get out of this town faster than I came in!"

4

The young blade was doing about eighty-five when the motorcycle policeman finally caught him. "Was I driving too fast, officer?" he asked apologetically. "Hell, no," growled the copper, getting out his book. "You wuz jist flyin' too low."

5

After a chase, Smith was finally flagged down by a traffic cop who demanded, "Whatsa idea doin' seventy in a twenty-mile-an-hour zone?" "But I wasn't doing seventy," protested Smith. "I wasn't doing sixty; no, nor fifty. Why I wasn't even doing forty. Shucks, I wasn't even—" "Hey, look out!" yelled the officer, springing back. "In a minute you'll be backing into somethin'!"

SPELLING

1

"You said you want to be a writer when you grow up, Danny," said teacher sadly, "but just look, you've misspelled half the words in your composition." "Aw, that won't make any difference," replied Danny calmly. "I'm gonna be a dialect writer."

2

The college professor's young wife was pretty, but whatever education she might have had had left her mind practically untouched. One evening while writing a letter, she looked up to ask, "John, dear, do you spell 'graphic' with one 'f' or two?" "Well, my sweet," he replied, "if you're going to use any, you'd might as well use two."

3

"I'm afraid I'll have to get another typist," complained the junior partner to the senior partner. "She's always interrupting my dictation to ask how to spell the simplest words." "Yes, it must be a great waste of time," sympathized the senior partner. "Oh, it's not the time I mind," replied the other. "It just gets embarrassing to have to keep saying, 'I don't know.'"

See also statue[2], synonym.

SPEND

See economy, millionaire[1], money[2], philanthropy[2], thrift.

SPINSTER

See old maid.

SPIRIT

1

A young lady was trying to sell a gentleman some tickets for a charity concert. "I'm very sorry," he said, smiling politely, "but I have a previous engagement for that evening. However, I admire your good work and I shall be with you in spirit." "How splendid!" exclaimed the girl. "And where would you like your spirit to sit? I have tickets from a dollar to twenty-five cents."

2

The minister opened the Sunday-school class by calling for the singing of the well-known hymn about "Little drops of water, little grains of sand." But the response was weak, so halfway through the first verse he stopped them. "Come, come, you can do better than that," he remonstrated. "Now try it again, 'Little drops of water,' and, for goodness sake, put some spirit into it!"

SPIRITUALISM

A recent widow visited a medium who promised to get her in touch with her deceased husband. When his shade had been evoked, she asked, "Are you happy, Henry dear?" "Very happy," she was assured. "Happier than when you were with me on earth?" "Far happier than when on earth with you," stated the spook emphatically. "Tell me, Henry," cried the widow, "what's it like in heaven?" "Heaven!" the ether crackled. "I ain't in heaven!"

See also ghost.

SPITTING

1

Mother cocked her ear as a suspicious noise issued from the living room. "Junior!" she cried. "Junior!" "Whatcha want, mom?" replied the boy's voice. "Are you spitting in the goldfish bowl?" demanded mother. "No, I'm not," came the answer. "But I'm comin' close."

2

A golfer had a reputation for never swearing regardless of how poor his game might be. "I hear that you never cuss your game," remarked an opponent to him one day. "Is that true?" "That's right,

I never cuss on the links," confirmed the other. "Instead, when I miss a shot I just spit; but, believe me, where I spit the grass won't *ever* grow again!"

3

The army recruit from the country was being given his physical examination. "Well, that's everything but the sputum test," said the doctor. "Just expectorate in one of those little bottles on that shelf down at the other end of the room." "What say, doc?" asked the boy. "Just spit in one of those little bottles down there," repeated the doctor. The boy still looked doubtful. "D'you mean all th' way from here, doc?" he inquired.

4

The city fathers were hotly discussing a proposal to build a bridge across a small stream near the town. Alderman Brown arose ponderously to insist, "It's a sinful waste of money to build a bridge over such a small stream. Why, I can stand on one bank and spit halfway across it." "Sit down, you're out of order!" cried several voices. "I know I'm out of order," agreed the alderman. "If I was in order I could spit clear across it easy."

See also bootblack[1], miss[1], volcano[1].

SPORTS

1

Mrs. Black drove into town from the farm with her husband one day and in passing through a park she saw several couples playing tennis singles. "Waal I declare to goodness!" she exclaimed unbelievingly. "Folks shore air gittin' careful these days when they keep 'em separated with a net!"

2

Jane had just returned from a vacation at a winter resort. Her friend Betty was questioning her about the trip. "I suppose you enjoyed the winter sports up there?" asked Betty. "Well, yes, most of them," replied Jane. "But one got pretty fresh and I had to slap his face."

See also amateur[1], games.

SPORTSMANSHIP

1

"Here, here!" the old gentleman told the lad who was sitting on another's chest hammering away vigorously at him. "You shouldn't be hitting that boy when he's down!" "Aw, g'wan!" scoffed the one on top, continuing to pummel. "What do you think I got him down for?"

2

A veteran huntsman took a young amateur hunter along on an expedition in the woods one day. He was horrified to see him drawing a careful bead on a pheasant running along the ground. "Hey, there!" he cried. "Don't you know you should never shoot a running bird?" "Think I'm crazy?" retorted the young fellow. "Can't you see I'm waiting for it to stop?"

3

"I like your sportsmanship," the stranger commended the captain of the village football team. "It was good to hear you cheer the visiting team after the sound beating they gave you." "Aw, 'tweren't nuthin'',"

declared the captain modestly. "We kin take a lickin' as good as the next." "By the way, where's the referee?" asked the stranger. "Oh, him?" said the other. "We threw him in the lake."

See also lose[2].

SPOTS

1

The landlady was showing a prospective tenant a dingy room with badly spotted wallpaper. "This is a very nice room," she declared. "The last man who lived here was an inventor—he invented some kind of explosive." "I see," said the prospect. "And I suppose the spots on the walls are the explosive?" "No," corrected the landlady, "they're the inventor."

2

"How come you're wearing glasses?" inquired Slim. "I've been having trouble with my eyes," explained Jim. "Kept seeing spots in front of them." "Do the glasses help?" asked Slim. "Oh, yes," was the reply. "Now I can see the spots much plainer."

3

"Whatever became of that valet you used to have?" Jack asked his bachelor friend. "I had to fire him," replied the other. "I caught him taking a spot from my gray suit." "But that was part of his job, wasn't it?" asked Jack. "Well, hardly," was the response. "You see, this was a ten-spot."

4

Little Ronnie was always getting stains on the tablecloth, so in order for him to be a little more careful his mother fined him a penny for each spot. The next day at dinner she saw him vigorously rubbing the cloth near his plate with his thumb. "You're wasting your time, Ronnie," she observed. "You can't rub out a spot that way." "I know," replied the boy. "I'm just trying to rub two spots into one."

SPRING

See season[2].

SPURNED

1

The girl shook her head regretfully but firmly, saying, "Sorry, George, but I can never be yours." "Okay," he took it calmly. "But how about all my presents?" "I'll return everything you gave me, of course," she assured him. "Oh, those things, sure," he cried hotly. "But how about all those cigars I gave your old man, those flowers to your mother, and all those dimes to your lousy kid brother?"

2

She had just refused him and was giving him elaborate reasons. "There, now," she concluded, "I hope I've made myself plain." "Don't take credit for that," he observed slyly, grabbing his hat. "Nature took care of that for you."

3

The girl had turned down his proposal as gently as possible, but still he looked sad. "Ah, me," he sighed. "I suppose I'll never marry now." "Silly boy," she said, flattered. "Just because I refused you it doesn't mean that other girls will do the same." "I'm not so sure," he retorted. "If you won't have me, who will?"

4

"You must marry me!" he insisted passionately. "For if you spurn me, I shall surely die!" "I'm sorry," she replied regretfully, "but I don't love you and can't marry you." "Very well," he declared tragically as he stalked out. "Be it on your head!" And sure enough, sixty-three years later he *did* die.

5

He was a romantic youth and was in love, and now he was moping about the house. "What's wrong, son?" asked father. "Oh, it's terrible," he moaned. "I finally proposed to Ethel, and I've been turned down." "Don't be downhearted, son," comforted father. "A woman's 'No' often means 'Yes.'" "That's just it," sighed the boy. "This woman didn't say 'No'—she said 'Nuts!'"

6

A girl found herself at the same party with a former sweetheart and she decided to snub him. "I beg your pardon," she murmured politely when the hostess introduced him, "but I didn't get your name." "I know you didn't," laughed her ex-sweetie. "But it wasn't because you didn't try like hell."

See also customary[3], forget[2], get[1], proposal[3], sarcasm[5], wedding[5, 8].

STAMP

See postage.

STAND

1

"Hey, you!" the policeman shouted at the drunk. "You can't stand there in the street like that." "Oh, but I can, offisher," insisted the drunk proudly. "Don' worry y'self 'bout me. Been stan'in' here 'nhour an' I ain't fell off yet."

2

It was the first time he was dating the girl, and she was telling him her rules about boyfriends. "And another thing," she warned him, "I don't stand for necking." "Don't you?" he replied weakly. "No, I don't," she affirmed. "Standing makes me tired."

See also posture, sitting.

STAR

1

A farmer in town was watching a sidewalk astronomer adjust his telescope on its tripod. Just as he swung the instrument around, a star fell. "By crackey!" ejaculated the farmer admiringly. "Thet feller shore is a slick shot!"

2

The astronomy class was out on the campus for a night lesson. "Oh, Professor," said a sweet young coed, pointing upwards, "is that Venus there?" "No, my dear," replied the professor patiently, "that is Jupiter." "Oh, Professor, what sharp eyes you have," exclaimed the young thing admiringly, "to be able to distinguish sex at that distance!"

See also direction[1].

STARVE

"The boss's wife is shore a stingy one," complained the farmer's hired man to a crony. "What'd she do now, Si?" asked the other. "Aw, she watches every bite I eat," pouted Si. "Jest this mornin' she sez, 'Si, do ye know how many pancakes ye've et?' an' I sez, 'No'm, I ain't had no call to count 'em,' an' she sez, 'Well, thet last wuz yore twenty-ninth,' an' it made me so durned mad thet I jest got up frum the table an' went to work without my breakfast!"

STATE

See birthplace[1], California, condition, Florida, Texas.

STATESMAN

1

The reporter was getting very little out of his interview with the politician, and finally he chided the man gently, "I always thought that a statesman should be familiar with all public questions." "He should," agreed the grafter, "but not necessarily with all the answers."

2

The statesman returned home after having delivered a public address. "How was the speech, John?" asked the wife. "Oh, fair," he replied. "But I'm certain that in discussing the revision of the tariff I said some things that were not generally understood." "But how can you be so sure of that?" said his wife. "Because," and the statesman lowered his voice to a confidential whisper, "I didn't understand them myself."

See also newspaper[3].

STATISTICS

1

"Here are some interesting statistics," remarked hubby, reading from the paper. "They show that graduates from Yale each have 1.3 children, while Vassar graduates have 1.7 children." "There you have it," declared wifey triumphantly. "That proves that women have more children than men."

2

"Traffic accidents are on the increase," observed an old gentleman. "It says here in the paper that in New York a man is run over every half hour." "My, my," murmured the wife sympathetically. "Poor fellow!"

3

"Here are some interesting figures," commented Mr. Black, looking up from his magazine. "According to these statistics, in New York a child is born every two minutes." "Good gracious, we'll have to change our vacation plans!" cried Mrs. Black in alarm. "We were going to stay there three weeks!"

4

The gentleman with the red nose paused in his excursions from one saloon to another and dropped into the library where he got to reading a volume on vital statistics. "Great God!" he commented, suddenly turning to the man on his right. "Do you know that every time I breathe a man dies?" "That's possible," conceded the other, moving farther away. "Why don't you chew cloves?"

5

The lecturer was ranting on his favorite subject—the evils of tobacco. "Carefully compiled statistics," he asserted, "demonstrate that every cigar a man smokes shortens his life by three days, and each cigarette by a week." A man in the audience arose to inquire, "Are those statistics accurate?" "Absolutely accurate, sir," declared the lecturer. "Why?" "It's quite important to me," replied the man, "for if they're accurate, I've been dead some 287 years."

See also clothes[1], insurance[3], recovery[3].

STATUE

1

A friend eyed the statue that the sculptor was just completing for the main square of the village. "Why in the world did you put the general in such an unusual pose?" he asked. "That couldn't be helped," explained the sculptor. "You see, the council first ordered an equestrian statue, but later they found that they couldn't afford the horse."

2

Mr. Newlyrich was just back from a trip abroad, and he was describing in glowing words the statue of a beautiful woman he had seen. "Man, the way she stood there so pert and on her toes was wonderful!" he declared enthusiastically. "They called her 'Posish,' and that was right because, man, that was some posish! But them ignorant foreigners," he added, "had it spelled 'Psyche!'"

3

The self-made man was now rich enough to take a trip abroad. In going through a museum, the guide paused before the statue of the Winged Victory, which the centuries have robbed of its head, and explained, "This, sir, is the famous statue of Victory." "Victory, is it?" grunted the visitor. "By golly, I'd sure like to see the other fellow!"

4

After returning from her tour of Europe, Mrs. Smith remarked to her neighbor, "I wonder what makes people so forgetful in this country? We don't have memories at all like those in Europe." "What makes you say that?" asked the other. "Because when I was abroad," replied the traveler, "I saw any number of statues erected to the memory of various famous people."

5

The grandson of a famous man was visiting the town of his grandfather's birth, and in walking down the street he passed two of the natives. "Who's the stranger?" inquired one of the other. "You don't know who that feller is?" exclaimed the other. "Why he's the grandson of that statue down in the town square."

STEAK

1

Regardless of how he tried, jabbing and sawing at it in every manner, the diner in the restaurant found himself unable to make any impression on his steak. At last he called the waiter and said, "I can't begin to cut this steak. You'll have to take it back and get me another." "Sorry, sir," replied the waiter, looking at the meat, "but I can't take this steak back now—you've bent it."

2

"Bring me a steak," ordered the tourist who had stopped in a small town restaurant. "Do you want the dollar or the dollar-and-a-half steak?" asked the waitress. "What's the difference, one bigger than the other?" asked the tourist. "No, they're the same," replied the waitress, "only with the dollar-and-a-half steak you get a sharp knife."

3

The cowpuncher in the big city chanced into a restaurant that specialized in rare meats. He ordered a steak, and the waiter brought him one that was very rare indeed. "Hey, take this meat back and cook it," he commanded. "It is cooked, sir," snapped the waiter. "Cooked, my eye!" retorted the cowboy. "I've seen cows hurt worse'n that an' git well."

4

After a struggle, the diner called the waiter over. "How was this steak cooked?" he demanded. "It was smothered in onions, sir," replied the waiter. "Humph!" said the customer. "It sure died hard."

See also find.

STEAL

The minister had a large strawberry patch. Thinking to point a moral lesson he invited all the village boys in for a strawberry party, then asked, "Now, boys, wasn't that better than breaking into my garden and stealing my strawberries?" "Oh, yes, sir," chorused all the lads. "And why was it better?" he demanded of one youngster. "Because that way we wouldn't have had sugar and cream with 'em," was the response.

See also burglar, joke[4], perfect[4], reform[3], robbery, thief.

STENOGRAPHER

1

"That girl looks familiar," observed a man as his friend tipped his hat to a young woman on the street. "Who is she?" "She used to be my stenographer," he was told. "She's lovely," declared the first. "Why did she leave you?" "Oh, I had to fire her because she was too conscientious in her work," explained the other. "One day I proposed to her and she took it all down in shorthand and brought it neatly typed to me to sign!"

2

After many mistakes in spelling and grammar in her letters, the boss finally lost patience and called his stenographer to him. "You look intelligent enough," he said, "so that it's hard to believe that you don't even know the King's English." "Of course, I know it," she retorted indignantly; "otherwise how could he be King?"

3

The boss's wife visited the office and in the anteroom she encountered his pretty stenographer. After telling the girl who she was, she added, "I'm really very happy to meet you, Miss Smith, as my husband has told me so little about you!"

4

The wife glared at the businessman after the pretty young stenographer had ushered her into his inner office. "I thought you told me your typist was an old maid?" she said accusingly. "Well, er, yes, my dear, I, ah, did," he faltered. "But you see she's, ah, sick today and she sent her, er, granddaughter in her place."

5

The applicant for the position of stenographer was very pretty. She was being interviewed by the junior partner when the senior partner chanced by. The latter called the other aside and whispered, "Say, I'd hire her." "I have," he was told. "Can she take dictation?" asked the senior partner. "Aw, I'll find that out later," was the reply. "I just didn't want any obstacles to crop up now."

See also feeling[2], flirt[1], interest[3], jealousy, mistake[2], sarcasm[2], typewriter.

STILL

See silence.

STINGY

1

"The stingiest man I know," remarked one fellow, "is the guy who told his little boy that the gas meter was a bank so that the kid put all his quarters in it." "I know a stingier one than that," declared another. "He gave his little girl a nickel not to eat any supper, sneaked the nickel away from her while she was asleep, and then wouldn't give her any breakfast because she'd lost it."

2

"Gosh, my husband is so tight,"

complained Mabel, "that the other evening when he opened his purse three moths flew out." "That's nothing," retorted Tilly. "Whenever my husband takes a penny out of his pocket the Indian blinks at the light."

3

Hubby was in an uproar because the wife had let someone give her a counterfeit dollar bill in change. "How in the world could you be dumb enough to let any one pass a counterfeit bill on you?" he shouted. "How could I tell?" she answered. "You never let me see real money often enough for me to know the difference!"

See also contribution[3], economy, nothing[2, 3], purpose, repay[3], starve, thrift.

STOCK MARKET

1

"Please lend me five hundred, dad," cried the broker's son, rushing into his office. "I've got a sure tip on the market." "How much might we make out of it?" asked the old man cautiously. "Two hundred anyway," asserted the boy. "That's a hundred apiece." "I can do better than that," said father, handing him some bills. "Let's assume you've made the deal and it worked out. Now there's your hundred, and I save four hundred."

2

A stockbroker was taken ill and rushed to the hospital. When the nurse had finished taking his temperature, he asked weakly, "What is it now, nurse?" "It was 101," she replied, "but now it's 102." "Fine!" he cried gleefully. "When it reaches 102½, sell!"

3

"Now, Johnny," teacher questioned the stockbroker's son, "can you tell us who the Puritans were?" "Huh?" asked Johnny. "The Puritans," repeated teacher. "You know, the people who were punished in stocks." "Oh, sure," replied Johnny. "They were the small investors."

4

"I sure made a good deal on a cheap little thing I picked up last winter," boasted a man to a stockbroker. "It stood at twenty-nine then, and yesterday it touched ninety-three." "Gosh, what luck!" exclaimed the broker. "What was it?" "A thermometer," replied the other.

See also bill[1], faithful[2].

STOCK RAISING

"Now, Hiram," teacher questioned the farmer's boy during the arithmetic lesson, "if there were nine sheep in a field and four jumped over the fence, how many would be left?" "None," replied Hiram. "But that's wrong," said teacher. "You don't know arithmetic." "No, it's not wrong," insisted the boy. "You don't know sheep."

STONE

1

The guide was giving the tourists an elaborate discourse on the topography of the surrounding country. "Now, those rock formations over there," he explained learnedly, "were piled up by the glaciers, and over there—" "But where are the glaciers now?" interrupted an elderly lady. The guide gave her a withering glance and replied, "They have gone back after more rocks, madam."

2

The prison guard had been watching a convict listlessly pecking at a rock for an hour without effect and finally lost patience. "Here, gimme that sledge!" he commanded, and with one mighty blow he shattered the stone. "See there!" he cried triumphantly. "Well, no wonder," said the prisoner; "look how I've been softening it up for you!"

STOP

1

A man was waiting in the bitter cold at the village railroad station for the local to take him to the city. But his train was evidently being held up by the non-stop express. The express finally came through and by some miracle stopped at the little station. The man was just climbing aboard when the conductor cried, "Sorry, sir, but you can't get on here. This train doesn't stop." "Oh, that's all right," answered the other. "If it doesn't stop, then I'm not on it."

2

It was evening when the tourist reached Boston and, wishing to find lodgings, he hailed a man on the street and asked, "Pardon me, sir, but could you tell me where I might stop at?" "I should advise," replied the Bostonian icily, "stopping just before the 'at.'"

See also boxing[2], bus[2], train[6].

STORE

1

Little Junior had accompanied mother to the grocer's. After the purchases were made the grocer gave the lad a piece of candy. "What do you say to the man, Junior?" prompted mother. "Charge it," was the reply.

2

"Gimme a dime's worth of asafetida," said the boy to the storekeeper. The man wrapped up the package and handed it to the boy, who then informed him, "Pop wants you to charge it." "All right," said the storekeeper; "what's the name?" "Schmertzkoppeldorfer," was the reply. "Aw, take it for nothing," instructed the proprietor. "I sure ain't gonna spell 'asafetida' and 'Schmertzkoppeldorfer' for no lousy dime."

3

A young clerk in a store was having trouble making ends meet on his meager salary, so he went in to ask his crusty old boss for a raise. "Humph!" growled the old sourpuss. "You're making plenty of money for a single fellow. Why, when I was your age I was supporting a family on a smaller salary than yours." "Maybe so," answered the young man. "But they didn't have cash registers in those days."

4

The manager of a large variety store happened to overhear a clerk telling a lady, "No, madam, we haven't had any for a long time." He rushed up and interrupted, "Oh, yes, we have. I'll have some brought from the warehouse at once." The lady departed laughing, and the manager turned and instructed the clerk, "Never refuse anything, but always send out for it. What did she want?" "Nothing," replied the smiling clerk. "She just said, 'We haven't had any rain lately.' "

See also business[3], butcher[1], candy, clothes[11], discharge[1], fruit[3], grocer, necessity[3], religion[3], shape[1], shopping, signs[4], weight[2].

STORK

A little girl at the zoo was tossing bits of bread to the stork who gobbled them up and bobbed its head at the girl for more. "What kind of bird is that, mamma," she asked. Mother read the sign on the cage and replied, "That's a stork, dear." "Oh, sure," said the girl. "No wonder it recognized me!"

STORM

1

Two hoboes slipped into the hayloft of a farmer's barn one night and went to sleep. During the night a terrible storm came up. Upon awakening in the morning, one bum said in surprise, "How come the hay's so wet?" "The roof leaks," the other told him. "Did it rain last night?" asked the first. "Boy, it sure did!" declared the second. "And I never did see such lightning and thunder." "Golly, why didn't you wake me?" cried the other. "Don't you know I never can sleep when it thunders!"

2

Little Jimmy shivered in terror as the thunderstorm raged on. "There's no need to worry, son," comforted mother. "The wind has to bring the clouds in so it can rain, and it must rain so that the trees and flowers and crops can grow. It's all part of God's work, dear." "Uh-huh," replied Jimmy, unconvinced, cringing at another thunderclap. "But, mom, when's God gonna quit work?"

See also radio[1], rain, wind.

STORY

1

It was about two-thirty in the morning when little Joan woke up. "Tell me a story, mamma," she pleaded. "Hush, dear," replied mother. "Daddy ought to be along pretty soon, now, and he'll tell us both one."

2

Uncle had been left to put little Betty to bed. His patience with children was not remarkable. "Please tell me a bedtime story, Uncle," Betty pestered him. "Please, please, please." "All right," growled uncle. "Once there was a little girl named Red Riding Hood and she met a wolf and the wolf ate up her grandmother. Now shut your mouth and go to sleep!"

3

It was one of those jolly little parties where every one had to do something to entertain. One guest had just finished singing in a squeaky voice, when they called on a minister who was present to sing also. "I'm afraid that I'm out of voice," he excused himself. "Then you must tell a story," they told him. "Well, if I *must* tell a story," he replied slyly, "I'll just say that

I'd like to hear our friend sing that song again."

See also convince[2], sermon[4].

STOUT

See fat.

STRANGER

1

The proprietor of a little backwoods hotel walked in one day and was shocked to see a new arrival standing with an arm around his daughter's waist. "Lands, Mary, tell that danged fool to take his arm from around you," commanded pappy. "Tell 'im you'se'f, paw," replied the girl. "He's a puffect stranger to me."

2

The preacher was back home after Sunday evening services. "Many folks in church tonight?" inquired the wife. "Yes, the attendance was pretty good," replied the preacher. "There was a stranger there, too, but I didn't see him." "Then how did you know he was there?" asked the woman. "There was a dollar in the contribution box," was the reply.

STRATEGY

1

Old Uncle Jim was watching his small nephew play soldiers with a chum, and finally he said, "I'll give you a nickel, Billy, if you take that fort from your friend in a quarter-hour." Within five minutes the boy was back demanding the nickel. "But how did you manage it so quickly?" asked Uncle Jim as he

took out the coin. "Easy," replied the lad. "I just gave Danny two cents to surrender."

2

Two housewives were talking shop over the back fence. "Do you ever nag your husband?" inquired one. "Only when he's beating the rugs," responded the other. "It gets him so thoroughly irritated and angry that he does a much better job."

STREET

See address, location[2, 3].

STREETCAR

1

The absent-minded professor was standing on a crowded trolley clinging to a strap with one hand while the other arm was full of bundles. As the conductor approached him, his face assumed a look of worry. "Can I be of any assistance, sir?" asked the conductor kindly. "Yes, thank you," the professor sighed in relief. "Just hold on to this strap for me while I get out my fare."

2

A lady boarded a streetcar and after a search through her purse, at last handed the conductor a twenty-dollar bill. "I'm sorry," she snapped, noting the conductor's disapproving glance, "but I don't have a nickel." "Oh, don't worry, lady," he reassured her, "you'll have just 399 of 'em in a minute."

3

"I'm sorry, lady," said the streetcar conductor apologetically as he examined the transfer she had given him, "but this transfer expired an hour ago." "And small wonder," she sniffed, rummaging in her purse for a coin, "with not a single ventilator open in this car!"

See also age[3], chivalry[2, 4], conductor[1], fat[2], polite[4].

STRENGTH

1

"Gee, I'll bet you're strong," commented little Junior admiringly to the pretty young widow who had come to call on mother. "Why, what makes you think I'm so strong?" asked the woman. "But you must be," insisted Junior, " 'cause daddy says you can wrap any man in town around your little finger."

2

"Gee, daddy, look!" cried little Bobby excitedly, running in from the garden. "I pulled up this big weed all by myself!" "Goodness, but you *are* strong!" replied father with admiration. "I should say I am," agreed Bobby. "The whole world had hold of the other end of it."

3

"Can you tell me, Willie," questioned teacher, "who were the two strongest men of old?" "Sure, they were Samson and Hercules," was the prompt answer. "Well, can you tell me anything more about them?" asked teacher. "Sure I can," said Willie. "Samson was a regular Hercules."

4

"Well, how are you feeling these days?" inquired a neighbor of an elderly gentleman. "Not so spry any more," complained the old man, "and my strength is failin' fast. Not so long ago I could walk around the block every afternoon, but lately I'm gettin' so weak that by the time I'm halfway around I get so tired that I have to turn around and come back."

See also convalescent[1], source[2].

STUBBORN

1

The parson was walking down the Main Street of the village when he met one of his parishioners. "And how's your cold, Mr. Brown?" he asked after greetings were over. "Very stubborn," reported Brown. "That's too bad," sympathized the preacher. "And how's your wife?" "About the same," was the answer.

2

A tourist in a remote section paused to watch a hillbilly struggling with a stubborn mule. Entreaties, curses, and beatings did no good. "What's the matter, is the mule stubborn?" inquired the tourist finally. "Stubborn!" exclaimed the hillbilly, mopping his brow with his sleeve. "Say, mister, thet danged critter is *so* contrary thet when his hind laigs air a-pushin' his front ones air a-walkin' back'ards!"

3

The jury had now been out for six days, and still the twelfth juror remained unconvinced by the others. As noon approached, the bailiff entered the jury room and asked, "Well, gentlemen, will it be twelve dinners as usual?" "No, I think not," said the foreman. "Better make it eleven dinners and one bale of hay."

STUDENT

1

A student's father was visiting the college and he was introduced to one of the professors. "I'm very glad to meet you," he said, shaking the professor's hand. "My son took algebra from you last year." "Pardon a slight correction," replied the professor; "your son was exposed to it, but it didn't take."

2

"Excuse me," said a caller to the landlady when she had answered his knock, "but does George Black, a student, live here?" "Well, there is a Mr. Black living here," admitted the landlady; "but I always thought he was a night watchman."

3

A student looking for a room stopped at a college town boarding-house. "What do you get for your rooms?" he asked the landlady. "Five dollars up," he was informed. "Whew! isn't that a little high?" he said. "You know, I'm a student." "In that case," retorted the landlady, "it will be five dollars down."

4

"Well, this is a fine welcome, I must say!" scowled father as he arrived to visit his son at college. "Here I hardly step off the train when you ask me for money." "Oh, it's not that bad, dad," the boy answered. "You must admit the train was fifteen minutes late."

5

The millionaire was questioning the private tutor about his son's progress in his studies. "Is my son getting well grounded in the classics?" he asked. "I'd put it stronger than that, sir," replied the tutor. "I'd say that your son is stranded high and dry on them."

STUDY

1

The high-school girl of the breezy manner was seated next to the famous astronomer at dinner and in the course of conversation she asked him, "Well, what are you doing with your life, pal?" "I study astronomy," the great man told her. "Golly, at your age!" exclaimed the girl. "Why, I finished astronomy last year."

2

The wealthy, self-made man visited his minister to express his concern over his son-in-law. "I'm worried about the boy," he confided. "All day long he does nothing but read, study, and pray." "But I see nothing wrong in that," protested the minister. "I do that myself." "I know," replied the other, "but this young fool takes it seriously."

3

"You look awfully tired, young man," observed a kindly old lady to a weary-looking fellow sitting on a bus with a lapful of books. "I am tired, ma'am," he informed her. "I'm studying for a doctor." "But that's outrageous!" she cried indignantly. "You tell that doctor to do his own studying and you get some sleep."

4

"I hope you all know your lessons

today," said teacher, looking over the class. "Tommy, how far have you studied?" "Just as far as the book is dirty, teacher," replied the boy.

STUPID

The moronic young man entered the washroom of the Pullman and noticed a sign over a pushbutton reading: "Ring bell for porter." He pushed the button, and when a man appeared he demanded, "Are you the porter?" "Yes, suh. What kin I do for you, suh?" was the reply. "Nothing," said the man. "I just saw the sign here, and I want to know why you can't ring the bell yourself?"

See also eating[6], fool, moron, professor[1], sarcasm[3].

STUTTERING

1

A certain actor was noted for his stuttering. His agent one day got in touch with him and said, "I've just got a five-minute spot for you on a big variety broadcast, Joe. What can you do in that time?" "W-w-w-we—uh—w-w-we-well," answered the comedian, "I-I c-can j-j-just c-clear m-my th-th-throat!"

2

A stuttering blacksmith had a helper who also stuttered. The blacksmith held a piece of red-hot iron on the anvil and commanded the other, "G-g-g-go on, h-h-h-hit it!" "W-w-wh-w-where sh-sh-shush-sh-shall I h-h-hit it?" asked the helper. "A-aw, h-h-heck!" cried the blacksmith. "N-n-now w-we'll h-h-

have to h-h-heat it a-all o-over again!"

3

A traveling salesman stopped in the railroad station of a small town to ask the agent, "How soon can I get a train for Detroit?" "W-wh-why, th-th-there's, uh, th-th-there's th-the t-t-train, uh, t-the t-train—H-heck!" exclaimed the agent, "i-if you h-hadn't a-asked m-me you c-could have c-caught it!"

4

"Well, Bill, I hear you've been to a school for stutterers," remarked Jim. "Did it help you?" Bill drew himself up and proudly recited, "She sells sea shells on the sea shore." "Say, that's marvelous!" approved Jim. "Yes, isn't it?" agreed Bill. "B-but it's s-so d-d-darned h-hard to w-work it into a c-conversation."

5

The prospective father wanted a son and he was pacing the hospital hall in agitation. "Tell me," he cried when the doctor finally appeared, "is it a boy?" "Tr-tr-tr—" stuttered the physician. The man paled. "What! Triplets?" he gasped. "N-no, qu-qu-qu—" stammered the doctor. "Oh, quadruplets!" groaned the new papa. "N-no!" barked the doctor. "Qu-qu-quite the c-contrary. Tr-tr-try to take it calmly. I-it's a g-girl."

6

There had been a bad accident on the construction job and one of the workmen had been killed. "Well, men," said the foreman sadly, "we'll have to let the poor guy's wife know, but we gotta send somebody who'll break the news to her gradual-like. Now, who'll we send?" "Send Clancy, he's just the feller to break it gradual," suggested someone. "Jist look how he stutters."

See also peculiarity.

STYLISH

See fashion, fashionable.

SUBSTITUTE

1

A passerby tossed a dime at the blind man's tin cup. The coin missed the cup and started rolling along the pavement, but the beggar quickly retrieved it. "Hey, I thought you were blind?" said the donor. "No, I'm not the regular blind man, sir," explained the wearer of the dark glasses. "You see, I'm just taking his place today while he's at the movies."

2

The grocer had just hired a new clerk and told him, "Now if a customer asks for something we don't happen to have, always suggest something else as nearly like it as possible." Soon a woman came in and asked the clerk, "Do you have any fresh green stuff today?" "No, madam, we haven't," replied the clerk politely, "but we just got in some nice bluing."

3

"Never turn a customer down because we happen to be out of something," said the grocer to his new clerk who had just let a woman walk out. "Always suggest a substitute of the same sort." Later, a lady asked the clerk, "Do you have any grapefruit?" "No, ma'am," he replied, "but we have grape-nuts, grape-jelly, grape-juice, and I think we have a new thing because I heard the boss whispering to the butcher about something that had just come in over the grapevine."

SUCCESS

1

"Could you please tell me, sir," pleaded the young college graduate of the hard-headed, self-made business magnate, "how to go about being a success in business?" "In a sentence, son," replied the other briefly: "Sell your wristwatch and buy an alarm clock."

2

"Two things, my son, are important to success in business," the big businessman lectured his son, "and they are: honesty and discretion." "But just what do you consider honesty, dad?" asked the boy. "Honesty is at all times—regardless of conditions or how it may affect you—keeping your word once you have given it," defined the old man. "And discretion?" asked the son. "Never giving it," was the reply.

3

A young man was seeking the successful businessman's advice. "I've just graduated from college," he said, "and I'd like to know what to do to make my way in this world." "Just keep your eyes open," instructed the other, "and marry the first girl you find who has a steady job."

4

A self-made millionaire was addressing a group of young college graduates. "My success in life," he stated pompously, "I owe to one thing—pluck, pluck, pluck." "That's fine, sir," interrupted a realistic young fellow down in front, "but could you tell us a little something about whom to pluck and how to go about it?"

See also ambition[1, 3], business[4], election[5], newspaper[6], soap.

SUFFER

1

The woman lecturer was a violent feminist. "For centuries women have been misjudged and mistreated," she declared emphatically, "and they have suffered in a thousand ways." As she paused to let this pronouncement sink in, a meek little man in front ventured, "But there is one way, madam, in which women never have and never will suffer." "And how is that, sir?" demanded the lecturer belligerently. "They have never suffered in silence," was the answer.

2

The farmer was wealthy and the city girl was suing him for breach of promise. "Now think carefully," said the attorney for the plaintiff, "when on the evening of the ninth you bade her good-by, did she suffer you to kiss her?" "Waal, reckon as how mebbe I did give 'er a kiss or two," admitted the farmer, "but there shore didn't seem to be much sufferin' about it, fur as I could see."

SUFFRAGE

"Come along and vote, dear," pleaded hubby to the wife. "Our candidate needs all the support he can get, and besides it's your duty to vote." But wifey shook her head. "You can call it bribery or not," she declared decisively, "but I insist I'll not vote unless you buy me a new hat to vote in."

See also help[7], vote.

SUGGESTION

1

The boss had spent a great deal to improve working conditions in his shop, and he now said to his men, "I wish that whenever I enter the shop I may see every man cheerfully performing his task. I am therefore putting up this box and inviting you to put in it any suggestions for bringing this about." When the box was opened a week later, it contained only one slip of paper on which was the suggestion: "Don't wear rubber heels."

2

The tourist had had tire trouble and was in an irritable mood when he stopped in a little roadside tea-room run by an aging spinster with a simpering manner. "What would you like with your tea?" she inquired coyly as she set the cup before him. "I suggest a lemon." "Boy, you sure do," he agreed.

3

The tramp leaned back with a sigh of satisfaction. He looked at the plate he had just cleaned. The lady of the house hinted, "Of course, it's merely a suggestion, but the woodpile is in the back yard." The bum raised his eyebrows in surprise. "Is that a fact, now?" he said politely. "What a perfectly splendid place for a woodpile!"

SUICIDE

1

A moron one day felt that life held nothing for him and decided to commit suicide. Sometime later, a friend entered his room and found him standing with a rope around his waist and the other end tied to the chandelier. "What are you doing?" he asked. "Committing suicide," was the reply. "Then why don't you put the rope around your neck?" asked the friend. "Oh, I had it there," said the moron, "but I couldn't get my breath."

2

"It says here in the paper," remarked wifey one evening "that marriage is the best preventive of suicide." "Maybe so," growled hubby, "but don't ever forget that suicide is the best preventive of marriage."

3

A melancholy old gentleman came out of his luxurious club and climbed stiffly into his elegant limousine. "Where to, sir?" asked the chauffeur. "Please drive to a suitable high cliff, James," instructed the old boy. "I'm committing suicide."

See also brains[1], customary[3], salesman[4].

SUITABLE

"Yes, grandma, I'm going to be married next month," confided the young girl happily. "Ah, but marriage is a serious business and you are very young, my dear," protested the old lady. "Do you feel that you're fitted for married life?"

"But I'm being fitted now, grandma," said the bride-to-be sweetly, "and my gowns are going to be simply marvelous."

SUITOR

1

"Quick, dear, get me my bag!" cried the doctor excitedly as he dropped the phone and grabbed his hat. "This man says he can't live without me." "Just a minute," called the wife, who had picked up the receiver. "This call is for our daughter."

2

"Ethel," father questioned his daughter, "is this young man of yours serious in his intentions?" "He appears to be, dad," replied the girl. "He's already asked me what my allowance is, what kind of meals we have, what brands of liquor and cigars you use, and how you and mother are to live with."

3

A millionaire, who was interviewing a prospective son-in-law, ended his questioning by asking, "Tell me truthfully, young man, would you love my Georgette just as much if she were poor?" "But of course, sir," declared the suitor ardently. "That settles it, then," decided the old man. "We don't want any fools in the family."

4

"Why, no, indeed," replied the millionaire genially to the young man with a title and nothing else, "I have no objection at all to your asking my daughter to marry you." "Ah, thank you, sir," replied the broken-down nobleman gratefully.

"Yes, go right ahead and ask her," continued the millionaire. "I've given her a good education, taught her to read the newspapers, and encouraged her to mix with people, and if she doesn't know enough to say, 'No,' she doesn't deserve any better luck."

See also brains[1], dust[1], father-in-law[1], income, meaning, salary[7], support[8], underwear, wealth[2].

SUMMER

See heat, vacation[1].

SUMMER BOARDER

1

"How does it happen," asked the summer boarder curiously of the farmer's young son, "that that one old hog keeps trying to come into my room? Do you think he's taken a liking to me?" "Naw, not that," replied the boy. "It's jest 'cause this is his room durin' the winter."

2

A city man who had enjoyed his stay on a certain farm the previous summer, wrote to ask the farmer if he might have the same room again this year, then added: "But I'd appreciate it if you'd move that pigpen from where it was under my window, as the noise bothered me." The farmer wrote in reply: "Keeping the same room for you. And don't let the pigpen bother you, because we ain't had no hogs on this farm since you left last year."

See also example[1].

SUN

Mr. Williams was a great traveler and never missed an opportunity to let folks know about it. While visiting a friend in the country, his host chanced to remark, "Lovely sunset, isn't it?" "Yes, but you should see the sunsets in the East!" raved the globe-trotter. "I'd certainly like to," asserted the other. "But it must seem very strange, as in this country the sun always sets in the west."

SUNDAY

1

The small boy was late for Sunday school and the teacher asked why. "I was going fishing," he replied, "but papa wouldn't let me." "Your father is a fine man," approved the teacher. "I suppose he explained to you why you shouldn't go fishing on Sunday?" "Yes, he did," responded the lad. "He told me there wasn't enough bait for both of us."

2

The minister called at the Browns' home one Sunday afternoon and little Junior opened the door. "Pop ain't home right now," he informed the caller. "He's gone over to the golf club." The preacher's brow began to cloud in disapproval, so Junior hastened to defend the old man. "But he ain't gone to play no golf, not on Sunday, pop ain't," he declared. "He just went over for a couple of highballs and a few hands of stud poker."

3

Little Tommy was trudging homeward from the lake one Sunday afternoon proudly carrying a large string of fish. He suddenly met the minister of his church. The clergyman's face showed disapproval, but before he could say anything Tommy quickly held up his string and said in a sanctimonious voice, "See, Reverend, what these heathen fish got for nabbin' at worms on Sunday?"

4

The quiet of Sunday afternoon was being shattered by a spirited ball game in the front yard. At last, the lady of the house came to the door and said, "Boys, don't you know you shouldn't play ball in front on Sunday? If you must play, go in back." "Hey, fellers, come on in the back yard," shouted one of the boys. "It ain't Sunday there."

See also hangover[3], morality[2].

SUNDAY SCHOOL

1

"Who can tell me," questioned the Sunday-school teacher, "what the rod of affliction is?" "I can," answered a boy whose father suffered from hay fever; "it's goldenrod."

2

"Now, Johnny," asked the Sunday-school teacher of one of her small pupils, "can you tell me what was the first thing the Israelites did after they crossed the Red Sea?" "I ain't sure," said the boy, "but I guess they dried themselves."

3

Little May had just trudged into her home after her first attendance at Sunday school. "Well, well," asked her father, "and what did my little girl learn this morning?" "That I'm a child of Satan," was the response.

4

The daughter of a newspaper editor returned from Sunday school carrying a picture card illustrating a Bible text. "What's that you have there, dear?" asked the editor. "What, this?" said the girl. "Oh, that's just a little illustrated handout of advance publicity for heaven."

5

A small girl had enjoyed going to Sunday school, being greatly interested in the accounts of Moses. But suddenly she lost all liking for attendance. "Why don't you care to go any more?" asked her mother. "Aw, I don' wike to go to Sunnay school no more," declared the tot firmly, "not since Moses died."

6

A missionary from darkest Africa was lecturing to a Sunday school. "Just think, my little friends," he said, "in that vast country there is not a single Sunday school for thousands of miles. Now who can tell me what little boys and girls should save their pennies for?" A little fellow in front raised his hand, and then spoke up, "To buy tickets to go to Africa."

7

A minister was telling a Sunday-school class the story about Elisha and the bears—how when on his journey to Bethel the children had mocked him, they were punished by having two she-bears come out and eat forty-and-two of them. "Now, children," he concluded, "what does this story show?" A little girl in front volunteered, "It shows how many children two she-bears can hold."

8

The Sunday-school teacher was telling her class the story of the Prodigal Son. "But amidst all this joy and celebration," she said, "there was one to whom the preparation of the feast for the return of the son brought no joy, who felt only bitterness and did not wish to attend the feast. Who was it?" After a moment's silence, a small voice answered, "It was the fatted calf."

9

"What can you tell us about King Solomon?" questioned the Sunday-school teacher. "He was very wise," replied a little girl, "and loved women and animals." "Loved women and animals?" gasped the teacher. "Who told you that?" "Why, the Bible says so," declared the child. "It says that he had seven hundred wives and three hundred porcupines."

10

"Now remember, children," explained the Sunday-school teacher, trying to make clear the meaning of a parable, "the tares represent the wicked people and the wheat the good ones." "Gee, that's funny," commented one little fellow thoughtfully. "Then how come it's always the wheat that gets threshed and the tares that don't?"

See also attendance[1], behavior[3], Bible[1, 3], commandment[2], foreigner[2], God[2], man[2], precocious[1], progress[1].

SUPERSTITION

The unfaithful wife had her boyfriend in her apartment when she heard hubby's key in the front door. "Quick, hide in the closet!" she told her lover. "Not enough room," he objected. "All right, then, jump out the window," she suggested. "But it's thirteen floors down," he protested. "Hmmm," she answered, "*now* he gets superstitious."

See also journey, prayer[7], protection, serving[2].

SUPPER

See eating, food, meals.

SUPPORT

1

"Poor old Jensen has two wives to support now," remarked the postman sympathetically as he handed Mrs. White her mail. "Merciful heavens!" gasped the lady. "Do you mean to tell me he's a bigamist?" "Oh, no, nothing like that," explained the postman. "It's just that his son got married a few days ago."

2

The girl was getting a little impatient, so at last she broached the subject of marriage to the fellow. "You know I love you, darling," he declared, "but marriage is, ah—well, it's simply out of the question. Why, I couldn't keep a goldfish." "You most certainly could, sweetheart," she insisted stoutly. "I love the little things."

3

"Well, Mandy, I hear you've been married," remarked the lady to her charwoman. "Yes'm," was the reply, "I got me a husband now." "That's fine," commented the lady. "Is he a good provider?" "Yes'm, he's a powerful good provider," asserted

Mandy; "only I'm awful skeered he's a-gonna git caught at it some day."

4

The neighborhood bum was up before the police judge on a peace disturbance charge. "I'm afraid I'll have to commit you for vagrancy," decided the judge, "as you don't have any visible means of support." "But indeed I have," protested the loafer. "Maggie, my darling, come here and stand up so that His Honor can see you!"

5

Bill had just married, and on his first payday he gave his bride twenty-eight dollars of his thirty-dollar salary and kept two dollars for himself. But on the second payday he gave his wife only two dollars and kept the rest for himself. "But, Jack," she protested, "how do you think I can get by a whole week on two measly dollars?" "Damned if I know," he replied. "I had a hell of a time doing it myself last week, and this week it's your turn."

6

The girl's father still hesitated in giving his daughter's suitor an answer. "I like you personally," he said, "but you must admit that you've never shown yourself capable of supporting a wife." The young man thought this over, then replied, "If, sir, you wish your daughter to marry a widower, then I must confess I cannot qualify."

7

The class was having a lesson in natural history and the teacher was trying to illustrate the difference between man-made and natural

wonders. "What," she questioned a small girl, "do you think is the most wonderful thing man ever made?" But the child's parents must have been hard-pressed by expenses, for she answered, "A living for a family."

8

"So you wish to marry Helen?" said the girl's father to daughter's suitor. "Yes, sir, very much," declared the young fellow. "Hmmm, I see," pondered father. "Well, can you support a family?" "Well, sir," the young man replied, "how many of you are there?"

See also courtship[3], salary[7], underwear.

SURGERY

1

"Heavens, dear," exclaimed the wife of the surgeon, "why did you tear out the rear portion of that book just now?" "I'm terribly sorry, darling," he apologized, "but that part was labeled 'Appendix' and I took it out without thinking."

2

An insurance agent was filling in an application blank for a policy. "Have you ever had appendicitis?" he inquired of the applicant. "Well, I'm not sure," was the reply. "I was operated on, but I've never been quite certain whether it was appendicitis or professional curiosity."

See also fee[1], mistake[4], operation[1], trust[2].

SURPRISE

1

The man was trying to choose a washing machine and was undecided. "You see," he informed the clerk, "I'm buying this for my wife for her birthday." "Oh, a surprise, eh?" said the clerk. "I'll say," answered the customer; "she's expecting a fur coat."

2

"Where are you going, mom?" asked the youngest of seven children. "To a surprise party for the Greens, dear," answered mother. "Are we all going along, mom?" the child wanted to know. "No, dear, only daddy and I are invited," he was told. The little fellow considered this for a moment, then piped up, "But, mom, don't you think they'd be lots more surprised if you took us all along?"

SUSPICION

A motorist was brought before the judge who demanded of the arresting officer, "What are the charges against this man?" "Suspicious actions, Your Honor," replied the policeman. "Suspicious actions?" echoed the judge. "Just what was he doing that seemed suspicious?" "Well, Your Honor," explained the officer, "he was traveling within the speed limit, sounding his horn and signaling properly, and trying to keep on the right side of the street—so I arrested him."

SWEARING

1

A wheel had just come off a truck and the driver was addressing it in no uncertain terms. A lady passing by was shocked by his language. She said, "Heavens, my good man, where did you learn such awful language?" "Learn it, hell, lady!"

he snapped. "I never learned it—it's a gift!"

2

A minister on a fishing trip chanced upon a young angler who was swearing. "My boy," he admonished him, "don't you know that the fish will never bite if you swear like that?" "Aw, I know I ain't very good at it," admitted the boy, "but I thought I might get some little ones on the few words I knew. Here, you take the pole and see what *you* can do."

3

"John, dear," requested the wife, "will you open that can of fruit in the kitchen, please?" When the husband reappeared with the opened can, she asked him sweetly, "What did you use to open it, John?" "A can-opener, of course," grunted hubby. "What did you think I opened it with?" "I wasn't sure," replied wifey, "but from some of the language I heard, I thought maybe you were opening it with prayer."

4

"Goodness, why is that man jumping about so frantically?" asked a passer-by of a youth lounging on a lumber pile. "Oh, he's a deaf-and-dumb carpenter," replied the other, "and he's just hit his thumb with the hammer for the third time in the same place and he can't find his pad and pencil."

See also almost[1], driver[3], grammar[4], language[1, 2], minister[1], oath[3], parrot[1], silence[2], spitting[2], Texas[1].

SWEATING

A medical student was taking his final examinations and each succeeding question proved increasingly difficult. At last, he reached one which asked: "How would you induce copious perspiration in a patient?" He thought a moment, then wrote: "I would have him take the medical examinations in this college."

See also honor.

SWEETHEART

1

"Won't you buy some flowers, sir?" pleaded the flower-woman on the street corner. "Can't use 'em," the gentleman refused her. "But why not buy some for your sweetheart?" the woman urged. The man hesitated, and then shook his head once more. "No, that wouldn't be right," he said. "You see, I'm a married man."

2

It was before Christmas and the young man was looking over some holiday greeting cards. "Do you have any of a sentimental nature," he asked the salesgirl, "such as would be suitable for one's sweetheart?" "Yes, sir," replied the girl. "Here's a pretty one that says, 'To the Only Girl I Ever Loved.'" "That's fine," he approved. "Give me five—no, let's see, give me about eight of them."

See also clock[2], heart[1].

SWIMMING

1

Teacher had just finished reading the class a story about a strong man who swam the river three times before breakfast, when she heard a snicker from the back row. "What's the matter, Billy," she asked, "don't you believe that a good swimmer could do it?" "Oh, sure he could," admitted Billy; "but why didn't he make it four times and get back to where his clothes were?"

2

The sergeant was questioning some rookies as to their abilities. "How many of youse guys kin swim?" he asked. "I can, sergeant," volunteered the meek little fellow at the end. "Fine!" approved the sarge. "Where did you learn?" "Why, er, in the water, of course," was the reply.

See also drowning[1], insurance[4], opportunity[4], size[3].

SYMPATHY

1

"Poor old Sam is down on his luck again and tried to borrow ten dollars from me today," remarked the prosperous man to his wife. "Poor fellow," she said. "I hope you were sympathetic." "Oh, yes," he replied; "I was touched."

2

Mother was showing little Janie a picture of the Christian martyrs being thrown to the lions and trying to instill in her a horror of man's inhumanity to man. "Now what do you think of this, dear?" asked mother gently. "Oh, mamma!" said the child, regarding the picture tearfully. "Just look, there's one poor little lion in the corner that doesn't have a Christian."

3

The woman was of a shrewish

disposition and none too good-looking, and her husband's friends were curious as to why he had married her. "Well, I didn't marry for beauty," he declared, "nor for wealth or position—I married for sympathy." "Well, I must say," one of his friends assured him, "you certainly have mine."

4

A tramp thought up a new scheme for winning sympathy. He rang the doorbell, then got down on his knees and started nibbling the grass. "What are you doing there?" asked the lady when she opened the door. The tramp got weakly to his feet, clutched his stomach in agony, and said, "Ah, madam, I'm so hungry that I just had to take to eating grass." "Why, you poor man, stop eating that dry old grass!" cried the woman sympathetically. "Go around in back where the grass is greener and longer."

5

A big business magnate was visited by a boyhood chum whom he had not seen for years. This man told him a long story of misfortune —bankruptcy, death of wife and children, long personal illness, and more—and ended with a plea for help. The big shot pushed a button on his desk, and a burly porter appeared. "Sam," he instructed in a sob-choked voice, "throw this poor fellow downstairs—he's breaking my heart."

6

The minister's old father had been ill, and one day a member of his congregation stopped to ask, "And how is your father today,

Reverend?" "Ah," sighed the preacher, rolling his eyes upward, "my dear father has passed away and is now in heaven." "Oh, dear me," answered the parishioner sympathetically, "I'm certainly sorry to hear it."

See also fur[2], landlord[4], poor.

SYNONYM

"Can you tell me, Billy," questioned teacher during the English lesson, "what a synonym is?" "A synonym," replied the boy, "is a word you use when you can't spell the one you started to use."

See also book[5].

SYSTEM

1

The office manager frowned at the elderly clerk. "Mr. Williams," he said, "I'm afraid you're ignoring our efficiency system." "Maybe I am, sir," admitted the clerk, "but somebody has to get the work done."

2

"See there, now," cried the efficiency expert triumphantly as he looked around the office. "Just look how many new men you've taken on since I installed my system." "Sure," growled the boss, "I had to hire them to take care of the damned system."

See also habit[3], teaching[3].

TACT

1

A widow who was no longer young, once put a young man on

the spot by asking him coyly, "How old do you think I am?" "I'm very poor at guessing age," he replied evasively. "Oh, come, you must have some idea," she insisted. "My difficulty, madam," he said, "is to decide whether to make you ten years younger because of your beauty, or ten years older because of your wisdom."

2

Little Willie had just returned from a birthday party and mother asked him, "Now, Willie, I hope you didn't ask for a second piece of cake?" "No, I didn't," replied Willie. "I only asked Mrs. Brown for the recipe so that you could make some of that awfully good cake, and she made me take two more pieces of her own accord."

3

"Now, sir," said the lawyer, looking severely at the young man, "you heard the last witness's testimony and how contrary it is to yours. Am I to understand that you wish to cast doubt upon the lady's veracity?" "Not at all," declared the young fellow. "I merely wish to make it plain what a liar I am if she's telling the truth."

4

In the days of the old West a young college graduate inherited a ranch and went out to run it. He soon discovered that his cattle was being rustled, and then found that it was his neighbor who was doing it. He also learned that the neighbor was a notorious killer. So he wrote the man a polite letter, saying: "I would appreciate it very much if you would be careful about leaving your hot branding irons around

where my stupid cattle can lie down on them."

5

Having heard no noise from the living room for awhile, hubby called down, "I say, Martha, has that old gossip gone yet?" The wife gulped, stole a glance at her guest sitting stiffly in her chair, then in a loud clear voice replied, "Yes, dear, she left over a half-hour ago. Mrs. Smith is here now."

6

Old Murphy didn't get out of the pit in time when the dynamite was set off, and Murphy was no more. "Too bad," said the foreman. "You'd better go tell his wife about it, John, but for heaven's sake, man, be tactful and break it gently." John rang the Murphys' doorbell, and when a woman appeared he asked politely, "Are you the Widow Murphy?" "My name's Murphy," replied the woman, "but I'm no widow." "Hmmm," said John, "you wanna bet?"

See also chivalry[1], complaint[3], dachshund[1], forget[1], hint[2], host[3], name[5], stuttering[6].

TACTLESS

It was a musical evening and as a woman was rendering a song one of the guests leaned toward the man next to him and muttered, "What an awful voice! I wonder who she is?" "She's my wife," replied the other. "Oh, I'm sorry," apologized the first. "Of course, it really isn't her voice, but that terrible stuff she has to sing. Wonder who wrote that horrible song?" "I did," was the reply.

See also resemblance[1].

TAILOR

1

A big business magnate was conversing with a group of men at a reception at which his tailor happened to be present. Someone started to introduce the tailor to the big shot, but the noise caused him to miss the name. "Your face looks familiar, sir," said the magnate, shaking hands, "but I can't recall your name." To assist his memory, the tailor whispered, "I made your pants." "Ah, to be sure," said the other heartily. "Gentlemen, meet my friend, Major Pants!"

2

A man came into the private office and dropped a bundle on the desk. "I'd like these clothes pressed right away," he said. "The fellow next door said you're an expert at pressing suits." "The man next door is quite right," confirmed the man behind the desk, "only this isn't a tailor's shop—it's a lawyer's office."

3

A tailor had been wrongfully accused of murder, but he had a fine lawyer and enough evidence to clear himself. Nevertheless, when he came up in court for trial he was very much dejected. "What's bothering you?" whispered his lawyer. "You haven't a thing to worry about." "I'm not so sure," replied the tailor; "there's not a man on that jury but owes me money for clothes."

See also craftsmanship[2].

TALENT

See ability, fame[1], genius.

TALK

1

The quarrel had reached the stage of personalities. "Men have no minds at all," she declared disdainfully. "Whenever you tell them anything it goes in one ear and out the other." "Maybe so," he retorted, "but when you tell a woman anything it goes in both ears and out her mouth."

2

"Henry," announced the wife gravely as she entered the living room and sat down, "I have a lot of things I want to talk to you about." "Well, fine," said Henry, "I'll certainly be glad to hear about them. Usually you want to talk to me about a lot of things you don't have."

3

"Why doesn't baby talk, mamma?" inquired little Joan. "He'll talk when he's about three, dear," replied mother. "Babies can't talk." "But they can," insisted Joan, "'cause Job talked when he was a baby." "Why, that's nonsense," scoffed mother. "No, it isn't," the child maintained. "It says in the Bible that, 'Job cursed the day he was born.'"

4

Two small boys were boasting of the abilities of their mothers, both of whom were prominent in club activities. "My mom's awful smart," insisted one proudly. "She can talk on just about any subject." "Aw, that's nothin'," jeered the other. "My mom can talk without any subject at all!"

5

It was a bright Sunday afternoon in spring and the farm boy had his girl out for a buggy ride. As they jogged along through the wine-like air, he suddenly turned to the girl and said, "Mandy, will ye marry me?" "Shore will, Hiram," was the immediate response. They drove along in perfect silence for about a quarter-hour, then Mandy asked, "Why don't ye say somethin', Hiram?" "Humph!" grunted the boy. "I've a'ready talked too damn much!"

6

Little Ronald was given to talking almost constantly in school, and there seemed nothing the teacher could do to discourage it. As a last resort, she made a notation under "Deportment" on his monthly report: "Ronald talks a great deal." The next day the report was returned signed by Ronald's father, and under her comment was an inscription in red ink: "You ought to hear his mother!"

7

Mrs. Smith was one of the doctor's regular patients. When she called this day, she, as usual, launched into a long recital of her ailments. The doctor endured it patiently to the end, then handed her another bottle of medicine. She started to leave, but suddenly stopped to exclaim, "But, doctor, you didn't look to see if my tongue was coated." "No need to," was the weary reply. "You never find grass on a racetrack."

8

"And you, sir," shouted the soapbox orator at the passing gentleman, "are you opposed to free speech?" "Not at all," was the reply, "unless I'm compelled to listen to it."

See also ass[2], baby[11], frank[2], interrupt, slow[1], woman[4], word[2].

TALL

See size.

TASTE

1

A hillbilly was visiting a friend in town and while out walking with him saw a bunch of bananas for the first time. "What's them?" asked the yokel. "They're bananas," and the town boy proceeded to explain what they were like. "Want to try one?" "Nope, reckon not," answered the hillbilly. "Done got too many tastes now thet I kain't satisfy, an' I ain't aimin' to take on any more."

2

"Henry!" said wifey sternly. "Don't you know it's bad form to dip your doughnuts in your coffee?" "It may be bad form," admitted Henry, happily dunking away, "but it's mighty good taste."

3

A famous traveler who was an authority on the Indians, was once asked by a dear old lady, "During your experiences with the Indians, sir, did you ever taste dog stew?" "Twice, madam," he replied. "Twice!" she cried in horror. "You must have liked it to eat it again?" "No, madam," he explained. "I tasted it once going down, and once coming up."

TATTOO

1

A sailor had been sitting moodily biting his nails for over an hour. "Aw, come on, shipmate," said a pal, slapping him on the shoulder. "Get it off your chest." "That's just what I'm tryin' to figger out how to do," moaned the sad one. "I got Mabel's name tattooed there, an' I'm engaged to marry Annie."

2

An elderly lady was examining the elaborate tattooing on the arms and chest of a grizzled old sailor. "My, aren't they curious!" she observed. "Do those marks wash off?" The sailor gave her a scornful glance. "How'n heck should I know, lady?" he snorted.

3

They were driving along a lonely road and the sweet young thing cuddled closer and asked, "Did I ever show you where I was tattooed, Bill?" "Gosh, no, but I'd sure like to see," returned Bill. "Then I'll show you," she decided, "if you'll just turn left at the next crossroads."

TAVERN

See saloon.

TAX

1

A man had sent in a claim to the income-tax department for $45 for repayment on his tax. He had, however, miscalculated and in checking over his figures the department discovered the error and sent him a check for $80. The taxpayer ac-

knowledged this by letter, saying: "Gentlemen, I am now sixty-eight years old, and at last I believe in Santa Claus."

2

"We should all be good citizens," declared the wealthy lady, "and pay our taxes with a smile." "I'd certainly like to," replied the pretty but poor girl, "but they insist on cash."

3

"Ah, me!" moaned Brown after he had had another disappointment. "Nothing is certain in this world but death and taxes." "That's true enough," agreed Black, "but at least death doesn't get worse every time Congress meets."

See also dog[8], mistake[2].

TAXI

1

A country woman arrived in the city and got into a taxi. It immediately took off at a breakneck speed, almost overturning at corners, and narrowly missing colliding with many cars. "Please be careful, driver," gasped the lady, holding her hat. "This is the first time I've ever ridden in a taxi." "That's nothin', lady," shouted the driver. "This is the first time I ever drove one!"

2

A farmer back from the city was telling his experiences to the boys around the store stove. "An' then they got autymobiles that ye kin rent to go ridin' in," he said. "They calls 'em taxidermy cabs on account o' they shore do skin ye."

3

With one deft twist of the wheel a taxi-driver ignored a red signal, missed a traffic officer's toes by inches, grazed a safety island standard by a hair, and scared a pedestrian half to death. The policeman shouted at him to pull over, and as he walked over toward him pulled a handkerchief from his pocket. "Look here, cowboy," he snarled, "on your way back I'll drop this, and you see if you can pick it up with your teeth."

4

The drunk had long since had enough, but apparently didn't know it. "Aw, be reasonable, Bill," pleaded his friend, "why don't you take a taxi home?" Great tears welled up in the drunk's eyes and he sobbed, "Sh'no use, pally, sh'no use a-tall. Th' wife wou'n't lemme keep the poor li'l thing inna houshe."

5

"What are you doing now, Jack?" asked Sam as the two met after a long separation. "Oh, I've got a taxi now," replied Jack. "Well, well. How're you doing?" asked Sam. "Not very good," admitted the other. "I'm making barely enough to pay for the damage I do to other cars."

6

A facetious man got into a taxi and flippantly ordered the driver, "Home, James." "Whaddaya mean, 'Home, James'?" growled the taxi man. "This here is a public taxi." "Okay," said the passenger agreeably. "In that case, Home, Jesse James."

7

The drunk had been riding around in the taxi for about an hour and at last the driver asked, "Just where did you want to go, sir?" "Oh, this'll do," said the drunk. "Whadda I owe you?" "Nine dollars and seventy-five cents," said the driver, reading the meter. "Oh, oh," he exclaimed. "You jus' better start backin' up an' keep going 'til you come to forty cents—tha'sh all I got."

8

It was the first time the old farm lady had ever ridden in a taxi. She became disturbed as she saw the driver keep putting his hand out to signal to the cars behind him. "Look here, young man," she at last commanded, "you jest tend to runnin' this here car and watchin' where it's a-goin', an' I'll tell you when it starts to rain."

See also nothing[1].

TEA

"A cup of tea, please," said the man to the waiter, "and make it weak." When the waiter set the cup before him, the customer looked at it. "Well, what's the matter?" demanded the waiter belligerently. "You wanted it weak, didn't you?" "Weak, yes," admitted the other gently, "but not helpless."

See also coffee[3], suggestion[2].

TEACHER

1

The gentleman was surprised when a pretty young lady he had never seen before greeted him on the street, saying, "Good evening, sir." She had evidently mistaken him for someone else. But his surprise increased when she exclaimed, "Oh, pardon me. For a moment I thought you were the father of two of my children." What he didn't know, of course, was that she was a teacher at a nearby school.

2

After struggling valiantly to keep little Junior in order, teacher at last wrote his mother a letter, saying: "Your boy is one of the brightest in the class, but he is also the naughtiest. What shall I do?" The reply the teacher received read: "You will just have to use your own judgment about Junior. I have my own hands full with his father."

3

"Now, Tommy," said teacher during the geography lesson, "please name all the states in the Union." Tommy started off glibly enough, but about halfway through he began to falter. "Come, come," prodded teacher, "I could name them all easily when I was your age." "Sure you could," Tommy defended himself; "there were only thirteen then."

4

A man was paying a visit to his native village after having been away for many years, and he paid a call at his old boyhood school. The aging schoolmaster failed to recognize his former pupil, saying, "You seem to know me quite well, but I have no recollection of having ever seen your face before." "That's not to be wondered at," replied the visitor smilingly, "for you were much better acquainted with my other end."

5

The speaker of the evening at a banquet of educators was waxing eloquent upon his theme of the civilizing effect of education. "And the agent in this great movement is the humble teacher," he declared sonorously. "I say, Long Live the Teachers!" A tall, emaciated man in the rear of the room arose and in a hollow voice inquired, "On what?"

6

Little Billy had his hand up, waving it. Teacher frowned disapprovingly and said, "Now, Billy, you must learn to be a gentleman. Put your hand down and presently I'll hear what you have to say." About five minutes later teacher asked, "All right, Billy, what did you wish to say?" "I was only going to tell you," said the boy, "that a man in the vestibule was taking your umbrella."

See also knowledge[3], salary[3].

TEACHING

1

"Timmy," mother scolded her small son, "are you teaching that parrot to use slang?" "Oh, no, mamma," answered Timmy innocently; "I'm just tellin' it what it shouldn't say."

2

His fiancee had left the dance floor with the handsome stranger and had been gone a long time. So he went to look for her. As they were returning, he demanded fiercely, "Did I see that man kiss you?" "Yes," she admitted. "The dog!" he stormed. "I'll teach him a thing or two!" "Oh, don't bother, darling," she sighed rapturously. "I don't think you could."

3

The faculty was discussing the manner in which the final examinations were to be given. It was decided to hold them in the order of their difficulty, the most difficult coming first. "That, of course, will make history come last," stated the head of the faculty. "I don't agree," the woman history teacher protested. "But surely history is the easiest subject," insisted the head. "Not the way I teach it," maintained the woman. "According to my system, it is the most difficult and perplexing of studies."

4

Little Janie brought home from school a pumpkin seed which she exhibited to her mother and proudly announced, "Teacher says that although this seed is white the pumpkins from it will be yellow." "That's right," confirmed mother. "And what will be the color of the vines?" "Oh, teacher didn't tell us that," said Janie. "But you ought to know, dear," insisted mother, "because we have pumpkin vines in our garden." "Of course I know," replied Janie, "but we ain't expected to know anything until we're taught."

See also school², Sunday school⁷.

TEETH

1

"Well, Johnny, how is everything at home?" inquired the minister as he met the boy on the street. "Oh, fine," said Johnny. "Pop's got a new set of false teeth." "Is that so?" commented the minister. "And what is he going to do with his old set?" "I ain't sure," replied the boy, "but I guess he'll have 'em cut down and make me wear 'em."

2

Mother and Junior paused to look at the display window of a dentist along the street. "Gee, mom," declared Junior, pointing, "if I ever have to wear false teeth, that's the pair I'd like." "Hush, Junior," admonished mother, "haven't I told you it's bad manners to pick your teeth in public?"

3

The revivalist was thundering his warnings of the retribution that would be the lot of the wicked. "And I tell ye, brethren," he roared, "that on the day of reckoning there will be wailing and gnashing of teeth!" "But, sir," objected a lady in the balcony, "I don't have any teeth." "Madam," rumbled the preacher, "teeth will be provided!"

4

Old Uncle Zeb hitched his buggy outside the village drug store and stamped inside in a rage. "Say," he snarled at the clerk, "be ye the smart-aleck youngster what sold me this stuff yesterday and said it was toothpaste?" "I did, sir; and it is," insisted the clerk. "Dang yore hide!" roared Zeb. "I tried fer a half-hour this mornin' an' I'll be durned if it would make my teeth stick in."

5

"Hem," announced the doctor as he concluded his examination of the woman. "It's quite plain, madam, that your arthritis is being caused by your teeth and that they'll have to come out. Let me see them please." "Sure, doc," said the woman, reaching toward her mouth; "just hold out your hand."

6

The family had to catch a two o'clock train, so mother urged them all to do everything as early as possible. After a hurried lunch, they were getting their wraps on when mother suddenly said, "Oh, Willie, you didn't brush your teeth." "Yes, I did, mom," declared the boy. "So as to save time, I brushed 'em before lunch."

See also clean[1], cold, dentist[1].

TELEGRAM

The proud new father sent his brother in a distant city this telegram: "Jane gave birth to a baby girl this morning. Both doing well." The brother received the news with rejoicing, but was rather puzzled by a sticker on the telegram, which read: "When you want a boy, call Western Union."

TELEPHONE

1

A gentleman pretty well along in his cups picked up a telephone and called into it, "Hello! Hic! Hello!" "Hello!" returned the operator's voice politely. "Hello!" repeated the drunk. "Hello!" came the voice again. "Hic! Gosh!" murmured the inebriate. "This damned thing sure echoes."

2

"Did you ever do any public speaking?" inquired the manager of the applicant for position of salesman. "Well, yes, in a way," was the reply. "I once proposed to a girl in the country over a party line."

3

The telephone rang and the new maid, fresh from the country, picked it up gingerly and said, "Hello!" "Hello!" came a cheery voice. "What number is this?" "Well!" cried the maid, exasperated. "You ought to know—you called it!"

4

The man had been trying for a half-hour to get his number, but without success. At last he lost patience and roared at the operator, "Say, am I crazy, or are you?" "I'm sorry, sir," replied the operator in her sweet voice, "but we do not have that information."

See also disturbance[2], drunk[12].

TEMPER

"Now, boys," admonished the old minister, lecturing the Bible class, "you must strive always to keep calm and never lose your tempers. You should never swear or get angry or excited. And it isn't hard," declared the old fellow, "because I never do it. For example, see that big fly on my nose? Now, most wicked men would be excited and swear, but I just say, 'Go away, fly,' and I—good God! It's a bee, damn it to hell!"

See also nerves.

TEMPERANCE

1

Having had some trouble with hecklers, the temperance lecturer hired a prize fighter to keep order at the meeting. "Now, my friends," the lecturer was ranting, "when we get home weary and spent from our labors, for what do we long to bring cheer to our hearts and a song to our lips and to lighten our burdens?" As he paused for effect, the pug stepped up and announced, "An' de foist mug what says 'a drink' gets t'rown out on his ear!"

2

"There's nothing like water," insisted the temperance fiend. "Aw, g'wan!" scoffed an intemperate. "Water has killed more people than liquor." "You're crazy," shouted the dry. "How can you say that?" "Well," retorted the other, "to begin with, there was the flood."

3

Dead-Eye Pete burst into the saloon waving his six-guns and commanded, "Everybody take a drink with me!" All hastened to comply save one meek-looking little man. "Why ain't you drinkin', podner?" demanded Pete menacingly. "For two reasons," explained the little man. "One is that I promised my old grandmother on her deathbed that I'd never touch the stuff." "An' what's the other?" asked Pete. "I've just had a drink," was the answer.

4

Old Sam was just getting over a drunk and felt repentant. So he was easy prey for the militant do-gooder who got him to go to the temperance society headquarters and sign the pledge. "Gosh," said Sam, looking admiringly at the elegant pledge card and pretty badge they had given him, "what must I pay for these?" "Not a cent," said the other magnanimously. "Gee, thanks," replied Sam gratefully. "Well, come across the street, then, and I'll buy a couple of drinks on it anyhow."

5

A doctor having heard that an inveterate drinker of his acquaintance had signed the pledge, decided to put him to the test. Meeting him one day, he invited him into a bar and ordered two drinks. After having put these down, and several more at the doctor's expense, he asked the teetotaler, "I thought you'd signed the pledge?" "Oh, I did," said the other, "but I wouldn't think of refusing to take what the doctor ordered."

See also adultery[1], ass[1], drinking[a], saloon[1].

TEMPERATURE

1

"Good morning, Mrs. Murphy," said the doctor as he stopped by to make his call. "Did you take your husband's temperature as I told you?" "Indeed I did, doctor," asserted Mrs. Murphy. "I borrowed a barometer and put it on his chest. It said 'very dry,' so I got him a bucket of beer and he's gone back to work."

2

A star athlete felt ill and went to see a doctor. "You have a temperature," announced the physician after examining him. "How much is it?" he wanted to know. "A hundred and one," said the doctor. "Gee, it is?" cried the athlete excitedly. "What's the record?"

3

The woman had just misread the fever thermometer and she rushed to the telephone. "Oh, doctor, come quickly!" she cried. "My husband has a temperature of 120!" "Don't get excited, madam," cautioned the doctor. "If that's true, it's too late for me—it's a job for the fire department."

4

The student nurse who had been caring for the influenza patient was not very bright. One day when the doctor was examining the patient he asked, "Nurse, what was this man's temperature at the onset?" "Gee, I don't know," replied the nurse, looking confused. "I've been taking it by mouth."

See also hereafter[2], stock market[2, 4].

TEMPT

1

A moralist was lecturing a group of modern young girls. "And remember, above all things, young ladies," he thundered, "to resist temptation when it comes." "I'd like to," sighed one of the girls regretfully, "but I'm always afraid it may never come again."

2

Little Danny had been strictly forbidden to go swimming in the river because of the danger. But one day he came home with wet hair. "You've been swimming, Danny," scolded mother. "Yes, I have," admitted the boy, "but I couldn't help it because I was so badly tempted." "But how did you come to have your bathing suit along?" demanded mother. "Oh, I took it with me,"

explained Danny, "because I thought I might be tempted."

See also attempt[1], feet[4].

TENANT

1

A man telephoned a pet shop and said, "I'd like to place an order for 25,000 cockroaches." "What in the world do you want with that many cockroaches?" exclaimed the clerk. "Well, I'm moving tomorrow," explained the man, "and my lease says that I must leave the premises in exactly the same condition I found them."

2

The landlord had been showing a prospective tenant a large residence, but after looking it over he decided, "No, I don't believe I care for it. I think, after all, an apartment would suit us better." "Well, as for me an apartment has always seemed like a prison," commented the landlord, "but then, of course, it all depends on what you're used to."

See also landlord[2,3].

TESTIMONIAL

1

"Do you get any testimonials on your product?" asked the woman of the peddler of patent-medicine. "Do we? Just look at this, madam," cried the peddler showing a letter which read: "A month ago I was so run down that I couldn't even spank the baby. Now, after taking four bottles of your marvelous tonic I am fully able to thrash my husband soundly, in addition to my other housework. God bless you and your wonderful medicine."

2

A life insurance company sent a check to the widow of one of their clients, and in a short time received from her the letter: "Dear Sirs, Thank you very much for the prompt payment. My husband took out his policy on July 7th, and less than one month later he was killed by a truck. I consider insurance a good investment."

TEXAS

1

"Here's an odd news item," remarked the wife, looking up from her paper. "It tells of a Texas man who was struck by lightning while he was swearing. Rather remarkable, don't you think?" "Oh, I don't know," observed hubby. "It would be a lot more remarkable if lightning had struck a Texas man when he *wasn't* swearing."

2

"Well, Tom, haven't seen you around lately," remarked one native of Brownsville, Texas, to another. "Where've you been?" "Had to take a little trip north," explained Tom. "Where'd you go?" asked his friend. "Up to Dallas," was the reply. "Have a good time?" was the next question. "Naw, I didn't," answered Tom disgustedly. "I never did like them damned Yankees anyway."

See also real estate[1].

THANKFUL

1

"Why, you ought to be ashamed when you say you haven't anything to be thankful for," the minister scolded the complaining man. "Just think of your neighbor Johnson who's just lost his wife by pneumonia." "Sure, but what good will that do me?" grumbled the other. "I ain't Johnson."

2

There were five churches in the small town and all of them had a difficult time getting by. "How is your church making out?" inquired a visitor of a deacon of one of the decaying institutions. "Oh, not at all well," was the mournful reply. Then more cheerily, "But, thank the Lord, the others aren't doing any better."

3

"Thankful! What have I to be thankful for?" grumbled the sour-looking man to the sunshine-spreader. "I can't even pay my bills." "In that case," prompted the other readily, "be thankful that you aren't one of your creditors."

4

A visitor to the poorhouse stopped to try to cheer a frail, old lady. "Thank you, ma'am, for your kind intentions," said the forlorn old pauper brightly, "but I really have a great deal to be thankful for. I have just two teeth left and they happen to be opposite each other."

THANKS

1

Little Tommy had been playing next door with the neighbor's boy and the neighbor called them into the house and gave them each a piece of bread and butter. "Thank you, ma'am," said Tommy politely.

"That's nice, Tommy," approved the woman. "I like to hear little boys say 'thank you.'" "Well," remarked Tommy hopefully, "if you'd like to hear me say it again, you might try putting some jam on the bread."

2

"Thank you, Billy," said the minister as the boy delivered the offering for the harvest festival. "I must make a point of seeing your mother and thanking her for these nine beautiful apples." "P-please, sir," faltered Billy, "but w-would it b-be too m-much trouble to thank her for t-twelve apples?"

3

With a magnificent flourish, the fruit peddler gave little Ronnie an orange. "What do you say to the kind man, Ronnie?" prompted mother. The boy extended the orange toward the peddler. "Peel it," he replied.

4

"Thank you so much, grandma, for the lovely necktie," said little Donald as he dutifully placed a kiss on the old lady's cheek. "Oh, that's nothing to thank me for," she murmured. "Well, that's what I thought, too," agreed Donald, "but mother said I had to do it."

5

Teacher was trying to give her small pupils some simple instruction in good manners. "Now, Nancy," she questioned, "can you tell me when you say 'Thank you'?" "Sure," replied Nancy promptly. "When we have company."

See also polite[2], store[1].

THEATER

1

The manager of a road show wired the proprietor of a small town theater where they were to appear next: "Would like to have rehearsal at three Monday afternoon. Have stage manager, electrician, carpenter, property man, and all stage hands present at that time." Several hours later he received in answer the wire: "All right. He'll be there."

2

A visitor to the big city decided to take in a show at one of the huge movie theaters on Saturday night. Naturally, the movie house was crowded and he was taken in tow by an usher who led him up ramp after ramp until they reached the floor level of the top balcony. Waving his hand upward toward the darkness, the usher said, "You'll find a seat up there somewhere. This is as far as I go. Above this level, my nose bleeds."

3

A small troupe of actors were touring the circuit with a revival of "Uncle Tom's Cabin." During the play on opening night, the villain stalked on the stage and in a hoarse whisper demanded of the heroine, "Are we alone?" From the gallery a bored voice called out, "Yuh ain't tonight, pal, but yuh will be tomorrow night!"

4

The lady purchasing a theater ticket wasn't at all certain that she was getting a good seat. "Are you quite sure," she asked the ticket seller for the fourth time, "that this seat is close enough to the stage?"

"Madam," replied the box office man, "if it were any nearer, you'd have to act in the play."

5

"How's Joan coming on with her theatrical work?" inquired the fellow who had been away for awhile. "Oh, she now has a leading part in a theater," the other informed him. "A star, eh?" said the first. "No," was the reply, "an usher."

6

The not-too-bright girl usher who was only doing her best was showing two sanctimonious women to their seats when one turned and demanded of her, "Is this show fit for church women to see?" "Well, I—I really don't know, ma'am," replied the girl. Then she brightened and added, "You see, I don't have no time to go to church."

See also audience[1, 3], critic[3], dying[2], play[3].

THEORY

"My goodness, but you have the strangest nickname for your husband," observed Mrs. Johnson to her neighbor. "Imagine calling a man 'theory'! Why do you call him that?" "It's quite obvious," was the reply. "It's because he so seldom works."

THIEF

A man was on trial for having attacked another and robbed him of his watch and chain, but the evidence against him was so meager that after a few minutes the judge declared, "Discharged!" The pris-

oner stood bewildered at the rapid turn of events. "You're discharged," repeated the judge. "You're free—you can go." "Gee, thanks," stuttered the man, "but does that mean I have to give him back his watch and chain?"

See also burglar, flattery, gas[2], lose[4], poet[4], reform[1], robbery, sentiment[1], steal.

THIN

1

A fat man encountered a thin man in a hotel lobby. "Haw, haw," he cried derisively, "from the looks of you there might have been a famine around here." "Oh, yeah?" retorted the other. "And from the looks of you, you might have caused it."

2

A fat man sharing a streetcar seat with a thin man was crowding him and the latter resented it. "It seems to me," he remarked, "that the fare on these cars ought to be charged according to weight." "Well, you're lucky they don't, sonny, or you'd have to walk," replied the fat one. "They couldn't afford to stop for you."

3

The farmer was trying to describe the new store clerk to a neighbor. "But what's he look like?" asked the neighbor. "Big feller?" "Naw, little dried-up feller," replied the other. "Looks like he always et at the second table."

See also leg[1].

THINK

1

The young man calling on the girl was very bashful. From across the room he made an attempt at polite conversation, asking, "Do you believe in telepathy, Miss Green?" "Telepathy?" responded the girl. "I don't believe I know what you mean." "Why, you know, thought transference," explained the boy. "Oh, heavens, no!" exclaimed the girl. "If there were any such thing, you wouldn't be sitting where you are."

2

The lawyer was attempting to browbeat the witness. "Just when did this robbery occur?" he demanded in an aggressive tone. "Well," began the witness meekly, "I think it—" "Stop!" interrupted the lawyer. "I don't want to know what you think. I want to know what you know." "In that case, I may as well leave the box," retorted the witness quietly, "because as I'm not a lawyer, I can't talk without thinking."

See also gift[1], politics[6].

THIRST

The explorer was relating some of his experiences to a breathless group. "There we were deep in the jungle with savage animals and hostile natives on all sides," he said. "Our ammunition, food, and whiskey had all run out, so we all were soon parched with thirst." "But couldn't you find water in the jungle?" asked a listener. "Oh, sure," was the reply; "but it was no time to be worrying about cleanliness."

See also drunk[2], homesick[1].

THREAT

It had taken much effort to get little Betty into the dentist's chair. Now as the dentist approached with forceps in hand it appeared that the girl was about to start screaming and kicking. "Now, Betty," threatened mother sternly, "if you let out just one cry, I'll never take you to the dentist's again!"

THRIFT

1

An old farmer who was the richest man in the neighborhood, was visited one evening by a young man who asked him the secret of his wealth. "Waal, it's a long story, son," replied the old man, "an' while I'm a'tellin' ye we'd as well put out the lamp an' save the oil." "Thanks, but you needn't tell the story," said the young fellow. "I think I understand."

2

Old Uncle Ned came and stayed with his nephew for over a month, and when at last he was leaving he gave his host a ten-dollar bill. "Now be careful with that money, William," he cautioned. "You know, a fool and his money are soon parted." "Yes, I know, Uncle," replied William. "But thanks just the same for parting with it."

3

A farmer was on one of his sprees and, coming home to change clothes to go out again, he heard the pigs squealing and remembered that he hadn't fed them for several days. Going to the pen, he threw in about five bushels of corn on the ear, muttering as he did so, "Thar, dang yore hides! If ye're prudent thet orter last ye 'til I git back."

4

The man was slowly but surely dying, and as he moaned and tossed about in his bed in agony his thrifty wife frowned disapprovingly upon him. "Now, see here, Henry," she rebuked him, "even if ye do be a-dyin', ye don't hev to go a-kickin' an' a-squirmin' so an' a-wearin' out my best sheets."

See also economy, emergency[3], stingy.

TIE

See necktie.

TIME

1

After talking for several hours, the speaker finally ended with the apology, "I'm sorry, my friends, if I have spoken too long—but, you see, I don't happen to have a watch with me." "What's that got to do with it?" shouted one of his victims from the audience. "There's a calendar behind you."

2

"Jed," said the farmer to his hired man, "all the clocks in the house hev stopped, so I wish ye'd hitch up an' drive to town to find out what time it be." "All right, but I ain't got no watch," replied Jed. "Kin ye lend me one?" "Watch? What d'ye want a watch fer?" cried

the farmer. "Jest write the time down on a piece o' paper."

3

The girl was in tears because her fond boyfriend had jilted her. "Now, now, dear," comforted her bony, wrinkled aunt, "it will all work out. Just remember that time is a great healer." "Maybe so," sobbed the girl, eyeing the other critically, "but it's certainly not much of a beauty doctor."

4

The lawyer was long-winded, but when he came to untangle a complex point in the case he outdid himself and rambled on and on until at last the judge yawned. The lawyer noted this and remarked, "I hope I'm not trespassing unduly on the time of this court." "My friend," sighed the judge, "there's a great difference between trespassing on time and encroaching upon eternity."

5

An engineer was trying to put through a railroad project in one of the Latin-American countries and he was seeking some local support for it. "How long does it take you to get your goods to market on a burro?" he inquired of a native. "Four days," he was told. "See there!" cried the engineer triumphantly, "with our road in operation you could get your goods to market and be back in one day." "But, señor," protested the native, "what would we do with the other three days?"

See also clock[1, 2], commuter[1], energetic[1], lecture[3], logic, moron[3], pig[2], punctual[2], sermon[11].

TIMETABLE

The man who was waiting for a train was becoming impatient. "What good are all those figures you have on those timetables, anyway?" he fumed. "But, sir," the station agent patiently explained, "if it wasn't fer them figures we wouldn't have no way o' findin' out how late the train is."

TIPPING

1

"I wonder why it is," said a diner in a restaurant, "that poor men usually give larger tips than rich men?" "The way I figure it out, sir," replied the philosophical waiter, "is that the poor man doesn't want anybody to find out that he's poor, and the rich man doesn't want anybody to find out that he's rich."

2

It was the lady passenger's first ocean voyage and she had wearied all the ship's officers with endless questions. One day she asked the steward, "Doesn't this ship tip a good deal?" "Perhaps it does, madam," replied that official, "but I imagine it is only trying to set a good example to the passengers."

TIRED

1

There were dark circles under his eyes and he looked worn out as he sank into the barber's chair. "Haircut," he grunted in response to the barber's cheery greeting. "Then you'll have to sit up a bit, please, sir," said the barber. "You're too far down in the chair for a haircut." The man didn't move, but merely mumbled wearily, "Then give me a shave."

2

It was the close of a strenuous day's electioneering and the political candidate's wife sighed, "Oh, dear, I'm *so* tired!" "Humph! Why should you be tired?" snorted her husband. "You haven't had to make five speeches today." "No," admitted the wife, "but I had to listen to them."

See also newspaper[2].

TOASTMASTER

See remark[2], speech[4].

TOBACCO

1

An inveterate smoker felt some vague pains about his heart and, fearing that his smoking might be the cause, consulted a doctor. "Do you believe, doctor," he asked, "that the use of tobacco tends to shorten a man's days?" "I most certainly do!" replied the doctor. "I once tried to stop smoking, and the days were about ninety hours long."

2

"My brother's certainly a smart one," boasted Marge to Myrt. "He's invented a smokeless tobacco." "Gee!" exclaimed Myrt. "What does he do to it to make it smokeless?" "He chews it," was the reply.

TOE

"Mummy, oh, mummy!" wailed little Joan as she ran into the room. "I've hurt my toe!" "Which toe is it, dear?" asked mother as she examined the foot. "It's my youngest toe," sobbed the child.

TOMBSTONE

1

A devoted husband, grieving over the death of his wife, had a tombstone erected in her memory bearing the inscription: "The light of my life has gone out." But Time got to doing its healing and after several years he decided to remarry. In something of a dilemma, he asked his minister if it would be proper to have this inscription removed. "Why bother?" asked the minister smilingly. "Why not just add another line: 'But I have struck another match'?"

2

The desolate widow had erected for her husband a tombstone bearing the words: "My grief is more than I can bear." Several months later, however, she was back asking the stonecutter how much it would cost to have this inscription removed and replaced by another. "No need of that, ma'am," replied the man. "You see, I figured on something like this and I left just enough room to add 'alone.'"

3

A few days after the erection of the business magnate's tombstone, one of the cemetery workmen rushed into the manager's office and cried, "Did you see what they did to Mr. Smith's tombstone?" "No, what?" asked the other. "Some one added the word 'friends' to the epitaph," said the workman. "Well, what was the epitaph?" asked the manager. "'He always did his best,'" was the reply.

See also dead[2].

TONGUE

"I'm moving out Saturday," announced the boarder to the landlady. "The bathroom is always a mess. I've never seen such dirty towels before; there's always a ring in the bathtub, and there's never any soap." "Well, goodness," snapped the landlady, "you've got a tongue in your head, haven't you?" "Sure I have," retorted the boarder, "but I'm no cat."

TOOTHBRUSH

1

"I'd like a toothbrush, please," said the customer to the druggist. "Yes, sir," said the other. "How about two of them? Give one to your wife." "No, thanks," refused the customer. "Whenever I buy a new toothbrush I always give the old one to my wife." As he became aware of the amazement on the druggist's face, he explained, "She uses it to clean her shoes."

2

A Pullman passenger was almost back to his berth when he discovered he'd left his toothbrush in the washroom. Hurrying back to get it, he found another man vigorously scrubbing his teeth with it. "Pardon me, but that's my toothbrush you're using," he said. "Gee, I'm sorry," apologized the other, handing over the brush. "I thought it belonged to the railroad."

TOUGH

1

A barefoot hillbilly woman, whose feet had been toughened by a lifetime of shoelessness, was standing before the cabin fireplace one day smoking her pipe when her husband entered. "Say, maw," he suggested, squinting at the hearth, "ye'd better move yore foot a mite—yore a-standin' on a live coal." "Be I, paw?" replied the woman coolly. "Which foot?"

2

The little farm boy trudging to school complained to a companion, "Golly, my feet sure gits sore from this here gravel road." "Why don't ye soak 'em in salt water?" suggested the other. "Thet'll toughen 'em up." The first thought this over, then said, "Waal, it's purty near time fer me to ketch a lickin', so reckon I oughta sit in it."

See also chicken[3], meat[1, 2].

TOURING

"How come Bill got turned down for that chauffeur's job?" asked one man of another. "I always thought he was a pretty good driver." "He is, but they gave him a pretty stiff examination," explained the other. "But even then he got along all right until they asked him if he'd driven much in other States. He told them he had, and then they said, 'All right, let's see you fold this road map.'"

See also distance[3], road[1, 2].

TOWEL

1

A tourist, who had stopped in a small town hotel for lunch, came out of the washroom provoked. "Look here," he said angrily to the hotelkeeper, "don't you know that roller-towels in hotels have been prohibited in this State for the past three years?" "Sure I know it," replied the other; "but that there towel was up there before the law was passed, an' I ain't a-takin' it down 'til it's dirty."

2

There were guests in for dinner and Junior had been sent upstairs to wash his hands. Suddenly he was heard crying down, "Mamma, oh, mamma!" "Yes, Junior, what is it?" called mother. "There's only clean towels in the bathroom, mamma," shouted the boy. "Shall I start one?"

3

"The towel's damp, mamma," complained the small boy who had been sent to wash. "Well, take it and dry it by the fire," instructed his mother. The boy did as he was told, but a short time later he wanted to know, "Mamma, is it done when it's brown?"

4

"Say, mom," asked the son one day, "was your name Pullman before you married daddy?" "No, dear, of course not," said mother. "Whatever made you think so?" "Oh, I just wondered," replied the boy, "'cause you've got that name on most of your towels."

TOWN

See country[2], location[2], village.

TRADE

See business.

TRAIN

1

A gentleman had just bought the last Pullman reservation. But when the elderly lady behind him found there was no reservation left and burst into tears, he gallantly surrendered his ticket to her. Stepping to the telegraph window, he wired his office: "Will not arrive until tomorrow. Just gave berth to an old lady."

2

A noted lecturer was traveling on one of the slow Southern trains and complaining bitterly. "Well, if you don't like it," cried the conductor at last, "why don't you get out and walk?" "I would," retorted the passenger, "but you see the committee isn't expecting me until this train gets in."

3

Every day for three years a certain train on a Southern line had been late. But one day to every one's amazement it rolled into the station exactly on time. In gratitude and to commemorate this historic event, the delighted passengers made up a purse which they presented to the engineer. But he refused it regretfully, saying, "I sure hate to do this, because I could use that money, but I gotta admit that this here is yesterday's train."

4

They were leaving on a trip, but despite all his pleadings wifey was a little late in getting ready. "You run ahead, dear," she suggested to hubby, "and hold the train." "Oh, yeah!" he retorted. "And do you prefer any particular hold—a headlock, scissors, or a half-nelson?"

5

As the train puffed into the station, the porter knocked on the door of a compartment. "This is Kansas City, ma'am," he announced. "Shall I brush you off?" "No, thank you," came the reply. "I'll just get off in the usual manner."

6

An old lady en route to New York for the first time was pestering the conductor with questions. "Tell me, conductor," she demanded, "does this train stop in Grand Central Station?" "I sincerely hope so, madam," replied the conductor, "as there'll be a horrible wreck if it doesn't."

7

"I was just reading about the terrible fate of a man captured by bandits down in Mississippi," remarked Brown to a friend. "What did they do, shoot him or hang him?" asked the friend. "Neither. They tied him to the railroad tracks," said Brown. "How horrible!" gasped the other. "The poor fellow was completely mangled, I suppose?" "Oh, no," corrected Brown. "He died a slow, agonizing death by starvation."

8

Two farmers were spending their first night in a Pullman. After having passed some time in the smoker, both retired at the same time. One was just settling himself in the upper berth when he heard a commotion from the other in the lower. Leaning out, he whispered, "Are ye all right there, Hiram?" "Waal, I don't know," replied the other. "I got my duds off all right, but durned if I kin git into this little hammock."

See also accident[3], clock[1], compromise[2], delay[3], importance[2], late[2], midget[1], moron[7], pronunciation[2], railroad[2], sarcasm[8], stop[1], transportation, tunnel[3], waiter[1].

TRAINING

1

A minister was making calls on some poor parishioners in the tenement district. In one home his attention was attracted to a grimy but cheerful little boy. "What's your name, son?" he asked. "Reginald Alphonso d'Autrefois Jones, sir," was the reply. "Goodness," cried the minister, turning to the boy's father, "why a name like that?" "It's because I want him to be a prize fighter," explained the father, "an' wid a name like dat he'll git plenty o' practice in school."

2

The father had decided that the time had come for his young son to learn about life. Piling several large boxes on top of each other, he placed the boy on top, stood below with outstretched arms, and commanded "Jump!" "But I'm afraid, papa," whimpered the boy. "Come on, jump," urged father. "Papa will catch you." The boy jumped, the man stepped aside, and the lad hit the floor with a thump. "Now let that be a lesson to you, son," instructed father, "and never trust anybody."

TRAMP

1

"Ah, madam," declared the ragged beggar with his arm in a sling, "I wasn't always as you see me now." "I know that," replied the woman sharply. "The last time I saw you you had a 'Blind' sign and a tin cup."

2

"Have you any idea, madam," inquired the bum of the lady of the house, "where I might get something to eat?" The lady compressed her lips and suggested, "You might try going in the woodshed and taking a few chops."

See also brief[2], charity[2, 4], convince[2], cooking[2], determination, grammar[2], lazy[2], medicine[6], rescue[1], self-made[3], smoking[4], suggestion[3], sympathy[4], unlucky[2], warning[2], wish[1], work.

TRANSPORTATION

A lady approached a ticket window in the railroad station in Chicago and requested, "I'd like a ticket for New York, please." "Certainly, madam," replied the ticket agent. "Do you wish to go by Buffalo?" "Heavens, no!" exclaimed the lady in horror. "I want to go by train."

TRAVELER

1

A group of tourists were gazing in awe down into the rumbling, smoking crater of Vesuvius. "Golly," observed an American breathlessly, "that sure looks a lot like the infernal regions." An English lady overheard this and remarked to a companion, "Mercy, but these Americans seem to travel every place!"

2

"We must get out to Stratford-on-Avon tomorrow," declared the American tourist in London. "Aw, why go 'way out there?" protested his friend. "We can buy Stratford picture postcards right here in London." "Don't be vulgar," advised the first scornfully. "Traveling means more than just sending picture postcards home. I want to write my name on Shakespeare's tomb and see if I can chip a piece off of it."

See also art[4].

TRAVELING

1

As a steamship was pulling away from Piraeus, the port of Athens, an elderly lady approached the captain and asked, "What's that white stuff on those hills there, Captain?" "That's snow, madam," was the answer. "Hmm, that's odd," mused the lady. "That gentleman over there told me it was Greece."

2

"What part of your trip did you enjoy most, Bill?" inquired a man of a friend who had just returned from abroad. "Well, I liked Paris and London a lot, and Rome was very educational," replied Bill, "but I think the best part of it all was the trip over. Whatever you do if you go to Europe, don't miss that!"

3

Mrs. Williams had just returned from a world tour with her husband, and her friends were questioning her about it. "Of course, you included Paris in your itinerary?" remarked one. "I really couldn't say," replied the traveler. "You see, my husband bought all the tickets."

4

A family was on a train in the course of a conducted, all-expense

tour of Europe. "Is this Rome, mamma?" asked daughter as the train pulled into the station. "What day is it, Angelina?" asked mother. "It's Thursday, mamma," said the girl. "Well, if it's Thursday," announced mother, "it must be Rome."

See also America[2], craftsmanship[3], hint[3], journey, newlyrich[3], seasick[6].

TREACHERY

See deceive.

TREATMENT

1

Betty, who had been suffering from a minor ailment had gone to the doctor's. On her return home her mother said, "Did the doctor treat you, Betty?" "He sure didn't," replied Betty. "He charged me two dollars."

2

The doctor shook his head gravely as he finished examining the patient and said, "First of all, sir, you must give up liquor." "But I never touch a drop, doc," was the reply. "Hmm. Then you must give up tobacco," ordered the medico. "Never used it in my life," the patient assured him. "Well, you'll have to stop coffee," the doctor tried again. "Never drink it," he was told. "Goodness!" exclaimed the doctor in exasperation. "If you haven't anything to give up, how do you expect me to treat you?"

TREE

1

A lady traveling down South saw for the first time a fig tree. "Can you tell me," she asked her guide, "what kind of tree that is?" "A fig tree, ma'am," was the answer. "But it can't be a fig tree," objected the lady. "But it is a fig tree, ma'am," insisted the guide. "Hmm," mused the lady. "I always thought its leaves were larger than that."

2

A wealthy man was inspecting his estate with his gardener and seemed much pleased with things. "My goodness," he remarked, "isn't it marvelous how fast the trees grow?" "Well, yes," admitted the gardener, "but you must remember, sir, that they don't have anything else to do."

3

A visitor from the city was examining the orchard with the farmer's little daughter. "This tree is certainly loaded with apples," he remarked. "Are all your trees as full of apples as this one?" "No, sir," replied the little girl. "Only the apple trees."

See also quarrel[7].

TRIAL

A lady opened a door and stepped into a large room filled with seats. "Is the professor in?" she inquired of a man who was sweeping up. "What professor?" he asked. "The professor of music, of course," she replied. "I've come to have my voice tried." "Well, you'd better not have it tried here, ma'am," advised the sweeper. "This is a court of justice."

TRIP

See journey, touring, traveling.

TRIPLETS

1

The small daughter of an auto tire dealer saw for the first time a set of triplets being aired by their mother. She rushed home in great excitement. "Oh, mamma," she cried breathlessly, "do you know what I just saw?" "No, dear, what was it?" asked mother. "I saw a lady with twins," she declared, "who was carrying a spare."

2

Smith who had recently become the father of triplets was stopped on the street one day by a friend who said, "Congratulations, old man, I hear that the stork has smiled on you." "Smiled on me, hell!" growled Smith. "He laughed out loud at me!"

3

The politician was pacing nervously up and down the corridor outside the delivery room. At long last the doctor appeared and with a smile announced, "Congratulations, sir, you are the father of triplets." "Impossible!" cried the politician. "I'll demand a recount!"

4

The farmer and his wife were sad because they had no children. So they prayed that their loneliness might be relieved, and after a year or so, they were blessed with triplets. "See there," remarked a friend upon hearing the news, "prayers are always answered." "Shore seem to be," agreed the farmer; "but I ain't never prayed fer no bumper crop like that."

See also economy[4].

TROUBLE

They had just become engaged and she was full of plans for their future life. "And just think, dear," she gurgled, "I shall always be there to share your troubles." "But, darling," he protested, "I don't have any troubles." "Oh, I know," she replied. "But I was talking about after we're married."

See also bachelor[1], help[2], husband[3, 6], wife[4, 7].

TRUANT

A small boy presented himself at the box office of a movie theater in time for the Wednesday matinee and asked, "Give me one children's ticket, please." The ticket seller eyed him suspiciously and asked, "Why aren't you in school, sonny?" "Oh, that's all right," the boy hastened to assure him. "I've got the measles."

See also catch[2].

TRUCK-DRIVER

1

The orator was in the midst of a lyrical outburst. "He of whom I speak drove straight on to his goal," he ranted on. "He looked neither to right nor left, but pressed ever onward, moved by a definite purpose. Nor friend nor foe could deter or turn him in his course, and all who crossed his path did so at their peril. What, my friends, would you call such a man?" "A truck-driver," called a voice from the rear.

2

"The case against you is quite plain," declared the judge to the truck-driver. "There's no doubt that you ran over the plaintiff with a loaded truck. Do you have anything to say in your defense?" "Yes, Your Honor," replied the truck-driver. "I didn't know it was loaded."

See also direction[2].

TRUST

1

"I used to know your cashier, Mr. Jensen," remarked a visitor to the boss. "I understand that he's a tried and trusted employee—" "Humph!" interrupted the boss. "He was trusted, all right, but he won't be tried until we catch him."

2

The woman had but recently moved into the neighborhood, so she asked a neighbor about a nearby doctor. "My little boy has swallowed a gold-piece and has to be operated on," she explained. "Do you think Dr. Smith is to be trusted?" "There's no doubt about it," the other assured her; "he's entirely honest."

3

A young politician had just made his first and very eloquent address and was receiving congratulations when an old farmer came up and drew him aside. "That was a real good speech ye made, son, up to the last sentence," he said. "But if ye don't retract that you're sure to git beat." "Why, what was wrong with it?" asked the amazed politician. "Waal, ye said if elected ye'd be true to yer Trust," explained the old man, "an' thet's jest what lots of us has been afraid of."

4

All week little Willie had tried hard to behave, and now he asked, "Have I been a good boy lately, mom?" "Yes, very good," said mother. "And do you trust me, mom?" the boy went on. "Of course, I trust you, dear," she assured him. "Why do you ask?" "Because," declared the boy, "if you really trust me, why do you keep on hiding the jam an' cookies?"

See also training[2].

TRUTH

1

Church services were over and several of the congregation were strolling leisurely along the street discussing the sermon. "There's one thing about our minister," asserted one, "he can undoubtedly dive deeper in the truth than any preacher I've heard." "Yes," put in a second, "and stay under longer." "Yes," a third joined in, "and come up drier."

2

The hillbilly about to be sworn in as a witness didn't look too intelligent. "Do you understand what you're to swear to?" asked the court. "Yes, suh," was the reply. "Ah'm to sweah to tell the truth." "That's right," said the judge. "And do you know what will happen if you don't tell the truth?" "Well, suh," the hillbilly hesitated, "ah reckon then that ouah side would win the case, suh."

3

"You're quite certain about your statement?" demanded the lawyer of the witness. "Quite certain," asserted the witness. "And you swear that it's true?" continued the lawyer. "I swear it," was the firm reply. "Would you be willing to bet on the truth of it?" asked the lawyer. "Well, er, yes, I might," answered the witness; "that is, of course, if I got the right odds."

4

The chorus girl had decided to get rid of her current sweetie, but couldn't make up her mind as to how to do it. "What's the matter, dearie," asked a friend, "afraid he might go around tellin' lies about you?" "Heck, he can lie about me all he wants," retorted the chorus girl scornfully, "but if he'd ever tell the truth I'd be sunk."

5

A newly-appointed judge in a small town found that one of his first cases was the village ne'er-do-well charged, as had often happened before, with chicken stealing. "Well, Sam, I see you're here again," he remarked. "Yes, sir," was the reply. "D'ya 'member last time you wuz my lawyer?" "That's right, Sam," agreed the judge. "Who's your lawyer this time?" "Ain't got none, judge," said Sam. "Reckon this time I'm jest gonna have to tell the truth."

6

The witness wore a baffled look when he appealed to the court. "I just don't know what I'm going to do, judge," he declared desperately. "Why, what seems to be the matter?" asked His Honor. "Well, I swore to tell nothing but the truth," explained the witness, "but every time I try it some lawyer objects."

See also hat[3], oil[2], sermon[4].

TRUTHFUL

1

The witness being sworn in to testify in court was a pretty tough-looking customer. "Do you swear to tell the truth, the whole truth, and nothing but the truth, so help you God?" recited the clerk. "Okay. Why not?" replied the tough mug, shrugging his shoulders. "I'll try anything once."

2

It was toward evening when a weary man in fisherman's garb and carrying a fishing rod entered a fish store. He picked out six nice plump trout, then asked the fish dealer, "Would you mind throwing the fish to me while I stand over there?" "Throw 'em to you! What for?" asked the shopkeeper. "So I can tell the family I caught them," was the reply. "I may be a bum fisherman, but I'm no liar."

See also compliment[1], dying[4], rent[1], soldier[3], tact[3].

TRY

See attempt.

TUNNEL

1

"My, that was certainly quite a tunnel, wasn't it?" observed the young man to his fair companion as the train emerged into the sunlight. "Did you know that it is over two miles long and cost fifteen million dollars?" "No, I didn't," she replied, rearranging her dress and straightening her hair. "But it was certainly worth it, wasn't it?"

2

Two moonshiners from deep in the hills were taking their first train ride. Having heard of soda pop but never having tasted any, they each bought a bottle when the vendor came by. One of the moonshiners tilted up his bottle and took a long swig—and just then the train went into a tunnel. "How ya like it, Zeke?" asked the other in the darkness. "Don't tech thet stuff, Jeff," warned the first. "It's jest struck me blind!"

3

A hillbilly was exploring the countryside, and as he stood at the top of a hill he saw an express train, the first he'd ever seen. It was dashing madly across the fields toward a rocky hill where it zipped into a tunnel and disappeared from sight. "Whew!" observed the man from the hills as he wiped his brow with his sleeve. "Wouldn't thet've been a mess if thet contraption hed missed thet little hole!"

TWINS

1

"Congratulations, Jim, my boy!" cried Uncle heartily. "I hear that you're engaged to one of those pretty Smith twins." "Yes, I am," replied Jim. "But they look exactly alike," said Uncle; "how do you ever tell them apart?" "Heck, they're both pretty, aren't they?" retorted Jim. "Why should I try?"

2

The maid met the man of the house as he entered the door. "We thought you'd never get back, sir," she exclaimed. "It's two o'clock. But I have news for you, sir. You're the father of two fine boys! Twins, sir, twins!" "Humph! quite a coincidence," grunted the young father; "two o'clock and two babies. Thank heavens I didn't come home at twelve."

3

It was just past bathing time, and from the nursery came a strange mixture of hearty laughter and bitter weeping. "What's going on in here?" demanded father, opening the door. "Oh, nuffin much," said one twin pointing to his tearful brother, "only nursie has gived Billy two baths an' ain't give me none."

See also identify[2], plural[1], repeat.

TYPEWRITER

"Say, Tom," asked a young businessman of a more experienced friend whom he met on the street, "where do you usually buy your typewriter ribbons?" "Aw, I don't go in for that corny stuff," replied Tom. "I always buy her flowers or silk stockings."

See also poet[1].

UGLY

The party was becoming dull, so the host, thinking to liven things up, announced, "We'll now have a contest for the ladies. I'll award a box of candy to the lady who can make the ugliest face." After observing the facial contortions, he declared, "Mrs. Adams wins the prize." "Well, I like that," said the lady. "I wasn't even playing your silly game."

See also angel[1], face[1], portrait, reform[4], resemblance[1].

UMBRELLA

There was a nasty drizzle falling when a man rushed into a restaurant. "Waiter, did I leave an umbrella in here yesterday?" he inquired. "What sort of umbrella, sir?" asked the waiter. "Oh, any kind," answered the man. "I'm not at all particular."

See also rain[1].

UNCONSCIOUS

1

"What are you doing to my husband?" asked the alarmed wife as the doctor placed a white cone over the man's face. "Giving him an anesthetic," explained the physician. "After he has this he won't know anything." "Then don't bother with it," advised the wife. "He doesn't need it."

2

Thinking to drive home a lesson after several trucks outside the psychology classroom had raised a terrific clamor in getting a heavy load up a hill, the professor asked a girl who had been reading aloud, "Now think, Miss Williams, did you unconsciously raise your voice while that noise was going on outside?" "But, Professor," asked the girl, "if I did it unconsciously, how can I tell?"

UNDERSTAND

See professor[2], statesman[2].

UNDERTAKER

1

"Say, what's the idea telling me your uncle's a doctor, Jim?" protested Jack. "I just found out that he's an undertaker." "But I never said he was a doctor," replied Jim. "I merely said that he followed the medical profession."

2

The new minister was meeting with the committee for the first time and he made an appeal for church funds. It was so eloquent that a quiet gentleman in black came up and made a donation of a hundred dollars. "I don't know your name, sir," cried the minister gratefully, "but I thank you sincerely and pray that your business may prosper." There was a startled hush and the committee looked at the preacher. "What's wrong?" he, asked of the chairman. "That donor was an undertaker," he was told.

See also education[2], price[5].

UNDERWEAR

"Marry my daughter!" the girl's father snorted derisively. "Why, young man, you couldn't even keep her in underwear." "Is that so!" retorted the suitor hotly. "Well let me tell you, sir, there are times when you don't do so well yourself!"

See also location[6].

UNFAITHFUL

"Bill doesn't seem to trust his wife any more," remarked Slim to Jim. "So I've noticed," agreed Jim. "Has anything happened?" "Well, nothing definite," replied Slim. "It's just that one morning, after he'd left, Bill slipped around into the kitchen and sneaked up behind her and kissed her on the back of the neck, and without turning around she said, 'Okay, babe, just leave a quart of milk and a pint of cream.'"

See also whisper.

UNFORTUNATE

See miserable, misfortune, unlucky.

UNIVERSITY

See college.

UNLUCKY

1

"Poor baby," sighed little Joan as she came into mother's room, "I'm afraid he's going to have seven years of bad luck." "What makes you say that?" asked mother. "He's just swallowed a piece of broken mirror," was the reply.

2

The tramp at the door was making a touching appeal. "Lady," he pleaded, "would you help a poor feller what lost his family an' all his property in the Florida flood?" "Say," demanded the lady, scrutinizing him, "aren't you the same man who lost his family in the Galveston flood, was shellshocked in the war, and lost everything in the crash?" "Yes, ma'am," admitted the tramp; "ain't I the unluckiest feller you ever saw?"

3

"Ah, me," sighed the man with

a large family, "one of my daughters has tonsilitis and the other has sprained her wrist." "That's certainly tough luck," sympathized a friend. "Golly, yes," growled the other. "Nothing ever works out right for me—the one with the hurt wrist sings, and the one with the bad throat plays the piano."

UNUSUAL

The old inn was crowded and the only room vacant was one with the reputation of being haunted. But the man was weary and decided he'd chance the room anyway. "By the way," he inquired of the evil-looking attendant conducting him, "has anything unusual ever really happened in this room?" "Not for over 50 years, sir," was the reply. "And what happened then?" asked the guest. "There was a gentleman who spent the night in it," related the other, "and he showed up for breakfast the next morning."

USE

Teacher was examining her class on their knowledge of industrial products. "Who can tell me what cowhide is chiefly used for?" she questioned. A small boy in front raised his hand. "It's chief use, ma'am," he stated, "is to keep the cow together."

See also flies.

USELESS

A traveling peddler was going through a backwoods district and stopped at a tumble-down cabin where he showed his wares and tried to make a sale. "All them things is foolishness an' a waste o' money," declared the man of the shack. "Oh, come now," encouraged the peddler, "we all spend a little money foolishly now and then." "Not me," insisted the hillbilly. "I only spent one dime in all my life fer foolishness, an' thet was fer a pair o' socks."

See also bird[1], economy[4].

VACATION

1

Summer vacation was over and the boys were beginning to gather in the fraternity house. "Well, Bill, what did you do this summer?" inquired one. "Oh, I worked in my dad's office," replied Bill. "What did you do?" "I loafed, too," responded the first.

2

"Heard from Bill on his vacation," remarked Brown to an acquaintance. "You did?" said the other. "How is he enjoying himself?" "Well, I can't exactly tell," replied Brown. "His postcard simply says: 'Having a wonderful time; wish I could afford it.'"

3

The meek bookkeeper approached the boss's desk hesitantly, cleared his throat nervously, and asked, "May I have a day off, sir, to get married?" "But you've just had a vacation," protested the boss. "Why didn't you get married then?" "Oh, I don't know," said the bookkeeper, "but I somehow just didn't want to spoil my vacation."

See also dressing, hotel[7], mosquito[8], summer boarder.

VALUE

1

A stranger, passing by, noticed a fine Jersey heifer grazing in a meadow. Driving around to the owner's house, he inquired of the farmer, "How much do you figure that Jersey cow of yours is worth?" The farmer scratched his head and pondered for a moment, then cautiously asked, "See here, be you the tax-assessor, or has thet cow been killed by the railroad?"

2

"How'd ye come out sellin' yore sheep, John?" asked a neighbor of a farmer. "Did ye git what they was wuth?" "Waal, I don't rightly know," replied John. " 'Course, I didn't git as much as I figgered I might, but then I never thought I would."

See also operation[4], price, salary[1], salt[2].

VANITY

The demure miss had become engaged to a noted actor and now she was nestling happily in his arms. "Ah," she sighed ecstatically, her head on his chest, "I'm the happiest person in the world." "And I," conceded the actor in a matter-of-fact tone, "am next to the happiest."

See also mistake[5].

VERSE

"Smith," questioned the English professor, "can you give us examples to illustrate the difference between prose and verse?" "Yes, sir," replied Smith. "An example of prose is: 'There once was a charming young lass, who waded out to her knees.' " "Very good," answered the professor. "And now for verse?" "Well," suggested the fellow, "just make the water about eighteen inches deeper, and you've got verse."

VICE

A student was applying for admission to a university. "Have you ever attended college before?" inquired the registrar. "Yes, sir," replied the applicant. "Did you matriculate?" was the next question. "What's that?" he questioned. "I said, did you matriculate?" repeated the registrar. "No, sir," denied the student stoutly. "I just smoked and chewed a little, but maybe some of the other fellows matriculated."

See also dissipation[1], wicked[2].

VIEW

1

An artist who wanted to buy a home in the mountains got in touch with a farmer who claimed to have a suitable house for sale. "The house is not as important to me as the view," explained the artist. "Is there a good view?" "Mebbe thet's the drawback," conceded the farmer. " 'Course, from the front porch yuh kin see Jim Brown's new red barn, but beyond thet there ain't a blasted thing but mountains, woods, an' lakes."

2

The newcomer looked out of his hotel-room window at a blank wall not ten feet distant. "But your advertisement said that at this hotel one could get a beautiful view for miles and miles," he complained. "And so you can," maintained the proprietor. "Just you stick your head out of that window and look up."

See also opinion[1].

VILLAGE

"Little do we know the trials and tribulations of others, Mrs. Smith," observed the visitor from the city. "Truly, one-half of the world is ignorant of how the other half lives." "Humph!" sniffed Mrs. Smith. "Not in this village."

See also amusement[1], curfew.

VIOLIN

1

Mr. Williams, a rich man, engaged a noted violinist to perform at his reception. The artist informed the host, "I wish you to know, sir, that the violin I shall use to entertain your guests is over two hundred years old." "Now, don't you worry about it a minute," said the rich man grandly. "We'll just dim the lights a bit and nobody'll notice it."

2

A violinist entered a small music shop in London and said to the young lady behind the counter, "I'd like to get an E string, please." Placing a large box of violin strings on the counter, the girl shyly requested, "Would you mind very much picking one out for yourself, sir? You see, I 'ardly knows the 'es from the shes."

See also appreciation[2].

VIRTUE

1

A captain was showing a visitor around camp when he saw a rookie sneaking along trying to conceal a fat chicken under his blouse. "Where did you get that chicken?" he demanded. Caught red-handed, the rookie answered frankly, "I stole it, sir." "See there!" cried the captain triumphantly to the visitor. "My men may steal a little, but they don't lie!"

2

"Well, you can say what you like," declared hubby during a brief lull in the quarrel, "but at least I don't parade my virtues." "Of course you don't," agreed wifey tartly. "Did you ever hear of a parade with nobody in it?"

3

Teacher had been lecturing at length on the beauties of kindness and charity, and now he wished to see if the lesson had reached home. "Tell me, Billy," he said, "if I happened to see a man beating a donkey and made him stop, what virtue would I be showing?" "Brotherly love," responded Billy promptly.

4

A big rowdy red rooster was chasing a frightened, fluttery little hen. Squawking shrilly, the little hen dodged hither and yon attempting to escape, finally running out in the road and directly into the path of a car. Two old maids seated on a nearby porch had witnessed the tragedy. "See there," declared one, nodding her head virtuously, "she'd rather die first!"

See also color[2], commandment[3], conceit[2].

VISITOR

See caller, guest.

VOICE

The village choir had just gained a new member. On the first Sunday of her participation the newcomer's voice sounded out shrilly above the organ and the singing of the rest of the choir and congregation much like a steam whistle above the gentle humming of bees. "Well, what do you think of our new singer?" one of the choir members asked another after services. "Goodness me!" declared the other. "That woman has the most selfish voice I've ever heard."

See also loud, trial.

VOLCANO

1

Mabel had got back from a trip abroad and she was telling a neighbor woman some of the marvels she had seen. "Then down in Italy, of course, we saw that famous volcano," she stated. "Saw what?" asked the neighbor. "A volcano," repeated Mabel. "You know, one of those big fiery things that's always belching and spitting. "Oh sure," said the other. "I ought to know—I married one."

2

"Here's a puzzle I just heard, pop," said Junior. "What does a volcano do with its lava?" "Hmm," he pondered, then said, "Give it up." "That's right," responded Junior.

See also traveler[1].

VOTE

It was well after dusk when a citizen rushed into a registration office. "Is it too late for me to register to vote?" he asked the registrar. That worthy looked him over critically. "That all depends," he declared. "What party?"

See also conscience[1], earn[1], suffrage.

WAGER

See bet, gambling.

WAGES

See salary.

WAITER

1

A passenger seated in a diner was waiting impatiently to be served his breakfast. But instead of taking his order, the waiter merely stood gazing out of the window at the scenery. "What's the matter?" he demanded at last. "Haven't you ever waited on table before?" "No, suh, I ain't nevah waited on table before," admitted the waiter with a cheerful grin. "Ain't nevah been on a train before, either. Sure is interestin', ain't it?"

2

"You must learn to mind your manners, Danny," mother scolded her young son. "Politeness doesn't cost anything." "Now, now, don't go putting such ideas in the boy's head," said father, slipping into his dress coat. "I've been planning to train the boy to take my place some day as head waiter."

3

Spoiled by having inherited a little money, the young man had become brusque and impatient with those who served him. One evening, in putting ice in the young fellow's water glass, a waiter splashed a few drops. "You're not fit to serve a pig!" snarled the young snob. "Sorry, sir," replied the waiter, frigidly polite, "but I'm doing my best."

See also misfortune².

WAITING

1

A sad-faced man sat quietly in the restaurant wearing a Job-like air. A waiter came by and remarked, "Your fish will be coming along any minute now, sir." "Tell me," asked the customer, "what are you using for bait?"

2

Once more the waiter returned to the table and inquired of the patron, "Let's see, sir, what was it you wanted now?" "Well, I originally came in for breakfast," the man explained, "but if lunch is about ready, I'll take supper."

3

A drunk was staggering around in front of a house when a policeman came up and asked, "Where do you live?" "Right here," said the drunk, indicating a house, "but I rang the bell and nobody answered." "How long since you rang?" the copper wanted to know. "Oh, over two hours," was the reply. "Then, why not ring again?" demanded the policeman. "Aw, to hell with 'em!" declared the drunk. "Let 'em wait!"

4

Mother turned a concerned face to father. "Our daughter will be twenty-six next month, John," she reminded him. "Don't you think it's time she got married and settled down?" "Oh, there's no hurry, dear," replied John. "Better let her wait until the right man comes along." "But why have her wait?" objected mother. "I didn't."

5

A farm boy was walking down a country road one evening when he spied an acquaintance sitting on a log beside the road. "Why you sittin' there, Ned?" he inquired. "Oh, I'm jest waitin' fer Molly to come along," explained Ned. "I'm gonna take her to prayer meetin'." "But meetin' ain't 'til tomorrow night," objected the other. "I know," agreed Ned. "But when a feller's in love, he don't mind waitin' a little."

6

After sitting unnoticed at a table for over twenty minutes, the diner finally snapped at a nearby group of waitresses who were chattering together, "Say, there! Who's waiting at this table?" One of the waitresses turned and answered, "Why, you are, of course!" and then resumed her conversation.

7

A doctor stuck his head out of his treatment room and addressed those assembled in the reception room, "Next patient, please. Which of you has been waiting the longest?" "I have, doctor," declared a little man, arising and presenting a slip of paper. "I'm your tailor, and

I delivered your clothes to you over two years ago."

See also delay[1].

WAITRESS

1

A grumpy old fellow came into a restaurant and began looking at the menu the pretty waitress handed him. Looking up at last, he demanded gruffly, "How's the duck today?" "Oh, I'm just fine," she assured him. "And how's the old pelican himself?"

2

He was studying the menu as the waitress came up to the table with a slight limp. "Do you have frog's legs?" he asked. "Oh, no, sir. It's just a touch of rheumatism that makes me walk like this," she answered.

3

The waitress was peeved this morning and didn't care who knew it. She swaggered up to the new customer's table, banged down the silverware, tossed a napkin in his direction, sailed a menu at him, then put her hands on her hips and snarled, "Whatcha want?" "Coupla eggs," he growled back at her. "How yuh wan' 'em?" she demanded impatiently. "Just like you are, babe," he told her.

See also kind[1], restaurant[2], waiting[6].

WALKING

1

A man and a woman were walking toward each other on a narrow sidewalk. As they tried to pass each other, one of those situations of mutual indecision developed whereby they both jockeyed back and forth, first to the right, then to the left, and so on. When at last they managed to untangle themselves, the man raised his hat and politely said, "Well, g'by, now. It's been fun knowing you!"

2

It was a pleasant summer evening and the young man had been parked on the girl's front porch for hours. "Would you like to take a walk?" she suggested at last. "I'd love to," he agreed. "Well, then," she retorted, yawning, "don't let me stop you."

3

"The younger generation expects too much," declared a self-made man to a young fellow. "I didn't always have this fine car, you know. When I first started out in life, I had to walk." "You were lucky at that," retorted the young man with a chuckle. "When I started out in life I couldn't even walk."

See also distance[4], experience[5], strength[4].

WANT

See desire, wish.

WAR

1

Teacher had been comparing the benefits of peace with the horrors of war, and now she asked, "How many of you children object to war?" A number of hands shot up, and picking one out she questioned,

"Will you tell the class, Tommy, why you object to wars?" "I hate war," announced Tommy with deep feeling, " 'cause wars make history."

2

The lecturer was full of reasons why every one else should be eager to make noble patriotic sacrifices. "As for me," he added importantly, "it is my proudest boast that during the war I was one of the men behind the guns." "Oh, yeah?" cried a voice from the crowd. "How far behind?"

3

"I'll never forget the day we were married," remarked the jolly-looking fellow reminiscently. "It was on that very day that the war started." "In that respect, sir," commented the meek-looking man in the corner, "you've nothing on the rest of us married men."

See also ancestor, army, navy, officer, soldier.

WARNING

1

"Say, there," demanded the big, burly man menacingly of the little fellow, "did you want to steal my girl from me without any warning?" "Why, not at all, sir," the small one hastened to assure him. "What warning about her did you wish to give me?"

2

A gentleman handed a tramp the coin requested, then in a friendly tone suggested, "In the middle of the next block right on down this street there's a woman who I know wants her leaves raked and grass

cut." "Gee, t'anks fer de warnin'," replied the bum gratefully. "I mighta passed by dere accidental-like."

3

Smith and his wife were sitting beside some palms on a hotel veranda one balmy spring evening, when a young couple came and sat on a bench on the other side of the palms. The young fellow at once began addressing the girl in passionate terms, and Mrs. Smith grew uneasy. "I think he's going to propose, John, and he doesn't know we're here," she whispered. "Whistle to warn him." "Why should I?" growled Smith. "Nobody whistled to warn me."

See also dog[1].

WASHING

1

"Johnny, your piano teacher will be here any minute," warned mother. "Have you washed your hands?" "Yes," replied the boy. "And your face?" persisted mother. "Yes," came the same answer. "And did you wash behind your ears?" questioned mother. "We-ell, yes," the assurance came more slowly. "That is, on her side I did."

2

The captain who was inspecting a group of rookies called the sergeant aside. "That third man looks very unkempt, sergeant," he declared. "Yes, sir," the sergeant agreed. "Does he ever wash?" the captain wanted to know. "Oh, yes, sir," the sarge assured him. "Are you positive he washes?" asked the captain doubtfully. "Absolutely, sir," asserted the sergeant. "He just dries a bad color, sir."

3

"You know, I think we misnamed our son," commented father thoughtfully. "We should have called him 'Flannel.'" "Good heavens, why 'Flannel'?" asked mother in amazement. "Because he shrinks from washing," explained father.

4

Invariably little Billy would come to the table with dirty hands and face and would, of course, be sent away to wash. One day mother lost patience and exclaimed, "Goodness, Billy, why do you always come to the table without washing? You know I always send you away and make you do it." "Well, you see," explained Billy, "once you forgot."

See also tattoo[2].

WASTE

The rich man was a gay old boy and he had just met a pretty young lady. "Do you know, my dear," he said, "I'd give five dollars for just one kiss from a sweet girl like you." "Oh, how awful!" gasped the girl. "I'm sorry," apologized the old boy contritely. "I didn't mean to offend you." "Oh, it's not that," explained the girl. "I was just thinking of the fortune I gave away last night."

See also economy[5], fruit[5], useless[1].

WATCH

1

A man had been boasting of his dollar watch until his listeners were bored. "Aw, that's nothing," interrupted one of his victims finally. "I dropped my watch into the East River over a year ago, and it's been running ever since." "What!" gasped the bore. "The same watch?" "No," was the reply. "The same river."

2

A man was seated on a bus beside a boy who was proudly playing with a cheap watch. "Does your watch tell the time, sonny?" inquired the man with an indulgent smile. "No, sir," was the serious response. "You gotta look at it."

3

It was a cheap watch that the gentleman brought into the jeweler's to have repaired. "I know it was a grave mistake," he confessed as the jeweler looked it over, "to drop it in the first place." "Well, no, you probably couldn't help that," the other reassured him. "Your mistake was in picking it up."

4

Two ministers were in a cab driving to the station to catch a train. Fearful that they were late, one pulled out his watch to consult it, but found it had stopped. "How vexing!" he cried in annoyance. "And I've always put such faith in this watch." "In this instance," remarked the other, "good works would probably have served better."

See also breakage[2], fee[4], payment[5].

WATER

Two clubmen were talking over the world situation as they stood at the bar. "If things continue to go as they are," observed one, "we may soon have to drink water." "Huh? Wha'sh 'at?" asked the other dimly. "Water. You know, water," repeated the first. "That stuff that the waiter brings you with your napkin."

See also ass[1], dirty[2], fraternity[1], ice[1], running, sense, spirit[2], temperance[2].

WEAK

1

The elephant in the zoo was in a peevish mood and was looking for an object upon which to vent his spleen. A tiny mouse happened into the cage. "Yah, yah!" he trumpeted. "You're the weakest, puniest, most helpless little thing I've ever seen! Why aren't you big and strong like me?" "Well," squeaked the mouse, "don't forget, I've been sick lately."

2

Two chorus girls were looking over a newspaper between acts. "Gee, look, Mame," pointed out one. "It says here that Mr. Adams, the octogenarian, has died. Now, what the heck is an octogenarian?" "I dunno," replied Mame, "but they're sure a puny, sickly bunch. You never hear about one but what he's dyin'."

See also seasick[5], tea[1].

WEALTH

1

"Well, well, it's good to see you again after all these years," said the man to an old school chum who had made good in the meantime. "And I'm glad to find that your great wealth hasn't changed you." "But it's changed me some in spite of myself," corrected the millionaire. "I'm now 'eccentric' where I used to be 'ill-mannered' and 'delight-fully witty' where I used to be 'damned rude.'"

2

"My dad has always had a natural ability for business," declared the young lady to a boyfriend. "While still very young he managed to make a large fortune. Would you care to hear how he did it?" "Oh, sure," assented the fellow. "But first tell me, does he still have it?"

3

"Ah, my sweet," he murmured passionately, "I gladly lay my fortune at your feet." "Your fortune?" she echoed. "I didn't know you had one." "Well, maybe it isn't much of a fortune," he admitted, "but it will look large beside those tiny feet."

4

"Papa," asked little Johnny, looking up from a book he was reading, "what is 'untold wealth'?" "That, my son," replied papa, "is the part of your earnings that doesn't show up on your income-tax return."

5

One of the younger sons of a large, poverty-stricken Ozark hillbilly family was dissatisfied with the outlook and wanted to go to town to seek his fortune. But the father was not in favor of it. "But what chancet I got here, paw?" complained the boy. "Ain't nuthin' fer me here 'cept bein' pore an' dirty all my life." "What chancet?" exclaimed the old man. "Why, jest look at me, son. When I come here frum Kaintucky twenty year ago I didn't have nuthin—now I got thirteen kids an' 'leven dawgs!"

6

Little Jackie had been listening to father complain, so now he in turn was complaining to teacher, "Aw, what chance has a poor man got anyway?" "All he needs is energy and ambition," declared teacher brightly. "Why, one of the richest men in the country came right here years ago without a shirt on his back, and now he has millions." "Gee, millions!" cried Jackie, much impressed. "How many does he wear at a time?"

WEAPON

A headwaiter in a swanky restaurant had to endure a certain amount of abuse from rude customers, but one arrogant, fat fellow had proved trying on occasion. Out of patience at last, he one day informed the person, with frigid politeness, "My position here, sir, does not permit me to argue with you or defend myself; but if it ever came to a choice of weapons between us, be assured I'd choose grammar."

See also music[1].

WEARY

See bore, tired.

WEATHER

Teacher had been telling her class about the weather in different seasons. Now she was talking about the variable March weather. "What is it," she questioned, "that comes in like a lion and goes out like a lamb?" A small girl raised her hand and volunteered, "Father."

See also agreement[1], California[1], London[1, 2], rain[1].

WEDDING

1

The speaker was eloquent on the beauties of marriage. "And it is most significant that the bride wears white," he declared. "White which is a symbol of happiness for her wedding day, the most joyous day of her life." "And why does the groom wear black?" cried a voice from the rear.

2

The eldest daughter was getting married and little Tommy was sitting with mother watching the ceremony. As the service progressed, the boy noticed some tears trickling down mother's cheeks. "Why are you crying, mamma?" he asked. "It's not your wedding."

3

A small girl was sitting with her mother watching a church wedding when suddenly she piped up, "What's the matter, mommy, did the lady change her mind?" "Hush, dear," reproved mother. "What makes you say that?" "Well, it sure looks like it," insisted the child. "She went down the aisle with one man and came back with a different one."

4

A young couple had requested the minister to marry them immediately following Sunday morning church services. So when the time came the minister arose and said, "Will those who wish to be united in the holy bonds of matrimony please step forward?" There was quite a stir among the congregation, and when it subsided sixteen women and one man stood before the altar.

5

It was a very elegant society wedding reception and a dear old lady was wandering aimlessly about trying to say the right and proper thing to every one. Encountering a young man in immaculate morning dress, she ventured brightly, "Ah, there, and you, of course, are the happy bridegroom." "Not quite, madam," was the response. "I was eliminated in the semi-finals."

6

A traveling parson got back to a certain village after a long absence and was met by a number of young couples eager to be married. Very tired, and wishing to get the business over with in a hurry, he told them all to join hands, read the marriage service over rapidly, and declared, "I now pronounce you man an' wife." The couples then discovered that in their haste they had paired off wrongly in holding hands, and appealed to the parson for help. "It's all right," he assured them. "I married ye all—now jest sort yourselves out."

7

"I'll never forget my wedding day," remarked Jack. "When the time came, I couldn't find the ring. Boy, did I get an awful fright!" "Yeah, I know," agreed his friend, "and you've still got her."

8

At the wedding reception after the ceremony the best man was circulating among the guests trying to keep things lively. Noticing a gloomy-looking young fellow in the corner, he approached and said cheerily, "Hope you're enjoying yourself. Have you kissed the bride?" The other gave him a far-away glance and replied, "Not lately."

9

A woman was describing to a friend a wedding she had attended a few days previously. "The bride was a veritable dream," she declared ecstatically, "all in white satin, with her long veil, slender slippers, huge bouquet, and everything." "And what did the bridegroom wear?" inquired the friend. "You know, that was a very strange thing," mused the other. "That dirty so-and-so never did show up."

10

A country couple presented themselves before a justice of the peace to be married. The ceremony was brief, but the couple continued to stand there as if expecting something more. Slightly embarrassed, the justice attempted to round things off with a religious flavor by stammering, "There, now, it's all over! Go and sin no more!"

See also appropriate[1], daughter[2], gift[1], horse racing[2], obedience[2].

WEEDS

1

A visitor from the city was looking over the farmer's well-kept land. "Which weeds are the easiest to kill?" he inquired. The farmer, who had recently remarried, smiled and replied, "Widow's weeds. All you have to do to them is say 'Wilt thou' and they wilt."

2

A man took great pride in his smooth, well-kept lawn, but one year dandelions cropped up and spoiled its appearance. He tried everything he had heard of to get rid of them, but they only increased. Finally, he wrote the Department of Agriculture, listing all he had done, and concluding: "What shall I do now?" In due time came a reply: "We suggest you learn to love dandelions."

WEEPING

1

"There, there," the kind lady comforted the weeping little girl, "I wouldn't cry like that if I were you." "Oh, y-yeah?" answered the child. "Well, you can cry any way you like, but this is my way."

2

An old lady was sad about things in general, and was telling an early visitor how life held nothing for her. "Ah, me," she sighed, "and just this morning I woke up a little after four and started crying, and I cried right on through until breakfast time. And just as soon as I finish my tea I'll start right in again and I'll probably be at it the rest of the day."

3

A lady paused to comfort a weeping little girl, and ended her arguments against crying by saying, "And, besides, crying makes little girls grow up ugly." The child looked at the lady through her tears and said, "Well, gee, lady, you sure must've cried a lot when you was a kid!"

See also laughter[1], wedding[2], widower[2].

WEIGHT

1

Two drunks were hanging onto a bar and exchanging confidences about their early lives. "D'ya know," remarked one, "when I wash born I on'y weighed a pound an' three-quarters!" "Gee, ya don' shay," replied the other. "Didya live?" "Did I live!" exclaimed the first. "Shay, fella, ya oughtta shee me now!"

2

The farmer's wife sold her butter to a grocer in a nearby town. One day when she came into the store the grocer complained, "Say, the butter you brought in last week was underweight." "That's odd," answered the woman. "The boy had misplaced my pound weight, so I just used that pound of sugar you sold me week before last."

3

The farmer's daughter was back from college for the summer vacation and the old man regarded her critically. "Don't ye be a lot fatter since ye went to school?" he asked. "Perhaps a bit, father," replied daughter. "I now weigh a hundred and thirty-eight pounds stripped for 'gym.'" "Hey what goes on?" cried the farmer. "Who in tarnation is Jim?"

4

"You fellows never believe me about the fish I catch," said the boastful fisherman, "so from now on I'm carrying this scale with me and I'll weigh every fish before witnesses." "Say, lend me that scale a minute, please," requested a doctor who had happened by. A short time later he returned the scale, shaking his head in bewilderment. "I can't understand it," he declared. "How can the Smiths' week-old baby already weigh forty-three pounds?"

See also baby[7], butcher[4].

WESTERN

1

A cowboy entered a saloon in a small Western town accompanied by his wife and five-year-old son. "Two shots o' whiskey, bartender," he ordered. "What's wrong, paw?" spoke up the boy. "Why ain't maw a-drinkin'?"

2

A college man vacationing in the West amused himself by trying to teach some cowboys how to play football. After explaining the rules of the game, he concluded, "Now remember, fellows, try to kick the ball, but if you can't, kick a man on the other team. Let's go. Where's the ball?" "T'hell with the ball!" shouted one of the cowboys. "Let's git th' game a-goin'!"

See also driver[5], celebration[1], justice[1], tact[4].

WHISKEY

1

"A glass of whiskey and soda, please," asked the customer of the bartender. The drink was set before him and he tasted it. "Which did you put in first, bartender, the whiskey or the soda?" he inquired. "I always put the whiskey in first, sir," was the reply. "I see," said the man. "Then maybe I'll come to the whiskey by and by."

2

A Kentucky colonel entered a bar with a friend, ordered a glass of Bourbon, then covered his eyes with one hand as he drank the liquor down. "Why do you do that?" asked his friend. "Bourbon is the noblest of mankind's boons." "Ah know thet well, suh," replied the colonel, "but every time Ah see Bourbon mah mouth begins to watah—and Ah'll be damned, suh, if Ah want mah whiskey diluted!"

See also bread[1], Christmas[1], dirty[2], fainting[1], judge[4], miracle[1], South[4].

WHISPER

The man had an acute case of laryngitis and could not speak above a hoarse whisper. Seeking relief, he stopped at the home of a doctor who had just moved into the neighborhood. In response to his ring, the doctor's young, pretty wife opened the door. "Is the doctor in?" he asked in his forced whisper. "No, he isn't," whispered the woman in reply. "Come on in."

WHISTLE

"Stop it!" cried the boss irritably to the office boy. "I won't have you whistling at your work!" "Oh, that's all right, sir," replied the boy cheerily. "I wasn't working."

See also bellboy[1].

WICKED

1

"Now, Timmy," the Sunday-school teacher questioned one of her small pupils, "can you tell us where the wicked eventually go?" "Sure," replied Timmy, who had been listening to father's complaints. "They practice law here for awhile, and then they go to the legislature."

2

A minister, visiting in a town famous for its horse racing, one Sunday preached a violent sermon against the sport. He was later informed that the principal supporter of the church was a wealthy man who was much interested in racing. He sought out the man and said rather sheepishly, "It seems that I've touched on one of your weaknesses, sir, but I assure you, it was unintentional." "Oh, that's all right," the sportsman cheerfully assured him. "It's a mighty poor sermon that doesn't hit me somewhere."

3

The spanking was a little more vigorous than usual, so Jimmy complained, "Gosh, mom, you're kinda hard on me." "It's because you've been very naughty and wicked," declared mother. "Well, gee, mom," Jimmy pointed out, "you oughtta remember that you didn't die young yourself."

See also christening[1], practical[2].

WIDOW

One of the ladies of the sewing circle was describing a recent wedding. "It was the strangest thing," she related. "Just as Sam and the widow were starting down the aisle toward the altar, every light in the church went out." "Goodness! And what did the couple do?" asked a listener. "Went right on going down the aisle," answered the other. "The widow knew the way."

See also proposal[4], tact[6], weeds[1].

WIDOWER

1

The farmer had been passing by the Widow Brown, a close friend of his recently deceased wife, without greeting her. One day she took him to task, saying, "I'm surprised at you, Mr. Smith. You don't even tip your hat to me any more." "Waal, you see, Mrs. Brown," explained the farmer, "you're a widow an' I'm a widower, but my pore wife ain't bin dead three weeks, an' I jest ain't started lookin' at women yit."

2

Old Mr. Johnson had lost several wives, but now his friends were gathered in his parlor to witness his taking a blushing young bride again. Suddenly there was the sound of sobbing from the next room and the guests all looked around. "Aw, that's only our Annie," explained his eldest daughter. "She always cries like that when paw's a-gittin' married."

See also consolation[2], support[6], tombstone[1].

WIFE

1

A nurse entered the office of the superintendent of a mental hospital. "There's a man outside who wishes to know if any of our male inmates have escaped lately," she announced. "No, certainly not," said the superintendent. "Why does he ask?" "He says that someone ran off with his wife," was the reply.

2

Two friends stopped to greet each other along the street. "Say, what's happened?" asked one. "Your hands are all covered with grease and soot." "I've just been down to the station seeing my wife off on a long trip," explained the other. "But how could that make your hands so dirty?" the first wanted to know. "I just had to pat the engine," he was told.

3

"Papa," asked Junior, looking up from his schoolbooks, "what is a monologue?" "A monologue, my son," answered father, "is a conversation being carried on by a man and his wife."

4

The henpecked plumber had received an emergency call from the Smith residence. In answer to his ring, both Smith and his wife met him at the door. Smith was a very methodical man, so he at once said to the plumber, "Now before you go up to the bathroom, I wish to acquaint you with my trouble." The plumber pulled off his cap, blushed shyly, and holding out his hand to Mrs. Smith said, "Pleased to meet yer, ma'am."

5

An excited man dashed into a fire station. "Sorry to interrupt your game, boys," he apologized, "but my wife's disappeared again." "That's too bad," remarked one of the firemen sympathetically, "but why tell us? Why don't you go to the police?" "Oh, no, I don't dare

tell the police," cried the man. "I told them the last time she disappeared—and they went out and found her and brought her back!"

6

Brown's wife was away on a trip and he was keeping bachelor quarters for himself. "But how can you live without your wife?" asked a friend. "Much cheaper," was the reply.

7

"I wish you'd tell me just what sort of person a wife is," asked a bachelor of an old married friend. "Some men I know say their wife is an angel, while others say theirs is a she-devil." "Well, I'll tell you," explained the other. "A wife is a woman who will stick by you through all the trouble you would never have got into if you hadn't married her in the first place."

8

The wives of an African chief were grouped about the missionary's wife questioning her curiously. "And you say you never let your husband beat you?" asked one of the natives. "Why, most certainly not!" declared the Christian lady indignantly. "He wouldn't dare!" The chief's oldest wife nodded her head knowingly and commented, "It's now plain why white man has only one wife."

9

The young husband had carelessly intimated that the wife might be wrong about something, and the first quarrel had started. "Oh, you brute!" she sobbed. "And to think that you used to say that you thought Heaven had sent me to you." "I still think so," he assured her. "Honestly?" she exclaimed. "Yes, indeed," he declared, "as a punishment."

NOTE: This subject has not been cross referenced because of its frequent occurrence throughout this dictionary.

WILL

1

A woman had been bitten by a dog and a doctor had been called in. After treating her, he advised, "As it's possible you may be carried off by hydrophobia, madam, it may be well to note down your last wishes." She busied herself with pencil and paper for such a long time that at last the doctor remarked, "That's rather a long will, isn't it?" "Will, nothing!" she retorted sharply. "I'm just making a list of the people I'm going to bite."

2

A wealthy man in a small town had died, and naturally speculation was rife as to how big was his fortune. "I bet I can find out," announced the village gossip, and she set out for the deceased's lawyer's office. "I understand you drew up old Smith's will," she began. "I wonder if you'd tell me how much he left?" "Why certainly," consented the lawyer. "He left everything he had."

3

A wealthy man with many relatives engaged a famous lawyer to draw up his will, instructing him to make it absolutely foolproof. When, after much labor, the document was completed, the client asked, "Have you made it so it can't be contested or broken?" "I've done my best," said the lawyer. "Well, now," continued the rich man, "I'd like to ask you another question—not professionally, but just man to man. Who do you really think stands the best chance of getting my fortune when I'm gone?"

WILLING

The village squire had been rude and grasping all his life and was heartily disliked. Now he was dying and one of the good, but rather simple-minded deacons, was paying him an official visit. "Are you willing to go, my friend?" asked the deacon. "Yes, I am," replied the sick man. "Well, that's fine," approved the deacon naively. "I'm glad to hear that you are, for all the neighbors are quite willing."

See also school[1].

WILL POWER

1

"Please gimme another piece of candy, mommy," pleaded little Bessie. "But you've already had four pieces," objected mother. "Aw, just one more, please, mommy," implored the child. "All right," consented mother, "but this is the last." "Thank you, mommy," said Bessie, "but, goodness, I must say you ain't got no will power."

2

Little Ronald had been begging father for permission to go to the movies, but was refused. "Now I've told you no, and I mean no!" cried father impatiently at last. "Just use your will power a bit and forget about the movies." "But I ain't got no will power, an' I don't want no will power," wailed Ronald. "I want to go to the movies."

3

Little Johnny refused to take his medicine and father was getting provoked. "Come, come, Johnny," said father, "it's just a question of a little will power. I don't like medicine any better than you, but I just make up my mind that I'll take it, and I do." "Well, when I've got medicine to take," retorted Johnny, "I just make up my mind that I *won't* take it, and I don't."

4

"When I married my husband less than a year ago, he was a heavy smoker," asserted the square-jawed lady, "but today he never touches tobacco." "Marvelous!" exclaimed a listener. "To break off a habit of a lifetime like that certainly requires a strong will power." "Indeed it does," agreed the other; "and that's just what I've got!"

See also conscience[3], determination.

WIN

"What's this I hear about your little sister being sick in bed, Jackie?" inquired a neighbor of the small boy. "I hope it's not serious." "Aw, it ain't much," answered Jackie. "We were just playin' a game to see who could lean out of the window farthest, an' she won."

WIND

1

The army was holding maneuvers in Texas near the Davis Mountains when one of the boys one day came drifting into camp and landed with a bump. Slightly bruised and cut up, he was taken to the commanding officer who commented, "You've really got nerve, son, to come down in a parachute with this 100-mile wind blowing. You might have been killed." "I didn't come down in a parachute, sir," replied the soldier. "I went up in a tent."

2

A stranger was walking about the residential district of a small Kansas town and looking all about him. One of the residents noticed him and asked, "Good mornin', mister, lookin' fer a house?" "Yep, I sure am," answered the stranger. "D'you reckon it could've blowed this fur?"

See also speaker[5].

WINE

A man who liked to drink, was invited to dinner at a friend's house. When it came time for the dessert course a large plate of grapes was offered him. "No, thanks," he refused, pushing the plate back; "I never take my wine in pills!"

WISDOM

"Oh, mamma," cried the small girl gleefully, "when I was at grandma's yesterday she let me have two pieces of pie." "She shouldn't have done that," commented mother. "One piece would have been plenty. Some day you'll find that the older you grow the wiser you'll become." The child considered this briefly, then pointed out, "Well, don't forget, mamma, that grandma is a good deal older than you."

WISH

1

The tramp had his usual story of being out of work, sick, and hungry all ready as he knocked on the back door. But he was taken aback when the door was suddenly flung open by a huge woman, angry at being interrupted in the midst of her baking. She demanded in a loud voice, "Well, did you wish to see me?" The bum gulped, backed warily down the steps, and said meekly, "I-I ain't s-sure, but if I d-did, I sure got my wish."

2

Little Betty had already had three helpings of the Thanksgiving turkey and was now asking for more. "You've had enough, dear," declared mother. "But I want more," demanded the child. "You've had all that's good for you," insisted mother. "But, here, you may pull the wishbone with mother." They pulled the bone, and mother exclaimed, "Ah, you've got the big end! Now, what do you wish for, Betty?" "More turkey!" was the prompt response.

See also selfish[2].

WITNESS

1

A witness in a suit for damages resulting from an accident was being cross-examined by a lawyer. "And just how far do you think you were from the accident when it occurred?" he demanded. "Exactly seventeen feet three and a quarter inches," was the unhesitating reply. "But how can you be so exact?" asked the lawyer. "Well," explained the witness, "I figured some fool would ask me that, so I just measured it."

2

"And what did you find when you arrived at the scene of the crime?" the lawyer asked the witness. "'Naught but barren nothingness,' as Shakespeare puts it," replied the witness poetically. The judge leaned forward. "Never mind what this here Shakespeare says," he directed severely. "If he knows anything about this case we'll summon him!"

3

The only witness to a railroad wreck was now on the stand in a suit resulting from it. "Now, you claim to have seen the two trains collide head-on at sixty miles an hour," roared the attorney for the defense. "Tell us, what did you say when that happened?" "Well," the witness shrugged his shoulders, "I just said to myself, 'Now ain't that a hell of a way to run a railroad!'"

4

It was the witness's first time in a courtroom and he was conducting himself awkwardly, speaking vaguely out toward the spectators. "If you please, sir," the judge leaned forward to advise him, "speak to the jury—to those men sitting behind you on the benches." The witness turned, bowed shyly, and said, "Good morning, gentlemen."

5

The defendant was already seated in the courtroom with his witnesses clustered about him before the trial opened, when the plaintiff bustled in. "Say, Sam," he asked, looking over the group, "are all those your witnesses?" "They are," Sam assured him. The plaintiff grabbed his hat and got ready to leave. "Then you win," he conceded. "I've had them witnesses twice myself, and they're good."

See also fee[3], truth[2].

WOMAN

1

The professor was giving a lecture on domestic relations, when someone in the audience asked him to give a definition of woman. "Well," the professor began leisurely, "woman is, generally speaking—" "Stop right there, professor," interrupted a married man in the crowd. "You could talk a hundred years and you'd never get a better answer than that."

2

"Daily I grow more conscious of God's greatest mistake," sighed the husband wearily. "What do you mean?" asked the wife. "Making Adam before He made Eve," was the reply. "Do you mean the woman should have come first?" asked the wife. "Why, certainly," asserted hubby. "As it is, who was there to boss the job of making Adam?"

3

The woman lecturer was a violent feminist. "Where, I ask you," she demanded belligerently, "would man be today if it were not for woman?" She paused for effect, looked around the auditorium, and repeated, "I ask again, where would man be today if it were not for woman?" "In the Garden of Eden eating strawberries," shouted a voice from the balcony.

4

The old sea captain had been dragged to an afternoon tea party by his wife. The women all gathered around him pestering him for a story of his adventures. Out of patience at last, he began, "Well, ladies, I recall once when I was shipwrecked off the coast of Africa, I came across a tribe of wild women who had no tongues." "Heavens!" gasped one of his listeners. "But then they couldn't talk." "Of course not," snapped the old sea dog, "and that's what made 'em wild!"

NOTE: This subject has not been cross referenced because of its frequent occurrence throughout this dictionary.

WOMAN-DRIVER

1

"Tell me, lady," asked the traffic cop after he had signaled the woman to stop her car, "how long do you expect to be out?" "Just what do you mean by that question, sir?" she demanded haughtily. "Well, it's this way, lady," he explained sarcastically, "there's just a couple of thousand other drivers who'd like to use this street when you get through with it."

2

A man was taking an examination for a driver's license and among the questions asked him was, "What would you do if the driver of a car in front of you put an arm out and moved it up and down?" "That all depends," replied the other. "Is the driver a man or a woman?"

3

The girl driving the car halted

by a traffic signal. She was evidently confused for when the signal changed to green she did not budge. Several times the signal changed from green to red and back, and still her car remained where it was. Finally a policeman strolled over and inquired, "What's the matter, Miss, don't we have any colors you like?"

4

The man's car had just collided with that of the woman-driver ahead of him, and they were both out discussing the situation. "What's wrong with you anyway?" demanded the woman indignantly. "I turned the way I signaled." "I know," admitted the man. "That's what fooled me."

5

Hubby was trying to teach his wife to drive the car and she was getting along fine until they reached a crowded intersection. Then she lost her head. "Quick, quick," she pleaded, "tell me what to do now!" "Now just relax and imagine that I'm driving the car," advised hubby, "and then you do what you'd tell me to do."

6

A man and wife were driving back to town after dinner in the country. As they got into the city traffic, the woman suddenly started directing, "Mind what you're doing, Henry! Look out for those cars! You're coming much too close!" "Say, are you crazy?" asked hubby. "Crazy? Just what do you mean?" demanded the wife. "Well," commented Henry, "have you forgotten that you're driving?"

7

A woman was driving along a country road when she noticed several linemen climbing telephone poles. "Silly fools!" she remarked to her companion. "They must think I've never driven before."

8

There was a screech of brakes as a man through heroic effort barely managed to prevent his car colliding with that of a woman ahead. "What's wrong with you?" he shouted angrily. "Why can't you signal when you're going to turn?" "Don't be silly!" the woman yelled back from her driveway. "I always turn here."

9

"What did you learn in Sunday school today, Junior?" asked mother as the boy came in. "Oh, they told us about how Lot's wife looked back and turned into a pillar of salt," replied the boy. "Humph!" grunted father from his armchair. "There's nothing so remarkable about that. Every time your mother looks back she turns into a lamppost or somebody else's car."

10

George had been patiently trying for weeks to teach the little woman how to drive the car, but without much success. They were out one afternoon and she was driving along a quiet country road when suddenly she screamed in fright, "Quick, George, you take the wheel! Here comes a big tree!"

See also parking, police[2].

WOMAN-HATER

"Just look at old Williams over there," remarked one guest at a party to another, "right in the midst of a bunch of girls and thoroughly enjoying himself. I've always understood that he was a woman-hater." "Oh, but he is," confirmed the other; "only she's not with him tonight."

See also enough[1].

WOOING

1

"Look here, daughter," said father, "that young man of yours invariably stays until a very late hour. Hasn't your mother said anything about this?" "Oh, yes, father," replied daughter. "Mother said that men haven't changed a bit since she was a girl."

2

"Now, Joan, I don't mind your going out with that young fellow," remarked father as daughter came in late, "but I do hope that you don't indulge in any of this silly petting." "Oh, of course not, father," replied the girl with sarcasm. "Now tonight we merely put our heads together and tried to figure out some way to help the President reduce the national debt."

3

The park driveway was crowded, but the young fellow could not resist slipping an arm about his fair companion as he drove along. "For heaven's sake!" squealed the girl, "use both hands!" "Sorry, babe," he replied regretfully, "but I need one for driving."

4

"See here, young feller," said the farmer as he met the visitor at the gate, "I ain't blind and I kin figger that ye've been a-sparkin' my gal Mandy a lot lately. Is it all on the square, or ain't it?" "No, 'tain't," admitted the young fellow, blushing. "It's mostly on the back porch, I reckon."

5

"Gee, Mame," asked one chorus girl anxiously of another, "what would you do if you had six dates with a guy an' he ain't never tried to kiss you or nothin'?" Without hesitation Mame replied, "I'd lie about it."

See also courtship, dating, delusion[3], feeling[1], go[1], invention[2], movies[1], plumber[3], recovery[4], signs[5], stand[2], tunnel[1].

WORD

1

The inveterate jokester met a serious man on the streetcar and fell into conversation with him. "Did it ever occur to you," he said with a chuckle, "that the word 'reviver' is spelled the same backwards or forwards? I'll bet you can't give me another such word." "Oh, tut-tut," replied the serious man.

2

A woman looked up from her newspaper to remark to her husband, "I doubt this statement here which says that the average woman has a vocabulary of only 500 words." "It does seem like rather a small stock," conceded the husband; "but just think of the turnover."

3

"I've a small favor to ask of you, dear," requested the proper old lady of her granddaughter, "and that is that you promise not to use two certain words. One is swell, and the other is lousy. Would you do that for me?" "Why, sure as you're born, Granny," agreed the girl. "What are the two words?"

4

"Ah, my fairest one," an ardent young man was pleading with the Hollywood actress, "say the words that will make you mine." "All right," she consented: "'One million dollars.'"

5

A husky, pugnacious foreigner, who considered himself quite a man with his fists, had recently come to a northern logging camp where a burly Canadian had long held sway. He soon challenged the other to a fight to determine the better man, saying, "Ve fight until vun man calls out 'Sufficient!'" So they began, and a terrific battle raged for an hour, when the foreigner called out, "Sufficient!" "Damn it!" exclaimed the Canuck, "I bin tryin' to t'ink o' dat word for a half-hour!"

See also work[6].

WORK

1

"Lady, have you got any work for a poor man to do?" inquired a tramp at the back door. "I'm sorry," said the woman regretfully, "but I couldn't give you enough work to keep you occupied." "Don't worry, lady," the tramp reassured her. "You'd be surprised what little work it takes to keep me occupied."

2

"I'll bet you haven't done a lick of work in your life!" declared the housewife angrily to the bum begging a handout at the door. "Look, lady," he retorted, "if youse t'ink askin' sour old dames like you fer a bite to eat ain't work, youse don't know what work is."

3

"You know, son," commented father to his boy just out of college, "hard work never killed anybody." "That's just the trouble, dad," rejoined the young fellow. "I'm the adventurous type and I want to engage in something with the spice of danger in it."

4

"The idea! A big man like you begging instead of working for a living!" the lady said to the tramp at her back door. "Hard work has never killed any one." "Oh, but that's where yer wrong, lady," the bum corrected her. "That's how I lost all three o' my wives."

5

The farmer not only kept his hired hand busy in the fields from dawn to dusk, but the fellow also had to do several hours of chores around the house by lantern light. Finally, he went to the farmer and said, "I'm afraid I'll have to quit. You know, you promised me steady work here." "Waal, ain't ye got it?" asked the farmer. "No, I haven't," was the reply. "Why, there's three or four hours every night when I ain't got a durned thing to do but fritter my time away sleeping."

6

"I say, my good man," said the lady to the tramp at the door, "would you care for some employment?" "Look, lady," replied the tramp patiently, "I know yuh means well, see, but yuh jest can't make work sound any more invitin' by usin' a word o' three syllables fer it."

See also business, inheritance[2], job, office[3], perseverance[2], reason[2], rescue[1], warning[2], whistle.

WORKMAN

1

The boss was interviewing an applicant for a job. "Are you a clock-watcher?" he asked. "No, sir, I don't like inside work," replied the other coolly. "I'm a whistle-listener."

2

The welder looked pretty mad when he came up to the foreman and announced, "I'm gonna quit." "But what's wrong, Pete?" asked the foreman. "Don't you like it here?" "Oh, the shop an' every-thing's fine," Pete assured him, "but I jist don't like to be spied on. Every place I go that guy's right behind me," and Pete pointed to a meek-looking little fellow standing nearby. "For gosh sakes, Pete!" cried the foreman, "that's no spy. He's your helper!"

3

The boss paused to remark to an old employee, "You've been with us quite a while, haven't you, Smith?" "Yes, sir," replied Smith. "Me an' that white horse there's bin workin' fer the company twenty years." "Fine, fine," commented the boss. "And you've both been very well treated, no doubt?" "Well, sir," was the reply, "last week we was both took sick an' they got a doctor for the horse, but they just docked my pay."

4

A pedestrian stopped and watched a laborer digging in the ground, and after awhile he asked, "What're you digging for, buddy?" "Money," replied the other briefly. "Money!" cried the spectator. "When do you expect to strike it?" "Saturday," said the workman.

See also day, haircut[3], painting[1], politics[1], suggestion[1].

WORKMANSHIP

See craftsmanship.

WORLD

1

"And thus," the lecturer on astronomy concluded, "I predict that the world will end in fifty million years." "How long?" cried an alarmed voice from the audience. "Fifty million years," repeated the lecturer. "Whew!" came the relieved voice. "I thought you said fifteen million."

2

The shipwrecked sailor had been on the desert island for over five years, but one morning he was over-joyed to see a ship standing offshore and a small boat being rowed in. As the boat touched shore, an officer tossed the castaway a bundle of newspapers. "The Captain's compli-ments," he cried, "and he asks that you please read through these and then let him know if you still want to be rescued."

3

"Is the world round, Jimmy?"

questioned teacher during the geography lesson. "No, ma'am," was the response. "Oh, isn't it?" returned teacher, surprised. "Is it flat, then?" "No, ma'am," came the answer again. "What's wrong with you, Jimmy?" asked teacher. "If the world isn't round and isn't flat, what is it?" "Pop says it's crooked," declared the boy.

See also craftsmanship[2], proof[3], shape[2].

WORM

1

Little Danny gulped hard and looked gravely at father. "Gee, pop," he said, "this apple had a worm in it an' I just ate it." "You did?" cried father. "Here, take a drink of this water and wash it down." But Danny shook his head and replied, "Aw, let 'im walk down."

2

"Gee, Bill," said Jack, peering into the tin can, "how did you ever get your little sister to find so many fishing worms for you?" "Oh, I had to bribe her a little," explained Bill. "Out of every ten worms she dug up, I let her have one to eat."

See also husband[2], imitation[5], lonely.

WORRY

1

A moral young man was talking to a friend who was quite a ladies' man. "When you go running around with women like you do," he asked, "doesn't your conscience ever bother you?" "Well, to tell the truth, I do worry for a while," admitted the young devil, "but if after a certain length of time I don't hear from their husbands, I feel all right again."

2

"Why so blue this morning, Bridget?" inquired the lady of her cleaning woman. "Oh, I've got me troubles, mum," replied the other, and began telling of her afflictions. "Come, come, cheer up, Bridget," consoled the lady. "There's no use in worrying." "How can you say that, mum?" asked Bridget. "It looks to me, mum, like when the Lord sends me tribulation He expects me to tribulate, don't He?"

3

"Golly," said Johnson to his friend. "I certainly feel worried about my wife. She's out in this awful rain." "Don't be concerned about it, old top," comforted the friend. "Surely she'll take shelter in some store." "That's just what's worrying me," grumbled Johnson. "She's got ten dollars of my money."

See also hair[4], tattoo[1], world[1].

WORSE

1

A golfer who was none too good was playing a particularly bad game on this day. "Good heavens!" he at last impatiently exclaimed. "I'm sure that there can't be any worse golfers than I!" "Oh, I wouldn't say that, sir," consoled the caddy. "I'm sure there must be worse players than you—it's just that they don't play."

2

No matter what the bad news

might be, a certain old fellow would invariably remark, "Oh, well, it might have been worse." One day an acquaintance stopped him and said, "I've something to tell you for which you can't use your pet expression. I dreamed last night that I died, went to hell, and was doomed to everlasting torment." "Oh, well, it might have been worse," commented the old boy. "For Pete's sake, man!" cried the other, "how could it have been worse?" "It might have been true," was the reply.

WORTH

See price, value.

WOUND

"Did you boys hear about Major Brown?" asked a soldier. "They say he's just been wounded." "Humph!" grunted another, who evidently didn't like the Major. "If he was it must have been by an accidental discharge of his duty."

WRITER

See author.

WRITING

1

The old hillbilly sat before his fireplace, tongue gripped between his teeth, intent with his pencil stub as he laboriously made scrawls on a scrap of paper. "Waal, tan mah hide!" he cried out in pleased surprise, "effin Ah ain't done gone an' larnt to write!" Maw looked admiringly over his shoulder and asked, "What's it say, pap?" "I dunno," replied the old boy. "Ah hain't larnt to read yit."

2

The writing lesson was in progress when little Betty raised her hand and said, "Teacher, Tommy Smith over there isn't doing the lesson right." "What do you mean?" asked teacher. "The lesson's on capital M's, but he's making capital P's." "But," objected teacher, "you can't see his paper from where you are." "I know," admitted the girl, "but I can see his tongue."

See also handwriting[1], literal.

WRONG

1

"Doctor," demanded the woman as she burst into the room, "I want you to be frank and tell me exactly what's wrong with me." "Well, madam," observed the man after surveying her critically, "I've just three things to say to you: first, you ought to take off about fifty pounds of that fat; second, you'd look better with about one-tenth the make-up; and third, I'm an artist—the doctor's upstairs."

2

The drunk was singing happily as he tried without success to fit his key into the front door lock. At last a man appeared at an upstairs window and cried, "Beat it, you fool! You've got the wrong house!" "Fool, yourself!" retorted the drunk. "You're lookin' outta the wrong window!"

YEAR

See season.

YELL

See loud, shouting.

YIELD

"Humbleness and submission are the keys to virtue," shouted the revivalist. "He who gives in when he's wrong is wise; but the man who gives in when he's right is—" "Married!" supplemented a voice from the audience.

YOUNG

See office boy[1], tact[1].

ZOO

1

Uncle had taken his little nephew Willie on his first visit to the zoo. After letting him look at all the cages, Uncle inquired, "Well, Willie, what do you think of the animals?" The boy gave this a moment's thought, then replied, "I think it would be a lot more sensible if the kangaroo and elephant changed tails."

2

Mother had little Willie to the zoo and he missed no opportunity to ask questions. Pausing before one cage, he inquired, "Does the giraffe get a sore throat if he gets his feet wet?" "Yes, I suppose so," replied the mother wearily, "but not until next week."

3

Teacher took the class on an educational trip to the zoo. Pointing at a deer, she asked little Tommy what it was. "I don't know," the boy replied. "Well," prompted teacher, "what does your mother often call your father?" Tommy's eyes opened in amazement. "Golly, teacher! Don't tell me that's a louse!"

See also coward[1], grief[1], hint[9], sex[1, 2], stork.